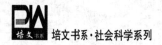

SOCIAL CHANGE

社会变迁

【美】史蒂文·瓦格 著
Steven Vago

第 5 版

北京大学出版社
PEKING UNIVERSITY PRESS

北京市版权局著作权合同登记图字：01-2004-5653 号

图书在版编目(CIP)数据

社会变迁(第5版)/(美)瓦格(Vago, S.)著. —影印本. —北京：北京大学出版社，2005.1
(培文书系·社会科学系列)

ISBN 7-301-08161-8

I. 社… II. 瓦… III. 社会发展-研究-英文 IV. K02

中国版本图书馆 CIP 数据核字(2004)第 112538 号

English reprint edition copyright © 2004 by PEARSON EDUCATION ASIA LIMITED and PEKING UNIVERSITY PRESS.
Original English language title from Proprietor's edition of the Work.

Original English language title: Social Change, Steven Vago
Copyright © 2004
ISBN: 0-13-111556-1
All Rights Reserved.

Published by arrangement with the original publisher, Pearson Education, Inc., publishing as Prentice Hall, Inc.

This edition is authorized for sale and distribution only in the People's Republic of China exclusively (except Hong Kong SAR, Macao SAR and Taiwan).
仅限于中华人民共和国境内(不包括中国香港、澳门特别行政区和中国台湾地区)销售发行。

书　　　　名：	社会变迁(第 5 版)
著作责任者：	[美] Steven Vago 著
责 任 编 辑：	戈含锋
标 准 书 号：	ISBN 7-301-08161-8/C·0299
出　版　者：	北京大学出版社
地　　　　址：	北京市海淀区中关村北京大学校内　100871
网　　　　址：	http://cbs.pku.edu.cn　电子信箱：pw@pup.pku.edu.cn
电　　　　话：	邮购部 62752015　发行部 62750672　编辑部 58874097 58874098
印　刷　者：	山东新华印刷厂临沂厂
发　行　者：	北京大学出版社
经　销　者：	新华书店
	850毫米×1168毫米　16 开　29.75 印张　525 千字
	2005 年 1 月第 1 版　2006 年 6 月第 3 次印刷
定　　　　价：	45.00 元

版权所有，翻印必究

本书封面贴有 Pearson Education(培生教育出版集团)激光防伪标签，无标签者不得销售。

出版说明

　　培文书系社会科学英文影印系列旨在面向社会科学领域的师生和广大社会科学的从业者和爱好者,推介国外社会科学领域的英文原版专著和教材,使我国读者能够接触到原汁原味的第一手资料。

　　需要重申的是,作者本人的有些观点和结论尚需商榷,有些甚至是不可取的,为此提请读者加以甄别。书中观点均不代表出版社观点。

北京大学出版社
2005 年 1 月

简明目录

前言　　　　　ix
1. 绪论：变迁的维度和源泉 …………………………… 1
2. 变迁理论 …………………………………………… 49
3. 变迁模式 …………………………………………… 85
4. 变迁领域 …………………………………………… 128
5. 变迁期间 …………………………………………… 190
6. 变迁应对 …………………………………………… 232
7. 变迁影响 …………………………………………… 279
8. 变迁成本 …………………………………………… 314
9. 变迁策略 …………………………………………… 357
10. 变迁评价 ………………………………………… 400

索引　　　　　437

Contents

Preface ix

1 Introduction: Dimensions and Sources of Change 1

The Organization of the Book 2
The Nature of Social Change 4
Conceptualizations of Social Change 7
Sources of Change 11
Technology 11
Ideology 15
Competition 19
Conflict 20
Polity 28
The Economy 31
Globalization 34
Structural Strains 37
Summary 39
Suggested Further Readings 41
References 42

2 Theories of Change 49

Evolutionary Theories 51
Conflict Theories 58
Structural-Functional Theories 64
Social-Psychological Theories 71
Summary 79

vi   Contents

> *Suggested Further Readings   80*
> *References   81*

3   Patterns of Change   85

> *Evolution   85*
> *Diffusion   88*
> *Acculturation   95*
> *Revolution   98*
> *Modernization   103*
> *Industrialization   108*
> *Urbanization   111*
> *Bureaucratization   116*
> *Summary   119*
> *Suggested Further Readings   120*
> *References   121*

4   Spheres of Change   128

> *The Family   128*
> *Population   139*
> *Stratification   148*
> *Power Relations   153*
> *Education   158*
> *The Economy   170*
> *Summary   178*
> *Suggested Further Readings   180*
> *References   181*

5   Duration of Change   190

> *Duration of Change from a Historical Perspective   191*
> *Transitory Social Changes   193*
> *Fads and Fashions   194*
> *Lifestyles   203*
> *Cults   217*

Summary 224
Suggested Further Readings 225
References 226

6 Reactions to Change 232

Social Stimulants 234
Psychological Stimulants 239
Cultural Stimulants 244
Economic Stimulants 247
Resistance to Change 251
Social Barriers 252
Psychological Barriers 259
Cultural Barriers 264
Economic Barriers 268
Summary 272
Suggested Further Readings 273
References 274

7 Impact of Change 279

The Social Impact of Technology 282
Responses to Change 288
Social Change and Social Disorganization 292
Unintended Consequences 297
Coping with Change 301
Summary 306
Suggested Further Readings 308
References 309

8 Costs of Change 314

Economic Costs 316
Social Costs 326
Psychological Costs 342
Summary 349

Suggested Further Readings 350
References 351

9 Strategies of Change 357

Targets, Agents, and Methods of Planned Social Change 358
Violence 368
Nonviolence and Direct Action 374
Social Movements 379
Law and Social Change 387
Summary 392
Suggested Further Readings 394
References 395

10 Assessment of Change 400

Assessment Techniques 400
Technology Assessment 406
Methodologies for Change Evaluation 411
Social Indicators 417
Policy Implications 425
Summary 427
Suggested Further Readings 429
References 430

Index 437

Preface

The fifth edition of this book is a response to the growing demands for timely and comprehensive sociological analysis of one of the most important concerns of our time, social change. This edition greatly increases contemporary multicultural and international components. At the same time, the book retains the classroom-tested, pedagogically sound features and the proven organizational framework of the previous editions and remains scholarly, comprehensive, informative, at times controversial, and quite readable. I have successfully resisted the temptation to make only cosmetic changes and verbiage alterations so common in revisions.

The book is designed to provide a clear, concise and up-to-date analysis of the major theoretical perspectives, sources, processes, patterns, and consequences of social change. It considers factors that stimulate or hinder the acceptance of change in a multi-cultural context, and it emphasizes unintended consequences and costs of both planned and unplanned change. It dwells on the ways of creating and on the methods of assessing change. Going beyond standard treatments of the topic, this text highlights those aspects of theory and research that have immediate practical implications for students of social change and uses contemporary examples, many of them flowing from the destruction of the World Trade Center towers by terrorists on September 11, 2001, that are relevant to the experience of the book's audience. Although the orientation of the book is sociological, I did not hesitate to incorporate theoretical and current empirical work from anthropology, social psychology, economics, political science, and history.

This edition reflects the many comments and recommendations made by students and colleagues both in the United States and abroad who have used the book in their classrooms and research. Whereas the basic organizational plan of the text remains unchanged, a substantial amount of new information has been included. Almost every page of this edition has been revised, not only for the purpose of updating, but also to increase its informative function, advance its analysis and minimize lapses into dry academic prose. New sections have been added, dated materials were dropped, and the list of suggested further readings at the end of each chapter has been expanded and updated. Key concepts and ideas have been developed in virtually every chapter. Most chapters have been reconsidered, refined and enlarged, or reduced when warranted, and all have been updated to reflect the latest theoretical and empirical advances and the most recent statistics, but not at the expense of the rich classical literature which provides the intellectual foundation for this book. Thus the reader will have a chance to learn what is new while being exposed to traditional sociological thinking. The novel features include discussions on terrorism, current developments in the former Soviet Union and Warsaw Pact nations, controversies on globalization, trends in higher education, the social impact of the proliferation of personal computers, and the steadily increasing economic and social costs of environmental alterations. A unique aspect of the book is its extensive use of cross-cultural illustrations.

Although any errors, inaccuracies, omissions, and commissions are accepted—and regretted—as my own responsibility, much of the book derives from many persons, mostly scholars at various universities in the United States and abroad and students, whose constructive criticism, help and cumulative wisdom I gratefully acknowledge. Special thanks go to my students in annual courses on social change over the past thirty-five years who patiently endured many earlier drafts of the various revisions and offered a variety of valuable suggestions. As with other books and scholarly endeavors, the Vago Foundation was once again instrumental in making this project feasible and went beyond all expectations in providing financial, research and secretarial assistance, inspiration and encouragement, and the requisite infrastructure for the preparation of this text.

To Pine Tree Composition, Inc., I extend my gratitude for their outstanding processing of the manuscript and for expertly preparing the index and to Karen Berry for superbly putting everything together.

Steven Vago
Bellingham, Washington
and Harrison Hot Springs,
British Columbia

Chapter 1

Introduction: Dimensions and Sources of Change

At the onset of the second millennium, change continues to be all-pervasive, ubiquitous, and at times disconcerting. People from all walks of life talk about it, want it, oppose it, fear it, and at times they even want to make sense out of it. But there is nothing new in the allure of change. From the beginning, social change has been an integral part of the human condition. Since the earliest times, there has been a fascination with change, a constant preoccupation with its ramifications, and prolonged agitation about its consequences. This book is about that age-old concern with social change, which is, with all due modesty, one of the most important, challenging, and exciting topics in sociology.

The science of sociology began in the quest for explanations for social change. The advent of this new science marked the beginning of a long and sinuous road toward making "sense" of change. Yet, in spite of the multitude of efforts since its inception, the discipline of sociology is still confronted with the questions of how society changes, in what direction, why, in what specific ways, and by what forces these changes are created. Considering the fact that social change has been ubiquitous and, from time to time, a dramatic feature of society, there is still a great deal to learn about its nature and scope. Today social change is a central concern of sociology, and it is likely to remain one of the most intriguing and difficult problems in the discipline.

The intention of this book is to draw attention to the complexities and concerns inherent in the understanding of social change. It will concentrate on the more salient features, characteristics, processes, and perspectives of change in the United States and cross-culturally. The purpose is to try to make "sense" of change and to consider what is changing—and where, why, and how.

The principal mission of the book is to serve as a text in undergraduate courses on social change. The comprehensives and the large number of references included also make the book a valuable resource for both graduate students interested in social change and instructors who may be teaching a course on the subject for the first time. Because the book has been written with the undergraduate student in mind, no one particular perspective or approach to change has been taken, nor has a specific ideology or theoretical perspective been embraced. To have done so would have been too limiting for the scope of this book, since important contributions to social change would have had to have been excluded or would have been subject to criticism that such contributions were out of context. As a result, the book does not propound a single thesis; instead, it exposes the reader to a variety of theoretical perspectives proposed to account for social change in the social science literature.

THE ORGANIZATION OF THE BOOK

The book deals with modes of social inquiry of change. It examines the principal theoretical, empirical, analytical, and evaluative aspects in the study of social change. The discussion of the various topics combines sociological classics with significant contemporary insights and balances the presentation of theory with useful and testable hypotheses. When warranted, theoretical insights are translated into practical applications in a variety of situations. To make the text more comprehensive and interesting, the sociological perspectives are supplemented with viewpoints drawn from other disciplines in the social sciences and an abundance of cross-cultural and historical illustrations. The following comments on chapter contents will provide a schematic orientation for the reader.

This chapter examines the nature and the basic concepts of the subject matter and presents an approach for the conceptualization of social change. Next, the sources of change are considered. They encompass the impetus for change, the driving force behind change, and the conditions that are sufficient to produce it. The principal sources of change chosen for analysis are technology, ideology, competition, conflict, political and economic forces, and structural strains.

Sociological explanations of why social change occurs are as old as the discipline itself. To introduce the reader to the diverse theoretical orientations, Chapter 2 reviews the most influential and important classical and contemporary theories of social change. They are discussed by principal perspectives and proponents. The review concentrates on evolutionary, conflict, structural-functional, and social-psychological explanations of social change.

After the identification and analysis of forces that produce change, we need to consider the question of how and in what form change takes place. In Chapter 3 the discussion focuses on such patterns of change as evolution, diffusion, acculturation, revolution, modernization, industrialization, urbanization, and bureaucratization.

One might comment at this stage of the discourse: "So far, so good, but what has really changed in our contemporary world?" In response to this question, Chapter 4 examines trends in such specific social arrangements and spheres as family, population, stratification, power relations, education, and economy.

Once a change is accepted at any level of the social system, it is appropriate to ask how long it is likely to be sustained. Thus, the question of duration becomes important; this is discussed in Chapter 5 in terms of both the long-term and transitory phenomena of change such as fads, fashions, lifestyles, and cults.

Social change contains varying dialectical modes. It is neither automatic nor unopposed. It affects individuals and groups in society in different ways, for whom change may mean different things. Chapter 6, on the reactions to change, looks at the social, psychological, cultural, and economic forces and conditions that facilitate or hinder the acceptance of change.

The question of what new social arrangements must be made, once change is brought about, has seldom been considered adequately in the literature on social change. The purpose of Chapter 7 is to examine the impacts and effects of change, its unintended consequences, and the methods of coping with change.

Any alteration of the social system and all forms of social engineering carry a price tag. But the price we pay for it is rarely mentioned. In Chapter 8, the discussion is concerned with the issues of the economics of change and the social and psychological costs of "progress."

How to bring about social change is among the most crucial and timely questions in the book. Thus, an analysis of strategies to create "desired" change is paramount. The aim of Chapter 9 is to analyze a series of social change strategies and tactics used in a variety of change efforts.

The last chapter is devoted to the current methodologies used in the assessment of the viability of change on social arrangements. Emphasis is placed on technology and environment assessment, techniques of change evaluation, and methodologies for forecasting change with applicable policy implications.

The study of social change is naturally eclectic. Knowledge about it has accumulated in shreds and patches. In attempting to explain social change—whether on the scale of major transformations in society or of a more specialized, localized kind—one is tempted to look for "prime movers" analogous to the forces of Newtonian physics. But there are no "laws" in sociology comparable to the laws of physics. At best, we have some good generalizations. Our investigations are guided by a number of theoretical perspectives resulting in a variety of strands of thought and research. In pulling them together, we will be guided by the following concerns:

1. What do we need to know about social change? What are the principal issues in the study of change?
2. What do we really know? What are the major theories and findings in the field? How much confidence can we have in them?
3. What remains to be known? What are the major gaps, "unknowns," or lacunae, in theory and research?

In a sense, more problems are raised than can be solved in this volume. One of the fascinating aspects of the study of social change is that there are so many loose ends, so many ways of considering the subject, and so much yet to be learned. It is hoped that this book will serve as a useful point of departure for further study of change.

THE NATURE OF SOCIAL CHANGE

Change is one of the central issues of our time. The Greek philosopher Heraclitus stated this in his oft-quoted proposition that one cannot step twice into the same river. The same observation in the words of a modern author: "The action in its repetition can never be the same. Everything involved in it has irrevocably changed in the intervening period" (Adam, 1990:168).

Everywhere, change has become central to people's awareness, and there is a commitment to change that is irreversible, irresistible, and irrevocable. In every society, there is technological change, demographic change, rapid ecological change, and change induced by internal incongruities in economic and political patterns and by conflicting ideologies. Since the beginning of the twenty-first century, Americans have had more than 4 million babies and 1.6 million abortions annually. Over 2 million couples wed every year, and a little over 1 million divorce. Life expectancy for Americans has reached a record level, while the infant mortality rate has fallen to a new low. Forty-three million Americans move in a given year, 10 million change occupations, 1.5 million retire, and 2.5 million die (Statistical Abstract of the United States, 2002). In the workplace, millions are hired, fired, promoted, demoted and sued. There is a dramatic decline in equities and personal wealth and unknown numbers of retirement plans are shattered. There is a growth in corporate corruption, large companies go bankrupt, new products appear on the market, and old skills become obsolete. New causes and abuses, issues, and excuses emerge with their appropriate slogans, politically correct vocabulary and blame targets and there is an unprecedented pedophilia scandal in the Catholic church with lawsuits by enraged victims and large-scale transfers of offending priests from parish to parish and secret out-of-court settlements with victims (Williams and Cooperman, 2002). Mass circulation magazines have special reports on the question of "What Has Changed" since the millennium, covering a slate of topics ranging from the impact of terrorism on our lives to the consequences of spending more time in cyberspace (see, for example, *Business Week*, 2002). Even the national girth is changing, along with food preferences and portion sizes, and in 2000, more than 65 percent of adult Americans were overweight as compared to 56 percent in 1999, and some 31 percent of them—55 million people—were obese (Shell, 2002; Spake, 2002). For our explorations, the fundamental questions relate to what is changing, at what level, and how fast. Further, we want to know what type of change is taking place—and what its magnitude and scope are.

An obvious first question in considering the nature of social change is, "What is changing?" For the layperson, it could be everything or nothing. The question as it is phrased is just too broad, too general to be meaningful. In the United States, the standard form of greeting someone is usually followed by the question, "What's new?" Invariably, we are at a loss to come up with a coherent and cogent response to this habitual but ridiculous question. Still, it is an everyday occurrence. As a rule, we fire back an equally ridiculous and meaningless response saying, "Not much," "Nothing," or remarks in that vein. To avoid this dilemma of uncomfortable ambiguity, we need to go beyond the original question and specify what it is that is assertedly changing. Change, when it exists, is change of something with a specific identity—whether this is a norm, a relationship, or the divorce rate. Failure to specify the identity or what is changing can easily lead to confusion.

Once we have established the identity of what is changing, the next consideration is the level at which change takes place. Even though the concept of social change is inclusive of all social phenomena, in reality, we cannot study and comprehend change without knowing where it takes place. Thus, we need to identify the location in the social system in which a particular change is occurring. We can establish several units of study and focus our attention, for example, on the following levels: individuals, groups, organizations, institutions, and society.

Thus, change is becoming "social" and we are also becoming a bit more specific with our question. We might now pose the question, "What is changing and at what level?" We are now talking about the scope of change in relation to the number of persons or groups whose norms or social arrangement change; that is, the location of a particular change in a social system as well as the type of norm, attribute, or relationship that has changed. For example, on the individual level we can talk about changes in attitudes, beliefs, aspirations, and motivations. On the group level we might consider changes in the types of interaction patterns—in communication, methods of conflict resolution, cohesion, unity, competition, and acceptance and rejection patterns. At the level of organizations, the scope of change would include alterations in the structure and function of organizations and changes in hierarchy, communication, role relationship, productivity, recruitment, and socialization patterns. At the institutional level, change may include alterations in marriage and family patterns, education, and religious practices. At the level of society, change may be seen as the modification of the social stratification, economic, and political systems. In the context of the discussion, the level at which change takes place will be easily discernible to the reader.

Now we are getting closer. We know roughly what is changing and at what level. So we might as well be a bit more specific and raise the question, "How long does it take for a certain type of change to come about?" In other words, we are referring to the rate of change. That is, at what rate does a specific change take place? The rate of change can be measured by a specific set of time intervals such as days, months, years, decades, or centuries; or, it can be designated as slow or rapid. Obviously, rate—that is, time in a comparative sense—enters into the study of social change through the use of words such as long-term or short-term, and will be an important consideration in discussing the duration of change.

The magnitude of change is somewhat more difficult to delineate. As an illustration, the classic three-part scheme proposed by Robert Dahl (1967) for measuring the magnitude of political change—incremental or marginal, comprehensive, and revolutionary—is suggested. Incremental or marginal changes would be those that expand, reduce, or otherwise modify the contours of a particular norm or behavior without altering or repudiating its basic substance or structure. There is consensus in the literature that incremental change is the most common and "normal" pattern of change in the United States. Comprehensive changes might represent the culmination of related incremental changes, or, in Dahl's terms, "sweeping innovations or decisive reversals of established" (1967:264) norms or behavior patterns. Changes of revolutionary magnitude would involve wholesale substitution of one type of norm or behavior for another and decisive rejection of the original behavior as well.

To round off our contemplations about the nature of change, we need to ask whether a particular change at a particular level is deliberate or unplanned. Deliberate or planned social change refers to inventing or developing social technologies consistent with existing social and behavioral knowledge and adequate to the practical and moral requirements of contemporary change situations. At the individual level, for example, it might be changing attitudes and behavior toward minorities. On the organizational level, it may entail attempts to increase efficiency and productivity. At the institutional level, the object may be to create more educational opportunities for disadvantaged students. At the level of society, change may entail the replacement of one political and economic system by another as evidenced by recent large-scale transformations in Eastern Europe.

The unplanned consequences of change, an important but often overlooked component, include the unanticipated and the dysfunctional results of a planned change. For example, the federal minimum wage law, set at $5.15 an hour in 1997 and still in effect in 2003 (state minimum wage laws vary and they tend to be higher: For example in Washington it was $7.01 in early 2003), was intended to provide unskilled laborers with an income slightly above the poverty level (see, for example, Neumark and Wascher, 2002). Unintentionally, however, this provision has contributed to an increase in teenage unemployment, particularly among black youth, and reduced job prospects for low-wage earners, and played a role in the increase in the gender wage gap (Shannon, 1996). When the minimum wage increased in the past, employers tended to hire more part-time than full-time workers and the overall level of hiring was lower (*The Wall Street Journal*, 1987:60).

There are other examples of unintended consequences. In an attempt to stop the rampant theft of expensive cars, manufacturers in the 1990s started to make ignitions very difficult to hot-wire. This lowered the chances that cars would be stolen from parking lots, but apparently contributed to the sudden appearance of a new and far more dangerous crime—carjacking. To help merchants to protect and verify the identity of their customers, financial institutions and marketing firms have created huge computerized databases of personal information: Social Security numbers, credit card numbers, telephone numbers, bank account numbers (checks, direct billing, etc.), home addresses, and the like. With these databases being increasingly interconnected by the Internet, they have become tempting targets for computer-savvy criminals. From 1995 to 2000 the incidence of identity theft tripled, with no signs of abatement (Mann, 2002)

In sum, when considering social change, it is helpful to specify its identity (what is changing), and to determine its level, rate of change, magnitude, causes, and consequences. With this in mind, let us examine various ways of looking at social change.

CONCEPTUALIZATIONS OF SOCIAL CHANGE

There are about as many ways of describing social change as there are ways of studying societies (Chirot, 1986:2). It is a ubiquitous buzz word for politicians, and change is the first thing newly hired academic administrators talk about. Economists, demographers, anthropologists, political scientists, historians, and sociologists bring their own special disciplines to the diverse conceptualizations of change (see, for example, Lindblom, 1997). Even among sociologists, discussions of social change often begin with complaints about the lack of uniformity concerning the definition of change. The point is well taken, for practically every book on social change has a section on definitions, conditioned by the author's theoretical and ideological orientation, in an attempt to narrow the concept. There is a multiplicity of such ventures emphasizing different features, and the following sample of definitions will focus on the principal areas of emphasis in post–Second World War social change literature. The elements that are variously highlighted over time are group activities, structure and functions, and social relationships.

Different Group Activities

In its most concrete sense, social change means that large numbers of people are engaging in group activities and relationships that are different from those in which they or their parents engaged in some time before. As stated by Hans Gerth and C. Wright Mills: "By social change we refer to whatever may happen in the course of time to the roles, the institutions, or the orders comprising a social structure, their emergence, growth and decline" (1953:398). Society is a complex network of patterns of relationships in which all the members participate in varying degrees. These relationships change, and behavior changes at the same time. Individuals are faced with new situations to which they must respond. These situations reflect such factors as the introduction of new techniques, new ways of making a living, changes in place of residence, and new innovations, ideas, and social values. Thus, social change means modifications of the way people work, rear a family, educate their children, govern themselves, and seek ultimate meaning in life.

Change in the Structure of Society

Many sociologists view social change as a change in the structure of society or alteration of the social structure, such as the structural transformation of small, isolated and illiterate societies (Riches, 1995). For instance, Morris Ginsberg (1958:205) writes: "By social change I understand a change in the social structure, for example, the size of a society, the composition or balance of its parts or the type of its organizations. Examples of such changes are the contraction in the size of the family . . . the breaking up of the domainal economy with the rise of the cities, the transition from 'estates' to social classes. . . ." Viewed from a somewhat different perspective, "Social change is the significant alteration of social structures (that is, of patterns of social action and interaction), including consequences and manifestations of such structures embodied in norms (rules of conduct), values and cultural products and symbols" (Moore, 1968:366).

It is understandable why social structure (patterns of social behavior that include statuses, roles, groups, and institutions such as the family, religion, politics, and the economic system) is being emphasized in change. Social structures are not stable, tightly integrated, or harmonious, but are unstable, loosely put together, and torn by dissension. To ignore this profound phenomenon and process is to miss a central fact about societies.

Change in the Structure and Functioning of Society

Others stress that social change is not only a change in the structure, but also in the functioning of society. "Social change comprises modifications in social systems or subsystems in structure, functioning, or process over some period of time" (Allen, 1971:39). Similarly, "By 'social change' is meant only such alterations as occur in social organization—that is, the structure and functions of society" (Davis, 1949:622). Harry M. Johnson (1960:626, 628) goes into some detail in observing that: "Social change is change in the structure of a social system; what has been stable or relatively unchanging changes. Moreover, of structural changes the most important are those that have consequences for the functioning of the system—for attaining its goals more (or less) efficiently or for fulfilling more (or less) efficiently the conditions that must be met if the system is to survive at all." These classic conceptualizations can be illustrated by the large-scale transformation taking place in Taiwan since the 1960s that have accompanied massive economic development, industrialization, and urbanization (Marsh, 1996).

Change in Social Relationships

Some authors consider social change principally in terms of a specific change in social relationships. For example, "By social change is meant changes in social relationships . . . the changing ways in which human beings relate to one another" (MacIver & Page, 1949:511). A generation later, in the same vein, Judson R. Landis (2000:229) writes: "Social change refers to change in the structure and functioning of the social relationships of a society."

Change in Social Structure and Social Relationships

Ronald Edari (1976:2) combines both elements, social structure and social relationships, in his definition: "When we talk of social change, we mean, at the very minimum, two things: a) the change in the constitution of social entities over time, and b) the change in the relations among entities over time." Taking a somewhat broader and more inclusive view, Robert A. Nisbet (1969:168) views social change as "a succession of differences in time within a persisting identity." Robert H. Lauer (1991:4) considers change as ". . . an inclusive concept that refers to alterations in social phenomena at various levels of human life from the individual to the global," and John J.

Macionis (2002:638) in a popular introductory text simply sums it up as "the transformation of culture and social institutions over time."

A Working Definition of Social Change

A common difficulty with these definitions of social change is the problem of reification, the tendency to equate conceptual abstractions of reality with an actual piece of reality. We can isolate the elements emphasized in the definitions, which include the social structure, the functioning of society, social relationships, forms of social processes, and time. But we still have difficulties in understanding what is changing. The term "change" is often used loosely, and as it has been illustrated, attempts at definitions are sufficiently numerous and conflicting as to be of much help.

At this point, I propose a different approach toward a workable definition of social change. For the present purpose, social change is conceptualized as the process of planned or unplanned qualitative or quantitative alterations in social phenomena that can be analyzed in terms of five interrelated components. For the sake of simplicity, these components are called identity, level, duration, magnitude, and rate of change.

> *Identity* of change refers to a specific social phenomenon undergoing transformation such as a definite practice, behavior, attitude, interaction pattern, authority structure, productivity rate, voting pattern, prestige, and stratification system.
>
> *Level* of change delineates the location in a social system where a particular change takes place. Several levels may be designated, such as individual, group, organization, institution, and society.
>
> *Duration* refers to the question of how long a particular change form endures after it has been accepted. It may refer to the life span of long-term or short-term (transitory) change phenomena.
>
> *Magnitude* may be based on the three-part scheme of incremental or marginal, comprehensive, and revolutionary changes, as discussed in the preceding section.
>
> *Rate* of change may be based on any arbitrary scale, such as fast or slow, continuous or spasmodic, orderly or erratic.

These dimensions of change are arbitrary and may be construed differently by those who are experiencing it or experimenting with it. However, when specific meanings are assigned to these dimensions, this conceptualization of social change can become a useful point of departure for empirical and theoretical endeavors in social change. With this background, we can now turn to the question: Why is social change inevitable? What is there in the nature of humans, society, and culture that demands and produces change? What are the reasons for the massive social changes we are facing today? What are the sources of change? Many different factors interact to generate changes in people's behavior and in the culture and structure of their society. Many of these factors are critical in making change inevitable, and a few of them will be considered briefly in the following pages.

SOURCES OF CHANGE

There are several specific factors that generate changes in society, and an understanding of the different factors relevant to any change is required to be able to initiate and manage them (Perkins, 1997). The ones considered important in the sociological literature include technology, ideology, competition, conflict, political and economic factors, and structural strains. All these sources of change are in many ways interrelated. Economic, political, and technological factors go hand in hand with ideology, competition, conflict, and structural strains. Consequently, one should be careful not to assign undue weight to any one of these causes of change. Admittedly, it is often tempting and convenient to single out one "prime mover," one factor, one cause, one explanation, and use it indiscriminately in a number of situations. But this can result in an incomplete and possibly erroneous explanation of the phenomenon under consideration. With this in mind, let us turn to the examination of the sources of change.

Technology

Modern social theory is concerned with the rapidly growing role technology plays in social change (MacKenzie, 1996). By way of illustration, let us turn to David M. Freeman's (1974:12) often cited description of the impact of technology (systematic knowledge, tools, and machines involved in the production of goods and services) by compressing it into a time frame. If we consider the approximately 5-billion-year lifetime of the earth scaled down to the past eighty days, then:

1. Life appeared sixty days ago.
2. Humans in their earliest forms appeared one hour ago.
3. The Stone Age started six minutes ago.
4. Modern humans appeared less than one minute ago.
5. The agricultural revolution occurred fifteen seconds ago.
6. Metals were utilized ten seconds ago.
7. The industrial revolution began three-tenths of one second ago.

Technology's capacity to change both the circumstances of human life and the character of social institutions is quite recent and, as the time frame indicates, is occurring at an increasingly rapid rate worldwide.

A noted characteristic of technology is exponential growth, as illustrated by the curve in Figure 1.1. It can be applied to such diverse phenom-

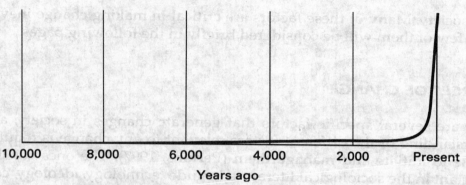

FIGURE 1.1 An exponential growth curve. This curve can be roughly applied to growth in several areas—for example, inventions, energy consumption, or population. For instance, world population growth clearly exhibits exponentiality. At the beginning of the Christian era, there were only 200 to 300 million persons on earth. By 1650, humankind totaled about 500 million. Three hundred years later, in 1950, the figure was more than 2,500 million, and, in 1994, it was over 5,600 million. By the year 2000, the world population was well over 6,000 million.

ena as the number of books written, energy consumption, and population growth. Exponential growth is growth that doubles within equal periods of time. Many aspects of modern development exceed this minimum requirement and are doubling in decreasing intervals of time, such as the consumption of energy or the depletion of certain natural resources, such as fossil fuels.

Positive and Negative Features of Technology It is easy to demonstrate that throughout history technological innovations have often been a moving force in social change. For example, changes in agricultural technology resulted in food surpluses necessary for the growth of cities. The introduction of steam power pushed the world into the Industrial Revolution, which altered gender, work and culture (see, for example, Goldstone, 1996). Changes in weapon technology often upset empires and nations (the long bow in Europe and the atomic bomb in Japan), and the discovery of the cotton gin revitalized a dying slave trade and helped to plant the seeds for the American Civil War.

The influence of technology reverberates in the lives of individuals in society, in social values, in the structure and functions of social institutions, and in the political organizations of society. Technology creates not only new alternatives and opportunities but also new problems for humans (Mesthene, 1986). It has both positive and negative effects that often occur at the same time. These ramifications can be seen even as a result of minor technological innovations such as the introduction of the snowmobile into northern areas such as Alaska and Lapland, where it remains the preferred mode of transportation (Brown, 2002). The snowmobile drastically changed patterns of reindeer herding and hunting. It shortened the work-week of the hunters and trappers dramatically, increased their leisure time, increased their earnings, established a new basis for stratification in the community (who owns and who does not own a snowmobile), and it generated a serious ecological imbalance as populations of snowbound game animals were wiped out (Pelto & Muller-Willie, 1987).

The Steel Ax among the Yir Yoront Even the introduction of less sophisticated technology—such as, for example, the steel ax—can create far-reaching and unforeseen effects in other aspects of the social system. Consider the example of the Yir Yoront tribe of southeastern Australia, who depended on the stone ax as their most basic and essential tool for many centuries (Sharp, 1952). For them the stone ax was more than a tool; it was a symbol of status, of male dominance, and of basic rights of ownership. It played a role in religious ceremonies and was considered as one of the tribe's most valued objects. When a person needed an ax, he would approach one of the leaders to ask permission to use it. Only if the leader considered him worthy would permission be granted. The very scarcity of this valuable tool made access to it a considerable privilege; thus, it served as a means of social control.

Then came the Caucasians, bringing modern technology in the form of steel axes. But instead of progress, the introduction of the steel ax resulted in a drastic upheaval of the social structure of the tribe. It had the following effects:

1. In order to get a steel ax, it was necessary to go to the mission or to a trader and act "deserving, industrious, and dependent." That resulted in a decrease in self-reliance.

2. Possession of the ax had been considered a status symbol and a sign of manhood, but the Caucasians at times gave them directly to young men and children, resulting in the upset of status relations between the young and the old.

3. Similarly, in the past no woman could own an ax. Europeans often gave axes to women to use as their own, thereby upsetting the status relations between males and females.

4. Prior to the introduction of the ax, there was no overall leader or chief of the tribe. However, when dealing with the whites, it was necessary to appoint one or two spokesmen, who gradually acquired more power than they were entitled to traditionally, creating a leader group form of organization in the tribe.

5. Easy access to axes diluted the entire notion of ownership and upset the norms of ownership, thus resulting in an increase in the incidence of stealing and trespassing.

6. Members of the tribe had explained the origins of every major artifact they possessed with some myth showing how the article was given to them by a distant mythical ancestor. Because they had very few artifacts and their technology was virtually stagnant, it was quite easy for them to believe in these stories. However, there was no mythical explanation for the origins of steel axes; the source was obvious. The result was to cast suspicion on the other myths and on the very structure of their religion.

In contemporary society, it is hard to find such dramatic changes in the social systems produced by one single piece of technology such as the steel ax among the Yir Yoront tribe. The closest we could come would be the number of changes followed by the series of technological innovations known as the Industrial Revolution. The basis of one's livelihood moved from the farm to the factory and from the country to the city. The size of individual enterprise changed as new methods of operation and financing became necessary to exploit technological innovation, resulting in the establishment of entirely new industries. The twentieth century has seen the rise of such mass complexes as the automobile, steel, rubber, glass, petroleum, and textile industries and, more recently, the chemical, aviation, and electronics industries. In a society increasingly dominated by mass industries, new social classes reflect the different productive functions. The big industrial unions are playing an important role in bringing about new power relations between labor and management.

Technology and Work The spread of technological and scientific developments in the workplace has been accompanied by a variety of changes. In analyzing how technological forces influence human activities, Neil J. Smelser (1976:96) suggests the following:

1. The technical arrangements of work determine in large part the amount of physical exertion required from the human organism.
2. The technical features of the job influence the degree to which work is paced and human activities are structured.
3. The technical arrangements of production influence the level of skills required of workers.
4. Technical aspects determine in part the degree of specialization of the division of labor and the structuring of authority.
5. Technological features of work influence the character of social interaction. . . . This influence often extends to off-the-job interaction as well.

The change from human to machine technology has transformed work in the industrial era. It resulted in the imposition of a steady pace or rhythm for work, bringing with it an increase in the discipline imposed on workers.

This was the result of the need for the uninterrupted flow of material and the fact that workers must be organized around the machines' schedule. Because of the imposition of a steady pace and discipline, workers and work became increasingly time-oriented, which in turn affected other aspects of nonwork time (Linder, 1970).

When the technical aspects of work are highly routinized, monotonous, and devoid of much personal interaction, such as on the assembly lines in an automobile factory, Robert Blauner (1964:15–34) notes that workers become alienated, to the extent that they are powerless at carrying out their work (that is, they have no control over quantity, quality, direction, and pace of work), or to the extent that their work is meaningless (that is, it has no clear relation to a broader life program or production program), or to the extent that they are self-estranged (they do not identify with their work or enjoy it or find it challenging), or to the extent that they are socially isolated from their supervisors and co-workers.

Technological developments can also bring about alterations in the composition of the workforce. Of the 19 million new jobs created in the United States during the 1970s, only a small percentage was in the manufacturing sector. Almost 90 percent of the jobs—some 17 million new openings—were in the service and information sectors (Naisbitt and Aburdene 1990:17). Many of the new jobs that were created in the nonmanufacturing sector are attributable to the significant advances made in computer technology during the past few years and the increased utilization of microcomputers in the workforce, which requires specially trained workers (*Economist*, 1994a: 2–22).

In addition to changes in the labor force, countless social effects can be attributed directly or indirectly to innovations in technology. For example, with the introduction of computers, microwave transmissions, television and satellites, we have moved from a state of information scarcity to one of information surplus, and now we are producing information much faster than we can process it. This creates what one author calls "data smog" (Shenk, 1997) and results in increased stress or "technostress" (Weil & Rosen, 1997), memory overload, compulsive behavior and attention deficit disorder. Many other effects will be discussed in detail in Chapter 7. Technology's capacity to contribute to social change is increasing worldwide, with a much more rapid rate of growth in developing countries (Bernard & Pelto, 1987). In the following section, another important source of change, ideology, will be examined.

Ideology

An ideology is a complex belief system that explains social and political arrangements and relationships (Baradat, 1999; Feuer, 1975; Funderburk & Thobaben, 1994; Gouldner, 1976; McCarthy, 1994) and underlies all social and political discourse and actions (Freire & Macedo, 1998). The functions of ideology are the legitimization and rationalization of behavior and social relationships; the provision of a basis for solidarity in a group or society; and the motivation of individuals for certain types of action. In social change, the role of ideology can be analyzed different ways. It can promote stability and support the status quo, or it can contribute to change. It may be either a dependent or independent variable in accounting for any process of stability or change. In this section, ideology will be examined only as a source of change.

Ideology and Change Max Weber's highly influential study of the development of capitalism represents one of the most thorough efforts yet made to establish a relationship between ideology and social change. As discussed in the section on social-psychological theories of change, Weber wanted to establish the principle that ideas as well as technological developments and economic structures could be determining factors in bringing about change. To do this, in *The Protestant Ethic and the Spirit of Capitalism,* he set out to identify the major factors responsible for the rise of capitalism as it had developed in Western societies—the type of capitalism characterized by double-entry bookkeeping, uniform pricing, systematic planning, and bureaucratic social organization.

Weber acknowledged that the development of industrial technology increased agricultural productivity, and improvements in sanitation, preventive medicine, and better methods of transportation had all been necessary to the development of capitalism, but he found the determining factor not in science or technology but in what he called "the Protestant ethic." Calvinism, Weber maintained, made possible the emergence of capitalism by providing people in Western societies with a new "this-worldly" orientation. In focusing their attention on such values as individualism, hard work, and frugality, it paved the way for a major restructuring of economic life.

Economic and sociopolitical changes are often associated with ideological shifts (Schatz & Gutierrez-Rexach, 2002). More than a century ago, Karl Marx argued that the ruling ideas of any society are the ideas of its ruling classes. His point was that ideologies do not fall from the sky, nor are they "things" that have a life of their own. Ideologies must be developed and maintained; an ideology must be transmitted to new generations or it will soon perish; and the implications of an ideology for specific issues and events must be determined and communicated because powerful groups and institutions are better able to succeed in this process than are less powerful groups. It is often their ideologies that are propagated.

Perhaps the best case for demonstrating the independent role of ideologies in social change at the macro level is Marxism.

> As an ideology, as an active critic of established "capitalist" values and norms, and as the active propagator of "socialist" values and norms, Marxism may

have caused more social change than any other force in the modern world. In both industrial and would-be industrial societies, its consequences have been very great. Only nationalist ideology, which is also a powerful and independent type of ideological system in the modern world and which the universalistic values expressed in Marxism have consistently neglected or underrated, might be said to have had an influence on modern social change of the same magnitude as Marxism. It can be argued that Marxist and nationalist ideologies together have caused as much social change as changes arising in the economy or polity. (Barber, 1971:260)

At this point, it should be noted that since the eighteenth century, social theorists are divided on the question of the relative importance of ideology and technology in social change, and the division has continued down to the present day. Many have argued for the dominance of ideology, others for the greater importance of technology (Nolan & Lenski, 1996).

The Ideology of the Conjugal Family At a somewhat lesser degree of comprehensives in social systems, in the structure of family systems "we can again see the independent influence of ideology on social change, in the case of the worldwide change toward prevalence of the conjugal family" (Barber, 1971:260). William J. Goode (1963:19) provides a great deal of evidence both for the change and for the influence of ideology.

One important source of change is the ideology of "economic progress" and technological development, as well as the ideology of the conjugal family, and spokesmen for both appear in non-Western countries before any great changes are observable either in industrial or family areas of life.

Elders may deplore both ideologies, but both appeal to the intellectuals, often trained in Western schools, and to the young, to women, and generally, to the disadvantaged. The ideology of the conjugal family is a radical one, destructive of the older traditions in almost every society. It grows from a set of more general radical principles which also arouse these groups politically in perhaps every underdeveloped country. Its appeal is almost as universal as that of "redistribution of the land." It asserts the equality of individuals as against class, caste, or sex barriers.

The ideology of the conjugal family proclaims the right of the individual to choose his or her own spouse, place to live, and even which kin obligations to accept, as against the acceptance of others' decisions. It asserts the worth of the individual as against the inherited elements of wealth or ethnic group. The individual is to be evaluated, not his lineage. A strong theme of "democracy" runs through this ideology. It encourages love, which in every major civilization has been given a prominent place in fantasy, poetry, art, and legend, as a wonderful, perhaps even exalted, experience, even when its reality was guarded against. Finally, it asserts that if one's family life is unpleasant, one has the right to change it.

Utopian Ideologies Sir Thomas More's famous book *Utopia* was published in 1516. It described an ideal society. Since that time, thousands of utopian schemes have been proposed on the basis of ideologies that "justify or criticize an imagined social system in which new values and norms prevail in a way that seems to current common sense knowledge or social science knowledge to be impossible" (Barber, 1971:262).

An example of utopian ideology is the Platonic ideology criticizing the conjugal family as a bastion of social inequality and recommending a familyless society. This system of sexual sharing has been tried repeatedly in contemporary communes. Among the several American communities that attempted to do away with sexual exclusiveness, only the Oneida community (we shall examine it in detail in Chapter 5), which flourished in upper New York State in the mid-nineteenth century, persisted for any length of time. Even though this Platonic ideology for a familyless society may not bring about the abolition of the conjugal family, it may aid in changes that could reduce the inegalitarian effects of the family, changes such as making property inheritance or access to education more equal.

A utopian ideology may still have considerable effects for social change, short of full realization of the utopia itself. "Utopian ideologies are exceptionally dramatic and often powerful systems of ideas that at least tell us the social directions our values and norms do or do not prefer" (Barber, 1971:262). Historically, several utopian ideologies contributed to major changes. The early ideology of Christianity is still with us; the Anabaptist ideology that preceded the Reformation in Germany generated a tradition that has survived to this day among pietist communities like the Amish and the Hutterites (Rise & Steinmetz, 1956). The Zionist ideology in the early twentieth century fostered the formation of a type of utopian community called the *kibbutz*, and there are more than 200 of these communities in modern Israel (Spiro, 1956). Finally, in recent years, utopian ideologies resulted in the formation of utopian communities in the United States for such diverse purposes as sexual sharing, political indoctrination, the practice of Buddhism, and the rehabilitation of drug addicts. There is even a historical dictionary of more than 600 entries about utopian communities and their founders (Trahair, 1999). The search for the "perfect place" continues in the literature on utopia (Schaer & Claeys, 2001).

Utopian ideology also plays an important part in the strategy of social change; ". . . inventing and designing the shape of the future by extrapolating what we know of in the present is to envision a direction for planning and action in the present. If the image of a potential future is convincing and rationally persuasive to men in the present, the image may become part of the dynamics and motivation of present action" (Chin & Benne, 1985:30). We shall return to this point in the discussion of strategies of social change.

Political Ideologies Of all types of ideologies, and there are many, political ideologies have an impact on the principal institutions of society

(Baradat, 1999; Funderburk & Thobaben, 1994). They are the source for action and, as such, perhaps the most important source of social change. The degree to which individuals ascribe to any political ideology affects their perception of the social structure and their notion of reality, which in turn guides their behavior. Examples of the main types of political ideologies include communism (a classless society in which private ownership of production ended, the state withered away along with other major institutions, and alienation ended); democratic socialism (a movement striving to attain the goals of socialism within the context of representative constitutional government); liberalism (there are two broad types: (1) classical, emphasizing the ideology of individualism, private property and limited government and (2) modern, which strives to use social programs to create conditions conducive to individual development in the context of private property and constitutional government); conservatism (contending that liberty, private property, and constitutional government is best conserved by emphasizing tradition, stability, and very gradual social and political change); and authoritarianism (in which power is concentrated in the hands of a few, usually military, clerical, or political elites).

Competition

Competition in society arises from the scarcity of goods, statuses, and services that are universally desired. In the struggle for scarce commodities, competition is usually restrained by tradition, custom, or law (see, for example, Waheeduzzaman, 2002). Because these limiting factors keep it within bounds, unrestricted competition is seldom found in actual behavior (Cvitkovic, 1993). Competition is an impersonal struggle for limited ends in accordance with socially prescribed rules. The goals of competition are likewise socially defined. Competition is both an effect and a cause of social change. It is an effect in that a changing society has more goals open to competition than a static society. It causes social change by forcing individuals to adopt new forms of behavior to attain desired goals.

Competition for scarce resources has been an ever-present feature of human societies. Marx and the socialistic philosophers condemned competition—in particular, capitalistic competition—as a means for exploiting the worker. On the other hand, evolutionists such as William Graham Sumner and Herbert Spencer, as will be discussed in Chapter 2, have lauded competition as the means whereby selection and progress were achieved. The renowned German sociologist Georg Simmel believed that "competition is endemic in any organization," and he seriously doubted "the ability of either capitalistic or socialistic organizations to reduce competition significantly" (Duke, 1976:107).

Competition is present in a number of social arrangements. Competition between business firms for markets and profits is an inherent part of capitalism. Historically, the concept of competition was used to justify reduced hours of work, business opposition to unions, wage increases, paid vacations, health and safety regulations, antipollution laws and so on (Rinehart, 1995). It is also evident among government agencies as they compete for a share of the tax dollar or among religious organizations as they compete for members and their support. (Religious and other voluntary organizations must also compete with alternative organizations for membership and money.) Competition to a great extent controls the organization's "choice of goals," in that its energies must be turned to their competitive activity.

Thus, competition can result in changes within the competing organizations. When there are competitors in the environment who could reduce the security, prestige, and profit of an organization, it can be expected that the organization will take action to overcome the threat from the competition (Hall, 2002:114–116). Such action would entail a greater emphasis on the security of the organization, evidenced in a variety of ways such as greater stress on employee loyalty, efficiency in the work process, and added emphasis on protecting confidential material. There is also a greater tendency to monitor the environment, especially the competing segments of that environment that can produce changes in the principal activities and the internal normative structure (policies, rules, departmentalization, positions) of the organization. It can also result in increased manipulation of the environment, which may be seen in the form of lobbying, political sabotage, or even in such efforts as contributing time and money to such civic efforts as the United Way campaign. It can also result in attempts either to absorb or banish the competition (Hetzler, 1969:250). Thus, competition can force an organization to change its character to become more complex and more dynamic, thereby influencing the internal structure of organizations.

In sum, when competition is carried out legitimately for the allocation of scarce resources, it can be seen as an effective instrument of social change with positive results: ". . . a regenerative force that interjects new vitality into a social structure and becomes the basis of social reorganization" (Blau, 1967:301). In the next section, we examine a form of competition called conflict.

Conflict

Both competition and conflict are characterized by an attempt of two or more parties to reach certain objectives. But the two terms are not identical. Parties in a competition are seeking the same goal, and they must abide by the rules. Parties in a conflict believe they have incompatible goals, and often it involves attempts by adversaries to threaten, injure, or otherwise coerce each other (Kriesberg, 1982:17; Rubin et al., 1994:5–6). Unlike competition, which is continuous and impersonal, conflict is conscious, intermittent, and personal. The emotions of distrust, hatred, suspicion, and fear are accentuated in conflict. Conflict emphasizes the differences between parties and minimizes their similarities (Fleming, 2000; Lulops, 1994).

Conflict is omnipresent in human societies. "The inevitability of conflict derives from mankind's innumerable and changing needs: if starvation is ended, men will fight for prestige; if one power system is destroyed, another emerges; if authority is eradicated, men will compete for precedence. There will be always a scarcity of 'commodities'—whether it be money, prestige, power, love—that will continue to set man against man. Therefore, all men will experience some form of conflict during their lifetime" (McCord & McCord, 1977:4). Conflict may occur among individuals in organizations, in institutions, in communities, in societies, or among nations. It is considered to be endemic to all social relations.

According to John Howard (1974:3–4), substantive conflict centers around the distribution of highly valued and scarce resources. He identifies three other bases of conflict: conflict over symbolic issues, as in the refusal to pledge alliance to the national flag; the conflict of ideologies, such as sexism and racism, which have been created to justify the advantages of various groups; and cultural conflict, resulting from differences in lifestyles and values, such as the repudiation of middle-class lifestyles by many American youth in the 1960s.

As it will be pointed out in the section on theories of conflict in Chapter 2, conflict should not be construed solely as having negative connotations. It can have many other consequences. For example, groups in conflict are likely to increase their internal solidarity and minimize intragroup disagreements. Conflict may also be a factor in the creation of innovative or creative strategies of benevolent intentions, and conflicting situations may result in various forms of accommodation or adjustment or other efforts to compromise or to alleviate tensions and underlying causes.

Conflicts are of primary significance in social change of and within a system (Coser, 1974). But the relationships between conflict and social change are neither simple nor always direct. Although conflict is an important source of change, change may occur without conflict. When conflict does result in change, that particular change may not be seen as desirable by those who are affected by it. The conditions under which conflict impels or impedes change, and those under which it impels change in a socially desirable direction, have yet to be indicated (Lauer, 1991). But, as Coser writes, "What is important for us is the idea that conflict prevents the ossification of the social system by exerting pressure for innovation and creativity" (1974:458). Conflict can generate new social norms and institutions and it may be directly stimulating in the economic and technologic realm (Carty & Singer, 1993). In the Marxian framework, total social systems undergo transformation through conflict.

In some conflict-laden situations, however, a relationship may be established between certain types of conflict conditions and the specific changes they have produced. Louis Kriesberg (2002; 1982:246–258), who systematically gathered evidence on the emergence of social conflicts and the processes of their escalation and de-escalation, gives some illustrative outcomes for conflict situations between workers and managers, university students and administrators, blacks and whites, females and males, and in the international arena. To Kriesberg's list, we can add the various conflicts that arose across Eastern Europe and the former Soviet Union as a result of the sudden economic and political changes that took place in the late 1980s and early 1990s and the religious and political conflicts that are currently happening in the Middle East and Africa (Amason, 1993; Wejnert, 2002; Sandole-Stratoste, 2002).

Workers versus Managers The principal objective of trade unions has been to improve the working conditions and raise the wages of their members. The turbulent years of the unionization movement have produced a series of changes (Jacobs, 1994). There has been a general increase in the material well-being of the workers in an absolute sense: Working conditions have improved; fringe benefits have increased; the number of hours at work has decreased; and, in general, the prestige of blue-collar workers has gone up over the years. For example, full-time West Coast dock workers who load and unload ships made on average nearly $100,000 a year in 2002, while clerks who keep track of cargo movements averaged $120,000. Not only does the medical coverage for active longshoremen require no out-of pocket expenses, but the same holds true for retirees. The benefit package averages $42,000 a year, more than many Americans make a year (Greenhouse, 2002).

Similarly, in Western European countries, there have been some important gains. In France, for example, truck drivers and employees of the national railroads can retire with full benefits at the age of 55; in the event of a lay-off in Germany, the former employee will receive 78 percent of wages for two years and generous benefits after that; in the Netherlands, workers with a 20 percent disability will receive 70 percent of their previous wage (Sawyer, 1997:4B). However, Kriesberg's observation of a generation ago is still accurate: "More fundamental changes in the structure of the economy, the role of workers in it, and income differentials between workers and managers, were not sought by most trade unions and did not occur" (1982:247).

University Students versus Administrators Although university students have been engaged in conflict over community, national, and international issues ever since the 1960s, there are also more recent conflicts about the role of the university in international, national, and community affairs. These include university investment policies, such as those involving South Africa; research activities that have military implications, such as the

Strategic Defense Initiative (the so-called Star Wars program aimed at developing a space-based defense against ballistic missiles); "sweatshop" stores and companies that use child labor at low wage at the overseas facilities in Asia and Latin America, and certain types of university expansions involving the relocation of impoverished local residents. Other conflicts are related to academic matters, such as the relevance of certain courses or programs, methods of teaching, grading, student involvement in promotion and tenure decisions, dormitory rules, censorship of student publications, control over university organizations, and the treatment of students from minority and "victimized" groups.

By the end of the 1960s, major changes had occurred on campuses. Dormitory rules were relaxed so that in many places members of the opposite sex were permitted not only to visit but to stay overnight; consumption of alcoholic beverages was allowed; administrative control over student publications declined (Vago, 2003:281–285); and important changes took place in curriculum and grading procedures. Special programs in black studies, women's studies, gay studies and environmental studies had been added to the curriculum on many campuses. A politically correct vocabulary has been introduced over the years with a growing list of words to be avoided along with sanctions for their use. (Even at faculty parties and in locker rooms, professors and administrators are becoming more and more sensitive and circumscribed in their choice of words and even the most brazen of them would think twice before using euphemisms such as "broads" for women or "pimples" for students.) Grading has been relaxed and there is a growing preoccupation with grade inflation in academic circles, language requirements for doctoral programs have been eliminated, and new options such as the pass-or-fail system, cyber courses, or credit for "real-life" experience were introduced. Some universities have terminated their contracts with the federal government or with private industries because of activities considered undesirable by students.

In general, students have gained more direct control of university affairs, particularly as they relate to internal matters. They serve on various committees, in some cases as voting members. More and more, they also participate in faculty recruitment, promotion, and tenure procedures. There is a growing legalism on campus: Students consider themselves buyers of education, they see their relationship with the university as contractual, they treat education like other consumer items, and there is insistence on the proper return for their educational dollars. In economic terms, the relationship of student to teacher is that of the buyer to seller or client to professional. Just like in the marketplace, the number of disputes over products is on the rise on campuses along with conflicts over grades (many professors are reluctant to fail a student or assign a low grade because of the probable complications, lengthy justifications, grievance committees and the possibility of litigation), utility, and relevance of course content (Vago, 2003:283).

But as Kriesberg (1982:249) warned, presciently, that "It would be an error . . . to regard all these changes as the product of a simple conflict between students and administrators and faculty in which coercion was the sole or even dominant way of changing the other side's position." To a considerable extent, these changes have reflected the dominant ideas in society, ideas that students have helped to formulate. Some of these changes also reflect non-conflicting forces, such as the change in the economy and in the population of students, who then instigated changes in the curriculum as a form of market response.

Blacks versus Whites As a consequence of the racial conflict of the 1960s, there have been important collective gains for blacks (Kriesberg, 1982:250–252). Examples of these aggregate gains include the increase in educational opportunities and attainment; a reduction of income differences between blacks and whites; and a drop in the proportion of blacks below the poverty level. In 2002, about 85 percent of blacks had finished high school, 32 percent attended college and 14 percent had a college degree. For whites, the figures are 92 percent high school graduates, 29 percent attended college, and 30 percent had a college degree. About 63 percent of blacks age 16 and over were in the labor force, compared with 67 percent of whites. Per capita income for the same period for blacks was $29,470, compared with $44,517 for whites.

Changes took place in the structure of dominancy (Moland, 1996), and there has also been an increase in the collective political power of blacks, especially in the South, in major urban areas, and in the Congress. Although it is true that the day-to-day life of many blacks has not changed, or has improved only marginally in spite of massive effort and major legislation, commentators maintain that many genuinely significant changes have taken place (see, for example, Jones & Morris, 1993). Still, according to a 2002 Gallup Organization poll, Black Americans' assessments of the current state of race relations in the U.S. have been slightly more negative in each of the last two surveys (37% currently characterize them as "somewhat" or "very" bad, compared to 27% in the fall of 1998). White evaluations have been stable over this period, with 29% currently giving a negative evaluation. Nearly four in ten whites, but only 9% of blacks, say that blacks are treated the same as whites in the nation. A majority of blacks express pessimism about whether a solution to the problems of black/white relations in the United States will ever be worked out. Indeed, black Americans are as pessimistic as they have been since the question was first asked in 1993, with 66% claiming that race relations will always be a problem in this country. At the same time, white Americans express less pessimism about the future of black/white relations than at any time since 1993. Currently, 45% of whites say that race relations will always be a problem, and the 21-point gap between white and black Americans' expectations for the future of race relations is the largest that Gallup has recorded.

Females versus Males Not long ago, it was argued without embarrassment that if a man was paid more than a women for doing the same job, it was because he had a family to support; that if a stewardess was fired at the age of 30, she shouldn't want to be flying anyway; and that women just weren't cut out to be cops, soldiers or marathon runners. That these arguments have been resolved in women's favor is one of the biggest changes of our times. In effect, the debate about whether women should have equal pay, opportunities and responsibilities is over.

The collective status of women in recent decades has changed in many ways as a result of their struggle for equality. Women, for the most part, have widened their choices to include not only the role of wife and mother but also a dazzling array of formerly male-dominated professions. Today, well over a third of all lawyers and physicians are women, as are nearly half of all managers and administrators. More than two-thirds of the nation's largest companies have at least one woman director. Women undergraduate and graduate students outnumber their male counterparts. For the first time in American history, a woman appeared on the presidential ticket of a major political party in 1984. As the Democratic vice-presidential candidate, Geraldine Ferraro heralded new opportunities for women in the political process. The number of women holding state and local public offices is rapidly increasing. For example, 21 percent of big city mayors, 20 percent of state senators and 24 percent of state representatives were women in 2002. At the beginning of the 108th Congress, 13.9 percent of congressional representatives and a fourth of the cabinet members were female.

Of course, not all of the changes have been positive. Women are still at a pay disadvantage, although from 1979 to 1993, women's median earnings rose from 62 percent of men's to 77 percent, reflecting women's greater opportunities, greater education and work experience. By 1997, the trend reversed and the median weekly earnings of full-time working women went down to 75 percent as a result of shifts in the work force, such as greater concentration of women in lower paying jobs, partly as a result of the welfare reform of 1997 (Lewin, 1997). By 2002, it went down further, to 72 percent. It is interesting to note that women make more than men in less than 16 percent of all couples (Roberts, 1994). Women's overall physical health has deteriorated relative to men's in recent years. Women are suffering from more ulcers and respiratory ailments than ever before. They also experience a higher incidence of stress and stress-related illnesses. In a sense, they are adopting lifestyles that affect adversely their longevity. American women in the early 2000s continue to perform more household tasks than men, and balance between caregiving and breadearning roles. Women still continue to respect their traditional roles at home in despite of increased gender equality. However, equal standing and economic independence led to an increase in divorce, out-of-wedlock childbearing and same-sex relationships (Bianchi & Spain, 1996).

International Conflicts The most obvious manifestation of conflict at the international level is war (see, for example, Betts, 2001; Fukuyama, 1997; Walt, 1996). The twentieth century has already had more than 200 wars, resulting in a loss of almost 80 million lives (and the twenty-first century has the military capability for even larger numbers of fatalities). This is in addition to the mass killings of 20 million in the former Soviet Union under Stalin's reign of terror, 1936–1953 (Westwood, 2003), and another 20 million during Mao's Cultural Revolution in China between 1966 and 1976 (Masland, 1994). The two world wars alone took over 50 million lives. Two-thirds of the countries of the world, some 97 percent of the global population, have been involved in at least one war in this century (Sivard, 1996:9).

There are many causes of such conflict: War may be triggered by a dispute over a soccer match, as was the case between Honduras and El Salvador. On the other hand, it could be the result of economic expansion; of scarcity of land or resources; or a series of other factors. Most of the armed conflicts that had arisen since the end of the Cold War have been within nations between peoples with ethnic or religious differences, seeking national identities (Shultz, 1995).

The consequences of such hostilities are too well known to catalogue here. However, some of the major change-producing effects of war can be seen in the development of new technologies, in the formation of new political systems, in the reorganization of existing institutions, in the redistribution of wealth, in the redrawing of political boundaries, and in the changes in the composition of the labor force.

Conflict in Eastern Europe and the Former Soviet Union The rapid collapse of the power structures and capitulations of the power elites in Eastern Europe and the Soviet Union in the late 1980s and early 1990s came as a surprise to most observers and analysts (see, for example, Westwood, 2003). The changes in Eastern Europe, from Communist control to multiparty democracy and from command economy to the free market, could not have been more extreme and more dramatic (Pridham & Vanhanen, 1994; Wejnert, 2002). Yet they happened in a very short time. One of the results of the rapid transformations was the emergence of political, economic, religious, and ethnic conflicts. Nationalistic extreme-right sentiments and prejudices are on the rise, and, when misused, they can lead to discrimination, "ethnic cleansing," and full-scale wars (Hockenos, 1994). In the case of Yugoslavia, these conflicts culminated in a vicious civil war in which tens of thousands of people were killed and injured and millions dislocated. Tensions between Romanians and ethnic Hungarians have erupted in fighting people's life chances—through the political process (Etzioni-Halevy, 1981:151). In the United States, polity is organized at three levels—federal, state, and local—and each consists of executive, legislative, and judicial branches. At a given time, any branch of government at any level may be actively seeking to maintain stability or to foster change in particular areas of American life. For the moment, only the latter will be considered.

Polity has traditionally played an important part in fostering change both nationally and internationally (Lebow, 1997). At times, the goals were specific and often were those being advocated by local or regional interests. They involved, among other things, land acquisition and suppression of native Americans; the building of roads and railroads; the encouragement of manufacturing; the irrigation of the land; the development of land grant colleges; the exploration of new lands; and the education of children. More recently, there have been attempts to provide financial security for the elderly and adequate health care for all. Attempts have been made also to alter long-standing patterns of inequality between whites and blacks, males and females, and to improve the economic status of recent immigrants (Issel, 1985).

The volume of activities undertaken by modern governments is greater, and the range of such activities is broader, than it ever was before. Governments bring about change through the processes of distribution, regulation, and redistribution (Lowi, 1964). This classification depends upon the number of people affected and their relationships with one another. Distribution may involve relatively small numbers of people; it may include government contracts, public works projects, and industries that will bring new wealth to an area. Regulation deals with the restriction or limitation of the actions of others; it may include issues such as labor-management relations and protection of the consumer and the environment. Redistribution calls for the transfer of resources among or between large groups or classes in society. Illustrations of this include graduated income taxes and other public policies intended to transfer resources from one group to another, for example, from the "haves" to the "have nots." There is, however, a tendency in political systems and subsystems to develop a "mobilization of bias" (Bachrach & Baratz, 1970)—that is, a set of predominant values, beliefs, rituals, and formal and informal institutional procedures that operate systematically and consistently to benefit some people and groups at the expense of others. Those who benefit most can defend and promote their vested interests. Usually, the status quo defenders are also the group with the most power. For example, the history of blacks' demands for access to effective problem-solving apparatus by polity validates this perspective.

It should also be noted that "The structures of power in which the political process takes place offer an explanation not only of how change originates and what direction it takes, but also why it is necessary. Power always implies non-power and therefore resistance. The dialectic of power and resistance is the motive force of history. From the interests of those in power at a given time we can infer the interests of the powerless, and with them the direction of change" (Dahrendorf, 1973:502). In the United States, this has been illustrated by several developments, such as the war, or attempted war, on poverty, the conflict that is intensifying among the haves and have-nots, and the existing contradictions among racial and ethnic groups.

At all levels and branches of polity, new programs and activities are initiated on a regular basis. The impetus for these may come from within the polity or from without. There are specific demands, such as hot-lunch programs in schools or increased regulation of insurance companies, or general demands requesting the polity to "get moving" to earn its keep, to work for the common good. In the United States, "Government is supposed to have programs. Agencies are supposed to do something, to advance toward some goals. A government with no program is a bad government. An agency without a program is a bad or stagnant agency. Government then takes great pains to show what it is doing. A flock of new programs are announced each year, guaranteed to help the nation or the world. When a new government takes office or when a new man takes the helm at an agency, program-mongering becomes more acute" (Friedman, 1975:190).

These activities may result in a series of palliative or placating measures, or they may produce creative incremental measures that may "breed new possibilities for subsequent radical change, although at the moment of adoption they appear quite modest" (Goulet, 1973:295).

The polity continuously fosters change in society at various levels. Its role obviously varies from situation to situation. On the institutional level, in the context of economic development, Szymon Chodak (1973:247) identifies three ways in which polity can induce change:

1. It can create conditions supportive of economic development without interfering in the actual course of economic activities. This would mean support of trade, business, entrepreneurial and other activities while safeguarding private capital, investments, and the rights of ownership. This takes place during the early stages of capitalism.

2. The polity can regulate some economic activities such as the protection of workers and farmers, but the market retains its competitive character. This is illustrative of advanced capitalism.

3. The polity engages directly in the planning and implementing of economic development by becoming owners of economic enterprises as evidenced by the former Soviet Union and Eastern European countries.

In addition to these activities, the polity can stimulate change in developing countries by regulating incentives, controlling prices and trade, and by helping individuals to liberate themselves from traditional kinship, village, or tribal ties. In essence, it entails the provision of welfare and related services that were traditionally provided by one's extended family. Finally, it facilitates integration of society through conflict regulation and accommodation of diverse demands.

In sum, some of the most far-reaching changes have occurred in recent decades in societies that are in the process of development. In modern industrial societies, changes instigated by the polity are principally distributive, regulative, and redistributive in nature.

The Economy

Economic systems have a variety of extra economic consequences and play a major role in social change (Lobao & Rulli, 1996). Their importance varies from theorist to theorist, but in general there is agreement that, indeed, economic forces shape and guide our lives. As will be discussed in Chapter 2, Marx argued that the manner in which people obtain their livelihood determines the way they establish their programs of justice, religion, kinship, education, and other social institutions. He pointed to the mode of production and stated that it determines the general character of the social, political, and spiritual processes in society. His idea of economic determinism is still an influential one with a substantial number of followers. However, economic forces are only one of the several factors that seem central in initiating and directing social change. Therefore, instead of describing how economic conditions are seen as "prime movers," the emphasis on the following pages will be on illustrating how economic factors foster change in specific walks of life rather than contributing to the transformation of entire societies.

In the United States, business, industry, and finance are considered to be the great sources of change and progress. They are supported by a strong ideology of free enterprise, which is evident throughout our economic institutions. In many ways, change is built into daily life as part of the economic system.

An important aspect of the economy is the division of labor. One's occupation, particularly in the middle class, is decisive, for it provides the person with a certain level of monetary reward, power, and prestige. Increased demand for products and increased specialization to meet those demands have greatly contributed to the growth in the division of labor and the number of occupations. The *1992 Dictionary of Occupational Titles*, the latest issued by the U.S. Department of Labor, for example, includes comprehensive descriptions of job duties and related information for over 20,000 occupations in the United States. The degree of specialization is almost as infinite, as is shown in the following illustration:

In the baking industry one can make a living as a cracker breaker, meringue spreader, a pie stripper, or pan dumper. In the slaughter or meat-packing industry one can specialize as: a large stock scalper, belly shaver, crotch buster, gut snatcher, gut sorter, snout puller, ear cutter, eyelid remover, stomach washer (sometimes called belly pumper), hindleg toenail puller, frontleg toenail puller, and oxtail washer. (Wilensky, 1967:78–79)

Increased differentiation in the economic sphere in turn brings about increased differentiation in stratification patterns. One's class position, in turn, determines one's lifestyle, values, interaction patterns, power, mobility—in short, one's life chances. Economic factors thus condition the distribution of rewards and the allocation of status and prestige. They also contribute to the differentiation between the haves and the have-nots (that is, inequality) both within and between societies. For example, the gap in per capita income between the industrial and developing worlds tripled between 1960 and 1993, from $5,700 to $15,400 (Speth, 1996), and has further widened in 2003. As it will be further discussed in Chapter 4, today the net worth of the world's 358 richest people is equal to the combined income of the poorest 45 percent of the world's population—about 2.8 billion people.

Economic factors contribute to inequality, which, in turn, begets other forms of inequality that are likely to increase further economic inequality. Economic surpluses have long been considered as a basis for stratification and in the creation of inequality (Lenski, 1966). Jonathan H. Turner and Charles Starnes (1976:3), using the United States as an example, note that economic surplus creates distribution problems, which lead people to compete for the surplus. Those who win in this competition are able to buy power that can be used to maintain or increase their advantage. Once power is bought, there is a decrease of reliance on force, and the emphasis switches to the legitimization of inequality by the use of ideas in order to mitigate inherent conflicts of interest between the privileged and those who are less privileged. Because those who are better off need not expend their resources on forcing acceptance of their privilege, they can now use their increased power to gather more of the economic surplus.

In addition to changes in the division of labor and stratification patterns, economic factors can literally make or break communities through the creation of markets, industries, employment opportunities, or through their manipulation. In a classic study, W. Fred Cottrell (1974) examines one change in the basic economic institution of a community and traces the effects of it throughout the social structure. He has chosen a one-industry town where other economic considerations would not enter to complicate the case.

Caliente, as Cottrell called the town, came into existence in order to service the steam locomotive, which, in the beginning, required frequent stops. The city grew and prospered with the railroad. People built homes, put in a water system using cast iron pipes, established businesses, and built a twenty-seven-bed hospital, school buildings, a theater, and even a park. They also established a number of civic organizations, such as the Chamber of Commerce and the Masonic lodge. The town was solid, growing, and optimistic.

The town was suddenly threatened with extinction in the mid-1940s when the railroad announced that it would no longer maintain its facilities there. "The location of Caliente, as far as the railroad was concerned, was a function of boiler temperature and pressure and the resultant service requirements of the locomotive" (Cottrell, 1974:683). The replacement of steam engines by diesel engines made the city obsolete from the perspective of the railroad.

Everyone in the town experienced some loss. The railroad company owned thirty-nine homes, a clubhouse, and a hotel in town that became virtually worthless. Workers who had seniority only in the local union had lost even more. One-fourth of the workers had to look for new jobs, as the diesel engine reduced overall labor needs. The local merchants also lost badly. The younger ones could move out, but even they lost because their property became worthless. Friendship patterns rapidly changed, and the community structure, built on a seemingly solid foundation, began to disintegrate. Attempts to attract new industry failed, and residents found it difficult to justify the cold-blooded, profit-motive decision of the railroad. But the town was dead, the victim of economic forces beyond the control of the community. Almost the same thing happened in 1988 with the closing of the Chrysler assembly plant in Kenosha, Wisconsin. When nearly six thousand workers lost their jobs in the shutdown, the community faced a series of economic crises, resulting in major changes in earning power, status, and power relations (Dudley, 1994).

Other economic forces also exert pressure on social life. John Kenneth Galbraith (1973) contends that large corporations, by virtue of their size and power, can create and control the market. Large corporations, he suggests, constitute a "planning system" in the American economy. They determine what customers shall eat, drink, wear, and smoke, and how their homes shall look, and, within broad limits, what price they shall pay for what they buy. The concentration of economic power in large corporations also involves the decline of countervailing power. When a firm buys its former competitors, it is removing checks on its power. An example of this is the beer industry (Currie & Skolnick, 1997:30–32). Over half of the domestic beer market is controlled by giant corporations such as Anheuser-Busch and Miller. Thousands of small breweries either went out of business or were bought up by a few large corporations. Local brands were taken over, the taste of beer became more standardized, and prices rose sharply. At the same time, production costs were reduced as a result of mass production and relocation to parts of the country with cheaper labor. Although some new jobs were created, many people became unemployed because of the buy-outs and relocations.

Globalization

The world economic landscape is changing dramatically as a result of globalization, the international integration of markets for goods, services and capital. More and more of the world has been drawn into a network of economic and social relationships which transcend conventional political, economic and cultural barriers (Schaeffer, 2003). Barriers to the global tradability of goods and services and the mobility of capital and labor are increasingly being eliminated by technological innovations, the widespread movement toward the liberalization of trade and capital markets, and the growing globalization of corporate production and distribution strategies. The trend toward internationalization is creating new opportunities as well as challenges at all levels in society (Cohen & Kennedy, 2002).

There is an integration of the world economy as the major players—large corporations that are "multinational"—draw more and more of the globe into networks of capitalist production and markets. For example, ITT employs over 400,000 workers in sixty-eight countries. Exxon operates in almost 100 countries, and its fleet of oil tankers constitutes a navy the size of Great Britain's. General Motors has facilities in thirty-nine countries and sells over $80 billion worth of products annually. Multinationals account for more than one-fourth of total world economic production, and their share is increasing. The different parts of the world economy are more interconnected, and people most everywhere are being affected by recent advances in telecommunications, transport, and the arrival of multinationals wishing to market a particular global brand of soap, foodstuff or cigarettes. Globalization is also seen as a cultural homogenization force (most easily summed up in words such as "Coca-Colaization" or "Hollywoodization" or in the powerful image of McDonalds' golden arches striding purposefully across the world) via consumerism (Hunter, 1995; Ritzer, 2002), creating similarities in social forms across political boundaries, resulting in the emergence of cultural cosmopolitanism (Stevenson, 1997). Globalization is also seen as an integrated international order conducive to American interests, which is guided by American rules and norms to satisfy the expectations for ever-greater abundance in the United States (Bacevich, 2002).

There are obvious "social contradictions" of globalization (MacEwan, 1996) and controversial economic consequences (Aaronson, 2001). Perhaps the most damaging social contradiction of globalization is its impact on democracy by limiting people's power to exercise political control over their economic lives because the power of government is limited in regulating private business. Critics argue that the globalization of business contributes to the decline of the power of labor as well as to the decline of small business as a result of its inability to compete in the marketplace (Harrison, 1984). The spread of free-market capitalism aggravates hostilities between the national ethnic majorities and the market-dominant minorities (Chua, 2003). Whether Jews in post-Communist Russia or the Chinese in many Southeast Asian nations, such minorities vastly outperform the indigenous majorities in production and consumption. It results in the rise of nationalism, ethnic tension and scapegoating.

Globalization makes it difficult for the U.S. government to keep up with the activities of such corporations, thus making regulatory agencies highly ineffective. The nationally oriented institutions are being replaced by globally oriented institutions under the legitimizing cloak of efficiency and financial credibility (McMichael, 1996). It reduces employment opportunities for American workers and undermines the power of the nation-state to maintain economic and political stability within its territory (Barnet & Cavanagh, 1994). Globalization also creates wage inequalities and falling relative wages among unskilled workers (Lee, 1996). In the United States, the earnings of unskilled labor fell, even as the economy enjoyed years of prosperity. The factors that account for the decline include stiff competition from Asia, a flood of immigrants, and automation in manufacturing (Wolman & Colamosca, 1997).

Highly paid workers in developed countries cannot compete with much lower paid, but equally skilled, workers in developing countries. This could lead to a breakdown of the international trading system and continued downsizing (Kennedy, 1997). Changes in the global economy also reshaped local labor markets, which tended to polarize labor demand into high-skill and low-skill categories. This polarization also reflects an emerging duality between a primary labor market of well paid, secure and pensionable jobs and a secondary labor market of poorly paid, insecure and often part-time employment and has obvious implications for international migration in terms of differential pull and push factors for "brain drain" versus "contract" migrants. For example, the United States, the biggest "skills-magnet," absorbs large proportions of the most educated people, and Western governments (e.g., Germany, Britain) encourage the skilled to migrate by expanding the availability of work permits for skilled migrants (*Economist*, 2002).

Finally, the forces of globalization and new technology threaten to weaken the power governments to tax their citizens. Modern tax systems were developed after World War II when cross-border movements in goods, capital and labor were relatively small. Now firms and people are more mobile and can exploit tax differences between countries. Globalization is a tax problem because firms have more freedom to decide where to locate and there are great variations in corporate taxes among countries; it makes it hard to decide where a company should pay tax; and it makes it harder to tax high-income individuals because of high mobility and the ability to carry out business in cyberspace (*Economist*, 1997).

Globalization has profound positive implications for developing countries (see, for example, Lewellen, 2002). It creates important new opportunities—wider markets for trade, an expanding array of tradables, larger private capital inflows, improved access to technology. Defenders of multinationals contend that they introduce great wealth and create jobs in poor countries (*Business Week,* 1994:92–93). They contribute to the economic development of third-world nations by introducing the latest manufacturing techniques, by upgrading the educational level of the labor force, by paying taxes and relatively high wages, by helping to modernize the infrastructure, and by providing jobs and promoting efficiency in the manufacturing and service sectors. Thus, the presence of multinationals is seen as a catalyst for modernization because the economies of the host societies will grow from wages and taxes paid by the corporations.

Globalization and economic factors foster change in society in many other ways. They play a role in the reduction of geographical and entrepreneurial frontier opportunities. They sharpen the dichotomy between the employed and the unemployed and contribute to the rise in higher expectations and keener perception of the gap between actualities and potentialities. Current economic conditions also play a role in the transition from a basic condition of labor scarcity to one of job scarcity, and the expanded power of the labor force induces wages to follow increasing productivity, which results in an inflationary force. They can also lead to the emergence of social problems triggered by competition and scarcities and to damages to the cohesion of civil societies (Dahrendorf, 1995). These in turn produce further changes in economic, political, and other institutional domains.

Economic problems can also create a chain of events that can set off changes in a number of ways. Examples of such problems include fluctuating currencies, foreign debts, and trade deficits (Silk, 1987). The almost 40 percent drop in the value of the United States dollar in the early 1990s in relation to Western European and Japanese currencies significantly increased the price of imported goods and brought in huge amounts of foreign investments in the mid-1990s. At the same time, the increase in the export of American goods remained negligible in spite of the passing by Congress of major trade agreements such as NAFTA (North American Free Trade Agreement) in 1993 and GATT (General Agreement on Tariffs and Trade) in November 1994. Because of domestic economic problems, several third-world debtor nations, such as Brazil and Argentina, suspended payment of the interest on almost $90 billion worth of debts (*Economist,* 1994b:95) in the early 1990s. To secure loans and debt relief from the World Bank, International Monetary Fund, and other national and international organizations, borrower nations had to rapidly privatize industries, cut deficits (and with them, possibly, social safety-net programs), and eliminate trade barriers. These developments culminated in political upheavals and economic crisis in the debtor nations and set the stage for the various antiglobalization protests on the streets of Seattle and Genoa (Stiglitz, 2002). It also shocked the financial world, and many American banks raised their prime interest rates in response in the mid-1990s. This brought about an increase in home mortgage loans, which, in turn, slowed down the housing industry. A decrease in new-home construction, in turn, reverberated in other aspects of the economy until the late 1990s. As a result of its huge trade deficit, the United States has become the world's largest debtor nation, and its net foreign debt is growing rapidly. Among other things, this trade deficit played a role in the economic downturn in the early 2000s and has resulted in a tighter domestic budget, with major reductions in many areas such as education, health care, and programs for the disadvantaged.

In sum, economic forces permeate all aspects of life in society. They are considered to be among the most potent inducements for social change.

Structural Strains

The concept of strain refers to a discrepancy between two or more elements of the social system. It is based on the assumption that the social system is made up of interrelated components. As long as the components are compatible and fulfill positive functions for each other, the social system is relatively stable. In situations where two or more components become incompatible, the equilibrium of the social system is upset, and this may result in social change. Several types of strains can be identified that produce incompatibility among the components of the social system and thus contribute to change of that system. They include population imbalances, anomie, certain forms of scarcity, role conflicts, inconsistencies between the ideal and the real, conflict of values, and status anguish.

Demographic imbalances are inherent in social systems, and they are likely to be manifested in change-producing strains (Brown & Kane, 1994). The aging of the baby boom generation may mean increased age discrimination litigation because of the size of the potential plaintiff pool, the baby boomers' self-centeredness, their history of rebelling against authority and the corporate downsizings and consolidations they are already confronted with (Stansky, 1997). Trends in birthrates, for example, may be out of phase with respect to plans for building and improving schools. Migration trends may be out of phase with the receiving area's ability to accommodate new arrivals. Changes in population composition can have an effect on labor force characteristics, for example, increasing or decreasing the size of nonworking or working populations. Population growth creates imbalances in food supply and distribution. It adversely affects resource utilization and depletion, and contributes to large concentrations in urban areas where the resulting strains may be seen in an overload of transportation facilities and traffic congestion (see, for example, Grant, 2001). The circadian rhythm impels nearly everyone to go to work at the same time, to take a break at the same time, and to impose demands on energy sources at the same time.

Change-producing strains are also created in a society by anomie, a condition of normative confusion in which the individual has few socially validated guides to behavior. According to Robert K. Merton's (1957:140) often-debated hypothesis, the source of this strain is the discrepancy between goals and means in a society. Individuals are uniformly committed to the goals society tells them to desire, but they encounter unequal access to the means socially defined as legitimate for achieving these goals. Many people in society are thus subject to intense frustration of their socially legitimate desires—for instance, to be successful, popular, and happy. By being poor, black, or otherwise disadvantaged, many individuals are severely handicapped in the race toward the goals society tells them they ought to value and pursue. Because of this frustration in finding access to legitimate means for achieving goals, individuals sometimes turn to illegitimate means—that is, deviance—to achieve them. Such deviance may include crime, alcoholism, drug addiction, or even suicide by those who cannot cope with the pressure; or rebellion by those who try to solve the problem by undermining the social order and establishing a new one.

Rebellion as a reaction to strain is considered an important source of social change. This kind of adjustment is characteristic of individuals who start social movements, and it has been used as an explanation for the student unrest in the late 1960s. This pattern also helps us to understand why individuals form communes, occupy buildings, destroy property, and formulate new ideologies in attempts to substitute new goals and norms for the dominant ones in society.

The presence of universal scarcities in society is another ubiquitous source of change-producing strains. "Any viable social system requires norms that determine allocation of these scarcities, but the latter remain omnipresent sources of potential strain in individual behavior in the relations between and among groups and social categories" (Moore, 1970:132). The allocation of scarce goods is always subject to challenge in society. If the challenge is successful and brings about alterations in the distribution of scarce resources such as in the Marxian perspective, it can have far-ranging consequences on all aspects of life. In modern societies, even time is considered as a scarce resource. "We are all of us compelled to read for profit, party for contacts, lunch for contracts, bowl for unity, drive for mileage, gamble for charity, go out for the evening for the greater glory of the municipality, and stay home for the weekend to rebuild the house" (Kerr, quoted by Linder, 1970:4).

Ambiguity in role expectations and conflict among social roles can also result in change-producing strains. A typical illustration of role ambiguity is the case of the modern American woman, whose traditional domestic duties have become uncertain. A commonly used illustration for role conflict is the situation of a black physician whose occupational role calls for deference from others but whose racial role traditionally has called for deference to others.

Moore (1974:20–21) suggests that a "ubiquitous source of change-producing strain arises from the inherent fact that social order is a moral order and from the associated fact that non-conformity to the moral order occurs in all societies." As a result, "the inconsistency between the ideal and the actual is tension producing and hospitable to change." For example, recent manifestations of changing moral standards among youth are indicative of changes in ideal patterns. In addition to discrepancies between expectations and actual situations, conflict in values can also result in strains, culminating in changes. Differences in values among social classes and among ethnic or religious groups often instigate changes, as evidenced by the consequences of efforts in school busing.

Finally, strains in a society can be produced by what Robert H. Lauer (1991) calls status anguish, which includes marginality, status inconsistency, status withdrawal, and relative deprivation. Marginality is existence in two or more social worlds without being fully a part of any of them. Illustrations of this would be the foreman, the black psychiatrist, and supervisor in industry. Marginality is also a ubiquitous factor of contemporary urban life as a result of conditions of poverty and destitution, ethno-racial divisions, and growing social inequalities (Wacquant, 1996). Status inconsistency refers to occupying statuses that have different implications for one's location in a system of stratification, as, for example, the rising number of unemployed and underemployed Ph.D.s (Hanson-Harding, 2002). Status withdrawal will be discussed in connection with Hagen's notion of economic development in Chapter 2. Relative deprivation is some kind of perceived or subjective deprivation in regard to some specific standards. These four types of status anguish have, in various degrees, contributed to change in society.

SUMMARY

Social change occurs constantly—although at varying rates—in society. An awareness of the components of change is essential to the understanding and explanation of change. Thus, attention must be paid to what is changing, at what level in a social system, at what rate and magnitude, and in which direction. A distinction needs to be made also between planned and unplanned changes and their consequences.

Social change may be defined a number of ways. For the present purpose, it is conceptualized as the process of planned or unplanned qualitative or quantitative alterations in social phenomena that can be analyzed in terms of the following interrelated components: identity, level, duration, magnitude, and rate of change. This conceptualization of social change is proposed as a heuristic device for the empirical and theoretical study of social change.

Change in society is produced by a number of factors, and it is important not to assign undue weight to any one of these factors in isolation. It is always tempting to have a "pet" theory or a unitary "prime mover," but to account for broad social changes such an exercise would be meaningless.

Among the mechanisms of change analyzed in this chapter, it was noted that technology creates new alternatives, but it also generates new problems, as evidenced by the introduction of the steel ax among Australian aborigines and the snowmobile among Eskimos. In modern society, technology is associated with changes at work and is considered a factor in alienation.

There are several types of ideologies. Max Weber (1958) contended that the Protestant ethic was instrumental in the rise of capitalism. On the other hand, Marxism is associated with large-scale societal transformations. The ideology of the conjugal family contributed to greater equality and freedom of family members. Some of the utopian ideologies are important instigators of change. One way or another, these ideologies all challenge existing social arrangements.

Competition is an endemic aspect of society. It contributes to social change in both ecological and organizational contexts. It stimulates innovation and has been effectively used as a motivating force for social change in development programs. When competitors do not abide by rules and regulations, the relationship turns into conflict. It may be substantive, or over ideological, symbolic, or cultural issues. Conflict should not be viewed as having only negative connotations. It plays an important role in social change, as illustrated by the outcomes of conflict between workers and management; university students and administrators; blacks and whites; females and males; in the international arena; and by some of the recent events in the former Soviet Union and Eastern bloc countries.

The polity has traditionally played a role in social change through its activities of distribution, regulation, and redistribution. Government is expected to "do something," and the result is often change at the various levels within society as well as among societies.

Economic factors have contributed to the increase in the division of labor, with concomitant changes in the stratification system. In small communities, change in the basic economic institution can have disastrous results, as illustrated by the case of the town of Caliente. Globalization refers to the international integration of markets for goods, services and capital, which has diverse social consequences. Finally, structural strains produced by population imbalances, anomie, scarcity, role and value conflicts, inconsistencies, and status anguish are also ubiquitous sources of change. In the following chapter, several prominent theories of change will be examined.

SUGGESTED FURTHER READINGS

AARONSON, SUSAN ARIEL. *Taking Trade to the Streets: The Lost History of Public Efforts to Shape Globalization*. Ann Arbor: University of Michigan Press. 2001. An overview of the activities and ideologies of the critics of the various international trade agreements.

AMASON, JOHANN P. *The Future That Failed: Origins and Destinies of the Soviet Model*. London: Routledge, 1993. One of the better sociological explorations of the sources of the crises and the reasons for the collapse of the Soviet Union.

FEUER, LEWIS S. *Ideology and the Ideologists*. New York: Harper & Row, 1975. A classic exploration of the social and emotional sources of ideological thought and their implications for change.

FLEMING, JOHN. *The War of All Against All: An Analysis of Conflict in Society*. Lanham, MD: University Press of America, 2000. A brief overview of the various facets of conflict in the context of territorial crowding and its relation to mass society.

FREIRE, PAULO, AND DONALDO MACEDO. *Ideology Matters*. Lanham, MD: Rowman & Littlefield Publishers, 1998. The title says it all.

FUNDERBURK, CHARLES, AND ROBERT G. THOBABEN. *Political Ideologies: Left, Center, Right*, 2nd ed. New York: HarperCollins Publishers, 1994. A good introduction to the world's major political ideologies.

HAY, COLIN S. *Re-Stating Social and Political Change*. Philadelphia: Open University Press, 1996. An insightful review of the social, political and cultural changes that have occurred in Britain since the Second World War.

JACOBS, DAVID J. *Collective Bargaining as an Instrument of Social Change*. Westport, CT: Quorum Books, 1994. A succinct analysis of the role of collective bargaining in labor-management relations nationally and internationally.

KRIESBERG, LOUIS. *Constructive Conflicts: From Escalation to Resolution*, 2nd ed. Lanham, MD: Rowman & Littlefield, 2002. A comprehensive analysis of all kinds of constructive conflicts and their role in social change.

LEWELLEN, TED C. *The Anthropology of Globalization: Cultural Anthropology Enters the 21st Century*. Westport, CT: Praeger, 2002. An analysis of the worldwide spread of neocapitalism from the perspective of cultural anthropology.

MARSH, ROBERT M. *The Great Transformation: Social Change in Taipei, Taiwan Since the 1960s*. Armonk, NY: M. E. Sharpe, 1996. A good attempt to capture changes at the level of society.

RITZER, GEORGE (ed.). *McDonaldization: The Reader*. Thousand Oaks, CA: Sage Publications, 2002. With an eye to the events of 9/11/01 and after, this reader proves insights into the way McDonaldization is affecting cultures and a wide range of social phenomena around the world with implications for globalization and social change.

RUBIN, JEFFREY Z., DEAN G. PRUITT, AND SUNG HEE KIM. *Social Conflict: Escalation, Stalemate, and Settlement*, 2nd ed. New York, McGraw-Hill: 1994. A contemporary review of the major theories and empirical works on conflict.

SCHAEFFER, ROBERT K. *Understanding Globalization: The Social Consequences of Political, Economic, and Environmental Change*, 2nd ed. Lanham, MD: Rowman & Littlefield Publishers, Inc., 2003. A good up-to-date introduction to the globalization process and its consequences.

SCHATZ, SARA, AND JAVIER JESUS GUTIERREZ-REXACH. *Conceptual Structure and Social Change: The Ideological Architecture of Democratization*. Westport, CT: Praeger, 2002. A novel theoretical approach that treats ideologies as complex cognitive systems that are internally articulated around prioritized principles and values.

TEICH, ALBERT H. (ed.). *Technology and the Future*, 9th ed. New York: St. Martin's Press, 2002. A collection of insightful articles devoted to the various facets of technology.

TRAHAIR, RICHARD C. S. *Utopias and Utopians: A Historical Dictionary*. Westport, CT: Greenwood Publishing Group, 1999. This reference provides more than 600 entries on a wide range of utopias and utopians around the world.

WEJNERT, BARBARA (ed.). *Transition to Democracy in Eastern Europe and Russia: Impact on Politics, Economy and Culture*. Westport, CT: Praeger, 2002. An overview of the difficult processes and components of transition to democracy from socialism and an examination of the impact of changes on a broad spectrum of societal life, from economy and politics to health, culture and art.

REFERENCES

AARONSON, SUSAN ARIEL. *Taking Trade to the Streets: The Lost History of Public Efforts to Shape Globalization*. Ann Arbor: University of Michigan Press. 2001.

ADAM, BARBARA. *Time and Social Theory*. Cambridge, MA: Polity Press, 1990.

ALLEN, FRANCIS B. *Socio-Cultural Dynamics: An Introduction to Social Change*. New York: Macmillan, 1971.

AMASON, JOHANN P. *The Future That Failed: Origins and Destinies of the Soviet Model*. London: Routledge, 1993.

BACEVICH, ANDREW. *American Empire: The Realities and Consequences of U.S. Diplomacy*. Cambridge, MA: Harvard University Press, 2002.

BACHRACH, PETER, AND MORTON S. BARATZ. *Power and Poverty: Theory and Practice*. New York: Oxford, 1970.

BARADAT, LEON P. *Political Ideologies: Their Origins and Impact*. 7th ed. Upper Saddle River, NJ: Prentice Hall, 1999.

BARBER, BERNARD. "Function, Variability, and Change in Ideological Systems." In Bernard Barber and Alex Inkeles (eds.), *Stability and Social Change*. Boston: Little, Brown, 1971, pp. 244–265.

BARNET, RICHARD J., AND JOHN CAVANAGH. *Global Dreams—Imperial Corporations and the New World Order*. New York: Simon & Schuster, 1994.

BERNARD, H. RUSSELL, AND PERTTI PELTO (eds.). *Technology and Social Change*, 2nd ed. Prospect Heights, IL: Waveland Press, 1987.

BETTS, RICHARD K. (ed.). *Conflict After the Cold War: Arguments on Causes of War and Peace*, 2nd ed. New York: Longman, 2001.

BIANCHI, SUZANNE M., AND DAPHNE SPAIN. "Women, Work and Family in America," *Population Bulletin*, 51 (3) December 1996, pp. 2–47.

BLAU, PETER M. *Exchange and Power in Social Life*. New York: Wiley, 1967.

BLAUNER, ROBERT. *Alienation and Freedom*. Chicago: University of Chicago Press, 1964.

BROWN, DENEEN L. "Starting Over," *The Seattle Times,* December 4, 2002, p. A3.
BROWN, LESTER R., AND HAL KANE. *Full House: Reassessing the Earth's Population Carrying Capacity.* New York: W. W. Norton, 1994.
Business Week. "The Winds of Change Blow Everywhere." October 17, 1994, pp. 92–93.
Business Week. "9.11. What Has Changed. The Economy, Homeland Security, The View from Abroad." Special Report, September 16, 2002, pp. 22–36.
CARTY, ANTHONY, AND H. W. SINGER (eds.). *Conflict and Change in the 1990s: Ethics, Law and Institutions.* London: The Macmillan Press, 1993.
CHIN, ROBERT, AND KENNETH D. BENNE. "General Strategies for Effecting Changes in Human Systems." In Warren G. Bennis, Kenneth D. Benne, and Robert Chin (eds.), *The Planning of Change,* 4th ed. New York: Holt, Rinehart & Winston, 1985, pp. 22–46.
CHIROT, DANIEL. *Social Change in the Modern Era.* San Diego: Harcourt Brace Jovanovich, 1986.
CHODAK, SZYMON. *Societal Development: Five Approaches with Conclusions from Comparative Analysis.* New York: Oxford, 1973.
CHUA, AMY. *World on Fire: How Exporting Free Market Democracy Breeds Ethnic Hatred and Global Instability.* New York: Doubleday, 2003.
COHEN, ROBIN, AND PAUL KENNEDY. *Global Sociology.* New York: NYU Press, 2002.
COSER, LEWIS A. "Social Conflict and the Theory of Social Change." In Philip Brickman (ed.), *Social Conflict: Readings in Rule Structures and Conflict Relationships.* Lexington, MA: Heath, 1974, pp. 458–466.
COTTREL, W. FRED. "Death by Dieselization: A Case Study in the Reaction to Technological Change." In Edgar A. Schuler, Thomas Ford Hoult, Duane L. Gibson, and Wilbur B. Brookover (eds.), *Readings in Sociology,* 5th ed. New York: Crowell, 1974, pp. 681–689.
CROSSETTE, BARBARA. "U.N. Study Finds a Free Eastern and Central Europe Poorer and Less Healthy." *The New York Times,* October 7, 1994, p. A7.
CURRIE, ELLIOTT, AND JEROME H. SKOLNICK. *America's Problems: Social Issues and Public Policy,* 3rd ed. New York: Longman, 1997.
CVITKOVIC, EMILIO. *Competition: Forms, Facts and Fiction.* London: The Macmillan Press, 1993.
DAHL, ROBERT. *Pluralist Democracy in the United States: Conflict and Consent.* Chicago: Rand McNally, 1967.
DAHRENDORF, RALF. "Market and Plan." In Amitai Etzioni and Eva Etzioni-Halevy (eds.), *Social Change: Sources, Patterns, and Consequences,* 2nd ed. New York: Basic Books, 1973, pp. 500–504.
DAHRENDORF, RALF. "Preserving Prosperity: Social Consequences of Economic Development," *New Statesman & Society,* 8 (383) December 15, 1995, pp. 36–42.
DAVIS, KINGSLEY. *Human Society.* New York: Macmillan, 1949.
DUDLEY, KATHRYN MARIE. *The End of the Line: Lost Jobs, New Lives in Postindustrial America.* Chicago: University of Chicago Press, 1994.
DUKE, JAMES T. *Conflict and Power in Social Life.* Provo, UT: Brigham Young University Press, 1976.
Economist. "The Computer Industry: The Third Age." September 7, 1994a, pp. 3–32.
Economist. "Bank Lending, Hidden Horrors." October 22, 1994b, p. 95.
Economist. "The Disappearing Taxpayer," May 31, 1997, pp. 15, 21–23.

Economist. "Outward Bound," September 28, 2002, pp. 24–25.
EDARI, RONALD. *Social Change.* Dubuque, IA: William C. Brown, 1976.
ETZIONI-HALEVY, EVA. *Social Change: The Advent and Maturation of Modern Society.* London: Routledge, 1981.
FEUER, LEWIS S. *Ideology and the Ideologists.* New York: Harper & Row, 1975.
FLEMING, JOHN. *The War of All Against All: An Analysis of Conflict in Society.* Lanham, MD: University Press of America, 2000.
FREEMAN, DAVID M. *Technology and Society: Issues in Assessment, Conflict, and Choice.* Chicago: Rand McNally, 1974.
FREIRE, PAULO, AND DONALDO MACEDO. *Ideology Matters.* Lanham, MD: Rowman & Littlefield Publishers, 1998.
FRIEDMAN, LAWRENCE M. *The Legal System, A Social Science Perspective.* New York: Russell Sage, 1975.
FUKUYAMA, FRANCIS. "Managing Global Chaos: Sources of and Responses to International Conflict," *Foreign Affairs,* 76 (2) March–April 1997, pp. 175–176.
FUNDERBURK, CHARLES, AND ROBERT G. THOBABEN. *Political Ideologies: Left, Center, Right,* 2nd ed. New York: HarperCollins Publishers, 1994.
GALBRAITH, JOHN KENNETH. *Economics and the Public Purpose.* Boston: Houghton Mifflin, 1973.
GERTH, HANS, AND C. WRIGHT MILLS. *Character and Social Structure.* New York: Harcourt, Brace Jovanovich, 1953.
GINSBERG, MORRIS. "Social Change." *British Journal of Sociology,* 4, 1958, pp. 205–229.
GOLDSTONE, JACK A. "Gender, Work and Culture: Why the Industrial Revolution Came Early to England but Late to China," *Sociological Perspectives,* 39 (1) Spring 1996, pp. 1–21.
GOODE, WILLIAM J. *World Revolution and Family Patterns.* New York: Free Press, 1963.
GOULDNER, ALVIN W. *The Dialectic of Ideology and Technology: The Origins, Grammar and Future of Ideology.* New York: Seabury Press, 1976.
GOULET, DENIS A. *The Cruel Choice: A New Concept in the Theory of Development.* New York: Athenaeum, 1973.
GRANT, LINDSEY. *Too Many People: The Case for Reversing Growth.* Santa Ana, CA: Seven Locks Press, 2001.
GREENHOUSE, STEVEN. "The $100,000 Longshoreman—A Union Wins the Global Game," *The New York Times,* October 6, 2002, pp. WK1 and WK3.
HALL, RICHARD H. *Organizations: Structures, Processes, and Outcomes,* 8th ed. Upper Saddle River, NJ: Prentice Hall, 2002.
HANSON-HARDING, BRIAN. "Scholars in a Teenage Wasteland: For Ph.D.s, Unexpected Joys in Teaching High School." *The New York Times.* Education Life, Section 4/A. November 10, 2002, pp. 18–19.
HARRISON, PAUL. *Inside the Third World: The Anatomy of Poverty,* 2nd ed. New York: Penguin Books, 1984.
HETZLER, STANLEY A. *Technological Growth and Social Change, Achieving Modernization.* New York: Praeger, 1969.
HOCKENOS, PAUL. *Free to Hate: The Rise of the Right in Post-Communist Eastern Europe.* New York: Routledge, 1994.
HOWARD, JOHN R. *The Cutting Edge: Social Movements and Social Change in America.* New York: Lippincott, 1974.
HUNTER, ALLEN. "Globalization from Below? Promises and Perils of the New Internationalism," *Social Policy,* 25 (4) Summer 1995, pp. 6–14.

ISSEL, WILLIAM. *Social Change in the United States, 1945–1983.* New York: Schocken Books, 1985.
JACOBS, DAVID J. *Collective Bargaining as an Instrument of Social Change.* Westport, CT: Quorum Books, 1994.
JOHNSON, HARRY M. *Sociology: A Systematic Introduction.* New York: Harcourt, 1960.
JONES, JAMES M., AND KIM T. MORRIS. "Individual Versus Group Identification as a Factor in Intergroup Racial Conflict." In Stephen Worchel and Jeffry A. Simpson (eds.), *Conflict Between People and Groups: Causes, Processes, and Resolutions.* Chicago: Nelson Hall, 1993, pp. 170–189.
KENNEDY, PAUL. "Globalization and Its Discontents. The Triumph of Capitalism Revisited," *New Perspectives Quarterly,* 13 (4) Fall 1997, pp. 31–34.
KRIESBERG, LOUIS. *Social Conflicts,* 2nd ed. Englewood Cliffs, NJ: Prentice Hall, 1982.
KRIESBERG, LOUIS. *Constructive Conflicts: From Escalation to Resolution,* 2nd ed. Lanham, MD: Rowman & Littlefield, 2002.
LANDIS, JUDSON R. *Sociology: Concepts and Characteristics,* 11th ed. Belmont, CA: Wadsworth, 2000.
LASSWELL, HAROLD. *Politics: Who Gets What, When, How.* New York: Harcourt, 1958.
LAUER, ROBERT H. *Perspectives on Social Change,* 4th ed. Boston: Allyn & Bacon, 1991.
LEBOW, RICHARD NED. "Theory and Practice in International Politics: Initiating Change," *American Behavioral Scientist,* 40 (3) January 1997, pp. 360–364.
LEE, EDDY. "Globalization and Employment: Is Anxiety Justified?" *International Labour Review,* 135 (5) September–October 1996, pp. 485–498.
LENSKI, GERHARD E. *Power and Privilege: A Theory of Social Stratification.* New York: McGraw-Hill, 1966.
LEWELLEN, TED C. *The Anthropology of Globalization: Cultural Anthropology Enters the 21st Century.* Westport, CT: Praeger, 2002.
LEWIN, TAMARA. "Wage Difference Between Women and Men, Welfare Laws Examined," *The New York Times,* September 15, 1997, pp. A1, A8.
LINDBLOM, CHARLES E. "Initiating Change: Modes of Social Inquiry," *American Behavioral Scientist,* 40 (3) January 1997, pp. 264–277.
LINDER, STAFFAN B. *The Harried Leisure Class.* New York: Columbia University Press, 1970.
LOBAO, L., AND J. RULLI. "Economic Change and its Extraeconomic Consequences," *Environment & Planning,* 28 (4) April 1996, pp. 606–611.
LOWI, THEODORE J. "American Business, Public Policy, Case Studies, and Political Theory," *World Politics,* 16, 1964, pp. 677–715.
LULOPS, ROXANA SALYER. *Conflict: From Theory to Action.* Scottsdale, AZ: Gorsuch Scarisbrick, 1994.
MACEWAN, ARTHUR. "Globalization and Stagnation," *Social Justice,* 23 (1–2) Spring–Summer 1996, pp. 49–63.
MACIONIS, JOHN J. *Sociology,* 9th ed. Upper Saddle River, NJ: Prentice Hall, 2002.
MACIVER, ROBERT M., AND CHARLES H. PAGE. *Society: An Introductory Analysis.* New York: Holt, Rinehart & Winston, 1949.
MACKENZIE, DONALD. *Knowing Machines: Essays on Technological Change.* Cambridge, MA: The MIT Press, 1996.
MANN, CHARLES C. "Homeland Insecurity," *The Atlantic Monthly,* November 2002, pp. 82–102.
MARSH, ROBERT M. *The Great Transformation: Social Change in Taipei, Taiwan Since the 1960s.* Armonk, NY: M. E. Sharpe, 1996.

MASLAND, TOM. "Will It Be Peace or Punishment?" *Newsweek,* August 1, 1994, p. 37.

MCCARTHY, DOLYE E. "The Uncertain Future of Ideology: Rereading Marx," *The Sociological Quarterly,* 35(3) 1994, pp. 415–429.

MCCORD, ARLINE, AND WILLIAM MCCORD. *Urban Social Conflict.* St. Louis: Mosby, 1977.

MCMICHAEL, PHILIP. "Globalization: Myths and Realities," *Rural Sociology,* 61 (1) Spring 1996, pp. 25–56.

MERTON, ROBERT K. *Social Theory and Social Structure.* New York: Free Press, 1957.

MESTHENE, EMMANUEL G. "The Role of Technology in Society." In Albert H. Teich (ed.), *Technology and the Future,* 4th ed. New York: St. Martin's Press, 1986, pp. 72–94.

MOLAND, JOHN R. "Social Change, Social Inequality, and Intergroup Tensions," *Social Forces,* 75 (2) December 1996, pp. 403–422.

MOORE, WILBERT E. "Social Change." In David Sills (ed.), *International Encyclopedia of the Social Sciences.* vol. 14. New York: MacMillan, 1968, pp. 365–375.

MOORE, WILBERT E. "A Reconstruction of Theories of Social Change." In S. N. Eisenstadt (ed.), *Readings in Social Evolution and Development.* New York: Pergamon, 1970, pp. 123–139.

MOORE, WILBERT E. *Social Change,* 2nd ed. Englewood Cliffs, NJ: Prentice Hall, 1974.

MYERS, STEVEN LEE. "Fighting International Crime: The Striped-Pants Crowd Gets Gumshoes," *The New York Times,* December 8, 1996, pp. 1E and 16E.

NAISBITT, JOHN, AND PATRICIA ABURDENE. *Megatrends, 2000: Ten New Directions Transforming Our Lives.* New York: Morrow, 1990.

NEUMARK, DAVID, AND WILLIAM WASCHER. "Do Minimum Wages Fight Poverty?" *Economic Inquiry,* 40 (3) July 2002, pp. 315–334.

NISBET, ROBERT A. *Social Change and History.* New York: Oxford, 1969.

NOLAN, PATRICK, AND GERHARD LENSKI. "Technology, Ideology, and Societal Development," *Sociological Perspectives,* 39 (1) Spring 1996.

PELTO, PERTTI J., AND LUDGER MULLER-WILLIE. "Snowmobiles: Technological Revolution in the Arctic." In H. Russell Bernard and Pertti J. Pelto (eds.), *Technology and Social Change,* 2nd ed. Prospect Heights, IL: Waveland Press, 1987, pp. 208–241.

PERKINS, EDWARD J. "An International Agenda for Change," *American Behavioral Scientist,* 40 (3) January 1997, pp. 354–360.

PERLEZ, JANE. "Fast and Slow Lanes on the Capitalist Road." *The New York Times,* October 7, 1994, pp. A1, A6.

PRIDHAM, GEOFFREY, AND TATU VANHANEN (eds.). *Democratization of Eastern Europe.* New York: Routledge, 1994.

REMNICK, DAVID. *The Struggle for a New Russia.* New York: Random House, 1997.

RICHES, DAVID. "Hunter-Gatherer Structural Transformation," *Journal of the Royal Anthropological Institute,* 1 (4) December, 1995, pp. 679–702.

RINEHART, JAMES. "The Ideology of Competitiveness," *Monthly Review,* 47 (5) October 1995, pp. 14–24.

RISE, CHARLES S., AND ROLLIN C. STEINMETZ. *The Amish Year.* New Brunswick, NJ: Rutgers University Press, 1956.

RITZER, GEORGE (ed.). *McDonaldization: The Reader.* Thousand Oaks, CA: Sage Publications, 2002.

ROBERTS, SAM. "When a Woman Earns Like a Man," *The New York Times,* November 6, 1994, p. 6E.

RUBIN, JEFFREY Z., DEAN G. PRUITT, AND SUNG HEE KIM. *Social Conflict: Escalation, Stalemate, and Settlement,* 2nd ed. New York: McGraw-Hill, 1994.

RYCKMAN, LARRY. "Russia Is Showing Hints of Stability," *St. Louis Post-Dispatch*, September 27, 1994, p. 9B.

SANDOLE-STRATOSTE, INGRID. *Women in Transition: Between Socialism and Capitalism*. Westport, CT: Praeger, 2002.

SAWYER, JON. "Europe on the Edge," *St. Louis Post-Dispatch*, June 22, 1997, pp. 1B–5B.

SCHAEFFER, ROBERT K. *Understanding Globalization. The Social Consequences of Political, Economic, and Environmental Change*, 2nd ed. Lanham, MD: Rowman & Littlefield Publishers, Inc., 2003.

SCHAER, ROLAND, AND GREGORY CLAEYS (eds.). *Utopia: The Search for the Ideal Society in the Western World*. New York: Oxford University Press, 2001.

SCHATZ, SARA, AND JAVIER JESUS GUTIERREZ-REXACH. *Conceptual Structure and Social Change: The Ideological Architecture of Democratization*. Westport, CT: Praeger, 2002.

SHANNON, MICHAEL. "Minimum Wage and the Gender Gap," *Applied Economics*, 28 (12) December 1996, pp. 1567–1577.

SHARP, R. L. "Steel Axes for Stone Age Australians," *Human Organizations*, 11, 1952, pp. 17–22.

SHELL, ELLEN RUPPEL. *The Hungry Gene: The Science of Fat and the Future of Thin*. New York: Atlantic Monthly Press, 2002.

SHENK, DAVID. *Data Smog: Surviving the Information Glut*. New York: Harper Edge/Harper Collins, 1997.

SHULTZ, RICHARD H., JR. "State Disintegration and Ethnic Conflict: A Framework for Analysis," *The Annals of the American Academy of Political and Social Science*, 541 September 1995, pp. 75–89.

SILK, LEONARD. "The Global Financial Circus: Everyone Is Growing Frantic," *The New York Times*, April 5, 1987, p. 3.

SIVARD, RUTH LEGER. *World Military and Social Expenditures, 1996*. Washington, DC: World Priorities, 1996.

SMELSER, NEIL J. *Sociology of Economic Life*, 2nd ed. Englewood Cliffs, NJ: Prentice Hall, 1976.

SPAKE, AMANDA. "America's 'Supersize' Diet Is Fattier and Sweeter—and Deadlier," *U.S. News & World Report*, August 19, 2002, pp. 41–48.

SPETH, JAMES GUSTAVE. "Global Inequality: 358 Billionaires vs. 2.3 Billion People. The Triumph of Capitalism Revisited," *New Perspectives Quarterly*, 23 (4) Fall 1996, pp. 32–34.

SPIRO, MELFORD E. *Kibbutz: Venture in Utopia*. Cambridge, Mass.: Harvard University Press, 1956.

STANSKY, LISA. "New Age Woes: Lawyers Are Preparing Now for a Possible Wave of Age Discrimination Suits by Baby Boomers," *ABA Journal*, 83 January 1997, pp. 66–70.

Statistical Abstracts of the United States: 2002, 122nd ed. Washington, DC: U.S. Bureau of the Census, 2002.

STEVENSON, MARK. "Globalization, National Cultures and Cultural Citizenship," *The Sociological Quarterly*, 38 (1) Winter 1997, pp. 41–67.

STIGLITZ, JOSEPH. *Globalization and Its Discontent*. New York: Norton, 2002.

TRAHAIR, RICHARD C. S. *Utopias and Utopians: A Historical Dictionary*. Westport, CT: Greenwood Publishing Group, 1999.

TURNER, JONATHAN H., AND CHARLES E. STARNES. *Inequality: Privilege and Poverty in America*. Pacific Palisades, CA: Goodyear, 1976.

VAGO, STEVEN. *Law and Society*, 7th ed. Upper Saddle River, NJ: Prentice Hall, 2003.

WACQUANT, LOIC J. D. "The Rise of Advanced Marginality: Notes on Its Nature and Implications," *Acta Sociologica*, 39 (2) July 1996, pp. 121–139.

WAHEEDUZZAMAN, A. N. M. "Competitiveness, Human Development and Inequality: A Cross-National Comparative Inquiry." *Competitiveness Review*, 12 (2) Summer–Fall 2002, pp. 13–30.

Wall Street Journal. "Hill Democrats Plan Efforts to Increase Minimum Wage Amid Employer Protests," March 25, 1987, p. 60.

WALT, STEPHEN. *Revolution and War*. Ithaca, NY: Cornell University Press, 1996.

WEBER, MAX. *The Protestant Ethnic and the Spirit of Capitalism*, trans. Talcott Parsons, foreword by R. H. Tawney. New York: Scribner's, 1958.

WEIL, MICHELLE M., AND LARRY D. ROSEN. *TechnoStress: Coping with Technology @Work @Home @Play*. New York: Wiley, 1997.

WEJNERT, BARBARA (ed.). *Transition to Democracy in Eastern Europe and Russia: Impact on Politics, Economy and Culture*. Westport, CT: Praeger, 2002.

WESTWOOD, J. N. *Endurance and Endeavor: Russian History 1812–2001*, 5th ed. New York: Oxford University Press, 2003.

WILENSKY, HAROLD. "The Early Impact of Industrialization on Society." In William A. Faunce (ed.), *Readings in Industrial Sociology*. New York: Appleton, 1967, pp. 78–79.

WILLIAMS, DANIEL, AND ALAN COOPERMAN. "Vatican Criticizes Rules on Misconduct," *The Seattle Times*, October 18, 2002, p. A2.

WOLMAN, WILLIAM, AND ANNE COLAMOSCA. *The Judas Economy: The Triumph of Capital and the Betrayal of Work*. Reading, MA: Addison-Wesley Publishing Company, 1997.

Chapter 2
Theories of Change

Attempts at sociological explanations of social change are as old as the discipline itself. This chapter shall draw on the rich literature of sociological theory to examine and illustrate the specific and complementary contributions to the study of social change that some of the major influential "classic" and contemporary theorists have made. We will consider their contributions to social change from the evolutionary, conflict, structural-functional, and social-psychological perspectives.

The chapter deals with only a few of the important classical and contemporary theories and theorists of social change in a rather brief fashion. By necessity, many of the giants in the field have been excluded (see, for example, Gould, 2002). This approach serves certain goals. It provides the reader with some conception of the content of the different theories and how the various theories relate to one another. The discussion of these theories clearly shows the complex and multifaceted nature of social change and also serves to provide, through classification and examination of the various theories, a way of differentiating, organizing, and understanding a great mass of material. Thus, although the concern is to suggest the magnitude of the field, an attempt is made also to lend order and diversity to that magnitude.

Over three decades ago, Wilbert E. Moore (1969:810) accurately noted that "The mention of 'theory of social change' will make most social scientists appear defensive, furtive, guilt ridden, or frightened. Yet the source of this unease may be in part an unduly awe-stricken regard for the explicitly singular, and implicitly capitalized word 'Theory.'" But the word "theory" in itself should not be that frightening. It is simply a network of interrelated hypotheses (statements of probable relationships between two or more variables—actions or attributes that can be measured or categorized) or propositions (statements of relationships between two or more facts or concepts) concerning a phenomenon (an observed or observable fact, occurrence or circumstance) or set of phenomena. Sociological theories are attempted models (abstractions of reality that are used for analytical purposes) of social reality. Some theories approach this reality more closely, but they are never an entirely accurate picture of it. What is essential to this conception is that theories are never true or false, right or wrong, but always more or less adequate.

At this point it will be useful to note the major purposes served by theory. First of all, theory is a convenient way of organizing experience. It allows one to handle large amounts of empirical data with relatively few propositions. It also enables one to go beyond the empirical data and to see implications and relationships that are not evident from any datum taken alone. Furthermore, a theory also provides a stimulus and a guide for further empirical research. Theory leads to predictions about events not yet observed and encourages the investigator to examine the consequences of these predictions. These, in turn, either may lead to further empirical data in support of the theory or may suggest needed modifications or possible rejection of the theory. Consequently, we cannot ignore theory; instead, we can only choose among alternative theories. All theories purport to say something about actual events and phenomena and are not merely fictitious representations of imaginary situations. The issue is not to use or ignore theories, but to decide among alternatives.

Prior to the discussion of specific theoretical approaches, a cautionary note is in order regarding the procedures followed in this chapter for classifying various theories. It will become clear that many theories of social change tend to overlap and, for all practical purposes, may fall under several different headings. For example, the reader may find that a theory that has been placed under the heading of "structural-functional" will contain elements similar to those embodied in "evolutionary theories." Any such effort at classification of theories should be viewed essentially as a heuristic device to facilitate discussion rather than to reflect the final status of the theories considered.

Any attempt to group or categorize theories under particular labels is open to question. The present effort should not be an exception. The categories used are in some ways arbitrary; the number of categories can be increased or decreased depending on one's objectives. These categorizations simply provide some semblance of order for the principal theoretical approaches to social change. In the schema employed, theories are presented in a chronological order and are classified under the general headings of evolutionary theories, based on assumptions of predictable, cumulative change from one stage to another, usually more complex, and in the direction of increasing adaptability; conflict theories, based on the assumption that conflict is endemic to all societies as a result of inequities and exploitation; structural-functional theories, devoted to the explanation of the function that a given structure performs in the maintenance of the stability of a social system or its subsystems; and social-psychological theories, focusing on individuals and their personalities.

EVOLUTIONARY THEORIES

In the second half of the nineteenth century, the concept of evolution assumed a central place in explanations of all forms of human development in both the social and biological sciences. The most influential among the biological evolutionists was Charles Darwin (1809–1882), whose theory of natural selection provided a solid base for the explanation of biological evolution. Just as biologists traced stages in the development of the organisms, sociologists envisioned society as proceeding inevitably through a fixed set of stages—for example, from savagery through barbarism to civilization. This evolution was believed to occur in response to a set of "natural laws" that explained each stage in the organization of a society in terms of the stage that preceded it (Timasheff, 1961:23). Moreover, the idea of evolution was tied with ideas of progress, development, and advancement; each stage represented a "higher" stage than the one before it, with the final stage in the series approximating societal perfection.

But Robert A. Nisbet (1969:161) warns us that it is a popular misconception to assume that nineteenth-century social evolutionism was just an adaptation of the ideas of biological evolutionism, as advocated by Darwin, to the investigation of social institutions. Many of the major works on social evolution appeared or were begun before the publication of Darwin's book, notably those of Comte, Spencer, and Morgan. Nisbet points out that there is a substantial difference between the theory of biological evolution and the theory of social evolution. Although the two approaches have some common features, the methodologies used in the biological and social sciences are different. The biological theory is mostly a statistical theory and deals with statistical abstractions of biological organisms.

By contrast, in evolutionary theories, typologies (ways of grouping or classifying data and ideas) are dominant. Nisbet (1969:162) notes that the object of inquiry in any theory of social evolution seems to be invariably social class, kinship, culture, law, society as a whole, or other classifications of institutionalized and structured behavior. The early sociologists all believed in social evolution, the progressive development of social patterns over long periods of time. Among others, Auguste Comte, Lewis Henry Morgan, and Herbert Spencer were particularly concerned with the identification of the types of stages through which they assumed all societies must pass. I will describe their theories in some detail.

Auguste Comte (1798–1857)

The theories of progress that developed broadly and loosely in the eighteenth century, particularly by Condorcet, and advanced in the early nineteenth century, particularly by Saint-Simon, formed the starting point for Comte's thinking, which centered in the explicit search for a law of progress. Comte (1915), like many of the philosophers of his period in France, believed in progress toward a perfect society. He insisted, however, that it would come about not by political revolution, but by the proper application of a new moral science, which he named "sociology" in 1839. Comte thus became known as the "father of sociology." The highest of all sciences, it would use the "positivist" scientific method of observation, experimentation, and comparison to understand order and promote progress.

The road to perfect society involved the human intellect passing through three historical phases of sophistication: the theological, the metaphysical, and the positive. The progress of knowledge, which is the underlying basis for his theory of evolution through the "law of the three stages," is not only inevitable but also irreversible. It is, in addition, asymptotic; that is, we always approach, but never attain, perfect positive knowledge.

Comte's description of each of the three stages is as follows: In the theological stage, people think inanimate objects are alive. This general view itself goes through three phases: animism or fetishism, which views each object as having its own will; polytheism, which believes that many divine wills impose themselves on objects; and monotheism, which conceives the will of one god as imposing itself on objects. The second, or metaphysical, stage is a period in which causality is explained in terms of abstract forces; causes and forces replace desires, and one great entity—nature—prevails. The third, or positive, stage is the scientific period, in which people develop explanations in terms of natural processes and scientific laws. At this point in a society's development, it becomes possible to control human events. Comte contended that Western civilization had already reached the positive stage in control of the physical environment and was on the verge of the positive stage with respect to social relations.

Each stage not only exhibits a particular form of mental development but also has a corresponding material development. In the theological state, military life predominates; in the metaphysical state, legal forms achieve dominance; and the positive stage is the stage of industrial society. Thus, Comte held that historical development shows a matching movement of ideas and institutions.

Lewis Henry Morgan (1818–1881)

Another influential nineteenth-century proponent of uniform evolutionary stages was Lewis Henry Morgan. After graduating from Union College in 1840, he practiced law in upstate New York for a few years, but he devoted much of his time to anthropological research, which eventually became his chief interest. He is among the most influential nineteenth-century anthropologists, and his writings are widely read today. His best-known work, *Ancient Society,* was published in 1877. Morgan's ideas of evolution made a strong impression on Marx and his coworker, Engels. The latter, following the advice of Marx, in 1884 published *The Origins of the Family, Private Property and the State,* a volume making extensive use of Morgan's theories and of his illustrations, taken largely from observations of native American tribes. Morgan is considered as a founder of Marxist anthropology and was more recognized in the former Soviet Union and China than in his native country (Tooker, 1992:357).

Morgan postulated that the stages of technological developments and kinship systems were associated with different social and political institutions. On the basis of historical data, he concluded that culture evolves in successive stages that are essentially the same in all parts of the world. The order of stages is inevitable, and their content is limited because mental processes are similar among all peoples under similar conditions in various societies.

He described the progress of humankind through three main stages of evolution: savagery, barbarism, and civilization. But he also subdivided savagery and barbarism into upper, middle, and lower segments. He distinguished these stages in terms of technological achievements. The seven stages are, in his words:

I. Lower Status of Savagery, From the Infancy of the Human Race to the commencement of the next Period.
II. Middle Status of Savagery, From the acquisition of a fish subsistence and a knowledge of the use of fire, to etc.
III. Upper Status of Savagery, From the Invention of the Bow and Arrow, to etc.
IV. Lower Status of Barbarism, From the Invention of the Art of Pottery, to etc.
V. Middle Status of Barbarism, From the Domestication of animals on the Eastern Hemisphere, and in the Western from the cultivation of maize and plants by Irrigation, with the use of adobe-brick and stone, to etc.
VI. Upper Status of Barbarism, From the Invention of the process of Smelting Iron Ore, with the use of iron tools, to etc.
VII. Status of Civilization, From the Invention of a Phonetic Alphabet, with the use of writing, to the present time. (L. H. Morgan, 1964:18)

Morgan contended that each stage and substage was initiated by a major technological invention. For example, he considered pottery to be characteristic of lower barbarism, domestication of plants and animals to be characteristic of middle barbarism, and iron tools to be characteristic of upper barbarism. Civilization was heralded by the invention of the phonetic alphabet, and the organization of political society on a territorial basis was the line of demarcation where modern civilization began. Each of these stages of technological evolution, Morgan maintained, was correlated with characteristic developments in the family, religion, political organization, and property arrangements. For example, he speculated that the family evolved through six stages. Human society began with indiscriminate promiscuity and without a real family structure. It was followed by cohabitation of brothers and sisters. In the third stage, group marriage prevailed, but brothers and sisters were not allowed to mate. Then came marriage between single pairs, followed by the patriarchal family in which the husband could have more than one wife. Finally, the stage of civilization was characterized by the monogamous family with a degree of equality between husband and wife. Morgan's ideas even influenced the evolution of marriage laws in the United States (Ottenheimer, 1990). In contrast to European countries, individual states enacted laws prohibiting cousin marriage, and currently some 60 percent of the states consider first-cousin marriage illegal. This is a reflection on a nineteenth-century evolutionary perspective that categorized cousin marriage as an early type of evolutionary institution—something to be avoided by so-called civilized peoples.

Herbert Spencer (1820–1903)

Herbert Spencer was an English railroad engineer who became "the second founding father of sociology" (Timasheff, 1961:30). Spencer saw evolution as a unilinear development—that is, as a steadily continuing accumulative process by which everything in the cosmos was continually being synthesized at ever higher levels of complexity. He maintained that human society had followed a course of natural development, from relatively simple patterns of organization to more complex structures, characterized by an increasing specialization of parts.

Spencer held that the process of societal evolution followed inexorable laws of nature in that it led inevitably toward progress, toward the development of increasingly desirable and just forms of society. But Spencer also posited that there is an equilibrium between population and food supply. Should the population growth exceed the needed resources for survival, a struggle for existence will occur. Those individuals who are best able to adapt to the new conditions will manage to survive. Crucial to an understanding of Spencer's evolutionary model is the basic analogy between change in both biological and social organisms. He suggested that an increase in mass or size in either of these organisms corresponds to an "increase in structure from a few like parts to numerous interrelated parts" (Appelbaum, 1970:30).

He also argued that although a particular stage of societal evolution might seem oppressive or undesirable, it was absurd to believe that society could be improved by legislation. The state should play the smallest possible role in regulation of society in order not to interfere with natural evolutionary processes.

Spencer had a strong influence on the young science of sociology. For example, in the United States at the turn of the century, William Graham Sumner (1840–1910), one of the most important American sociologists, became an outspoken theorist of social evolution. In a famous dictum, Sumner (1896:87–88) argued that stateways could not change folkways. That is, social improvement could only come about through natural evolution of society and not by legislation. His arguments are still echoed today by those who oppose laws providing for more equitable treatment of minorities on the ground that morality cannot be legislated. But to equate his ideas wholly with right-wing ideology is a mistake largely caused by sociologists' misunderstanding of his work. That would be too simple a portrayal of Spencer's genius (Turner, 2003:442).

Other Evolutionists

Other vanguards of American sociology accepted part of the evolutionary theory of social change while embracing the notion that society could be improved by deliberate effort. Lester Frank Ward (1841–1913), a paleontologist who became the first president of the American Sociological Society in 1906, for instance, believed that both human beings and human society had developed through eons of evolution, but he maintained that once intellect had evolved in humans, they gained the ability to help shape the subsequent evolution of social forms (Ward, 1911:451). Through the application of intelligence, people could effect desired changes in society (although desired changes to some may not be desired by others). In this respect Ward was following in the tradition of Auguste Comte, who maintained that human intelligence had reached the point where society could be reconstructed through application of the scientific method.

Several other sociologists have taken an evolutionary approach to social change. In Germany, Ferdinand Toennies (1855–1936) described the trend from what he calls Gemeinschaft to Gesellschaft as one in which small, primitive, traditional, homogeneous, closely knit communities are eradicated and replaced by a large, urbanized, industrial society in which human relations are impersonal, formal, contractual, utilitarian, realistic, and specialized. The Gemeinschaft relationship is an intimate one, not unlike that found in primary groups such as the family. The close interpersonal ties that bind lifelong friends and neighbors in a rural village provides one familiar example. Because members of the community are concerned with each other's well-being, they do things for each other without consideration of repayment or personal gain. The Gesellschaft relationship, on the other hand, is based on individualistic and mutual distrust. In Toennies' (1957:65) words:

> Here everybody is by himself and isolated, and there exists a condition of tension against all others. Their spheres of activity and power are sharply

separated, so that everybody refuses to everyone else contacts with and admittance to his sphere, i.e., intrusions are regarded as hostile acts.

In the Gesellschaft relationships, people are competitive and struggle with each other to gain a personal advantage. There is no common sentiment that generates trust or concern for one another. Contract becomes instrumental in defining relationships: "For everything pleasant which someone does for someone else, he expects, even demands, at least an equivalent" (Toennies, 1957:78). Urbanization of society is considered as the main reason for the increase in Gesellschaft relationships.

Similarly, Howard P. Becker (1899–1960) saw the transition as being one from a sacred, traditionally oriented society to a secular society that evaluates customs and practices in terms of their pragmatic outcomes (1950). In anthropology, Robert Redfield (1897–1958) put the transition as being from folk to urban (folk-urban continuum). He described folk society as

> small, isolated and homogeneous with a strong sense of group solidarity. The ways of living are conventionalized into that coherent system which we call a "culture." Behavior is traditional, spontaneous, uncritical and personal. There is no legislation or habit of experiment and reflection for intellectual ends. Kinship, its relationships and institutions are the type categories of experience and the familial group is the unit of action, the sacred prevails over the secular, the economy is one of status rather than of market. (Redfield, 1947:294)

Change for Redfield is the consequence of an "increase of contacts bringing about heterogeneity and disorganization of culture" (1941:369).

Judging from this representative sample of evolutionary theories, there seems to be agreement among theorists that change is natural, directional, imminent, continuous, and necessary and proceeds from uniform causes (Nisbet, 1969:159–189). These theories also contained, as all theories do, an implicit ideological component. The general evolutionary approach, because of its emphasis on natural laws and its fixed series of stages, perhaps had a special appeal to political conservatives. Sumner, for example, used it to justify the social class system of the time, maintaining that the operation of natural selection had placed the most able groups at the top of the structure. He also believed that people should not interfere with the operation of natural laws and the evolution of society, and thus he opposed all ideas of the possibility of guided social change.

By the early part of the twentieth century, enough information had been gathered by social scientists on societies throughout the world to make it appear unlikely that societies everywhere had passed through the same series of stages. Thus, the idea of a unilinear evolution was generally discarded. Furthermore, both ideas—(1) that present societies represent the highest stage in any evolutionary sequence and (2) that there is a necessary link between social change and progress—were discredited.

The evolutionary approach is, however, still with us in more contemporary forms such as attempts to account for long-term economic growth (Hodgson, 1996) or the emergence of a new word system (Schafer, 1996, Schaeffer, 2003). The renewed interest in evolutionary theory is also evidenced, for example, by Gerhard and Jean Lenski's and Patrick Nolan's analysis of the evolution of societies. They maintain that continuity, innovation, and extinction are basic aspects of the evolutionary process and that evolution is fundamentally cumulative change because it involves a gradual addition of new elements to an already established base (Lenski, Nolan, & Lenski, 1999:66–77). But the idea of unilinear evolution—that is, all societies inevitably passing through the same set of fixed stages—has given way to the idea of a multilinear evolution (Stewart, 1953:313–336). Those who hold this view reason that, because societies were often very different to begin with, they may have appropriately undergone varying patterns of change and that the same patterns of change may produce slightly varying products in a society that started from different beginnings.

Remnants of the classical, evolutionary theories of social change can still be found in some of the contemporary anthropological theories such as those of Leslie White and Julian Steward (Lauer, 1991); perspectives on sustainability (Jeffrey, 1996), and theories dealing with economic development or societal modernization. An example of the latter point would be Walt W. Rostow's (1961) classic and still controversial and provocative sketch of the stages of economic growth, which is also illustrative of the duration of change (Chapter 5). His basic assumption is that the lengthy process of economic development can be depicted according to various stages and that uniformities tend to occur in the sequence of development. Rostow postulates that the overall process of economic growth proceeds through the following five stages:

1. *The Traditional Society.* Agriculture is predominant, there is little capital accumulation, savings are practically nonexistent, and the traditional mentality and attitudes of people hamper development.

2. *The Preconditions for Takeoff.* They include a population increase, the existence of entrepreneurs, an increase in agricultural production, and "reactive nationalism." The idea spreads that economic progress is not only possible but necessary. Education is geared to substantiate the new economic outlook. Banks and other economic institutions are formed, and the state is becoming more centralized.

3. *The Takeoff.* Economic growth becomes the normal condition. The main features of the takeoff are: (a) an increase in the ratio of savings and investment to national income from perhaps 5 to 10 percent or more; (b) the development of one or more substantial manufacturing sectors with high rates of growth; and (c) the existence or quick emergence of a political, social, and institutional framework to exploit the impulses to expansion in the modern sector. The takeoff period began in Britain after 1783, in France and the United States around 1840, and in India around 1950.

4. *The Drive to Maturity.* The application of modern technology becomes evident in all sectors of the economy. From 10 to 20 percent of the national income is steadily reinvested, permitting output regularly to outstrip the increase in population. It takes about sixty years to reach this stage "in which an economy demonstrates the capacity to move beyond the original industries which powered its take-off and to absorb and to apply efficiently over a very wide range of its resources—if not the whole range—the most advanced fruits of (then) modern technology" (Rostow, 1961:10).

5. *The Age of High Mass Consumption.* The economy shifts toward the production of consumer goods and services. More and more funds are allocated to welfare in the society, and there is a striving for power in the international arena. Rostow thinks that the United States entered this stage of high mass consumption around 1920, followed by Western Europe and Japan in the 1950s.

In sum, we may turn to the main assumptions to which, according to Smith (1973:27–28), evolutionists subscribed:

1. *Holism*—studying the whole unit rather than its parts.
2. *Universalism*—change is natural, universal, perpetual, and ubiquitous, and requires no explanation.
3. *Potentiality*—change is inherent and endogenous in the unit undergoing change.
4. *Directionality*—change is progressive.
5. *Determinism*—change is inevitable and irreversible for all units.
6. *Gradualism*—change is continuous, cumulative growth.
7. *Reductionism*—"laws of succession" are uniform and the basic topic of change is everywhere the same.

CONFLICT THEORIES

Conflict theory assumes that social behavior can best be understood in terms of tension and conflict between groups and individuals. It suggests that society is an arena in which struggles over scarce commodities take place. Conflict theorists consider change, rather than order, as the essential element of social life (see, for example, Fleming, 2000). Change is viewed as an intrinsic process in society, not merely the outcome of some improperly functioning or imbalanced part of the social system. Structural differentiation is felt to be the source of conflict, and social change occurs only through this conflict. A number of social theorists have espoused this approach, and in this section we shall focus on the main ideas of three important conflict theorists: Karl Marx, Lewis Coser, and Ralf Dahrendorf.

Karl Marx (1818–1883)

Of all the social theorists, few were as important, brilliant, original, or influential as Karl Marx. Part philosopher, part economist, part sociologist, and part historian, Marx combined political partisanship with deep scholarship in his work. His writings are generally considered among the most basic and most crucial in the study of conflict theory with regard to social change. In his words: "Without conflict, no progress: this is the law which civilization has followed to the present day" (Marx, quoted by Dahrendorf, 1959:27).

Marx postulated that every society, whatever its stage of historical development, rests on an economic foundation. He called this the "mode of production" of commodities. The mode of production, in turn, has two elements. The first is "the forces of production," or the physical or technological arrangement of economic activity. The second is "the social relations of production," or the indispensable human attachments that people must form with one another in carrying out this economic activity. In Marx's words:

> The sum total of these relations of production constitutes the economic structure of society—the real foundation, on which rise legal and political superstructures and to which correspond definite forms of social consciousness. The mode of production in material life determines the general character of the social, political, and spiritual processes of life. It is not the consciousness of men that determines their existence, but, on the contrary, their social existence determines their consciousness. At a certain stage of their development the material forces of production in society come into conflict with the existing relations of production, or—what is but a legal expression for the same thing—with the property relations within which they had been at work before. From forms of development of the forces of production these relations turn into their fetters. Then comes the period of social revolution. With the change of the economic foundation the entire immense superstructure is more or less rapidly transformed. (Marx, 1959:43–44)

The determinant or independent variable for Marx is the mode of production. Changes in this produce changes in the relations of production; that is, changes in the way in which groups of people are attached to this production technology. To illustrate this point, Marx divided history into five major stages, each characterized by a type of economic production. These stages are: (1) tribal ownership, a type of primitive communism; (2) ancient communal and state ownership accompanied by slavery; (3) feudalism; (4) capitalism; and (5) communism, which is divided into a dictatorship of the proletariat and "pure" communism. With the exception of pure communism, each stage is characterized by economic and other conflicts between two or more opposing economic groups with separate and opposing economic interests. The economic conflict between these groups inevitably leads to further social and political conflicts, as each group seeks to further its own interests at the expense of other groups. This is epitomized in the opening lines of the famous Communist Manifesto of 1848:

> The history of all hitherto existing society is the history of class struggles. Freeman and slave, patrician and plebeian, lord and serf, guild-master and journeyman, in a word, oppressor and oppressed, stood in constant opposition to one another, carried on an uninterrupted, now hidden, now open, fight, a fight that each time ended, either in a revolutionary reconstitution of society at large, or in the common ruin of the contending classes. (Marx & Engels, 1955:1)

For Marx, conflict is a normal condition of social life whose nature and variations are some of the most important things to be described and analyzed by social science. Conflict and change for him are inseparable. The economic production is the substructure upon which the rest of society, the superstructure, is built. Social institutions—such as the government, the family, education, and religion—are dependent on the mode of economic production in a given society. Variations and changes in economic production give rise to variations and changes in other social institutions with their associated values, attitudes, and norms.

In a capitalistic society, all individuals will move from intermediate groups to become either proletarians (workers) or bourgeoisie (property owners). The struggle is inevitable between these two classes and will result, as class consciousness and militant class action develop, in the overthrow of the existing system. It will culminate in the establishment of a new form of economic production—communistic production—and the new historical stage, communism. The proletariat, having won the revolution, will become the dominant group in this final historical stage.

In brief, the series of events leading to an ultimate proletariat revolution is as follows: "(1) the need for production; (2) the expansion of the division of labor; (3) the development of private property; (4) increasing social inequality; (5) class struggle; (6) creation of political structures to represent each class's interests, and finally, (7) revolution. Each event leads inevitably to the next event" (Duke, 1976:28). And, according to Marx, no person or group of people can stop the revolution from occurring.

The Marxian approach to social change has been attacked on a number of grounds. One group of criticisms deals with the fact that it overemphasized economic determination and ignored ideological, political, and other factors that influence social change. Others maintain that it insisted on the dialectical model of change through thesis, antithesis, and synthesis (action, reaction, and combination) and did not allow for regressive change or for change to occur in other ways. Some sociologists have criticized Marx, saying he placed too much emphasis on conflict and economically based power and rank. They argue, instead, that conflict is often integrative, as we shall see in the writings of Coser; and that consensus, integration, and cooperation are much more frequently in evidence than is conflict. These critics argue that shared values are common to normative systems, and functional and economic interdependence all tend to gloss over or reduce class conflict to a minimum. Finally, many critics have challenged his formulations regarding revolution. They have stressed that most revolutions, especially those in the twentieth century, have been middle-class revolutions. They argue that, aside from Marx's inadequate predictions of the place of revolution, he misjudged the depth of alienation and frustration of the average worker. Marx also failed to see the tendency of workers to identify with national, community, religious, racial, sexual, and occupational groups.

Notwithstanding these limitations, scholars felt compelled to develop and expand his ideas and, in so doing, often produced some of their most important work. Each succeeding generation has had sociologists working directly in the Marxian tradition and Marxism continues to meet a religious or teleological need among Western intellectuals (Sherman, 1995). More recently, in the mid-1990s, neo-Marxism has become one of the most important theoretical schools in American sociology (McQuarie, 1995:121) and it remains influential in the 2000s. The study of Marxism remains relevant in contemporary times in many areas. For example, many economic theories, including the computation of national income, accounting and input-output models, are based on Marxist theories (Hollander, 1995). His approach remains an important, influential, and viable one in contemporary social, economic and political thought.

Lewis A. Coser (1913–)

The conflict approach to social change gained additional momentum during the middle of the twentieth century, prompted by race conflicts, class struggles, and the warring of interests. Undoubtedly, the best-known conflict theorist among contemporary American sociologists is Lewis A. Coser. In his widely read book, *The Functions of Social Conflict*, Coser (1956) holds that conflict has both positive and negative effects. He explains that conflict is part of the socialization process and that no social group can be completely harmonious. Conflict in society is inevitable because individuals have a predisposition to hate as well as love. Thus, conflict is part of the human condition. But conflict can be constructive as well as destructive because it frequently resolves disagreements and leads eventually to unity. He believes that conflict makes for an increase in adjustment and adaptation as groups learn to live side by side. Moreover, conflict encourages "in-group" cohesion because the members of the group have a common enemy and a common cause.

Coser views conflict as a means of promoting social change. People who feel that their society satisfies their needs are not likely to want to alter anything in it. Those whose needs are not satisfied will attempt to change the situation by confronting the dominant group that has suppressed their goals. An obvious example is the civil rights movement in the United States. But Coser maintains that conflict can lead to change in a number of ways, including the establishment of new group boundaries, the drawing off of hostility and tension, the development of more complex group structures to deal with conflict and its accompaniments, and the creation of alliances with other parties. Each of these can result in a new distribution of social values, with the concomitant formation of a new social order. Therefore, conflict is seen as a creative force that stimulates change in society (Coser, 1956:153).

Ralf Dahrendorf (1929–)

Another influential contemporary conflict theorist is Ralf Dahrendorf (and the only sociologist who has been knighted and addressed as Sir Ralph). He rejects the Marxian notion of social class as determined by the relations to the means of production and defines it in terms of the unequal distribution of authority. All groups in society are seen as divided into those who have authority and those who do not. He maintains that social conflict has a structural origin and is to be "understood as a conflict about the legitimacy of relations of authority" (Dahrendorf, 1959:176). In any organization, roles and positions can be dichotomized into two "quasi-groups" whose members have opposed "latent interests." The group in position of power or authority is interested in preserving the status quo, whereas the subordinated group is interested in change. These two "quasi-groups" are potential antagonists, in that their members share common experiences, roles, and interests, whether or not they are aware of them.

Under proper "conditions of organization," interest groups emerge out of quasi-groups as the members develop a leadership cadre, effective intragroup communication, a consistent ideology, and an awareness of their common interests. Dahrendorf suggests that the more the subordinate interest groups become organized, the more likely they will be in conflict with the dominant group. The "conditions of conflict," such as opportunities for social mobility and the responses of the agents of social control, will determine the intensity and violence of conflict. By "intensity" he refers to the emotional involvement and animosity felt by the participants. He proposes that the more organized the interest groups and the more regulated their conflict, the less violent the conflict will be. Conflict, in turn, leads to structural change as a result of a change in dominance relations. The type, speed, and magnitude of change depend on the "conditions of structural change." These conditions include the capacity of those in power to stay in power and the pressure potential of the dominated interest group. Conflict between workers and management, the unionization process, and the changes brought about by the unions are used by Dahrendorf to illustrate his theory.

He concluded that "the great creative force" that leads to change in society is social conflict. "The notion that wherever there is social life there is conflict may be unpleasant and disturbing." But ". . . societies and social organizations are held together not by consensus but by constraint, not by universal agreement but by the coercion of some by others . . . and as conflict generates change, so constraint may be thought of as generating conflict. We assume that conflict is ubiquitous, since constraint is ubiquitous wherever human beings set up social organizations" (Dahrendorf, 1967: 479–480).

Dahrendorf altered Marx's theory in several ways. He saw conflict as a problem of unequal authority in all sectors of society, in contrast to the strict Marxian notion of classes. Then, he suggested the importance of dealing with external conflict while, in the Marxian conception, conflict is identified as its primary source in the internal workings of society. Furthermore, Dahrendorf pointed out that conflict in a given society results not from internal contradictions arising in historical development but from pressures exerted by other societies. Finally, Dahrendorf contended that many of the conflicts are not capable of resolution as Marx has suggested, but most frequently are controlled through "compromise" (Dahrendorf, 1990).

Unlike other conflict theorists, Dahrendorf argued that ". . . it is the task of sociology to derive conflicts from special social structures and not to relegate these conflicts to psychological variables (aggressiveness) or to descriptive historical ones (the influx of Negroes into the United States) or to chance" (Dahrendorf, 1973:102).

The conflict perspective has proved to be a lasting contribution to sociological theory. With the recent collapse of the Soviet Union and the Eastern European socialist states and the consequent ethnic and political turmoil, conflict theory has reemerged as a viable perspective albeit without its pronounced traditional Marxist flavor. The past few years witnessed the rise of a series of middle-range conflict perspectives that are variously referred to in the sociological literature as "radical," "activist," "critical," "humanist," and the like. Examples of these include the Critical Legal Studies Movement and Feminist Legal Theory, which are currently prevalent in progressive law schools (Vago, 2003:65–71). These theoretical approaches are greatly influenced by the writings of C. Wright Mills, whose polemic attacks on "the power elite" gave direction to a whole group of (generally younger) sociologists who reject the concept of value-free science and use their research and teaching to promote what they believe to be desirable—what some define as radical social change (Mills, 1956). For these sociologists, directed social change is the primary goal of scientific endeavors.

STRUCTURAL-FUNCTIONAL THEORIES

Although many scholars now accept the theory that all industrialized societies eventually develop institutions, traits, structures and cultures with certain similarities, controversy rages over the way in which these changes come about (see, for example, Pettit, 1996). In sociological theorizing, there is a group of thinkers who emphasize the so-called functionalist, or structural-functional, approach. The word *structure* generally refers to a set of relatively stable and patterned relationships of social units, and *function* refers to those consequences of any social activity that make for the adaptation or adjustment of a given structure or its component parts. In other words, structure refers to a system with relatively enduring patterns, and function refers to the dynamic process within the structure. The structures are the various parts of the social system. In the case of society, the principal structures are usually considered to be the societies' institutions—family, government, economic system, religion, and education—and the analysis focuses upon the interrelations among these institutions. Each structure and each part within the larger structure is conceived to have a function in helping the society to operate and preserving it intact.

Historically, structural-functional theorizing was brought into sociology by borrowing directly, and developing analogies for, concepts in the biological sciences. Biology, since the middle of the nineteenth century, frequently referred to the structure of an organism, meaning a relatively stable arrangement of relationships between the different cells, and to the function of the organism, which considered the consequences of the activity of the various organs in the life process. The principal consideration of this organic analogy was how each part of the organism contributes to the survival and maintenance of the whole.

Sociologists of the structural-functional school usually distinguish between the latent function and the manifest functions of social relationship (Merton, 1957:19–84). Manifest functions are those that are built into a social system by design; like manifest goals, they are well understood by group members. Latent functions are, by contrast, unintentional and often unrecognized. They are unanticipated consequences of the system that has been set up to achieve other ends. For example, the system of free public education in the United States has the manifest function of opening educational opportunities to all citizens and thereby increasing their ability to participate equally in a democratic society. In practice, however, the system has had the unintended effect of opening opportunity for some and closing it for others based on financial considerations.

Despite Spencer's adoption of the word *function*, the first systematic formulation of the logic of a structural-functional approach in sociology can be found in the works of Emile Durkheim (1858–1917). In the sociological classic, *The Division of Labor in Society*, Durkheim (1947) makes a clear distinction between the function of the division of labor and its efficient cause. Its basic function is the integration of society; its cause was the increase in "moral density" induced by population pressure. Function, for Durkheim, is a contribution to the maintenance of social life and society, as it can be seen further in his discussions on the social significance of religion, punishment, and ceremony.

In addition to Durkheim, structural-functional analysis in the United States was greatly influenced by the works of two British anthropologists: A. R. Radcliffe-Brown and Bronislaw Malinowski. Function was seen by Radcliffe-Brown (1956:189) as a contribution to the continuing existence of the social structure. Institutions and individuals alike worked toward this goal. "The continuity of structure is maintained by the process of social life, which consists of the activities and interaction of the individual human beings and of the organized groups into which they are united. The social life of the community is here defined as the functioning of the social structure. The function of any recurrent activity, such as the punishment of a crime, or a funeral ceremony, is the part it plays in the social life as a whole and therefore the contribution it makes to the maintenance of the structure continuity." Maintenance of the structure, for him, entails harmonious relationships between groups, social continuity or the nurturing of tradition and the existence of those institutions necessary for survival.

Malinowski's (1926) theoretical perspective was built around the assertion that cultural items exist to fulfill basic human and cultural needs: "The functional view of culture insists therefore upon the principle that every type of civilization, every custom, material object, idea and belief fulfills some vital function, has some task to accomplish, represents an indispensable part within a working whole." Such a theory, by its very nature "aims at the explanation of anthropological facts at all levels of development by their function, by the part which they play within the integral system of culture, by the manner in which they are related to each other within the system . . ." (1926:132–133).

The early structural-functional theorists viewed the world in systematic terms (Turner & Maryanski, 1995:49–55). For them such systems were considered to have needs and prerequisites that had to be met to assure survival. They tended to view such systems with needs and requisites as having normal and pathological states, thus connoting a system of equilibrium and homeostasis. The social world was seen as composed of mutually interrelated parts, and the analysis of these interrelated parts focused on how they fulfilled the requisites of the systems as a whole and how, therefore, system equilibrium was maintained.

Some of these ideas are incorporated in contemporary structural-functional analysis, especially the notion of systems of interrelated parts. To account for social change in a structural-functional context, let us now look at some of the principal tenets of this approach:

1. Societies must be analyzed "holistically as systems of interrelated parts";
2. Cause and effect relations are "multiple and reciprocal";
3. Social systems are in a state of "dynamic equilibrium" such that adjustment to forces affecting the system is made with minimal change within the system;
4. Perfect integration is never attained, so that every social system has strains and deviations, but the latter tend to be neutralized through institutionalization;
5. Change is fundamentally a slow, adaptive process, rather than a revolutionary shift;
6. Change is the consequence of the adjustment of changes outside the system, growth by differentiation and internal innovations; and
7. The system is integrated through shared values. (Van den Berghe, 1967: 294–295)

One way to examine the structural-functional approach to social change is in terms of the negative or unintended or, as Merton would say, dysfunctional elements. Merton (1968:40) is suggesting that the dysfunctional elements that tend normally to be a part of any social system may themselves, in their accumulation, culminate in the more overt types of change that affect the structure itself. Accordingly, "By focusing on dysfunctions as well as functions, this approach can assess not only the bases of social stability but the potential sources of change. . . . The stresses and strains in a social structure which accumulate as dysfunctional consequences of existing elements . . . will, in due course, lead to institutional breakdown and basic social change. When this change has passed beyond a given and not easily identifiable point, it is customary to say that a new social system has emerged."

Stability and change in society are basically complementary processes. Parsons (1966:21) argues that "At the most general theoretical levels, there is no difference between processes which serve to maintain a system and those which serve to change it." Or, as Kingsley Davis (1949:634) put it, "It is only in terms of equilibrium that most sociological concepts make sense. Either tacitly or explicitly, anyone who thinks about society tends to use the notion. The functional structural approach to sociological analysis is basically an equilibrium theory." The widespread use of equilibrium approaches is characteristic not only of sociology but of other social sciences as well.

In essence, equilibrium theory seeks to uncover the general conditions for the maintenance of a social system in stable equilibrium and specify the mechanisms by which that stability is preserved or reestablished after the occurrence of internal or external disturbances with implication for macro-analysis of action systems and social movements (see, for example, DeWitt, 2000).

Talcott Parsons (1902–1979)

The most influential and best-known representative of contemporary American sociologists embracing this approach is Talcott Parsons. Detailed examination of Parsons's complex ideas concerning social change that appeared in a number of this publications over time [for example, *The Social System* (1951); *Societies: Evolutionary and Comparative Perspectives* (1966); *The System of Modern Societies* (1971); and *The Evolution of Societies* (1977)] is beyond the scope of this discussion. The ensuing analysis will only consider some of his ideas of change in the context of equilibrium theory.

Parsons considers stability ". . . as a defining characteristic of structure . . . equivalent to the more specific concept of stable equilibrium—which in another reference may be either 'static' or 'moving.'" For him, "a system then is stable or (relatively) in equilibrium when the relation between its structure and the processes which go on within it and between it and its environment are such as to maintain those properties and relations, which for the purposes in hand have been called its structure, relatively unchanged. Very generally, always in 'dynamic' systems, this maintenance is dependent on continually varying processes, which 'neutralize' either endogenous or exogenous sources of variability which, if they went far enough, would change the structure." By analogy, "A classic example of equilibrium . . . is the maintenance of nearly constant body temperature by mammals and birds—in the face of continuing variation in environmental temperature and through mechanisms which operate either to produce heat, including slowing up its loss, or to slow down the rate of heat production or accelerate its dissipation." Therefore, "Contrasted then with stability or equilibrating processes are those processes which operate to bring about structural change. That such processes exist and that they are of fundamental scientific importance is nowhere in question" (Parsons, 1973:73).

In "An Outline of the Social System," which succinctly summarizes functionalism, Parsons (1961) views society as a system surrounded by three other systems (personality, the organism, and culture). He considers a society in equilibrium when its boundaries with the other three systems are not breached. Social equilibrium consists of "boundary maintenance"; social change consists of boundary breaking. "If a subboundary is broken, resources within the larger system counteract the implicit tendency to structural change" (Parsons, 1961:71).

Social change considered as boundary destruction and equilibrium restoration has two sources: endogenous (that is, affecting boundaries within the system) and exogenous (that is, initiated from one of the systems outside the social system). The external (exogenous) forces of social change are internal to the other systems (personality, the organism, culture), which are said to delineate society. "The exogenous sources of social change consist in endogenous tendencies to change in the organisms, personalities, and cultural systems articulated with social systems in question" (Parsons, 1961:71). Many kinds of exogenous changes affect the social system—for example, genetic changes in the population, changes in the technique of exploiting nature, and the impact of other social systems, as in war or in the form of cultural influences. These changes are external to the social system, but they have an impact on it.

Endogenous changes are caused by "strains" within the system itself. In Parsons's (1961:71) words: "The most general, commonly used term for an endogenous tendency to change is a 'strain.' *Strain* here refers to a condition in the relation between two or more structured units (i.e., subsystems of the system) that constitute a tendency or pressure toward changing that relation to one incompatible with the equilibrium of the relevant parts of the system." In other words, these strains result from certain disequilibria between inputs and outputs across the boundaries of subsystems. Several things can happen to these stresses and strains: they can be resolved, they can be arrested, they can be isolated, or they can be compensated for by changes in the structure of the system.

There are two main types of changes, depending on the source (exogenous or endogenous) of the model for reequilibrium once the forces to repair boundary destruction are underway. "The first . . . is the one where the principal model component comes from outside the society. This has been true of the contemporary underdeveloped societies. . . . The second . . . is that occurring when the cultural model cannot be supplied from a socially exogenous source, but must . . . be evolved from within the society" (Parsons, 1961:78).

Adjustments within the system will generally be associated with the reorganization of roles. This can take several forms, involving the disappearance, the creation, or the modification of roles. Changes of this kind tend to be more complex and continuous than changes where roles are not affected. Based on Parsons's theoretical framework, Neil J. Smelser (1959) recognizes a sevenfold sequence in which the reorganization of roles leads to other kinds of structural differentiation within the social system. In his famous study of the British cotton industry, Smelser characterized advanced societies as differing from underdeveloped or traditional societies in their degree of complexity and structural differentiation of basic institutional roles.

The process of structural differentiation is seen as a sequence of steps or stages, including the following:

1. Dissatisfaction with the goal-achievement of the social system or subsystem in question and a sense of opportunity for change in terms of the potential availability of facilities.
2. Symptoms of disturbance in the form of "unjustified" negative emotional reactions and "unrealistic" aspirations on the part of various elements in the social system.
3. A covert handling of these tensions and mobilization of motivational resources for new attempts to realize the implications of the existing value system.
4. Encouragement of the resulting proliferation of "new ideas" without imposing specific responsibility for their implementation or for "taking the consequences."
5. Positive attempts to reach specification of the new ideas and institutional patterns which will become the objects of commitments.
6. Responsible implementation of innovations carried out by persons or collectives which are either rewarded or punished, depending on their acceptability or responsibility in terms of existing value systems.
7. If the implementations of Step 6 are received favorably, they are gradually routinized into the usual patterns of performance and sanction; their extraordinary character thereby diminishes. (Smelser, 1959:15–16)

William F. Ogburn (1886–1959)

As one of the most influential early American sociologists, William F. Ogburn, in his presidential address to the American Sociological Society (ASS) in December 1929, told colleagues that sociology was "not interested" in improving the world. Science, he suggested, is interested only in discovering new knowledge. For him society was simply a term for the collective responses of the individuals who comprised it, and he maintained that sociology should be confined to the measurement and tabulation of environmental change and responses to it.

His cultural lag theory may be considered a kind of equilibrium theory. As Appelbaum (1970:73) notes, however, this is the case only "with respect to nonmaterial culture. With respect to material culture—that is, technology—cultural lag theory is closer to evolutionary theory in positing smooth, cumulative change in the direction of ever increasing complexity." Ogburn's theory reasons that societies operate as homeostatic mechanisms, in that changes that upset equilibrium in one part tend to produce compensating changes to restore that equilibrium. In this situation, however, the new equilibrium condition differs from the old one and there is a lag between the two equilibrium states. The unequal rates of change produce a strain or maladjustment, which in turn produces a lag, until the more slowly changing, usually nonmaterial, culture catches up. For example, if technology changes, the curriculum may be out of date, and students will be less able to get jobs. Unemployment may then be a problem until education is modernized. In Ogburn's words (1964:86): "A cultural lag occurs when one of two parts of culture which are correlated changes before or in greater degree than the other part does, thereby causing less adjustment between the two parts than existed previously."

In essence, Ogburn argues that material culture and nonmaterial culture change in different ways. Change in material culture is considered to have a marked directional or progressive character. This is because there are generally agreed-upon standards of efficiency that are used to evaluate material inventions. To use airplanes as an example, designers keep working to develop planes that will fly higher and faster and carry more payload at a lower unit cost; and because airplanes can be measured against these standards, inventions in this area appear both rapidly and predictably.

In the area of nonmaterial culture (knowledge and beliefs, norms and values), on the other hand, there are often no generally accepted standards. The obvious directional character of change in material culture is lacking in many areas of nonmaterial cultures.

In addition to the differences in the directional character of change, Ogburn believes that material culture tends to change faster than nonmaterial culture. This difference in rate of culture change gives the basis for the concept of cultural lag. Material inventions bring changes that require adjustments to be made in various areas of nonmaterial culture. The invention of the automobile, for instance, freed young, unmarried men and women from direct parental observation, made it possible for people to work at great distances from their homes, and, among other things, facilitated crime by making escape easier.

In sum, the structural-functional approach and its ramifications really became dominant in American sociology in the second half of the twentieth century. Indeed, as Kingsley Davis (1959) pointed out, functionalism became almost synonymous with sociological theory. Almost from the beginning, however, the functionalist approach was attacked both for alleged theoretical shortcomings and on ideological grounds. Questions such as "Functional for whom?" were raised—valid questions in that the interests and needs of different groups in society are often in conflict, and what may be functional for one group may be dysfunctional for another. Thus, the model is unable to explain social conflicts and social change because it assumes consensus on basic societal values and goals and it minimizes the importance of power and coercion as a mechanism of social integration (Eisenstadt, 1985:13).

Others argue that functional analysis deals far more adequately with the problem of social order than with the problem of social change. They argue that it is a static, antihistorical mode of analysis with a bias toward conservatism and that the theory cannot adequately account for social change. Some sociologists even suggest that there is an implicit teleology in functional analysis, in that this mode of analysis inappropriately attributes purposes to social institutions as if they were conscious beings. As expected, a sizable literature in the field has been devoted to both making and refuting these charges (Turner & Maryanski, 1995:55–58).

SOCIAL-PSYCHOLOGICAL THEORIES

In a changing society it is important to remember that it is, after all, people who change (see, for example, Ward, 2003). It is not surprising, therefore, that the social-psychological approach gained much attention over the years due primarily to the ground-breaking contributions of David McClelland and Everett E. Hagen to the study of change and, in particular, development. The underlying assumption is that societies develop as a result of the workings of certain psychological factors. Where such factors are present, change will take place; where they are absent, stagnation will prevail. Instead of concentrating on technological and environmental factors, ideas, structural conditions, or social conflict, this approach focuses on individuals with unique personality attributes. It deals with psychological determinants that drive people to act, to push forward, to invent, to discover, create, acquire, build, or expand. The German sociologist Max Weber (1864–1920), who had a stronger influence on Western sociology than any other single individual, was among the first to use this approach in his study of the Protestant ethic and capitalism. Hagen's theory of status withdrawal and McClelland's theory on achievement motivation are examples of the modern social-psychological approach to change and development.

Max Weber (1864–1920)

In *The Protestant Ethic and the Spirit of Capitalism*, Weber's theme is that the development of modern industrial capitalism was possible because of specific psychological states that occurred after the sixteenth century in Western Europe, prompted by the spread of the Protestant ethic. He pays much attention to the spirit of capitalism, stating that "development of the spirit of capitalism is best understood as part of the development of rationalism as a whole, and could be deduced from the fundamental position of rationalism on the basic problems of life" (Weber, 1958:76). The spirit of capitalism is characteristic of situations in which people are preoccupied by the idea of making money, and the acquisition of goods becomes the ultimate purpose in life. Idleness, wastefulness, or continuous enjoyment of life are not tolerated. Life is to be devoted to achieving. In the relentless pursuit of acquisitions, greater efficiency is advocated because this leads to more results. We are under a constant pressure to rationalize our activities and to organize our lives so that credibility, punctuality, honesty, inventiveness, and adaptability to new circumstances become integral parts of our behavior. Because such qualities are instrumental in efforts of achieving,

"Capitalism is identical with the pursuit of profit and forever renewed profit by means of continuous rational capitalistic enterprise" (Weber, 1958:17).

Weber emphatically argues that people, dominated by the capitalist spirit, have little regard for traditions that would impede their climb to greater and greater wealth. "The most important opponent with which the spirit of capitalism . . . has had to struggle was the type of attitude and reaction to new situations which we may designate as traditionalism" (Weber, 1958:58–59). Therefore, the capitalist, the acquisition seeker, is an innovator by nature. Acquisition and profit making become a preoccupation. But greed is not the motivation. The capitalist spirit requires that both the acquisition and the spending of money be strictly rational, calculated, and directed toward the goal of progressive, optimal accumulation.

Weber asserts that modern Western civilization is a product of the Protestant ethic. There is a strong attitude of respect for work in the Protestant ethic. Weber points out that "the god of Calvinism demanded of his believers not single good works, but a life of good works combined into a unified system" (Weber, 1958:117). From this perspective, instead of being punishment for sin, work was worshipful activity through which man glorified God. Rationality and calculation were means to salvation in the next world as well as to success in this one. The world was a place of sin, and the individual must not be trapped by its pleasures. These beliefs constitute the core of what Weber called the doctrine of worldly asceticism, a crucial prerequisite of capitalism.

When people work hard, they may accumulate wealth. When they are prohibited from indulging in worldly pleasures, they do not spend it. They save, and savings are one of the foundations of capitalism. Simply by embracing the Protestant ethic, postfeudal citizens began acting in ways that made them more successful members of the rising capitalistic economy. Merchants and manufacturers, ill at ease with the conflict between their traditional beliefs and business behavior, found comfort and reinforcement in the Protestant ethic. The Protestant ethic, as a way of life, was one of piety, frugality, prudence, discipline, devotion to work which became one's calling, and postponement of gratification. It also generated the right atmosphere for the spread of the spirit of capitalism. But Weber assumed that although the impulse to profit and gain is present in all societies, only in the West did capitalism, as a rational organization of production and the calculable balance sheet of costs, emerge (Bell, 1996).

Max Weber, as most great and provocative thinkers usually are, is challenged, questioned, and criticized on a number of grounds (see, for example, Weinert, 1997). A number of questions centered around the alleged direct causal connection between the Protestant ethic on the one hand and the development of capitalism on the other. "Others have cast doubt on the specific 'mechanism' through which, according to Weber, Calvinist belief became transformed into or linked to motivation for this—worldly economic activities, namely, the psychological derivatives of the idea of predestination, the great anxiety which this idea created among believers, urging them to undertake in a compulsive way this-worldly activities to prove their being of the elect" (Eisenstadt, 1973:215).

There are also arguments suggesting that Weber's linking of capitalism to the Protestant work ethics fails to explain the success of Confucian ethics–based Asian countries and areas such as Singapore, Taiwan, and Hong Kong and the great economic success of overseas Chinese. Confucius, who lived in the sixth century, denounced the profit motive as unworthy of an ethical citizen. He states in one of his more famous aphorisms that "The gentleman understands what is moral. The small man understands what is profitable." Confucius was a stern moralist who advocated filial piety, reverence for ancestral customs, and emperor worship. His main concern was that people fulfill their "heavenly decree" and learn to live honorably within a static and hierarchical society. The virtues he recommended were magnanimity, propriety, moderation, persistent striving, respect for one's superiors, and honest dealings with one's inferiors. He said nothing about competition, risk taking and trade. But Francis Fukuyama (1995) argues in his provocative book *Trust* that something very interesting happens when Confucian values are transplanted into a free market environment. Fukuyama points out that many of the virtues of Confucianism, such as close-knit family structure, frugality and striving for excellence, are not premodern, but are precisely those values that are best adapted to modern capitalist success. He concludes that when the Chinese migrate to other parts of the world with competitive and free markets, their Confucian values helped them to out-perform the natives.

On the other hand, in the past three decades or so, with the surge of the great interest in development and modernization, interest in his thesis has arisen once more. Inspired by Weber's contentions, for example, Robert N. Bellah (1975) found that the Japanese religion's promotion of diligence and frugality was instrumental in generating the spirit of entrepreneurship and the fruitful activity that were essential elements in Japan's industrialization.

Everett E. Hagen (1906–1993)

Everett E. Hagen (1962, 1991) became interested in economic growth when he wrote a paper on the panic of 1907 for a graduate course. After working for the National Resources Planning Board during World War II, he chaired the economics department at University of Illinois at Urbana, and then went to Burma as an advisor to the government. Subsequently, he became a professor at the Massachusetts Institute of Technology. His theory is concerned, just like Weber's, with the beginnings of economic development.

He asserts that change from traditional to modern society will not come about without a change in personalities. He develops his ideas within a framework of contrast between traditional and modern societies, positing that each of these societies is a product of a different type of personality.

In Hagen's view, traditional societies are characterized by fixed status levels (such as peasants and elites) and the personalities in such social groupings are authoritarian, uncreative, and noninnovational. A member of a traditional society is uncreative because he or she sees the world as an arbitrary place rather than one that is subject to analysis and control. A person's unconscious processes are both inaccessible and uncreative. Interpersonal relations are solved on the basis of "ascriptive authority," and people avoid anxiety by resorting to authority. Such a type of society has a great degree of stability in its institutions and there may be no social change for centuries, for "the interrelationships between personality and social structure are such as to make it clear that social change will not occur without change in personalities" (Hagen, 1962:86).

Modern society is a product of what Hagen calls innovational personality. This personality type is characterized by attributes such as creativity, curiosity, and openness to experience. A person with this type of personality persistently looks for new solutions and does not take generally accepted evaluations for granted. Such a person sees the world as having a logical and coherent order that can be understood and explained. In spite of sporadic doubts, individuals such as these are confident that they can evaluate the order of things by themselves and solve the problems they are confronted with. Such people are not necessarily happy and may be driven to creativity by a continual anxiety that causes them to feel satisfaction only when they are striving and achieving and when their accomplishments are acknowledged and favorably evaluated.

Following this discussion of the two personality types, Hagen poses the key question: How can a stable traditional society dominated by authoritarian personalities be transformed into a modern society characterized by innovational personalities? Hagen's answer is that change comes about if and when members of one particular social group perceive that their purposes and values are not respected by other groups in the society whom they respect and whose esteem they value. The phrase he uses for this is withdrawal of status respect (Hagen, 1962:185). He considers several situations of status withdrawal; for example, when a traditional elite group is replaced by another group, when symbols and beliefs that a subordinate group considers vital are depreciated or even prohibited by a superior group, inconsistency of economic and other statuses, nonacceptance of a migrant group in a new place of residence, and the delegation of institutional activity without change in the power structure.

Status withdrawal, for Hagen, means disregard for one's role in society or for one's beliefs and aspirations. He argues that it is painful to be disregarded. People without a role in society become alienated and frustrated. Groups with a low status, or groups that are forced to accept a lower status, become disenchanted with the established order. Their accumulated resentment is then transferred to their children. As a result, frustration and rage continue to be accumulated from one generation to another. Following Merton's typology of modes of individual adaptation, retreatism, he believes, is the typical reaction to withdrawal of status. The retreatist person, he says, "is not free of rage." On the contrary, the rage is intense, but held in leash, with occasional outbursts. But

> retreatism is not a dead end. As retreatism deepens in successive generations, it creates circumstances of home life and social environment that are conducive to the development of innovational personality. The historical sequence seems to be: authoritarianism, withdrawal of status respect, retreatism, creativity. (Hagen, 1962:217)

Hagen considers child-rearing practices in developing countries a decisive factor in the transformation of societies. Following Freud, he assumes that childhood determines what people will become and how they will react to values and events. Values inculcated in a person's mind in early childhood remain for life. Assuming that, he argues, there is reason to expect that the men in a group suffer more from loss of status than do women. Thus, because of loss of status, men will despair, become weak, and adopt an attitude of retreatism. Women, on the other hand, resenting the weakness of their husbands, will do everything to instill in the minds of their sons a desire to be better off than their parents. Hagen posits that the mothers will bring up their sons in a spirit of self-reliance in a yearning for achievement and ardent aspiration to prove their worth to others. The innovational personality characterized by creative imagination is likely to come into being if the boy's

> experiences of infancy and early childhood give him a firm and satisfying impression of the loving nurturance of his mother, but that repeatedly he is unable to achieve as she seems to wish him to. He may then feel that the fault must lie in him, and there may become built into him anxiety that he may not accomplish enough, anxiety that drives him all his life to achieve in order to regain fleetingly that temporary feeling of security conveyed by his mother's praise and caresses. In this case, little rage and hatred may be provoked in him, and his unconscious processes will remain accessible to him. (Hagen, 1962:94)

Hagen assumes that the home environment and the lessons of the mothers should, in due time, inspire their sons to become innovators and reformers. They will acquire and establish new roles challenging the actual elite. This will come about, in Hagen's view (1962:242), when two conditions are fulfilled: "a requisite for economic growth in a traditional society is not merely that upward social mobility by new means is possible, but also that upward social mobility by traditional channels is not possible."

He illustrates his theory with case studies of Japan, Burma, and Colombia, with sporadic reference to the situation of the blacks in the United States. His attempts to account for the importance of personality in development are ambitious and revealing. There are, nevertheless, problems with his theory.

Some of the criticisms deal with the fact that he paid little attention to social structure features that changed the fashion in which socialization impinges upon different members of the same society. Others question his appraisal of the authoritarian personality in traditional society and the innovational personality in modern society. His description of the authoritarian personality could easily fit any Prussian Army officer, members of the prewar Japanese military, or any typical bureaucrat who avoids the anxiety of independent, creative, innovative thinking. Still, in spite of some of these criticisms, Hagen is right in telling us that psychological factors and the rearing of a new generation, in general, are important elements in promoting change and development.

David C. McClelland (1917–1998)

David C. McClelland was a renowned and controversial psychologist who spent long periods at Wesleyan and Harvard and taught at Boston University until his death. His grandfather was the presiding judge of the U.S. Court of Customs, and his father, a minister, was the president of a small Methodist women's college in Jacksonville, Illinois. He did not start school until the third grade because of illness, but by the time he finished high school, he spoke four languages. He was inspired by Max Weber's *The Protestant Ethic and the Spirit of Capitalism*, which posits, as noted earlier, that a change in social psychological orientation (the Reformation) was the cause of an economic change—the birth of industrial capitalism. Like Hagen, he has been primarily concerned with a specific kind of change—economic development. He focused his interest on the investigation of what he called achievement motivation, which subsequently was changed to the need for achievement (symbolized by n Achievement). He asserts that economic development, both in historical and contemporary societies, results from a preceding development of the n Achievement. And, the greater the development of the n Achievement, the more likely that economic development will be intense. He and his colleagues developed several methods of analyzing and measuring the n Achievement in historical societies and for cross-cultural purposes in existing societies. His results led him to suggest that "a society with a generally high level of n Achievement will produce more rapid economic development" (McClelland, 1961:205). The lesson is obvious, for rapid economic growth helps to ". . . encourage and develop those . . . who have a vigorous entrepreneurial spirit or a strong drive for achievement. In other words: *invest in a man, not just in a plan*" (McClelland, 1973:16).

McClelland's *n* Achievement means individual economic achievement that produces economic growth. It is similar to what Max Weber emphasized many times. It is not greed for riches, it is action ". . . on the basis of rigorous calculation, directed with foresight and caution toward the economic success which is in sharp contrast to the hand-to-mouth existence of the peasant, and to the privileged traditionalism of the guild craftsman and too of the adventurers' capitalism, oriented to the exploitation of political opportunities and irrational speculation" (Weber, 1958:76). Similarly, McClelland is talking about accumulation of money, but not about money for its own sake. Accumulation of money is but one measure of success for the *n* Achievement seekers: ". . . it is *not* profit per se that makes the businessman tick but a strong desire for achievement, for doing a good job. Profit is simply one measure among several of how well the job has been done, but it is not necessarily the goal itself" (McClelland, 1973:162). More specifically, the *n* Achievement is manifested in behavior characterized by preferences for tasks with moderate difficulties for moderate calculated risks, and energetic innovative activity, especially when it results in personal achievement. Also exhibited are a degree of individualism, manifested in a high degree of responsibility and a tendency for prospective planning of individual actions, combined with a better performance if there is a knowledge of the results of the action and an evident probability of success.

Most of McClelland's work and that of his associates was devoted to the analysis of ethnographic accounts of numerous cultures in an attempt to determine the percentage of adult males engaged in entrepreneurial activity. They analyzed the content of folktales and children's stories of twenty-three nations for content and conditions of *n* Achievement, and correlated them with subsequent indicators of economic growth. Ancient Greek literature in different periods was analyzed. The findings suggested that such literature written before periods considered prosperous in Greece, as a rule, contained stimulation toward entrepreneurial activity. They also established that persons with a high *n* Achievement have a tendency to doodle in multiple or diagonal waves and "S" shapes. Thus, the ceramic patterns of different cultures at different times were compared from that angle. A number of other examinations were made, special psychological tests were constructed to evaluate *n* Achievement, and people in various countries were tested.

Having established the pattern of *n* Achievement, the question is raised: How can achievement motivation be induced? The answer is simple: by learning. In the classic Freudian tradition, McClelland and his colleagues believed that motives are learned in reference to both external and internal stimuli. Because most of the motivations are learned in early childhood, the kind of motivations learned at that time and the stimuli experienced in childhood are of crucial importance for subsequent behavior. In other words, the desired motives may be elicited by properly selected stimuli. Achievement motivation could be inculcated in training of self-reliance, high praise for hard work, persistence in goal attainment, and interest in excellence for its own sake. Education and child-rearing practices that emphasize such values are instrumental in creating a foundation for a strong *n* Achievement. "Studies of the family have shown, for instance, that for a boy three factors are important in producing high *n* Achievement—parents' high standards of achievement, warmth and encouragement, and a father who is not dominating and authoritarian" (McClelland, 1973:172).

In another publication, *Motivating Economic Achievement* (McClelland, Winter, & Winter, 1969), however, he reiterates his belief that achievement motivation is the major stimulant of economic growth. He provides evidence that even adults who were educated in a traditional setting can acquire a strong desire for modernity (see also Carleheden & Jacobsen, 2002) and can achieve in economic undertakings if they are properly induced in the direction by external agencies. The key is to change their attitude. This can be accomplished when they are put under special training that rewards their prowess and stimulates their desire for acquisition. McClelland argues that they soon start to behave as modern entrepreneurs—that is, they promote economic activities that cumulatively will produce the effect of economic growth, creating more jobs, and, subsequently, raising the general standard of living. The book deals with activities and the results of special courses in raising achievement motivation organized in India. In his conclusion, he repeats his earlier advice: "sow achievement motivation to harvest economic development."

The work of McClelland and his associates generated much subsequent research and interest on *n* Achievement, much of it translated into practical and empirical applications (see, for example, Nathawat, Singh, & Singh, 1997). McClelland also carried out further work in a variety of settings: he set up achievement motivation courses in India, trained U.S. Navy personnel in a program to improve leadership and management, and gave achievement-motivation training to workers at the Gdansk shipyard in Poland, including the future leader of Solidarity, Lech Walesa, who was subsequently elected president. The "War on Poverty" and related activities also benefited from his efforts (Lemann, 1994). On the other hand, there have been some concerns raised about his work. One is the question of "who trains the trainer"—that is, what motivates parents or teachers to train children for achievement rather than for something else, such as power of affiliation. Another is the question of explanatory completeness. Can McClelland's thesis account for economic growth in a causal sense (Sztompka, 1994:243)? Others contend that motivational theories in general have fallen into relative disfavor and researchers have turned to other questions concerning the supply of entrepreneurship (Smelser, 1976:128).

SUMMARY

In the history of sociology, few theories have been so passionately pursued as that of social change. These efforts of explaining social change should be seen in the context of the intellectual, political, and social climates of the particular theorists. In each historical epoch, every interpretation of social reality posits certain questions and provides certain answers, thereby effectively excluding the possibility of other questions and other answers. According to S. N. Eisenstadt (1972), tension is inherent in intellectual life because of the tendency to challenge the intellectual construction of social reality. If a theory of society is developed by one group of intellectuals, this will provide an incentive for others to view the matter in another way. Eisenstadt's insight accounts, in part, for the diverse explanations of social change.

Some of the principal theories attempting explanation have been reviewed, and their weaknesses have been noted. Evolutionary theories tried to show that all societies in all spheres of social life pass through similar stages of development, moving from less complex, less differentiated stages to more complex and differentiated stages—culminating in the modern industrial, secular society.

Conflict theorists view change as the outgrowth of inescapable competition for scarce resources among groups in society. Conflict is considered inevitable in social systems and is seen by some as a creative source of change and by others as the only possible means of change.

The structural-functional theorists have sought in various ways to account for change within the overall framework of their theory that society consists of interrelated parts that work together for the purpose of maintaining internal balance.

Social-psychological theories posit that activities of people constitute the essence of change in society and modifications in the behavior can facilitate change and play an essential role in societal development.

Although the study of social change has been the focus of attention of sociologists since the beginning of the discipline, agreement on a general theory is not yet in sight. A satisfactory theory of social change should indicate what elements are changing, what direction the change is taking, and how and why it is occurring. Such a theory should also provide an explanation for both the internal dynamics of society and the relationship between the society and its external environment. In the literature on social change, no theory realizes these objectives.

The quest for such comprehensive theory may well be futile. A concentration on narrower theories of change that seeks to explain transformations in particular domains, such as economic or family life, may be more productive in the future.

SUGGESTED FURTHER READINGS

APPELBAUM, RICHARD P. *Theories of Social Change.* Chicago: Markham, 1970. A clear, concise and now almost classic review of evolutionary, equilibrium, conflict, and rise-and-fall theories of social change.

CARLEHEDEN, MIKAEL, AND MICHAEL HVLID JACOBSEN (eds.). *The Transformation of Modernity: Aspects of the Past, Present and Future of an Era.* Burlington, VT: Ashgate, 2002. A multidisciplinary volume on the various perspectives of modernity with an emphasis on historical and specific social, political and philosophical issues.

COSER, LEWIS. *The Functions of Social Conflict.* New York: Free Press, 1956. Building on the earlier work of Georg Simmel, Coser elaborates the many ways in which conflict strengthens rather than weakens group life. Even after close to half a century, it remains one of the most widely quoted and influential books on conflict.

DEWITT, M. ROSS. *Beyond Equilibrium Theory: Theories of Social Action and Social Change Applied to a Study of Power Sharing in Transition.* Lanham, MD: University Press of America, 2000. An intriguing attempt at a fundamentally new interpretation of social reality that introduces theories of social formation and transformation for micro and macro analysis of action systems and social movements.

GOULD, STEPHEN J. *The Structure of Evolutionary Theory.* New York: Belknap, 2002. A paleontologist's approach to evolutionary theorizing, replete with refreshing and thought-provoking insights.

JANOS, ANDREW C. *Politics and Paradigms: Changing Theories of Social Change in Social Science.* Stanford, CA: Stanford University Press, 1986. A critical evaluation of the major theoretical perspectives on social change with special emphasis on the controversial Marxist model.

McQUARIE, DONALD (ed.). *Readings in Contemporary Sociological Theory: From Modernity to Post-Modernity.* Englewood Cliffs, NJ: Prentice Hall, 1995. A collection of important articles on, among other topics, functionalism, conflict theory, Marxism and neo-Marxism.

NISBET, ROBERT A. *Social Change and History.* New York: Oxford, 1969. A lucid and highly readable analysis of many of the influential theories of social change.

SHERMAN, HOWARD J. *Reinventing Marxism.* Baltimore, MD: Johns Hopkins University Press, 1995. An attempt to show that Marxism has not been tainted or discredited by the political–institutional practices pursued in its name or on its behalf.

SZTOMPKA, PIOTR. *The Sociology of Social Change.* Cambridge, MA: Blackwell, 1994. The author combines theoretical approaches with major issues of social change to demonstrate how change may be analyzed at different levels of society.

TURNER, JONATHAN H. *The Structure of Sociological Theory,* 7th ed. Belmont, CA: Wadsworth, 2003. A good overview of the major classical and contemporary sociological theories with multiple applications to social change.

WARD, STEVEN C. *Modernizing the Mind: Psychological Knowledge and the Remaking of Society*. Westport, CT: Praeger, 2003. A social and cultural history of the spread of psychological knowledge and its impact on our conception of self and society.

REFERENCES

APPELBAUM, RICHARD P. *Theories of Social Change*. Chicago: Markham, 1970.
BECKER, HOWARD P. *Through Values to Social Interpretation: Essays on Social Context, Actions and Prospects*. Durham, NC: Duke University Press, 1950.
BELL, DANIEL. "The Protestant Ethic," *World Policy Journal*, 13 (3) Fall 1996, pp. 35–40.
BELLAH, ROBERT N. *Tokugawa Religion: The Values of Pre-industrial Japan*. New York: Free Press, 1975.
CARLEHEDEN, MIKAEL, AND MICHAEL HVLID JACOBSEN (eds.). *The Transformation of Modernity: Aspects of the Past, Present and Future of an Era*. Burlington, VT: Ashgate, 2002.
COMTE, AUGUSTE. *The Positive Philosophy*, trans. and ed. Harriet Martineau. London: George Bell, 1915.
COSER, LEWIS A. *The Functions of Social Conflict*. Glencoe, IL: Free Press, 1956.
DAHRENDORF, RALF. *Class and Class Conflict in Industrial Society*. Stanford, CA: Stanford University Press, 1959.
DAHRENDORF, RALF. "Out of Utopia: Toward a Reorientation of Sociological Analysis." In N.J. Demerath III, and Richard A. Peterson (eds.), *System, Change, and Conflict: A Reader on Contemporary Sociological Theory and the Debate over Functionalism*. New York: Free Press, 1967, pp. 465–480.
DAHRENDORF, RALF. "Towards a Theory of Social Conflict." In A. Etzioni and Eva Etzioni Halevy (eds.), *Social Change: Sources, Patterns, and Consequences*, 2nd ed. New York: Basic Books, 1973, pp. 100–113.
DAHRENDORF, RALF. *The Modern Social Conflict: An Essay on the Politics of Liberty*. Berkeley, CA: University of California Press, 1990.
DAVIS, KINGSLEY. *Human Society*. New York: Macmillan, 1949.
DAVIS, KINGSLEY. "The Myth of Functional Analysis as a Special Method in Sociology and Anthropology." *American Sociological Review*, 24, 1959, pp. 757–772.
DEWITT, M. ROSS. *Beyond Equilibrium Theory: Theories of Social Action and Social Change Applied to a Study of Power Sharing in Transition*. Lanham, MD: University Press of America, 2000.
DUKE, JAMES T. *Conflict and Power in Social Life*. Provo, UT: Brigham Young University Press, 1976.
DURKHEIM, EMILE. *The Division of Labor in Society*, trans. George Simpson. New York: Free Press, 1947.
EISENSTADT, S. N. "Intellectuals and Tradition," *Daedelus*, 101 (2), 1972, pp. 1–19.
EISENSTADT, S. N. *Tradition, Change and Modernity*. New York: Wiley, 1973.
EISENSTADT, S. N. "Macro-Societal Analysis—Background, Development and Indication." In S. N. Eisenstadt and H. J. Helle (eds.), *Micro-Sociological Theory: Perspectives on Sociological Theory*, vol. I. London: Sage Publications, 1985, pp. 7–24.
FLEMING, JOHN. *The War of All Against All: An Analysis of Conflict in Society*. Lanham, MD: University Press of America, 2000.

FUKUYAMA, FRANCIS. *Trust: The Social Virtues and the Creation of Prosperity.* New York: Free Press, 1995.

GOULD, STEPHEN J. *The Structure of Evolutionary Theory.* New York: Belknap, 2002.

HAGEN, EVERETT E. *On the Theory of Social Change: How Economic Growth Begins.* Homewood IL: Dorsey Press, 1962.

HAGEN, EVERETT E. "My Life Philosophy," *American Economist,* 35 (1) Spring, 1991, pp. 10–18.

HODGSON, GEOFFREY. "An Evolutionary Theory of Long-Term Economic Growth," *International Studies Quarterly,* 40 (3) September 1996, pp. 391–411.

HOLLANDER, SAMUEL. "Comment: The Relevance of Karl Marx," *History of Political Economy,* 27 (1) Spring 1995, pp. 167–173.

JEFFREY, PAUL. "Evolutionary Analogies and Sustainability: Putting a Human Face on Survival," *Futures,* 28 (2) March 1996, pp. 173–188.

LAUER, ROBERT H. *Perspectives on Social Change,* 4th ed. Boston: Allyn & Bacon, 1991.

LEMANN, NICHOLAS. "Is There a Science of Success?" *The Atlantic Monthly,* 273 (2) February 1994, pp. 82–95.

LENSKI, GERHARD, PATRICK NOLAN, AND JEAN LENSKI. *Human Societies: An Introduction to Macrosociology,* 8th ed. New York: McGraw-Hill, 1999.

MALINOWSKI, BRONISLAW. "Anthropology," *Encyclopaedia Britannica,* 1st supplementary volume. Chicago: Encyclopaedia Britannica, 1926, pp. 132–133.

MARX, KARL. "A Contribution to the Critique of Political Economy." In L. S. Feuer (ed.), *Marx and Engels: Basic Writings on Politics and Philosophy.* New York: Doubleday (Anchor Books), 1959, pp. 42–46.

MARX, KARL, AND FRIEDRICH ENGELS. *The Communist Manifesto.* New York: Appleton, 1955 (originally published in 1848).

MCCLELLAND, DAVID C. *The Achieving Society.* Princeton, NJ: Van Nostrand, 1961.

MCCLELLAND, DAVID C. "Business Drive and National Achievement." In A. Etzioni and Eva Etzioni-Halevy (eds.), *Social Change: Sources, Patterns and Consequences,* 2nd ed. New York: Basic Books, 1973, pp. 161–174.

MCCLELLAND, DAVID C., DAVID G. WINTER, AND SARAH K. WINTER. *Motivating Economic Achievement.* New York: Free Press, 1969.

MCQUARIE, DONALD (ed.). *Readings in Contemporary Sociological Theory: From Modernity to Post-Modernity.* Englewood Cliffs, NJ: Prentice Hall, 1995.

MERTON, ROBERT K. *Social Theory and Social Structure.* New York: Free Press, 1957.

MERTON, ROBERT K. *Social Theory and Social Structure,* rev. ed. New York: Free Press, 1968.

MILLS, C. WRIGHT. *The Power Elite.* New York: Oxford, 1956.

MOORE, WILBERT E. "A Reconsideration of Theories of Social Change," *American Sociological Review,* 25(6), 1969, pp. 810–818.

MORGAN, LEWIS HENRY. *Ancient Society.* Cambridge, MA: Harvard University Press, 1964 (originally published in 1877).

NATHAWAT, S. S., RAM SINGH, AND BHIM SINGH. "The Effect of Need for Achievement on Attributional Style," *The Journal of Social Psychology,* 137 (1) February 1997, pp. 55–63.

NISBET, ROBERT A. *Social Change and History.* New York: Oxford, 1969.

OGBURN, WILLIAM F. *On Culture and Social Change.* Chicago: University of Chicago Press, 1964.

OTTENHEIMER, MARTIN. "Lewis Henry Morgan and the Prohibition of Cousin Marriage in the United States," *Journal of Family History,* 15 (3) July 1990, pp. 325–335.

Parsons, Talcott. *The Social System.* New York: Free Press, 1951.

Parsons, Talcott. "An Outline of the Social System." In Talcott Parsons, Edward A. Shills, Kaspar D. Naegele, and Jesse R. Pitts (eds.), *Theories of Society,* vol. 1. New York: Free Press, 1961, pp. 30–79.

Parsons, Talcott. *Societies: Evolutionary and Comparative Perspectives.* Englewood Cliffs, NJ: Prentice Hall, 1966.

Parsons, Talcott. *The System of Modern Societies.* Englewood Cliffs, NJ: Prentice Hall, 1971.

Parsons, Talcott. "A Functional Theory of Change." In A. Etzioni and Eva Etzioni-Halevy (eds.), *Social Change: Sources, Patterns and Consequences,* 2nd ed. New York: Basic Books, 1973, pp. 72–86.

Parsons, Talcott. *The Evolution of Societies.* Englewood Cliffs, NJ: Prentice Hall, 1977.

Pettit, Philip. "Functional Explanation and Virtual Selection," *The British Journal for the Philosophy of Science,* 47 (2) June 1996, pp. 291–303.

Radcliffe-Brown, A. R. *Structure and Function in Primitive Society.* New York: Free Press, 1956.

Redfield, Robert. *The Folk Culture of Yucatan.* Chicago: University of Chicago Press, 1941.

Redfield, Robert. "The Folk Society," *American Journal of Sociology,* 52, 1947, pp. 293–308.

Rostow, Walt W. *The Stages of Economic Growth: A Non-Communist Manifesto.* New York: Cambridge, 1961.

Schaeffer, Robert K. *Understanding Globalization: The Social Consequences of Political, Economic, and Environmental Change,* 2nd ed. Lanham, MD: Rowman & Littlefield Publishers, Inc., 2003.

Schafer, Paul D. "Towards a New World System: A Cultural Perspective," *Futures,* 28 (3) April 1996, pp. 285–300.

Sherman, Howard J. *Reinventing Marxism.* Baltimore, MD: Johns Hopkins University Press, 1995.

Smelser, Neil J. *Social Change in the Industrial Revolution.* London: Routledge, 1959.

Smelser, Neil J. *The Sociology of Economic Life,* 2nd ed. Englewood Cliffs, NJ: Prentice Hall, 1976.

Smith, Anthony D. *The Concept of Social Change: A Critique of the Functionalist Theory of Social Change.* London: Routledge, 1973.

Stewart, Julian. "Evolution and Progress." In A. L. Kroeber (ed.), *Anthropology Today.* Chicago: University of Chicago Press, 1953, pp. 313–326.

Sumner, William Graham. *Folkways.* Boston: Ginn, 1896.

Sztompka, Piotr. *The Sociology of Social Change.* Cambridge, MA: Blackwell, 1994.

Timasheff, Nicholas S. *Sociological Theory: Its Nature and Growth,* rev. ed. New York: Random House, 1961.

Toennies, Ferdinand. *Community and Society: Gemeinschaft und Gesellschaft,* trans. and ed. Charles P. Loomis. East Lansing: Michigan State University Press, 1957.

Tooker, Elizabeth. "Lewis H. Morgan and His Contemporaries," *American Anthropologist,* 94 (2) June 1992, pp. 357–376.

Turner, Jonathan H. *The Structure of Sociological Theory,* 7th ed. Belmont, CA: Wadsworth, 2003.

Turner, Jonathan H., and Alexandra R. Maryanski. "Is 'Neofunctionalism' Really Functional?" In Donald McQuarie (ed.), *Readings in Contemporary Sociological*

Theory: From Modernity to Post-Modernity. Englewood Cliffs, NJ: Prentice Hall, 1995, pp. 49–62.

VAGO, STEVEN. *Law and Society*, 7th ed. Upper Saddle River, NJ: Prentice Hall, 2003.

VAN DEN BERGHE, PIERRE L. "Dialectic and Functionalism: Towards a Synthesis." In N. Demerath and R. A. Peterson (eds.), *System, Change, and Conflict: A Reader on Contemporary Sociological Theory and the Debate over Functionalism*. New York: Free Press, 1967, pp. 294–310.

WARD, LESTER FRANK. *Dynamic Sociology*, 2nd ed. New York: Appleton, 1911.

WARD, STEVEN C. *Modernizing the Mind, Psychological Knowledge and the Remaking of Society*. Westport, CT: Praeger, 2003.

WEBER, MAX. *The Protestant Ethic and the Spirit of Capitalism*, trans. Talcott Parsons, foreword by R. H. Tawney. New York: Scribner's, 1958.

WEINERT, FRIEDEL. "Weber's Types as Models in the Social Sciences," *Philosophy*, 72 (279) January 1997, pp. 73–94.

Chapter 3

Patterns of Change

The preceding chapters have been devoted to causes and principal theories of change. Thus far, the discussion has been guided by the questions of why and in what context change takes place, and what the driving forces are behind change. In this chapter, the question of how change occurs will be considered. The objective is to examine the major processes and dimensions of change, not as "causes" but as "intermediaries" or "carriers" of change, and to analyze the various forms or patterns by which change comes about.

In the sociological literature there have been many attempts to analyze, both qualitatively and quantitatively, the emergence of change patterns in societies. This chapter will describe, compare, and contrast several of the major patterns. In this discussion, the emphasis will be on both cultural and societal forms. Among the former, three seem to be of particular importance: evolution, diffusion, and acculturation. Among the latter, the major ones considered are revolution, modernization, industrialization, urbanization, and bureaucratization.

EVOLUTION

In Chapter 2, the various evolutionary theories of change were discussed in some detail. It was noted that many of the earlier theories were based on the idea that it was possible to improve society through deliberate human effort and that society, especially Western society, was moving inexorably from one stage or phase toward another, usually a better and more desirable one. For example, for Marx and Engels, evolution was to make manifest destiny of the *Communist Manifesto*. Others, in a similar vein, also saw the evolution of societies toward greater complexity, which, they believed, inevitably produces greater human happiness.

Some go as far as to argue that changing social structures and global processes seem to signify the emergence of the first global civilization with a new world order and shared values, structures, and processes (Perlmutter, 1991).

Contemporary anthropologists, in an attempt to revitalize evolutionary theory, have focused on culture and technology to show how evolutionary changes take place in society. They have tried to demonstrate that the major source of change is a shift in a society's basic means of subsistence—for instance, from agricultural to industrial. Because each subsistence level is more productive than its predecessor, the result is a greater economic surplus. That makes possible larger populations, more affluence, greater cultural diversity, the emergence of new statuses and roles, faster economic development, and an ever-increasing complexity and efficiency (see, for example, Lenski, Nolan, & Lenski, 1999). In all evolutionary approaches, a recurrent theme is the search for a universal "law" of change. The orientation of this section is different. Instead of considering broad theories of evolutionary change, the emphasis will be on specific evolutionary forms or patterns. These can be characterized by directionality in time, which in its course generates greater variety and complexity.

Directionality, novelty, variety, selectivity, and increased complexity are key aspects of evolutionary patterns (Chattoe, 2002; Richerson & Boyd, 1992). Some of the so-called revolutions with the "r" removed could be illustrative of this. Consider the agricultural revolution, for example, which could be more appropriately termed agricultural evolution. Similarly, we can talk about the industrial revolution as industrial evolution. In both instances, there are discernible evolutionary patterns in the use of energy, technology, work skills, and materials. Of course, their emergence was based on already established foundations in the cumulative sequence. Each improvement required novelty, directionality, and variety, and each resulted in increased complexity.

It is plausible and possible to isolate individual change forms and talk about their evolution. For example, Richard Schwartz and James C. Miller (1970) used anthropological data to try to draw a pattern of legal evolution. They posited that legal organization seems to develop with a degree of regularity, and elements of such organization emerge in a sequence such that each constitutes a necessary condition for the next. The preliminary findings show "a rather startling consistency in the pattern of legal evolution. In a sample of fifty-one societies, compensatory damages and mediation of disputes were found in every society having specialized legal counsel. In addition, a large majority (85 percent) of societies that develop specialized police also employ damages and mediation" (Schwartz & Miller, 1970:157). The findings of the study lend support to the belief that "an evolutionary sequence occurs in the development of legal institutions" (p. 171).

A similar sequence of evolution was discussed by Robert N. Bellah (1970) in his paper, "Religious Evolution." He views evolution "as a process of increasing differentiation and complexity of organization which endows the organism, community, or whatever the unit in question may be, with greater capacity to adapt to its environment so that it is in some sense more autonomous relative to its environment than were its less complex ancestors" (Bellah, 1970:213). In light of this conceptualization of evolution, he traced the emergence of religion in terms of the evolution of religious symbol systems, which moved from "compact" to "differentiated"; religious collectivities, which became more differentiated from other social structures; and increased consciousness of the self as a religious subject. On these grounds he delineated five stages, to which he referred as the primitive, archaic, historic, early modern, and modern religious stages. Bellah noted, however, that these ideal typical stages are not inevitable, and that actual cases may include features that cannot be neatly characterized in terms of any one stage.

But evolution is not characterized merely by qualitative changes in organizations, as was illustrated in the case of legal systems and religion; it is also characterized by quantitative cumulation. The quantitative approach in the study of evolutionary patterns implies that the emergence of certain forms can be ranked along some scale ranging from small to large numbers. Such quantitative scaling is implied, for example, in the study by Morton Fried (1976) of the evolution of stratification. He used two measures: (1) a ratio between positions of prestige available for any given age-sex grade and the number of persons capable of filling them and (2) a ratio between strategic resources and persons possessing impeded or unimpeded access to them. In another study, Raoul Naroll (1964) used the number of people in the most populous building cluster of the ethnic unit study as an index of social development, and showed that this measure can be related systematically in a mathematical formula to the number of occupational specialties and to the number of organizational types.

In his classic study, *The Science of Culture,* Leslie White (1949) proposed a potentially quantifiable measure of the emergence of energy utilization and posited that culture evolved as the amount of energy harnessed per capita per year is increased or as the efficiency of the instrumental means of putting the energy to work is increased. From a different perspective, Marshall Sahlins (1958) used surplus production of food commodities and the degree of their redistribution as a measure of technological efficiency in his stratification study in Polynesia. He demonstrated that the amount of stratification was directly correlated with the size of the group involved in the redistribution of the surplus and with how frequently the food was distributed.

Thus, it is possible to study the evolutionary change forms or patterns in societies both qualitatively and quantitatively. Change patterns such as those of legal systems, religion, stratification, energy utilization, food production, and the like can be isolated and looked upon in an evolutionary or emerging context. These change patterns tend to evolve in a cumulative and incremental fashion, usually with directionality, increased variability, and complexity as a result of the incorporation of novel features.

DIFFUSION

Diffusion is the process by which innovations spread from one culture to another or from a subculture into the larger culture (see, for example, Howells, 2002). Diffusion theory emerged as an alternative to evolution. It is based on the idea of culturally dominant centers, which was made into a theory of social change by G. Elliot Smith (Kroeber, 1973:143). According to Smith, an unusual constellation of circumstances resulted in a great spurt in cultural development in Egypt. Around 3000 B.C., agricultural technology was rapidly improved, geometry was invented, metal-working and tool-making processes were developed, and a new and effective political order was devised. From that center of cultural innovation, cultural elements were carried throughout the Mediterranean and to all peoples of the world. Smith argued that the inventiveness of the Egyptians of that period was the "cause" of social change in various parts of the world, and what the Egyptians invented was diffused to and adopted by most societies.

To document his theory, Smith attempted to locate cultural similarities between the early Egyptians and societies far removed in space and time, such as the Incas of Peru and the people of India and Mexico. He convincingly argued that the bone fishhook in Melanesia was based on a bronze spear developed by the Egyptians, and the Mayan practice of building pyramids out of stone derived from the Egyptian practice of mummifying the dead and burying them in great pyramids. This theory provided an alternative to evolutionary theories in positing that social change was the result of contact and diffusion among societies.

In the United States, the anthropologists of the mid-1940s greatly emphasized diffusion as a pattern of change. In Kroeber's words, "whatever else diffusion does or does not involve, it does always involve change for the receiving culture. The total part played by diffusion in human culture is almost incredibly great" (Kroeber, quoted by Lauer, 1982:165). Kroeber posited that the development of cultural complexes is inversely related to the distance from "high centers" of civilizations. That is, the more isolated and the farther away societies are from such centers, the more retarded or marginal they will be in their development.

George Murdock (1934) estimated that about 90 percent of every culture known to history has acquired its elements from other peoples. Ralph Linton (1936:326–327) provides a now-classic illustration of this point by describing the beginning of the day for a typical American in terms of the origins of the objects he or she uses. Among other things, the bed came from the Near East via northern Europe, the cotton from India, the silk from China, the pajamas from India, and the shaving ritual for men originated in Egypt. The custom of wearing a necktie came from seventeenth-century Croatia, the umbrella was invented in southeastern Asia, and coins originated in ancient Lydia. While eating breakfast, a typical American uses plates invented in China, a knife from southern India, a fork from Italy, and a spoon derived from Roman society. The orange came from the eastern Mediterranean, cantaloupe from Persia, and coffee from ancient Abyssinia. Wafers are derived from a Scandinavian technique from wheat domesticated in Asia Minor. The after-breakfast cigarette comes from Mexico, from a tobacco plant that originated in Brazil. The newspaper that is being read was imprinted in characters invented in Germany, and "As he absorbs the accounts of foreign troubles he will, if he is a good conservative citizen, thank a Hebrew deity in an Indo-European language that he is 100 percent American" (Linton, 1936:327). And, the same 100-percent American that Linton talked about sixty years ago is surrounded today by products that originated elsewhere (Baker, 1987). Some examples: This text is being composed on a laptop computer with components made in Japan and assembled in Mexico while the author is listening to classical music composed in Austria on a radio built in Hong Kong while sipping the 2003 Christmas blend espresso made with coffee beans from Kenya and Ethiopia. The paper clips on the Danish desk came from Taiwan, the pens from France, and the stapler was made in Korea. And, I have not even looked at the labels in my shirt or shoes.

Anthropologists estimate that in the past and at present, there have been some 4,000 different human societies (Murdock, 1957). A considerable amount of borrowing goes on among these societies. The processes of diffusion, reinterpretation of borrowed or introduced elements, innovation, and synthesis of the old and new are ongoing and are present in all of them to varying degrees. Diffusion is not always a one-way process, as was implied by Linton's illustration; it can be reciprocal as well. In the United States one might assume that the borrowing between Indians and Caucasians has been a one-way process, but this is not the case. "Our borrowings from the native American culture have been numerous and can be found in many different areas and segments of our culture, and, perhaps, even in our personalities" (Spindler, 1984:23). Many of the things borrowed from native American culture are evident throughout the world. The plants domesticated by native Americans provide close to half of the world's food supply today. They include "Irish" potatoes, corn, beans, squash, and sweet potatoes. A number of drugs can be traced back to them, such as coca in cocaine and Novocain, curare in anesthetics, and cascara in laxatives. Other examples include the woolen poncho, the parka, moccasins, and the commercial cottons used today, all of which had their origins in native American culture.

Diffusion is evident also within complex societies. Many of the cultural items can be traced back to specialized groups in society as a component of a specific subculture, which are later taken over by other groups. To illustrate, jazz was developed by American blacks in the South, but as blacks moved north to Chicago and to other urban centers, they carried their music along, and today jazz is an important part of the American cultural heritage. Many currently popular dance forms have African origins (Newman, 1997). Similarly, attributes of popular culture such as hairstyles, clothes, dance forms, and slang spread from distinct subcultures to society at large.

Over the years, a sizable body of literature has developed on diffusion (see, for example, Bengtsson & Soderholm, 2002). In addition to works on how new ideas and practices spread from one society to another (McAdam & Rucht, 1993), sociologists have studied the institutionalization of world views (Kirby & Kirby, 1996) and the diffusion of new values and styles within societies. In particular, rural sociologists have studied the spread of new agricultural technology among farmers (Cernea, 1991) and adoption of new wheat varieties (Fischer, et al., 1996) and medical sociologists have been concerned with the spread of drugs such as tetracycline (Strang & Tuma, 1993), vaccinations, and family-planning methods. Educators have studied school adoption of new teaching methods and equipment. Economists have been concerned with the imitation process by which firms adopt new technological and production processes in cost-reduction attempts (Jovanovic & MacDonald, 1994). Communication researchers have focused on the diffusion process to better understand the dynamics of persuasion, propaganda, and interpersonal influence (Valente, 1993). Marketers have studied diffusion implicitly for many years as they attempted to guide and control the spread of new products and technologies such as optical scanners in supermarkets (Edmonds & Meisel, 1992).

In his influential book *Diffusion of Innovations*, Everett M. Rogers (1995) reports on over 500 diffusion studies that suggest some remarkably similar findings. Based on this enormous body of research, Rogers developed a theoretical framework on the diffusion of innovations, which has been widely adopted and is well worth examining in detail. For Rogers, the crucial elements in diffusion are (1) the innovation (which may be a technological development, a fad, a social movement, or a new product), (2) which is communicated through certain channels (word of mouth, advertising), (3) over time, and (4) among members of a community. On the basis of research evidence, he then identifies five stages of the adoption process. They are:

1. *Awareness Stage.* The individual knows of the new idea but lacks sufficient information about it.
2. *Interest Stage.* The individual becomes interested in the idea and seeks more information.

3. *Evaluation Stage.* The individual makes a mental application of the new idea to his or her present and anticipated future situation and makes the decision either to try it or not.
4. *Trial Stage.* The individual uses the innovation on a small scale to determine its utility.
5. *Adoption Stage.* The individual accepts the innovation and commits oneself to its use.

One of the major factors affecting the rate of adoption of an innovation is the characteristics of the innovation itself. Rogers suggests five characteristics that have a major influence on the rate of adoption of an innovation. They are:

1. *Relative advantage* refers to the degree to which an innovation is considered superior to the ideas or products it supersedes. It is determined in terms of efficiency, cost, novelty, or perceived advantage. An example of a product with a high perceived relative advantage is the transistor radio as opposed to the tube-type radio.

2. *Compatibility* is the degree to which an innovation is seen as consistent with the existing values, past experiences, and the needs of the recipients. For example, Eskimo hunters can readily grasp the advantages of the steel blade over the slate knife, but they are very uncertain of the alleged advantages of Christianity over their own religion. Similarly, birth-control practices may be seen as incompatible with existing traditions, values, and beliefs.

3. *Complexity* refers to the extent to which an innovation is seen as relatively difficult to understand and use. The rate of adoption may be put on a complexity-simplicity continuum, and, as a rule, the adoption rate of an innovation will be slower when it is perceived as complex by members of a community.

4. *Tryability* is the degree to which an innovation may be experimented with on a limited basis. Certain things can be tried on a small scale; others cannot. Certain inventions, such as the automobile or television, have to be accepted as they are. It is considered advantageous for the adoption rate if an item can be tried out first.

5. *Observability* refers to the extent to which the results of an innovation are visible to others. The fact that certain items such as clothes or durable goods are highly observable facilitates the rate of adoption. The crucial point, according to Rogers, is how these characteristics are perceived by members of a community, for this is what governs their response.

Rogers suggests that the type of innovation decision is related to an innovation's rate of adoption. He outlines three types: (1) optional, whereby an individual has a choice whether or not to adopt an innovation; (2) collective, whereby a majority needs to be convinced about an innovation; and (3) authoritarian, whereby a decision has been superimposed upon a community, such as in the case of water fluoridation. Communication channels are also considered as affecting the rate of adoption, and interpersonal channels are considered more effective with more complex innovations than mass media channels. Finally, both the nature of the community, whether or not it is modern or traditional, and the extent of the change agents' promotional efforts influence the rate of adoption.

As ideal types, Rogers identifies five adopter categories. They are:

1. *Innovators*, who are eager to try out new ideas. They are daring, risking, and willing to take the consequences for their actions.
2. *Early adopters*, who are more integrated in the community than innovators and tend to be more prominent, successful, and respected.
3. *Early majority*, who adopt new ideas just before the average in a community. They tend to be deliberate and they aid in legitimizing innovations, although they are seldom leaders.
4. *Late majority*, who follow after the average community members; at times, adoption results from social pressures or economic necessity.
5. *Laggards*, who are suspicious of innovators and change agents and have traditional values. They are the last to accept an invention.

The derivative effects of diffusion may be illustrated by the changes in the United States resulting from the invention and adoption of the automobile. These changes were first apparent in the economic institutions directly related to the manufacture of automobiles, such as the steel, rubber, glass, and petroleum industries. Government institutions were affected in a variety of ways, ranging from the revenues from the sale of gasoline to the detection and control of crime. Religion has felt the impact of the automobile in a number of ways, with the automobile often competing with the church for time and energies of the people. Moreover, the family has seen the automobile bring about new patterns of recreation, social control, and economic expenditure, not to mention sexual morality and adolescent discipline.

The concept of planned diffusion has become an important one over the years in the context of modernization, economic development, and aid to third-world countries. Diffusion has both a temporal and spatial component and often begins in centers of innovation, spreading outward to the periphery (Grubler, 1996). In one of his earlier books, *Beyond the Stable State*, Donald A. Schon (1971) describes two models of diffusion of innovation. The first he calls the center-periphery model, which is characterized by one source of innovation and multiple receivers of that innovation. The second is referred to as the proliferation-of-centers model, which describes the situation in which the receivers of innovations become innovators in their own right. These two models can be used also to indicate the direction of diffusion and the alterations produced by the acceptance of innovations. This is a more pragmatic view of change advocated primarily by policy-makers and others involved in planned social change (Schon & Rein, 1994). Schon contends that the two systems of diffusion evolve simultaneously with the technological infrastructure in society.

The center-periphery model rests on three basic elements:

1. The innovation to be diffused exists, fully realized in its essentials, prior to its diffusion.
2. Diffusion is the movement of an innovation from a center out to its ultimate users.
3. Directed diffusion is a centrally managed process of dissemination, training, and provision of resources and incentives.

Proponents of the center-periphery model view diffusion as a form of interaction in which one person transmits a new idea to another person. At the most fundamental level, the process consists of (1) a new idea, (2) individual A who knows about the innovation, and (3) individual B who does not yet know about the innovation. Examples of diffusers would be agricultural extension agents, those who introduce new pharmaceuticals to physicians, doctors and nurses, and college professors. Studies on diffusion deal with the spread of, for example, public health practices, drugs, insecticides, and ideologies.

Schon argues that the effectiveness of a center-periphery system depends on the level of resources and energy at the center, on the number of points at the periphery, the length of the radii or spokes through which diffusion takes place, and the energy required to gain a new adoption (1971:82). He uses as an illustration the diffusion capability of an agricultural extension agent, which depends upon the agent's own energies, the number of location of farmers served, and the time and effort devoted to each farmer.

The scope of the model "varies directly with the level of technology governing the flows of men, materials, money and information" (Schon, 1971:82). The scope of the model also depends on its capacity for generating and managing feedback. He suggests that there are two important variants to this model. The first he calls Johnny Appleseed:

> Here the primary center is a kind of bard who roams his territory spreading a new message. Into this category fall the traveling scholars, saints and artisans of the Middle Ages; Voltaire and Thomas Paine; and contemporary bards of radical activism like Saul Alinsky. (Schon, 1971:83)

The second variant he calls the magnet model. For this, he gives the illustration of nineteenth-century universities in Germany, to which students came from all parts of the world; afterward they returned to their own countries to teach and practice what they had learned. Today, in technology and in economics, the United States and Great Britain are magnet countries, especially to developing nations.

The Johnny Appleseed model allows the innovation to be adapted to the special conditions of the recipient's locality. The magnet model may establish new centers.

An elaboration of the center-periphery model is the proliferation-of-centers approach. Although it retains the basic center-periphery structure, it tends to differentiate the primary from the secondary centers. The primary centers manage and support the secondary centers, which, in turn, engage in the diffusion of innovations. Schon uses the illustration of the activities of the Roman army for this model. Regiments of the Roman army moved out from Rome to occupy new territories, subjugated their occupants, and established colonies. The task of these advanced guards was war and government. Once an area was occupied, the military established an approximation to the Roman way of life based on centrally established doctrine and a centrally established method for diffusing it. Similarly, missionaries followed the proliferation-of-centers model in disseminating their message.

Schon contends that industrial expansion came about on a worldwide scale through a form of specialization resembling that of the Roman army. "The central message now took the form of technology both for production and for the management of the business firm. These spread throughout the world as industrial centers established decentralized networks of distribution, marketing, production, manpower and financial control" (Schon, 1971:86–87).

Even though there are many variants of this model, a dominant pattern prevails in the primary center's relationship to secondary centers. The primary center oversees policies and methodology. It selects territories for expansion; develops methodologies for diffusion; trains new agents for diffusion; sustains decentralized outposts through finances, information, and know-how; monitors decentralized operations; and maintains information throughout the network of outposts.

To varying degrees, the spread of colonialism, Christianity (Montgomery, 2001), Coca-Cola, and communism all followed this model. In today's world, this model is used as a technique of business expansion, and the unfolding of the various multinational corporations (large corporations that operate in many nations) would be a good illustration of its operation (Barnet & Cavanagh, 1994). In the area of marketing, in particular, a series of new models have been developed that describe the spread of products, repeat purchase patterns, and technical innovations (Furnham, 1994). In policy making, it is used to study how states change policy innovations as they diffuse—a process known as reinvention (Hays, 1996). Among demographers, the diffusion of contraceptive technology in underdeveloped countries is receiving substantial attention. Understanding diffusion is an important consideration in planned social change. It is a fruitful subject of investigation that barely has been sampled thus far.

ACCULTURATION

Acculturation refers to taking on material and nonmaterial attributes from another culture as a result of prolonged face-to-face contact. Such contact can come about in several ways. It can be the result of war, conquest, military occupation, or colonization; or it may be through missionaries or cultural exchanges. It may be produced by migration or the transportation of labor, such as through slavery or penal deportations. Voluntary labor movement is another factor in creating contact, as is the case in Europe where "guest workers" from less developed European countries move to France, Germany, and Switzerland. Trade, technical exchange, and the spread of ideas and institutions represent other sources of contact. Contacts of shorter duration have been brought about by travel and tourism in recent years. Indirect forms of contact include mass communication and the transfer of knowledge.

Diffusion is considered as only one aspect of acculturation. Even though diffusion occurs in all cases of acculturation, since attributes and ideas have to be transmitted before they can have an impact on recipient cultures, it is usually considered as a component of the broader process of acculturation. Diffusion usually deals with one or a small number of attributes, whereas acculturation provides the group with many possible new ways of behaving, which might be quite different from those dictated by their own cultures, traditional norms, and beliefs. In most cases, acculturation is also more rapid and more observable than diffusion. Acculturation is produced by contact, whereas contact may not be required in diffusion. Acculturation brings about greater similarities between two cultures, whereas diffusion usually refers to a lesser influence or impact. Acculturation plays a role in a variety of activities and behaviors ranging from Russian refugee adaptation (Birman et al., 2002), language use (Brown, C., 1994), frequency of sexual partners and condom use among Hispanic unmarried adults (Marin et al., 1993), delinquency among Cuban American adolescents (Vega et al., 1993), to explanations of Asian-American living arrangements in later life (Burr & Mutchler, 1993).

In general, two cultures that are in contact rarely acculturate reciprocally and to the same degree. Rather, the politically subordinate or technologically inferior group adopts cultural attributes from the dominant group. Acculturation, in a sense, is cultural borrowing in the context of subordinate-superordinate relations (Bodley, 1999:14,43). Often status enhancement is considered an inducement to accept new ideas or elements.

Those groups that are considered "inferior" in society feel that by assuming the characteristics of a "superior" group they will, in consequence, also become superior and receive the same respect that is given to members of that superior group. In situations in which neither group is clearly "superior," there may be a standoff in the adoption of attributes, and thus each group tends to retain its identity (DeVos, 1976:4).

Acculturation may be voluntary or involuntary. The former occurs when members of a group in contact with another group accept some of their attributes, characteristics, norms, and values without force or pressure for compliance by the other group. This situation happens when neither group is superior to the other. Involuntary acculturation, on the other hand, seems to be much more widespread. Let us now examine some of its ramifications.

In the United States, most native American tribes have made adjustments through acculturation. A few have been assimilated, and others have suffered annihilation as a result of social and cultural contact with whites. It should be noted, though, that the early contacts were the kind that led to diffusion; trappers, traders, and missionaries carried new traits to the native peoples and borrowed in return such things as buckskin clothes, kennels, snowshoes, tobacco, corn, and maple syrup. Diffusion was stimulated but there was not yet acculturation. Acculturation began in earnest with the arrival of white settlers, soldiers, and administrators. The result was the disorganization of the ecological, economic, and political bases of traditional tribal life. The whites continued to borrow ideas and attributes from the native Americans, but, by virtue of the whites' dominant position, there was no reciprocal acculturation. Instead, the dictum seemed to have been: "Acculturate—or else!"

At times, acculturation can be both forced and planned. Consider the attempts of the British colonial office to "civilize" the "backward" native Africans. This entailed the teaching of the English language and the transmission of rudimentary skills and technologies. Provisions for medium-level opportunities to encourage limited mobility were made; at the same time, however, colonizers continued to maintain strict boundaries between themselves and the "inferior" groups. Similarly, the Portuguese and Spanish conquerors of Latin America were successful in undermining the native Indian cultures and, with a few exceptions, in imposing their Iberian cultures on these people. Through violence, disease, overwork, and forced migration, they succeeded in weakening the native social structures that might have preserved the traditional cultures. This is similar to what happened to slaves in the New World. Even though the measures are less dramatic, the recent attempts at acculturation that took place between the former Soviet Union and the Eastern European countries is indicative also of planned and forced acculturation. In the former Eastern European countries, the instruction of the Russian language traditionally had been mandatory. In many cases, the history of Russia took precedence over their native histories. The study of political philosophy and Marxism was required both at the high school and university levels. The dominant Soviet group attempted also to "encourage" the acceptance of a series of other cultural attributes and traits such as literature, art, cinematography, and music that came from the socialistic ideological mold.

Acculturation can also be seen as the interaction between a constant and a variable—that is, between an essentially stable receiving culture and an adapting immigrant group (Petersen, 1965:220). The acculturation of immigrants can be depicted on a continuum ranging from total assimilation to total nonassimilation, with most cases falling somewhere in between. This continuum may be analyzed in terms of a tripartite typology devised by Ralph Linton (1936:271–287). He considered social roles in any culture under three categories: universals, specialties, and alternatives. Universals include attributes that are common to all members of a society. Specialties are shared by the members of certain socially recognized categories but not shared by the total population. Alternatives include roles shared by certain individuals that are not common to all members of the society or even to all members of any one of the socially recognized categories (Linton, 1936: 272–273). Conformity is expected of immigrants only with respect to those ideas and behavior patterns to which all members of society must conform. In the United States, this includes the learning of the English language, self-support, and political alliance. Alternatives refer to the selective acceptance of attributes and the simultaneous retention of certain old-country habits. Food preferences among the various immigrant groups in America are illustrative of this. Specialties pertain to the kind of work an individual does, which, in turn, is a factor in his or her social status. Thus, total acculturation for immigrants is seen only in terms of Linton's "universals" category, whereas social roles in the "specialties" and "alternatives" categories retain a degree of uniqueness and flexibility.

The most famous case of acculturation at the level of society discussed in the literature is perhaps the transformation of Manus society as a consequence of the occupation of the island by American troops during World War II. The Manus community of the Admiralty Islands in the South Pacific was revisited by Margaret Mead after twenty-five years. The first time she studied the community, it comprised people with no contact with the outside world and no known writing. The problems of social interaction and reciprocal obligation were handled in terms of kinship. The natives wore G-strings and grass skirts and had a very primitive economic system. When she returned twenty-five years later, she was "greeted by a man in carefully ironed white clothes, wearing a tie and shoes, who explained that he was the 'counsel,' one of the elected officials of the community" (Mead, quoted by Spindler, 1984:35). A few days after her return, she was asked by another elected official to make up a list of rules for modern child care—feeding, discipline, sleeping, and so forth. "When she explained that her comments would be based on the latest thinking of the International Seminar on Mental Health and Infant Development, held at Chichester, England, in 1952, under the auspices of the United Nations, this man, who was born into what was then a primitive 'stone age' society, understood what she was saying" (Spindler, 1984:35).

When she had left the island twenty-five years earlier, she had left a primitive, isolated, nonliterate "stone age" society. When she returned, she found them moving rapidly into the mainstream of the modern world, with concerns that would allow them to accelerate this process even more. Why did it take place? During World War II, more than a million Americans managed to reshape the island completely. The Manus natives worked for them and were treated as equals. The Americans furnished a kind of model for the Manus as well as providing them with a vision of American technological and material culture. Using the "American model," the Manus rapidly threw away their own culture and modeled their lives after that one. Contrary to traditional anthropological thinking, the change took place without disruptive effects on the society. This is accounted for by the fact that the change was desired by the entire society. It is interesting to note that today the area is an unusually valuable tourist property offering some of the best scuba diving in the world (Kristof, 1997).

In sum, acculturation is a form of change that is conditioned by various degrees of convergence among cultures. Acculturation is not necessarily disruptive and painful. On the contrary, because it is more rapid than other forms of change, it may well be less upsetting than gradual change. At times, as Mead suggested, it is easier to embrace a new culture in its entirety—since it is a meaningful, integrated whole—than to try to splice two cultures together. Substituting clothes for grass skirts (to use Mead's own example) without introducing soap produces dirt and disease; without sewing machines, starch, and irons, it creates a society of ragamuffins; without closets, it produces huts that are cluttered with hanging clothes, and so on. As Mead (1961:374–377) points out, it is easier for a Samoan to become a New Yorker than to become a half-acculturated, or perhaps "deculturated," Samoan.

REVOLUTION

By definition, *revolution* is a fundamental, rapid, and violent change in political organization, power relationships, stratification, economic property control, and the predominant myth of a social order within a society (Goldstone, 2003:1–17; Neumann, 1971:122). In a classic sense, revolution is a forcible transfer of political power from one block of contenders to another in a society and is considered the most radical form of social change

(Kimmel, 1990:6; Tilly, 1993). Revolutions intensify security competition and increase the probability of war by altering each side's perceptions of the balance of threats (Walt, 1996).

As compared to other patterns, revolutions are distinguished by the following characteristics: they induce changes of the largest scope involving all levels and dimensions of society, including the economy, polity, culture, and social organization; the changes in these areas are radical; and these memorable events evoke unusual intellectual and emotional reactions from the participants that range from exhilaration to utopian visions of the immediate future (Sztompka, 1994:301). Revolutions are often classified into one of two ideal types: leftist or rightist (DeFronzo, 1996:9–10). In a left-wing revolution, the goal is to change major social and political institutions. It involves the redistribution of resources and wealth between the rich and poor, provision of basic services such as health and education, land reform, and the nationalization of industries and commerce. The Russian, Chinese, and Cuban revolutions are illustrative of this pattern. In a right-wing revolution, the objective is the restoration of traditional institutions. The emphasis is on maintaining social order and traditional authority rather than on trying to achieve greater social equality through institutional change. The 1979 revolution in Iran is an example of a predominantly right-wing revolution.

Before we proceed further with the patterns of revolutionary change, it should be noted that not all such change can be equated with force or violence, nor does it always entail initiation by antiestablishment forces or radical alteration in social structure or political organization (see, for example, Foran, 2002). For example, many of the revolutions in Latin America prior to World War II consisted of overthrowing Colonel A by General Y and his followers, but nothing after the overthrow changed in the basic structure of society. Similarly, Max Gluckman studied what he calls "rebellion cycles" in a number of precolonial African kingdoms. He found that periodic rebellions and replacement by one clan over another served to strengthen rather than weaken the established political and economic structures. Their community persisted for generations with minor modifications until truly radical changes were introduced by Western colonial powers (Gluckman, in Gerlach & Hine, 1973:19).

Similarly, there have been what may be designated as "revolutionary" changes in science. "A change in the thought-system, or world view, is revolutionary in the extreme and has wide ramifications in technological, economic, political, and religious spheres of life" (Gerlach & Hine, 1973:20). For example, when Nicholas Copernicus (1473–1543), the Polish astronomer, described the sun as the center of a great system with the earth revolving around it, revolutionary changes in astronomy resulted. Johann Gutenberg (1397–1468) invented movable printing type in 1437, thus revolutionizing the technique of disseminating knowledge. The names of Isaac Newton or Albert Einstein do not require commentaries in terms of their revolutionary contributions to science. In medicine, we need only consider some examples such as Louis Pasteur (1822–1895); Conrad Wilhelm Roentgen, who discovered x-rays (1845–1923); or Ignaz Philipp Semmelweis (1818–1865), a Hungarian physician who, through the use of antiseptic methods in obstetrics, significantly reduced deaths from puerperal fever. These are just a few illustrations to show that revolutionary and radical forms of social change need not always be violent or involve the basic structures in society. For the remainder of the discussion, the term "revolution" will be used in the context of the original definition.

The patterns of revolution, according to Chalmers Johnson (1964), can be analyzed in terms of (1) the targets selected for attack—government personnel, political regime, the community as a social unit; (2) the nature of the carriers of the revolution—mass or an elite; and (3) its goals and ideologies—reformist, nostalgic, nation-forming, elitist, or nationalist. On the basis of these, he identified six patterns:

1. *The Jacquerie.* The name comes from a French peasant insurrection in 1358 against the nobility and the pillaging English soldiers. It is a spontaneous mass peasant uprising, generally carried out in the name of the traditional authorities, church, and king, and with the limited objectives of purging local or national elites.

2. *The Millenarian Rebellion.* This pattern is similar to the first one but with the extra feature of a utopian dream fostered by a strong leader. This pattern is rather widespread and found in all parts of the world. An illustration of this would be the Sioux Ghost-Dance Rebellion, which will be discussed in some detail in Chapter 7. In more recent times, Hitler offered overwhelming proof of the power of a charismatic leader.

3. *The Anarchistic Rebellion.* This pattern reflects a nostalgic reaction to progressive change that involves a romantic idealization of the previous order, for example, the Boxer Revolt.

4. *The Jacobean Communist Revolution.* This pattern is a rather rare phenomenon, which has been defined as "a sweeping fundamental change in political organization, social structure, economic property control, and the predominate myth of a social order, thus indicating a major break in the continuity of development" (Neumann, quoted by Johnson, 1964:2). This pattern of revolution can occur only in a highly centralized state with good communications and a large capital city, and its target is the government or the regime. Revolutions of this nature serve to increase national consciousness and to create a more rational and stronger state and social structure. Such revolutionary patterns occurred in France, Russia, and China.

5. *The Conspiratorial Coup d'État.* The coup d'état is a calculated and highly organized undertaking of a small elite and is instigated by an

oligarchic sectarian ideology. It is considered a revolutionary pattern only if it in fact anticipates a social movement and inaugurates social change. Examples include the Nasser revolution in Egypt or the Castro revolution in Cuba. Johnson contends that this pattern of revolution must be distinguished from palace revolts, banditry, assassination, strikes, dynastic succession-conflict, and other forms of violence, none of which would entail social change.

6. *The Militarized Mass Insurrection.* This pattern is a deliberately planned mass revolutionary war guided by a dedicated elite. The outcome of guerrilla warfare is determined by political attitudes, not by military strategy or materiel, and the rebels are wholly dependent on broad popular support. In the examples found in Yugoslavia, Algeria, Vietnam, and China, the ideology that attracted mass following has been a combination of xenophobic nationalism and Marxism, with a somewhat heavier emphasis on the former.

Like any categorization of historical processes, Johnson's typology of patterns of revolution is concerned with ideal types. In reality, individual revolutions may, at times, display characteristics of several different patterns conditioned by the targets, carriers, and ideologies of the revolution. A difficulty with Johnson's schema is his distinction between rebellion and revolution. The former tends to concentrate on individuals, rather than institutions, with a retrospective outlook, whereas the latter seeks to change institutions and social structures and is innovative. To simplify the distinction between rebellion and revolution, Smith (1973:113) proposed a fourfold typology:

1. Simple rebellion, such as the Jacquerie, which is nonideological and attempts changes only in the governing personnel.
2. Ideological rebellion, such as anarchism, which attempts to restore the old order as well as change the present elite.
3. Simple revolution, such as the early American Revolution, in which the ideology attempts alterations in some values, such as governmental or economic values, while leaving others intact.
4. Total revolution, such as in France in 1789, Russia in 1917, or China in 1949, which attempts to restructure the entire society.

For each revolutionary pattern, it is possible also to establish quantitative changes in several domains. Basically, all revolutionary patterns deal with the class, status, and power systems. Mark N. Hagopian (1974) suggests, as summarized in Table 3.1, that the intensity of a revolution pattern on the class, status, and power systems can be ascertained as ranging from negligible to moderate and from radical to total abolition. Thus, a revolution could include only a moderate change in one aspect of the stratification

TABLE 3.1 A Scale of Measuring the Intensity of Revolution

	Negligible Change	Moderate Change	Radical Change	Total Abolition
Class systems				
Status systems				
Power systems				

SOURCE: Mark N. Hagopian, *The Phenomenon of Revolution*. New York: Dodd, Mead, 1974, p. 100.

Negligible change = 0   Moderate change = 1
Radical change = 2   Total abolition = 3

system (Score 1) to a revolution that would succeed in abolishing all three aspects (Score 9). For illustrative purposes, the English Revolution may be classified toward the lower end of the scale and the Russian and Chinese revolutions toward the upper end.

Although revolution is seen as affecting all three components of the stratification system (class, status, and power), the transfer of power from one social group to another is usually considered the most crucial. Various significant factors have been considered to precede such transfer of power on a wide scale, but there seems to be a substantial disagreement in the literature about which of these are of paramount importance. Marx, Crane Brinton, and others see economic fluctuations and the increasing illegitimacy of the existing government as necessary preconditions for revolution. Even among these theorists, however, there is some disagreement. The Marxists argue that economic conflict between classes plays the primary causal role in revolution. Brinton (1959) advocates the argument of "relative deprivation," or rising expectations. Others argue that economic decline and status crises bring about revolution, and still other observers suggest that military pressures, large-scale corruption, and conflict among the elites are the primary source of major social upheavals (Close & Bridge, 1985; Goldstone, 2003).

In sum, revolutions are best studied in retrospect. Although the objectives of revolutions are generally clearly stated and couched in emotional and ideological terms, it is very difficult to predict their outcomes accurately. There will always be a discrepancy between ideals and reality. In Mao Zedong's words, "Anything can grow out of the barrel of a gun." As Jack A. Goldstone (2003:207) notes, revolutions have many accomplishments. They include redistribution of land and elimination of oppressive systems of land tenure and of hereditary privileges of traditional aristocracy. Revolutions have also brought about increases in literacy, improvements in education and medical care, greater equality and economic opportunities, and independence to hundreds of millions of people. But revolutions have not generally delivered their main promises: greater freedom, equality for all, and significantly improved material well-being. In fact, revolutions in many countries resulted in more powerful and authoritarian regimes than the ones they replaced, such as Iran in the 1980s. And, let us remember the high price of wars and severe economic dislocations that are often part of revolutionary changes. Some examples from this century include: internal strife and efforts to collectivize agriculture in Russia resulted in the deaths of tens of millions of people; the revolution in Nicaragua caused over 50,000 deaths in a population of 2.5 million; and the bodies are still being counted following the aftermath of Iran's revolution (DeFronzo, 1996).

MODERNIZATION

Modernization is the process by which agrarian societies are transformed into industrial societies. This transition entails the development of advanced industrial technology and the political, cultural, and social arrangements appropriate to sustaining, directing, and utilizing that technology. The aim of modernization is to approximate the characteristics of economically developed and relatively stable nations (Chirot, 1985; Germani, 1981:10–14; Moore, 1974:94). This transition seldom, if ever, takes place smoothly or evenly (see, for example, Tilly, 1997). Still, it affects every social institution, touches every community, and is felt in all walks of life (see, for example, Savelsberg, 2002). Evidence from both objective and subjective measures indicates that modernization is associated with an improved quality of life for most people (Inkeles, 1993). Modernization is a comprehensive term that describes many simultaneous changes at several levels. Industrialization, urbanization, and bureaucratization are closely related to modernization. For the purpose of analysis, however, these interrelated change patterns will be discussed separately.

In a sense, modernization is a form of imitation, emulation, and transplantation of patterns, products, and technologies from Western countries to less developed countries. Thus, a prerequisite of modernization is communication and contact among the various cultures and societies. It is usually the leaders of developing countries who set the plans and policies for changing a particular society in motion in the direction of contemporary societies. Industrialization is not always a crucial factor in modernization. For example, African and Asian nations usually start the process of modernization with nation building and the development of modern political systems. The object is the transformation of their social structure and the dissemination of new norms and values through education. The development of industry usually follows later.

By contrast, in Europe in the eighteenth and nineteenth centuries, industrialization gave birth to modernization (Chodak, 1973:259; Kerr, 1983). For some theorists, modernization is seen in terms of humans' increased knowledge and mastery of the environment. Cyril E. Black (1967) suggests that modern societies are characterized by the growth of new knowledge, and this presumes the existence of an individual with an increasing capacity to understand the secrets of nature and to apply this new knowledge to human affairs. Robert N. Bellah (1965) regards modernization as the ability of "learning to learn" and the increased capacity of a community to process information in a society and to respond to it appropriately. From a different perspective, Marion Levy, Jr. (1966:35) considers modernization as gradable because it appears in different forms. "A society will be considered more or less modernized to the extent that its members use inanimate sources of power and/or use tools to multiply the effects of their efforts. Neither of these elements is either totally absent from or exclusively present in any society." Even though a continuum of modernization may not be established, Levy suggests that one can safely distinguish between relatively modernized countries, such as the United States and England, and relatively nonmodernized countries, such as India and some of the Latin American countries.

In *The Politics of Modernization*, David E. Apter considers modernization as a particular case of development. In his words:

> Modernization implies three conditions—a community that can constantly innovate without falling apart (and that includes among its essential beliefs the acceptability of change); differentiated, flexible social structures; and a social framework to provide the skills and knowledge necessary for living in a technologically advanced world. Industrialization, a special aspect of modernization, may be defined as the period in a society in which the strategic functional roles are related to manufacturing. It is possible to attempt the modernization of a given country without much industry, but it is not possible to industrialize without modernization. (1965: 67)

Based on historical phenomena and modernization processes in developing countries, it is possible, according to Szymon Chodak (1973:261), to generalize that modernization occurred in one of three ways: (1) as a result of industrialization of a country, which, in turn, generates changes in attitudes and behavior, producing a new value orientation, which sets the motivation to generate further industrialization; (2) spontaneously, as a result of contact between the more developed and less developed societies and cultures; and (3) as a consequence of purposeful planned governmental activity to modernize the economy. On the basis of these generalizations, Chodak (1973:263–271) identified three patterns of modernization that occurred in sub-Saharan Africa: industrial, acculturative, and induced.

1. *Industrial Modernization.* The process of industrialization creates new material conditions and needs, contributes to the formation of new attitudes and value orientations, and increases the division of labor. It increases interdependence in society and new roles, organizations, and systems of activity become more differentiated. Chodak states that "Modernization of this type arises out of the necessity to adapt the social organization to the requirements of industry" (1973:263).

2. *Acculturative Modernization.* This process is based on the convergence of two different cultures and is manifested through the acceptance of behavior patterns, information about lifestyles, and educational practices of a different culture. The selective transplantation of cultural elements does not lead to the replacement of traditional institutions but "very often it leads to its impoverishment, deformation and, in some instances, to all kinds of cultural and social abnormalities" (1973:263). Chodak suggests that during the process of colonialization of Africa, acculturative modernization was typical.

3. *Induced Modernization.* The third pattern of modernization entails modeling a country's organizations, institutions, and value orientations after those of Western countries. "Induced modernization consists of introducing modern forms of government and administration, education, universities, research institutes, universal suffrage, and communications media into an industrially underdeveloped country, without having previously industrialized the country. Induced modernization arises primarily out of the desire to catch up with the more developed societies, especially in the spheres of political organization and education, and partly because of the desire to have easy accessibility to the products of modern technical progress" (1973:267). In a sense, in modern African countries, induced modernization can be equated with nation building through the processes of educational, administrative, and governmental reforms. In all cases of induced modernization, however, it should be noted that the government, the ruling political party, and the elite are the principal organizers and implementers (Chirot, 1985).

Each of these forms of modernization develops through a differentiation of roles, the establishment of specialized institutions, and the generation of specific kinds of interdependencies. For example, the key roles in industrial modernization are those of entrepreneur, worker, inventor, and innovator; in acculturative modernization, the key roles are of the tradesman, migrant, student, and liberated members of the tribal society; in induced modernization, the roles of politician, intellectual, and the bureaucrat are important (Chodak, 1973:269–270).

As modernization gains momentum, new characteristics accompany it. They include the "development of a high extent of differentiation; the development of free resources which are not committed to any fixed, ascriptive (kinship, territorial, etc.) groups; the development of specialized and diversified types of social organization; the development of wide nontraditional, 'national,' or even supranational group identification; and the concomitant development, in all major institutional spheres of specialized roles and of special wider regulative and allocative mechanisms and organizations, such as market mechanisms in economic life, voting and party activities in politics, and diverse bureaucratic organizations and mechanisms in most institutional spheres" (Eisenstadt, 1973:23).

These have developed concomitantly with basic changes in all major institutions. In the economic sphere, these developments were characterized by a greater specialization of economic activities, the influx of external capital and the resulting external debt (Pattnayak, 1996), and the growth of scope and complexity of the principal markets—markets for goods, labor, and money. In social organization, it resulted in the growth of the population in urban areas in which the more specialized types of economic, professional, and civic activities and enterprises became concentrated and expanded. This gave rise to a change from traditional ascriptive status to the development of a more open form of stratification, with greater opportunities for upward social mobility through economic, occupational, and educational channels (Germani, 1981:173–195).

In the political sphere, modernization is characterized by a development of a more differentiated political structure; by a growing extension of the scope of central legal, administrative, and political activities; by the continuous spread of potential political power to wider groups in society; and by the weakening of traditional elites.

In the cultural sphere, modernization is characterized by a greater differentiation between principal aspects of major cultural and value systems such as religion, philosophy, ideology; by an increased secularization and, concomitantly, the weakening of traditional, cultural elites; by an increase in literacy and secular education; and by the rise of a new secular intelligentsia.

These developments have been closely related to an extension of print and electronic communications and their penetration of various local groups. The resulting growing awareness among the various strata of the population has created greater participation in social life and increased consumption of "culture" (Eisenstadt, 1973:23–25).

These institutional changes are accompanied by marked transformations in attitudes and personality, which have been characterized as "modern" in the literature. According to Alex Inkeles and David H. Smith, "The modern man is not just a construct in the mind of sociological theorists. He exists and he can be identified. . . ." (1974:290). Inkeles and Smith propose that the modern individual's character may be summed up under four major headings:

1. He or she is an informed participant citizen,
2. Has a marked sense of personal efficacy,
3. Is highly independent and autonomous of his or her relations to traditional sources of influence,
4. Is ready for new experiences and ideas; that is, the individual is relatively open-minded and cognitively flexible. (1974:290)

As an informed participating citizen, the individual identifies with newer, larger aspects of regions and state, partakes in public affairs, joins local and national organizations, votes, and keeps informed through the mass media about major events. A sense of efficacy is seen in the conviction that the individual can take actions that affect his or her life and that of the community. One knows that an individual can improve one's conditions in life and, as a result, rejects passivity, resignation, and fatalism. The advice of public officials and trade-union leaders concerning public issues is followed rather than that of the priests or village elders. One's openness to new experience is reflected in the exploration of formerly sacred objects and the individual's willingness to meet strangers and to allow women to take advantage of opportunities outside of the home.

In addition, as evidenced by the writings of Max Weber, Hagen, and McClelland in Chapter 2, the modern individual is also efficient, diligent, orderly, punctual, and frugal. One is rational in decisions on action, and is prepared for change and alert to opportunities as they arise in a changing world. One finds that scrupulous honesty pays in the long run and is a condition for improving efficiency in all social and economic relations (Myrdal, 1968:61). One is also energetic and cooperative; one also accepts responsibility for the welfare of both the community and the nation and is willing to take the long view and forgo short-term profiteering. One favors the subordination of speculation to investment and of commerce and finance to production. In a sense, "the hallmark of modernity is an existential conviction that man can select and can achieve his own future; that he has indeed many futures, that all he must do—to begin with—is to write his own scenario of the future as he himself dreams it and then to live his drama" (Meadows, 1971:21).

In sum, modernization has no end product. To embark on the modernization process is to accept the fact of continual and prolonged change. Its uniqueness lies in the fact that it is based on the assumptions of the possibility of the active creation by humans of a new social and political order, an order based on premises of universalism and equality, and the spread of these assumptions is combined with the development of far-reaching structural and organizational changes, especially in the economic and political fields (Eisenstadt, 1973:209). In the next section, industrialization, which is an important component of modernization, will be examined.

INDUSTRIALIZATION

Industrialization is the process by which technology is substituted for manual labor as the basis of production of goods. The most commonly used index of industrialization is the proportion of the nation's labor force engaged in agriculture. As the proportion declines, a nation can be considered as becoming more industrial. Clark Kerr (1983:5), for example, considers industrialized nations as those with 25 percent or less of the labor force engaged in agriculture. It should be noted, however, that this is an index and not a measure of industrialization. The reduction in the agricultural labor force can be seen more appropriately as a consequence of technological, economic, and organizational changes accompanying industrialization, as is the case, for example, in today's China (Liang et al., 2002). As indicated in the preceding section, the concept of modernization is a more comprehensive term that subsumes industrialization and other concepts such as economic growth or development and the political, social, religious, educational, and other institutional changes that accompany industrialization.

Great Britain is considered the first and the classic case of industrialization (Kerr et al., 1964:14). By 1830, it had seen the development of workers who were acclimatized to factory conditions and were able to move from place to place, from employment to employment, as required. Prior to World War I, industrialization had spread widely from England to the Western world and to Japan. It spread largely by diffusion rather than by independent social inventions. Today, much of the interest in industrialization is focused on the changes taking place in economically underdeveloped areas where the pattern of industrialization is based on flexible, small-scale production, rather than on the more typical large-scale technology of mass production (James & Bhalla, 1993).

There are many descriptions in the literature of the various patterns of industrialization (see, for example, Gulati, 1992; Hall, 1993; Kerr, 1983; and Lenski, Nolan, & Lenski, 1999).The most commonly used distinctions entail the differences among preindustrial, early industrial, and mature industrial societies, occasionally with the term postindustrial added to account for highly advanced societies such as the United States or certain Western European countries. They all have in common very developed international commodity, capital, and labor markets; a disciplined industrial labor force; a highly developed technology; and sophisticated professional, technical, and managerial personnel.

Industrialization is accompanied by a growing degree of complexity in the division of labor and the concomitant distribution of the labor force among occupations. At the most general level, industrialization involves a shift from labor force concentration in agricultural employment to manufacturing employment and eventually to employment in service industries. Wilbert Moore (1969) describes some of the factors that result in increased division of labor. One of these considerations is the growth in size of economic organizations, which encourages the efficiencies that result from occupational specialization. Another is technological change, which brings about new occupational specialties, such as computer programmer, and can also result in the further subdivision of skills, as is the case of specialized machine operators who replaced the skilled dressmaker. A third consideration is the development of new products and services, resulting in occupations that previously did not exist. The changes in the size and complexity of the labor force engaged in manufacturing and service are usually accompanied by a growth of unions and management power and a growth of class consciousness among workers. The division of labor is also related to occupational and geographic mobility as well as to higher levels of educational attainment that are more closely related to industrial functions. There is also a relationship between industrialization and racial inequality. A study of seventy-five Brazilian metropolitan areas concluded that industrialized areas have lower occupational inequality, especially in blue-collar occupations; at higher occupational levels, racial inequality is either greater or is unaffected by industrialization (Telles, 1994).

Change in population patterns (birth, death, marriages, migration) is also closely linked with industrialization. The sequence of events, often referred to as the "demographic transition," first occurred and proceeded to the greatest degree during the industrialization of Europe. The essence of the demographic transition is a move from a situation in which both birth rates and death rates are high to a situation in which both of these are low. Thus, many of the first European countries to industrialize (for example, England and France) have been characterized by low population growth for a number of years, in which replacement through fertility equals population losses through deaths. Contemporary developing societies, however, present a different picture. Demographic changes are taking a very different—and highly problematic—form. This is due to the fact that reduction in death rates has been brought about relatively rapidly, whereas a corresponding drop in birth rates lags far behind (Daugherty & Kammeyer, 1995).

Rapid reductions in death rates can be achieved through such relatively simple procedures as using insecticides to control mosquitoes, flies, and other disease-transmitting insects. For example, dramatic reductions in world deaths from malaria have been achieved in this fashion. Widespread immunization programs and the greater availability of antibiotic drugs also contributed to the lowering of mortality rates. Birth control, however, is a different matter. In many societies, fertility is a source of social prestige. In the context of industrialization, traditional attitudes may remain a strong positive sanction for bearing children, possibly in keeping with religious values, possibly for practical considerations, such as the economic value of children; or possibly for other complex interrelated reasons. Such societies are generally characterized by a high fertility rate and low or rapidly falling mortality rates, resulting in a rapid population growth and subsequent changes in the economically dependent or nonproductive segments in the population, such as the very young or the old.

Industrialization is also accompanied by changes in family form. Traditional societies are typically characterized by an extended family system. But the more industrialized a society becomes, the more likely it is to move toward the nuclear family (husband, wife, and their children) (Goode, 1963; Germani, 1981:87–90). The nuclear family form presents numerous advantages from the perspective of geographical mobility and increased urbanization, which are associated with industrialization. Traditional patterns in mate selection and parent-child relationships have been replaced by contemporary forms; and, as the family ceases to be an economically productive unit, the social position of women has changed. There is also some evidence to indicate that the rate of divorce and other indicators of family breakdown increase with industrialization. However, it would be erroneous to say that "family disorganization" is a concomitant of industrialization. Instead, at least in the United States, the modern family has undergone major changes—changes associated with urbanization and industrialization, although these are not signs of deterioration. Parsons (1955) argues that the family has become a more specialized structure. Even though it has lost some of its functions, such as producing economic goods and services and educating the children, it has also become a more exclusive guardian of other functions, such as socializing the very young and providing a setting for emotional tension management for adults. Furthermore, the roles of the husband-father and wife-mother have become more specialized relative to one another. Parsons contends that these new features of the family signify the opposite of disintegration and concludes that the nuclear family is more effective than its predecessor in socializing children for adult roles in industrial society.

Industrialization is related to the increased need for literacy, for education is a determining factor in labor force participation and for social mobility. There is a greater reliance on mass communication channels both as a source of information and as a means for breaking down the previous forms of isolation. Industrialization also results in the development of a popular culture, replacing some of the traditional forms of recreation. There is also a sharp division between "work" and "leisure," a distinction that did not exist in agrarian or tribal societies. Time becomes a scarce commodity (Szalai, 1972). There is an increased participation in voluntary associations, an increase in secular attitudes, and the rise of clearly differentiated political and administrative structures.

In sum, industrialization is an important pattern of change. In analyzing it, we often find it difficult to determine where best to "draw the line." Any examination of this pattern of change can be almost indefinitely extended in continuing to discover ways in which its presence makes itself known. In the next section, a close associate of industrialization, urbanization, will be considered.

URBANIZATION

The term *urbanization* refers to the process by which an increasing proportion of a country's population comes to live in cities, with a concomitant concentration of economic activity, administrative and political organization, and communication networks in these urban areas (Friedmann, 2002; Germani, 1981:203; Iverson, 1984). The term *population implosion* is sometimes used to describe this increased concentration of the world's peoples in urban or metropolitan areas (Hauser, 1973:430). Urbanization also refers to how people live—that is, their patterns of behavior and social relationships. These two aspects—where people live and how they live—are interrelated (see, for example, Feagin, 1997). Modernization, industrialization, and urbanization often occur in combination. It is clear, however, that the city and the factory systems are separable. Large urban areas existed in antiquity, and many factories are located in otherwise rural areas (Sjoberg, 1960). The world's earliest cities appeared some 5,000 to 6,000 years ago in Sumer, the southern part of Mesopotamia, and various types of ceremonial cities such as Mecca existed long before the advent of modernization and industrialization (Pfeiffer, 1977:149–170). Even today, urbanization is taking place in less developed societies without simultaneous industrialization (Brown, L., 2001; Hardoy, 1975:xi). For example, in Latin America, urbanization has not been accompanied by simultaneous industrialization or by better distribution of opportunity, income, and consumption (Germani, 1981:231–261; Linn, 1983). Consequently, most Latin American countries are not in a position to provide the employment opportunities, or even the basic urban infrastructure such as housing, sewer and utility services, medical care, and education, necessary to maintain an extremely large urban population.

In 2002, the world's population was over 6.25 billion, and 48 percent lived in urban areas (Population Reference Bureau, 2003). "Urban place" is defined somewhat differently from one country to another, with the bottom limit usually in the range of 2,500 to 5,000 people. Still, the percentage of the population that dwells in urban places would not change by more than 5 percentage points even if the bottom limit were 10,000 (Davis, 1972:31). Urbanization as a process clearly has a beginning and an end. For example, three-fourths of the United States' population of close to 260 million is now urban, and the maximum level of urbanization for any country is probably about 90 percent. Even after a nation achieves a high level of urbanization, its cities and metropolitan areas can continue to grow. This is the situation in North America and Western Europe. Although there is a limit to the percentage of urbanization possible, there is not yet agreement on the practical limit concerning the size of metropolitan areas. By the start of the next century, developing countries will contain eight of the world's ten megacities (cities with 10 million or more inhabitants), with Mexico City, São Paulo, Bombay, Calcutta and Shanghai at the top of the list. By 2015, there will be twenty-seven such metropolitan centers, twenty-three in developing countries (Piel, 1997).

Historically, it seems that the urbanization of *Homo sapiens* has occurred almost overnight. As recently as 1850, no country in the world was as urbanized as the world as a whole is now. Only about 2 percent of the world's population lived in cities of more than 100,000 inhabitants. The most rapid urbanization of both England and the United States occurred in the nineteenth century, and the twentieth century has witnessed an acceleration of this process in many other countries. Cities are growing because they provide, on the average, greater social and economic benefits than do rural areas and they reflect the enormous changes in the nature and scale of economic activity worldwide. Basically, cities are very efficient, they optimize the use of energy, they allow for fast and cheap transportation, they provide flexible and productive labor markets, and facilitate the diffusion of products, ideas, and human resources (World Resources Institute, 1999:10).

It is possible to depict both the level and rates of urbanization on a continuum. At the lower end of an urbanization level are the countries that have less than 10 percent of their populations located in cities; for example, countries such as Yemen, Saudi Arabia, Afghanistan, Chad, and Uganda. On the other end of the continuum, there are countries such as Belgium, Australia, and Uruguay that have more than 80 percent of their populations in urban areas. In terms of the rate of urbanization, the highest rates are found in Japan and Uruguay, whereas the lowest rates are in Israel and the United Kingdom, where much of the countryside has been already devoured by the urban sprawl (Pearce, 1993).

Urbanization has been a highly significant factor in both modernization and industrialization, and the three forces, different as they are, contain a number of parallel features, many of which have already been discussed under the headings of modernization and industrialization. For present purposes, the emphasis will be on how people live in urban areas. The question is this: Is there something inherent in the settlement patterns of cities that produces a distinctive "urban way of life"?

Well over six decades ago, Louis Wirth (1938:9) answered affirmatively. He started by assuming that "the larger, the more densely populated, and the more heterogeneous a community, the more accentuated the characteristics associated with urbanism will be." For him, a city is a permanent settlement, characterized by large size, density, and heterogeneity, which leads to correspondingly more transitory, anonymous, formalized, and specialized interrelationships—that is, to a more urbanized way of life. He reasoned that the greater the number of people interacting, the greater the potential for differentiation, bringing about lesser dependence on particular persons, less intimate relations, more freedom from the personal and emotional control of intimate groups, and no individual alliance to a single group. Density results in further differentiation and specialization, a separation of residence from the workplace, and the functional specialization of areas in the city. The city thus becomes "a mosaic of social worlds." Because of a high degree of heterogeneity, no common set of values exists in the city, and money tends to become the measure of all things. Cities become "heteropolises" with a diverse blend of ethnic groups, economic activities and lifestyles (Jencks, 1996). Formal controls replace informal controls, and it becomes necessary to adhere to predictable routines.

As a consequence of these factors, urban dwellers develop characteristic personality attributes and attitudes. Because of the many lifestyles and kinds of people, they develop a relativistic perspective. They become secularized and free of intimate ties; they lack a strong sense of integration and participation. Thus, the city is characterized by anomie; in the middle of the crowd, individuals feel lonely, sense friction and irritation, and experience personal frustration and nervous tension. Because of the mobility and diversity in the city, they accept instability and insecurity in the world at large as a norm because of their segmental roles and alliances. Their personal integrity is constantly threatened, and they are vulnerable to manipulation by the mass media. For these reasons, Wirth suggested that the incidence of personal disorganization, mental breakdown, suicide, delinquency, crime, corruption, and disorder tend to be higher in cities than in rural communities.

Obviously, other factors have an impact on social patterns in urban areas in addition to heterogeneity, density, and large size (Rosen, 1986: 68–73). However, there is not yet enough evidence to prove or disprove that number, density, and heterogeneity have the social consequences Wirth observed. In fact, social isolation and insularity similar to what has been described above has been found within the cultural and ethnic enclaves of contemporary American cities. Herbert Gans (1982) found that the Italians of Boston's North End formed a tight and homogeneous folk group having minimal contact with the remainder of the metropolitan area. In this traditionally based subculture, primary groups still retain a dominant social position. In spite of their cosmopolitan residence, people in this area of the city remain urban villagers. A similar pattern of cultural isolation is portrayed in Elliot Liebow's (1967) study of black street-corner men in Washington, DC.

Robert Redfield (1941) argues that all occasions of urbanization repeat a particular series of events—that there is a unilinear continuum from a folk to an urban form of organization. He describes folk societies as small, isolated, and homogeneous, with no division of labor except according to sex and age roles. Face-to-face communications prevail and these societies are marked by a high degree of solidarity. Religion is important, and social control is exercised through the sacred. Cultural patterns are based upon sentiment and tradition; there is no writing, no complex technology; status is ascribed at birth; and members of the society follow folkways uncritically and spontaneously. The family is the central social group. Redfield maintains that the transformation of an isolated folk community into an urban society occurs through a transmission of influences from the latter, resulting in cultural heterogeneity, disorganization, secularization, and individuation in the former. Redfield's approach is evolutionary, and for him the transformation of the world is accomplished by the spread of urbanization into more and more backward areas.

Both Redfield and Wirth argue that urbanization initiated a long-term historical process of detaching individuals from the comprehensive and familiar shared network of interrelations embedded in rural folk communities and that urban society is marked by a greater degree of functional interdependence. The nature of these changes and new conditions suggest that urbanization and its associated social changes probably increased the problems of social instability, raised conditions of class interest and conflict, and began to lay the foundations for the appearance of new and competing ideologies.

Currently, urbanization is more highly visible in the underdeveloped nations. Few aspects of international social change have generated as much scholarship as patterns of urbanization in the third world (Kasarda & Crenshaw, 1991). Many of these nations have already large proportions of urban populations, but it should be noted that the recent pattern of urbanization in these countries contrasts with the earlier experience of Western Europe. The cities of the underdeveloped nations have grown by the transfer of the rural unemployed and underemployed to the cities, which have offered little more than the countryside in the way of economic opportunities. The European experience was more a phenomenon of urban growth reflecting a general pattern of industrialization, with the cities characterized by expanding economic opportunities (DeVries, 1984).

The rapid rate of urbanization in developing countries gave rise to the concept of "overurbanization" (Graves & Sexton, 1984). It implies the belief that a particular developing country has too high a proportion of its population residing in cities, where high densities are considered detrimental to health and general well-being. The urban population of developing countries will exceed 4 billion by 2015, and five years later half of them—80 percent in Latin America—will be living in cities, and about a fourth of them in poverty (Annez & Friendly, 1996; Piel, 1997).

Moreover, overurbanization is often indicative of the fact that the urban population of a nation is too large in relation to the extent of its economic development. There are already some calls in the literature for rural development programs to prevent rural-urban migration and reduce population growth rates in urban areas (see, for example, Amani, 1992).

Overurbanization is usually the result of migration from rural areas at a rate higher than the expansion of employment opportunities in the city. This migration is prompted by high rural densities and lack of economic opportunities for peasants. Life seems difficult in the city, and, for many of the migrants, it is not better than the countryside. However, at least in the city, there is always hope and the possibility of something better. All over the world, peasants are voting with their feet in favor of city life. It may be argued that insofar as urbanization is associated with the development of a modernized mode of life and general economic progress, the problem in much of the developing world is not overurbanization, but possibly underurbanization.

As migrants flock to urban areas in developing countries, the diversity and heterogeneity of urban areas further increase. Ways of life in the city differ enormously in the various areas. Traditional lifestyles exist side by side with Western ways, and they often mingle. In Asian countries, occidental technology sometimes clashes with oriental mentality. New arrivals often identify more closely with their native villages or with such sociocultural groupings as caste, tribe, race, or religion than with the city and what the city can offer. They have the bare necessities for survival, but some do not have even those. Their culture is primarily a culture of poverty rather than a distinctively urban way of life. This phenomenon is referred to by Joel Halpern (1967:34–35) as the "peasantization of the cities." For example, in cities of former Yugoslavia, rural migrants constructed new houses identical to those they left behind, with a garden, a chicken coop, and (despite city ordinances) a pig or two. For at least a couple of generations, they retained ties to their villages. If they lived in modern apartment buildings, they created maintenance problems, being unfamiliar with plumbing and central heating, and kept domestic animals inside. In most cases, the assimilation of migrants into the urban culture and way of life is a long and tedious process.

Kingsley Davis argues that the recent trend in world urbanization "cannot have existed very long in the past and certainly will not endure long in the future." It began somewhat slowly "in the 16th and 17th centuries, with the entire world probably between one and two percent urban . . . The pace picked up some in the 18th century, but really got under way rapidly in the 19th, continuing and perhaps accelerating a bit around the middle of the 20th century. Within another century—certainly by the year 2100—the entire process of world urbanization should be finished" (Davis, 1972:48, 52–53). In view of Peter Hall's (1996) argument that the current growth of cities is determined by four finite factors—(1) the shift from manufacturing to the service factor, (2) the use of information as a basis of the economy, (3) the spatial separation of command-control functions from production, and (4) innovations in manufacturing and information that keep the economy active—Kingsley Davis' view may just be prescient about the end of urbanization. Chances are that the next change pattern, bureaucratization, which will be examined in the next section, will be here longer than urbanization.

BUREAUCRATIZATION

The onset of the twenty-first century did not improve the image of bureaucracy. The word bureaucracy still carries strong negative connotations. It is blamed for inefficiency, inflexibility, and general inhumanity (Heckscher & Donnellon, 1994; Keiser et al., 2002). It conjures up images of officiousness, red tape, and the endless filling out of forms—such as one or more of the 4,987 different kinds used by the federal government (*Time*, 1978). For sociologists, the term *bureaucracy* simply means a hierarchical social structure for administering large-scale organizations rationally, efficiently, effectively, and impersonally. The topic of this section, bureaucratization, refers to changes within an organization, public or private, toward greater rationality in decision making, improved operating efficiency, and more effective attainment of common goals (Lorsch, 1987). As the size and complexity of an organization increase, there is a greater need for coordination if efficiency and effectiveness are to be maintained or improved. Organizational efficiency can be maximized when there is a hierarchical line of authority, with each role in the chain having clearly defined and stated duties and responsibilities; when all decisions are made on the basis of technical knowledge, not personal considerations; when members are judged solely on the basis of technical knowledge, and discipline is impartially enforced; and when the members are recruited on the basis of their abilities and there is a system of assured tenure and promotion based on merit (Weber, 1947:329–341).

In a truly fascinating book, *The Bureaucratization of the World*, Henry Jacoby (1973:9) cites Alfred Weber, who wrote that "the history of all great civilizations begins with the formation of a bureaucracy which supports and shapes men's whole existence." In ancient Egypt and Babylon, it was the priestly, hierarchically organized class of scribes who created and guarded the magic and sacred character of life. "This class, founded on the economic productivity of the canal system, was probably the most totalitarian bureaucracy ever to have existed in history" (Jacoby, 1973:9–10). The early civilizations of China and India also exhibited similar strong bureaucratic tendencies, and the Inca Empire used a bureaucratic system to administer the construction of agricultural terracing and established a rather efficient communication network that was dependent on suspension bridges. When the Spaniards invaded Peru, they discovered a well-organized system of statistical information using differently colored twines to indicate objects and knots in the twines to represent numbers. Record keeping was also present in ancient Egypt, and taxation was determined by record offices with centralized information about citizens and their living conditions. Periodically, a census was taken by the government and "all of Egypt was inventoried" (Jacoby, 1973:10). All of this obviously required an experienced administrative bureaucracy whose structure was subjected to various changes.

As early as the thirteenth century in France, a number of functions came under the jurisdiction of the state and gave rise to a class of people whose position in society was determined by office rather than by ascribed status. By the end of the sixteenth century, they became known as the Fourth Estate. The bureaucracy became a separate class, recognizable by special long gowns (Jacoby, 1973:19). At that time, bureaucracy was associated with absolute monarchy. "It is bureaucracy which represents absolute authority, the monarch being the symbol at its head. . . . When powerful political leaders occupy the throne of an absolute monarchy they themselves are the bureaucratic heads" (Frolich, quoted by Jacoby, 1973:25). By that time, the state bureaucracy never doubted that all economic activities were controllable. In 1577, industry and commerce became regulated by a royal decree in France. New industries were created, and the quality and quantity of goods produced were controlled. Wage and price controls were introduced and severe sanctions were imposed to maintain them. A new department was created to inspect and supervise these activities.

It is evident from the above historical sketch that the origin of the state and the development of the bureaucracy are closely intertwined. While examining American democracy in 1832, Alexis de Tocqueville also looked into the origin of the bureaucratic state. He concluded that the disappearance of traditional institutions and the development of an economy under which individuals concentrated exclusively on their own affairs led to greater state control of economic and social functions. General apathy toward public affairs "must almost compulsorily concentrate the direction of all men and the management of all things in the hands of the administration" (de Tocqueville, quoted by Jacoby, 1973:53). Marx shared de Tocqueville's observation that although the forms of government changed, administrations continued uninterruptedly to accumulate more functions and responsibilities.

Not everyone looked upon the growth of bureaucratization favorably. For example, the Revolution of 1917 in Russia brought the entire administrative machine to a standstill and gave rise to an optimistic idea that a new way of organizing society is possible without the hated bureaucracy. Lenin predicted that the principle of sound government would be carried so far in the future that any cook could govern the state. "Since *everyone* was to participate in the government, *everyone* would become a temporary 'bureaucrat,' and thus *no one* would be a real bureaucrat" (Jacoby, 1973:124). Thus he predicted that bureaucracy would die out. But this dream of Lenin's never came true. In 1917, approximately 1 million people were employed in administrative offices in Russia. By 1921, this number of increased to almost

2.5 million and kept growing at a very rapid pace until the demise of the Soviet system in the early 1990s.

In developing countries, a stable and efficient system of taxation is the precondition for the permanent existence of bureaucratic administration (*Economist*, 1997). A highly interdependent relationship exists between bureaucracy and taxation. "The efficiency of the bureaucracy depends upon the effectiveness of its taxation system; and the effectiveness of the taxation system depends on the efficiency of the bureaucratic apparatus" (Lockwood, 1976:380). When a taxation system cannot provide adequate support for the bureaucracy in a developing country, members of bureaucratic organizations will rely on graft and corruption to supplement their income (Ockey, 1994). This is why the concept of white-collar crime is simply not applicable to many of these societies. Public servants, police, custom officials, and others in general are dependent on graft, and, in a sense, "the system is tantamount to a labyrinth of informally levied and collected surcharges in substitution of formal taxation and accounting" (Hetzler, 1969:47).

When there is a more or less stable form of taxation system in developing countries, the bureaucracy can facilitate economic development by rendering the needed legal and public service preconditions for development, including law and order, money and banking organizations, and the administrative apparatus essential for economic enterprises. "The bureaucracy can help modify 'the resource-structure of a country, together with its exploitation, as to make it more favorable to economic growth' . . . can form public corporations or other types of enterprises that will furnish the initiative for economic development, [and] . . . can fashion tax, fiscal, and investment policies that will sustain and enhance economic growth" (Spengler, quoted by Lauer, 1982:324).

In contemporary societies, bureaucracies represent significant concentrations of resources and power without being directly accountable to the public at large. Even though this concentration of power and resources is essential to the business of modern industrial society, there is also a sense in which such concentrations raise public anxieties. In third-world countries, bureaucracies are characterized by high salaries and interdependent structure, making the officials dependent on the system for survival. When their positions are threatened, they will often support a coup d'état in order to maintain the bureaucratic structure on which they depend (Riggs, 1993). Not surprisingly, there are questions occasionally raised as to what extent bureaucracy is compatible with democracy. There is a tendency in bureaucratic organizations for power to be concentrated in the hands of a few, exemplified by what Roberto Michel (1949) calls the "iron law of oligarchy." Admittedly, as demonstrated by Seymour M. Lipset and his associates (1956), under some conditions democratic processes can be maintained in large bureaucratic organizations, but still the relationship between bureaucracy and democracy is an uncomfortable one. In an age of increasing "bigness" of government, business (Meyer, 1985:34–40), and university (indeed, every kind of organization), one may speculate on how the individual and the democratic process fit into the picture. It is a growing concern in the light of increasing bureaucratization, which pervades all aspects of life.

Although the efficiencies of large-scale organizations have made possible the unprecedented material growth of the twentieth century, the scope of their power and influence has come to threaten basic social and political values, particularly individual freedom (Fischer & Sirianni, 1984:3). There is a disturbing growth of centralized bureaucratic control with technological surveillance and centralized data banks resembling what Bertram Gross (1980) characterizes as "friendly fascism." There is also a waste of intelligence because organizations use only a small fraction of the capacity of its members as a result of the practice of slotting people into predefined offices, a failure to control informal organizations, and a pronounced tendency to resist change (Heckscher, 1994:20–24).

In sum, as Otto Hintze writes, "Bureaucratic organization is a first-class sociological work of art which has been fashioned over many centuries. It is an illusion to maintain that it could be suppressed and replaced by 'self government.' . . ." Or, in Joseph Schumpeter's words, bureaucracy ". . . grows everywhere, whatever the political method a nation may adopt. Its expansion is the one certain thing about our future" (Hintze & Schumpeter, quoted by Jacoby, 1973:199, 191).

SUMMARY

In this chapter, several change patterns were considered. The object was to describe the principal forms that change can take. Evolution was seen in the context of directionality, novelty, increased variety, and complexity. Such change patterns are cumulative. These patterns can be investigated both qualitatively, as illustrated by the evolution of legal systems and religion, and quantitatively, as in the case of stratification and food production or energy consumption.

Diffusion theory developed as an alternative to evolutionary theories. It deals with the spread of cultural elements. Historically, it was posited that ancient Egypt was the source of civilization, and from there elements spread to all parts of the world. The process of diffusion refers to the acquisition of elements from other cultures or social groups. The diffusion process includes the stages of awareness, interest, evaluation, trial, and the adoption of an innovation. It is conditioned by the perception of relative advantage, compatibility, complexity, tryability, and observability of an element by members of a culture. The adopter categories include innovators, early adopters, early and late majority, and laggards. The center-periphery and the proliferation-of-centers are the principal models of diffusion. Diffusion is considered an important component of planned social change.

Diffusion is subsumed under acculturation, which is a result of contact among cultures. However, cultures in contact seldom acculturate reciprocally, as illustrated by the case of Native Americans. Acculturation can also be planned and involuntary, as happened in Africa during colonization. Immigrants in the United States undergo selective acculturation. The process of acculturation can be rapid and nondisruptive, as evidenced by the Manus.

Revolution usually entails rapid and fundamental changes, but such changes may or may not be violent. Several patterns were discussed, such as the Jacquerie, the Millenarian and Anarchistic Rebellions, Jacobean Communist Revolution, Conspirational Coup d'État, and Militarized Mass Insurrection. Most revolutionary forms bring about alterations in the class, status, and power systems, and the intensity of changes can be ascertained in a continuum.

Modernization refers to the transition from traditional to contemporary society and may take place without industrialization. Three types were identified: industrial, acculturative, and induced. Modernization is accompanied by increased differentiation in the economic, organizational, political, and cultural spheres. Modern people are portrayed as informed, efficient, and independent beings willing to experiment.

Industrialization involves the development of a factory system under mechanical power. An index of industrialization is the proportion of the labor force in agriculture. Industrialization is accompanied by a growing division of labor, a shift from agriculture to manufacturing and service industries, the creation of new specialties and occupations, greater literacy, and demographic changes.

As with modernization, urbanization may take place without industrialization. Living in cities produces a distinctive "urban way of life." The process of urbanization can be depicted on the folk-urban continuum. Currently, urbanization is most rapid in developing countries, where it is associated with distinct lifestyles and with the concept of overurbanization.

The final change pattern examined in this chapter is bureaucratization. It refers to greater rationality in decision making and increased efficiency in the attainment of organizational goals. The section concluded with a not-too-cheerful note that bureaucracy, regardless of the form of government, is here to stay. In the next chapter, a series of specific spheres of change will be considered.

SUGGESTED FURTHER READINGS

FEAGIN, JOE R. *The New Urban Sociology.* Lanham, MD: Rowman & Littlefield Publishers, Inc., 1997. A collection of articles by Feagin on contemporary urban themes that shape cities.

FORAN, JOHN (ed.). *The Future of Revolutions: Rethinking Political and Social Change in the Age of Globalization.* New York: Zed Books, 2002. An examination of the many theoretical and disciplinary frameworks through which revolutions can be understood.

FRIEDMANN, JOHN. *The Prospect of Cities.* Minneapolis: University of Minnesota Press, 2002. A survey of global urbanization and a review of models of development.

GERLACH, LUTHER P., AND VIRGINIA H. HINE. *Lifeway Leap: The Dynamics of Change in America.* Minneapolis: University of Minnesota Press, 1973. A highly readable book, with chapters on evolutionary and revolutionary patterns of change.

GERMANI, GINO. *The Sociology of Modernization.* New Brunswick, NJ: Transaction Books, 1981. Studies on the historical and theoretical aspects of modernization with an emphasis on Latin America.

GOLDSTONE, JACK A. (ed.). *Revolutions: Theoretical, Comparative, and Historical Studies,* 3rd ed. Australia; Belmont, CA: Wadsworth, 2003. A selection of readings by major thinkers and writers on the various facets of revolution and social change.

HAFERKAMP, HANS, AND NEIL J. SMELSER (eds.). *Social Change and Modernity.* Berkeley: University of California Press, 1992. A collection of seventeen articles by sociology's foremost theorists on modernity and its manifestations—industrialization, social differentiation, rationalization, and capitalism.

HECKSCHER, CHARLES, AND ANNE DONNELLON (eds.). *The Post-Bureaucratic Organization: New Perspectives on Organizational Change.* Thousand Oaks, CA: Sage Publications, 1994. A collection of articles on the various facets of bureaucracy with recommendations for alternatives.

IVERSON, NOEL (ed.). *Urbanism and Urbanization: Views, Aspects, and Dimensions.* Leiden: E. J. Brill, 1984. A collection of informative and provocative articles on urbanism and urbanization.

KERR, CLARK. *The Future of Industrial Societies.* Cambridge, MA: Harvard University Press, 1983. An interesting discussion of the process of industrialization and the prospects for industrial societies.

KIMMEL, MICHAEL S. *Revolution: A Sociological Interpretation.* Philadelphia: Temple University Press, 1990. An excellent synthesis of the existing concepts and theories of revolution.

MONTGOMERY, ROBERT L. *The Lopsided Spread of Christianity: Toward an Understanding of the Diffusion of Religions.* Westport, CT: Praeger, 2001. Comparing the spread of Christianity in the East to its more successful spread to the West, the book illustrates the uneven diffusion of one of the world's most influential religions.

ROGERS, EVERETT M. *Diffusion of Innovations,* 4th ed. New York: Free Press, 1995. An authoritative and comprehensive statement on the current status of diffusion research and theory.

SPINDLER, LOUISE S. *Culture Change and Modernization: Mini-Models and Case Studies.* Prospect Heights, IL: Waveland Press, 1984. An informative and entertaining discussion on culture change with good illustrations of acculturation and diffusion patterns.

REFERENCES

AMANI, MEHDI. "The Urban Explosion," *UNESCO Courier,* January 1992, pp. 34–37.

ANNEZ, PATRICIA, AND ALFRED FRIENDLY. "Cities in the Developing World: Agenda for Action Following Habitat II," *Finance & Development,* 33 (4) December 1996, pp. 12–15.

APTER, DAVID E. *The Politics of Modernization.* Chicago: University of Chicago Press, 1965.

BAKER, RUSSELL. "Made Elsewhere," *The New York Times Magazine*, April 26, 1987, p. 18.
BARNET, RICHARD J., AND JOHN CAVANAGH. *Global Dreams: Imperial Corporations and the New World Order.* New York: Simon & Schuster, 1994.
BELLAH, ROBERT N. *Religion and Progress in Modern Asia.* New York: Free Press, 1965.
BELLAH, ROBERT N. "Religious Evolution." In S. N. Eisenstadt (ed.), *Readings in Social Evolution and Development.* New York: Pergamon, 1970, pp. 211–244.
BENGTSSON, MARIA, AND ANDERS SODERHOLM. "Bridging Distances: Organizing Boundary-Spanning Technology Development Projects." *Regional Studies*, 36 (3) May 2002, pp. 263–275.
BIRMAN, DINA, EDISON J. TRICKETT, AND ANDREY VINOKUROV. "Acculturation and Adaptation of Soviet Jewish Refugee Adolescents: Predictors of Adjustment Across Life Domains." *American Journal of Community Psychology*, 30 (5) October 2002, pp. 585–608.
BLACK, CYRIL E. *The Dynamics of Modernization.* New York: Harper & Row, 1967.
BODLEY, JOHN H. *Victims of Progress*, 4th ed. Mountain View, CA: Mayfield Pub. Co., 1999.
BRINTON, CRANE. *The Anatomy of Revolution.* New York: Vintage, 1959.
BROWN, CECIL H. "Lexical Acculturation in Native American Languages," *Current Anthropology*, 35 (2) April 1994, pp. 95–118.
BROWN, LESTER R. *State of the World 2001.* London: Earthscan, 2001.
BURR, JEFFREY A., AND JAN A. MUTCHLER. "Nativity, Acculturation, and Economic Status: Explanations of Asian-American Living Arrangements in Later Life," *Journal of Gerontology*, 48 (2) March 1993, pp. 855–864.
CERNEA, MICHAEL M. (ed.). *Putting People First: Sociological Variables in Rural Development*, 2nd ed. New York: Oxford, 1991.
CHATTOE, EDMUND. "Developing the Selectionist Paradigm in Sociology," *Sociology*, 36 (4) November 2002, pp. 817–834.
CHIROT, DANIEL. "The Rise of the West," *American Sociological Review*, 50, 1985, pp. 181–195.
CHODAK, SZYMON. *Societal Development.* New York: Oxford, 1973.
CLOSE, DAVID, AND CARL BRIDGE (eds.). *Revolution: A History of the Idea.* Totowa, NJ: Barnes & Noble, 1985.
DAUGHERTY, HELEN GINN, AND KENNETH C. W. KAMMEYER. *An Introduction to Population.* New York: Guilford Press, 1995.
DAVIS, KINGSLEY. "World Urbanization 1950–1970: Analysis of Trends, Relationships and Developments," *Population Monograph*, 2(9), 1972. Berkeley: University of California Press.
DEFRONZO, JAMES. *Revolutions and Revolutionary Movements*, 2nd ed. Boulder, CO: Westview Press, 1996.
DEVOS, GEORGE A. (ed.). *Responses to Change, Society, Culture, and Personality.* New York: Van Nostrand, 1976.
DEVRIES, JAN. *European Urbanization 1500–1800.* Cambridge, MA: Harvard University Press, 1984.
Economist, "Disappearing Taxes," May 31, 1997, pp. 21–23.
EDMONDS, RADCLIFFE G., AND JOHN B. MEISEL. "Explaining Rates of Technology Diffusion: A Need for Caution," *Quarterly Review of Economics and Finance*, 32 (2) Summer 1992, pp. 85–100.
EISENSTADT, S. N. *Tradition, Change, and Modernity.* New York: Wiley, 1973.

FEAGIN, JOE R. *The New Urban Sociology.* Lanham, MD: Rowman & Littlefield Publishers, Inc., 1997.

FISCHER, A. J., A. J. ARNOLD, AND M. GIBBS. "Information and the Speed of Innovation Adoption," *American Journal of Agricultural Economics,* 78 (4) November 1996, pp. 1073–1082.

FISCHER, FRANK, AND CARMEN SIRIANNI (eds.). *Critical Studies in Organization and Bureaucracy.* Philadelphia: Temple University Press, 1984.

FORAN, JOHN (ed.). *The Future of Revolutions: Rethinking Political and Social Change in the Age of Globalization.* New York: Zed Books, 2002.

FRIED, MORTON. *The Evolution of Political Society.* New York: Random House, 1976.

FRIEDMANN, JOHN. *The Prospect of Cities.* Minneapolis: University of Minnesota Press, 2002.

FURNHAM, ADRIAN. "When Change is S-Shaped," *New Scientist,* 141 (1908) January 15, 1994, pp. 46–48.

GANS, HERBERT. *The Urban Villagers,* rev. ed. New York: Free Press, 1982.

GERLACH, LUTHER P., AND VIRGINIA H. HINE. *Lifeway Leap: The Dynamics of Change in America.* Minneapolis: University of Minnesota Press, 1973.

GERMANI, GINO. *The Sociology of Modernization.* New Brunswick, NJ: Transaction Books, 1981.

GOLDSTONE, JACK A. (ed.) *Revolutions: Theoretical, Comparative, and Historical Studies,* 3rd ed. Australia; Belmont, CA: Wadsworth, 2003.

GOODE, WILLIAM J. *World Revolution and Family Patterns.* New York: Free Press, 1963.

GRAVES, PHILIP E., AND ROBERT LOUIS SEXTON. "Overurbanization and Its Relation to Economic Growth for Less Developed Countries." In Pradip K. Ghosh (ed.), *Urban Development in the Third World.* Westport, CT: Greenwood Press, 1984, pp. 160–166.

GROSS, BERTRAM. *Friendly Fascism.* New York: Evans, 1980.

GRUBLER, ARNULF. "Time for a Change: On the Patterns of Diffusion of Innovation," *Daedalus,* 125 (3) Summer 1996, pp. 19–43.

GULATI, UMESH C. "The Foundations of Rapid Economic Growth: The Case of the Four Tigers," *The American Journal of Economics and Sociology,* 51 (2) April 1992, pp. 161–163.

HAGOPIAN, MARK N. *The Phenomenon of Revolution.* New York: Dodd, Mead, 1974.

HALL, PETER. "Forces Shaping Urban Europe," *Urban Studies,* 30 (6) June 1993, pp. 833–849.

HALL, PETER. "The Global City," *International Social Science Journal,* 48 (1) March 1996, pp. 15–24.

HALPERN, JOEL. *The Changing Village Community.* Englewood Cliffs, NJ: Prentice Hall, 1967.

HARDOY, JORGE E. (ed.). *Urbanization in Latin America: Approaches and Issues.* New York: Doubleday (Anchor Books), 1975.

HAUSER, PHILIP M. "The Chaotic Society: Product of the Social Morphological Revolution." In Amitai Etzioni and Eva Etzioni-Halevy (eds.), *Social Change: Sources, Patterns, and Consequences,* 2nd ed. New York: Basic Books, 1973, pp. 428–442.

HAYS, SCOTT P. "Influences on Reinvention During the Diffusion of Innovation," *Political Research Quarterly,* 49 (3) September 1996, pp. 631–651.

HECKSCHER, CHARLES. "Defining the Post-Bureaucratic Type." In Charles Heckscher and Anne Donnellon (eds.), *The Post-Bureaucratic Organization: New Perspectives on Organizational Change.* Thousand Oaks, CA: Sage Publications, 1994, pp. 14–62.

HECKSCHER, CHARLES, AND ANNE DONNELLON (eds.). *The Post-Bureaucratic Organization: New Perspectives on Organizational Change.* Thousand Oaks, CA: Sage Publications, 1994.

HETZLER, STANLEY A. *Technological Growth and Social Change: Achieving Modernization.* New York: Praeger, 1969.

HOWELLS, JEREMY R. L. "Tacit knowledge, innovation and economic geography," *Urban Studies,* May 2002, pp. 871–875.

INKELES, ALEX. "Industrialization, Modernization and the Quality of Life," *International Journal of Comparative Sociology,* 34 (1–2), January–April 1993, pp. 1–23.

INKELES, ALEX, AND DAVID H. SMITH. *Becoming Modern: Individual Change in Six Developing Countries.* Cambridge, MA: Harvard University Press, 1974.

IVERSON, NOEL (ed.). *Urbanism and Urbanization: Views, Aspects, and Dimensions.* Leiden: E. J. Brill, 1984.

JACOBY, HENRY. *The Bureaucratization of the World,* trans. Eveline L. Kanes. Berkeley: University of California Press, 1973.

JAMES, JEFFREY, AND AJIT BHALLA. "Flexible Specialization, New Technologies and Future Industrialization in Developing Countries" (Special Issue: The Future of Industrialization) *Futures,* 25 (6) July–August 1993, pp. 713–733.

JENCKS, CHARLES. "The City that Never Sleeps," *New Statesman,* 125 (4290) June 28, 1996, pp. 26–29.

JOHNSON, CHALMERS. *Revolution and the Social System.* Stanford, CA: Hoover International Studies, vol. 3, 1964.

JOVANOVIC, BOYAN, AND GLENN M. MACDONALD. "Competitive Diffusion," *Journal of Political Economy,* 102 (1) February 1994, pp. 24–53.

KASARDA, JOHN D., AND EDWARD M. CRENSHAW. "Third World Urbanization: Dimensions, Theories, and Determinants," *Annual Review of Sociology,* 17 Annual 1991, pp. 467–502.

KEISER, LAEL R., VICKY M. WILKINS, KENNETH J. MEIER, AND CATHERINE A. HOLLAND. "Lipstick and Logarithms: Gender, Institutional Context, and Representative Bureaucracy," *American Political Science Review,* 96 (3), September 2002, pp. 553–565.

KERR, CLARK. *The Future of Industrial Societies.* Cambridge, MA: Harvard University Press, 1983.

KERR, CLARK, JOHN T. DUNLOP, FREDERICK H. HARRISON, AND CHARLES A. MYERS. *Industrialism and Industrial Man.* New York: Oxford, 1964.

KIMMEL, MICHAEL S. *Revolution: A Sociological Interpretation.* Philadelphia: Temple University Press, 1990.

KIRBY, ERIC G., AND SUSAN L. KIRBY. "On the Diffusion of International Social Values: Institutionalization and Demographic Transition," *Social Science Quarterly,* 77 (2) June 1996, pp. 289–301.

KRISTOF, NICHOLAS D. "An Atomic Age Eden (but Don't Eat the Coconuts)," *The New York Times,* March 5, 1997, p. A4.

KROEBER, A. L. "Diffusionism." In Amitai Etzioni and Eva Etzioni-Halevy (eds.), *Social Change: Sources, Patterns, and Consequences,* 2nd ed. New York: Basic Books, 1973, pp. 140–144.

LAUER, ROBERT H. *Perspectives of Social Change,* 3rd ed. Boston: Allyn & Bacon, 1982.

LENSKI, GERHARD, PATRICK NOLAN, AND JEAN LENSKI. *Human Societies: An Introduction to Macrosociology,* 8th ed. New York: McGraw-Hill, 1999.

LEVY, MARION, JR. *Modernization and the Structure of Societies*, vol. 1. Princeton, NJ: Princeton University Press, 1966.

LIANG, ZAI, YIU POR CHEN, AND YANMIN GU. "Rural Industrialization and Internal Migration in China," *Urban Studies*, 39 (12), November 2002, pp. 2175–2188.

LIEBOW, ELLIOT. *Tally's Corner*. Boston: Little, Brown, 1967.

LINN, JOHANNES F. *Cities in the Developing World*. New York: Oxford, 1983.

LINTON, RALPH. *The Study of Man: An Introduction*. New York: Appleton, 1936.

LIPSET, SEYMOUR M., MARTIN TROW, AND JAMES COLEMAN. *Union Democracy*. New York: Free Press, 1956.

LOCKWOOD, DAVID. "Social Integration and System Integration." In George K. Zollschan and Walter Hirsch (eds.), *Social Change: Explorations, Diagnoses, and Conjectures*, 2nd ed. New York: Wiley, 1976, pp. 370–383.

LORSCH, JAY W. (ed.). *Handbook of Organizational Behavior*. Englewood Cliffs, NJ: Prentice Hall, 1987.

MARIN, BARBARA VANOSS, JEANNE M. TSCHANN, CYNTHIA A. GOMEZ, AND SUSAN M. KEGELES. "Acculturation and Gender Differences in Sexual Attitudes and Behaviors: Hispanic vs. Non-Hispanic White Unmarried Adults," *The American Journal of Public Health*, 83 (12) December 1993, pp. 1759–1762.

MCADAM, DOUG, AND DIETER RUCHT. "The Cross-National Diffusion of Movement Ideas," *The Annals of the American Academy of Political and Social Science*, July 1993, pp. 56–75.

MEAD, MARGARET. *New Lives for Old*. New York: Mentor, 1961.

MEADOWS, PAUL. *The Many Faces of Change: Explorations in the Theory of Social Change*. Cambridge, MA: Schenkman, 1971.

MEYER, MARSHALL W. *Limits to Bureaucratic Growth*. Berlin: Walter de Gruyter, 1985.

MICHEL, ROBERTO. *Political Parties*. New York: Free Press, 1949.

MONTGOMERY, ROBERT L. *The Lopsided Spread of Christianity: Toward an Understanding of the Diffusion of Religions*. Westport, CT: Praeger, 2001.

MOORE, WILBERT E. "Changes in Occupational Structures." In William A. Faunce and William H. Form (eds.), *Comparative Perspectives on Industrial Society*. Boston: Little, Brown, 1969, pp. 107–125.

MOORE, WILBERT E. *Social Change*, 2nd ed. Englewood Cliffs, NJ: Prentice Hall, 1974.

MURDOCK, GEORGE P. *Our Primitive Contemporaries*. New York: Macmillan, 1934.

MURDOCK, GEORGE P. "Word Ethnographic Sample," *American Anthropologist*, 59, 1957, pp. 664–687.

MYRDAL, GUNNAR. *Asian Drama: An Inquiry into the Poverty of Nations*, vol. 1. New York: Pantheon, 1968.

NAROLL, RAOUL. "On Ethnic Unit Classification," *Current Anthropology*, 5 (4), 1964, pp. 283–312.

NEUMANN, SIGMUND. "The International Civil War." In Clifford T. Paynton and Robert Blackey (eds.), *Why Revolution? Theories and Analyses*. Cambridge, MA: Schenkman, 1971, pp. 110–123.

NEWMAN, RICHARD. "American Culture's African Roots," *Black Issues in Higher Education*, 13 (25) February 6, 1997.

OCKEY, JAMES. "Political Parties, Factions, and Corruption in Thailand," *Modern Asian Studies*, 28 (2) May 1994, pp. 251–278.

PARSONS, TALCOTT. *Family, Socialization and Interaction Process*. New York: Free Press, 1955.

PATTNAYAK, SATYA R. "Modernization, Dependency, and the Stage in Asia, Africa, and Latin America," *International Journal of Comparative Sociology*, 37 (3–4) December 1996, pp. 274–289.

PEARCE, FRED. "Urban Sprawl Devours Britain's Countryside," *New Scientist*, 140 (1901) November 27, 1993, pp. 8–9.

PERLMUTTER, HOWARD V. "On the Rocky Road to the First Global Civilization," *Human Relations*, 44 (9) September 1991, pp. 897–921.

PETERSEN, WILLIAM. *The Politics of Population*. New York: Doubleday (Anchor Books), 1965.

PFEIFFER, JOHN E. *The Emergence of Society, A Prehistory of the Establishment*. New York: McGraw Hill, 1977.

PIEL, GERARD. "The Urbanization of Poverty Worldwide," *Challenge*, 40 (1) January–February 1997, pp. 58–69.

POPULATION REFERENCE BUREAU. *Population Data Sheet 2003*. Washington, DC: Population Reference Bureau, 2003.

REDFIELD, ROBERT. *The Folk Culture of Yucatan*. Chicago: University of Chicago Press, 1941.

RICHERSON, PETER J., AND ROBERT BOYD. "Darwinian Models of Culture: Toward Replacing the Nature/Nurture Dichotomy," *World Futures*, 34 (1–2) June 1992, pp. 43–58.

RIGGS, FRED W. "Fragility of the Third World's Regimes," *International Social Science Journal*, 45 (2) May 1993, pp. 199–244.

ROGERS, EVERETT M. *Diffusion of Innovations*, 4th ed. New York: Free Press, 1995.

ROSEN, CHRISTINE MEISNER. *The Limits of Power*. Cambridge, England: Cambridge University Press, 1986.

SAHLINS, MARSHALL D. *Social Stratification in Polynesia*. Seattle: University of Washington Press, 1958.

SAVELSBERG, JOACHIM J. "Dialectics of Norms in Modernization," *The Sociological Quarterly*, 43 (2) Spring 2002 pp. 277–307.

SCHON, DONALD A. *Beyond the Stable State*. New York: W. W. Norton, 1971.

SCHON, DONALD A., AND MARTIN REIN. *Frame Reflection: Toward the Resolution of Intractable Policy Controversies*. New York: Basic Books, 1994.

SCHWARTZ, RICHARD, AND JAMES C. MILLER. "Legal Evolution and Societal Complexity." In S. N. Eisenstadt (ed.), *Readings in Social Evolution and Development*. New York: Pergamon, 1970, pp. 155–172.

SJOBERG, GIDEON. *The Preindustrial City: Past and Present*. New York: Free Press, 1960.

SMITH, ANTHONY D. *The Concept of Social Change: A Critique of the Functionalist Theory of Social Change*. London: Routledge, 1973.

SPINDLER, LOUISE S. *Culture Change and Modernization: Mini-Models and Case Studies*. Prospect Heights, IL: Waveland Press, 1984.

STRANG, DAVID, AND NANCY BRANDON TUMA. "Spatial and Temporal Heterogeneity in Diffusion," *The American Journal of Sociology*, 99 (3) November 1993, pp. 614–640.

SZALAI, ALEXANDER. *The Use of Time*. The Hague: Mouton, 1972.

SZTOMPKA, PIOTR. *The Sociology of Social Change*. Cambridge, MA: Blackwell, 1994.

TELLES, EDWARD E. "Industrialization and Racial Inequality in Employment: The Brazilian Example." *American Sociological Review*, 59 (1) February 1994, pp. 46–64.

TILLY, CHARLES. *European Revolutions, 1492–1992*. Cambridge, MA: Blackwell, 1993.

TILLY, CHARLES. *Roads from Past to Futures*. Lanham, MD: Rowman & Littlefield Publishers, Inc., 1997.

Time. "Paper Chase, The Battle Against Red Tape," July 10, 1978, p. 26.

VALENTE, THOMAS W. "Diffusion of Innovations and Policy Decision-Making," *Journal of Communication,* 43 (1) Winter 1993, pp. 30–46.

VEGA, WILLIAM A., ANDRES G. GIL, GEORGE G. WARHEIT, AND RICK S. ZIMMERMAN. "Acculturation and Delinquent Behavior among Cuban American Adolescents: Toward an Empirical Model," *American Journal of Community Psychology,* 21 (1) February 1993, pp. 113–126.

WALT, STEPHEN. *Revolution and War.* Ithaca, NY: Cornell University Press, 1996.

WEBER, MAX. *The Theory of Social and Economic Organization,* trans. A. M. Henderson and Talcott Parsons. New York: Free Press, 1947.

WHITE, LESLIE. *The Science of Culture.* New York: Grove Press, 1949.

WIRTH, LOUIS B. "Urbanism as a Way of Life," *American Journal of Sociology,* 44, July 1938, pp. 1–24.

WORLD RESOURCES INSTITUTE. *World Resources, A Guide to the Global Environment: The Urban Environment, 1998–99.* New York: Oxford University Press, 1999.

Chapter 4

Spheres of Change

To say that the modern world in the early years of the twenty-first century is in the throes of dramatic changes is an obvious understatement. The sense and feeling of change permeates social arrangements at all levels of society. This chapter will examine some of the more important changes in society and show the context in which they are taking place. The specific changes occurring in such spheres as the family, population, stratification, power relations, education, and the economy will be considered. Changes in these spheres are interrelated; they influence each other as well as the course of society; they often occur more or less simultaneously; and they are set in motion by the social forces discussed in previous chapters.

THE FAMILY

The major changes in the structure and functions of the family can be traced to the Industrial Revolution and to the resulting urbanization, modernization, and economic development of society (Gelles, 1995; Goode, 1968; Janssens, 1993; Leslie & Korman, 1989; and Ruggles, 1994, Schwartz & Scott, 2003). Industrialization was instrumental in transforming the traditional large, authoritarian, relatively stable rural family system into a more egalitarian, emotionally free, and less sexually stratified nuclear family. This is not to say that industrialization had the same immediate effect on family systems in every society [see for example, Thornton & Lin (1995) on the family in Taiwan]. Cultural and social forces determine the rate of family changes under the impact of industrialization, and there is substantial variation from society to society concerning the direction and magnitude of changes in specific family attributes such as the incidence of divorce or age at marriage.

Although at varying rates, there are a number of specific changes occurring worldwide in family patterns (Goode, 1968:59; Leslie & Korman, 1989:61–75; Zarnowska, 1997). These include an increased freedom of marital choice, in which marital bargaining is taken from the hands of elders. Both the dowry and bride price are disappearing in most parts of the world. In India, for example, the 2001 census found a rather lopsided sex ratio (820 girls for every 1,000 boys) due to a cultural preference for boys and the use of modern medical technology, particularly ultrasound exams, which allow couples to indulge their preference for sons by using abortion to avoid having girls. This cultural preference for boys has drastically reduced the number of girls and now parents of some sons are dropping demands for wedding dowries (Lancaster, 2002). Dowry is further being replaced by, among other things, an increase in the proportion of working wives.* Young couples are more economically independent; the age of females at first marriage is increasing; and great discrepancies between the ages of spouses are becoming rarer. There is also a decrease of marriage between close kin, such as between cousins. Illegitimacy rates are on the increase. There is a significant decline in infanticide. The institutions of concubinage and polygamy are on the decline. Although the divorce rate is on the increase, the trend in any given society depends on its prior level (see, for example, Jones, 1997). Remarriage after divorce or after the death of one's spouse is becoming more common in areas where it was once rare. Let us now consider some of the specific changes in the American family.

The Changing Functions of the American Family

In a classic essay written some seven decades ago, William F. Ogburn (1934) contended that the American family is ill-adapted to modern industrial society, as evidenced by the loss of many of its traditional functions to other agencies such as the school, church, and the state. More recently, historian John Demos (1970:193) reached a similar conclusion.

---

*Although it is outlawed in India, the practice of dowry payment is still widespread among Hindus, who account for about 80 percent of the country's over 1 billion people. Brides are increasingly being killed for providing dowries deemed inadequate by their husbands' families. Between 1990 and 1994, close to 21,000 brides were put to death, often by being set on fire (*Wall Street Journal*, 1994:A8). In addition, wife-beating is widely accepted as an integral part of the patriarchal social structure in India, under which women are still considered inferior and dependent. In a recent study of 1,842 Indian women in 1993–1994, about 40 percent had been beaten by their husbands and three out of four women in the survey considered wife-beating necessary for punishment and discipline (Jejeebhoy & Cook, 1997).

> Broadly speaking, the history of the family in America has been a history of contraction and withdrawal; its central theme is the gradual surrender to other institutions of its functions that once lay very much within the realm of family responsibility.

In the early days of the United States, the family functioned in several spheres—economic, productive, religious, recreational, educational, status conferring, and reproductive. With industrialization, production was taken out of the home and the economic function of the family declined. Prior to industrialization, the family, according to Demos (1970:183), "was first of all a business agency of economic production and exchange. Each household was more or less self-sufficient; and its various members were inextricably united in the work of providing for their fundamental material wants. Work, indeed, was a wholly natural extension of family life and merged imperceptibly with all of its activities." Children were economic assets, and marriage was a kind of business relationship. With the advent of the factory system, the woman's traditional economic contribution declined, her status as wife and mother diminished, and children became liabilities rather than assets. Today, the consumption of goods and services has replaced production, and all members are encouraged to participate. Once they worked together; now they shop together—for food, clothing, sporting goods, TV sets, and the like.

Traditionally, the family was the principal source of protection for the individual. In addition to physical protection, it provided medical care and economic security. These functions have been largely transferred to the state through the operation of such agencies as the police, welfare departments, the medical profession, and insurance companies.

The religious function of the family is also on the decline. Religion once served as an integrating force, one that complemented other institutional controls in the maintenance of a cohesive family system. The home was the center of religious activities. Today, the church is often taking over many of these functions, and even marriage is becoming a secular matter devoid of religious overtones.

In the early American family, education was considered to be a function of the home. Children were likely to follow the footsteps of their parents, and education was usually of short duration and vocational in nature. Now the education of children, both academic and vocational, is more formal and has passed on to the hands of professionals.

The status-conferring function of the family has also declined, and individuals are evaluated on the basis of their own performance rather than on the basis of ascribed status. A family's status is more often than not ascertained in terms of the husband's occupation, and usually the man leaves his status when he leaves his job. Finally, even the reproductive function of the family has not remained an exclusivity of the family, as evidenced by illegitimacy rates.

"In the past, stability has been the great value exemplified by the family and that expected of it by society. This was true because the family was the basic institution in a static society" (Burgess, 1973:195). Today, the American society is not static but dynamic, and the family is characterized not by its stability but by its adaptability to a rapid tempo of social change. It is becoming a more specialized structure, but the loss of functions should not be construed as signs of deterioration. They are only indicative of changes that have taken place.

Current Trends

In addition to the disappearance of traditional family functions, other changes have occurred in the American family. There is a pronounced trend among young people to delay marriage over time (Russell, 1997; Schwartz & Scott, 2003; Witwer, 1993). The median age at first marriage in the United States has risen from 20.2 for women in the mid-1950s to 24.5 and from 22.6 for men in 1955 to 26.5 in 1994. In 2000, the median age for males was 26.8 and for females 25.1 The figures represent the highest median age for both men and women since 1890. In part, this is prompted by the desire among some, particularly women, to finish their education and start careers prior to marriage. The delay in marriage is greatest among blacks, with 22 percent of black women age 40–44 never having been married, compared with 7 percent of white and 9 percent of Hispanic women. There is also a growing preference among many people to forgo marriage altogether, and the percentage of men and women who have never married nearly doubled between 1970 and 1993, to 72.6 million from 37.5 million (Holmes, 1994) and to over 76 million in 2000. During the same time, one-person households as a percent of all households increased from 13 to 25 percent (one in nine adults lives alone in the United States), and the number of unmarried couples living together increased from about one-half million to well over 3.5 million in 2000 (U.S. Bureau of the Census, 2002:56).

Over time, family size has also decreased. The number of live births for an average American woman declined from eight at the end of the eighteenth century to three in 1970 (Winch, 1970), and to 1.9 in 2000. This was accompanied by a drop in the size of the average household to 3.1 in 1970 (Eshleman, 2003:6) and to 2.5 persons in 2000. There is also a growing tendency among American women to postpone childbearing because of their concern with careers, economic security, and personal freedom (Leslie & Korman, 1989:463). The decline in family size and delayed parenthood are accompanied by what may be called "the streamlined family"—that is, the nuclear family without children. Planned childlessness is on the increase. The percentage of couples without children has doubled in the last few decades. Today, motherhood is just one of the many options for married women. In 2000, one out of four married women between the ages of 25 and

34 had never had a child—a total of nearly 3.6 million women—compared to one out of ten in 1960. Economic factors play a crucial role in the decision to forgo parenthood, and there is also a desire to avoid being part of the "sandwich generation"—those that must take care of elderly parents and raise children at the same time (Nemeth, 1994). Childlessness has increased as women have moved in record numbers into well-paying careers. Faced with new options, many wives have decided that motherhood is not an essential, or even desirable, role. And, in the absence of widespread governmental or corporate support for working parents, many feel compelled to choose between children and jobs (Campbell, 1986). The fact that childless couples are happier and more satisfied with their lives than are couples with children may also play a role in the decision to forsake parenthood (Leslie & Korman, 1989:463).

After rising dramatically during the half century from 1940 to 1990, out-of-wedlock childbearing leveled off, or slowed its rate of increase during the 1990s. Between 1940 and 1990, the number of births to unmarried women rose thirteen-fold, from 89,500 to 1.17 million, with the increase over this period averaging more than 5 percent per year. During the 1990s, this rate of increase slowed, to about 1 percent per year. The birth rate for unmarried women increased more than six times between 1940 and 1990, from 7.1 births per 1,000 unmarried women to 43.8 births. The rise in the birth rate was most rapid during the late 1970s through the 1980s, when the rate increased about 4 percent per year. Between 1994 and 1999 the rate declined about 6 percent overall.

A key factor contributing to the rising numbers of out-of-wedlock births through the 1990s was the steep increase in the number of unmarried women of childbearing age. This was due in part to a change in the overall size of the population, which swelled during the postwar baby boom, and the fact that women and men began postponing marriage from the mid-1960s, a trend that shows no sign of abating (National Center for Health Statistics, 2000).

Illegitimacy is most pronounced in the inner city, but the phenomenon is not exclusive to any race or sector of society. More white children than black are born and raised out of wedlock, and it is among whites, college graduates, and women with high-paying jobs that illegitimacy is rising most rapidly (Murray, 1994). Some of the reasons contributing to the increase in this sector is due to a shift in values and an increase in earning power among women. In 1993, 6.3 million children, or 27 percent of all children under the age of eighteen, lived with a single parent who had never been married, up from 243,000 in 1960, and from 3.7 million in 1983 (Holmes, 1994). In 2000, almost 8 million children lived with a single parent. Another 10.5 million children lived in "blended families"—that is, with stepparents and half-bothers and half-sisters.

The increased work responsibility of women has also tended to bring about changes in the structure of the family. The percentage of working women has almost doubled since 1940. In the mid-1980s, more than half of all adult women were working, and six out of ten of these were married (Williams, 1987:367); by 2000, close to 80 percent of adult women were in the labor force. In addition, there has been a substantial increase in the number and types of occupations in which women are employed and greater involvement on their part in high-paying, prestigious occupations and professions. Changes in career patterns and employment opportunities for women bring about such adaptations as the commuter, or long-distance, marriage, in which the spouses live some distance from one another. In such families, either the wife or husband assumes primary responsibility for the children. In the early 1990s, approximately 1 million couples had commuter marriages (Maines, 1993), by the early 2000s, over 1.5 million couples had such marital arrangement (Roehling & Bultman, 2002).

Divorce

The American divorce rate today is more than twice that of 1960, but has declined slightly since hitting the highest point in our history in the early 1980s. Divorce trends are shown in Figure 4.1. Although the long-term trend in divorce has been upward since colonial times, the divorce rate was level for about two decades after World War II during the period of high fertility known as the baby boom. By the middle of the 1960s, however, the incidence of divorce started to increase. It more than doubled over the next fifteen years, to reach an historical high point in the early 1980s. Since then the divorce rate has declined modestly, a trend described by many experts as "leveling off at a high level." The decline in the 1980s may be partly attributable to compositional changes in the population, for example the aging of the baby boomers and a decrease in the number of people of

FIGURE 4.1 Number of Divorces per 1,000 Married Women Age 15 and Older, by Year, United States

Year	Divorces
1960	9.2
1965	10.6
1970	14.9
1975	20.3
1980	22.6
1985	21.7
1990	20.9
1995	19.8
2000	18.9

SOURCE: *Statistical Abstract of the United States, 2001*, p. 87, table 117; *National Vital Statistics Reports*, August 22, 2001; *California Current Population Survey Report: 2000*, table 3, March 2001; and calculations by the National Marriage Project based on preliminary data.

marriageable age. The continuing decline in the 1990s, however, apparently represents a slight increase in marital stability.

Although a majority of divorced persons eventually remarry, the growth of divorce has led to a steep increase in the percentage of all adults who are currently divorced (Figure 4.2). This percentage, which was only 1.8 percent for males and 2.6 percent for females in 1960, quadrupled by the year 2000. The percentage of divorce is higher for females than for males primarily because divorced men are more likely to remarry than divorced women. Also, among those who do remarry, men generally do so sooner than women.

Overall, the chances remain very high—still around 50 percent—that a marriage started today will end in divorce. The likelihood of divorce has varied considerably among different segments of the American population, being higher for blacks than for whites, for instance, and higher in the West than in other parts of the country. But these and many other variations, such as in social class level, have been diminishing. The trend toward a greater similarity of divorce rates between whites and blacks is largely attributable to the fact that fewer blacks are marrying. Divorce rates in the South and Midwest have come to resemble those in the West, for reasons that are not well understood, leaving only the Eastern Seaboard and the Central Plains with significantly lower divorce.

At the same time, there has been little change in such traditionally large divorce rate differences as between those who marry when they are teenagers compared to those who marry later, and the non-religious compared to the religious. Both teenagers and the non-religious who marry have considerably higher divorce rates.

About one out of every two marriages continues to end in divorce in the United States (Powers, 1997:4). Sociologists generally attribute the high divorce rates to changing family functions, casual marriages, shorter courtship, prevalence of premarital sex, increases in teenage pregnancies

FIGURE 4.2 Percentage of All Persons Age 15 and Older Who Were Divorced, by Sex and Race, 1960–2000, United States

Year	Males			Females		
	Total	Blacks	Whites	Total	Blacks	Whites
1960	1.8	2.0	1.8	2.6	4.3	2.5
1970	2.2	3.1	2.1	3.5	4.4	3.4
1980	4.8	6.3	4.7	6.6	8.7	6.4
1990	6.8	8.1	6.8	8.9	11.2	8.6
2000	8.3	9.5	8.4	10.2	11.8	10.2

SOURCE: U.S. Bureau of the Census, *Current Population Reports*, Series P20-537: *America's Families and Living Arrangements*, March 2000 and earlier reports.

with subsequent "shotgun" weddings, increased job opportunities with economic and sexual freedom for women, a decline in moral and religious sanctions, the prevailing philosophy of "happiness," the phenomenal growth in "starter" marriages where couples have no children and much joint property, (while they do not wed with the intention of divorcing, their temporary stay in marriage is similar to the starter home of a generation ago, shed as the family outgrows it) (Schupack, 1994), and, of course, more liberal divorce laws.

The high rate of divorce in the United States has spawned a new industry for lawyers, counselors, divorce psychologists, accountants, and other experts, along with an assortment of new conservative anti-divorce writers (DeWitt, 1992; Sarno, 2002; Talbot, 1997). Among the many consequences of divorce for children, it is interesting to note that students with divorced parents are less likely to apply to, be accepted by, and attend the fifty most selective universities and colleges in the country. The researchers argue that children of divorced parents have fewer resources for higher education because neither parent assumes sufficient financial responsibility for the offspring (Powers, 1997).

The Sexual Revolution

The much publicized "sexual revolution" of the 1960s and 1970s has important ramifications for the structure of the family. The term has multiple meanings. It refers to a shift toward a higher incidence of all kinds of heterosexual activity and more permissive attitudes toward homosexuality and variety in the sexual act. Same-sex marriages are legal and unremarkable in countries such as Denmark (Ingrassia, 1994), and although homosexual marriages are not recognized in the United States, there are already legal problems of "gay divorce," that is, dissolving fairly and equitably in court messy property issues at the end of a turbulent relationship (Johnson, 1994).

Although there are only two sexes, there are numerous genders, and as society changes so do the numbers and nuances of gender (Gray, 1996). Gender transgressions allow for an infinite variety of role-play scenarios, from night clubs to advertisement campaigns. The concept of sexual revolution also alludes to sexual liberation, greater freedom for women, alternatives to marriage, and, at the same time, to trivialized sex, diminished intimacy, and fewer lasting commitments among partners (Williams, 1987:249–253). There is no doubt that major changes in sexual mores and behavior have occurred. But to call these changes "revolutionary" is questionable. Regardless of how it is described, sex today is no longer tied to reproduction or marriage, nor domestic life to a large family of children. Sex is increasingly liberated from the bonds of matrimony and even heterosexuality. For a contemporary young woman, for example, the choices are:

> Have sex or don't. Have it with a man, or a woman. Use the pill, the IUD, the diaphragm. Have an abortion. Marry, or don't. Do have children. Don't have children. Have a career. Have a career and a child. Have a husband, but no child. Have a child, but no husband. (Rivers, 1975:144)

Among unmarried young people, sexual activity is on the increase, and they start at younger ages today than in earlier times. A quarter of the new HIV cases today occur in those 21 years and younger (*Time*, 2002:65). Surveys show that about half of the women aged fifteen to nineteen have had intercourse, and about one-fifth, at age fifteen, had already experienced coitus. It is revealing to note that 56 percent of the teens state that they had sex at their family's home or at the home of their partner's family—often during the late afternoon or early evening, before 10 PM (so much for the 11 PM weekday curfew . . .). Close to one-half in this age group had more than one sexual partner and slightly over 14 percent of high school students in 2001 reported that they had more than four partners (Lewin, 2002.) In 1994, the median age for first intercourse was 16.6 years for boys and 17.4 for girls. Approximately 20 percent of both sexes remain virgins throughout their teenage years (Laumann et al., 1994), but about 10 percent of those who are still virgins engage in oral sex—and both girls and boys are equally likely to be the receiving partner (Lewin, 1997).

More girls are experimenting sexually today than a generation ago, and young women's sexual experiences are increasingly becoming like young men's in both homosexual and heterosexual situations (Marano, 1997). A study suggests that geographic mobility is positively related to premarital sex, and that weakened community bonding, parental supervision, and increased loneliness play a role in the high incidence of sexual activity in the fifteen-to-nineteen-year-old age group (Stack, 1994). As an outgrowth of the abstinence movement in sex education and evangelical Christian churches in the late 1990s and early 2000s, some women who did not delay sexual experience until marriage started to engage in a period of abstinence for a couple of months or so prior to the wedding. Nowadays, a period of "secondary virginity" as the practice is sometimes called, is increasingly the norm for many brides-to-be across the South, an accommodation to the modern reality of premarital sex and the traditional disapproval of it in the Bible Belt (Hayt, 2002).

Although there is a decline in births among teens, more than 1 million teenagers get pregnant annually and slightly more than half give birth. About eight in ten pregnancies among teenagers (and 60 percent of all pregnancies in the United States) are unintended. America's yearly teen-pregnancy rate—one girl in every ten—remains the highest of any developed country (and so is the legal abortion rate of about 1.6 million per year), mostly as a result of lack of knowledge about effective contraceptive use and technologies (World Population News Service, 1997). By age twenty, nearly 40 percent of young white women and 63 percent of young black women become pregnant, although the abstinence movement ("just say no") is beginning to change young people's attitude toward premarital sex. Whether or not changing attitudes will have an impact on behavior remains to be seen (*Time*, 2002).

There are other derivatives of the changes of sexual mores and behavior. They include alternatives to family living, such as group marriage and communal living. Group marriage is based on the principle of sharing, variety in sexual experience and partners, and interpersonal intimacy. Group marriage involves three or more people. The most common pattern involves four adults, usually the members of two former couples (Leslie & Korman, 1989:129). Members are motivated by personal growth opportunity and by an interest in having multiple sex partners. Because of its egalitarian structure, sex roles are much less differentiated in group marriage than in the average nuclear family (Williams, 1987:363). Communal living arrangements are characterized by lack of private property, financial self-sufficiency, and open sharing of sexual partners. Communal living may involve up to 200 or more people (Leslie & Korman, 1989:131). Although their numbers have diminished drastically since the mid-1970s, group marriages and communal living arrangements still exist in the United States.

Another alternative to family life is cohabitation. As indicated in Figure 4.3, between 1960 and 2000, the number of unmarried couples in America increased by over 1,000 percent. Unmarried cohabitation—the status of couples who are sexual partners, not married to each other, and sharing a household—is particularly common among the young. It is estimated that about a quarter of unmarried women aged 25–39 are currently living with a partner, and an additional quarter have lived with a partner at some time. Over half of all first marriages are now preceded by living together, compared to virtually none earlier in the century (Bumpass & Lu, 2000).

For some, cohabitation is a prelude to marriage, for others, an alternative to marriage, and for still others, simply an alternative to living alone. Cohabitation is more common among those of lower educational and

FIGURE 4.3 Number of Cohabiting, Unmarried, Adult Couples of the Opposite Sex, by Year, United States

Year	Number (in millions)
1960	.439
1970	.523
1980	1.589
1990	2.856
2000	4.736

SOURCE: U.S. Bureau of the Census, *Current Population Reports, Series P20-537: America's Families and Living Arrangements*, March 2000 and earlier reports.

income levels. Recent data show that among women in the 19 to 44 age range, 60 percent of high school dropouts have cohabited, compared to 37 percent of college graduates. Cohabitation is also more common among those who are less religious than their peers, those who have been divorced, and those who have experienced parental divorce, fatherlessness, or high levels of marital discord during childhood. A growing percentage of cohabiting couple households, now more than one-third, contains children (Smock, 2000). Cohabitation is rapidly gaining legitimacy as a family form in the United States, as evidenced by recent court decisions stating that long-term, unmarried partners may have a claim on each other's property. Such decisions make the legal distinction between cohabitation and marriage somewhat blurred. Similarly, in Canada couples living together without being married in 2001 represented almost 14 percent of families as contrasted to 6 percent 20 years ago (O'Brian, 2002).

But the so-called sexual revolution may be over—if it ever really existed outside of Hollywood and popular publications. Despite living in a culture that seems saturated with sex [see, for example, the 2002 reissue of the 1972 groundbreaking book, *The Joy of Sex* (Comfort, 2002); triple X-rated DVDs; cyber-porn; ubiquitous television and Internet advertisements for breast enhancements and penis enlargement, Viagra, ad infinitum], Americans lead fairly conventional sex lives, with people who are married and monogamous the most satisfied, according to repeated surveys on sexual attitudes and behavior. Similarly, several campus surveys reported a renewed interest in the value of virginity. The decrease could be attributable to a more conservative campus mood, an increase in women's assertiveness in saying no, a wariness to commitment and to pairing off (resulting in pack dating), and the fear of sexually transmitted diseases (Gabriel, 1997). The growing incidence of herpes was instrumental in changing sexual patterns. The concern that casual sex may lead to incurable genital herpes prompted many people to be more cautious about their sexual behavior. Shortly after the herpes scare, a far more serious disease appeared: AIDS (McCoy & Inciardi, 1995). First diagnosed in the United States in 1981, by the mid-1990s, an estimated 15 to 23 million people had been infected worldwide, with half of its victims already dead [by contrast, malaria kills roughly twice as many people each year worldwide than AIDS (Shell, 1997:48)]. HIV is now spreading more rapidly than ever, resulting in an estimated 2.4 million new infections each year among adults. By the mid-1990s, close to one of every 100 people in the world was HIV positive (Brown, Kane, & Roodman, 1997:102); by 2003, it was over one per 100. It has reached pandemic proportions, and the fear of catching this incurable, dreaded disease has altered sexual norms and restricted sexual activities among both heterosexuals and homosexuals in most parts of the world, but more so in developed than in underdeveloped countries. At the same time, controlling AIDS is not only a moral imperative, but is rapidly becoming a practical necessity (Cowley, 2003).

In sum, the options have indeed increased for the family. Family life is no longer confined to a traditional, approved form of family in the conjugal type. In the real world, a wide range of family patterns can be observed, from homosexual unions to mothers living with their illegitimate children, from open sex communes to the Shakers' total rejection of sexuality, from living together without any ceremony to living separately in spite of a ceremony; the list is nearly endless. Whether or not these changes now occurring within the family will inaugurate a totally new system of family is just too early to tell. Regardless, changes in the sphere of the family have been and are dramatic. In the next section, changes in population will be examined.

POPULATION

Assuming that the first human being appeared between 1 million and 2 million years ago, it is estimated that between 60 billion and 100 billion representatives of *Homo sapiens* have lived on planet Earth. It is estimated that the world population in 1650 was one-half billion, and it took approximately 200 years to double. In 1850, it was 1 billion, with a doubling time of 80 years. By 1930, it reached 2 billion, with a doubling time of 45 years (Ehrlich & Ehrlich, 1972:5–6). In 2003, the world's population was expected to double in 45 years (Population Reference Bureau, 2003). In only sixteen years, from 1987 to 2002, world population grew from 5 billion to over 6.25 billion, adding more bodies to feed, house, clothe, and educate than the present combined populations of Europe and Latin America. To put these numbers in some kind of perspective, in 2002, the world population increased 3.1 people every second. Globally, this translates to 186 people per minute, 11,160 per hour, 267,840 per day and well over 8 million per month, for a total of close to 98 million new people annually. By the time you finish reading this page, 160 additional people have been added to the world population. The daily increase equals roughly the population of Dayton, Ohio.

World population growth is the result of natural increase—the excess of births over deaths. For individual countries, net migration—the difference between out-migration and in-migration—is also a factor. Rapid population growth is the result of great declines in death rates along with continuing high birth rates. Mortality rates in Europe began to decline in the eighteenth and nineteenth centuries. The great reductions in mortality did not reach two-thirds of humankind in the developing nations in Asia, Latin America, and Africa until after World War II, primarily as a consequence in the rise of the general level of nutrition, improvements in sanitation, and health care delivery. Today, more than 90 percent of the growth is in developing countries, much of it in the poorest nations of South Asia and Africa. The developing countries add 1 million people every five days to lands that are often already overcrowded and depleted of water and cheap sources of energy (Crossette, 1994:4). In 2002, China had a population of almost 1.3 billion and is growing at a steady rate of just over 1 percent, or 13 million, annually. Due to the relaxation of the "one child" rule, this number is expected to increase.

In contrast, the United States, Canada, and many European countries are experiencing a decline in fertility since the 1960s (Teitelbaum & Winter, 1998:81–87; Wattenberg, 1989). Six European countries (Denmark, Sweden, Austria, Germany, Luxembourg, and Hungary), about 4 percent of the world population, are actually experiencing a zero or negative population growth (Population Reference Bureau, 2003).

Consequences of Rapid Growth Rates

In many developing countries the rate of population growth is at least half the rate of economic growth and, in some cases, almost equal to the latter. Because of the high birth rate, the ratios of children to adults are very high when compared with industrialized countries, and the number of young people reaching the age of labor-force participation is rapidly increasing. These factors can produce serious economic consequences. Rapid population growth slows down the growth of per-capita income in developing countries and tends to perpetuate inequalities of income distribution (Grant, 2001).

Income and wealth inequality actually harms economic growth (Wesimann, 1996). The statistics are alarming. Half the world's population lives on less than $2 a day; and a billion people survive on less than $1 a day. The population in the poorest countries will grow three times faster than the world as a whole over the next 50 years. Some 14,000 people are infected each day with HIV, the virus that causes AIDS. So grim is the picture painted by a late 2002 United Nations Population Fund report entitled *State of World Population 2002: People, Poverty and Possibilities*, that it is difficult to know how to respond to the challenge of world poverty. The UN's Millennium Development Goals, endorsed by the General Assembly in September 2000, seem more elusive than ever. Halving global poverty by 2015 is itself an enormous task. But other goals, such as the provision of universal primary education by the same date, are now at risk because of the impact of AIDS.

Controlling fertility is crucial to bridging the gap between rich and poor, according to the *State of World Population 2002* report from the United Nations Population Fund. Poor young women in Latin America and East Asia have more than five times as many children as the rich. Unwanted pregnancies can undermine mothers as well as babies; women in poor countries, such as Liberia, are 600 times more likely to die in pregnancy and birth than women in rich countries. The report argues that greater access to contraception and more female education would help to lower birth rates.

The recipe might seem simple, but implementing it more widely is still an uphill struggle. The failure to invest sufficiently in the prevention of disease, instead of, as so often happens, focusing solely on curative care, means that birth rates will remain high. A rapidly rising population is usually accompanied by poverty and inequality—especially for women. The UN reckons that better family planning accounts for a third of the decline in fertility between 1972 and 1994. But lower-income countries only spend, on average, $21 per person per year on health care—and much of that goes to short-term curative care rather than to prevention and family planning. International donors, says the report, have failed to deliver what is needed: they provided only $10.9 billion for such spending in 2000, which is less even than their own target of $17 billion. Poverty is an obvious consequence of rapid and unsustainable population growth. So is inequality, both among different income groups and between men and women. Both gaps are widening. Expenditures in certain areas can also widen the gap—for example, spending on education tends to benefit relatively better-off groups in society, says the report.

Women are the biggest losers. More women live in poverty than men—and the gap continues to widen. Women now account for half of all adults infected by HIV, up from 41 percent five years ago. The report points out that, in the poorest countries, weak economic performance is closely related to gender inequality. It cites South Asia as a region where the gap between the genders has narrowed more slowly than in others—and where, as a consequence, the region has fallen even further behind. But inequality is a problem in rich countries too. America's infant mortality rate is the same as Cuba's and higher than rates of most European countries. This is because, although America spends more per head on health care than any other country, its expenditure is distributed unevenly across the population. How to tackle the increasing problems of poverty, inequality and rising populations? Rich countries are making more money available, but only if poor countries spend it wisely and do so more transparently. Ironically, says the report, the countries that are setting the highest standards are often those receiving the least amount of help.

Food supplies and agricultural production must be increased to meet the needs of rapidly growing populations, which affects resource allocation to other economic and social sectors. Because of the rapid increase in the size of the labor force, unemployment and underemployment are becoming increasingly serious and challenging problems (see, for example, Lassonde, 1997). Large supplies of cheap labor tend to hold back technological improvements, and industrialization is slowed by mass poverty, which, in turn, reduces the demand for manufactured goods. It is important to note that population growth at a given level tends to require economic growth at some higher level just to maintain a constant per-capita income. This is due to the fact that additional population requires additional production, each production addition being, after the point of diminishing returns is reached, more costly than the previous one.

Rapid population growth is also associated with internal migration and urbanization. It places increased demands for government services in the areas of health, education, welfare, among others. It also places heavy burdens upon resources and the environment (Brown, 2001; Harf & Trout, 1986; Kuznets, 1973).

Demographic Transition

In stark contrast to trends in developing countries today, over the past 200 years, the now-industrialized nations have experienced what demographers refer to as demographic transition, moving from high fertility rates to low mortality rates and low fertility rates. Death rates started to drop before birth rates did, causing population growth rates to rise rapidly for a time. Gradually, however, birth rates also began to fall, and rates of growth in most industrialized nations seem to be stabilizing at relatively low levels. For example, in 2002, the United States had a growth rate of 0.6 percent, whereas Western European countries had a growth rate of −.01 percent (a decline, in fact), compared with 1.7 percent in Latin American countries, and 2.8 in Africa and Western Asia. Demographic transition essentially predicts the patterns of change that occur over a long time (Szreter, 1993).

Let us now consider the major variables in population dynamics. They are mortality, or death rate, that is, the number of deaths per 1,000 population; fertility, which refers to the number of births in a population relative to every thousand women of childbearing age (usually between the ages of fifteen and forty-five); migration, which indicates the movement of segments of the population from one geographic area to another; and age-sex composition, or population composition—that is, a proportion of males and females in various age groups in a given population.

Mortality In the United States, accidental injury is the leading cause of death for people from age one to age forty-four, and over half of these are the result of motor vehicle accidents. Since 1968, however, the number of deaths from firearms has increased 60 percent, while vehicle deaths have fallen 21 percent (*Morbidity and Mortality Weekly Report*, 1994). Globally, in a recent report, the World Health Organization estimates that 40 percent of the world's 56 million deaths in 2001 were caused by such preventable risks as unsafe sex, high blood pressure and cholesterol levels, obesity, tobacco and alcohol consumption, indoor smoke from solid fuels, poor sanitation, iron deficiency and child malnutrition (*Economist*, 2002a).

Turning to other indicators, in any given group of 1,000 infants, mortality rates are relatively high in the first year of life, rapidly decline in early childhood, reach their minimum around the ages of four to ten, and then rise gradually but steadily until they reach their maximum at old age. In all countries of the world, mortality rates through the life cycle are declining, though at different rates, as evidenced by a decrease in infant mortality and an increase in life expectancy. Since World War II, health programs involving the use of antibiotics, vaccines, and insecticides have contributed to the decline of mortality rates in developing countries. The most noticeable is the drop in infant mortality rates—that is, the number of deaths per thousand during the first year of life. The decline in infant mortality is most rapid in industrialized countries. In the United States, for example, it declined from 99.9 in 1915 to 20 in 1970 and to 8.1 per 1,000 births in 2003 (*JAMA*, 1994; Population Reference Bureau, 2003). The rates are even lower for other developed nations, for example, 4.4 for Japan, 4.8 for Sweden, and 4.4 for Finland. In developing countries, the decline in infant mortality rates is much slower. In Afghanistan, the rate is 168, and it is not unusual to see rates between 110 and 120 per 1,000 births in African countries such as Mali and Chad. Even in certain industrialized countries, such as Brazil, the rate is about 66 per 1,000 births. For the world, the rate is 64 (Population Reference Bureau, 2003). Life expectancy is increasing, but much more rapidly in the developing countries. For the United States, it increased from 47.3 years at the turn of the century to over 78 years in 2002. In the developing countries, an extremely rapid rise in life expectancy occurred during the first two decades after World War II and is still continuing, though probably at a slower rate. However, in Russia, mortality levels have climbed since the fall of Communism in 1989, with the average life expectancy declining to levels lower than those in many developing countries with high mortality rates. This decline is attributed to factors that include environment hazards, deterioration of medical care, economic decline, fiscal insecurity, social inequality, political instability and earlier risk exposure (Chen et al., 1996).

There are several changes associated with the decline in mortality rates (Heer & Grigsby, 1992; Pritchett & Summers, 1996; Teitelbaum & Winter, 1998:88–89). In general, wealthier nations are healthier nations with lower mortality rates. Per capita income reflects both on infant mortality and life expectancy. In societies in which there is a high mortality rate, the family is more likely to be dependent on some larger kin group. By contrast, in low-mortality societies such as Western countries, the nuclear family often lives at a great distance from other relatives, as there is a smaller likelihood for children to become orphaned and require the support of extended kin. In high-mortality societies, individuals are more likely to have a stronger present orientation than when mortality is low. It may have an effect on the achievement motivation, for achievement is usually associated with a sacrifice of present values for future goals. There is also a decline in the emphasis placed on how religion will benefit one in the next world with the decline in mortality. The concern with afterlife is waning, and the accent is on how religion will help one in this world (Schneider & Dornbusch, 1958). Finally, there are also changes in the institutions of mourning as a result of the decrease in mortality. Geoffrey Gorer (1965) points out that at the turn of the century, there were strict rules of etiquette that the bereaved must observe, as well as rules that dictated what others must show toward them. Today, people are unsure of how to confront bereavement, and the general tendency is to try to deny its very existence.

Fertility There is an extensive body of literature describing fertility among nations at a given time, within a single nation over time, among geographic areas within a single nation, and among such social categories as educational attainment, income, occupation, religion, or ethnic group. In general, the nations with the lowest per capita income have the highest fertility, and vice versa. In developed countries, the level of fertility is lower than it was a hundred years ago, but the change leading to a decreased demand for children has not been a regular process (Starke, 1994). In most nations, fertility in general is higher in rural than in urban areas, and in some countries, including the United States, unmarried women exhibited a higher fertility level than married women in recent years (Althaus, 1994). In developed nations, it is usually highest among persons of the lower socioeconomic classes and lowest in the middle and upper classes.

In addition to these variations, there is a general downward trend in fertility in most countries, primarily as a result of the confluence of a series of economic and social factors. They include:

- An overall increase in the educational attainment of women and the concomitant changes in their values and roles.
- An increase in the proportion of women in the nonagricultural labor force.
- Continued decline in infant mortality.
- Increasing cost of raising and educating children.
- Decline in traditional religious beliefs in favor of high fertility.
- Decline in the economic utility of children.
- The weakening of the extended family system.
- Widespread availability of contraceptive technology and abortion.
- Development of welfare and old-age systems outside of the home.
- Increased mobility opportunities.
- Lack of faith in the future.

Obviously, this is only a partial list, even though it indicates many of the changes that have been associated with the decrease in fertility. This list could be supplemented by questions of individual motives, such as, "Why do you want to have x number of children?" or "Why do you use (or not use) a certain contraceptive method?" In that case, one would be led to conclude that the reasons for a given fertility level are as many as the number of individuals who have borne children. Still, on a worldwide basis, literacy, increased wealth, urbanization, economic development, and industrialization have all contributed to the decrease in fertility. Some demographers and social commentators are even complaining that the United States and other Western countries are not reproducing fast enough to replace themselves (Teitelbaum & Winter, 1998; Wattenberg, 1989). In his rather alarmist book, *The Birth Dearth,* Ben J. Wattenberg (1989) fears that the decline in fertility in the West will bring about economic problems, a weakening of the military might of the West, a decline in the productivity of the aging labor force, and an inevitable bankruptcy of social security systems. He also alludes to the eventual overtake of the West by "inferior" races. Time will tell whether Western civilization is endangered by the "birth dearth."

In addition to the decline in actual fertility rates, there are also changes in the preference system that affects the decision to have children (Spengler, 1966). The preference system simply describes the value a couple puts on an additional child relative to the value of all other goals they might achieve without having that child. The changes affecting the preference system include the reduction in infant mortality, the decrease in the productive labor of children, changes in the institutions that provide support for the elderly, the decline in rewards that could be expected from society at large for bearing large numbers of children, and the shift from allocation of status by ascription to allocation by achievement.

Migration It is much easier to discuss general trends in mortality and fertility than in migration. Relevant data for migration often are not available. Furthermore, trends in migration vary from nation to nation, and there has been no generalized change such as those occurring in mortality and fertility. For the sake of brevity, the discussion will be confined to trends in the United States.

Americans migrate more often than people of other developed, industrialized countries, with many moving several times in their lives. Since World War II, approximately one-fifth of the total population has moved every year, about 6 percent have changed their country of residence, and roughly 3 percent have moved to a new state (Gober, 1993).

Based on various census estimates, some 60.5 million immigrants entered the country since the turn of the century (U.S. Bureau of the Census, 2002:10). In 2002, there were more than 24 million legal immigrants in the United States, and they made up 9.3 percent of the population. If current trends persist, some 45 million immigrants will have arrived by 2050, and post-1970 immigrants and their descendants will then make up about a third of the population. In 2002, some 36 percent of New York's population was foreign born (*Economist,* 2002b:5).

The period up to about the turn of the century corresponds to the wave of "old immigrants," predominantly composed of Irish leaving their native land because of the potato famine. The second large wave of "new immigrants," made up of individuals from southern Europe and eastern Europe, occurred roughly between 1900 and 1921, when restrictive legislation greatly reduced the flow of immigrants to the United States. World War II and its aftermath brought some 20 million refugees from eastern and central Europe (Harf & Trout, 1986:102). In recent years, some 1 million immigrants entered the country annually. Contrasted with the older waves of immigration, they came primarily from Latin American and Asian countries. In addition to legal immigration, there has been a substantial growth in illegal immigration since the 1970s. In 2002, an estimated 9 million illegal aliens were residing in the United States; about 60 percent of them entered illegally and 40 percent overstayed their visas (*Economist*, 2002b:7) In 1987, Congress passed legislation authorizing those who entered the country illegally prior to 1982 to remain and obtain citizenship should they so desire. Still, the flow of illegal immigrants continues, fueled by, among other things, an anticipation of comparable legislation in the future. It is worth noting that immigration and children born to immigrants after their arrival in the United States, predominantly from developing countries, account for 50 percent of the population growth, and this share is projected to increase steadily (Abernethy, 1994). The changes in immigration origins are expected to alter the country's racial makeup. In 1995, the American population was 74 percent white, 12 percent black, 10 percent Hispanic and 3 percent Asian. If the countries of origin remain the same, in 2050 it will be 51 percent white, 14 percent black, 26 percent Hispanic, and 8 percent Asian (Cassidy, 1997:41) There is already a growing sense of xenophobia, as evidenced by, for example, the passing by a large majority of Proposition 187 in California in November 1994, a measure that denies non-emergency health care, education, and social services to illegal immigrants (*Newsweek*, 1994:57) and the restrictions imposed upon international migration following the events of September 11, 2001, in New York (*Economist*, 2002b:3.)

Age-Sex Composition The final variable of population dynamics is the age-sex composition, which is determined by the population's sex ratio at birth (sex ratio is the number of males divided by the number of females times 100) and the population's past history of births, deaths, and migrations. As a result of the decline in birth rates, the proportion of the population less than fifteen years of age has been steadily declining in industrialized countries. In the United States, it declined from 41.6 percent in 1850, to 34.4 percent in 1900, and to 21 percent in 2002 (Smith & Zopf, 1976:182; Population Reference Bureau, 2003). By contrast, the world population under fifteen years of age is 33 percent; Latin America's population under fifteen years of age is 36 percent, and it exceeds 49 percent in Eastern African countries such as Kenya and Zimbabwe.

The current "aging" of the population has been widely publicized over the years, both in the United States and abroad (Eyetsemitan and Gire, 2003; Menken, 1986; Wattenberg, 1989). This refers to the increase both in the median age and in the number and proportion of those sixty-five years of age and over, which is another characteristic of developed countries. In 1994, the median age in the United States was close to thirty-four years (half the population older, half younger), and, for Canada, one study predicts that the median age in 2036 will be 49.9 years (McKie, 1993). About 13 percent of the population was over the age of sixty-five. In Latin American countries, the figure was 4 percent, and, in a number of countries in Asia and Africa it ranged between 1 and 2 percent.

Changes in the sex ratio in the United States are usually attributed to immigration, as more males than females tend to immigrate. Changes in both the age and the sex structures tend to bring about changes in other domains.

Changes in the age structure alter the dependency ratio, which is the ratio of persons in dependent ages (that is, ages under fifteen and over sixty-five). In general, the lower the ratio, the easier it is for persons in the economically productive ages to support those in the dependent age category. Age structure changes also relate to the age of persons in the labor force, and developed countries generally have an older labor force as compared to underdeveloped countries. This, in turn, is reflected on patterns of consumption and money allotted to education.

Changes in age-sex structure also affect marriage rates. Assuming that men usually marry women a few years younger than themselves, then females in any population in which the age structure has a downward slope will have more difficulty in finding mates than will men. Rapid change in the rate of population growth can also affect the sex ratio at marriageable ages. In the United States, there were somewhat more boys born between 1941 and 1943 than girls born between 1944 and 1946. In contrast, the number of girls born between 1947 and 1949 was 14 percent greater than the number of boys born between 1944 and 1946. Thus, girls born right after World War II and reaching marriageable age in the later 1960s had substantially poorer prospects for marriage than girls born during World War II who reached that age in the mid-decade. To conclude on a more cheerful note, women born in the late 1970s and at the beginning of the 1980s will have an excellent chance to marry (statistically) in the early 2000s and they can further improve their matrimonial odds by moving to small towns and rural areas in states such as Alaska, Montana and Wyoming.

In sum, the principal changes in the population include a general upward trend in terms of absolute numbers, accompanied by a slow decline in fertility and a rapid decrease in mortality. This is particularly evident in developing countries. Worldwide, the gap between birth rates and death rates is still wide enough to cause some alarm. In the next section, changes in the sphere of stratification will be examined.

STRATIFICATION

Stratification refers to a system of ranking individuals and families into levels (strata or class) that share unequally in the distribution of status, wealth, and power or other scarce, highly valued and cherished objects in communities and societies (Gilbert, 2002; Gilbert & Kahl, 1993; Rossides, 1997; Spector, 1995). In all societies, differences exist between some individuals and others in terms of a number of factors. For example, the chief of a tribal society may be differentiated from tribesmen by receiving a greater degree of deference, living in a larger house, and having more wives. The president of a large university in a modern society is also likely to be differentiated in a number of ways from other members of the academic community—for example, a larger office, a much larger income, more secretaries, a reserved parking place and a generous travel and entertainment budget.

Types of Stratification Systems

There are three general types of stratification systems. At one extreme is the caste system, in which the strata are hereditary, endogamous (marriage partners must be chosen within the group), and permanent. An individual is born into a caste, marries in it, and dies in it. The best-known caste system is that of traditional India. However, with the introduction of modern forms of technology and economic organization, together with the diffusion of ideologies favorable to social change and the integration of village life with the outside world, the traditionally rigid status system has been greatly undermined, although not necessarily abandoned (Mendelsohn, 1993). Much of this change has occurred in cities, not in rural villages, but the values and lifestyles associated with a more flexible status system have filtered into the rural sectors, planting the seeds of a "revolution of rising expectations" (Mandelbaum, 1970).

At the other extreme is the open class system, in which only individual achievement matters, and one rises or falls in social class according to his or her own accomplishment. Class frees individuals from the accident of birth more than any other ranking system. The class system does not remove the disadvantages or advantages of birth but does allow more room for achievement. Class is a relatively open system that allows for maximum social mobility in either direction (Berger, 1996). The United States is considered to have the most open and mobile class system in the world. In the third, the estate system, strata are defined by law and are relatively rigid and permanent. But there is some opportunity to shift one's status. Feudal Europe is the most notable example of an estate system. Changes from estate and caste stratification systems to open systems are indicative of changes of type, whereas changes in the open class system are changes within the stratification system (Barber, 1973:199–209).

Toward Greater Equality

The economic difference between the top and bottom strata of society is greater in underdeveloped and developing countries than in developed nations. The richest 358 people in the world—the global billionaire club—possess assets which exceed the combined income of countries accounting for 45 percent of the world's population (Weismann, 1996). Gerhard Lenski's (1966:309) observation of almost four decades ago is still correct: the top 1 or 2 percent of the population in nonindustrial societies as a whole usually receives not less than half of the total income of the country. In industrial societies the comparative figure is much less.

In developed countries, the gap between the rich and the poor narrowed between 1930 and 1960. Because of changing economic realities, this trend has been reversed, income inequalities are growing, and they are greater than any time in the past fifty years (*Economist*, 1994:19–21)—although wealth inequalities (a less frequently used indicator of inequality defined as assets owned at a given time such as land, stocks, retirements benefits, homes and cars) have remained relatively unchanged (Weicher, 1997) and the median family wealth in the United States has stayed around $52,000 for the last 15 years, with some minor fluctuations as a result of the 2002 recession.

The biggest increases in income inequalities occurred in the United States, the United Kingdom, and New Zealand, where free market policies have been pursued most zealously. For example, the average salary of a chief executive officer of a major American firm is over $3 million per year, not including stock options and special benefits—about 149 times as much as an ordinary production worker (Sanders, 1997). Between 1970 and 2000, the average real annual compensation of the top 100 chief executive officers went from $1.3 million—39 times the pay of an average worker—to $37.5 million, more than 1,000 times the pay of ordinary workers (Krugman, 2002:64).

In the United States, for example, in late 1990s, the top 20 percent of households received eleven times as much income as the bottom 20 percent. The effect is to give the richest 20 percent of the households a 45-percent share of the country's net income—the highest since World War II—and the poorest 20 percent of households a mere 4-percent share. Slightly more than 10 percent of American households had incomes of $100,000 or more in 1995. In the same year, the median family income from wages was $25,480 (it reached $42,228 in 2002). The number of those with incomes in excess of

$1 million has increased fourfold since 1995. This trend is succinctly captured in an article title in a business magazine: "The Rich Get Richer, and That's O.K." (Mandel, 2002:88).

The bottom 80 percent of the population receives a smaller share of the nation's total income than it did 20 years ago, when the median earning of men began dropping. Adjusted for inflation, the average pay for four-fifths of American workers plummeted by 16 percent between 1973 and 1993 (Sanders, 1997). Middle-income households avoided downward mobility only by sending wives to work, by postponing both marriage and children, and by taking on part-time jobs. At the same time, the poor have become poorer (Hacker, 1997). Income inequalities are likely to remain with us in the same proportions in the foreseeable future (see, for example, Nielsen & Alderson, 1997). But then there are those who argue that "It's better to have a wide income gap but few people in poverty than greater equality and a high poverty rate" (Mandel, 2002:90).

The publication of a controversial book, *The Bell Curve*, by Charles Murray and the late Richard Hernnstein (Hernnstein & Murray, 1994) has highlighted the concern with income inequality by renewing a claim that intelligence as measured by IQ tests plays a major role in deciding society's winners and losers, and that genetic inheritance may be a main determinant of IQ. As may be expected, critics were not very kind to their thesis (see, for example, Reese, 1996; Schwartz, 1997).

Aside from income gaps, in many industrialized societies, the long-term trend is toward equalization of rights and privileges for all classes and toward the reduction of the power of the elite. Voting rights were extended to all levels, minimum wage laws were enacted to improve the economic position of the working classes, and graduated income taxes were utilized in an attempt to moderate glaring inequities in wealth. Other attempts to equalize opportunities included social security for the unemployed, children, and the physically handicapped; education for the masses; free public recreational facilities; and a judicial system to protect the rights of individuals regardless of their class position.

Industrialization and urbanization have profoundly altered the economic basis of stratification. As a result of economic and technological changes, many Western countries have experienced a general improvement in the overall income for the masses, both urban and rural, and a significant increase in the standard of living. The emphasis shifted to consumption, and there is considerable preoccupation with both what and how to consume and under what circumstances. In the United States, large-scale changes in major patterns of stratification have been associated with industrialization, creating a large urban working class. Well into the twentieth century, the urban proletariat was generally underpaid and overworked, and the lifestyle imposed upon it reflected its underprivileged position in the economy. In recent decades, however, a substantial proportion of the urban working class has adopted a middle-class lifestyle. The basic change making this possible has been the rise in their relative incomes and the shorter workweek. With higher incomes and more leisure time, many workers acquired consumer "needs" of the middle class, such as modern homes and household equipment, an annual vacation and travel, leisure-time activities, and so on. For a while, the American dream became a reality. Workers got used to a rapidly growing standard of living in the 1960s and most of the 1970s, but the gains took a turn in the opposite direction starting in about 1978 (Koten, 1987). With a concomitant increase in the length of the workweek, the average American is working longer for less income (Sanders, 1997). Suddenly, a generation raised with great material expectations has discovered there is a big gap between its reach for more satisfaction and what is within its grasp. In view of current trends, it is doubtful that the new urban working class can maintain the highly cherished middle-class style of life. And, it is little consolation for them that their "real" middle-class counterparts are not faring much better.

Rising income inequality and the concomitant class segregation is creating geographical localization of affluence and poverty across the world. The localization will likely cause an increase in the density of poverty and expose the disadvantaged to increased disease, crime, violence and family disorganization. On the other hand, the affluence concentration will improve the privileges of the rich and we are likely to see further polarization, snobbery (Epstein, 2002), gated communities, and class segregation through ecological mechanisms (see, for example, Massey, 1996).

Social Mobility

The United States is frequently described as a "mobile society." Because stratification really involves a series of steps, one can consider mobility with regard to a number of variables such as income, educational achievement, housing, neighborhood status, occupational prestige, and so forth (see, for example, Smith, 2000). There is consensus in the stratification literature that occupation is the best single indicator of one's overall stratification position. Changes in a stratification position are brought about by vertical mobility, that is, either upward or downward movement on an occupational scale. Moreover, mobility can be plotted across various periods of time, which would include two possible forms: intergenerational and intragenerational. Intergenerational mobility concerns changes in occupational prestige between generations and specifically involves the mobility of the offspring relative to the parent. Intragenerational mobility has to do with mobility within a single generation or movement following the individual's first major job (Blau & Duncan, 1967). Such mobility patterns may involve changes from manual to non-manual occupations or movements into and out of the occupational elite at the top of some kind of occupational scale. Several studies claim that patterns of social mobility have not changed in recent decades (Rose, 1996).

As the economy changed in the United States in the nineteenth century, so did the nature of the occupational roles to be filled. The rise of industrialization and the increasing technological development of the society had an enormous impact in creating not only "room at the top" but actual "demand at the top," requiring a new supply. The greatly increased need for business executives, research scientists, lawyers, and financial managers exerted a demand on the education system that led, in turn, to a need for more teachers at every level. This change considerably altered the ratio of nonfarm to farm and even the ratio of elite to nonelite jobs.

During the same period, American society was playing host to waves of immigrants who entered the American stratification system near the bottom and had the effect of pushing those already in the system toward the top. Irish, Italian, and Eastern European immigrants were all initially restricted to the less prestigious slots on the occupational ladder, whereas those workers already on the ladder were encouraged and even prodded to move up the rungs and fill the new occupational opportunities that were developing. Widening educational opportunity acted as the crucial mechanism for the transformation. The rise of public universities with low tuition made possible a massive surge of occupational mobility on the part of ethnic immigrants previously at the bottom of the stratification ladder.

Urbanization also contributes to changes in stratification patterns and to an increase in social mobility. Urbanized societies, or even those moving in this direction, commonly have expanding economies and thus increased job opportunities and rising income. Growing cities, in particular large cities, have a complex division of labor, which involves the creation of new occupations or more jobs and a need for personnel to fill these positions. Thus, there are opportunities for upward occupational mobility—or prospects for downward mobility. For the United States and other highly industrialized societies, however, data indicate that in recent decades the rates of total mobility have not changed all that much (Gilbert & Kahl, 1993).

Patterns of social mobility vary from one society to another, with perhaps the most marked differentiation to be made between industrial and nonindustrial societies. Moreover, variations among nations in mobility rates can be interpreted in different ways, depending on which aspect of mobility one examines. S. M. Miller (1960) suggests that chances for long-term upward mobility from blue-collar to elite appear to be greater in the United States and Japan. To illustrate, in America children of high school graduates are almost as likely to get a college degree as children of college graduates (Mandel, 1996). When all possibilities of entry into the elite from other levels are considered, Sweden and the Netherlands may be more open than the United States or Japan. Australia has a very low inheritance of occupational status and hence the highest general mobility figures. Blue-collar to white-collar moves seem to be most prevalent in France, Switzerland, and Great Britain.

Regardless of the prevalence, frequency, and type of social mobility, movement through the class system, either up or down, is an experience that profoundly affects many aspects of an individual's life (Tumin, 1985). For many, upward social mobility may be a disruptive experience. Through education or other forms of achievement, they realize occupational attainments that place them into lifestyles substantially different from those of their parents. In certain situations, lifestyle differences that stem from occupational factors may be accentuated by considerations of ethnic culture. To illustrate, the upwardly mobile children of immigrant parents may be under considerable pressure to reject or abandon parental beliefs, values, and way of life in order to become assimilated into their new social class. In some cases, upward mobility is associated with guilt and anxiety and may result in the breakdown of relations with the parents. It has also been suggested that those who are upwardly mobile into the middle class are generally more politically conservative than those born into middle-class circumstances (Tumin, 1985:93–95).

POWER RELATIONS

Few people would disagree with Olsen's often cited truism (1970) that like "energy in the physical world, power pervades all dynamic social phenomena." Although power has been variously defined, most sociologists would agree with Max Weber's definition of power as "the chance of a man or a number of men to realize their own will in a communal action even against the resistance of others who are participating in that action" (Gerth & Mills, 1946:180). Implicit in this definition is the notion that power cannot be considered an attribute of any individual or group. Rather, it is defined as a relationship between individuals or groups. Invariably, power has at least three components: force, authority, and influence (Bierstedt, 1974:220–241).

Force means the application of sanctions to, or the elimination of alternatives from, one group or individual by another. "Surrender or die," "Your money or your life," "Publish or perish," "Behave or get spanked"; all of these are examples of the elimination of possibilities. In earlier days, for example, force used to be an inherent part of the student-teacher power relation. In one instance, a schoolteacher tells that during his fifty-one years of teaching, he administered "911,527 blows with a cane; 124,010 with a rod; 20,989 with a ruler; 136,715 with the hand; 10,295 over the mouth; 7,095 boxes on the ear; [and] 1,115,800 slaps on the head. . . ." (Coleman, quoted by Rogers & Skinner, 1968:335).

Authority is a legitimate power, an established right to make decisions and order the actions of others. Weber (Gerth & Mills, 1946:196–252) identifies three main types of authority:

1. *Charismatic authority*, or the authority of an extraordinary person who is obeyed because of charisma—his image of wisdom, saintliness, or invincibility—such as Christ, Napoleon, or Hitler.
2. *Traditional authority*, resting on a belief of sacred norms and traditions that one must obey; for example, prince, priest, or chief.
3. *Bureaucratic or rational legal authority*, resting on formal office or rank; for example, a general or a president of a university.

Finally, *influence* is the ability to affect the decisions and actions of others beyond any authority to do so. For example, professors have authority to command certain work assignments and to assign grades, but they do not have the authority to compel students to accept their opinions, even though they can influence students to do so. In brief, power is implied because when challenged, it becomes force; when legalized, it becomes authority; and influence rests on some combination of personality attributes and authority.

Power is a universal phenomenon in human societies, and there is an infinite number of power relations—the power of the parent over the child, the master over the slave, the teacher over the student, the warden over the prisoner, the employer over the employee, the general over the lieutenant. In short, it pervades all social relationships (see, for example, Nadler, 2002).

The Dynamics of Power Relations

In *Power and Privilege*, Gerhard Lenski (1966) contends that the variety of inequality a society exhibits depends upon the existing power relations and upon how the power system distributes material surplus, especially food. Focusing his analysis on the basic techniques of subsistence, he develops a typology of societies, each type having a distinguishable degree of inequality and different power relations. The five types of societies are as follows:

1. *Hunting and gathering societies* are characterized by pronounced equality as a result of universally shared economic scarcity. Any superiority that exists is based on personal skills and abilities, a form of superiority that cannot be transmitted socially to children.

2. In *simple horticultural societies*, institutionalized inequality first emerges with farming based on the digging stick, a fundamental tool of a gardening economy. Domestication of plants results in a more dependable supply of food, which, in turn, is related to the emergence of a division of labor, wherein specialized economic occupations and full-time occupations in politics and religion develop. As a result of functional specialization, new social statuses and power relations emerge.

3. In *advanced horticultural societies,* there is a noticeable increase in inequality, which accompanies the development of the hoe, permitting a greater utilization of the soil, and of terracing, irrigation, fertilizers, or metallurgy. The higher level of technology leads to an increase in economic specialization and to the development of political power. There is an elaboration of formal statuses, accompanied by an increase in property rights (including rights over human beings, or slavery) and the availability of transferable assets such as money, cattle, and slaves. From the perspective of power relations, this level of technological and social development sees the emergence of well-defined hereditary strata.

4. In *agrarian societies,* there is a significant increase in food production and food surplus that leads to advances in transport, communication, engineering, and military technology. New forms of power relations emerge in the form of a city-state, a bureaucratic empire, or feudalism. In such a society there is a well-developed, superior, hereditary social group, and the causes of inequality are primarily economic.

5. In *industrial societies,* the development of an industrial technology represents a significant change in the means of subsistence available to society. As a result, sharp increases take place in production and in specialized economic activity. But the subsequent material surplus, according to Lenski, does not lead, as in the past, to increases in inequality but to a reversal of this historic trend. Although economic prestige and political inequality is still substantial, it is less marked than in agrarian societies. Economic resources are more equitably distributed, and there is an emergence of universal suffrage, representing a diffusion and popularization of political power. The major reason for this trend toward increased equality is that industrial society is too complex to be run personally or arbitrarily. The ruling groups find it in their interests to involve the lower and intermediate groups in economic and political processes.

The contention that industrial society is characterized by a decrease in economic and political inequality as compared to agrarian society is a major theme in Lenski's work. It is important to note that the economic elite in industrial society claims a smaller portion of the economic pie than the economic elite of agrarian society, and there is a greater willingness of the political elite to involve the masses in political processes. Moreover, unlike in agricultural societies, in industrial societies, at least in the West, ownership in corporations has more or less become separated from control: Power has passed into the hands of managers (Zeitlin, 1982).

A similar point is made by Gaetano Mosca, who suggests that while wealth may still facilitate recruitment to the ruling class or political elite, in modern industrial societies access to the political or ruling elite has become open to wider and wider strata of the population. Mosca came to this conclusion by tracing the changes in the relations between the ruling minority and the majority that is being ruled. He pointed out that the structure of the ruling class and the criteria of recruitment into it change with the changes in its predominant societal function. Historically, one change was the shift from military skills, first to land ownership and then to wealth, as a criterion of access to the ruling class. At first, the ruling warrior classes acquired ownership of the land, which is the principal source of production and wealth in premodern societies. As revenue from the land increases, accompanied by the growth of population and the development of urban centers of consumption, an important societal transformation occurs: "Wealth rather than military valor comes to be the characteristic feature of the dominant class: the people who rule are the rich rather than the brave" (Mosca, 1973:214).

He further suggests that "If a new source of wealth develops in a society, if the practical importance of knowledge grows, if an old religion declines or a new one is born, if a new current of ideas spreads, then, simultaneously, far-reaching dislocations occur in the ruling class" (Mosca, 1973:215). The ruling classes inevitably decline when they can no longer render the services they once rendered and when their talents lose in importance in the environment in which they live. This is further facilitated when scattered smaller units become integrated into large-scale tightly knit political entities. This brings an ever-increasing concentration of power in the hands of a state that carries out and regulates more and more functions. This is related to a change in the mode of organization of the political structure, the transition from feudalism to bureaucracy. Political bureaucracy first came into being in seventeenth-century France under the reign of Louis XIV, and then, according to Mosca, evolved into the democratic and totalitarian bureaucratic state where the potential political power of nonpoliticians has increased significantly.

Suzanne Keller (1963) contends that industrialization brought about the development of many "strategic elites" defined as "a minority of individuals designated to serve a collectivity in a socially valued way" (1963:4). In addition to a political elite, an economic elite, and a military elite, Keller discusses cultural, moral, intellectual, scientific, religious, and diplomatic elites among others. She writes (1963:277–278):

> In highly industrialized societies . . . power has become less arbitrary and personal and is increasingly shared among various groups and institutions. . . . The current strategic elites are not as free to exercise their powers as were the aristocracies and ruling classes of the past because in being functionally

specialized they are themselves subordinate in spheres not relating to their specialty, and because they are now far more dependent on the good will of the public. . . . Today, no single strategic elite has absolute power or priority . . . and none determines the patterns of selection and recruitment of the rest . . . their more varied skills and experiences result in the formation of a more complex and many-sided social core, one in which a number of personalities must coexist.

Decentralization of Power

In addition to changes in power relations at the societal level, changes are taking place at the level of community. In most American communities, power is diffused to a considerable degree. Thomas R. Dye (1986:49) contends that the community's most important resource is land, and those who control land use are the community's power elite. They include mortgage bankers, real estate developers, builders, and landowners. Community elites, Dye argues, are different from national elites in their economic function. At the local level, the elites' function is to prepare land for capital investment. But their power is limited, for they cannot control the destinies of their communities. Their power is limited to economic development decisions, and they secure mass support for their policies by emphasizing prospects for more jobs and small business opportunities. There is no single center of power, and Paul E. Mott (1970:85–86) cites the factors or conditions that favor an increase in the number of local centers of power and in the number of power relations. "The number of centers of power is to increase as (1) the population (of the community) increases, (2) the ethnic composition becomes more heterogeneous, (3) functional specialization increases, (4) the number of self-conscious social classes increases, (5) as immigration increases."

Law and Power

Changes in power relations are also brought about by law. As J. O. Hertzler (1961:421) points out, ". . . the law in effect structures the power (superordinate-subordinate) relationships in the society; it maintains the status quo and protects the various strata against each other, both in governmental and non-governmental organizations and relationships." The law affects power relations by stating who may do what to whom. For example, prior to the passing of the National Labor Relations Act of 1935, employers were legally entitled to fire employees who joined unions. This law established workers' legal right to join unions and prohibited employers from penalizing workers for union activity. Civil rights legislation also changed the power relations between blacks and whites by enabling the former to obtain goals more efficiently, pursue goals that otherwise they would not pursue, and act out values more effectively. It resulted in the acquisition of new opportunities and in the formation of new attitudes such as increased self-esteem, courage, and political awareness (McClusky, 1976:393).

In sum, it should be noted that when talking about political power relations, an organized minority generally can control an unorganized majority. Even though there have been important changes in power relations, indicating a trend toward a more egalitarian distribution of power, it is probably true, contrary to popular myth, that "the people" neither possess nor dispense power. It should also be remembered that "it is quite impossible for the government of a society to be in the hands of any but a few . . . there is government for the people; there is no government by the people" (Aron, quoted by Bottomore, 1993:120).

EDUCATION

In traditional societies, individuals can acquire the knowledge and skills necessary for the successful performance of adult roles without formal education. In more complex societies, parents are unable to pass on to their children the knowledge and skills they will need as adults. As a society becomes more industrialized, there is an ever-increasing demand for general skills—reading, writing, and arithmetic—and for specialized vocational and technical training for specific occupational roles. Nowadays, an increasing supply of highly educated people has become the absolute prerequisite of social and economic development.

Schools were invented several thousand years ago to prepare a select few for leadership. They educated only an elite class, which was supposed to "carry" the culture for the whole society. The education provided was theoretical, consisting of the trivium (grammar, rhetoric, and logic) and the quadrivium (arithmetic, geometry, astronomy, and music). While describing education in medieval Europe, Phillippe Ariés (1962) points out that schools lacked a gradation of subjects according to difficulty. There was a very broad age dispersion of students, ranging from age nine to age twenty-four in the same class; an absence of standard age for beginning school; instruction from a few to several hundred students by one teacher; and the maintenance of control by corporal punishment, humiliation, and reliance on informers. The notion of schooling as preparation for adulthood was foreign to the medieval tradition. Schooling of this nature, largely consistent with training a clerical elite, endured for a long time.

A century or more ago, public schools were created to teach the three Rs to the masses. Today, education is a dominant institution that touches almost every member of a society at some time, consumes a large portion of a society's financial resources, and is one of the largest employers of the workforce. Universal education became a right, if not a mandate, at least up to age fifteen in most countries of the world.

During the late twentieth and at the beginning of the twenty-first century, school enrollments at the primary, secondary, and college levels have increased dramatically. In 2002, more than 72 million Americans between the ages of three and thirty-four were enrolled in educational institutions. Some examples of changes: Of those aged twenty-five years and over in 1940, 24.5 percent had completed high school and 4.6 percent college. The median school years completed was 8.6. By 2002, 80.2 percent had completed high school and 21.9 percent college, and the median school years completed grew to 12.6. Between 1960 and 2002, school expenditures rose almost fivefold, to $438 billion for all levels (U.S. Bureau of the Census, 2002:154, 157, 151). This figure represents around 7 percent of the total value of the nation's annual output of goods and services. Public elementary and secondary schools spend about $4,700 per student, public colleges $13,200, and private institutions $22,000. Full-time tuition income covers between one-half and three-fourths of the per-pupil expenditures of colleges. For example, one top college, Swarthmore in Pennsylvania, estimates that it spends more than $40,000 per student, which is far more than the $29,900 fee it receives for actual tuition, room and board. At University of Iowa, the school's annual in-state tuition and fees charge of $4,191 covers less than half of educating a student (Schodolski, 2002). [It should also be noted that university education is the best investment most people can make, and the annual returns to students in the United States average around 15 percent while globally it ranges from 6.5 percent in Italy to almost 18 percent in Britain (*Economist*, 2002d). The calculation treats the costs of study, including earnings foregone, as the investment, and the gains in post-tax earnings above those of school leavers as the payoff. Shorter university courses are one reason why returns are so high in Britain.]

The difference is made up from gifts and endowment income. At this point, it should be noted that the perennially "soaring tuition" image of higher education has little to do with reality. In 2002, of the more than 4,100 colleges and universities in the United States, only some 36 charged more than $30,000 in tuition and fees. More than a quarter of all colleges are public, where the average cost is $2,860; two-thirds of all students, around 6 million, attend them. Another 5.3 million attend two-year junior colleges with an average tuition of $1,359. Public colleges and universities enroll more than 80 percent of all students, and they pay on the average $3,506 for their education. (Out-of-staters typically pay two or two and a half times the tuition and fees charged to residents). Those who attend private colleges pay an average of $18,273 in tuition and fees, and less than 6 percent of all students pay more than $24,000 (Hershey, 2002; Neusner, 2002:86). These figures do not take scholarships into account: 41 percent of all students at public and 60 percent at private four-year colleges receive financial aid. A related point is that the nation's public four-year colleges and universities are increasingly serving the economic elite, who, as a group, no longer place a high premium on private education and star-studded faculty who are often unavailable to undergraduates. The proportion of students from affluent families increased sharply at public institutions over the past 15 years, to 38 percent of the freshmen coming from families earning more than $200,000.

Several reasons account for these phenomenal increases both in the number of students and in expenditures. One explanation is the high birth rate following World War II. Another factor is the lengthening of the educational time span, as communities add kindergarten at one end and community colleges at the other. A third explanation is the rising popularity of a college education. But beyond these, the average cost per pupil at every level has been rising faster than either the price or level of the gross national product. This is due, in part, to a national drive to improve education with the customary prescription being a generous diffusion of money, although there is little empirical evidence that spending more money makes for better students (*Economist*, 1997a) and the debate on the issue of whether public spending is related to school performance continues (Burtless, 1996; Zernike, 2002). Let us now consider some specific changes in elementary, secondary, and higher education.

Elementary and Secondary Education

Since about the turn of the century, the main change in American elementary and secondary education has been from curriculum-oriented subject matter to an emphasis on the child as a growing personality. Under the former, more weight was given to content and to the capacity to reproduce what had been read or heard. Today, schools are more and more child-centered, with emphasis on self- and social development. This change has been accompanied by a shift from a rather severe authoritarianism to a more permissive practice in teaching methods in which the child has a larger degree of participation. There is greater emphasis on matters of motivation, cooperative learning, mental hygiene, and the like.

The number of public and private school students reached 52.2 million in 1997, and current demographic trends suggest that enrollment will peak at 54.3 million in 2007. During this period, high school enrollment is projected to increase by 13 percent (an additional 1.7 million students), while elementary enrollment is projected to increase by less than 1 percent. This continued enrollment spiral reflects the "echo boom" of the children of baby boom generation, increased immigration, more children in pre-kindergarten and kindergarten, and more students staying in school longer. The shift from elementary to high schools has spatial and fiscal implications—some 6,000 new schools will be needed along with some 2 million new teachers to accommodate the growing number of high school students and there is a cost estimate of $112 billion for just the repair and maintenance of existing buildings (Applebome, 1997).

The rapid rise in high school population over the years has also led to a proliferation of separate courses, and to such varied courses of study as liberal or college preparatory, commercial, vocational, and fine arts. The trend has been away from the courses designed to prepare the pupil for higher education toward those that have more practical use in jobs or in the home and that give the future citizen some orientation to his or her public and political rights and duties. Ancient languages, algebra, geometry, trigonometry, and formal political history have tended to give way to modern languages, simplified or "new" mathematics, and social studies that emphasize current issues. These changes have been accompanied by a series of educational innovations, such as the use of teaching machines and closed-circuit television, the creation of open classroom environments, and a widespread reliance on computers both as a teaching and learning aid.

As increasingly large proportions of young people attend schools at all levels, concern has grown that the quality of education has been declining. A number of shortcomings have captured the public's attention. Examples of these include the relatively high rate of functional illiteracy among young adults (as high as 40 percent among minority youths); inadequacies in the teaching of science, mathematics and foreign languages, and the general decline on test performance (Ravitch, 2003). Studies indicate that American high school students average lower test scores in mathematics, science, and other subjects when compared to their counterparts in Japan, Germany, Russia, Singapore, and other industrialized nations. For example, in a 1997 survey of math achievement scores of students from 41 countries, the United States ranked 28th. Top on the list were students from Singapore, South Korea, Japan and Hong Kong (*Economist*, 1997b). It is interesting to note that second-ranked South Korea and sixth-ranked Czechs spend only a third as much per pupil as the United States. Once again, teaching methods are more crucial than education spending. In teaching mathematics, both countries spend more time on basic arithmetic than on deeper mathematical ideas, emphasize mental arithmetic, rely on standard teaching manuals and favor whole-class (as opposed to group) teaching.

Further, some of the differences are also due to greater emphasis on the hard sciences and languages and to the length of the school year. For example, German students routinely study physics and algebra for five years, chemistry and biology for four years, and calculus for two years. Most American high school students do not take even a year of either physics or chemistry. Only 6 percent study calculus. With a 180-day school schedule, the United States is one of the few countries with classrooms idle over half the year. Japanese schools operate more than 240 days, including half-days on Saturdays. Most Japanese high school students do not date, drive cars, hold part-time jobs, or even do household chores. In the United States, 76 percent of high school seniors spend fewer than five hours per week on homework; in Japan, less than 35 percent do. In 1994, one-third of high school seniors reported that they were not required to do daily homework in all school subjects and over half of them could not write a narrative essay (Manegold, 1994). This is reflected in the SAT (Scholastic Achievement Test) scores, which have declined from their postwar high in 1956. In 1997, math scores showed some overall improvement, while the verbal scores remained relatively unchanged (Honan, 1997) and leveled off for the next five years (Barnes, 2002). Asian Americans continued to have the highest averages in mathematics, and whites scored highest in the verbal test. Blacks had the lowest average in both the verbal and mathematics parts. But low test scores are not limited to students. In a well-publicized case in 1997, school officials in the Connetquot school district on Long Island were not surprised when they received hundreds of applications for 35 openings. What surprised them, however, was the number of candidates who could not pass a new test—50 multiple-choice reading comprehension questions from old Regents exams in English given to *high school juniors*. Of the 758 applicants, only about a quarter passed: Just 202 correctly answered at least 40 questions (*New York Times*, 1997:A12). It should be noted that all applicants had at least a baccalaureate, and several a master's degree and New York State certification to teach. In this connection, it is also interesting to note that while colleges readily publish SAT scores of incoming high school students, none publish test scores (LSATs, GMATs, GREs or MACTs) for their graduates.

There are several reasons for the long-term decline of SAT scores. They include the fact that more lower-scoring minorities and disadvantaged students have been taking the tests since the mid-1960s; that learning standards in schools are down, as evidenced by an increase in absenteeism, grade inflation, and easier textbooks; that changing family structures, notably the increase in one-parent homes, have hurt the children's learning ability; and that easier access to colleges, along with a growing lack of motivation, may have resulted in less preparation by students for college entrance examinations. The decline in scores are further attributed to an increase in disciplinary problems in schools, high rates of truancy, and the substantial amount of time spent viewing television on school days. But there is good news for those who had problems with the current SAT format. The College Board, a nonprofit organization that owns SAT, has begun the biggest overhaul ever of the test in late 2002. By 2005, the board plans to strip out the analogies section, ask questions based on more advanced math, and add a grammar and essay-writing test (Barnes, 2002:56). This may be the most important change in the SAT since its inception in 1926.

Generally, these are the reasons given for the school systems' inability to teach the fundamentals to America's poor children. It is interesting to note that "The same school system that had taught the fundamentals to the children of immigrants from provinces in southern Italy, where from 67 percent to 79 percent of the adult populations could not read or write Italian, now presumably could not do the same for the children of native-born Americans, all of whom spoke English and most of whom were at least literate" (Armbruster, 1977:11).

Armbruster (1977:54) further points out that the lack of academic climate in high schools, the proliferation of elective courses, less homework, and lax attendance requirements, in many instances, have resulted in a discouraging situation in which

> many schools have tended to educate children for a nonexistent world. Certain things in life simply cannot be avoided or blamed on someone else; actions have personal consequences; outside the school environment one normally has to produce to be promoted; work must satisfy the needs of the economy to be profitable to the worker; many trades and professions require work that gives no credit for good intentions or for being nearly accurate—much work, and advanced study, must be explicit, meticulous and correct every time; it is important to be well informed and logical, not just spontaneous and talkative. To let students believe otherwise is to mislead them dangerously—especially if they are underprivileged.

Higher Education

Today's universities have their origins in the institutions that developed in eleventh- and twelfth-century Europe. They began in Italy, spread to Spain and France, from there to Germany and Scandinavia, then to England, Scotland, and finally to America. The contemporary American university is an amalgam borrowed from Western Europe, particularly England and Germany. The assumptions underlying the undergraduate curriculum originally came from England, whereas graduate education is grounded in German scholarship and science. The English influence can be dated from the founding of the first college, Harvard, in 1636. The German influence did not take hold until more than two centuries later. The curriculum was designed to produce a learned clergy and cultivated gentlemen and to impart an aristocratic lifestyle to the well born. In the seventeenth century, more than half of the college graduates became ministers, and most college professors were clergymen, or at least were trained in theology. Before the Civil War, almost all college presidents were ministers.

In the early American college, the principal method of instruction was recitation. This is a process in which students repeat from memory, often verbatim, textbook assignments. (Remnants of this method are still found in Eastern European and Russian universities.) For disputation, students defended or attacked a proposition in Latin, the required language of instruction. Later on, the lecture by teachers supplemented student recitations.

Because of the limited number of books, students often copied down word for word what the instructor said. As the size of classes increased, the lecture method slowly replaced recitation and disputation. The blackboard was first used at Bowdoin College around 1823. The seminar method was imported from Germany in the mid-nineteenth century. Finally, the discussion class, designed to supplement lectures, was introduced at Harvard in 1904 (Boyer, 1987:149).

The early colleges were for male students only. Higher education did not become a reality for women until the early 1800s. (Now women make up over 55 percent of the undergraduate student body.) By 1860, there were 246 colleges and universities in the United States and 17 state universities. In 1862, higher education gained support from the passage of the Morrill Act by Congress. This act granted each state a large area of land for the purpose of endowing at least one agricultural college. These "land-grant colleges" contributed greatly to the expansion of agricultural and engineering education. Further support for higher education came from the passage of the GI Bill by Congress in 1944, and its extension in 1952. The Economic Opportunity Act of 1964 authorized grants for college work-study programs, and, in 1972, the Higher Education Act authorized, for the first time, direct all-purpose aid to colleges and universities. The greater financial support by the government resulted in the greater involvement of the government in higher education.

As college has become more central to society, higher education has grown into a $180 billion industry, nearly three percent of the gross national product, from 2.4 billion, less than 1 percent, 50 years ago (Arenson, 1997). By 2002, there were 4,182 institutions of higher education in the United States: 2,450 were classified as four-year (which includes 159 universities), and the remaining 1,732 as junior colleges (*Chronicle of Higher Education Almanac*, 2002:12). The number of two- and four-year colleges almost doubled during the last generation. A similar increase took place among the number of college students. By the fall of 2002, total college enrollment in institutions of higher learning was close to 14.8 million, and college students today can choose from a list of more than 6,000 different majors (Boyer, 1987:102) and take courses on a huge variety of subjects such as democracy and gender, introduction to herbs and spices, even including the fundamentals of circus skills, the "Madonna phenomenon," and the theory and techniques of windsurfing—all for credit (Frank, 1994). The percentage of U.S. high school graduates who enrolled in college or completed at least one year also grew steadily over the years, reaching almost 69 percent in 2002. This is the highest in the world.

A phenomenal increase has occurred in the number of junior colleges. In 1960, there were 521 such institutions; by 2002, there were 1,732. In 1960, there were 451,000 junior college students; today there are more than 5.5 million. From 1965 to 1970, there were 194 new junior colleges that opened up in America, about one every nine days for half a decade. The junior college diploma is rapidly replacing the high school diploma as a minimum credential for entrance into the "educated" middle class.

Concomitant with the growth in the number of colleges has been the steady increase in the number of types of degrees conferred. The number of bachelor's degree recipients increased from 839,730 in 1971 to 1,237,875 in 2002 (*Chronicle of Higher Education Almanac*, 2002:12). But there were some major changes in the field of study. The number of business majors more than doubled. There were significant increases in the number of students majoring in psychology, communications, criminal justice and corrections and education. Fields with notable declines included communications technologies, computer and information sciences, library science, theology and nursing. Just one specific case: The number of nursing school graduates taking the national license exam for entry level registered nurses declined from 96,438 in 1995 to 68,759 in 2001 (U.S. Department of Health and Human Services, 2002), creating a national nursing shortage of over 110,000 people, or six percent of the nurses needed. The projected shortage for 2020 is in excess of 808,000 people, or 29 percent of the nurses needed.

Between 1971 and 1978, the number of M.A. degrees conferred increased from 230,509 to 311,620. From 1978, however, there was a gradual decline to 286,251 in 1985, followed by a pronounced increase to 352,838 in 1992 that reflected generally poor employment prospects for college graduates. This trend continued during the past ten years and in 2002, 457,056 M.A. degrees were awarded. There is an uneven trend among doctoral recipients; their number rose in 1975 to 34,083, declined in 1985 to 32,943, and increased again to 44,808 in 2002 (U.S. Bureau of the Census, 2002:190; *Chronicle of Higher Education Almanac*, 2002:12). In 2002, over half of all M.A. degrees were earned by those majoring in business and education, and close to one-fifth of Ph.D. recipients were in education, closely followed by engineering.

America educates one-third of all foreign students, and, not surprisingly, about half of all students who get Ph.D.s in the United States are still there five years later. The proportion rises to over 60 percent for those with doctorates in mathematics, computer science, and the physical sciences. In the early 2000s, students from India and China were especially likely to stay on after they completed their studies (*Economist*, 2002c:24). In economics, 40 percent of doctorates went to foreign-born students (Bhagwati and Rao, 1994).

As the population of the United States became increasingly well educated, women made significant gains (Bianchi & Spain, 1986:137). In terms of enrollment, women represent 55.5 percent of the college population. In 1997, more women than men earned both bachelor's and master's degrees. But women represented slightly more than a third of Ph.D. recipients. Differences still exist between men and women in their major fields of study.

More than two-thirds of students in majors such as architecture, engineering, physical sciences, and religion are men. Those fields in which over two-thirds are female include education, foreign languages, library sciences, and health professions. But women made significant inroads in traditional "male" areas of study. For example, women recipients of medical and law degrees have more than tripled since the 1970s, and the number of women has increased substantially in fields such as mathematics and engineering.

Data show that overall minority enrollment has also continued to grow. Between 1984 and 2002, the total enrollment in higher education increased by about 2.8 million. Not one of the students contributing to this rise was a white American male. Seventy-one percent were students classified as African American, Native American, Asian American and Hispanic American. The remaining 29 percent were nonresident aliens and white women. The number of "white men" actually declined. By 1997, the number of minority students in two- and four-year colleges had risen to over 23 percent of the total college enrollment. The patterns, however, vary widely by race. Black enrollment is up to 10 percent of the college population, which reflects a gradual upward trend, but is still lower than the proportion of blacks in the population. Hispanic students gradually increased from 3.5 percent, in 1976, to about 12.5 percent of the college population in 2002. Enrollment of Native American students increased slightly in that same period. The one ethnic minority to show substantial gains was Asian Americans. Their representation increased to 7.1 percent of all students in 2002, up from 1.8 percent in 1976 (*Chronicle of Higher Education Almanac*, 2002:19).

Traditionally, the objectives of higher education were to make available to students the tools of learning, to open up new horizons for them to explore, and to help them to understand their cultural heritage. Today, by contrast, as a 1987 Carnegie Foundation report foresaw more than a decade ago, "careerism dominates the campus" (Boyer, 1987:102). Students view general education as an irritating interruption—an annoying detour on their way to their degree. The report finds that most students go to college to pursue a special field of study that leads to a career, comfortable living, and security from unemployment. For example, in 1999, 45,000 students applied for the approximately 16,000 spots in the nation's 125 medical schools, partly as a response to the decline in career opportunities in the high-paying fields of law and investment banking (Thomson, 1999). One-third of undergraduates would drop out if college did not increase their prospects of employment.

Most students (and parents) want to translate their education dollars into marketable skills. As a result, career-related education continues its dramatic increase, which began about a generation ago. Almost all colleges (see, for example, Steinberg, 2002), in response to the demand and competition for students, added new vocational majors and split up old ones into smaller pieces. New programs were created such as medical technology, computer programming, and police science. Colleges, which in the past had one major in business administration and limited M.B.A. programs, in response to marketplace demands have a dozen or so business-related majors such as fashion merchandising, foods and nutrition in business, and health services administration (see, for example, *Business Week*, 2002a). Gerontology, which hardly existed as an academic subject in the early 1970s, has become one of higher education's fastest-growing disciplines, and colleges and universities offer more than 1,300 different programs as growing numbers of elderly people create demands for practitioners and retraining opportunities as happened, for example, in the recently undersubscribed nursing profession (*Chronicle of Higher Education Almanac*, 2002). The vocationalization of higher education is being promoted both in two- and four-year colleges and universities. The emphasis seems to be on technically competent workers, not on a corps of free-thinking liberal arts graduates. The shift away from liberal arts and toward career-oriented vocational majors is not limited to American campuses. A similar trend prevails in European universities. It has even reached China, where there are "three ways"—black, gold and red—for students to pursue a career. The "black way" is to leave China to study abroad, to earn a black graduation cap and gown. "Gold" involves going into business in the hope of becoming rich. And, "red" refers to joining the Communist party and becoming a government official. In all three cases, students are driven by "blatant opportunism instead of devotion to the socialist ideals" in their academic work (Gargan, 1987).

The Great Training Robbery

Most Americans believe college is a necessity and a right and that the more education a person has, the better he or she will do in life (Arenson, 1997). Education seems to be the most popular solution for the individual's desire for success and social mobility. This idea is reflected in the growing trend toward "credentialism." The more society relies on formal education as its basic training device, the more individuals find that educational credentials are essential if they are to have access to jobs and opportunities for promotion. In fact, as noted earlier, the individual benefits are clear, getting a college education makes one richer. As these credentials become more and more important, mere experience in the labor market is downgraded. An emphasis on educational credentials has been said to be justified in that, because the economy has become more technical and complex, a more highly educated work force is necessary. Ivar Berg (1970) attacks this notion and argues that on every occupational level Americans tend to overestimate the value of education, denying employment opportunities to those with less education and demanding more education than most jobs require. Berg finds no relation between formal education and work productivity, turnover rates, work satisfaction, promotion, and success in business. Berg's observations are well documented in the literature. For example, a 1994 study already concluded that although a college degree has became a virtual prerequisite for getting ahead in the corporate world or the professions, only 46 percent of the wealthy business owners surveyed completed their college education; 29 percent never went to college, and 25 percent started but did not finish. Even those who can boast academic achievements do not put much faith in them, and only 33 percent said that educational background was important to their financial success (Bowers, 1994). This feeling is perhaps most pronounced among college professors and a 1995 Carnegie Foundation international survey of 20,000 faculty members in 14 countries concluded that most of them were unhappy about their salary—along with the lack of student preparation (Altbach & Lewis, 1995).

If anything, there is an inverse relation between amount of formal education and occupational performance. Berg notes that formal education plays one single role for blue-collar, white-collar, and engineer-scientist workers: It determines where one enters the occupational system. What is important, in other words, is that employers believe that formal education makes better workers and therefore use it as a criterion for hiring. But once hired, workers with more or less formal education exhibit no significant difference in work performance. The only apparent difference is in income, because workers with more formal education enter the labor force at higher levels and change jobs more often. There are questions being raised both at the marketplace and in the literature regarding the importance placed on credentials by both colleges and employers, especially when it can be shown that the educational requirements for entry into an occupation have little bearing on the activities of that occupation (see, for example, Ray & Mickelson, 1993).

Publish or Perish

Traditionally, the emphasis in colleges was quite clearly on teaching. The goal was to preserve and transmit existing truths rather than to advance knowledge. "Even as late as 1857, a committee of the Columbia College board of trustees attributed the poor quality of the college to the fact that three professors 'wrote books'" (Lewis, 1998:3). However, with the spread of graduate education modeled after German universities, faculty advancement and promotion soon became dependent on scholarly research rather than on teaching. A number of universities advocated "productive" work in an attempt to establish a "national reputation" (Lewis, 1998:7). By the turn of the century, many academics in universities lived by the code of "publish or perish," and they were judged only according to the merit of their research, rather than on their teaching. Today this trend is becoming even more pronounced. Evidence of publication and research is a crucial factor both in hiring as well as in retention and promotion, even though it is getting harder and harder to get one's ideas into print (Shapiro, 1996). Today, it seems that when the chips are down, it's published research, not classroom skills, that is likely to determine one's professional fate. An important preoccupation on campus is the attempt to determine the proper balance between research and teaching. Ideally, good teaching and quality research should flourish side by side (Boyer, 1987:127).

Publish and Perish

For several decades, the shift from unskilled labor to skilled, technical, and professional employment appeared to have created an inexhaustible demand for education. But by the 1970s, higher education caught up with the demand, and competent college graduates in many fields were unhappily scanning the help-wanted ads. For example, in 1965, there were two teaching vacancies for each new Ph.D. In 1972, graduates and vacancies were about equal. Two years later, the bottom fell out of the academic job market for newly minted Ph.D.s. Those in the humanities and the social sciences were particularly affected by it, and many graduates were unable to find jobs in academia. It was commonplace to have hundreds of qualified applicants for an assistant professorship at a small college in English, history, or even in sociology. Many departments were closed, and M.A. and Ph.D. programs were phased out, with a concomitant reduction in the number of tenured positions. For the few lucky ones who obtained an academic appointment, it was more often than not for a specified short time period, ranging from one to five years. At many colleges, it became very difficult (if not impossible) to get tenure. Many qualified graduates became frustrated by the shortage of academic jobs and sought placement outside of academia or kept seeking postdoctoral or part-time appointments. This is not the best of times in academe—many, indeed, would argue that it is the worst of times (see, for example, Altbach & Lewis, 1995). The academic job market for Ph.D.s remains bleak, especially in humanities and life sciences. For example, in 2000, 1,070 new Ph.D.s in English competed among themselves and with former graduates for 528 tenure-track assistant professorships (Hanson-Harding, 2002:17). The outlook in other fields is also discouraging. Typically, those who do not land good jobs remain as research assistants or poorly paid adjuncts (a nice word for part-time), or they try to break into industry. But despite poor job prospects and fiscal problems, the number of Ph.D.s has kept rising.

By the early 2000s, the days of glut in a growing number of academic fields are expected slowly to moderate as professors hired in the 1950s and 1960s start to retire. A major portion of academia's 526,000 full-time faculty members were hired during that period to teach the baby-boom generation. They have now started to retire or cut back—right at the time that the baby boom's boomlet and the early waves of the boomlet's boomlet begin to pour into colleges. It is estimated that between now and 2015, institutions of higher education will have to hire between 450,000 and 500,000 new faculty members. But many of the them will be part of the "invisible faculty" (Gappa & Leslie, 1993) and can look forward to only part-time work. Currently almost half of four-year faculty and 65 percent of two-year faculty are part timers.

Many are the campus equivalent of migrant workers, with no stake at all in the institutions for which they work. They earn about $1,500 per course, with no benefits or pension, and are considered higher education's working poor (Merik, 1996). Many of them hold several jobs at once, and spend the week rushing from one campus to the next. The growth in part-time faculty is, to a degree, a response to the tenure system, which had grown cumbersome and expensive, particularly for colleges with small endowments and shrinking revenues. Even though early retirement incentives have substantially lightened college payrolls, many institutions continue to replace retirees with adjunct faculty. Increasingly, undergraduates can expect to be taught by part-timers and adjuncts, leading to what some educators call "faceless departments" (Leatherman, 1997). In some instances, they may even end up with graduate students from other departments who lack formal training and experience in the discipline they are assigned to teach.

In sum, education over the years has undergone drastic changes. Universities have been transformed into huge complexes with enormous power, college students now far outnumber farmers in the United States, and there are some 1.8 million full-time employees in colleges and universities. The education level of the American population is steadily growing; more and more people graduate from high school; there is a steady decline in the proportion of dropouts; more and more high school graduates go on to college and professional schools; and, ironically, more and more people find it harder and harder to find a job after graduation. This situation is not unique to the United States. In Italy, many young people just keep studying—the average age of graduation is 28. Universities have become "parking lots" for young Italians unable to crack into the job market (Rhoads, 2002:A6). While the level of education goes up in the United States (not necessarily the quality), there are still over 1 billion people worldwide who cannot read or write, which represents an estimated illiteracy rate of 18.5 percent. The growth of population in the world still outpaces the advance in literacy rates.

THE ECONOMY

The structure of an economic system is based on production, distribution, and consumption. *Production* involves the assembling and applying of resources, and it requires land, capital, and labor. *Land* refers to physical territory and resources; *capital* consists of the means of production—of money, equipment, and tools; and *labor* pertains to people who produce goods and services. *Distribution* entails some system of exchange in which goods and services have some equivalent values. Finally, *consumption* refers to the utilization of goods and services produced by the economy.

Production

In traditional societies, production is located in family units. Subsistence farming is predominant, and other industry is supplementary—but still attached to the family and village. Neil J. Smelser (1976:151) points out that as the economy develops, many of the production activities are removed from the family-community complex. In agriculture, the introduction of money crops differentiates between the social contexts of production and consumption. The use of agricultural wage labor separates work roles from what previously might have been a family productive unit. In industry, there are several levels of differentiation. In the simplest form, household industry, only the workers' own needs are supplied, and there is no surplus to enter the market. "Handicraft production" differentiates between production and consumption, even though the latter may take place in the local community. On the other hand, "cottage industry" usually involves a differentiation between consumption and community because production is for unknown consumers in the market, usually through wholesalers. In manufacturing and factory systems, the worker is segregated from capital and frequently from his or her family. It brings about a structural differentiation in the labor force as a response to the exigencies of production and marketing. More specialized and efficient roles and organizations are required than the one found in traditional family and community structures. Changes in the production process bring about an increase in the division of labor, with concomitant alterations in the composition, size, and variety of the labor force.

Most economies today, whether fully industrialized or not, contain three basic sectors, with the proportion of labor force in each sector depending on society's technological development. The primary sector refers to that part of the economy that directly generates raw materials from the natural environment, such as fishing, mining, or agriculture. The primary sector dominates the economies of preindustrial societies, where virtually the entire population is engaged in hunting, gathering, or agricultural activities. The secondary sector refers to that part of the economy that transforms raw materials into manufactured goods. Examples of this sector include the refining of petroleum, the manufacture of wood into furniture, metals into tools, building materials, and automobiles. Most of the labor force is engaged in "blue-collar" occupations in this sector. The tertiary sector refers to that part of the economy that generates services rather than goods. The

United States became the first country in the 1950s to have more than half of its labor force engaged in the tertiary sector—providing services and processing information (Naisbitt & Aburdene, 1990:14–15) in locations such as offices, hospitals, universities, and restaurants. After considering some changes in the labor force of the United States, I will return to this point.

The civilian labor force has grown from 22 million in 1890 to over 135 million in 2002 (U.S. Department of Labor, 1987:9; U.S. Bureau of the Census, 2002:396). Although the proportion of the population represented in the labor force remained relatively constant at about 66 percent of the civilian noninstitutional population over sixteen years of age, there have been significant changes in its composition over the years.

The percentage of blue-collar (manual) workers was a close second to those employed on farms at the turn of the century. Between World War I and World War II, because of the growth of industrialization and the accelerated decline of farm employment, blue-collar workers comprised almost 40 percent of the labor force. But by the mid-1950s, the percentage of white-collar workers exceeded those in blue-collar occupations, and this gap has increased greatly between 1960 and 1987. Technological advances that increased production also contributed to reducing the number of manual workers. The decline in steel and automobile industries, due primarily to competition from abroad, cost the country hundreds of thousands of blue-collar jobs. The shift from producing goods to service industries, to be discussed shortly, also played a significant role in the long-term decline in the number of blue-collar workers. In 1997 there were some gains as more and more people with higher education filled traditional blue-collar jobs, which reached 32.8 million (Hershey, 1997).

Those in clerical and related occupations represented 3 percent of the labor force in 1900. By the mid-1990s, they represented over 20 percent. This category includes such occupations as word processors, clerks, typists, proofreaders, and office machine operators. Some are in entirely new fields. For example, in 1960 there were approximately 12,000 "computer specialists" in America. By 1970, the number had grown to 260,000, and today it is close to 2 million. Contrary to popular belief, the introduction of new technology, such as, for example, computers for office data application, does not necessarily result in the reduction of employees. When computers were introduced in the mid-1950s, some experts predicted that large numbers of clerical and kindred workers would be displaced and that job opportunities for millions of people, in one of the largest occupational employment categories, would be curtailed. Yet over the last three decades, employment of clerical workers has continued to increase, and between 1972 and 1986, the number of such workers grew by 40 percent (Mark, 1987:27). Office computerization made possible work that previously had been impractical because it would have been too costly and time-consuming. It gave rise to new kinds of data analyses, extending the scope of activities for many industries, thus creating new jobs. In addition, it created new occupations such as tape and disk librarian and console operator. New industries were also created to manufacture computers and related paraphernalia. As a result, thousands are employed in manufacturing microelectronics devices, advanced communication equipment, and other technologies that are gaining prominence (Perrolle, 1987).

The percentage of people in the professions and related occupations also quadrupled since the turn of the century. One reason for the growth in the number of professionals is the greater sophistication in knowledge, techniques, and machinery, resulting in a growing demand for technically trained people (Adler, 1992). There is also a growing demand for services from such diverse occupations as accounting, divorce law, and psychiatry. Many occupations are also becoming professionalized (Ritzer & Walczak, 1986). Their members are changing their names to something more prestigious; for example, "beautician" becomes "hairstylist," and "mortician" becomes "funeral director." They are also developing codes of ethics and rights of passage whereby members may gain access to the occupation as professionals. This trend is accompanied by an increase in licensing requirements for many occupations.

There was also a dramatic increase in the number of women in the labor force since 1900—from about 5 million then to over 59 million today. Around the turn of the century, few married women entered the work force because their wages were much lower than those of single women (Bianchi & Spain, 1986:166). As the wage differential started to narrow, more and more married women increased their participation in the workplace. Rising educational attainment of women, along with economic growth during the 1950s, the increasing divorce rate, the women's movement, changing attitudes about the desirability (and necessity) of working outside the home, and the rising consumption aspirations are among the main factors bringing about the current high level of labor-force participation among women.

Another major trend is the aging of the labor force. After rising less than 3 percent between 1979 and 1992, the number of U.S. workers fifty-five and over is expected to increase 38 percent by 2005—more than either blacks or women (Shellenbarger & Hymowitz, 1994:1). As America ages, older workers are increasingly perceived as a management problem—rigid, hard to retain, and expensive. Gray hair may be a fixture of executive suites, but is becoming unfashionable in middle management and lower down in the ranks. Instead of a fifty-year-old, employers often want younger people who cost much less and who are considered more flexible and less demanding. The current corporate downsizings have greatly affected workers aged fifty and over, with many companies making heavy use of early retirement offers or outright terminations. As a result, a new class of permanently unemployed or underemployed middle-aged workers is emerging. There is also a surge in age-bias lawsuits as more and more older workers are being laid off.

Distribution

In traditional societies, goods and services are exchanged on a noneconomic basis without the use of money or a clearly delineated market system. In such a society, one does not necessarily exchange scarce goods or labor in order to get what one needs. A self-regulating price market for the exchange of goods and services is brought about by the advent of economic surplus and the introduction of money as a means of exchange. It should be noted, however, that not all exchanges of goods and services take place in a market situation. For example, the redistribution of wealth through charity or progressive taxation is an exchange of potentially marketable commodities outside of the market. Furthermore, "The mobilization of economic resources for public goals—through eminent domain, taxation, direct appropriation, and selective service—involves the transfer of economic goods and services without the intrusion of an economic market" (Smelser, 1976:119).

The economist Karl Polanyi and his associates (1957) suggest that economic activities fall into three main patterns of exchange. The first pattern is reciprocative, which is illustrated by the ritualized gift giving among families, clans, and tribes. Farmers in many societies help each other at harvest. Goods and services are given because it is traditional to do so. The only principle of calculation is the loose principle that the giving and receiving of goods or services should "balance out" in the long run.

The second form of exchange is redistributive. This involves bringing economic goods and services to a central source—usually governmental—and then redistributing them throughout the populace. Several examples of this form occurred in ancient Asian and African civilizations. Modern examples are organized charity or progressive taxation. Like reciprocative exchange, redistributive forms are characterized by an absence of economic calculation and price payment. In this situation, the principle of calculation seems to be one of justice or equity based on a traditional notion of what the recipients deserve.

The third form of exchange, the one that is most common in the Western world, is simply referred to as exchange. In this type of distribution, economic goods and services are brought into a market context. Prices are not standardized on the basis of tradition but result from bargaining for economic advantage. Formal economic analysis is equipped to handle only this type of exchange. In modern societies, distribution can also be seen as a one-way exchange, whereby goods and services are given to individuals without receiving an exchangeable market value in return. Examples of this one-way exchange would include redistribution through taxation, donations, public support of children, welfare, Medicaid, and legal aid (Boulding, 1973).

Consumption

"Production not only supplies the need with an object," wrote Marx, "but also supplies the object with the need" (quoted by Anderson, 1976: 164). In traditional societies, the limited production obviously does not supply the object with too many needs for consumption. By contrast, modern economic systems depend on the sustaining and creating of needs. Growth in the economic domain is based upon the continuous expanding of consumption, and . . . "consumption, rather than being the privilege of the elite, is becoming the duty of the masses" in modern societies (Kando, 1975:14). In a fascinating book entitled *Land of Desire*, William Leach (1993) contends that 1880 was probably the last year one could live in America without trying to be persuaded to want more things. By the end of the nineteenth century, merchants have developed a sophisticated system of enticement to turn their fellow citizens into shoppers, and a new consumer culture was developed—supported by hundreds of magazines with full-page ads aimed at turning the country into a "land of desire," awash in consumer goods.

Traditional societies often have sumptuary laws, or laws that lend the power of the "state" to moral and religious norms governing consumption. Such laws establish differential consumption by, for example, stipulating that only aristocrats can wear fur or silk or carry a sword. In caste, multireligious, or multiethnic societies there are strong normative traditions that define appropriate forms of consumption for each level or segment of society, especially in the areas of food, drink, and clothing.

In the United States, a unique feature of consumption is that a large proportion of the American population consumes the same items and services. A tendency of industrial economy is to create a national or international market for products and services and to transform all citizens into equivalent consumers. A mass-production economy obviously does not seek to restrict consumption according to social position or religious or ethnic factors. The only restriction on consumption is income. Marketers have long recognized this, and a variety of advertising messages are targeted at children to ask for specific products. [The food industry alone spends an estimated $33 billion a year on ads and promotions, much of it targeted at children (*Business Week*, 2002b:112), and for contrast, Americans spend $34 billion annually on various diet products, from sugar-free sodas and weight-loss supplements to diet programs.] In fact, children are what might be called "surrogate salesmen" who persuade their parents to buy what they want. In an interesting book, *Kids as Customers,* James U. McNeal (1992) describes the various techniques children use to nag their parents. He classifies juvenile nagging tactics ("pester power") used by kids in various major categories. A *pleading* nag is the one accompanied by repetitions of certain words such "please," or "mom, mom, mom." A *persistent* nag involved prolonged requests for a desired product and may include comments such as "I am going to ask one more time." *Forceful* nags are rather pushy and may include subtle threats such as "I am going to ask Grandfather, Dad, etc." *Demonstrative* nags are often characterized by temper tantrums, throwing things, breath-holding, tears, a refusal to leave the store, grabbing items, and other forms of public nuisance. *Sugar-coated* nags offer affection in return for the purchase and include declarations such as "you are the best mom." *Threatening* nags are juvenile forms of blackmail, vows of eternal hatred, and running away if something is not bought. Finally, *pity* nags imply that the child will be heartbroken, teased, or socially shunned if something is not bought by the parent. These appeals are used in various combinations, and children soon learn which ones work. They seem to stick to those that prove to be effective.

Of course, the various economic classes spend different amounts in their overall consumption. Differences in consumption, and the resulting sharp distinctions in prestige, do not exist in the United States to the same degree as in other developed countries. The primary reason is that the majority of the population consumes a wide range of similar products, often brand-name goods with national prestige: food (staples as well as nonstaples); beverages (milk, beer, soft drinks); household products (soap, waxes); household appliances (refrigerators, vacuum cleaners); clothes; and such items as computers, entertainment products, and sporting goods. The important point is that a vast portion of the public consumes these goods in common, regardless of income and often on credit, since only 64 percent of American households have any income left after paying for the necessities of life such as food, clothing, housing, and taxes (McLaughlin, 1994).

Personal consumption expenditures (food, clothing, household operation, medical care, transportation, etc.) more than doubled in the United States in the past ten years, to more than $7,300 billion (U.S. Bureau of the Census, 2002:452). In addition to inflation, this increase in expenditure is associated with an increase in per-capita disposable income; continued improvement of technology generating new products available to be demanded; and an increase in leisure time, due partly to the availability of various labor-saving devices, which, of course, increases the capacity to consume various leisure-related products such as travel, TV, and entertainment.

While personal consumption expenditures doubled, personal disposable income increased from $2,254 billion to over $6,500 billion for the same time period. The average adult in the United States has 2,650 leisure hours per year. This comes to over 110 days per year. Much of the increase in leisure time is spent on consumption. Needs and desires for new products are constantly being created by advertisements and reinforced by increased time spent watching television. In the United States, 99 percent of all households have TV sets, almost all in color. The average American between the ages of three and sixteen spends more time in front of the television set than in school. The average adult woman spends more than thirty hours a week, and the average adult man some twenty-five hours per week, watching TV. This is in contrast to the roughly two hours a week spent reading books (which explains why many of the 62,000 or so new titles published annually remain unread) and 3.5 hours a week devoted to newspapers and magazines (Carvajal, 1997).

John Kenneth Galbraith (1973:33–37) points out that the ideal consumers are nonworking middle- and upper-class women, a group with day-long TV exposure. He sees these women as serving a crypto-servant function in household administration and maintenance that involves goods, food, child care, social enjoyment, and social displays. He observes that "The servant role of women is critical for the expansion of consumption in modern economy. . . . In few matters has the economic system been so successful in establishing values and moulding resulting behaviour to its needs as in the shaping of a womanly attitude and behaviour. . . . Thus it is women in their crypto-servant role of administrators who make an indefinitely increasing consumption possible." The role of youth and women in maintaining consumption is evident in the manner in which advertising promotion and TV content are fixed. Youth and women are more likely than men to have the time to consume, and consumption does require large amounts of time. For many, consumption becomes an entire way of life.

Adjusting for inflation, the percentage of American households with annual incomes of $75,000 or more rose to 18.6 percent in 1995, the latest for which data are available, from 13 percent in 1982. About 39 percent of all the households have incomes of $50,000 or more, up from 32.8 percent in 1982. And the upper 40 percent of households account for 60 percent of the nation's consumer spending (Uchitelle, 1997). This segment of the population is increasingly becoming the target for marketers who push the sale of higher profit and higher priced luxury or gadget-laden merchandise, such as electric toothbrushes with a timer—for an extra $20. This process is called product differentiation and has been around for some time in different versions. For example, blue collar workers moved up from Chevrolets to Pontiacs, while middle-level managers made the jump from Pontiacs to Oldsmobiles, and upper-echelon executives from the Olds to Cadillac.

As disposable income increases in society, consumption patterns undergo drastic alterations. The proportion of income spent on food, housing, and religious and welfare activities diminishes while there is an important increase in expenditures on foreign travel, tourism, pets, recreation, private education, and personal care. For example, expenditures for overseas travel increased from $3.9 billion in 1970 to more than $35 billion in 1994, and

Americans spend over $15 billion (more than the GNP of many small countries) on pet supplies. The bare-bones costs of owning a pet are, for example, $8,665 and $11,580, respectively, during the average life span of a cat and dog (Eaton, 1994). Health insurance around $100 per year for pet HMOs.; grooming; special diets and spas are additional and for many, necessary, expenses (Kelley, 1997). In 1993, 42 percent of the U.S. households had at least one pet to keep them company (Crispell, 1994). Finally, while the way Americans dissolve their unions has become cheaper and easier with no-fault divorces and pre-nuptial agreements, wedding costs are escalating; the average is around $16,000. In New York City, a wedding can cost $1 million and nuptials costing $100,000 are common enough that caterers consider them mid-range; the lower end is around $25,000. Bridal gowns are extra (White, 1997).

In addition to the general increase in expenditures by consumers, there seems to be a moderate decline of ostentatious display by the rich in the United States (but not by the *nouveaux riches* in sports and entertainment) and an increase in what David Caplovitz (1963:13) calls compensatory consumption. Compensatory consumption refers to the purchase of selected items of the standard middle-class package by the poor, such as an expensive pair of shoes, an expensive hat, or a color TV. This is their way of compensating for lack of other symbols of success and status.

Changes in consumption patterns are accompanied by the growth of consumer-based activities. In the public sphere, Alan Gartner and Frank Riessman (1974:76–78) point out that in 1960 no state had consumer affairs offices. However, thirty-three did by 1970; and by mid-1973, all fifty states had such offices. Nationally, a number of consumer protection laws have been passed, and 138 public interest groups with over 400,000 dues-paying members were formed to work on consumer issues. Membership in consumer credit unions more than doubled during the course of the late 1980s and mid-1990s.

In sum, these are some of the changes that occurred in the triad of production, consumption, and distribution in the economic sphere. The general trend in developed countries seems to be the continuous increase in production, accompanied by a growing general level of income and an increase in consumption expenditures. There is also a trend toward the reduction of extremes in consumption among the various segments in society.

SUMMARY

This chapter examined changes that have occurred in several specific spheres. It should be recalled that social change may originate in any institutional area, bringing about changes in other areas, which, in turn, make for further adaptations in the initial sphere of change. Changes that have taken place in the various spheres are interrelated; they influence each other as well as the course of society.

Many of the dramatic trends have slowed down or halted in some areas, while in others, new currents have set in. The decline in the functions of the American family has been compensated for by an ascent of its "companionship" function. The trend is toward a nuclear family with egalitarian conjugal roles. The size of the family is decreasing, and there is an increase in childless families. The divorce rates are up and the new morality seems to reverberate in the family structure.

The population of the world is expected to double in about forty-three years at the 2002 rate of annual natural increase. In developing countries, the consequences of this rapid growth rate are felt in economic, social, and political institutions. Mortality rates are declining, and life expectancy is on the increase. The trend in fertility is downward, but with little effect on growth rates as a result of more rapid declines in mortality rates. As a result of the demographic transition, modern societies have both low mortality and fertility rates, and several European countries are experiencing a zero or negative population growth. There is an increase in migration and a change in the place of origin of immigrants into the United States. There has been a pronounced increase in the dependency ratio in developed countries in recent years.

In the sphere of stratification, an important change is the opening up of opportunities for much higher rates of mobility. The trend is toward equality, but it is questionable whether absolute equality can ever be attained.

In power relations, important changes have occurred in the ruling elite over time. Access to the political elite has became open to wider and wider strata of the population, and there is a proliferation of "power elites." The political power of nonpoliticians has increased enormously, and this has been accompanied by the decentralization of power. The scope of political participation has been widened, but there is still room for expansion for minorities and ethnic groups.

Education is now separated from the family and, to a great extent, from community life. The development of schools and universities spread education from a monopoly of a few to the property of the masses. This trend was associated with changes in curriculum and the lengthening of the education process for more and more students. Today there seems to be too much emphasis on credentials by employers. Test scores are declining in high schools, and college education is becoming increasingly vocationalized. The marketability of a liberal arts degree is on the decline, and the market for Ph.D.s remains tight. For some younger faculty members, the credo of "publish or perish" is slowly changing to "publish and perish."

In the economic sphere, changes in production have been associated with alterations in the size and composition of the labor force. Farming has declined dramatically, but there have been important increases in the categories of craftspeople and kindred workers and in professional and technical jobs. The number of women in the labor force is rapidly increasing, and the composition of the labor force changed from predominantly goods-producing to predominantly service-producing workers. With the advent of economic surplus and money, forms of distribution have changed from reciprocative to redistributive and exchange. The trend in consumption is toward more leisure and recreational goods, accompanied by a decline in the proportion of expenditures for the basics such as food or housing. There is an increased concern with the protection of consumers, as evidenced by the number of recent laws and organizations. In the next chapter, the duration of change will be examined.

SUGGESTED FURTHER READINGS

ECONOMIST. "The Longest Journey, A Survey of Migration," November 2, 2002, pp. 1–16. An excellent current overview of global migration trends.

EYETSEMITAN, FRANK E., AND JAMES T. GIRE. *Aging and Adult Development in the Developing World: Applying Western Theories and Concepts.* Westport, CT: Praeger, 2003. A thought-provoking review of the attempts to use Western theories and perspectives in the study of aging in the developing world.

GILBERT, DENNIS. *The American Class Structure in an Age of Growing Inequality*, 6th ed. Belmont, CA: Wadsworth Publishing Company, 2002. An up-to-date synthesis of the most pertinent social science research on stratification patterns and changes in the United States.

GRANT, LINDSEY. *Too Many People: The Case for Reversing Growth.* Santa Ana, CA: Seven Locks Press, 2001. A convincing argument against the notion of many politicians and businessmen that the more the merrier.

JANSSENS, ANGELIQUE. *Family and Social Change: The Household as a Process in an Industrializing Community.* Cambridge, England: Cambridge University Press, 1993. An empirical study on the influence of industrialization on family relationships in a Dutch community between 1850 and 1920 from the structural–functionalist perspective.

RAVITCH, DIANE. *The Language Police: How Pressure Groups Restrict What Children Learn.* New York: Knopf, 2003. Comments on the swings of the educational pendulum from one extreme to another.

RITZER, GEORGE, AND DAVID WALCZAK. *Working: Conflict and Change*, 3rd ed. Englewood Cliffs, NJ: Prentice Hall, 1986. A sociological overview of work in America.

STEINBERG, JACQUES. *The Gatekeepers: Inside the Admissions Process of a Premier College.* New York: Viking, 2002. An eye-opener on how the college crapshoot works. The book describes the complex and little understood processes involved in college admission.

TEITELBAUM, MICHAEL S., AND JAY M. WINTER. *A Question of Numbers: High Migration, Low Fertility, and the Politics of National Identity.* New York: Hill & Wang, 1998. In addition to a good review of the basic demographic trends and concepts, this book raises a number of controversial issues.

UNITED NATIONS POPULATION FUND. *State of the World Population 2002: People, Poverty and Possibilities*. New York: United Nations Population Fund, 2002. A statistical overview of the various deleterious consequences of population growth, with some projections at various time horizons and recommendations for trying to cope with anticipated demographic developments.

WASTE, ROBERT J. *Independent Cities: Rethinking U.S. Urban Policy*. New York: Oxford University Press, 1998. A discussion of the various facets of power relations, particularly at the community level.

REFERENCES

ABERNETHY, VIRGINIA. "Changing the USA's Population Signals for a Sustainable Future," *Futures*, 26 (2) March 1994, pp. 138–146.

ADLER, PAUL S. (ed.). *Technology and the Future of Work*. New York: Oxford University Press, 1992.

ALTBACH, PHILIP G., AND LIONEL S. LEWIS. "Professorial Attitudes—An International Survey," *Change*, 27 (6) November–December 1995, pp. 50–58.

ALTHAUS, FRANCES A. "U.S. Birthrate Decreased in 1991, but Nonmarital Fertility Continued to Rise," *Family Planning Perspectives*, 26 (1) January–February 1994, pp. 13–15.

ANDERSON, CHARLES H. *The Sociology of Survival: Social Problems of Growth*. Homewood, IL: Dorsey Press, 1976.

APPLEBOME, PETER. "Record School Enrollments, Now and Ahead," *The New York Times*, August 22, 1997, p. A8.

ARENSON, KAREN W. "Rationing Higher Education. Why College Isn't for Everyone," *The New York Times*, August 31, 1997, p. E1.

ARIES, PHILLIPPE. *Centuries of Childhood*, trans. Robert Baldick. New York: Knopf, 1962.

ARMBRUSTER, FRANK E. "The More We Spend, the Less Children Learn," *The New York Times Magazine*, August 28, 1977, pp. 9–11, 53–60.

BARBER, BERNARD. "Change and Stratification Systems." In Amitai Etzioni and Eva Etzioni-Halevy (eds.), *Social Change: Sources, Patterns, and Consequences*, 2nd ed. New York: Basic Books, 1973, pp. 199–209.

BARNES, JULIAN A. "The SAT Revolution: The New Test Spells the End of IQ—and Big Changes for American Education," *U.S. News & World Report*, November 11, 2002, pp. 51–60.

BERG, IVAR. *Education and Jobs: The Great Training Robbery*. New York: Praeger, 1970.

BERGER, PETER L. "Two Cheers for Class," *First Things: A Monthly Journal of Religion and Public Life*, 64 June–July 1996, pp. 18–21.

BHAGWATI, JAGDISH, AND MILIND RAO. "Foreign Students Spur US Brain Gain," *The Wall Street Journal*, August 31, 1994, p. A8.

BIANCHI, SUZANNE M., AND DAPHNE SPAIN. *American Women in Transition*. New York: Russell Sage, 1986.

BIERSTEDT, ROBERT. *Power and Progress: Essays on Sociological Theory*. New York: McGraw-Hill, 1974.

BLAU, PETER, AND OTIS DUDLEY DUNCAN. *The American Occupational Structure*. New York: Free Press, 1967.

BOTTOMORE, TOM. *Elites in Society*, 2nd ed. New York: Routledge, 1993.

BOULDING, KENNETH E. "Urbanization and the Grants Economy: An Introduction." In Kenneth E. Boulding, Martin Pfaff, and Anita Pfaff (eds.), *Transfers in an Urbanized Economy*. Belmont, CA: Wadsworth, 1973, pp. 1–6.

BOWERS, BRENT. "Sheepskin Isn't a Requirement for Success in Business," *The Wall Street Journal*, November 1, 1994, p. B2.

BOYER, ERNEST L. *College: The Undergraduate Experience in America*. New York: Harper & Row, 1987.

BROWN, LESTER R. *State of the World 2001*. London: Earthscan, 2001.

BROWN, LESTER R., HAL KANE, AND DAVID MALIN ROODMAN. *Vital Signs, 1997*. New York: W. W. Norton, 1997.

BUMPASS, LARRY, AND HSIEN-HEN LU. "Trends in Cohabitation and Implications for Children's Family Contexts in the U.S.," *Population Studies*, 54, 2000, pp. 29–41.

BURGESS, ERNEST W. "The Family in a Changing Society." In Amitai Etzioni and Eva Etzioni-Halevy (eds.), *Social Change: Sources, Patterns, and Consequences*, 2nd ed. New York: Basic Books, 1973, pp. 191–198.

BURTLESS, GARY (ed.). *Does Money Matter? The Effect of School Resources on Student Achievement and Adult Success*. Washington, DC: Brookings Institution Press, 1996.

Business Week. "The Best B-Schools," October 21, 2002a, pp. 85–110.

Business Week. "Why We're So Fat—Fast Food at School, Huge Portions, and Relentless TV Ads Make It Easy," October 21, 2002b, pp. 112–114.

CAMPBELL, ELAINE. *The Childless Marriage: An Exploratory Study of Couples Who Do Not Want Children*. New York: Tavistock, 1986.

CAPLOVITZ, DAVID. *The Poor Pay More: Consumer Practices of Low-income Families*. New York: Free Press, 1963.

CARVAJAL, DOREEN. "You Can't Read Books Fast Enough. Read Faster. You're Already Another 166 Books Behind," *The New York Times*, August 24, 1997, pp. E1, E3.

CASSIDY, JOHN. "The Melting-Pot Myth," *The New Yorker*, July 14, 1997, pp. 40–43.

CHEN, LINCOLN C., FRIEDERIKE WITTGENSTEIN, AND ELIZABETH MCKEON. "The Upsurge of Mortality in Russia: Causes and Policy Implications," *Population and Development Review*, 22 (3) September 1996, pp. 517–531.

Chronicle of Higher Education Almanac. August 30, 2002. (Annual Supplement to *The Chronicle of Higher Education*.)

COMFORT, ALEX. *The Joy of Sex*. Revised ed. New York: Crown Publishers, 2002.

COWLEY, GEOFFREY. "Fighting Poverty, Fighting AIDS," *Newsweek*, January 6, 2003, p. 72.

CRISPELL, DIANE. "Pet Projections," *American Demographics*, 16 (9) September 1994, p. 59.

CROSSETTE, BARBARA. "U.N. Meeting Facing Angry Debate on Population," *The New York Times*, September 4, 1994, pp. 1 and 4.

DEMOS, JOHN. *A Little Commonwealth: Family Life in Plymouth*. New York: Oxford, 1970.

DEWITT, PAULA MERGENHAGAN. "Breaking Up Is Hard to Do," *American Demographics*, 14 (10) October 1992, pp. 52–57.

DYE, THOMAS R. "Community Power and Public Policy." In Robert J. Waste (ed.), *Community Power: Directions for Future Research*. Beverly Hills, CA: Sage Publications, 1986, pp. 29–51.

EATON, LESLIE. "Hey, Big Spenders," *The New York Times*, September 11, 1994, pp. 1F and 6F.

Economist. "For Richer, for Poorer," November 5, 1994, pp. 19–21.

Economist. "The Costs of Learning: Research Indicates that Quality of Education is Unrelated to Amount of Money Spent on Education," February 15, 1997a, pp. 26–27.
Economist. "Education and the Wealth of Nations," March 29, 1997b, pp. 15–17.
Economist. "Healthy Life Expectancy," November 2, 2002a, p. 98.
Economist. "The Longest Journey: A Survey of Migration," November 2, 2002b, pp. 1–16.
Economist. "Returns to Education," November 2, 2002c, p. 96.
Economist. "Outward Bound," September 28, 2002d, pp. 24–25.
EHRLICH, PAUL R., AND ANNE H. EHRLICH. *Population, Resources, Environment*, 2nd ed. San Francisco: Freeman, 1972.
EPSTEIN, JOSEPH. *Snobbery: The American Version*. Boston: Houghton-Miffin Company, 2002.
ESHLEMAN, J. ROSS. *The Family*, 10th ed. Boston: Allyn & Bacon, 2003.
EYETSEMITAN, FRANK E., AND JAMES T. GIRE. *Aging and Adult Development in the Developing World: Applying Western Theories and Concepts*. Westport, CT: Praeger, 2003.
FRANK, STEPHEN E. "Dear Mom and Dad: Today at College I Learned How to Spit Wine in a Spittoon," *The Wall Street Journal*, October 5, 1994, p. B1.
GABRIEL, TRIP. "Pack Dating: For a Good Time, Call a Crowd—On College Campuses, Many Avoid Pairing Off," *The New York Times*, January 5, 1997, p. E22.
GALBRAITH, JOHN KENNETH. *Economics and the Public Purpose*. Boston: Houghton Mifflin, 1973.
GAPPA, JUDITH M., AND DAVID W. LESLIE. *The Invisible Faculty: Improving the Status of Part-Timers in Higher Education*. San Francisco: Jossey-Bass, 1993.
GARGAN, EDWARD A. "Students in China Turn Cynical and Apathetic," *The New York Times*, July 5, 1987, p. 3E.
GARTNER, ALAN, AND FRANK RIESSMAN. *The Service Society and the Consumer Vanguard*. New York: Harper & Row, 1974.
GELLES, RICHARD J. *Contemporary Families: A Sociological View*. Thousand Oaks, CA: Sage Publications, 1995.
GERTH, HANS H., AND C. WRIGHT MILLS, eds. and trans. From Max Weber, *Essays in Sociology*. New York: Oxford, 1946.
GILBERT, DENNIS. *The American Class Structure in an Age of Growing Inequality*, 6th ed. Belmont, CA: Wadsworth Publishing Company, 2002.
GILBERT, DENNIS, AND JOSEPH A. KAHL. *The American Class Structure: A New Synthesis*, 3rd ed. Chicago: Dorsey Press, 1993.
GOBER, PATRICIA. "Americans on the Move," *Population Bulletin*, 48 (3) November 1993, pp. 2–41.
GOODE, WILLIAM J. "Industrialization and Family Change." In S. N. Eisenstadt (ed.), *Comparative Perspectives on Social Change*. Boston: Little, Brown, 1968, pp. 47–62.
GORER, GEOFFREY. *Death, Grief, and Mourning*. New York: Doubleday, 1965.
GRANT, LINDSEY. *Too Many People: The Case for Reversing Growth*. Santa Ana, CA: Seven Locks Press, 2001.
GRAY, LOUISE. "After Vice and Versa—Social Change and Evolution of Multiple Gender Identities," *New Statesman & Society*, 9 (393) March 8, 1996, pp. 31–32.
HACKER, ANDREW. *Money: Who Has How Much and Why?* New York: Scribner, 1997.
HANSON-HARDING, BRIAN. "Scholars in a Teenage Wasteland. For Ph.D.s, Unexpected Joys in Teaching High School," *The New York Times*, Education Life, Section 4/A, November 10, 2002, pp. 18–19.

HARF, JAMES E., AND B. THOMAS TROUT. *The Politics of Global Resources: Population, Food, Energy, and Environment.* Durham, NC: Duke University Press, 1986.

HAYT, ELIZABETH. "It's Never Too Late To Be a Virgin; No More Sex Till the Wedding, Some Brides-to-Be Say," *The New York Times,* August 4, 2002, Section 9, pp. 1 and 6.

HEER, DAVID M., AND JILL S. GRIGSBY. *Society and Population,* 3rd ed. Englewood Cliffs, NJ: Prentice Hall, 1992.

HERNNSTEIN, RICHARD J., AND CHARLES MURRAY. *The Bell Curve: Intelligence and Class Structure in American Life.* New York: Free Press, 1994.

HERSHEY, ROBERT D., JR. "The Rise of the Working Class: Blue-Collar Jobs Gain, but the Work Changes in Tone," *The New York Times,* September 3, 1997, pp. C1, C2.

HERSHEY, ROBERT D., JR. "Suddenly State Universities Have More Allure," *The New York Times,* November 10, 2002, p. 8BU.

HERTZLER, J. O. *American Social Institutions.* Boston: Allyn & Bacon, 1961.

HOLMES, STEVEN A. "Birthrate for Unwed Women Up 70% Since '83, Study Says," *The New York Times,* July 20, 1994, pp. A1 and A7.

HONAN, WILLIAM H. "S.A.T. Math Scores Improve, But Verbal Results Stay Flat," *The New York Times,* August 27, 1997, p. A12.

INGRASSIA, LAWRENCE. "Danes Don't Debate Same-Sex Marriages, They Celebrate Them," *The New York Times,* June 8, 1994, pp. 1A and 8A.

JAMA, The Journal of the American Medical Association. "Infant Mortality—United States, 1991," 271 (1) 1994, pp. 15–17.

JANSSENS, ANGELIQUE. *Family and Social Change: The Household as a Process in an Industrializing Community.* Cambridge, England: Cambridge University Press, 1993.

JEJEEBHOY, SHIREEEN J., AND REBECCA J. COOK. "State Accountability for Wife-Beating: The Indian Challenge," *The Lancet,* 349 (9052) March 1, 1997.

JOHNSON, KIRK. "Gay Divorce: Few Markers in This Realm," *The New York Times,* August 12, 1994, p. A16.

JONES, GAVIN W. "Modernization and Divorce: Contrasting Trends in Islamic Southeast Asia and the West," *Population and Development Review,* 23 (1) March 1997, pp. 95–115.

KANDO, THOMAS M. *Leisure and Popular Culture in Transition.* St. Louis: Mosby, 1975.

KELLER, SUZANNE. *Beyond the Ruling Class: Strategic Elites in Modern Society.* New York: Random House, 1963.

KELLEY, TINA. "See Spot Run. See Spot Fall. Call Spot's H.M.O.," *The New York Times,* July 20, 1997, p. F10.

KOTEN, JOHN. "Steady Progress Disrupted by Turbulence in Economy," *The Wall Street Journal,* March 11, 1987, p. 33.

KRUGMAN, PAUL. "For Richer—How the Permissive Capitalism of the Boom Destroyed American Equality," *The New York Times Magazine,* October 20, 2002, pp. 62–78 and 141–142.

KUZNETS, SIMON. *Population, Capital, and Growth.* New York: W. W. Norton, 1973.

LANCASTER, JOHN. "Frantic Search for a Bride in India," *The Seattle Times,* December 3, 2002, p. A11.

LASSONDE, LOUISE. *Coping with Population Challenges.* London: Earthscan, 1997.

LAUMANN, EDWARD O., ROBERT T. MICHAEL, JOHN H. GAGNON, AND STUART MICHAELS. *The Social Organization of Sexuality: Sexual Practices in the United States.* Chicago: University of Chicago Press, 1994.

LEACH, WILLIAM. *Land of Desire: Merchants, Power, and the Rise of a New American Culture.* New York: Pantheon Books, 1993.

LEATHERMAN, COURTNEY. "Reliance of Lecturers Said to Produce 'Faceless Departments'," *The Chronicle of Higher Education*, March 28, 1997, p. A12.

LENSKI, GERHARD. *Power and Privilege: A Theory of Social Stratification.* New York: McGraw-Hill, 1966.

LESLIE, GERALD R., AND SHEILA K. KORMAN. *The Family in Social Context*, 7th ed. New York: Oxford, 1989.

LEWIN, TAMAR. "Fearing Disease, Teens Alter Sexual Practices," *The New York Times*, April 5, 1997, p. Y7.

LEWIN, TAMAR. "More in High School Are Virgins, Study Finds," *The New York Times*, September 29, 2002, p. 27.

LEWIS, LIONEL S. *Scaling the Ivory Tower: Merit and Its Limits in Academic Careers.* New Brunswick, NJ: Transaction Publishers, 1998.

MAINES, JOHN. "Long-Distance Romances," *American Demographics*, 15 (5) May 1993, pp. 47–48.

MANDEL, MICHAEL J. "The Great Equalizer, Education and Economics," *Business Week*, July 22, 1996, pp. 74–76.

MANDEL, MICHAEL J. "The Rich Get Richer, and That's O.K.," *Business Week*, August 26, 2002, pp. 88–96.

MANDLEBAUM, DAVID G. *Society in India: Continuity and Change.* Berkeley: University of California Press, 1970.

MANEGOLD, CATHERINE S. "Students Make Strides But Fall Short on Goals," *The New York Times*, August 18, 1994, p. A9.

MARANO, HARA ESTROFF. "Sexual Issues Fan Parents' Fears," *The New York Times*, July 2, 1997, p. B14.

MARK, JEROME A. "Technological Change and Employment: Some Results from BLS Research," *Monthly Labor Review*, 110 (4) April 1987, pp. 26–29.

MASSEY, DOUGLAS S. "The Age of Extremes: Concentrated Affluence and Poverty in the Twenty-First Century," *Demography*, 33 (4) November 1996, pp. 295–313.

MCCLUSKY, JOHN E. "Beyond the Carrot and the Stick: Liberation and Power Without Control." In Warren G. Bennis, Kenneth D. Benne, Robert Chin, and Kenneth E. Corey (eds.), *The Planning of Change*, 3rd ed. New York: Holt, Rinehart & Winston, 1976, pp. 382–403.

MCCOY, CLYDE B., AND JAMES A. INCIARDI. *Sex, Drugs, and the Continuing Spread of AIDS.* Los Angeles, CA: Roxbury, 1995.

MCKIE, CRAIG. "Population Aging: Baby Boomers into the 21st Century," *Canadian Social Trends*, 29, Summer 1993, pp. 2–7.

MCLAUGHLIN, PAT. "Clever Businessmen Taught Us to Shop," *St. Louis Post-Dispatch*, June 2, 1994, p. 2WF.

MCNEAL, JAMES U. *Kids as Customers.* New York: Lexington Books, 1992.

MENDELSOHN, OLIVER. "The Transformation of Authority in Rural India," *Modern Asian Studies*, 27 (1) October 1993, pp. 805–843.

MENKEN, JANE (ed.). *World Population and U.S. Policy.* New York: W. W. Norton, 1986.

MERIK, SUNNY. "Helping Higher Education's Working Poor," *The Chronicle of Higher Education*, July 26, 1996, p. B1.

MILLER, S. M. "A Comparative Social Mobility," *Current Sociology*, 9 (1) 1960, pp. 1–66.

Morbidity and Mortality Weekly Report. "Deaths Resulting from Firearms and Motor-Vehicle-Related Injuries—United States, 1968–1991," 43 (3) January 28, 1994, pp. 37–43.

MOSCA, GAETANO. "The Varying Structure of the Ruling Class." In Amitai Etzioni and Eva Etzioni-Halevy (eds.), *Social Change: Sources, Patterns, and Consequences*, 2nd ed. New York: Basic Books, 1973, pp. 210–222.

MOTT, PAUL E. "Configurations in Power." In Michael Aiken and Paul E. Mott (eds.), *The Structure of Community Power*. New York: Random House, 1970, pp. 85–86.

MURRAY, DAVID W. "Poor Suffering Bastards: An Anthropologist Looks at Illegitimacy," *Policy Review*, 68 (9) Spring 1994, pp. 9–16.

NADLER, ARIE. "Inter-Group Helping Relations as Power Relations: Maintaining or Challenging Social Dominance Between Groups Through Helping," *Journal of Social Issues*, 58 (3) Fall 2002, pp. 487–503.

NAISBITT, JOHN, AND PATRICIA ABURDENE. *Megatrends 2000: Ten New Directions Transforming Our Lives*. New York: Morrow, 1990.

NATIONAL CENTER FOR HEALTH STATISTICS. *National Vital Statistics Reports*, 48 (16) October 18, 2000.

NEMETH, MARY. "Sandwich Generation," *Maclean's*, 107 (2) January 10, 1994, pp. 34–36.

NEUSNER, NOAH. "Paying for College. Why Does It Cost so Much? Special Report," *U.S. News & World Report*, September 30, 2002, pp. 85–111.

New York Times. "Student Hurdle Foils Teachers," July 8, 1997, p. A12.

Newsweek. "'It's Our Turn Now,' Prop 187: As California Cracks Down on Illegals, Blacks and Hispanics Fight a Deeper Ethnic War," November 21, 1994a, p. 57.

NIELSEN, FRANCOIS, AND ARTHUR S. ALDERSON. "The Kuznetz Curve and the Great U-Turn: Income Inequality in the U.S. Counties, 1970 to 1990," *American Sociological Review*, 62 (1) February 1997, pp. 12–34.

O'BRIAN, AMY. "Vancouver Gays Come Out in Census," *The Vancouver Sun*, October 23, 2002, pp. 1 and 4.

OGBURN, WILLIAM F., AND CLARK TIBBITTS. "The Family and Its Functions: Reports on the President's Research Committee on Social Trends in the United States." In *Recent Social Trends in the United States*. New York: McGraw-Hill, 1934, pp. 661–708.

OLSEN, MARVIN E. (ed.). *Power in Societies*. New York: Macmillan, 1970.

PERROLLE, JUDITH A. *Computers and Social Change: Information, Property, and Power*. Belmont, CA: Wadsworth, 1987.

POLANYI, KARL, CONRAD ARENSBERG, AND HARRY PEARSON. *Trade and Market in the Early Empires*. New York: Free Press, 1957.

POPULATION REFERENCE BUREAU. *Population Data Sheet, 2003*. Washington, DC: Population Reference Bureau, 2003.

POWERS, MIKE. "The Hidden Costs of Divorce," *Human Ecology Forum*, 25 (1) Winter 1997, pp. 4–8.

PRITCHETT, LANT, AND LAWRENCE SUMMERS. "Wealthier is Healthier," *Journal of Human Resources*, 31 (4) Fall 1996.

RAVITCH, DIANE. *The Language Police: How Pressure Groups Restrict What Children Learn*. New York: Knopf, 2003.

RAY, CAROL AXTELL, AND ROSLYN ARLIN MICKELSON. "Restructuring Students for Restructured Work: The Economy, School Reform, and Non-college-bound Youths," *Sociology of Education*, 66, January 1993, pp. 1–20.

REESE, WILLIAM A. II. "Review Essay: The Shaped Bell Curve and the Social Sciences," *The Social Science Journal*, 33 (1) January, 1966, pp. 113–120.

RHOADS, CHRISTOPHER. "Short Work Hours Undercut Europe in Economic Drive. Culture That Values Leisure Now Finds It an Obstacle; Jobs Are Going Elsewhere. Taking 9½ Weeks of Vacation," *The Wall Street Journal*, August 8, 2002, pp. A1, A5.

RITZER, GEORGE, AND DAVID WALCZAK. *Working: Conflict and Change*, 3rd ed. Englewood Cliffs, NJ: Prentice Hall, 1986.

RIVERS, CARYL. "The New Anxiety of Motherhood." In Uta West (ed.), *Woman in a Changing World*. New York: McGraw-Hill, 1975, pp. 141–152.

ROEHLING, PATRICIA V., AND MARTA BULTMAN. "Does Absence Make the Heart Grow Fonder? Work-Related Travel and Marital Satisfaction," *Sex Roles: A Journal of Research*, May 2002, pp. 279–294.

ROGERS, CARL R., AND B. F. SKINNER. "Some Issues Concerning the Control of Human Behavior: A Symposium." In Robert Perrucci and Mark Pilisuk (eds.), *Social Problems in Depth*. Boston: Little, Brown, 1968, pp. 331–335.

ROSE, STEPHEN J. "The Truth about Social Mobility," *Challenge*, 29 (3) May–June 1996, pp. 4–9.

ROSSIDES, DANIEL W. *The American Class System: The Interplay of Class, Race and Gender*, 2nd ed. Upper Saddle River, NJ: Prentice Hall, 1997.

RUGGLES, STEVEN. "The Transformation of American Family Structure," *American Historical Review*, 99 (1) February 1994, pp. 103–128.

RUSSELL, CHERYL. "The Rorschach Test—Demographics of Marriage among People in Their Twenties," *American Demographics*, 19 (1) January 1997, pp. 10–12.

SANDERS, BERNARD. "What's Really Going on with the Economy? Unequal Distribution of Wealth and Income," *USA Today* (magazine), 135 (2622) March 1997, pp. 18–21.

SARNO, ANGELO. "Look for Hidden Assets in Computer Files; Next Generation Discovery Techniques are Coming of Age in Divorce Litigation," *New Jersey Law Journal*, 169 (6) August 5, 2002, pp. 4–8.

SCHNEIDER, LOUIS, AND STANFORD M. DORNBUSCH. *Popular Religion: Inspirational Books in America*. Chicago: University of Chicago Press, 1958.

SCHODOLSKI, VINCENT J. "Colleges Working to Hasten Graduation," *The Seattle Times*, October 22, 2002, p. A6.

SCHUPACK, DEBORAH. "Young Love, Brief Marriage, Early Divorce," *The New York Times*, July 7, 1994, pp. B1 and B5.

SCHWARTZ, JOEL. "Inequality by Design: Cracking the Bell Curve Myth" (book reviews), *The Public Interest*, 126, Winter 1997, pp. 113–119.

SCHWARTZ, MARY ANN, AND BARBARA MARLIENE SCOTT. *Marriages and Families: Diversity and Change*, 4th ed. Upper Saddle River, NJ: Prentice Hall, 2003.

SHAPIRO, JAMES. "Saving 'Tenure Books' from a Painful Demise: 'Publish or Perish vs. Sink or Swim'," *The Chronicle of Higher Education*, 43 (10) November 1, 1996, p. 86.

SHELL, ELLEN RUPPEL. "Resurgence of a Deadly Disease," *The Atlantic Monthly*, 280 (2) August 1997, pp. 45–60.

SHELLENBARGER, SUE, AND CAROL HYMOWITZ. "Over the Hill? As Population Ages, Older Workers Clash with Younger Bosses," *The Wall Street Journal*, June 13, 1994, pp. 1 and A8.

SMELSER, NEIL J. *The Sociology of Economic Life*, 2nd ed. Englewood Cliffs, NJ: Prentice Hall, 1976.

SMITH, SANDRA S. "Mobilizing Social Resources: Race, Ethnic, and Gender Differences in Social Capital and Persisting Wage Inequalities," *The Sociological Quarterly*, 41 (4) Fall 2000, pp. 509–548.

SMITH, T. LYNN, AND PAUL E. ZOPF, JR. *Demography: Principles and Methods*, 2nd ed. Port Washington, NY: Alfred, 1976.

SMOCK, PAMELA J. "Cohabitation in the United States," *Annual Review of Sociology*, 26, 2000.

SPECTOR, ALAN J. "Class Structure and Social Change: the Contradictions of Class Relations in Advanced Capitalist Society," *Sociological Inquiry*, 65 (3–4) Fall 1995, pp. 329–339.

SPENGLER, JOSEPH J. "Values and Fertility Analysis." *Demography*, 3 (1) 1966, pp. 109–130.

STACK, STEVEN. "The Effect of Geographic Mobility on Premarital Sex," *The Journal of Marriage and the Family*, 56 (1) February 1994, pp. 205–209.

STARKE, LINDA. "Fertility Rates: The Decline is Stalling," *World Watch*, 7 (2) March–April 1994, pp. 37–39.

STEINBERG, JACQUES. *The Gatekeepers: Inside the Admissions Process of a Premier College.* New York: Viking, 2002.

SZRETER, SIMON. "The Idea of Demographic Transition and the Study of Fertility Change: A Critical Intellectual History," *Population and Development Review*, 19 (1) December 1993, pp. 659–772.

TALBOT, MARGARET. "Love, American Style: What the Alarmists about Divorce Don't Get about Idealism in America," *The New Republic*, 216 (15) April 14, 1997, pp. 30–39.

TEITELBAUM, MICHAEL S., AND JAY M. WINTER. *A Question of Numbers: High Migration, Low Fertility, and the Politics of National Identity.* New York: Hill & Wang, 1998.

THOMSON, SUSAN C. "Medicine Lures Record Number of Aspiring MDs," *St. Louis Post-Dispatch*, September 6, 1999, pp. 1 and 4.

THORNTON, ARLAND, AND HUI-SHENG LIN (eds.). *Social Change and the Family in Taiwan.* Chicago: University of Chicago Press, 1995.

Time. "An Rx for Teen Sex," October 7, 2002, pp. 64–65.

TUMIN, MELVIN M. *Social Stratification: The Forms and Functions of Inequality*, 2nd ed. Englewood Cliffs, NJ: Prentice Hall, 1985.

UCHITELLE, LOUIS. "Profits Rise with Taste for Comfort," *The New York Times*, September 14, 1997, pp. Y1, Y16.

UNITED NATIONS POPULATION FUND. *State of the World Population 2002—People, Poverty and Possibilities.* New York: United Nations Population Fund, 2002.

U.S. BUREAU OF THE CENSUS. *Statistical Abstracts of the United States: 2002*, 122nd ed. Washington, DC, 2002.

U.S. DEPARTMENT OF HEALTH AND HUMAN SERVICES. "Projected Supply, Demand, and Shortages of Registered Nurses: 2000–2020," Washington, DC: National Council of State Boards of Nursing: American Association of Colleges of Nursing, 2002.

U.S. DEPARTMENT OF LABOR. "Employment and Earnings," 34 (5) May 1987.

Wall Street Journal. "Dowry Deaths in India," August 25, 1994, p. A8.

WATTENBERG, BEN J. *The Birth Dearth*, rev. ed. New York: Pharos Books, 1989.

WEICHER, JOHN C. "Increasing Inequality of Wealth?" *The Public Interest*, 126, Winter 1997, pp. 15–26.

WEISMANN, ROBERT. "Grotesque Inequality," *Multinational Monitor*, 17 (9) September 1996, pp. 6–7.

WHITE, CONSTANCE C. R. "The Price a Woman Pays to Say 'I Do'," *The New York Times*, June 29, 1997, p. E5.

WILLIAMS, JUANITA H. *Psychology of Women: Behavior in a Biosocial Context*, 3rd ed. New York: W.W. Norton, 1987.

WINCH, ROBERT S. "Permanence and Change in the History of the American Family and Some Speculations as to the Future," *Journal of Marriage and Family*, 1970, pp. 173–179.

WITWER, M. "U.S. Men and Women Now Have the Highest Mean Age at Marriage in This Century," *Family Planning Perspective*, 25 (4) July–August, 1993, pp. 190–192.

WORLD POPULATION NEWS SERVICE. "60% of U.S. Pregnancies Unintended," *Popline*, 19, July–August 1997, p.1.

ZARNOWSKA, ANNA. "Social Change, Women, and the Family in the Era of Industrialization: Recent Polish Research," *Journal of Family History*, 22 (2) April 1997, pp. 191–204.

ZEITLIN, MAURICE. "Corporate Ownership and Control: The Large Corporation and the Capitalist Class." In Anthony Giddens and David Held (eds.), *Classes, Power, and Conflict: Classical and Contemporary Debates*. Berkeley: University of California Press, 1982, pp. 196–223.

ZERNIKE, KATE. "Tests Are Not Just for Kids. Accountability Hits Higher Education. The Rallying Cry: Show Me the Learning," *The New York Times Magazine*, Education Life, Section 4A, August 4, 2002, pp. 26–29.

Chapter 5

Duration of Change

Every social phenomenon lasts for some time; every event has some duration. The process of social change is directional in time: It has a beginning, a middle, and an end. This temporal component of change is called *duration*. It refers to the life span of a social phenomenon, event, or innovation after its introduction. It is concerned with the question of how long a change will be sustained after it is accepted at any level of the social system without major modification or replacement by a functional alternative. The goal of this chapter is to examine the notion of duration, which is a key dimension in social change.

Nineteenth-century evolutionary thinkers were already preoccupied with the duration or temporality of change (Ingold, 1986:128–133). They were concerned with spans of time in their study of growth or decay, progression or retrogression. But localizing events in time—that is, the study of duration—can be, and often is, a complicated and difficult undertaking. The investigation of the temporal dimension of a phenomenon requires information on its initial point of occurrence, the time frame during which it becomes established, and on its termination. On occasion, changes enter social life so slowly and imperceptibly that we remain unaware of them until they have been fully institutionalized. In other instances, the introduction of an innovation can set off a chain reaction of subsequent changes in a very short time. For example, at the organizational level, the introduction of a new technology in a factory may alter existing work groups, which, in turn, leads to worker demands for union control over job assignments, which causes the union to grow in size and strength, which forces management to revise many of its policies and programs, which ultimately changes the structure and functioning of the whole organization.

TABLE 5.1 Approximate Duration of Change Phenomena

Types of Change	Representative Change Phenomena		Approximate Duration
Broad historical change	Horticultural era		10,000 years
	Agrarian era		4,800 years
Industrial technology	Modern craft age		285 years
	Machine age		85 years
Societal revolutions	Commercial revolution		200 years
	Scientific revolution		100 years
Economic development	"Takeoff" for the United States		60 years
Transitory social changes	Fashion	Clothing and adornment	6 months–60 years
		"Scientific" theory	2–50 years
		Material objects	1–30 years
	Fads		1 month–1 year
	Lifestyles		4–40 years
	Social movements		1–25 years
	Cults		1–15 years

Notwithstanding the difficulties, it is possible to isolate and study the duration of a variety of change phenomena. For some time now, social scientists have been analyzing social change processes of disparate duration and in a wide range of societies (Boskoff, 1972:245). Such analyses are valuable and have potentially relevant implications for planning, forecasting, and making business decisions and marketing choices by providing an approximation of how long and under what circumstances a similar change phenomenon may be sustained in the future (see, for example, *Fortune*, 1996; Glenn and Gordon, 2002). One can even talk about the duration of certain change patterns such as diffusion, discussed in Chapter 3. Perhaps the most famous case of technological substitution is the automobile for horses. In this case, the diffusion of one technological artifact, the passenger car, began simply by replacing another, the riding horse and the carriage. Millions of horses and mules used for transport disappeared in less than 30 years. Similarly, diffusion trajectories can be established for other technologies (Grubler, 1996).

We shall begin this chapter with a brief discussion of the duration of broad historical trends. It is followed by a study of such transitory social changes as fads and fashion, lifestyles, social movements, and cults, and a related analysis of the conditions that have contributed to their demise. Table 5.1 provides a synoptic overview of the types of changes that will be considered and an indication of their approximate duration.

DURATION OF CHANGE FROM A HISTORICAL PERSPECTIVE

Social change always occurs in historical settings, and any sociological analysis of change must take account of sequences of events through which change becomes manifest. Moreover, most instances of broad-scale social change are directional in nature, and thus societies are seen as evolving along identifiable lines and evidencing new forms. Social scientists for a long time have identified historical eras with distinct characteristics. Some even assign dates to them. For example, Gerhard and Jean Lenski and Patrick Nolan (1999) suggest one way of designating human history:

Hunting and gathering (from the origins of *Homo sapiens* to circa 7000 B.C.)
Horticultural (from circa 7000 B.C. to circa 3000 B.C.)
Agrarian (from circa 3000 B.C. to A.D. 1800)
Industrial (since circa A.D. 1800)

In a similar fashion, one may talk about the duration of technologies in industry or agriculture. In a historical context, Delbert C. Miller (1957a: 245–277), for example, identifies four major stages in the evolution of modern technology and calls them the modern craft age, the machine age, the power age, and the atomic age. Each age is unique and has left a technical heritage that remains in various forms even as the new emerges and becomes dominant. The principal elements in technology that shape a pattern are: power, tools, work skills, material, transportation, and communication.

The *modern craft age* in industry is dated as beginning with the fifteenth century, "which is often regarded as the threshold of modern civilization" (Miller, 1957a:253). The *machine age* was inaugurated by Watt's invention of the steam engine in 1785 and its application to the textile industry. The *power age* is characterized by the widespread use of electricity, which began in 1953 and is still in progress. Miller contends further that the evolution of machines in agricultural technology parallels the four-stage patterns of industrial technology. The dates and duration of each stage are somewhat different. The modern craft age began in the year 1000, the machine age in 1830, the power age in 1920, and the *atomic age* in 1960 (Miller, 1957b:336–337). It is also possible to ascertain the duration of specific shorter-term technological innovations in the context of the four ages of industrial and agricultural technologies and the reasons for their discontinuities. For example, one could establish how long the steam press for printing books and newspapers was sustained in a particular society and why and under what circumstances it was replaced by a more modern version.

Finally, let us recall Walt M. Rostow's (1961) idea that the lengthy process of economic development can be depicted by a series of five stages. Each stage, for the analysis of duration, may be considered as representing the acceptance of a unique configuration and constellation of novelties with more or less identifiable and designatable life spans. Rostow estimates that, for example, the mature economy is attained roughly sixty years after the beginning of "takeoff" (stage three). Thus, for the United States, the takeoff was around 1840, and the mature stage was attained around the turn of the century. It remained in that stage until approximately 1920, when it entered into stage five, the age of high mass consumption. In the Rostowian framework of stages, the duration of each stage or phase of development is indicated. Using a crude analogy, his five stages may be compared to five flights in a staircase, which entail both a continuous progression upward and stops at the intervening. The length of the stay at each floor prior to embarking to the next one would be, in this analogy, the duration of change. Let us now turn to the consideration of short-term transitory changes.

TRANSITORY SOCIAL CHANGES

As Richard T. LaPiere (1965:66) points out: "To constitute a socially significant change, the new must be not only adopted by a sufficient number of the members of a social population to give it currency, but so integrated into the social system that it will endure. . . . No change may justly be deemed socially significant until the new has been so effectively transmitted from the generation in which it occurs to the next generation that it is thereafter considered as the normal and is taken for granted as an integral part of things as they are." Obviously, not all changes are socially significant and sustained for generations. Many social changes are transitory and of relatively short duration. Often "the new is in many instances adopted with great rapidity until the majority of the members of at least a class of the population have become involved; its appearance and spread are invariably recognized; and, like births and deaths and other events, it is usually the subject of much reporting and comment. At the time of its occurrence the new may have a considerable impact on social life; but it may be abandoned even more rapidly than it came into use, with the result that it never becomes an established part of the social system and rarely leaves any durable imprint" (LaPiere, 1965:59).

In the following pages, several forms of transitory changes will be examined, such as fads and fashion, lifestyles, and cults. Although it is argued that any given transitory change generally contributes little, if anything, to changes in the social system, "the occurrence of transitory changes in a society is symptomatic of conditions that are conducive to the appearance of significant changes in that society. In the modern world trying out something new is one way in which individuals attempt to resolve their frustrations or to secure satisfactions that are not otherwise forthcoming; and the occurrence of a great number of transitory changes is thus an indication that the felt needs of many of the members of the society are not being satisfied by the established practices of social life, that for many of the members of society life is in some respects frustrating or inadequate" (LaPiere, 1965:65).

At times, transitory changes operate as a substitute for important changes or socially significant changes by reducing tension and discontent and by diverting energies and abilities that might otherwise be applied to something else. It is also possible that "a social population may become so much engrossed in the excitements of transitory changes that it tends to ignore and neglect the inadequacies of the social system itself" (LaPiere, 1965:66).

Transitory changes tend to be of shorter duration than the changes LaPiere calls "socially significant." People are more conscious and more aware of short-term transitions than of long-enduring and continuous patterns of social life. Transitory changes also provide a good opportunity for social scientists to investigate events that influence the course of society and shape our lives. In the following pages, several such events of relatively short duration will be examined in the context of fads and fashions, lifestyles, and cults.

FADS AND FASHIONS

As Rolf Meyersohn and Elihu Katz (1957:594) aptly remark, "The study of fads and fashions may serve the student of social change much as the study of fruit flies has served geneticists: neither the sociologist nor the geneticist has to wait long for a new generation to arrive." Fads and fashions provide an extraordinary opportunity to study the duration of change, the processes of influence, the diffusion of innovation, and a whole series of other social phenomena. For the present purposes, however, the discussion of fads and fashions will be limited principally to the duration of change.

Can fads be distinguished from fashions? Fashions are of a cyclical nature and typically exhibit a diffusion process resembling an S-shaped pattern, though more pronounced and more condensed in time. Fads, in contrast, tend not to repeat themselves and tend to exhibit much more rapid growth followed by generally complete collapse, although occasionally adoption can stabilize at a lower residual level. Figure 5.1 shows generalized diffusion patterns for fads and fashions. Fashions are culture patterns that are adopted by a given segment of a society for a relatively brief period of time and then abandoned. Fads, on the other hand, are culture patterns of even shorter duration that tend to appear suddenly and disappear as suddenly. Thorstein Veblen (1911) linked fashion to conspicuous consumption—the practice of spending money to display one's wealth occasionally in the form of unostentatious luxuries such as diamond studded watches that can cost up to $500,000 or ultra-expensive furs or sports cars (Brown, 1997).

Persons lacking the means to buy exactly what the rich can afford obtain less expensive imitations. For example, those who cannot afford a currently popular form of cosmetic surgery—nipple enhancements—resort to cheaper and less invasive ways to achieve the look; they buy synthetic rubber nipples meant to be tucked inside the bra (Spencer, 2002). Fashion often

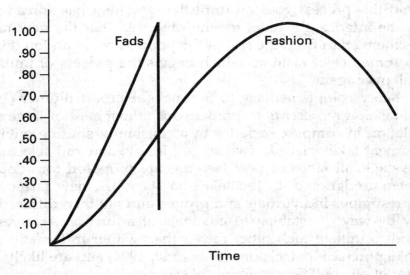

FIGURE 5.1 Generalized Diffusion Patterns for Fads and Fashions

signals social status or rank (Coelho & McClure, 1993) and, as a particular fashion trickles downward in society, the rich move on to something else. Thus, fashion originates at the top of the social hierarchy then moves to mass popularity. This contention is not always tenable; for example, Elihu Katz and Paul F. Lazarsfeld (1955:247–270) found in their study of personal influence and fashion behavior that there were as many fashion leaders among women in the middle class as in the upper class, and only low-status women were underrepresented in fashion leadership. Furthermore, in recent decades, some fashions have originated in the lower classes and have been adopted subsequently by the more affluent. Witness, for example, the popularity of blue jeans, which were worn initially by manual laborers. For the purpose of analyzing duration patterns, fads and fashions will be treated separately in the next two sections.

Fashion

Fashion operates only in societies with an open class system. According to Georg Simmel (1957:541–558), the elite in such societies are engaged in a prolonged effort to set themselves apart from individuals of lower classes by distinctive customs, mannerisms, and lifestyles. But because individuals of slightly lower status who are closest to the elite are eager to raise their statuses, they no sooner become aware of a new pattern of elite behavior than they adopt it for themselves. Individuals on the next lower rung of the status ladder are drawn into adopting the new fashion next, for similar reasons, and this process goes on until the new item has spread to all the classes. In the interim, the elite, having observed that the new fashion no longer sets them apart from the rest of the population, abandon it in a hurry to take up some newer fashion, which begins the process of imitation and diffusion all over again.

In a theory complementary to Simmel's, Herbert Blumer (1968) proposed that fashion represents a spontaneous adjustment of large segments of a population in complex societies to a constantly shifting environment. This adjustment takes place in two stages: innovation and selection. In the innovative stage, all kinds of new fashions are proposed for adoption, but most of them are ignored. In the selection stage, the new fashions are selected by prestigious individuals and groups and are then diffused through the society by way of established channels of influence. As a result, consumers tend to imitate each other rather than gather information on their own to make purchasing decisions (*Economist*, 1994) and are likely to follow the behavior of others (Bikhchandani, 1992).

The transitory nature of fashion is evidenced by the intrinsic relationship of two common expressions to the concept of fashion—in fashion and outmoded. Blumer (1968:341–342) observes that "These terms signify a continuing pattern of change in which certain social forms enjoy temporary acceptance and respectability only to be replaced by others more abreast of the times." Fashion under capitalism exhibits certain features such as planned obsolescence due to mass production and competition (Craik, 1994:6). Although most pronounced in the area of adornment and tonsorial patterns (see, for example, Innes-Smith and Webb, 2003, on hair styles over the years), fashion changes occur in many other aspects of social life "that are relatively independent and that can therefore change without seriously affecting other aspects of society" (LaPiere, 1965:61).

Changes in fashion are most noticed in clothing and adornment. Changes in dress and decoration patterns can be described in terms of a "fashion cycle." However, the notion of "cycle" is misleading. It implies a repetitive rise and fall, as if a wheel had turned and the fashions that were "in" had to go "out" for a time and then reappear at predictable intervals. Of necessity, there are some recurrent variations of specific elements of style—such as dress length and width, which is cyclical within the limits of practicality and morality (see, for example, Hollander, 1994). There are revivals of styles from time to time, but the fashions of another day never quite come back in their entirety; neither history nor fashion ever plays itself back completely unchanged. For example, A. L. Kroeber's (1919) studies of fashion have shown that the periodicity of cycles in dress styles during recent centuries is different for different dimensions of the dress. Similarly, the ubiquitous and ever popular T-shirt was originally part of sailor's uniforms in the 1800s and has endured through several fashion trends. In the 1950s T-shirts were a sign of conformity among youth, and in the 1960s they became a form of self-expression. By the late 1990s, the T-shirt became hip among the fashion elite (Jones, 1997).

Fashions are cyclical, however, to the extent that they go through stages of increasing and decreasing popularity. James M. Carman (1966) used mathematical time-series models to study fashion trends in women's clothes from 1786 to 1965. The predictive accuracy of his models is good, based on two cyclical theories. One of these posits three cycles lasting approximately 100 years: a bell, or full-skirt, cycle; a bustle cycle; and a tubular, or sheath, cycle. The other theory suggests shorter cycles of thirty to fifty years. In a study by Dwight E. Robinson (1976:1136–1137) of fashions in shaving and trimming of the beard in England between 1842 and 1972, he found a "most remarkable" correspondence with "Kroeber's width of skirt wave, which rose and fell between 1811 and 1926, and the beard wave, which rose and fell between 1842 (or very possibly 1840) and 1956." The reasons that skirt width and beard frequency fluctuate together are open to speculation, and the new millennium did not bring forth new hypotheses.

Marvin Harris (1973), in an article entitled "What Goes Up May Stay Up," suggests that fashions reflect the dominant interests and values of a society at a particular time. Throughout history, clothing has been designed to show the social position of its wearer (Lurie, 1987:193). For example, in the eighteenth century, elaborate clothing reflected an ornate and decorative upper-class culture. The end of the eighteenth century, however, saw some unusual fashions. To illustrate: "The last time well-bred Western women bared their nipples was during that elegant, albeit short-lived, period called the Directoire, a time of stylish Graecisms ranging from neopagan piety to pseudo-Pompeian household furniture, when women, at least those who could afford to do so, dressed as goddesses and also, for the first time since antiquity, showed their bare feet" (Rudofsky, 1984:44). The fashion of women baring their nipples lasted for four years, from 1795 to 1799. Its demise may have been brought about by the early signs of the upcoming Victorian era and Victorian prudishness.

There are many other instances in fashion in which the duration can be more or less specified. For example, the corset [the topic of a fascinating study of cultural history by Valerie Steele (2001)], which was fashionable for approximately sixty years, operated on three levels—mechanical, aesthetic, and moral. "The corset," wrote Thorstein Veblen (1911:172), "is in economic theory substantially [an instrument of] mutilation for the purpose of lowering the subject's vitality and rendering her personally and obviously unfit for work. It is true, the corset impairs the personal attractiveness of the wearer [Veblen, of course, refers to the naked woman], but the loss suffered on that score is offset by the gain in reputability which comes of her visibly increased expensiveness and infirmity." The corset was a hallmark of virtue and its use marked an advanced technique of disfigurement. Rustproof summer corsets were advertised as a necessity for summer wear and for swimming, and unbreakable electric corsets guaranteed quick cures for all kinds of diseases such as paralysis, rheumatism, spinal complaints, constipation, liver and kidney troubles, and so forth. According to the 1880s advertisements, the corsets were constructed on scientific principles, with an emphasis on their therapeutic values (Craik, 1994:121–126).

One would never guess what freed women from the corset. What brought about the corset's disappearance was the necessity of conserving steel for armaments during World War I. In view of this patriotic objective, women decided that corsets were nonessential. "Subsequently, a member of the War Industries Board revealed that the American women's sacrifice released 28,000 tons of steel during World War I, enough to build two battleships" (Rudofsky, 1984:189). But the demise of the corset was of relatively short duration; it returned at the beginning of the twenty-first century dubbed as "sensual scaffolding" (La Ferla, 2002) and was made out of non-ferrous materials.

After World War I, there are other illustrations of fashion change with more or less specific duration. For example, "Following World War I and until about 1929, the female torso became a flattened tube, and the body was as wide at the waist as at the hips. . . . This was the era of the 'flapper' fashions, and the bust disappeared altogether in an effort to achieve a 'boyish flat appearance'. . . . Women with large breasts were forced to wear correctors or flatteners in an attempt to conform to prevailing fashion" (Morrison & Holden, 1973:571). Prior to attempting to acquire a male front, women enthusiastically accepted a "sweeping homogeneous front bulge, a highly artificial protuberance that I shall call the monobosom, to distinguish it from the double-breasted chest. It embodied a new concept of corporeal modesty—the merger of two pointed secondary sexual characteristics into a single mass of flesh that has no organic precedent in human history. Apparently, one bulge seemed less immodest than two" (Rudofsky, 1984:44).

In the context of fashion, almost every generation has its own ideas on supporting some part of the human anatomy. For about two decades around the turn of the century, almost everyone went through life ankle-supported. Young and old wore laced boots. A shoe that did not reach well above the ankle was considered disastrous to health. Then ankle-support gave way to arch support. For almost another generation, "Western woman, whom nature forgot to endow with a magnificent rear end, had at times to rely on make-believe to render herself desirable; witness the bustle of the eighteen-seventies, a gross illusion of steatopygia" [extreme accumulation of fat on and around the buttocks] (Rudofsky, 1984:99–100). And the illustrations could go on and on. The important point is that no part of the human anatomy is free of fashion, there is a tendency among people to "accentuate the appropriate," and, in many instances, changes in adornment patterns are documentable with more or less exact life spans.

Although it would be interesting to continue with illustrations of changes in clothes and adornment patterns, fashion is not limited to these aspects of social life. Fashionlike changes in technique, theory, academic styles (Yagoda, 1994), college curriculum (Stark & Lattuca, 1997), and the use of certain concepts such as "social capital" (Greeley, 1997) and interests occur in every field of science and in almost any aspect of group life. For example, the publication of *The Principles of Scientific Management* by Frederick W. Taylor (1911) started a fashion that lasted for almost four decades, with a tremendous impact on the entire field of organizational management. Taylor believed that a maximization of efficiency in organizations could be achieved by the segmentation of all tasks involved in production into a series of simple movements and operations. Each worker could be trained to perform a few simple operations, and the combined efforts of all workers laboring for the common good would maximize efficiency and productivity. Taylor also believed that the average workers were interested in doing only what is minimally required by management. Therefore, in addition to the redesigning and simplifying of tasks, increased productivity could be achieved by the creation of incentives to work harder during a specified time period. He suggested that workers could be directed, like robots, to perform at command in a predetermined manner. He posited that if workers could be made to adhere to a mandatory schedule of rest pauses and work periods, the worker would be at peak efficiency at all times during the workday. This is basically the idea of scientific management, which was discredited, regretfully, too late.

Certain fashions in science not only are influential but can have serious implications. This is the case with phrenology. It is associated mainly with the work of Franz Joseph Gall (1758–1828), who investigated the bumps and other irregularities of the skulls of inmates of penal institutions and asylums for the insane. The theory of phrenology is based on the notion that the exterior of the skull corresponds to the interior and to the brain's conformation. The brain can be divided into faculties or propensities that are related to the shape of the skull. Furthermore, each proportion in the brain represents a distinct mental or moral disposition and, depending upon the relative concentration of these propensities or faculties, they determine the conformation of the skull, which, in turn, can be detected by touching it (Schafer, 1969:110–115).

Phrenology spread rapidly in Europe. It had its own journal, called the *Phrenological Journal*, and "the art of reading bumps," as it was called in the United States, was so successful that an American university established a professorship of phrenology. Observed *The Encyclopedia Americana* (1998:22): "The most necessary thing for a professor of phrenology was a happy faculty for flattering everybody, and the more they flattered, the more people paid to have their heads charted to get information as to other characteristics." As long as phrenology was concerned with squeezing heads in the form of a crude aptitude test, it was relatively harmless. But not so when it was adopted in prisons toward the end of the nineteenth century in the United States. At that time phrenological profiles of inmates were a part of the prison records, and phrenology was used as an important criterion in probation and parole. It was even used in New York's Sing Sing prison until about 1910, when it was finally discredited.

When fashion centers around a material object, one of its most important characteristics is that replacement of that object is made before its life span ends. Quite often, such objects are acquired without regard for their durability. In modern societies, the public is ready to accept anything new, anything different; in fact, there is a demand for novelty and for continuous refinement of existing products. The greatly accelerated stylistic changes have been used to create technological obsolescence, which is perhaps most pronounced in the United States in terms of trading automobiles in every couple of years or so.

Fads

"The more trivial, unpredictable, rapidly spreading, and rapidly disappearing changes are those of a faddish character. Changes of this sort occur when the value of the new to the individual who adopts it arises, not from what the new is or does, but from the fact that, being new, it attracts favorable attention from others. As more and more adopt it, its value rapidly diminishes, so that within weeks or months of its initial appearance, the new has become old and uninteresting; and the change has come to an end" (LaPiere, 1965:59–60). In many instances, the duration of fads can be determined with a fair degree of accuracy.

Although the terms fad and craze are frequently linked and both are instances of culture patterns of very short duration, they can, at times, be distinguished by "the quickness with which they alternate, the utter superficiality of their content, and the irrationality and intensity of the temporary fascination for them" (Davis, 1949:79). Neil J. Smelser (1963) notes that the craze may be superficial (hula hoops, celebrity fan clubs) or serious (war crazes); it may be political (bandwagons), expressive (dance steps), religious (revivals), or economic (speculative boom), just to mention a few types.

A fad often provides a way of ascertaining personal identity (Turner & Killian, 1987:146–148). It is a way of demonstrating that one is different and is worth noticing. Observe the popularity of punk attire and hairdo among some teenagers or wearing baseball-type caps backwards on college campuses (Trinkhaus, 1994), the wearing of striped, spotted and floral-patterned pajamas on the streets and at workplaces in Shanghai, China (Faison, 1997), or the ever-lowering waistbands of young women exposing the navel with its attendant piercings along with the trousers cut so low as to reveal jutting hipbones, the descending V of the groin and the top of the pubis (Smith, 2002). (I really feel for the teachers in high schools and professors at colleges who have to teach women in these states of undress in an atmosphere of caution and constant fear of sexual harassment charges—which also have a faddish character.)

Fads seem to be more numerous in periods of group crisis, which implies that certain recreational fads divert attention from the problems at hand. Many fads have little significance for participants beyond identifying them with an in-group and thus giving them prestige, such as various forms of body piercing (Gladwell, 2002). Fears and belief in special formulas (megadoses of vitamin C against the common cold) may also have a faddish character. There are, of course, more serious fads such as war crazes, or those found in the social sciences where fads determine the intellectual domination of ideas, as evidenced in the fluctuating distribution of publications over time (Peng, 1994).

For the present purposes of attempting to ascertain the duration of change, economic crazes are of particular interest. They are also unique because they involve a risk that other fads and crazes do not. Individuals are willing to risk their entire fortunes because of the belief that they will get rich quickly if they only seize the opportunity. The Florida land boom of 1925–1926 is an excellent illustration of economic crazes.

At the turn of the century, the southern part of Florida was rather isolated and thinly populated. With the advent of the railroad and automobiles, it entered a period of steady growth. This growth greatly accelerated during the early 1920s; for example, the population of the city of Miami grew from 30,000 in 1920 to an estimated 75,000 by 1925. It was a period of general prosperity in the United States, during which it seemed that everybody could become rich. Plans were announced for grandiose real estate development, and lots were offered for sale. One financier proposed to build a settlement on land dredged up from Tampa Bay. He sold $3 million worth the first day, even before the dredging operation had begun. Rumors of tremendous profits spread, and the demands for lots for resale were so great that realtors could sell land that was still under water. Thousands of people flocked to Florida to participate in the boom, and lots were bought and sold, sight unseen, all over the United States. During the summer of 1925, a race was on to get into the market before prices increased, and eager buyers were easy to find. By January 1926, confidence in the boom began to falter, prices started to decline, and many people defaulted on their promises to buy land. In September 1926, a hurricane hit the Miami area, killing more than 400 people. "Now the rush to unload land began in earnest; buyers defaulted on their binders, and developers and realtors went bankrupt. There was an exodus of forlorn speculators from the state, most of them with scarcely enough money to get home. Promoters who, a few months previously, had been regarded as public servants, showing small investors the route to Eldorado, were now denounced as charlatans. Investors who had been envied by their neighbors as bold, shrewd adventurers were now pitied as gullible fools who had been fleeced" (Turner & Killian,

1987:150–151). The craze lasted for approximately one year, from the summer of 1925 until September 1926.

At times a craze can become an obsession for its followers. For example, the use of LSD became a craze among a small number of college students, with an estimated 5 or 6 percent having tried it at least once at the peak of the craze in 1967 (Meyer, 1969:201). With Timothy Leary as its main prophet, LSD was to bring the world into a new nirvana of peace, love, creativity, and ultimate salvation. However, the growing fear of the hazards of LSD seems to have reduced its users to no more than 1 percent of college students by 1969 (Meyer, 1969:201).

Many other fads are of much shorter duration than the LSD craze. For example, in the popular music industry, the life span of a "hit" is about one month (Meyersohn & Katz, 1957:598). The pet-rock craze lasted a couple of months, as did the attempts by college students to set new records by crowding into telephone booths or Volkswagens. Pac Man, Cabbage Patch dolls, and "Trivial Pursuit" did not fare much better. In late 1997, Beanie Babies (tiny beanbag animals) incited frenzies at toy stores for a short time along with the Tamagotchi, an electronic gadget that mimics something like a baby chick. It eats, sleeps, poops, gets cranky and screeches—actually, beeps—for attention. If the owner does not intervene electronically to coddle it or clean up its messes, the creature dies (Wudunn, 1997). All this for about $17.00, if one could get it. Then came Pokemon, followed by Yu-Gi-Oh! (roughly translated as "king of games" from Japanese, which started out as a comic book in 1996 and gained popularity as a television series four years later) collectable cards (some at $50 or more per card). By the end of 2002, it turned into a $2 billion industry. As with all comparable fads, this, too will face a predictable point of waning interest (Tsai, 2002).

Rubik's Cube endured a bit longer, possibly due to the challenge it posed. In some instances, fads catch on and become a permanent part of a culture. For example, three decades ago soccer was limited to a handful of devoted, predominantly male, aficionados, mostly of European or Latin American origin. Today it is played by both sexes all over the United States. Some other games caught on, such as "Monopoly" and backgammon, but many more lasted only for a short period of time. Fads of varying duration are present in diets, mission statements by universities, and in words and phrases such as "information superhighway" (1993), "millennium bug" (1997), "Y2K" (1999), and "chad"—as in voting cards (2000) (Metcalf, 2002). One even finds fads in health care. In psychiatry, for example, more than 450 different forms of psychotherapy were purveyed a generation ago in the marketplace (Hunt, 1987:30). How many of these will be around next year, or even next month, is open to conjecture.

One of the most widely publicized fads of the twentieth century was "streaking" (racing nude through a public place)—practiced by few, but enjoyed by many. It lasted approximately four months in 1974. Let us examine it in the context of the natural history of fads, which "seeks to determine the origin of a given item, the conditions of acceptance by the first participants (the 'innovators'), the characteristics of those whom the innovators influence, the shifts from minority to majority acceptance, its waning, and where it goes to die" (Meyersohn & Katz, 1957:597).

Streaking was spearheaded by college students and spread like wildfire to all parts of the country. It was not confined to the United States; in later stages, the fad was also found in Europe and Latin America. The fad cut across class lines and appealed to diverse age and sex groups. Granted, the incidence of nudity on college campuses is nothing new, but the sheer numbers of those who became involved (one study analyzed data on 1,016 recorded incidents of streaking at colleges and universities) (Aguirre, Quarantelli, & Mendoza, 1988:569), the publicity they received, and the cycle of unbelief to mild indignation to popularity is unprecedented in modern times.

How, when, and where it all started is difficult to determine. The first mention of streaking in a national magazine appeared in a *Newsweek* (1974a:63) article dated February 4, 1974. By March 18, 1974, the streaking fad was at its peak. At college campuses around the country, categories of streaking activity were being devised and competition over a totally absurd phenomenon was clearly evident and highly publicized (*Newsweek*, 1974b: 41–42). But streaking was no longer limited to the college campus; junior and senior high school students were emulating their elders in greater and greater numbers. En route to New York from London, an adult male streaker jogged up and down the aisles of a Pan American jumbo jet, and a senior citizen was arrested in Lima, Ohio, for taking a bare stroll in the public square, which the participant called "snailing" (*Time*, 1974:58–59).

By April 1974, streaking was on the decline, and altogether the fad lasted roughly four months. The postmortem for streaking in the popular literature endured for another month or so, and then interest rapidly waned. Streaking as an activity became too diffused, too popular, and was no longer differentiated by age, sex, or occupational groups. Because everyone could participate in it, the fad, in its later stages, left no one astounded. Positive rewards and reinforcement for the activity were no longer forthcoming and because of mass participation, its novelty value quickly wore out. In the next section, the duration of various changes in lifestyles will be considered.

LIFESTYLES

The term *lifestyle* was introduced into the sociological literature by Max Weber. He posited that social status was determined primarily by one's style of life, how one consumed, rather than how one produced. "Certain goods become objects for monopolization by status groups. . . . The decisive role of a 'style of life' . . . means that status groups are the specific bearers of all 'conventions.' In whatever way it may be manifest, all 'stylization' of life either originates in status groups or is at least conserved by them" (Weber, 1966:26). The notion of lifestyles, however, goes beyond the differences in consumption patterns (Bogenhold, 2001). Lifestyles also include specific sets of values which provide the grounds for classifying populations. For instance, in one often-cited study, three broad categories were identified: the *Traditionalists* or *Heartlanders*, who believe in small town life and strong churches; *Modernists*, who advocate features of modern economy; and the *Cultural Creatives*, who support globalism and environmental issues (Ray, 1997). The term also refers to those patterns of conduct over which individuals have options or choices, although they may have the same resources. These options include modes of dressing, utilizing leisure time, spending vacations, using drugs, joining groups, and pursuing health lifestyles (Cockerman, Abel, & Luschen, 1993; Bensman & Vidich, 1987: 101–151; Gilbert & Kahl, 1993; Ray, 1997; Tumin, 1985:99). Lifestyles often pervade many aspects of life and imply a central life interest (Feldman & Thielbar, 1975:2).

Social Class and Lifestyles

To a great extent, lifestyles are determined by one's social class. "To the extent that the various classes live apart from one another, they develop recognizable subcultures with values that give a special and unique flavor to life" (Kahl, 1957:186). Lifestyles based on class position are temporal and tend to be of relatively short duration. The major traditional lifestyles of the nineteenth century are now defunct and have been replaced by new sets of living patterns. Consider, for example, the traditional aristocratic lifestyle of the American South, which emphasized elegance, leisure, noblesse oblige, chivalry, and slavery. Over time, this lifestyle was subjected to a continuous process of dilution and has all but disappeared (Bensman & Vidich, 1987:123–124).

Similarly, class-based lifestyles (described in the section on stratification in Chapter 4) between the Great Depression and the 1960s are all but passé. The wealthy can no longer be characterized by charity work or elaborate codes of etiquette. For them, there is more to life than selective social ties and membership in exclusive clubs. They do not follow the pattern of European feudal aristocracy and have their children study liberal arts rather than vocational subjects. By the same token, lower-middle-class lifestyles are no longer dominated by respectability, religion, home ownership, and patriotism, nor can the poor be characterized as apathetic or fully resigned to a life of relative misery and deprivation.

The lifestyles of professionals and managers, as epitomized by William H. Whyte's (1957) *The Organization Man*, endured about four decades. As Whyte paints the portrait of the organization man, he emerges as a rather frightening character, totally identified with organizational goals, a belief in the group as the source of creativity, rather than in the individual, a belief that belongingness is the ultimate need of the individual. The "organization man" was satisfied to devote his entire life to one organization, with no thought of changing employers and with no concern for family. The problems of society were decidedly secondary. This particular lifestyle again may have had its beginning during the post-Depression years, climaxing in the 1950s, and, to a great extent, coming to an end by the mid-1960s. Today, it seems that more and more individuals view their work life as one part of a broader life experience, which involves not only job but family, community, social responsibilities, and concern for political and economic issues. In other words, one's commitment to careerism, to an organization, appears to be on the decline (see, for example, Fleishman, 2003).

Since the 1960s, the American class structure has undergone some important changes. Proportionately, the size of the working class has declined, while the upper-middle and middle classes, working poor, and underclass (formerly known as the poor) have expanded. In 1996, American sociology witnessed an epochal moment, the birth of a new class: "the overclass," representing the top 5 percent of household income of 12.5 million people, starting at around $132,000 (Lind, 1996). This is more than three times the median household income and may seem a tad extravagant to most, but business magazines proclaimed in the same year that the new standard for executive pay is "four times your age"—in other words, $120,000 at the age of 30. The overclass is national, even transnational, in outlook, although its members are primarily concentrated on both coasts. They judge each other on the basis of merit and value competitive achievement: books published, products launched, mergers completed, elections won. They are, in the catchy terms of *Newsweek* (1997), the "cyber-rich," the "Wall-Street rich," the "entrepreneurial rich," the "media rich," and the "info-rich."

The overclass is composed primarily of the baby boom generation, people born between 1946 and 1964. The baby boomers, some 77 million strong, are being followed by the "baby busters," or "Generation X" as they were dubbed in the early 1990s, and there are some 44 million X'ers (Losyk, 1997). In the mid-1990s, they were mainly in their 20s, about 40 percent were products of divorce, and many were brought up in single-parent homes. They have a negative view of the world shaped by events such as escalating crime, riots, AIDS, environmental concern, the Gulf War, and economic uncertainty. They see their economic prospects as gloomy and feel that they may not get the job and pay they want. They look upon jobs as temporary instead of part of a career and feel that there is no such thing as job security. This is also the first generation of workers that is truly computer literate—

they grew up with information technology. Authority figures and bosses are an anomaly. The twenty-somethings also average $2,400 in credit card debt and are more likely to file for bankruptcy than earlier generations (Ellerson, 1997). By 2003, Generation X was being replaced by Generation Y. This group, born between 1978 and 1995, is almost as numerous as the "boomers." This generation is made up of bull market babies, the products of doting parents who enacted helmet laws, spent money on tutors, and stocked the house with electronics. They tend to have a more global, cosmopolitan outlook, thanks to increased travel opportunities, the pervasiveness of the Internet, and the increasing number of immigrants. They are experts at multitasking, change careers more often than their predecessors, and want the workplace to be fun, relaxed, and nontraditional, with minimal constraint on manners and attire (Hakim, 2002).

The distinction between white-collar and blue-collar workers has all but disappeared. Generally, those in the top half of the class structure seem to be gaining privilege and power at the expense of those in the bottom half (Gilbert & Kahl, 1993:340). These changes have been accompanied by a decline in the monolithic class-based lifestyles. New lifestyles, and a much greater variety of them in any one socioeconomic group, have replaced or supplemented older ones. We no longer talk about the lifestyle of, say, the upper middle class. Rather, the emphasis is on several (although overlapping) characteristic lifestyles. An interesting approach to the lifestyles of the upper middle class and segments of the overclass, for example, might include the following (Bensman & Vidich, 1987:145–148):

1. The style of the *Country Gentleman*, where the emphasis is on sports or on nautical activities. An advocate of this lifestyle spends a considerable amount of his income on his chosen pleasure. He may build his life around a boat, nautical dress styles, and involvement in cup races. This may be combined with elaborate entertainment in country or golf clubs involving all members of the family. Fresh air, sun, and fun are preferred to books and intellectually demanding activities.

2. The style of the *Culture Vulture* involves intellectual and cultural activities. Books, talk, theater, music, and museum attendance are part of daily activities. Publishers, book and record clubs, dance, theater, and music groups all depend on the cultural demand created by this segment of the upper middle class.

3. The *Cultured Academic*, who may not be a professor, but finds the university community to be an ideal place of residence. Many professionals, business persons, and managers have opted to live in the vicinity of universities such as Cambridge, MIT, or Princeton. They participate in university-sponsored cultural events, maintain old school ties, and tend to blend into the academic environment. The Ph.D. nouveau riche (a scientist turned entrepreneur who became rich because of a good idea related to space, computers, electronics, etc. or the author of a successful college text) contributes to this lifestyle because it offers a compromise between an intellectual past and newly gained economic success.

4. The *Fun-Lover* prefers to be a participant in sports, parties, dancing, safaris, flying, and skiing. In this group, the accent is on "fun" of the jet-set variety. This type of person prefers to be continuously on the move and conveys the impression of being "in." He or she likes to think of himself or herself as being influential in science, technology, and administration. Examples of this lifestyle would include the world-traveling junior executive, the international consultant, or the youthful college president.

5. The old upper-middle-class *Vulgarian* who emphasizes conspicuous consumption. For the most part, these are people who own their own businesses and have succeeded beyond their expectations. They have plenty of money but they do not exactly know what to do with it, such as real estate speculators, developers, etc. So they spend it on Cadillacs and Caribbean cruises and other symbols of material success.

Another interesting development is the emergence of so-called lifestyle enclaves that have sprung up around the country and where people who share interests live together—an affluent retirement village, a yuppie neighborhood in a big city, a DINK (double-income, no kids) condominium development around a golf course, or a community of pilots who build homes around a shared airstrip. Thus, lifestyles are not solely class-based. The term lifestyle essentially implies a focus in life, and a number of things can be of central interest to the individual: work, ethnic heritage, politics, or sexual orientation. A distinctive lifestyle is evident when one single activity dominates a person's other interests and activities, such as lifestyles of openly lesbian women (Buenting, 1992).

There have been several lifestyles of relatively short duration in the past two decades in the United States for which it is fairly easy to ascertain temporal dimensions. Of these, the ones under the general label counterculture have received a great deal of scholarly and popular attention.

Counterculture Lifestyles

The term counterculture refers to a subculture with distinct beliefs, values, symbols, and norms that stand in opposition to those of the larger culture and is often used to embrace a cluster of lifestyles of relatively short duration (see, for example, Schwendener, 2001). These lifestyles represent a distinct subculture, and the term counterculture is used because it is "so radically disaffiliated from the mainstream assumptions of our society that it scarcely looks to many like a culture at all, but takes on the alarming appearance of a barbaric intrusion" (Roszak, 1995:42). A well-known spokesman for the merits of this counterculture is Charles Reich (1970), who in his book, *The Greening of America,* analyzes and cites some of the alternatives that are emerging and affecting the overall society. Central themes of Reich's analysis are that America has veered from its original humanistic purpose and that the "corporate state" has become a death-dealing machine. In examining America's earlier "levels of consciousness," he describes the manner in which America has moved off course. He first analyzes the drive that made it a corporate state and led it into becoming a death-dealing, machine-enslaved society. In Reich's terminology, *Consciousness I* involved the enormous promise of America and *Consciousness II* relates to the lifestyle that emanated from the rise of the corporate state. *Consciousness III,* according to Reich, is the adaptation of the new young revolutionary and dropout. It rests, he asserts, on various premises: respect for each individual, for his or her uniqueness and for his or her privacy; abstention from coercion or violence against any individual; abstention from killing or war; respect for the natural environment; respect for beauty in all its forms; honesty in all personal relations; equality of status between all individuals; genuine democracy in the making of decisions; and freedom of expression and conscience.

"There is a revolution coming," he writes. "It will not be like revolutions of the past. It will originate with the individual and with culture, and it will change the political structure only as its final act." He asserts that "the revolution will not require violence to succeed and it cannot be successfully resisted by violence" (Reich, 1970:2). One characteristic of the revolution, on the part of the young, affluent dropout, is the development of lifestyles that are alternatives to the status quo, and is based on opposition to the status quo. Hippies [or "zippies," the counterculture of hippies in England (Caniglia, 1994)]; yippies; Weathermen; committed psychedelic drug trippers; and black-, brown-, and white-power advocates, are all characterized by a disenchantment with the dehumanization of the larger society and a subsequent involvement with alternative lifestyles which, they believe, are more humanistic (although it should be noted that the Weathermen, yippies, and similar groups could hardly be considered as humanists).

Both in the United States and abroad, the 1960s witnessed the rise of several alternative lifestyles challenging mainstream values and embracing antimaterialistic and pacifist nonaggression ideals (Harrison, 1993). Sixties activists confronted the institutions of American postwar culture (Farrell, 1997). This was a period of turbulence, an era of rapid social change, when many American youth played important roles of challenger and innovator. They viewed the so-called "establishment" as threatening, and its institutional norms and traditional values were seriously questioned. Many rejected the material values of their parents, and "In phrases redolent of nearly all utopian thought of the past, they proclaim[ed] that happiness and a meaningful life are not to be found in things, but in the cultivation of the self and by intensive exploration of inner sensibilities with like-minded others" (Davis, 1971:106).

There were several ways of exploring "inner sensibilities." Many began to experiment with mind-altering substances, such as LSD, peyote, and, especially, marijuana. Timothy Leary's admonition to "Turn on, tune in, and drop out" progressively captured the imagination of millions of young people during this period. An important consequence of these experiments was the evolution and development of alternative lifestyles and a different perception of the world. Hippie communal colonies began to emerge in both urban and rural areas. The best known of these is the Haight-Ashbury district in San Francisco, initially populated by the so-called "flower children." It lasted about two years, and "The Haight, as a youth community, was dead. However, the anti-values expressed and acted out by those in the Haight of 1966 were diffused (even as they were romantically distorted) across America by both under- and overground media" (Lewis, 1974:379). Many hippies later formed tribes and lived in communes, some lived near Native American tribes or in simulated Native American styles, and others established nonviolent subgroups. However, some groups dedicated to violence developed as the original hippie lifestyle waned.

In the quest for a new humanistic community, a militant and sometimes violent lifestyle became, for some, a methodology for change. Unlike the more retreatist classic hippies, such diverse and transient groups as the yippies, white panthers, Weathermen, and various self-labeled "freaks" are more apt to engage in aggressive behavior against a system they find oppressive. In the optimistic words of Abbie Hoffman (1969:77):

> In the past few years our numbers have grown from hundreds to millions of young people. Our conspiracy has grown more militant. Flower children have lost their innocence and grown their thorns. We have recognized that our culture in order to survive must be defended. Furthermore we have realized that the revolution is more than digging rock or turning on. The revolution is about coming together in a struggle for change. It is about the destruction of a system based on bosses and competition and the building of a new community based on people and cooperation. That old system is dying off all around us and we joyously come out in the streets to dance on its grave. With our free stores, liberated buildings, communes, people's parks, dope, free bodies and our music, we'll build our society in the vacant lots of the old and we'll do it by any means necessary. Right on!

The yippies, perhaps more than the other groups, epitomized this lifestyle of militancy and violence. The "formal" origin of this lifestyle was clearly spelled out by Jerry Rubin (1970:86):

> We started yippee with an office, a mailing list, three telephone lines, five paid staff organizers, weekly general meetings and weekly Steering Committee

meetings. We were the hardest workers and the most disciplined people you ever met, even though we extol sloth and lack of discipline. We are a living contradiction, because we're yippies. Marijuana is compulsory at all yippee meetings.

Yippies take acid at breakfast to bring us closer to reality. Holden Caulfield is a yippee. The Old Nixon was a yippee; the New Nixon is not. Yippies believe every nonyippie is a repressed yippee. We try to bring out the yippee in everybody. Yippies proclaim: Straights of the world, drop out! You have nothing to lose but your starched shirts! . . . America says: DON'T! The yippies say: DO IT.

The goal of the yippies was to turn on everybody who can be turned on and turn off everybody else. In the words of Abbie Hoffman (1968:157):

Our message is always: Do what you want. Take chances. Extend your boundaries. Break the rules. Protest is anything you can get away with. Don't get paranoid. Don't be uptight.

The lifestyles of the counterculture persisted for a relatively short time along with the unsuccessful attempts to try to revive them (see, for example, Marks, 1997). Their celebrated prophets are today part of the "establishment," and many former advocates of these lifestyles have embraced more pragmatic middle-class values and jobs—Jerry Rubin in his later years embraced capitalism and had a lucrative Wall Street job at the time of his death in 1994. Abbie Hoffman, who committed suicide in 1989, became a reporter. In general, lifestyles endure as long as they serve a set of more or less clearly identifiable needs. These needs may be emotional and personal for the individuals involved, or they may be dictated by utilitarian or ideological principles and objectives. In some cases, it may be a combination of both. But regardless of whether a particular lifestyle is more personal or utilitarian, one is concerned with how long it may be expected to endure. Some lifestyles may persist for a period of many years, while others may dissolve in a relatively short time. At the most general level, the duration of a lifestyle can be ascertained in terms of the functions it performs for the society of which it is a part, the degree to which it provides certain satisfactions to its advocates, and the extent to which new adherents to that lifestyle can be recruited.

At present, there are many ongoing countercultures with known beginnings but with no demise in sight. They include Skinheads, the Unification Church, the Ku Klux Klan, the Church of Scientology, and Survivalists (Zellner, 1995). In the future, duration of lifestyles may be established with a greater degree of accuracy. But for now, the analysis of the duration of class-based or counterculture-based lifestyles is hampered by the lack of reliable data. One can only assign rough temporal dimensions, and even then questions of reliability pop up. Even in the cases of hippie or yippee lifestyles, the life span can vary from analyst to analyst. In some instances, however, the duration of lifestyles can be approximated with a great degree of accuracy. This is the case with experiments in communal living. There have been several such ventures of discernible duration. The Oneida community is one of the most successful American experiments in communal living to date. It began in the 1840s, its radical family form lasted about thirty years, and, at its peak, it served 288 persons. It is an excellent sociological example of unique lifestyles and will be examined in some detail in the following pages.

The Oneida Community

William M. Kephart and William W. Zellner (2001) provide a comprehensive account of religious community known as Oneida. The beginnings are traced back to Putney, Vermont, in 1831, where a fierce religious revival was in progress (White, 1996). One of those deeply affected was John Humphrey Noyes, a young Dartmouth graduate intent upon the practice of law. He gave up law for the ministry, and was licensed to preach after graduation from Yale's Theological Seminary in 1833. He had been a minister only a short time when he announced that he was perfect—sinless. This statement alienated him from the mainstream of Christian orthodoxy, cost him his license, and forced him to reexamine his own principles.

His doctrine of "Perfectionism"—the attainability of the sinless or perfect state—attracted a small group of followers. Noyes began to publish Perfectionist literature, and began to develop a complex marriage system—a form of group marriage that was to be the basis of Oneida's social structure. Monogamous marriage was considered a sign of selfishness.

In 1846, the Putney community was formed, and members followed a "share-the-wealth" type of economy in which private ownership was condemned. They also practiced group marriage; that is, every adult male had marital privileges with every adult female, and vice versa. As might be expected, the citizens of Vermont were up in arms, and in 1847, Noyes was arrested and charged with adultery. He did not want to stand trial and escaped to New York State, followed by his flock. In 1848, they took up residence on the banks of the Oneida Creek in New York. The small group had some difficulties surviving the first few winters. Fortunately, one of the members invented a steel trap, which turned out to be a very profitable venture. A substantial part of the Oneida economy came to be based on the manufacture of the steel traps, and the group became free of financial worries.

The entire community was housed under one roof, the famous Mansion House. Although each adult had his or her own small room, the building was designed to encourage a feeling of togetherness, hence the inclusion of a communal dining hall, recreation rooms, library, concert hall, and the like. The community was a close group, with members seldom going very far from home. The system of sustained cultural enclosure served as a solidifying force. They raised their own food, made all their own clothes, did their own laundry, ran their own school, and performed a number of other collective tasks. But their unique social organization was not the only thing that held the Oneida community together. As the membership increased, three basic principles of Noyes' teaching combined to form the very heart of the Perfectionist lifestyle: (1) economic communism; (2) mutual criticism; and (3) complex marriage.

Economic Communism A principal feature of the Oneida Community was its adherence to economic communism. Throughout their existence, members rejected all forms of individual wealth and private property. They had no concept of private ownership, not even in the realm of personal belongings such as clothes, trinkets, or children's toys. The needs of individual members were taken care of, and they never once had second thoughts about private property.

In addition to the manufacture of steel traps, members of the community found a ready market for their crops, and their prosperity slowly increased. At one point it became necessary to hire outside help, and, eventually, the Perfectionists were employing several hundred local workers. Beginning in 1877, they embarked on the manufacture of silverware. It proved so successful that when the community dissolved, the silverware component was perpetuated as a joint stock company (Oneida, Ltd.), whose product is still widely used today.

The various jobs within the community were rotated from year to year in order to prevent feelings of discrimination. It was quickly pointed out to members that at one time or another almost everyone took a turn at the necessary menial tasks. Still, although jobs were generally rotated, individual variations in ability were recognized, and members were not placed in positions beyond their capacities. Any kind of social differentiation by occupational status was played down. Plant superintendents and farm laborers, as a result, had the same status.

Members of the community, in their efforts to promote equality, were required to eat the same kind of food, wear the same type of clothing, and live in the same home. For both sexes, dress was uniformly simple, and no adornments or jewelry were allowed. It is interesting to note that Noyes was responsible for a genuine innovation in the women's clothing style. Being dissatisfied with ordinary female attire, he set up a committee to work on the problem of designing an appropriate dress. The costume they decided upon—a short, knee-length skirt with loose trousers down to the shoes— became the standard dress of all Oneida women.

Mutual Criticism The community had neither laws nor law-enforcing officers, but there was little need for them as major infractions were nonexistent. As in any organization, however, problems of human conduct are likely to occur. And even though the Oneidans considered themselves to be Perfectionists, they acknowledged that individual idiosyncrasies did exist. Mutual criticism was the method by which such problems were handled. When someone deviated from the group norms, whenever there was a manifestation of a personality or character witness, a committee of peers would meet with the offender to discuss the matter. The experience was, at times, traumatic for certain members. Some, in fact, left the community rather than submit to what they considered unwarranted censure. There is no question that mutual criticism served as a measure of social control. The only exception was Noyes, who was never criticized by the community.

Members of the community were so convinced of the effectiveness of mutual criticism that they actually used the technique as a cure for illness. Known as *krinopathy*, the criticism cure was applied to both adults and children and was often used for everything from common colds to more serious diseases. According to their organ, the *Circular*:

> It is a common custom here for everyone who may be attacked with any disorder to send for a committee of six or eight persons, in whose faith and spiritual judgment he has confidence, to come and criticize him. The result, when administered sincerely, is almost universally to throw the patient into a sweat, or to bring on a reaction of his life against disease, breaking it up and restoring him soon to usual health. (Quoted by Kephart & Zellner, 2001:67–68)

Even death did not necessarily put a stop to the process. "Deceased members whose diaries or letters were found to be incriminating might find themselves subjected in absentia to a 'rousing criticism'" (Kephart & Zellner, 2001:68).

Complex Marriage The world remembers the Oneida community not for its social and economic system, but for their practice of complex marriage. Just as the term Mormon brings to mind polygamy, so the name Oneida conjures up thoughts about unique and advanced sex practices. It was the founder, Noyes, who coined the term free love, but it was discarded in favor of complex marriage. Noyes had no time for romantic love or monogamous marriage, and he considered such practices as signs of selfishness and personal possession. Romantic love, or "special love" as it was referred to in the community, was considered to give rise to jealousy and hypocrisy and made spiritual love impossible to attain.

Consequently, the Perfectionists promulgated the idea of complex marriage because it was natural for all men to love all women and all women to love all men. It followed that every adult should consider himself or herself married to every other adult of the opposite sex. In extolling the virtues of group marriage, Noyes stated:

> The human heart is capable of loving any number of times and any number of persons. This is the law of nature. There is no occasion to find fault with it. Variety is in the nature of things, as beautiful and as useful in love as in eating and drinking. . . . We need love as much as we need food and clothing, and God knows it; and if we trust Him for these things, why not for love? (Quoted by Kephart & Zellner, 2001:75)

It should be pointed out, however, that the members of the community abided by the doctrine of complex marriage, not for reasons of lust, as it was sometimes charged, but because of the conviction that they were following God's word.

The system of complex marriage was relatively uncomplicated. As everyone lived in the Mansion House, sexual relations were easy to arrange. If a man desired sexual intercourse with a certain woman, he simply asked her. If she agreed, he would stay with her overnight in her room. In case of a shortage of single rooms, the couples could use one of the "social" rooms set aside for that purpose.

Even in complex marriage, sex is never a simple matter. And, from the very beginning, there were a number of prohibitions and restrictions. Sex was not to be considered a "wifely duty," that is, something accepted by the female to satisfy the male.

Noyes preached the separation of the "amative" from the "propagative" functions of sex. He believed that only when the two were separated could the true goals of Perfectionism be attained. "In practice, this meant that males could have sexual intercourse up to, but not including, ejaculation. (Females, of course, could achieve sexual climax at any time.) There were two exceptions to the nonejaculatory rule: (a) when the male was having intercourse with a female who was past menopause, and (b) when a child was desired" (Kephart & Zellner, 2001:76). As the community grew, men became more enthusiastic than women in the sexual domain, and the practice of having the man ask the woman for sexual relations was replaced by a new system.

Under the new system, if a man desired sexual relations, he would transmit the message to a central committee member, usually an older woman, who would thereupon make his request known to the woman in question. In practice, the use of a go-between served a number of purposes, such as sparing women the embarrassment of voicing a refusal or conjuring up an excuse. The use of a go-between also provided a measure of control over the sexual system. It helped to prevent their members from falling in "special love," and when a particular couple were having too-frequent relations, the go-between would simply disallow further meetings between them. The Oneidans were presumed to act like ladies and gentlemen at all times; inappropriate behavior, suggestive language, and overt displays of sexuality were not tolerated. Sexual behavior was not openly discussed within the community, and the subject of "who was having relations with whom" never became common knowledge. A male member who became too inquisitive on this score was literally thrown out of the community. He "found himself, one winter night, suddenly, unceremoniously, and horizontally propelled through an open window, and shot—harmlessly but ignominiously—into the depths of a snowdrift. It was the first and only forcible expulsion in the history of the community" (quoted by Kephart & Zellner, 2001:77).

As may be expected, John Humphrey Noyes also had some "advanced" ideas about the subject of children. He felt that only those who possessed superior physical and mental abilities should have children. In the words of the *Circular*:

> Why should not beauty and noble grace of person and every other desirable quality of men and women, internal and external, propagated and intensified beyond all former precedent by the application of the same scientific principles of breeding that produce such desirable results in the case of sheep, cattle, and horses? (Quoted by Kephart & Zellner, 2001:83)

The term eugenics had not yet been coined. However, he proposed, in effect, a eugenic program in which specially chosen adults would be utilized for breeding purposes. A committee would decide on the individuals who could become parents, and there would be no appeal. Noyes called this program *stirpiculture*, and it was not long before the scientific world was discussing the implications of this unique experiment.

For the first two decades, members of the community had largely refrained from bearing children. They reasoned that procreation should be delayed until such time as the group had the facilities for proper child care. Noyes rejected all forms of contraception and advocated the birth control technique of *coitus reservatus*, that is, sexual intercourse up to, but not including, ejaculation on the part of the male. Until they had mastered the necessary coital control, younger men in the community were required to limit their sexual relations to women who had passed menopause.

At the beginning of the eugenics program, fifty-three women and thirty-eight men were chosen to be parents by the committee. During the decade or so of the program, there were fifty-eight live births. Noyes himself fathered upwards of a dozen children. For the first fifteen months, children remained under the care of their mothers. After that, they were transferred to a special section of the Mansion House, called the "children's house," where they were raised communally. They would spend most of their childhood in age-graded classes. Although they were treated with kindness by their parents, sentimentalizing was frowned upon, the feeling being that under Perfectionism all adults should love all children, and vice versa. The children were well adjusted, and as a group they were remarkably healthy. Mortality comparisons indicate that the products of stirpiculture had a significantly lower death rate than children born outside the Oneida community.

The Breakup Outside pressures against the community, as might have been predicted, were becoming irresistible. Professional crusaders and self-appointed watchdogs of American morals complained about such practices as "free love," "lust," and "animal breeding," and were successful in creating a storm of adverse public criticism. As a result of ever-increasing pressure campaigns, the Oneidans were forced to give up their practice of complex marriage. In 1877 Noyes resigned, and in 1879 he left the community for the same reason that he had fled Putney thirty-two years before: to escape the law. No new leader appeared, and, during 1880, plans for dissolution were discussed and approved. On January 1, 1881, the Oneida community officially ceased to exist.

At that time the community gave up its distinctive style of life, its complex form of marriage, and its stirpiculture children. The members entered into monogamous marriages, retained their accumulated capital, and launched Oneida Company, Ltd., a venture in silversmithing that continues today. The style of this corporation was much influenced by idealism, and its board of directors and managerial staff frequently took cuts in salary in order to help the company. This practice, along with the habit of generally low wages for executives, has disappeared as the company had to compete in the larger markets for top executives. Today, Oneida Ltd. is a worldwide organization with thousands of employees, and its stocks are traded on the New York Stock Exchange.

Explanations for the community's disintegration vary. Internally, the aging Noyes was apparently unable to turn the leadership over to his son. The son was more interested in biology than in experimental communities. Although the power of the community was formally vested in the council of elders, Noyes usually tipped the balance of power in matters that concerned him. He was, however, unable to provide for his succession. The community also outraged official morality, and worsening community relations may have contributed to the disbanding. Noyes also had a habit of initiating young virgins into the sexual life of the community, and apparently some girls were under the age of consent. As a result, he was charged with rape and fled the community in an attempt to avoid prosecution. There was also conflict between the generations; some younger members objected to the principle of ascendancy, and some preferred monogamous marriage over complex marriage. This conflict between the generations may have contributed to the internal tension. However, any explanation offered must be less than adequate because much of the data—the diaries and the personal accounts of the community—were burned to protect the reputation of those involved after the establishment of the corporation. All that remains are in the recollections of children of members and the published accounts of the community's life. Thus, the case of the community raises questions that must finally remain unanswered.

Still, the case of Oneida is perhaps the best-documented illustration of a lifestyle of specific duration. Its complex marriage, economic communism, mutual criticism, and unique child-rearing program lasted approximately thirty years. It had a high degree of internal cohesion; it was highly homogeneous, dominated by upper-middle-class literate people; and it drew on the prior organization of Perfectionist circles. The commitment to remain aware of the community's development and one's own progress toward becoming a more perfect being further contributed to social solidarity and to its distinctive character. Although this venture in utopia was not durable, it provided an excellent case study of unconventional lifestyles. In the next section, duration of another type of transitory social phenomena, cults, will be examined.

CULTS

Cults and social movements are considered transitory social phenomena because of their relatively short duration (LaPiere, 1965:59–66). In the sociological literature, both cults and social movements are generally subsumed under the heading of *collective behavior*. A cult is a religious group that advocates a belief that is new and unconventional in society (Curtis & Curtis, 1993). It has the continuity of a social movement and usually makes demands only on the behavior of its members. A social movement, by definition, is a collectivity acting with some continuity to promote or resist change at various levels in society (McAdam & Snow, 1997:xxiii). Leadership in a movement is determined by the informal response of participants rather than by formal procedures legitimizing authority (Turner & Killian, 1987:223). Often, social movements are expressed through new trends in literature, art, the popular press, and the adoption of novel lifestyles. Thus, as a collective activity, successful social movements have an identifiable life span. For example, William A. Gamson (1990), in a study of fifty-three "challenge" groups in the United States between 1800 and 1945, in addition to analyzing the strategies and outcomes of these movements, also indicated the approximate duration of each. As we shall discuss in Chapter 9, social movements cover an extremely broad spectrum of human activities. Important social movements in the United States and abroad to a lesser extent have focused on the abolition of slavery, temperance, civil rights, resistance to war, environmentalism (Halsey, 2001; Oberschall, 1993) and feminism and the "gendered" experience of the femocrats in Australian politics (Eisenstein, 1996). But there have been literally hundreds of other social movements in the United States aimed at solving a wide range of problems using a variety of strategies and tactics (see, for example, Tarrow, 1996). Even though in this section the emphasis is on cults, let us for a moment consider the nature of social movements.

There are several types of social movements based on the objectives of participants. Some examples:

1. *Revolutionary Movements.* Participants in these movements are deeply dissatisfied with the existing social order and promote change in accordance with their ideology. Such movements can bring about sweeping social changes, as happened, for example, in countries such as Russia, China, Cuba, and Iran.

2. *Reactionary Movements.* These are social movements whose members oppose certain changes and aim to return to the "good old days." Examples include the Moral Majority, the Ku Klux Klan, the John Birch Society, and the American Nazi Party. They all oppose social changes advocated by other movements.

3. *Reform Movements.* Participants are generally satisfied with the existing social order but feel that certain reforms are necessary in specific areas. Reform movements generally work with the system, often through the legislative process. Examples include the consumer, environment, and anti-nuclear movements.

4. *Expressive Movements.* Instead of changing external conditions in society, followers of expressive movements are concerned with the modification of the attitudes and behavior to enable them to cope better with the outside world. They accept society as is, and any change must come from within. Many expressive social movements have a religious focus, seeking to transform people's lives radically, as is the case with the various fundamentalist Christian sects. Participants in such movements seek to achieve mastery over their feelings and emotions and search for inner ways to accept current conditions.

Like all transitory social phenomena, every cult and social movement has a life cycle, a series of stages in its natural history, during which it arises, develops, goes through various phases, decays, and comes to some kind of end (Sztompka, 1994:285–292). Armand L. Mauss (1975:61) calls these stages (1) incipiency, (2) coalescence, (3) institutionalization, (4) fragmentation, and (5) demise. In the *incipient* phase, early advocates of the movement formulate its essential definition and orientations. This is accompanied by a period of popular excitement in which the goals and orientations of innovators gradually spread through relevant segments of the population. The next stage is *coalescence,* in which one or more groups form around leaders and develop patterns of formal organization, specifying goals, norms, a division of labor, social controls, and so forth. As these groups interact with the larger society, *institutionalization*, the process of "strengthening, stabilizing, and perpetuating a pattern of social ordering" (Olsen, 1978:117) gradually occurs through the establishment of definite norms that assign status positions and role functions. The movement becomes a recognized part of society that must somehow be taken into account by the public. But "an irony in the natural history of social movements is that their very success leads to fragmentation" (Mauss, 1975:64). *Fragmentation* in turn leads to the final stage of movements, to their eventual *demise*. A social movement to promote change may reach this final stage for various reasons. Its goals may become official policy, as happened to the Townsend movement of the 1930s, when Social Security provided its goal of old-age pensions.

A movement may become part of the establishment itself; for example, organized labor movements and unions for a long time have been the recognized bargaining agents with management. A movement can also be repressed by the larger society; for example, the New Left, or its leaders, are co-opted, or "bought off." Finally, it should be noted that not all movements pass through stages. A movement may collapse and vanish at any stage, and a large number of movements—because of their objectives, strategies, or internal makeup—never reach the institutionalization stage of stability and recognition and thus fail to exert any effect on the larger society. The life span of a movement that passes through these five stages can be determined with some degree of accuracy.

Two cults, the Ghost Dance and the Cargo cult, which will be considered here, have proved to be objects of intense fascination for students of social movements and social change, and they have received a great deal of attention both from anthropologists and sociologists. Of course, there have been many other examples of cults in the annals of anthropology (see, for example, Willigen, 2002) and sociology, and their numbers vary from 700 to 5,000, depending on who does the counting (*Newsweek*, 1993:60). They range from the religious cults at the dawn of human civilization to, for example, the belief in the ultimate salvation through drugs during the Middle Ages, to Normal Vincent Peale's "power of positive thinking" in modern times. More recently, the International Society for Krishna Consciousness (a cult of purported Indian origin), Reverend Sun Myung Moon's Unification Church (whose members are called Moonies), Bhagwan Shree Rajneesh's now-defunct communal cult in Oregon, and Los Angeles Church of Christ have attracted many followers. After the grisly events at the People's Temple in Guyana, where more than 900 cult members committed mass suicide in late 1978; the storming of the Branch Davidians in Waco, Texas, in 1993; the mass murder-suicide of fifty-three members of Solar Temple in Switzerland in fall of 1994 (Serrill, 1994); and the suicide of 39 people in San Diego in 1997 linked to a cult called Heaven's Gate (Purdum, 1997), many such cults are viewed with skepticism and encounter strong opposition, especially when they start recruiting children from middle-class families (see, for example, Wright, 1993).

The Ghost Dance Cult

A cult that has received considerable attention from social scientists is the well-known Ghost Dance religion (Hittman, 1992; Kracht, 1992; Mohrbacher, 1996; McNeil, 2001). This cult, which lasted only a short period of time and involved relatively few Indians, has generated an inordinate amount of interest among sociologists and anthropologists. "The reason seems to be that it now acts as something of a symbol or representational drama of the agony of the Native Americans, faced with the inevitability of defeat at the hands of the predatory white and feeling that his old gods had failed him" (Wilson, 1973:48).

By the 1870s, the plight of the Plains Indians of North America had reached its lowest ebb. They had been driven into the most barren wastelands as reservations; the white man had killed many of their finest warriors (along with a number of women and children). Venereal disease, tuberculosis, and alcoholism had greatly diminished the population, and near-starvation was commonplace.

In 1870, a prophet appeared to the Paiute Indians of Nevada. He called himself Wovoka, the Messiah. When he was twenty years old, the sun went into an eclipse and Wovoka fell asleep and was taken into the spirit world.

> After showing him all, God told him he must go back and tell his people they must be good and love one another, have no quarreling, and live in peace with the whites, that they must work, and not lie or steal . . . that if they faithfully obeyed his instructions they would at least be reunited with their friends in this other world, where there would be no more death or sickness or old age. He was then given the dance which he was commanded to bring back to his people. By performing this dance at intervals, for five consecutive days each time, they would secure this happiness to themselves and hasten the event. (Mooney, 1965:14)

There was a strong belief that the white man and his destructive ways would disappear. How was this to occur? As the Ghost Dance spread from tribe to tribe, different answers were given to this question. Although it originated among the Paiute, the more warlike and proud Sioux gave this belief a more militant interpretation, believing that they themselves must participate in some way in the expulsion of the whites—with the help of "ghost shirts," which would make the wearer invulnerable to the white man's bullets:

> . . . the white man's gunpowder would no longer have power to drive a bullet through the skin of an Indian. The whites themselves would soon be

overwhelmed and smothered under a deep landslide, held down by sod and timber, and the few who might escape would become small fishes in the rivers. (Mooney, 1965:29)

There were rumors of increasing belligerence among the Sioux, which caused the white settlers to take precautionary military measures. The conflict between whites and the Sioux escalated, and the whites attempted to arrest the leader of the Ghost Dance cult among the Sioux, Sitting Bull. In one of the bloodiest encounters between any Native American tribe and whites, the Battle of Wounded Knee on December 29, 1890, more than 350 Sioux, including many women and children, were massacred. This massacre was triggered by a tragic misunderstanding. While the Indians were surrendering their weapons to federal troops, a great deal of tension arose in the camp as soldiers overturned teepees, beds, and furniture in their search for guns. A medicine man kept walking among the warriors assuring them that the whites would be helpless against the ghost shirts and, therefore, the Sioux should resist the troops. Somehow, a shot was fired at the soldiers. Their retaliation resulted in the well-known massacre.

This defeat signaled the end of the Ghost Dance cult among the Sioux. Before the battle with the federal troops at Wounded Knee, the cult had lasted slightly over one year.

The occurrence of the Ghost Dance is explained in the literature as the result of the wholesale disintegration of Sioux social organization, which had followed the arrival of the white man to the plains (Wilson, 1973:49–50). The loss of their hunting grounds, the influx of settlers, the extension of the railroads, the steady and often illegal takeover of land by federal authorities, and the official encouragement of the decimation of the buffalo herds all contributed to a severe strain on the Native American community. The loss of the buffalo was particularly devastating to the Sioux. It was a source of food, shelter, clothing, and an article of trade. Social status was measured in terms of buffalo-hunting skills. The buffalo also represented a sacred significance in the culture of the Sioux, acting like a totem animal to the tribe. The loss of the sacred aspects of a culture, particularly when it is brought about by outsiders, can be very disturbing to any community, and this particular event further enhanced the receptivity of the Sioux to the Ghost Dance. The Ghost Dance, with its belief in imminent extinction of the white man and its magical belief in the protective powers of the ghost shirt, seems to have met the needs of the Sioux during this stage of disorganization.

After this defeat at Wounded Knee, large numbers of Indians turned to the use of peyote, a carrot-shaped cactus that produces visual and auditory hallucinations. It was no accident that the popularity of the peyote cult followed the demise of the Ghost Dance. "The Ghost Dance promised redemption and liberation at a time when the Indians were ready for rebellion, and provided the motivating force for uprisings such as that of the Sioux; the peyote cult emerged when the Ghost Dance was being snuffed out and the Indians were forced to admit defeat, but when, however, the white man had changed his attitude and substituted assimilation in place of destruction" (Lanternari, 1965:59).

The Cargo Cult

Cargo cult is the designation of a kind of movement, primarily restricted to Melanesia, which is centered on a belief in the coming of a cargo ship, staffed by ancestral spirits, which would contain European goods such as radios, tobacco, steel axes, alcohol, trucks, and occasionally arms (Dalton, 2000). The arrival of the Cargo ship, the natives believed, would initiate a new era of plenty and would release them from their present sufferings. The Cargo cultists devoted their lives to preparations for the arrival of the Cargo; they built piers for the ship and warehouses for the goods; they imitated European ceremonials; and renounced their old lifestyles and destroyed the crops and livestock in the belief that these would hasten the coming of the Cargo (Kempf, 1992).

One of the most spectacular of these Cargo cults was the Vailala Madness, which broke out in the Gulf of Papua after World War I. It was supposedly initiated by an old man named Evara. Evara went into a trance at the death of his father and awoke giving forth prophesies.

> He prophesized the coming of a steamer carrying the spirits of dead ancestors on board, who would bring them the "cargo". . . . The spirits had revealed that all the flour, rice, tobacco, and other "trade" belonged to the Papuans, not the whites. The latter would pass into the hands of its rightful owners, the natives. To obtain these goods it was necessary to drive out the whites. (Worsley, 1957:81)

Once started, the cult

> involved a kind of mass hysteria, in which numbers of natives were affected by giddiness and reeled about the villages. So infectious was it that almost the whole population of a village might be affected at one time. The leaders of the movement poured forth utterances in "djaman" ("German"), which were in fact a mixture of nonsense of syllables and pidgin English. Sometimes these were incomprehensible, but sometimes the leaders gave intelligible utterances to prophesies and injunctions. The central theme of the former was that the ancestors would soon return to the gulf in a ship, bringing with them a cargo of good things. The leaders of the movement communed with them by means of flag-poles, down which messages were transmitted to the base where they were received by those who had ears to hear—an obvious adaptation of the idea of a wireless mast. Elaborate preparations were made to receive the ancestors, and offerings of food for them were placed in special houses under the control of the leaders. (Piddington, 1957:739)

The leaders of the cult claimed that they were told by their ancestors to have the people abandon the old ceremonial customs and to burn their noisemakers and ceremonial masks. The Vailala Madness, in its intense form, lasted only about three years. It was unrealistic and therefore ineffective in coping with the stressful situation in which the natives found themselves.

Another version of the Cargo cult, the Taro cult, started about 1914, when a native prophet, Buninia, emerged from a trance in which he had been visited by a Taro or food spirit. The "Taro men" designed dances, singing, and community eating rituals that were followed by trances, seizures, and ecstatic experiences. Followers of the cult were assured that their ancestors would bring them food as well as European garments and tools. The natives were reacting to the relative wealth of their new white neighbors, and the Taro cult was able to offer them what they lacked—that is, hope for material improvement. Whites came into the area around the turn of the century in search of gold. Gold mines were established with the aid of native labor. The working conditions of the natives were anything but ideal, resulting in the development of hostility toward the white man. The cult helped them to channel this hostility and, at the same time, contributed to the development of some unity among the traditionally antagonistic tribes in the area. By 1930, however, the Taro cult started to decline in importance. Its decline was facilitated by the perception of the British administrators of the Taro cult as an antiwhite, antigovernment organization. However, it was not seen as a great enough threat to the colonial system to be harshly suppressed.

Another New Guinea Cargo cult resulted in unanticipated consequences. The disciples of the cult went to the mission station and presented the missionary with their belief, asking him what he thought of it. In the words of Ward Goodenough (1963:314–315):

> He did not sneer, but expressed approval of its obvious Biblical content, of the aspirations it revealed, and what it was they were trying to conceptualize within the outwardly fantastic myth. Finding that he was not hostile, they asked him if he could show them the road by which they might achieve their aspirations. By agreeing to teach them the way, he came to occupy the position of "prophet" for the revitalization movement, at least in the people's eyes. In this way he acquired considerable control over its adaptation and transformation phases. He succeeded, accordingly, in getting the several villages in the movement to revise a number of their marriage and family customs in the direction endorsed by his religious denomination.

In this particular instance, the missionary had found a way of working from the "inside" to the "out," introducing many changes in the pattern of village life that were in keeping with the aims of his mission. This entailed the co-optation of cult leaders, which, in turn, resulted in the rapid demise of the original belief system.

There have been a number of other Cargo cults that have made their presence felt in a wide variety of locales throughout Melanesia. The principal theme of the cults is that the returning ancestors will drive out the whites—in some cases with the help of the cultists, in other cases, by themselves (Wilson, 1973:51–52). In the former instance, which marks a more militant interpretation of the Cargo cult, the Cargo is always thought to contain artifacts of war, such as weapons, radios, and trucks. All of the Cargo cults were basically anti-European in character, and they rarely lasted for long. "They have succumbed either to the frustrations of repeated failure of the Cargo to arrive or to the antagonism of fearful colonial authorities" (Wilson, 1973:51). In addition to its bizarre manifestations, the Cargo cult has attracted attention because of the fact that it often erupted in a relatively stable and homogeneous community. Just as in the case of American Indians, the coming of the white man meant the loss of land and the disruption of native social organizations. Social disorganization was also brought about by the use of native labor in mines and plantations, which often resulted in a separate residence away from their villages. This, in turn, affected the network of family obligations to which the islanders felt traditionally bound. Finally, the coming of the white man meant the arrival of highly divisive Christianity. There were competing missionaries, but they managed to renounce uniformly many traditional sacred practices as sinful. Simultaneously, they preached the value of obligations and associations that ignored the old tribal and kinship ties. On top of this, the Europeans brought a new lifestyle and new models of consumption, which the natives were able to envy but not to emulate.

In the words of a frustrated old villager: "When we followed our customs, we lived in peace and honor. Now everything is new and pulls us in different directions. We are confused" (Kristof, 1987:6). At the same time, the unrealistic, bizarre, and fanatic nature of cults greatly contributed to their own demise. One can only wait so long for the Cargo to arrive.

SUMMARY

In this chapter, we have considered the question of how long change will be sustained after its introduction and before its demise or drastic alteration in a social system. In a historical context, the study of the duration of change is problematic because of the broad and amorphous time dimensions. Still, it is possible to talk about general longevity patterns for historical periods in terms of distinct eras of considerable life span.

The discussion of the duration of change becomes more concrete and meaningful in the framework of transitory social changes. Here we are dealing with datable, recognizable, and, in many instances, measurable events of relatively short duration.

Fads and fashions provide an extraordinary opportunity to study the life span of changes. Both are culture patterns that are adopted by a given segment of a society for a relatively brief period of time and then abandoned. Of the two, fads are of shorter duration; they tend to appear suddenly and disappear as suddenly. Fashion and faddish changes are present in most aspects of group life, and some, such as phrenology or the Florida land boom, can have serious implications.

The study of lifestyles affords another occasion for the analysis of the duration of change. Class-based lifestyles tend to endure longer than the so-called counterculture lifestyles of hippies or yippies. An excellent sociological example of a unique lifestyle of discernible duration is found among the members of the Oneida community, which endured approximately three decades.

Cults and social movements are considered transitory social-change phenomena because of their relatively short duration. Both have a life cycle, a series of stages in their natural history. The Ghost Dance and the Cargo cults, both of short duration, proved to be objects of intense fascination for social scientists. In the next chapter the various strategies of change will be examined.

SUGGESTED FURTHER READINGS

AGUIRRE, B. E., E. L. QUARANTELLI, AND JORGE L. MENDOZA. "Streaking," *American Sociological Review*, 53, August 1988, pp. 569–584. The major collective behavior themes on the effect of participation, identification, and career of fads are tested with data on 1,016 incidents of streaking on college campuses.

BENSMAN, JOSEPH, AND ARTHUR J. VIDICH. *American Society: The Welfare State & Beyond*, rev. ed. South Hadley, MA: Bergin & Garvey, 1987. See, in particular, Part III on emerging lifestyles and the new classes.

CRAIK, JENNIFER. *The Face of Fashion: Cultural Studies in Fashion*. London: Routledge, 1994. An entertaining and insightful treatment of fashion changes and the prejudices and inhibitions that entrap the human body.

DIANA, MARIO, AND DOUG MCADAM. *Social Movements and Networks: Relational Approaches to Collective Action*. New York: Oxford University Press, 2002. An up-to-date compendium and source material on the diverse facets of social movements.

FARRELL, JAMES J. *The Spirit of the Sixties: The Making of the Postwar Radicalism*. New York: Routledge, 1997. A good account of the 1960s activists in various contexts such the civil rights movement, Ban-the-Bomb protests and the Beat generation lifestyles.

GLADWELL, MALCOLM. *The Tipping Point*. Boston: Bay/Little, Brown, 2002. A journalist's study of social epidemics, otherwise known as fads. The book is slightly more readable than the standard academic treatise on the subject but is equally informative.

KEPHART, WILLIAM M., AND WILLIAM W. ZELLNER. *Extraordinary Groups: An Examination of Unconventional Life-Styles*, 7th ed. New York: Worth, 2001. A highly readable account of the Old Order Amish, the Oneida community, the Gypsies, the Father Divine Movement, the Mormons, and some other contemporary lifestyles.

SIMMEL, GEORG. "Fashion," *American Journal of Sociology*, 62, May 1957, pp. 541–558. A classic statement of the role of fashion in society.

STEELE, VALERIE. *The Corset: A Cultural Study*. New Haven, CT: Yale University Press, 2001. A fascinating study of the corset in the context of the Victorian obsession with sex.

TURNER, RALPH H., AND LEWIS M. KILLIAN. *Collective Behavior*, 3rd ed. Englewood Cliffs, NJ: Prentice Hall, 1987. See particularly the outstanding sections on cults and social movements.

WORSLEY, PETER. *The Trumpet Shall Sound: A Study of "Cargo" Cults in Melanesia*. London: Macgibbon & Kee, 1957. One of the most comprehensive treatments of cults in print.

ZELLNER, WILLIAM W. *Countercultures: A Sociological Analysis*. New York: St. Martin's Press, 1995. A fascinating review of some of the ongoing countercultures such as the Skinheads, Satanism, the Unification Church, Ku Klux Klan, the Church of Scientology, and Survivalists.

REFERENCES

AGUIRRE, B. E., E. L. QUARANTELLI, AND JORGE L. MENDOZA. "Streaking," *American Sociological Review*, 53, August 1988, pp. 569–584.

BENSMAN, JOSEPH, AND ARTHUR J. VIDICH. *American Society: The Welfare State & Beyond*, rev. ed. South Hadley, MA: Bergin & Carvey, 1987.

BIKHCHANDANI, SUSHIL, DAVID HIRSHLEIFER, AND IVO WELCH. "A Theory of Fads, Fashion, Custom, and Cultural Change as Informational Cascades," *Journal of Political Economy*, 100 (5) October 1992, pp. 992–1027.

BLUMER, HERBERT. "Fashion." In David L. Sills (ed.), *International Encyclopedia of the Social Sciences*, vol. 5. New York: Macmillan/Free Press, 1968, pp. 341–345.

BOGENHOLD, DIETER. "Social Inequality and the Sociology of Life Style: Material and Cultural Aspects of Social Stratification (Focus on Economic Sociology)," *The American Journal of Economics and Sociology*, 60 (4) October 2001, pp. 829–848.

BOSKOFF, ALVIN. *The Mosaic of Sociological Theory*. New York: Crowell, 1972.

BROWN, ED. "$79 K—And It Keeps Score," *Fortune*, 135 (4) March 1997, p. 42.

BUENTING, JULIE A. "Health Life-Styles of Lesbian and Heterosexual Women," *Health Care for Women International*, 13 (2) April–June 1992, pp. 165–171.

CANIGLIA, JULIE. "Summer of Raving Love, 1994. (British alternative culture)," *Utne Reader*, 64 (2) July–August 1994, p. 26.

CARMAN, JAMES M. "The Fate of Fashion Cycles in Our Modern Society." In Raymond M. Haas (ed.), *Proceedings of the American Marketing Association, 1966*. Chicago: American Marketing Association, pp. 722–737.

COCKERHAM, WILLIAM C., THOMAS ABEL, AND GUNTHER LUSCHEN. "Max Weber: Formal Rationality and Health Lifestyles," *The Sociological Quarterly*, 34 (3) Fall 1993, pp. 413–426.

COELHO, PHILIP R. P., AND JAMES E. MCCLURE. "Toward an Economic Theory of Fashion," *Economic Inquiry*, 32 (4) October 1993, pp. 595–606.

CRAIK, JENNIFER. *The Face of Fashion: Cultural Studies in Fashion*. London: Routledge, 1994.

CURTIS, JOHN M., AND MIMI J. CURTIS. "Factors Related to Susceptibility and Recruitment by Cults," *Psychological Reports*, 73 (2) October 1993, pp. 451–461.

DALTON, DOUG, "Cargo Cults and Discursive Madness," *Oceania*, 70 (4) June 2000, pp. 345–369.

DAVIS, FRED. "Why All of Us May Be Hippies Someday." In Dennis Pirages (ed.), *Seeing Beyond Personal, Social and Political Alternatives*. Reading, MA: Addison-Wesley, 1971, pp. 102–113.

DAVIS, KINGSLEY. *Human Society*. New York: Macmillan, 1949.

Economist. "Ten Million People Can Be Wrong: Research on Consumer Fads," February 19, 1994, p. 81.

EISENSTEIN, HESTER. *Inside Agitators: Australian Femocrats and the State*. Philadelphia, PA: Temple University Press, 1996.

ELLERSON, AMY. "X Marks Spot in Credit Card Game," *St. Louis Post-Dispatch*, August 8, 1997, p. 6C.

Encyclopedia Americana. International edition. "Phrenology," vol. 26. Danbury, CT: Grolier: 1998.

FAISON, SETH. "A City of Sleepwalkers? No, They Just Like PJ's," *The New York Times*, August 6, 1997, p. A4.

FARRELL, JAMES J. *The Spirit of the Sixties: The Making of the Postwar Radicalism*. New York: Routledge, 1997.

FELDMAN, SAUL D., AND GERALD W. THIELBAR (eds.). *Life Styles: Diversity in American Society*, 2nd ed. Boston: Little, Brown, 1975.

FLEISHMAN, AVROM. *New Class Culture: How an Emergent Class Is Transforming America's Culture*. Westport, CT: Praeger, 2003.

Fortune. "Why People Often Act Like Sheep: The Theory of Fads," 134 (7) October 14, 1996, pp. 49–51.

GAMSON, WILLIAM A. *The Strategy of Social Protest*, 2nd ed. Belmont, CA: Wadsworth, 1990.

GILBERT, DENNIS, AND JOSEPH A. KAHL. *The American Class Structure: A New Synthesis*, 4th ed. Belmont, CA: Wadsworth, 1993.

GLADWELL, MALCOLM. *The Tipping Point*. Boston: Bay/Little, Brown, 2002.

GLENN, JEROME C., AND THEODORE J. GORDON. *2002 State of the Future*. Washington, DC: American Council for the United Nations University, 2002.

GOODENOUGH, WARD HUNT. *Cooperation in Change*. New York: Russell Sage, 1963.

GREELEY, ANDREW. "Coleman Revisited: Religious Structures as a Source of Social Capital," *American Behavioral Scientist*, 40 (5) March–April 1997, pp. 587–592.

GREENE, BOS. "Abbie Hoffman Ready to Join 'Heroes' of One-Man Shows," *St. Louis Post-Dispatch*, October 26, 1977, p. 3H.

GRUBLER, ARNULF. "Time for a Change: On the Patterns of Diffusion of Innovation," *Daedalus*, 125 (3) Summer 1996, pp. 19–43.

HAKIM, DANNY. "Talk About Generation Gaps—This One's 38 Million Strong," *The New York Times*, November 10, 2002, p. 2WK.

HALSEY, RICHARD S. *The Citizen Action Encyclopedia: Groups and Movements That Changed America*. Westport, CT: Praeger, 2001.

HARRIS, MARVIN. "What Goes Up May Stay Up," *Natural History*, 81, January 1973, pp. 18.
HARRISON, BENJAMIN T. "Roots of the Anti-Vietnam War Movement," *Studies in Conflict and Terrorism*, 16 (2) April–June 1993, pp. 99–111.
HITTMAN, MICHAEL. "The 1890 Ghost Dance in Nevada," *American Indian Culture and Research Journal*, 16 (4) Fall 1992, pp. 123–166.
HOFFMAN, ABBIE. *Revolution for the Hell of It*. New York: Dial, 1968.
HOFFMAN, ABBIE. *Woodstock Nation*. New York: Vintage, 1969.
HOLLANDER, ANNE. *Sex and Suits*. New York: Knopf, 1994.
HUNT, MORTON. "Navigating the Therapy Maze: A Consumer's Guide to Mental Health Treatment," *The New York Times Magazine*, August 30, 1987, pp. 28–49.
INGOLD, TIM. *Evolution and Social Life*. Cambridge, England: Cambridge University Press, 1986.
INNES-SMITH, JAMES, AND HENRIETTA WEBB. *Bad Hair*. London: Bloomsbury, 2003.
JONES, MARIAN A. "The Model T: Enduring Popularity of T-Shirts," *Psychology Today*, 30 (2) March–April 1997, pp. 14–15.
KAHL, JOSEPH A. *The American Class Structure*. New York: Holt, Rinehart & Winston, 1957.
KATZ, ELIHU, AND PAUL F. LAZARSFELD. *Personal Influence*. New York: Free Press, 1955.
KEMPF, WOLFGANG. "'The Second Coming of the Lord': Early Christianization, Episodic Time, and the Cultural Construction of Continuity in Sibog," *Oceania*, 63 (1) September 1992, pp. 72–87.
KEPHART, WILLIAM M., AND WILLIAM W. ZELLNER. *Extraordinary Groups: An Examination of Unconventional Life-Styles*, 7th ed. New York: Worth, 2001.
KRACHT, BENJAMIN R. "The Kiowa Ghost Dance, 1894–1916: An Unheralded Revitalization Movement," *Ethnohistory*, 39 (4) Fall 1992, pp. 452–478.
KRISTOF, NICHOLAS D. "Space Age Succeeds Stone Age on Pacific Isle," *The New York Times*, July 19, 1987, p. 6.
KROEBER, A. L. "On the Principle of Order in Civilization as Exemplified by Changes of Fashion," *American Anthropologist*, 21, 1919, pp. 235–263.
LA FERLA, RUTH. "Those Naughty Victorians Find New Takers," *The New York Times*, October 6, 2002, pp. 1 and 6 ST.
LANTERNARI, VITRIOL. *The Religious of the Oppressed: A Study of Modern Messianic Cults*. New York: New American Library (Mentor Books), 1965.
LAPIERE, RICHARD T. *Social Change*. New York: McGraw-Hill, 1965.
LENSKI, GERHARD, PATRICK NOLAN, AND JEAN LENSKI. *Human Societies: An Introduction to Macrosociology*, 8th ed. New York: McGraw-Hill Book, 1999.
LEWIS, GEORGE H. "Capitalism, Contra-Culture, and the Head Shop: Explorations in Structural Change." In Marcello Truzzi (ed.), *Sociology for Pleasure*. Englewood Cliffs, NJ: Prentice Hall, 1974, pp. 374–387.
LIND, MICHAEL. *The Next American Nation: The New Nationalism and the Fourth American Revolution*. New York: Free Press Paperbacks, 1996.
LOSYK, BOB. "Generation X: What They Think and What They Plan to Do," *The Futurist*, 31 (2) March–April 1997, pp. 39–44.
LURIE, ALISON. "Fashion and Status." In John Stimson and Ardyth Stimson (eds.), *Sociology: Contemporary Readings*, 2nd ed. Itasca, IL: F. E. Peacock Publishers, 1987, pp. 193–202.

MARKS, JOHN. "Woodstock (!) Cracks Down on the Hippies," *U.S. News & World Report*, 122 (14) April 1997, pp. 32–33.

MAUSS, ARMAND L. *Social Problems as Social Movements*. Philadelphia: Lippincott, 1975.

MCADAM, DOUG, AND DAVID A. SNOW (eds.). *Social Movements: Readings on Their Emergence, Mobilization, and Dynamics*. Los Angeles: Roxbury Publishing Company, 1997.

MCNEIL, LYNDA D. "On 'Ghost Dancing the Grand Canyon'," *Current Anthropology*, 42 (2) April 2001, pp. 277–299.

METCALF, ALLAN. *Predicting New Words: The Secrets of Their Success*. Boston: Houghton Mifflin, 2002.

MEYER, ROGER E. "LSD: The Conditions and Consequences of Use and the Treatment of Users." In J. R. Wittenborn et al. (eds.), *Proceedings of the Rutgers Symposium on Drug Abuse, 1969*. Springfield, IL: Charles C. Thomas, pp. 199–208.

MEYERSOHN, ROLF, AND ELIHU KATZ. "Notes on a Natural History of Fads," *American Journal of Sociology*, 62, May 1957, pp. 594–601.

MILLER, DELBERT C. "Influence of Technology on Industries." In Francis R. Allen, Hornell Hart, Delbert C. Miller, William F. Ogburn, and Meyer F. Nimkoff (eds.), *Technology and Social Change*. New York: Appleton, 1957a, pp. 245–277.

MILLER, DELBERT C. "Impact of Technology on Agriculture." In Francis R. Allen, Hornell Hart, Delbert C. Miller, William F. Ogburn, and Meyer F. Nimkoff (eds.), *Technology and Social Change*. New York: Appleton, 1957b, pp. 324–351.

MOHRBACHER, B. C. "The Whole World Is Coming: The 1890 Ghost Dance Movement as Utopia," *Utopian Studies*, 7 (1) Winter 1996, pp. 75–86.

MOONEY, JAMES. *The Ghost-Dance Religion and the Sioux Outbreak of 1890*. Chicago: University of Chicago Press, 1965.

MORRISON, DENTON E., AND CARLIN PAIGE HOLDEN. "The Burning Bra: The American Breast Fetish and Women's Liberation." In Robert R. Evan (ed.), *Social Movements: A Reader and Source Book*. Chicago: Rand McNally, 1973, pp. 564–583.

Newsweek. "Blue Streak; Streaking," February 4, 1974a, p. 63.

Newsweek. "Streaking: One Way to Get a B.A.," March 18, 1974b, pp. 41–42.

Newsweek. "Cultic America: A Tower of Babel," March 15, 1993, pp. 60–61.

Newsweek. "The New Rich," August 14, 1997, pp. 48–59.

OBERSCHALL, ANTHONY. *Social Movements: Ideologies, Interests, and Identities*. New Brunswick, NJ: Transaction Publishers, 1993.

OLSEN, MARVIN E. *The Process of Social Organization: Power in Social Systems*, 2nd ed. New York: Holt, Rinehart & Winston, 1978.

PENG, YALI. "Intellectual Fads in Political Science: The Cases of Political Socialization and Community Power Studies," *Political Science and Politics*, 27 (1) March 1994, pp. 100–109.

PIDDINGTON, RALPH. *An Introduction to Social Anthropology*, vol. 2. London: Oliver & Boyd, 1957.

PURDUM, TODD S. "Tapes Left by 39 in Cult Suicide Suggest Comet Was Sign to Die," *The New York Times*, March 28, 1997, pp. 1A and 11A.

RAY, PAUL H. "The Emerging Culture: Nearly One in Four American Adults Lives by a New Set of Values," *American Demographics*, 19 (2) February 1997, pp. 28–35.

REICH, CHARLES. *The Greening of America*. New York: Random House, 1970.

ROBINSON, DWIGHT E. "Fashions in Shaving and Trimming of the Beard: The Men of the Illustrated London News, 1842–1972," *American Journal of Sociology*, 81 (5) 1976, pp. 133–141.

ROSTOW, WALT W. *The Stages of Economic Growth: A Non-Communist Manifesto.* New York: Cambridge, 1961.

ROSZAK, THEODORE. *The Making of a Counterculture: Reflections on the Technocratic Society and Its Youthful Opposition.* (Originally published in New York: Doubleday, 1969.) Berkeley, CA: University of California Press, 1995.

RUBIN, JERRY. *Do It!* New York: Simon & Schuster, 1970.

RUDOFSKY, BERNARD. *The Unfashionable Human Body.* New York: Van Nostrand Reinhold Co., 1984.

SCHAFER, STEPHEN. *Theories in Criminology.* New York: Random House, 1969.

SCHWENDENER, PETER, "We Are All Bohemians Now," *American Scholar*, 70 (2) Spring 2001, pp. 103–113.

SERRILL, MICHAEL S. "The Remains of the Day," *Time*, October 24, 1994, p. 42.

SIMMEL, GEORG. "Fashion," *American Journal of Sociology*, 62, May 1957, pp. 541–558.

SMELSER, NEIL J. *Theory of Collective Behavior.* New York: Free Press, 1963.

SMITH, RUSSELL. "Cleavage, Fine. Bellies, Well, Okay. But Groins?" *The Globe and Mail*, September 21, 2002, p. R6.

SPENCER, JANE. "The Next Cosmetic-Surgery Frontier—Nipple Enhancements," *The Wall Street Journal*, August 1, 2002, p. D3.

STARK, JOAN S., AND LISA R. LATTUCA. *Shaping the College Curriculum, Academic Plans in Action.* Des Moines, IA: Longwood Division, Allyn & Bacon, 1997.

STEELE, VALERIE. *The Corset: A Cultural Study.* New Haven, CN: Yale University Press, 2001.

SZTOMPKA, PIOTR. *The Sociology of Social Change.* Cambridge, MA: Blackwell, 1994.

TARROW, SIDNEY. "Political Process and Social Change: Analyzing Politics" (book reviews), *American Political Science Review*, 90 (4) December 1996, pp. 74–84.

TAYLOR, FREDERICK W. *The Principles of Scientific Management.* New York: Harper & Row, 1911.

Time. "Streaking, Streaking Everywhere," March 18, 1974, pp. 58–59.

TRINKHAUS, JOHN. "Wearing Baseball-Type Caps: An Informal Look," *Psychological Reports*, 74 (2) April 1994, pp. 585–587.

TSAI, MICHALE. "The Next Pokemon, Yu-Gi-Oh! Cards Are Here," *The Bellingham Herald*, October 15, 2002, pp. C1, C4.

TUMIN, MELVIN M. *Social Stratification: The Form and Functions of Inequality*, 2nd ed. Englewood Cliffs, NJ: Prentice Hall, 1985.

TURNER, RALPH H., AND LEWIS M. KILLIAN. *Collective Behavior*, 3rd ed. Englewood Cliffs, NJ: Prentice Hall, 1987.

VEBLEN, THORSTEIN. *The Theory of the Leisure Class.* New York: Random House (Modern Library), 1911.

WEBER, MAX. "Class, Status and Party." In Reinhard Bendix and Seymour Martin Lipset (eds.), *Class, Status, and Power: Social Stratification in Comparative Perspective*, 2nd ed. New York: Free Press, 1966, pp. 21–28.

WHITE, JANET R. "Designed for Perfection: Intersections Between Architecture and Social Programs at the Oneida Community," *Utopian Studies*, 7 (2) Spring 1996, pp. 113–129.

WHYTE, WILLIAM H., JR. *The Organization Man.* New York: Doubleday, 1957.

WILLIGAN, JOHN VAN. *Applied Anthropology*, 3rd ed. Westport, CT: Praeger, 2002.
WILSON, JOHN. *Introduction to Social Movements*. New York: Basic Books, 1973.
WORSLEY, PETER. *The Trumpet Shall Sound: A Study of the "Cargo" Cults in Melanesia.* London: Macgibbon & Kee, 1957.
WRIGHT, LAWRENCE. "Orphans of Jonestown," *The New Yorker*, 69 (39) November 22, 1993, pp. 66–89.
WUDUNN, SHERYL. "Tokyo Toy Sensation: A Pet Lover's Hatchling," *The New York Times*, September 7, 1997, p. Y6.
YAGODA, BEN. "Retooling Critical Theory: Buddy, Can You Spare a Paradigm?" *The New York Times*, September 4, 1994, p. 6E.
ZELLNER, WILLIAM W. *Countercultures: A Sociological Analysis*. New York: St. Martin's Press, 1995.

Chapter 6

Reactions to Change

We have various reactions to change. This chapter will consider the conditions that facilitate or hinder the acceptance of change. Those involved in social change at the theoretical and practical levels recognize the proclivity of individuals, groups, organizations, institutions, and even entire societies to seek and ward off change at the same time. At every level in society, there are forces that seek to promote change, and there are those that strive to maintain the status quo. Change is both sought and opposed, and in the long run the forces that promote change in society will have an edge over those that strive toward conservatism. Change often involves disruption, the reorganization of behavior patterns, and requires some alterations of values, attitudes, and lifestyles. Very few changes of any magnitude can be accomplished without impairing the life situations of some individuals or groups. As Donald Klein (1985:98) aptly notes, "It is probably inevitable that any major change will be a mixed blessing to those undergoing it in those instances when the status quo or situation of gradual change has been acceptable to many or most people. The dynamic interplay of forces in social systems is such that any stable equilibrium must represent at least a partial accommodation to the varying needs and demands of those involved. Under such circumstances, the major change must be desired by those affected if it is to be accepted."

To a great extent, the structure of a society dictates whether change will be opposed or advocated. When a society is highly integrated so that each element is tightly interwoven with all the others in a mutually interdependent system, change is difficult and costly. For example, among a number of Nilotic African societies, such as the Pakot and Masai, the culture is integrated around the cattle complex. Cattle are not only a means of subsistence; they are also a necessity for bride purchase, a measure of status, and an object of intense affection (Schneider, 1959). Such a system is strongly resistant to social change. But when the culture is less highly integrated, so that work, play, family, religion, and other activities are less dependent on one another, change is easier and more frequent. A tightly structured society, in which every individual's roles, duties, and privileges are clearly and precisely defined, is less given to changes than a more loosely structured society, where social roles, lines of authority, privileges, and obligations are more open to individual rearrangement. For example, the structure of American society is highly conducive to social change. The prevailing individualism, lack of rigid social stratification, great emphasis on achieved status, high level of educational attainment, and institutionalization of research all tend to encourage rapid social change (Bensman & Vidich, 1987; Naisbitt & Aburdene, 1990; Sztompka, 1994; Toffler, 1980).

In the Western world, change seems normal, and most people pride themselves on being progressive and up to date. By contrast, the Trobriand Islanders off the coast of New Guinea had no concept of change and did not even have any words in their language to express or describe change. When Western visitors tried to explain the notion of change, the islanders could not understand what they were talking about. Societies obviously differ greatly in their outlook toward change. Those who revere the past, who worship their ancestors, honor and obey their elders, and are preoccupied with tradition and rituals, will change slowly and unwillingly (see, for example, Heinze, 2000). When a culture has been relatively static for a long period of time, individuals are likely to assume that it should remain so indefinitely. They consider their customs, culture, and technique as correct and everlasting. The accent is on the status quo, and change is never consciously or seriously considered. Still, change occurs in such a society, but in most cases it is too slow and too gradual to be noticed.

Although the rate of change varies from society to society, and within society among its various subgroups, it is possible to identify and analyze factors that inhibit or promote change in a variety of domains and levels. We shall now examine the conditions that play a role in the acceptance or rejection of change. A number of cross-cultural illustrations of actual situations will be considered to demonstrate the influence of specific factors in concrete change situations.

As a convenient way of organizing the diverse sources, conditions, and causes of acceptance and rejection of change, they will be considered in terms of social, psychological, cultural, and economic factors. Obviously there is a fair amount of overlapping among these factors, and the conditions of acceptance and rejection can only be separated for analytical purposes. They are the opposite sides of the same coin. The factors that are found in the nature of the social structure of the group or society are simply referred to as social; those dealing with perception, learning, and motivation are designated as psychological; factors that are culture-based are called cultural; and those with an economic base are termed economic. Clearly, economic factors set the limit of change in many situations. As it will be shown, individuals are often reluctant to change their ways because of cultural, social, and psychological factors. But equally as often they are aware of the benefits of change and are anxious to alter their traditional ways, but the economic cost is just too great. If the economical potential is not present, attention to the other three factors will be meaningless. With these introductory remarks in mind, let us now turn to the stimulants to change.

SOCIAL STIMULANTS

All societies are constantly changing—some rapidly and some very slowly. A number of factors influence the rate of change and facilitate the acceptance of an innovation. The ones that play an important role in stimulating change include the desire for prestige, contact with other peoples, friendship obligations, social class, authority, problems of "fit," timing, degree of participation in decision making, and competition. In the following paragraphs, these social stimulants to change will be examined.

Desire for Prestige

In every society, certain types of behaviors and activities are emulated because they confer prestige and status. The forms of behavior that are considered prestigious obviously differ from society to society (Zagorski, 2000). In the United States, for example, individuals with high parental and other nonwage income tend to choose high-status occupations that often produce low earnings (Fershtman & Weiss, 1993). In traditional societies, certain nonmaterial and symbolic achievements are rewarded with high status, such as religious asceticism, chastity, and fulfillment of ritual obligations. In the contemporary world, prestige is increasingly sought through the acquisition of certain visible material symbols such as clothes, food, housing, and automobiles or being listed in certain publications such as the *Botin* in France (*Economist*, 1996). There are many illustrations of how the prestige factor is significant in bringing about social change. For example, in modern Indian villages, Western clothes, cigarettes, sunglasses, and tea are popular, both because of utility and because they possess prestige value. In Zambia (formerly Northern Rhodesia), the refrigerator confers a great deal of prestige and is usually placed in the center of the living room. Egyptians find status in costly cellular phones (Mekay, 1997). In Melanesia, the prestige factor to a great extent accounts for the use of corrugated iron roofs on the better homes, which, although more durable, are less comfortable than the old fashioned sago-palm thatch. In India, mothers of lower socioeconomic groups increasingly spend money on highly advertised, patented, powdered carbohydrate foods, which have prestige value, rather than on milk and other locally produced foods that represent better nutritional value for the same price (Foster, 1973:155–158).

Felix M. Keesing (1958:400) points out that an innovation will be accepted more readily if it will add to the prestige of the acceptors. For example, in Latin America, latrines frequently are installed not because of an appreciation of the desirability of environmental sanitation, but because they add an extra note of elegance to a man's home; he thereby rises in importance in the eyes of his peers. Similarly, in rural Egypt, modern medicine is making some progress because it is becoming a sign of social prestige to bring a physician into one's home. In the same vein, using a tractor, even though it may not be economical, is a symbol of being modern in many areas. For example, Foster saw in Zimbabwe many tractors whose use was clearly not economic—as a matter of fact, many of them were inoperable—but they were valued and prominently displayed for the prestige they conferred upon the owner (Foster, 1973:157).

Contact

It is frequently proposed in the social-change literature that contact with other societies stimulates change (Bochner, 1982; Keesing, 1958:401). Because many new attributes and traits come through diffusion, those societies in closest contact with other societies are likely to change most rapidly. During the period of overland transportation, the land bridge connecting Asia, Africa, and Europe was the center of civilizing change. With the introduction of sailing vessels, the center shifted to the fringes of the Mediterranean Sea and still later to the northwest coast of Europe. Areas of greatest intercultural contact are centers of change. Traditionally, war and trade have always led to intercultural contact, and today, travel, tourism, and the mass media are adding to the contact between cultures. Through contacts, behaviors are modified, new practices are introduced, and new symbols of prestige are established. For example, as a result of increased tourism and contact with Westerners, young people in the former Soviet Union sought to emulate certain Western practices and attires. Frequently, a pair of faded blue jeans sold on the black market for $120 to $140, which approximated a month's income of an average factory worker (although such transactions carried a heavy penalty). While on the topic of jeans, a *New York Times* article (Hofmeister, 1999) reports that a vintage pair of Elvis jeans is a status symbol that "can fetch $3,000" and used Air Jordan athletic shoes from the 1980s, sweaty and soiled, can sell for "$800 or more in Japan." In general, there are certain conditions of contact that facilitate the acceptance of a novelty. They include situations in which there is equal status between members of different cultural groups, when the contact is of an intimate rather than casual nature, and when the contact is pleasant and rewarding (Jaspars & Hewstone, 1982:128).

Friendship Obligations

Friendship patterns and organizational and institutional bases and conceptions of trust in much of the world are more carefully worked out and balanced than they are in the United States (see, for example, Cook, 2000). In addition to liking and free association with someone of a person's choice, friendship implies mutual obligations and reciprocal favors. Friendship in this context provides the basis for cooperation in many societies. As a result of this type of friendship bond, many changes and innovations are accepted in order to please the proponent or those friends who have already accepted them. For example, authorities on international business emphasize the importance of friendship ties in business ventures in Africa. Friendship comes before business, and trust must be established before Africans enter business deals or consider the acceptance of new products or practices (Harris & Moran, 2000:518–519).

Social Class

Different social classes in a society react to change in different ways (see, for example, Fleishman, 2003). For example, individuals in the upper and upper middle classes will be more likely to accept modern medical practices because they can more likely to afford them, are better educated, and are in closer contact with clinics and physicians (see, for example, Stroneger et al., 1997). They also have the means to obtain many innovations inaccessible to members of the other classes.

One would think that the poorest people in a society would be most receptive to change. However, this is not the case, and they tend to be the most reluctant to adopt new ways. As pointed out by T. R. Batten:

> This is because they of all people can least afford to take risks. They have no reserves to tide them over failure. They know that they can just make a living by doing as they do, and they need to be very sure before they do anything differently. (Batten, quoted by Foster, 1973:170–171)

The people most receptive to change, in general, are those in the middle class. They have enough that they can take limited risks without threatening their well-being, but their situation is not so secure that the attraction of greater income, and the satisfaction of other felt needs, would not be a strong motivation to action. Moreover, they do not usually represent vested interests that may be threatened by major innovations, nor are they in a state of apathy, believing that no change is possible.

Authority

There are at least two kinds of authority that can be recognized as influencing receptivity to change. The first is the kind in which a respected leader vouches for, or approves, a proposed change. He or she is not actually forcing the people to change; rather, the person is using the authority inherent in his or her position to reassure others that it is, indeed, safe, advantageous, and desirable. For example, a respected leader in the community, a well-liked teacher, or a popular coach, because of his or her prestige and moral authority, can facilitate the introduction of innovations in many areas of life.

When dealing with the welfare of the majority, at times the use of authority is required over the beliefs of a dissident minority. For example, compulsory vaccination and chlorinating of water have brought about important health benefits over the protest of vocal minorities. Similarly, the introduction of the New World potato in Europe required the initial use of authority for the benefit of all concerned. When the potato was first introduced in Europe in the late eighteenth century, it was opposed and was considered poisonous in that it would cause diarrhea and would otherwise be harmful. But in Germany, the head of the army ordered every soldier to plant potatoes to care for, harvest, and eat. Apparently the length of the military service was sufficiently long to give the soldiers time to learn how to cultivate potatoes and to develop a taste for them. When the men returned to their farms after their military duty, they started to grow potato crops. It soon became a staple food in Germany and later spread to other parts of Europe.

The Problem of "Fit"

Acceptance of change is greatly facilitated when it can be integrated into the existing configuration of culture (Keesing, 1958:398). If a new form can be integrated or associated with traditional patterns, it has a greater chance of being accepted than if there is nothing to tie it to. For example, the horse fitted easily into the hunting culture of the Apaches, as it enabled them to improve their hunting techniques. Also, many non-Western societies have readily accepted the procedures and materials of scientific medicine—inoculations, antibiotics, and even surgery—where these were consistent with their traditional folk medicine. It was easier for the ill Navaho to swallow the doctor's pill while the Navaho's healing dance continued. By contrast, Western-type toilets are still being rejected (to the greatest consternation of many American tourists) in many parts of Thailand, Vietnam, Turkey, China and other countries because they are not suitable for the preferred squatting position.

The acceptance of an innovation is further facilitated when new tools and techniques can be adapted to preexisting ways of using the body.

Traditional and established motor patterns are important, and if a new innovation can fit into this existing framework, the possibilities for successful introduction are multiplied. For example, at times it is easier to modify a tool than the motor pattern. When Mexicans were furnished with modern wheelbarrows at railroad construction sites, they removed the wheel and lifted the barrow proper to their backs, supporting and carrying it with a forehead tumpline. This is owing to the fact that Mexicans for centuries have moved earth by carrying it in a basket supported on their backs in this fashion. As a matter of fact, even today, the tourists in Mexico City may see earth from the foundations of new skyscrapers being carried out of the ground in the same fashion.

Timing

The timing of the presentation of an innovation is a crucial, and obvious, consideration in its acceptance. For instance, in rural areas the acceptance of an innovation is conditioned by the right time within a yearly cycle. This is particularly true when one's pocketbook is involved. In rural communities the amount of available cash fluctuates during the year. During the harvest time people have the most cash available. This is the period for weddings, fiestas, and other activities that involve large expenditures. If new material items or practices come to the attention of people during this period, they are more likely to spend money on it than a couple of months before or after harvest time.

Participation in Decision Making

In the United States, an innovation will be more readily accepted if the people who are to change are involved in planning and execution even if the decision-making process involves adversary proceedings in which supporters of an opposing view are given an opportunity to influence the eventual decision (Helmer, 1994). In a classic study by Kurt Lewin (1965), conducted during World War II, the object was to change meat consumption patterns to less desirable, but more plentiful, cuts such as kidneys and sweetbreads. In Lewin's study, two experimental conditions were employed. In one, housewives heard a lecture of the benefits of these foods; in the other, a discussion was initiated among women. The same information was relayed in both cases. Results gathered at a later date indicated that 32 percent of the individuals participating in the discussion used the unfamiliar meats, compared to only 3 percent of the individuals who heard the lecture. It has since been repeatedly suggested in the social-science literature that change is effected more readily and with more relative permanence if the mass of the people involved participate in some way in the change program, although it is recognized that the notion of participation is class- and culture-specific.

Similarly in formal organizations, employees' participation in planning and implementing change tend to capture their excitement. It may result in better decisions because of employee input, and it may create more direct communications through personal involvement (Nadler, 1987:365). If employees feel deprived, bringing them into the decision-making process will augment their involvement in the acceptance of the decision that is made. In general, if the decisions are important for the subordinates in terms of their own work, the acceptance of change will be aided through their involvement (Hall, 2002).

Competition

As already noted in Chapter 1, competition often spurs people to make changes. It may take place between individuals, between groups, or between communities. Competition as a stimulant to change is perhaps most pronounced in the contemporary marketplace (see, for example, Teisberg, Porter, & Brown, 1994). Consumers increasingly expect and prefer new products. Nowadays more than ever before, the flow of goods and services consists of innovations. Consumers not only expect a constant change in the items available to them, but they have come to consider such change desirable. The continuous production of new automobile models and the growth of the range of personal computers are two obvious illustrations. The process of continuous innovation, invention, and new technologies under the impetus of competition also create new demands for investment and capital. This provides a basis for renewed expansion, thus further promoting change in the economic sphere.

PSYCHOLOGICAL STIMULANTS

When individuals are confronted with new opportunities, acceptance of those opportunities is conditioned by a number of psychological factors. In this section motivation, perceived needs, communication patterns, attitudes, and forms of personal influence are examined as facilitators in the acceptance of change.

Motivations to Change

Motivation is a purposive or goal-directed behavior that is acquired through experience by learning. It is a way of gratifying needs and desires, and thus there are many different types and levels. Certain kinds of motivations seem to be universal or nearly universal in that they cut across all kinds of societies and cultures and are found in some degree almost everywhere. These motivations for stimulating change are universal in nature and include such things as the desire for prestige, economic gain, and the wish to comply with friendship obligations.

The element of play, the fascination with a novel or unusual toy, has long been recognized as an important factor in invention and also seems to be significant as motivation in change. As an illustration, consider the effect of the play motive in East Bengal as a stimulant to change. Nearly 80 percent of all families in a village had built bore-hole latrines, all within the course of several weeks. This kind of success rate was highly unusual for the prevailing environmental sanitation programs in that area. A bit of probing revealed that in that part of East Bengal there is a thick covering of rich alluvial soil, which permits the use of an auger for drilling the latrine pit. Four men can bore through as much as 20 feet of this soil in an hour and the results are little short of miraculous. It turned out that the villagers were enchanted with this marvelous new tool and wanted to try their hand at it. Competition between groups of men were informally organized, and records were set and broken for latrine drilling in rapid succession. "For several weeks this was undoubtedly the happiest village in the country. And, at the end of the time, a good job of environmental sanitation had been done—but not for the reason the health team thought" (Foster, 1973:163). Of course, the element of play stimulates the acceptance of innovations in many other ways. For example, the current fad among youngsters playing computer games increases their computer literacy and, at the same time, helps their parents to accept and use personal computers.

Perceived Needs

Acceptance of change in a society is greatly affected by how its members perceive their needs. "Needs" are obviously subjective and time and culture bound; they are real if people feel that they are real (see, for example, Perkins et al., 1995). In many underdeveloped and malnourished parts of the world, individuals not only need more food, they also need different foods, especially vegetables and legumes. Agricultural changes that bring more food are more readily accepted than those bringing different foods for which they feel no need (Arensberg & Niehoff, 1971:155).

It is often argued that changing conditions tend to create new needs—genuine objective needs, not just subjectively "felt" needs. For example, urbanization created a need for sanitary engineering; the modern factory system created a need for labor unions; and the high-speed automobile created a need for superhighways. A culture is integrated, and therefore any change in one part of the culture creates a need for adaptive changes in related parts of the culture. Individuals can also develop a need when they learn that an improved method, an innovation, exists. "Therefore, innovations can lead to needs, as well as vice versa. Some change agents use this approach to change by creating needs among their clients through pointing out the desirable consequences of new ideas" (Rogers & Shoemaker, 1971:105).

Communication Patterns

Communication is a circular interaction that involves a sender, a message, and a receiver. Several characteristics of the sender can promote the acceptance of change (Williams, 2002). If the person is considered an expert in a particular field, he or she is likely to exert a favorable influence. Closely related to the question of expertise is the source of credibility. In general, the more credible the source, the greater the persuasive impact (Weyant, 1986:83–86). Credibility is often determined by level of education, social status, and professional attainment. Other sender characteristics that are likely to influence the receiver include trustworthiness, power, attraction, likeability, and similarity.

Several characteristics of a message may stimulate the acceptance of change. One is the use of the arousal of fear as opposed to more rational, less emotional, appeals. For example, the highly emotional and fear-arousing appeals to combat AIDS through what is popularly referred to as "safe sex" seem to be effective in altering sexual practices and behavior. Similarly, over the years, some politicians who have employed negative campaign tactics that attempt to discredit their opponents have been more successful than those who stick to more traditional issue-oriented campaigns (*Newsweek*, 1994a:22–42).

A second characteristic is the organization of the message. In terms of stimulating acceptance of change, is it more effective to present one side of an argument or both sides? In a classic and oft-replicated study by Carl Hovland and his associates it was found that presentation of both sides was more effective in converting the highly educated. The presentation of only one side of the argument was more effective among the poorly educated and those originally favoring the advocated view. Two-sided communications, it has been discovered, appear to be more effective "inoculators" than are one-sided communications. In summarizing the relative merits of one and two-sided communications, they say this:

1. A two-sided presentation is more effective in the long run than a one-sided one (a) when, regardless of initial opinion the audience is exposed to subsequent counter-propaganda, or (b) when, regardless of subsequent exposure to counter-propaganda, the audience initially disagrees with the commentator's position.
2. A two-sided presentation is less effective than a one-sided presentation if the audience initially agrees with the commentator's position and is not exposed to later counter-propaganda. (Hovland, Lumsdaine, & Sheffield, 1949:109)

Finally, there is the question of primacy-versus-recency effects in the delivery of a message. There are arguments in support of both sides of the question. Those in favor of recency contend that an audience is more likely to recall material that is presented last. Those in favor of primacy argue that attention span of an audience declines by the time the second speaker presents the argument. The key seems to be the time interval between the presentations. If there is little time between the two, the first speaker will have an advantage. If the time interval is greater, it is more likely (assuming that the speakers are equal in characteristics such as expertise, trust, attractiveness, and so on) that the second speaker will be more effective. It should be noted, however, that these are broad generalizations, and the question of primacy versus recency should be seen as just one of the many variables stimulating the acceptance of a message.

Receiver characteristics also need to be taken into consideration. For example, research shows that many voters do not respond directly to appeals by politicians. These appeals, instead, are evaluated in the context of their memberships in groups and organizations such as social clubs and labor unions. If a person is supported by a group holding similar views, the individual will be more resistant to change than when such support is absent. By contrast, when group ties are weak or lacking, one is more susceptible to persuasive appeals. This explains, to an extent, why new immigrants, who lack family, community, and group ties, are more likely candidates for extremist political and religious organizations. Such organizations provide the individual with a sense of solidarity, identity, and belongingness. Extremist organizations, such as the John Birch Society, capitalize on this through their appeals to the uprooted, and are relatively successful in areas with large migrant populations. Related to this is the idea that when individuals make a public commitment before a group, the probability of their acceptance of a change will increase. For example, Alcoholics Anonymous and the various quit-smoking and weight-reduction groups rely heavily on such public commitments (Albrecht, Chadwick, & Jacobson, 1987:232–237).

Attitudes

In the acceptance of a change, one would tend to think that information must precede attitudes and that favorable attitude toward the change must precede behavior. However, empirical research as of the early 2000s has not clearly specified these relationships. Although many studies examine attitude change, little research exists to document the relationship of attitude change and behavior change. In fact, the relationship between the two has been subject to considerable debate. Arthur R. Cohen (1964:137–138) pointedly concluded:

> Most of the investigators whose work we have examined make the broad psychological assumption that since attitudes are evaluative predispositions, they

have consequences for the way people act toward others, for the programs they actually undertake, and for the manner in which they carry them out. Thus attitudes are always seen as precursors of behavior, as determinants of how a person will actually behave in his daily affairs. In spite of the wide acceptance of the assumption, however, very little work on attitude change has dealt explicitly with the behavior that may follow a change in attitude.

Leon Festinger, in support of Cohen's conclusion, suggested that when attitudes are changed on the basis of persuasive communication, this change "is inherently unstable and will disappear or remain isolated unless an environmental or behavioral change can be brought about to support and maintain it (1964:415). His main point is that unless environmental change to support the new opinion occurs, "the same factors that produced the initial opinion and the behavior will continue to operate to nullify the effect of the opinion change" (p. 416). Thus attitude change may not serve as a sufficient condition for a behavioral change, and it seems reasonable that the probability of behavioral change would be greater as environmental circumstances also change.

Personal Influence

Personal influence refers to a change in an individual's attitude or behavior as a result of interpersonal communication. A theory of particular importance regarding the acceptance of personal influence is that of Herbert C. Kelman (1961). He elaborates three processes by which individuals respond to personal influence. These are compliance, identification, and internalization. *Compliance* occurs when the person accepts influence in the hope of achieving a favorable reaction from another person or persons. The individual does not accept the influence because he or she believes in its content but because of an anticipated gratifying social effect. Influence based on identification occurs when the opinion or behavior accepted is associated with a "satisfying self-defining relationship" to a person or a group. *Identification* is basically role imitation, whereby influence results from admiration of another person, or role maintenance, whereby acceptance is necessary to maintain a role relationship with another person. The motivational basis for identification is different from that of compliance in that the person is not primarily concerned with pleasing the other individual, but with meeting the other's expectations—or at least perceived expectations—for his or her own role performance. *Internalization* occurs when an individual accepts influence congruent with his or her particular value system. The content of the advocated opinion or behavior is of major concern and becomes integrated with the individual's existing values. Kelman's theory is very helpful in understanding the role of personal influence in facilitating the acceptance of change. It also helps to create similarity, and it has been shown in the literature that the more similar an actor is to a neighbor, for example, the more likely the actor will follow the adoption patterns of that neighbor (Axelrod, 1997).

Individuals facing a new life experience—such as migrants, newlyweds, or new college students—tend to be more susceptible to personal influence because, in such states of life, habits for handling many situations are not yet established and the individual is open to new information. Similarly, individuals aspiring to membership in certain groups may be inclined to emulate the behavior of persons already in these groups and be susceptible to their influence. Merton (1957:265) calls this "anticipatory socialization"; that is, an individual tends to adopt the attitudinal and behavioral characteristics of group members before he or she actually belongs to the group. For example, the medical student at the first opportunity dons the white coat of the profession and runs to the nearest medical supply store to buy his or her symbolic stethoscope. Among consumers, anticipatory socialization entails the development of expectations regarding product ownership and adaptive patterns of consumer behavior (Moschis, 1987:26–28). Such aspirational behavior might be seen in the social climber, who drives the "right" kind of car, buys the "right" kind of clothes, joins the "right" clubs, and sends his or her children to the "right" schools. In all of these cases, the individual who lacks actual membership acquires the visible symbols of that membership and is more prone and willing to accept changes than those who are already in the group.

These are the more important psychological factors that stimulate the acceptance of change. However, it should be noted that the list is not exhaustive. In the next section we shall consider some of the principal cultural stimulants to change.

CULTURAL STIMULANTS

The term culture refers to a set of knowledge, beliefs, attitudes, and rules for behavior that are shared by members of a society. In general, the existing culture base largely determines what new traits will be accepted. Different cultures exhibit different degrees of capability and readiness for accepting change. Both the context of culture and the degree of cultural integration not only play a role in the receptivity for the new, but encourage innovation. This section will focus on these cultural conditions to show under what circumstances they facilitate the acceptance of change.

High- and Low-Context Cultures

Edward T. Hall (1989), a renowned anthropologist, has suggested the concept of *high and low context* as a way of understanding different cultural orientations. Cultures differ widely in the extent to which unspoken, unformulated, and inexplicit rules govern how information is handled and how people interact and relate to each other. In high-context cultures, much of human behavior is covert or implicit, whereas in low-context cultures much is overt or explicit. The amount of contexting required for understanding everyday life extends from low in some cultures to high in others. Hall, for example, places Germany, Switzerland, Scandinavia, and the United States at the low end of the continuum; France in the middle; and China, Japan, and the Arab countries at the high end of the scale.

In a low-context culture, messages are explicit; words carry most of the information in communication. Bonds between people are often fragile, formal, and legal. Involvement of people with each other is low, and there are fewer distinctions made between insiders and outsiders. In such cultures, Hall contends, change is easy, rapid, and welcomed by most people.

In high-context cultures, less information is contained in the verbal part of the message, as much more information is in the context of communication, which includes the background, associations, and basic values of the communicator. Who you are—that is, your values and position or place in society—is crucial in the high-context culture, such as Japan or the Arab countries. Bonds between people tend to be strong, and there is a deep involvement of people with each other. They get along with much less legal paperwork than is deemed essential in low-context cultures such as the United States. In a high-context culture, a person's word is his or her bond. There is less need to anticipate contingencies and provide for external legal sanctions in a culture that emphasizes obligation and trust as important values. In these cultures, shared feelings of obligation and honor take the place of impersonal legal sanctions. Greater distinctions are made also between insiders and outsiders; and cultural patterns are enduring and slow to change. In such cultures, an awareness of the cultural environment is essential to create receptivity for an innovation coming from the outside (Vago, 1982).

Cultural Integration

The extent of cultural integration plays a role in the acceptance of change (Eriksen, 1992; Holli, 2002). Highly integrated and harmonious cultures tend to produce a sense of security and satisfaction among their members. On the other hand, a culture with a lower degree of integration in which the various themes and patterns are less perfectly coordinated adapts more easily to circumstances that bring about change. In a highly integrated culture, change, even if it begins in only one aspect of culture, may cause the whole culture to disintegrate. For example, when the British abolished headhunting in Melanesia, the results were dramatic. The people lost their interest in living, and the birthrate dropped rapidly; on one island, the number of childless marriages increased from about 19 percent to 46 percent, on another from 12 percent to 72 percent. Why? Headhunting was the center of social and religious institutions; it pervaded the whole life of the people. They needed to go on headhunting expeditions because they needed heads to appease the ghosts of their ancestors on many occasions, such as on making a new canoe, building a house for a chief, or making a sacrifice at the funeral of a chief. Although their headhunting expeditions lasted only a few weeks, and the actual fighting only a few hours, preparations lasted for years. They had to build new canoes and celebrate numerous rites and feasts, which stimulated horticulture and the breeding of pigs. The number of festivities and celebrations increased as the date for the expedition neared. Other activities commenced when the successful hunters returned. With the integrating pattern of their lives denied them, the Melanesians lost interest in their lives (Montagu, 1968:94).

In a society in which there is little harmony and integration of cultural norms and understandings, there is usually much conflict, confusion, waste, insecurity, and social unrest. These conditions provide a fertile ground for the acceptance of change. Moreover, such a culture tends to be more rational and more secular, with a high emphasis on achievement orientation and individualism. There is a higher degree of social mobility, high rates of literacy, and strong occupational differentiation. Personal obligations to family and friends are minimal, and contractual relations tend to prevail. Religion is superficial for most people, the nuclear family dominates, the outlook is cosmopolitan, and the emphasis is on innovativeness. In such a climate, novelty is not only encouraged but eagerly sought after.

In highly integrated cultures, receptivity is stimulated when the change is seen in the context of a religious framework. When the recipients of a change are aware that the proposed innovation has the support of the existing deities, acceptance of it will be greatly enhanced. For example, in development programs in Arab countries it helps to introduce a given innovation with the phrase, "In the name of Allah" (Patai, 2002:143–155).

Different groups in a society may show differing receptivity to change. Obviously, in every changing society there are liberals and conservatives. In general, literate and educated people tend to accept changes more readily than the illiterate and uneducated. And a group may be highly receptive to change of one kind, but highly resistant to changes of other kinds. For example, there are many churches of strikingly modern architecture where the sermons have remained basically unchanged since the days of Luther.

The characteristics of a social group obviously influence the acceptance of a new idea or practice, as has been demonstrated in a now-classic study by Saxon Graham (1956) on the acceptance of five innovations in the United States—television, canasta, supermarkets, hospital insurance, and medical service insurance—across social-class levels. His research revealed that no single social class was consistently receptive in adopting all five innovations. Television, for example, diffused more quickly among lower social classes, while the card game canasta diffused more quickly among upper social classes. Graham argues that the critical factor in acceptance is the extent to which the attributes of the innovation are compatible with the attributes of the culture of the receiving social system. The "cultural equipment" required for the adoption of television, according to Graham, included an average education, a minimum income, and a desire for passive spectator entertainment. This cultural pattern coincided with a lower social-class level.

Finally, the perception of the relative merits of a novelty is considered as influential in facilitating acceptance. On the lighter side, this may be illustrated by the promotion of movies by film distributors. If the movie is good, it usually is placed in a small number of theaters and not distributed on a mass basis for a considerable period of time. This results in a fairly slow process of diffusion, which often relies heavily on personal influence. If the movie is bad, it is shown in multiple runs in neighborhood theaters, with heavy advertising in order to secure as much acceptance as possible before word spreads among moviegoers as to the film's true merits (Katz & Lazarsfeld, 1955:180). Let us now examine some of the economic conditions and factors that stimulate the acceptance of change.

ECONOMIC STIMULANTS

Convincing evidence exists that the desire for economic gain is an important stimulant to change. If something has a purely utilitarian value (that is, if it is valued because of what it will do), change may be accepted quite readily. Frederic C. Fliegel and Joseph E. Kivlin (1966), in a study of the acceptance of new farm practices by American farmers, found that those that are perceived as most profitable and least risky are most readily accepted. However, if some feature of the traditional culture is valued intrinsically aside from what it will do, change is less readily accepted. To illustrate, for the American farmer, cattle are a source of income, to be bred, culled, and butchered whenever most profitable. In contrast, cattle are considered sacred in India, and there is a prohibition on the slaughter and consumption of beef among Hindus (Nair, 1987). For many of the Nilotic peoples of Africa, cattle represent intrinsic values. The owner recognizes and loves each cow. To slaughter one would be like killing one of the family. The average Westerner, who takes a rational and unsentimental view of economic activities, may find it hard to accept the sentiments and values of non-Western peoples. (By the same token, many non-Western peoples resent and find hard to accept a great variety of Western sentiments, values, and practices.) Westerners may be irritated by the Biaga of central India, who refused to give up their primitive digging sticks for the far-superior moldboard plow. Why? The Biaga loved the earth as a kindly and generous mother; they would gently help her with the digging stick to bring forth her yield; but could not bring themselves to cut her "with knives."

Perception of Economic Advantages

However, economic forces ultimately tend to override many traditional values and practices. Lucy P. Mair, for example, suggests that the modern African's actions increasingly are determined by a perception of economic advantage and not by "an abstract theory of the sacredness of land which inhibits . . . recognition of its economic potentialities," and she proposes as a generalization of wide application that: "the conservative force of tradition is never proof against the attraction of economic advantage, provided that the advantage is sufficient and is clearly recognized. In the case of land it is abundantly clear that the emotional and religious attitudes towards it which are inculcated by native tradition have not prevented the development of a commercial attitude" (Mair, quoted by Foster, 1973:154–155).

Cost

Change is always costly. In general, the very poor resist all change because they cannot afford to take any risk (Arensberg & Niehoff, 1971: 149–150). However, cost is a relative judgment. It is generally a function of an individual's economy of preferences:

> The price of a novelty in goods or labor is measured by a prospective acceptor's reference to his total wealth, by his comparison of its cost with the cost of some alternative, and also by his estimate of the pressures of his need for it. The man who can afford a yacht may still find the price of a new lawn mower excessive; yet the sick man considers that any sacrifice is not too great to secure relief. An American mortgages his salary to buy an automobile, whereas the English workingman considers this price too high for him to pay. (Barnett, 1953:361)

The restraining effect of novelty costs is also evident when they are absent. It is fairly easy to get individuals to try something if doing so entails no financial cost to them. Initially they may think that it is worthless or harmful just because it is free, but they are more likely than not to accept it because it is free. The practice of giving away free things is widespread in the United States, and advertising campaigns often include giving away samples and "free" gifts. Only those individuals who are suspicious that there might be some strings attached to such a sample will reject it and fail to give it a trial. Obviously, trying something does not commit them, so what can they lose? Sponsors of TV and radio giveaway shows, box-top contests, and the like capitalize on this appeal and win often enough to make the gamble a sound business practice. Such activities have often resulted in the adoption of a given product.

At the organizational level, cost is one of the most obvious dimensions influencing the acceptance of change. In formal organizations the financial cost can be divided into (1) initial cost and (2) continuing cost. When the outcome of cost-benefit analysis is favorable for the organization in question, the likelihood of accepting a given innovation is enhanced (Hall, 2002:206–208). Social cost is another form of expense and is an important factor in explaining the rate of adoption, particularly in developing countries. Gerald Zaltman and his associates (1973:34–35) cite an international management consulting firm in which it was observed that even seemingly minor management changes (from the consulting firm's viewpoint) in power and status within the organization, resulting from the adoption of more efficient management science techniques, produced sufficient internal conflict to cause a substantial number of medium-size business firms in developing areas to discontinue the newly adopted practices.

Social cost may come in the form of ridicule, isolation, ostracism, or even exclusion or expulsion from some important reference groups. As Zaltman and his colleagues wrote:

> Social position within a group influences the degree to which such a cost may occur and how serious the individual may perceive this cost. The marginal member of a group may have little to lose by innovating; therefore, even in the presence of considerable disapproval, he may proceed to adopt an innovation. There is always the possibility that the decision might prove to be a wise one, and he may gain stature as a consequence. . . . A high-status member of a group may also adopt, again, even in the presence of potential or actual ridicule. The high-status person can do so because he generally has an inventory of goodwill or social credit upon which he can draw, and he will suffer little if the innovation does not succeed. (Zaltman, Duncan, & Holbek, 1973:35)

In many instances, the cost factor is also related to the efficiency of a given product or article. At the time of their initial introduction, most machines and articles are crude. For example, the first airplane barely got off the ground, the first computer was the size of a small classroom, and the first automobile barely exceeded the speed of a horse-drawn carriage. The first radio was hardly audible, and the first television set was barely visible. Indeed, imperfections are part of discoveries and are to be expected to exist. If any invention, however, meets a need and persists, it tends to be steadily improved. Today's airplane is a far cry from the Wright Brothers' flying machine of 1903. Similarly, today's automobile, usually a smoothly functioning machine, bears little resemblance to the contraptions of the turn of the century. Mass production usually brings about an increased efficiency and a lowering of the cost as evidenced by, for example, the continuous refinements and power increases in personal computers at rapidly decreasing prices (*Economist*, 1994:99). Once the mechanical imperfections are removed, accompanied by a decline in cost of the article, the likelihood of its acceptance will be increased.

Vested Interests

Vested interests also relate often to economic concerns and growth patterns (Krusell & Rios-Rull, 1996). They appear as promoters of change whenever proponents believe the proposed change will be profitable to them. Over time in a society, certain interests tend to be more successful than others. They manage to have their views accepted by the society at large, and they accumulate money, organization, and power. In so doing, they become vested interests: interest groups that derive special advantage from maintenance of the status quo, that seek to protect their special advantages, and that oppose all further changes except those favorable to them. The railroads, for example, have opposed the growth of the trucking industry and at the same time promoted innovations in engines and passenger cars as well as improvements in organization and delivery of services. In the social-change literature, more emphasis is placed on the opposition than the promotion of change by vested interests, perhaps because, in part, opposition to change is more dramatic and widespread than support of change. The changes that vested interests make are mainly improvements in existing practices, whereas the opposition they show is directed against major—and, for them, threatening—innovations. More will be said about the role of vested interests in social change in the discussion of social barriers to change in the next section.

To recapitulate, social scientists have placed much more emphasis on the reasons for opposing rather than accepting change (Bennis, 1987:37–39; Germani, 1981:167–172; Hall, 1989:197–211; Zaltman & Duncan, 1977:61–89). Still, by pulling together the social, psychological, cultural, and economic stimulants to change, it is possible to come up with some generalizations concerning the conditions of acceptance. There is sufficient evidence in the social-science literature to indicate that change will be more readily accepted if it is adopted by consensus group decision; when people have an opportunity to empathize with opponents; when there is an opportunity to recognize and discuss valid objections and to take appropriate measures to relieve unnecessary fears or hardships. The likelihood of acceptance is further increased when people feel that the change is not going to threaten their autonomy or security; when it does not clash with prevailing values and ideas that have long been cherished; and when it is seen as reducing rather than increasing present burdens. When these conditions are met, readiness to accept change gradually becomes a characteristic of many individuals, groups, or institutions in a society. The good old days are no longer nostalgically cherished; instead, there is an anticipation of a better life in the days to come. The spontaneity of youth is cherished, and innovations are protected until they have had a chance to establish their worth. In such a situation the ideal is more and more seen as possible.

In the contemporary world, however, situations of resistance to change are much more numerous than situations of acceptance. Even within rapidly changing societies, there is considerable resistance to new ideas, new scientific and technological developments, and new patterns of social life. Often change is resisted because it conflicts with traditional values and beliefs, or a particular change may simply cost too much money. Sometimes people resist change because it interferes with their habits or makes them feel frightened or threatened. In the following pages, the various conditions of resistance to change will be examined.

RESISTANCE TO CHANGE

The concept of resistance has become one of social science's dominant theoretical and practical preoccupations in social change analyses (Brown, 1996). One can always find a justification in some more or less pragmatic terms for active resistance to change. The peasant in a developing country will find reasons for refusing to try out a new tool, a new technique, a fertilizer, or a different mode of cultivation. The new, the different, the peasant may insist, will only poison the soil, produce inferior grain, upset God, or cause his wife to bear only girls. A modern businessperson may single out ventures with new things or practices that have failed to produce a profit. Bureaucrats will have a body of rules and precedents to justify their conservatism; a scholar, the whole of history to protect him or her from new ideas. "And for everyone, primitive, peasant, and modern layman and expert alike, there is always as the final and ultimate defense against anything new some version or other of the thesis that what was good enough for father is good enough for son" (LaPiere, 1965:175–176). Anything new or novel can be the object of resistance. It can be a social or cultural innovation, a scientific discovery, or mechanical or social invention. Regardless of the type of novelty, its unqualified acceptance can in no way be assured regardless of how socially or otherwise beneficial it may be seen. For example, western Europeans commonly regard maize as fit only for animal fodder, avoiding human consumption to an extent that could be considered a food taboo (Brandes, 1992). Many things that are new are opposed, and whenever change is attempted, resistance is likely to appear. Although the term resistance conjures up a pejorative connotation in general, this is not always the case. In fact, resistance can be a healthy phenomenon. It is a positive force when, from some objective perspective, the proposed change is harmful to society. In situations in which an intended change is subjectively harmful to a person or a group, resistance is justifiable (Zaltman & Duncan, 1977:62).

With this in mind, let us now turn to the social, psychological, cultural, and economic barriers to change.

SOCIAL BARRIERS

Many social factors act as barriers to change. The ones that will be examined in the following pages include vested interests, status interests, social class, ideological resistance, group solidarity, authority, fear of the unfamiliar, forms of rationalization, and organized opposition.

Vested Interests

Change may be resisted by individuals or groups that fear a loss of power, wealth, or prestige should an innovation gain acceptance. "A particularly potent obstacle to change is the opposition to innovation by strong, organized groups that stand to lose by the change.... Such groups [are] called vested interests.... A realistic inventory of the sources of resistance to social change needs to give prominence to vested interests" (Nimkoff, 1957:68). There are many different types of vested interests for whom the status quo is profitable and preferable. Students attending state universities have a vested interest in tax-supported higher education. Divorce lawyers constitute a vested interest and for a long time have fought efforts to reform the divorce laws. Physicians opposing various forms of "socialized medicine" constitute a vested interest. In fact, nearly everyone has some vested interests—from the rich with their tax-exempt bonds to the poor with their welfare checks.

Many of the social and economic changes that have been promoted in developing countries threaten the security of some groups or individuals. "Witch" doctors and midwives may resent medical programs because they fear that the competition will be injurious to them. Landlords may oppose education of their tenants for fear that it will promote unrest and may result in land redistribution. Moneylenders in villages may oppose low-interest, government-managed credit programs, and merchants may object to consumer cooperatives. In such instances, "untrue rumors are among the most common techniques used by individuals who feel threatened by proposed changes" (Foster, 1973:117). For example, when a census of the inhabitants was taken in Indian villages, there were rumors that anyone who gave his age as over sixty-five would be killed. In another instance, when an expert appeared in the village, there were rumors that the villagers would be driven out and all the land would be used for setting up an American colony.

Closer to home, residents in a community often develop vested interests in their neighborhood. When zoning changes, they often organize to resist it. Objections are made against new interstate highways or the construction of correctional facilities in one's neighborhood. Parents may resist busing their children, or residents may organize in opposition to allowing the supersonic Concorde to take off or land nearby.

Contrary to popular impressions, the American university is a strong bastion of resistance to change. Curriculum changes may be viewed as trivial matters by many individuals, but the departments that are to be affected adversely by the proposed changes are quite likely to resist as long as they can. For well over 120 years, the American Ph.D. program, which was transplanted from Germany, remained unaltered. Only recently have there been some minor modifications and dilutions in the requirements such as the elimination of foreign language requirements.

Throughout history new ideas have often met with entrenched resistance by vested interests. The astronomical theories of Copernicus and Galileo were long suppressed because they challenged beliefs about the central position of human beings in the universe. *On the Revolutions of the Celestial Orbs* was published by Nicholas Copernicus in 1543. However, a license to print a book exposing the heliocentric hypothesis was refused until 1822 by the Roman Catholic church, and only then was a decree quietly issued by the Holy Office:

> There is no reason why the present and future Masters of the Sacred Palace should refuse license for printing and publishing works treating of the mobility of the earth and the immobility of the sun, according to the common opinion of the modern astronomers. (Smith, quoted by Bierstedt, 1974:213)

Now and then, there are vested interests in skills and knowledge. Artisans, for example, are usually reluctant to adopt a new tool or material because doing so would render their existing skills obsolete and demand that they learn to utilize new ones. At the organizational level, change can threaten occupational groups (Hall, 2002). Resistance is likely to come about when some specialties foresee that they will not be needed if certain changes are implemented. There was a fair amount of resistance to the adoption of the early typewriter because it devaluated the skill of handwriting, which had been a prized ability of the educated person. LaPiere (1965:192) suggests that "no man . . . will passively accept a change that destroys the value of hard-won skills and knowledge and that demands that he acquire a complex of new and different skills and knowledge if he is to hold his own." Thus, in many cases, those who must adapt to a new innovation may find it to be a personal disadvantage to do so.

Status Interests

The acceptance of almost any innovation will adversely affect the status of some individuals in society; and, to the degree that those whose status is threatened consciously recognize the danger, they will resist adopting it. In most societies, through time, individuals made some improvements in their social status, became a known artisan, a tribal elder, a wise old parent, and this rise in social status was a recognition of the person's increased value to society. In rapidly changing societies, past experience often has little bearing on the present, and those who have earned a high status often see that status jeopardized by an innovation, and as a result, they resist its adoption. Today, occupational status and age are no longer correlated. The modern business prefers highly educated employees. Downsizing and the possibility of underemployment or unemployment are real concerns in many occupations and professions (Jensen, 1996). Not surprisingly, fear of loss of status associated with seniority and not with education may prompt resistance. People who benefited from the existing order are unlikely to welcome anything that will lower their self-esteem (Bennis, 1987:37) or threaten their economic well-being.

Resistance stemming from the fear of status depreciation can take many forms. For example, Raphael Patai (2002) calls attention to one the basic features of the Bedouin ethos, which is a contempt for any kind of physical labor with exception of tending of the livestock and raiding, considered the only proper occupations for a free person. He comments that among the many despised varieties of work, agricultural labor is the one most emphatically rejected. For Bedouins, to engage in cultivation would not only result in an irreparable loss of status, but it would also dishonor them. As a result of this disdain for agriculture, attempts in several Arab countries to have the Bedouins settle in one place have met with little success. The same fear of loss of status compels young people in many Arab countries to be clerks for inadequate wages rather than helpers at construction sites with considerably more pay.

Social Class

In general, rigid class and caste patterns tend to hinder the acceptance of change. However, different social classes in a society tend to react to and alter the course of change in different ways. In highly stratified societies, individuals are expected to obey and take orders from those in superior positions of authority or power. Those in position of superiority, in turn, dictate to those below them. This reduces the free interplay of ideas and opinions that is so important in so many change situations (Foster, 1973:127). The prerogatives of the upper strata are jealously guarded, and attempts to infringe upon them by members of lower socioeconomic groups are often resented and repulsed. For example, under the rigid traditional Indian and Pakistani caste system, which was declared illegal only recently, members of different castes could not draw water from the same well, go to the same schools, eat together, or otherwise mingle. The types of work one could do were rigorously prescribed, and any violation of rules was condemned. Until the mid-1960s, a somewhat similar situation existed in the United States concerning the position of blacks.

Members of the upper classes, in general, are more likely to accept innovations, whereas those in the lower classes or those who are downwardly mobile tend to resist them (see, for example, Fleishman, 2003). Occupation is one of the bases of stratification, and rarely, if ever, have any considerable proportion of the members of an occupational group willingly renounced their established skills and knowledge in favor of some innovation that required the development of new skills and understandings (LaPiere, 1965: 191). In most cases there is a tendency to cherish the old ways of doing things and to adhere to the status quo.

Ideological Resistance

Resistance to change on the grounds of ideological traditionalism is quite prevalent (Germani, 1981:169–172; Zaltman & Duncan, 1977:66). At the individual level, traditional ideology is an inhibitor of sexual behavior (Brody et al., 1996). At the level of society, many non-Western societies are reluctant to accept innovations that they see as Westernizing influences. This nationalistic fear is very common, and even many Europeans and Canadians worry about the "Americanization" of their societies. For a while, the expression "the Coca-Colaization of Europe" was in vogue. These attitudes are not against change as such, but against the perceived political implications of certain changes. To illustrate: In Islamic countries, anti-Western sentiments derive, in part, from a fear that the adoption of Western technology will destroy the ancient faith (Patai, 2002). Or, a nationalistic ideology rationalizes that rapid population growth contributes to the strength of a nation and any attempt at family planning or fertility moderation is a neocolonialist plot.

There are many other types of ideological resistance to change. The Catholic church opposes birth control and abortion on ideological grounds. The medical profession uses ideological arguments to resist anything suggesting socialized medicine, and fought against the enactment of the Medicare Law of 1965 (Allen, 1971:278–279). Thus, it may be concluded that the basic intellectual and religious assumptions and interpretations regarding existing power relations, morality, welfare, and security tend to be rather consistent and adversely disposed to change.

Group Solidarity

Previous work suggests that group solidarity influences the nature of social change (Moxley & Proctor, 1995). In traditional societies, there is usually a strong sense of solidarity, which is reflected in bonds of mutual obligation in the context of family and friendship patterns, a preference for small-group identification, a pronounced sense of belonging, and a willingness to criticize anyone who deviates from customary norms.

When economic well-being is roughly at the same level and individuals have generally the same access to resources, reciprocal obligations are effective in maintaining a society. Conditions of equality and cooperation are incompatible with trends toward individualization, migration, and changes in the division of labor. In villages, those who make economic progress no longer find their relationships in balance. Progressive individuals must be prepared to disregard many of the traditional obligations and ties that their societies expect of them. The prevalence of mutual obligations, the accent on self-esteem and prestige, factors that in part make up solidarity and hold societies together, can effectively curb the acceptance of innovations (Zaltman & Duncan, 1977:72).

Identification with small groups provides a sense of psychological security and satisfaction for most people both at the organization level (Zetka, 1992) and at the community level. Frequently, innovations that upset such traditional groups meet with strong resistance, and people will often forgo comfort, convenience, and economic gain in return for more enjoyment in life. For example, in many Latin American villages women wash clothes under conditions that are anything but comfortable. The pleasures of working in the company of others and the discussions and joking compensate for the hardship. They resist efforts to alter this pattern of working regardless of the hardships involved. In a far corner of Africa, the village well serves the same function, and women resented the builders, putting running water into all houses and rebelled because they were taken away from their only excuse for social contact.

Authority

Whenever an established pattern of authority is threatened or even questioned by the promoters of an innovation, resistance is likely to occur. This is perhaps most pronounced at the level of organizations (Aghion & Tirole, 1997; Zaltman & Duncan, 1977:75). For example, when two or more departments at a university merge, one of the most difficult problems to overcome is the feeling on the part of individual departments that they are going to lose control over decision making and be subjected to a reduction in influence. Chairpersons, whose authority is likely to diminish, will be the most vocal (and frustrated) opponents of such reorganization.

At community level, authority figures play a decisive role in the acceptance or rejection of change (Waste, 1998). However, in many societies, leadership and authority patterns as an institution are not fully developed and insufficient to guide group decisions that are needed in order to make major changes. Often, individuals who speak out for a new project or idea or volunteer their services will be criticized rather than praised for their efforts, and their neighbors will suspect that they see opportunity for personal gain at their own expense. Roger M. Keesing (1968) describes the Kwaio of the Solomon Islands, who have chiefs only on Tuesdays. Their social organization included no chiefs, but it became necessary to invent some to handle dealings with white officials after World War II. To avoid conflict between these new chiefs and the traditional holders of authority and influence, they simply agreed that the chiefs would "reign" only on Tuesdays when the white officials called.

At times, authority within the family is a deterrent to acceptance of change. For example, among the Navaho, the decision to enter the hospital is reached only after a family conference. A wife and husband alone are not free to exercise their discretion in this context. Similarly, among some traditional Spanish-speaking Mexicans in California, hospitalization is a grave and serious step and is a family, not an individual, problem. In such situations, resistance to medical practices, among other types of change, can be anticipated.

Fear of the Unfamiliar

A good deal of the initial resistance to any innovation stems from apprehension, from fear of the unknown, of a new technology (Miller, 1996). Even today, many individuals in Western countries are still afraid of air travel. Although carefully gathered government studies indicate that flying is many times safer than traveling by automobile, these individuals are petrified by the idea of getting into an airplane and taking off. Fear is also a factor in resistance to change that threatens individuals with a loss of status, income, or power. Individual opposition to both the civil rights movement and the women's movement has often reflected the fear of the dominant group members—whites on the one hand, men on the other—that gains for a minority would mean losses for them. In such situations, stereotyped thinking is likely to act as a further barrier to the acceptance of change. Fear has often prevented the use of particular plants as food; for example, in parts of the United States, the tomato was considered poisonous as recently as a century ago. Even such a minor change from the familiar as the use of aluminum in place of iron in cooking pots and pans has aroused considerable apprehension; housewives were afraid that the new metal would contaminate the food cooked in it, and even experts doubted the use of aluminum as kitchenware (LaPiere, 1965:178–179).

Often, even the name of a given product can elicit a negative reaction from people. Some years ago, the Colgate Palmolive Company introduced a new toothpaste called Cue into French-speaking districts in Canada. The product was never accepted, for the word has an obscene connotation in French (it means "ass"). McDonald's Big Mac hamburger did not fare much better in parts of Vancouver—Big Mac is a slang expression there for "big breasts."

Forms of Rationalization

At times, resistance to change occurs for quite plausible reasons when the proposed change is seen as being possibly deleterious for a social system, or when the outcomes are impractical or highly debatable (Warren, 1977:51). New forms of social organization may also be resisted for a while on the grounds that they do not work, or do not work well enough to justify their cost in time, effort, or money. On occasion, however, some of the rationales for opposing change are anything but logical and reasonable, and alibis or excuses are created in all parts of society to ward off new developments (Zelby, 1992). For instance, when the railroad could not exceed 30 miles per hour, people in opposition to it argued that the speed was more than the human body could endure. Today, possibly, their great-grandchildren claim that people cannot endure supersonic speeds. Doctors disapproved of the use of early automobiles because it would lead to atrophy of the human legs, and some argue today that cellular phones cause cancer.

Organized Opposition

At times, widespread individual resistance to change may become mobilized into organized opposition that can assume formal organizational structure (for example, the National Rifle Association [NRA], which opposes gun control), or it may be channeled through a social movement (such as recent pro-life activities) or political action committees and lobbyists (Thompson, Cassie, & Jewell, 1994; Ainsworth and Sened, 1993). In other instances, organized opposition may take the form of a letter-writing campaign. For example, the Occupational Safety and Health Administration received over 50,000 letters in August 1994, in opposition to proposed regulations that would severely restrict workplace smoking. This massive mailing initiative is believed to be organized by tobacco companies. Of course, their spokesmen would neither confirm nor deny involvement in a letter campaign (Swisher, 1994). Or it may be channeled through demonstrations and various forms of civil disobedience as evidenced by the various antiglobalization groups from Seattle to Davos in Switzerland in the late 1990s and early 2000s.

In traditional societies, the existing social organizations are often strong enough to delay, if not prevent, the acceptance of change. Through much of the Middle Ages, family, church, guild, and state cooperated in maintaining the existing order. In modern societies, by contrast, with a multiplicity of informal and formal organizations often in conflict with each other, new organizations have developed to combat particular threats to the status quo. For example, the Ku Klux Klan developed in opposition to the early efforts of reformers to bring the blacks of the South something of that equality with whites that was their constitutional right (LaPiere, 1965:197), and a nativist group, the League of Deliverance, attempted to mobilize West Coast workers to prevent the employment of Chinese labor (Gamson, 1990). These and similar organizations have resisted change that was under way, and although most of them have fought a losing battle, their delaying effects have often been considerable.

At times, however, when organized opposition to change is not forthcoming, the consequences can be disastrous. For example, more than 6 million Jews were slaughtered in concentration camps during World War II, in part because they did not organize resistance to the changes beginning in the early 1930s in Nazi Germany. In the next section, the psychological factors in resistance to change will be considered.

PSYCHOLOGICAL BARRIERS

It is a well-established proposition in the social-change literature that "All of the forces which contribute to stability in personality or in social systems can be perceived as resisting change" (Watson, 1969:488). Any detailed account of these forces is obviously beyond the scope of this book. For the present purposes, the emphasis will be on selected psychological barriers to resistance. They include habit, motivation, ignorance, selective perception, and ineffective communication.

Habit

From the psychological perspective, an initial impediment to change is the matter of habit. Once a habit is established, its operation often becomes satisfying to the individual. Habits, once formed, resist change. Individuals become accustomed to behaving in a certain manner and they feel comfortable with it. A person who is accustomed after dinner to his or her chair, a glass of red wine, and a newspaper, may resist any change in the details of this routine.

The customs of a society may be seen as collective habits, and especially where sentiment pervades custom, custom is slow to change when challenged by new practices and ideas. Habits of individuals that impede social change are derived from social experience and can often be modified by using a group approach to the problem. For example, the dietary patterns of humans change very slowly (Popkin, 1993), and new foods are introduced into a diet with great reluctance, but when the individuals have a chance to discuss the relative merits of the proposed substance in the interest of better nutrition, the likelihood of its acceptance is increased (Lewin, 1965).

Motivation

The motivational forces stimulating the acceptance of change may be handicapped by the active or potential resistance of different sectors of society. How these different sectors influence motivation has been described by Clark Kerr and his associates (1964) in their study of industrialization processes in developing countries. They identify five such sectors: (1) the family system, (2) class and race, (3) religion and ethical evaluations, (4) legal concepts, and (5) the concept of the nation-state. The manner in which these sectors of society control change and affect motivation may be seen in the following evaluations.

1. The extended family system, they argue, weakens industrial incentives to work, save, and invest, and reserves key managerial positions for family members, regardless of relative competence of insiders and outsiders.
2. A class structure based on traditional social status does not encourage motivation keyed to economic performance.
3. Traditional religious and ethical values, which emphasize "peace" and "duty" unrelated to economic gain or advancement and which oppose change, particularly in science and technology, do not enhance the cause of innovation.
4. Traditional customs and social norms that deny individual and property rights and fail to guarantee contracts do not facilitate the processes of acceptance of novelty.
5. Finally, divisive groups in developing society that hinder or prevent the emergence of a strong nation-state system do not serve the cause of accelerated acceptance of change.

Collectively, these five sectors reinforce the traditional motivational forces in society geared to the preservation of the status quo.

Ignorance

Ignorance is another psychological factor associated with resistance to change. Ignorance often goes hand in hand with fear of the new and is a product of cognitive impairment (Dunn, 1997). This has often been the case with new foods. Not long ago, many individuals assumed that citrus fruit brought an acid condition to the digestive tract. Once it was proved otherwise, resistance based on the concern about acid has faded. Many examples abound of products and procedures that failed to be accepted by people for whom they would seemingly have been beneficial as a result of their misconceptions and ignorance about them. For example, in a rural village in Peru, an effort was made to reduce the incidence of typhoid and other water-borne diseases by introducing the hygienic measure of boiling contaminated water. But, in spite of efforts to convince the residents of the advantages of the innovation and the great benefits to their health, most refused to take it up. Their beliefs about the origins of disease and their association of boiled water with illness prevented them from accepting this new kind of behavior (Wellin, 1955).

Selective Perception

Once an attitude has been formed, an individual responds to other suggestions within the framework of his or her established outlook. Situations may be perceived as reinforcing the original attitude when they are actually dissonant. In a classic experiment, a common stereotype associating blacks with carrying razors led observers of a cartoon to think they had seen the razor in the hands of a black rather than of a white person (Allport, quoted by Watson, 1969:491). It is a well-known fact in the social sciences that individuals prefer news sources, whether in print or broadcast, with which they are already in agreement. "By reading or listening to what accords with their present views; by misunderstanding communications which, if correctly received, would not be consonant with preestablished attitudes; and by conveniently forgetting any learning which would lead to uncongenial conclusions, subjects successfully resist the possible impact of new evidence upon their earlier views. There are relatively few instances in which old prejudices have been changed by better information or persuasive arguments" (Watson, 1969:491).

Perception is to a great extent conditioned by culture (Moody-Adams, 1994). Individuals in different cultures frequently perceive the same phenomenon in different ways. For example, in rural Mexico, the Indians are reluctant to call the priest for the last rites for a sick relative, even though they are Catholics. They have noticed that on entirely too many occasions the patient dies shortly after the priest visits. In another instance, an anthropologist was unable to measure his subjects for his anthropometric records: The only time an Indian was measured was for a coffin, and if they permitted the anthropologist to measure them, they knew they would die (Foster, 1973:130).

George Foster (1973:131–141) examines a number of situations in which selective perception hinders the acceptance of change. In one instance, he describes a case of perceptual misinterpretation. A linguist missionary couple was living in a village in southern Mexico in a native house with stick walls and thatched roof. For decoration, they placed on their wall a picture of the black and white Scottie dogs that advertised the whiskey of the same name. The Indians showed enormous interest in the picture; as a matter of fact, their fascination bordered on veneration. It dawned on the couple that the only pictures the Indians had ever seen were of Christ, the

Virgin, and the saints. Not wanting to create the belief that Americans worship dogs, they quickly removed the Scotties from the wall.

The perception of health issues can be problematic. Physicians started lancing the gums of teething infants in the 16th century. Soon, cutting the gums of infants to encourage dentition, a period of discomfort and fever, became standard procedure. Lancets became more sophisticated and ornately decorated, often sporting elaborate handles. Few physicians argued against the practice, and dental textbooks as late as 1938 continued to make references to the benefits of the procedure. As dentistry evolved, teething was considered as a natural process best left alone. There were no complications and justification for it and lancing no longer exists in the developed world (Dally, 1996).

In much of the developing world, hospitals are perceived as places where people go to die, not to get well. As a result, there is much resistance to hospitalization because the patient perceives it as meaning his or her family has lost all hope for the person. Foster (1973:132) cites a famous saying about the largest hospital in Egypt: "He who enters it will be lost (dead) and he who comes out of it is born (as a new man)."

Another aspect of differential perception has to do with gifts. Many aid programs offer commodities and services without cost. However, acceptance of such programs often has been negligible. For example, when free powdered milk was first distributed in Chilean health centers, very few women would use it. They suspected that it was of poor quality, or downright harmful. A free gift, in their experience, was suspect. However, when a token charge was made for the milk, they perceived that in the eyes of the clinic personnel the milk had some value, and, shortly thereafter, they started to use it in great quantities. Making a nominal charge for goods or services has been found effective to facilitate acceptance.

At times, there are misperceptions about the objectives of a given proposal or project for change. For example, contraceptive devices had been rejected by many Indian villagers because they feared that family planning change agents were trying to stop birth completely. Occasionally, similar objects intended for different purposes result in the same use as a consequence of misperception. For instance, one of the earlier forms of birth control that was tried in a village in India was the "foaming tablet" that produced contraceptive effects when placed in a woman's vagina. Unfortunately, these tablets were similar in appearance to aspirin and other pills that the village women had received from public health workers. The similarity of the foaming tablets with a previous innovation led to their eventual rejection, for women simply swallowed the tablets (Rogers & Shoemaker, 1971:150). While on the topic of contraceptives, it is worth noting that in many parts of the world, the condom is associated with prostitution. Its purchase is perceived by others, such as the seller, that the buyer is planning to have an encounter with a prostitute. Strong norms against prostitution, especially in Latin America, carry a negative connotation regarding anything associated with prostitution. As a result, it is difficult to promote condoms among certain groups for the purpose of family planning (Zaltman & Duncan, 1977:74).

Ineffective Communication

A basic principle of human communication is that the transfer of ideas occurs most frequently between a source and a receiver who are alike, similar, homophilious. *Homophily* refers to the degree to which individuals who interact are similar in certain attributes, such as beliefs, values, education, social status, and the like (Rogers & Shoemaker, 1971:14). In homophilious situations, communication of ideas is likely to have greater effects in terms of knowledge gained, attitude formation, and change, and overt behavior change. "One of the most distinctive problems in the communication of innovations is that the source is usually quite heterophilious to the receiver." [*Heterophily* is the mirror opposite of homophily and is defined as the degree to which pairs of individuals who interact are different in certain attributes (Rogers & Shoemaker, 1971:15).] Such a situation results in ineffective communication which, in turn, hinders the acceptance of change. In other words, they simply do not speak the same language. In this sense, the effectiveness of the mass media as an instrument of social change can be impaired (see, for example, Comstock, 1983; Washburn, 2003).

In a large, complex, and heterogeneous society, the language problem is multiplied by the presence of a number of subgroups within societies who in expressing themselves use specialized vocabularies that are not fully comprehensible to nonmembers. For example, American teenage slang is to some degree unintelligible to most parents. Similarly, members of the various professions and occupations, such as physicians, lawyers, and carpenters, all use specialized words and expressions.

Medical personnel appear to be among the worst offenders with respect to poor communication. For example, in a Spanish-speaking community in the United States, a physician gave a young mother with limited command of English the following instruction: "Apply a tight pectoral binding and restrict your fluid intake." At a Mother's Club meeting in Temuco in Chile, a physician advised expectant mothers to walk "three kilometers a day." However, this instruction was meaningless, for the women simply were not trained to think in terms of distance in the same way that an educated person would (Foster, 1973:143). These two illustrations simply show how communication can be a factor in resistance to change. The problem is further compounded in cross-cultural communication. For instance, many business people abroad assume that, because their counterparts speak good English, they are probably familiar with American business jargon such as "ballpark figures," "front-end money," and "the bottom line." But when someone from France, for example, tries to translate "bottom line," it can have a completely different meaning. (Une ligne du derrière?)

There are sometimes problems with symbolic communication. The meaning of an action or a gesture often can be quite different from what it was intended to elicit. For example, in New Zealand, a successful health-education poster designed to encourage students to brush their teeth depicted a whale jumping out of the water in pursuit of a tube of toothpaste. The same poster was reproduced for use in Fiji. The response was immediate and overwhelming! Fiji fishermen sent a rush call to New Zealand for large quantities of this wonderful new fish bait (Foster 1973:144)! In another instance, a well-meaning gesture by an American labor-relations expert created a great degree of embarrassment. In Micronesia a few years back, our expert sought to recruit Palauan workers for a mining operation. He first demanded to see the "chief"—a request that posed a problem because they have no chief in their social structure. Finally, they produced a person with whom the American expert sought to establish rapport by throwing an arm around his shoulders and laughingly tousling his hair. In Palauan culture this little gesture was an indignity comparable in our culture to opening a man's fly in public (Useem, 1952). Needless to say, this expert was not very successful. In the next section, cultural barriers to change will be examined.

CULTURAL BARRIERS

Resistance to change is usually most pronounced when traditional values, beliefs and strongly entrenched world views are involved (see, for example, Singer, 2003). In Ireland, cultural values, derived in part from the material conditions of life in a small-scale rural society, and, in part, from antimaterialistic religious ethics, combined to produce a value system that put little premium on dynamic and innovative entrepreneurship, and this held back economic development in the country (Keating, 1992). In India, much of the population is ill fed or even starving, yet over 500 million cows, sacred to the Hindus, are not only exempt from being slaughtered for food, but are also allowed to roam through villages and farmlands, often causing extensive damage to crops. However, it is unlikely that the raising of cattle for food will be acceptable in India in the near future, as the eating of beef runs counter to long-held religious beliefs. Many factors influence values and beliefs in a culture. They include fatalism, ethnocentrism, norms of modesty, the degree of cultural integration, notions of incompatibility, prevailing motor patterns, and superstitions.

Fatalism

Fatalism is an important impediment to change. "In many parts of the world we find cultures adhering to the belief that man has no causal effect upon his future or the future of the land; God, not man, can improve man's lot. . . . It is difficult to persuade such people to use fertilizers, or to save the best seed for planting, since man is responsible only for the performance, and the divine for the success of the act" (Mead, 1953:201). Fatalism is a belief that all events are determined by fate and are hence inevitable. It entails a feeling of a lack of mastery over nature and one's surroundings. It is present in a variety of situations ranging from accounting for illness and misfortune (Davison, Frankel, & Smith, 1992) to hypothesizing that Communist rule in eastern Europe was predicated on hierarchies that encouraged widespread fatalist attitudes among citizens that helped to preserve the status quo (Taras, 1991). One has no control over one's life, and everything that happens to a person is caused by gods, evil spirits, fate or forces beyond one's control. Expressions such as "it was my fate" or it is the "will of Allah" are common reactions to problems such as epidemics and crop failures (Harris & Moran, 2000; Patai, 2002).

Religious beliefs and sacred writings often contribute to fatalistic attitudes. For example in rural Brazil it is difficult to persuade mothers to seek help for their sick children during the month of May. In Catholic theology, May is the "Month of the Virgin Mary," and, in parts of Brazil, it is believed that when a child dies in May, it is particularly fortunate because the Virgin is "calling" her child to come to be with her. To obtain medical aid during this time would be contrary to the will of the Virgin. In Egypt, some authorities consider high infant mortality rates related to the perception of that as "Allah's will" and the belief that no one can extend life because the Koran says: "Wherever you are, death will seek you, even if you are in strongly built castles."

Ethnocentrism

Americans are not the only ones who consider themselves superior, possessing the only "right" way of thinking about the world and of coping with their environment. Similarly, most primitive peoples before extensive contact with the Western world were extremely ethnocentric, thinking that they were the people, and their ways were the only correct ones dealing with the environment. Feelings of superiority about one's culture make people unreceptive to the ideas and methods used in other cultures. A version of ethnocentrism is also found in some organizations where one encounters resistance often referred to as NIH, or "Not Invented Here" (Bennis, 1987:37). For example, some faculty members may balk at a new teaching method because it originated outside of their department or school.

Related to ethnocentrism are pride and dignity, which also constitute barriers to change. Quite frequently, adults feel that "they will lose face" if they go back to school. Often older women resist modern maternal and child health care programs on the grounds that if young pregnant women attend clinics, for example, such would reflect on the ability and judgment of the older ones.

Norms of Modesty

Ideas about modesty, like ideas about most everything else, are culturally conditioned. Proper behavior in one setting may be highly shocking in another. In many parts of the world nudity or seminudity is taken for granted, as on many beaches of Europe, and modest dress is not always associated with covering the sex organs. For example, in the Amazon Basin, Indian women were observed at close range in a state of nature. When seen by travelers, they were highly embarrassed, but this embarrassment usually disappeared when the women retired for a moment to reappear wearing a string of beads or some other kind of ornament (Foster, 1973:90).

In many cultures, medical examination and treatment may be resisted by native women when it is done by a male physician, and frequently the husband may object to the treatment. Ideally, this resistance could be overcome by having it done by female physicians. However, this is not always the case. Women on the island of Yap in Micronesia are resistant to genital examination by a male physician, but they are even more resistant to examination by a female. The reason: women regard all other women, regardless of age, as potential rivals for men's attention; at the same time, they believe their own genitals are their strongest power over men. Exposing their source of power to potential rivals, they feel, weakens their competitive advantage and threatens them with loss of masculine attention (Schneider, cited by Foster, 1973:91).

Cultural Integration

Anthropologist R. A. Manners (1952) uses an interesting metaphor in comparing highly integrated cultures with a delicate watchlike mechanism. He suggests that the rapid introduction of new elements into such a culture acts very much like the dropping of a grain of sand into the delicate works of a watch. The watch runs poorly or the culture becomes disorganized and anomic. Thus, he points out, highly integrated cultures tend to be resistant to change, whereas less delicately balanced cultures tend to assimilate change better if the change is not too radical or sudden.

Incompatibility

Resistance is often due to the presence in the recipient cultures of material and systems that are, or are considered to be, irreconcilable with the invading traits or systems and, as a result, tend to block them, checking their further diffusion (Kroeber, 1973:141). When such incompatibility exists in a culture, change comes about with difficulty. For example, the contrast between a monotheistic and a polytheistic religion underlines this point. Monotheistic peoples can accept a new deity only by rejecting the previous incumbent, which would be asking a great deal from them. Many missionaries have found this out the hard way.

Motor Patterns

Motor patterns and customary body positions are conditioned by culture and learned in childhood. Culture dictates the positions in which we sleep, stand, sit, and relax. Culture determines what gestures we use, how we hold and use tools and carry objects (i.e., on the head, shoulder, or in the hands) and how we manipulate our bodies in variety of situations. In many cases unfamiliar muscular activity involved in a new activity may underlie its rejection. To change established motor patterns is difficult and tiring. For example, as part of a community development program in the Cook Islands, a raised cooking stove was devised so that food would be protected from animals and dirt, and women would not have to stoop continually in preparing the meals. However, the raised stove was generally rejected because it was very uncomfortable to have to stand on one's feet while cooking. In another instance, an attempt was made to introduce latrines in rural El Salvador (the outhouse version, which was considered an improvement over disposing of bodily wastes in the traditional fashion). A coffee planter built the standard American model, that is, a square wooden structure with a raised seat, perforated by one or more holes, for each house. However, he was quite upset when his employees refused to use them. "Finally, an old man offered a suggestion. 'Patron, don't you realize that here we are squatters?' The planter ripped out the seats, replaced them with a perforated slab floor, and was gratified to find that public acceptance was much greater. He had learned what has had to be learned independently time after time, in many parts of the world: for psychological or physiological reasons, latrines with raised seats seem to cause constipation among people who customarily defecate in a squatting position" (Foster, 1973:103).

Superstitions

Superstition is an uncritical acceptance of a belief that is not substantiated by facts. Throughout the world, many people start the day by consulting their horoscopes in the morning paper. Some consider the arrangement of stars a factor in decision making. Former presidents Ronald Reagan and Boris N. Yeltsin have been known to consult astrologers for guidance. It is noteworthy that in the United States alone, there are 15,000 astrologers and only 1,500 astronomers (Specter, 1997). Residents of Hong Kong are particularly obsessed with lucky numbers and fortune telling. Bankers and lawyers regularly consult fortune tellers, as do housewives and delivery boys, and the 200 or so fortune-tellers in the Soothsayer's Arcade may be the largest such grouping in the world (Faison, 1997). In China (and many other parts of the world), there are people trained in feng shui, the Chinese practice of placing man-made structures in harmony with natural surroundings. In fact, such experts were called in to look at the ill-fated Denver International Airport, which was plagued by a series of construction difficulties that delayed its long awaited opening until 1995. They concluded that it was a feng shui disaster, rife with images of death and grief (*Newsweek*, 1994b). This New Age fad spawned an industry over the past few years that finds a niche in such fields as interior design, real estate, urban planning, architecture and landscaping. There is now an International Feng Shui Guild and it is "in the beginning stages of becoming a profession" (Heyemoto, 2002), with a mission to create harmonious space which equals happy people and good karma. In Russia, the most popular weekly television programs deal with straight, factual discussions of how sorcery and witchcraft can improve one's daily life. Major newspapers advertise the services of clairvoyants, witches and warlocks. Well-trained physicians at respected hospitals see nothing unusual in recommending that their patients see a *babka*, an old woman with the power to heal (Specter, 1997).

In many instances, superstitions act as important barriers to change. Some examples: In Zimbabwe (formerly Southern Rhodesia), nutrition-education efforts were hampered because many women would not eat eggs. According to widespread belief, eggs cause infertility, they make babies bald, and they cause women to be promiscuous. In the Philippines, it is widely believed that eating squash and chicken at the same time produces leprosy. In some places, women are not given milk during late pregnancy because of the belief that it produces a fetus too large for easy delivery, and, in other places, a baby may not be given water for several months after birth because water's "cold" quality is upsetting to the infant's heat equilibrium. Finally, in areas of Ghana, children are not given meat or fish because it is believed that they cause intestinal worms (Foster, 1973:103–104). Obviously, where such superstitious beliefs prevail, the acceptance of novelty, which is contrary to traditional ideas, will be greatly hampered. In the final section, economic barriers to change will be considered.

ECONOMIC BARRIERS

Resistance to change stemming from economic factors mostly relates to technological innovations, machines, and gadgets, although it can apply to social inventions and scientific discoveries as well. The cost of an invention can prevent its adoption, at least for a while. A society of limited economic means cannot afford to initiate programs involving nuclear energy nor can the majority of its citizens afford to adopt such modern appliances and conveniences as central heating, refrigerators, or automobiles (see, for example, Weisskoff, 1994). Even in the most affluent societies, limited economic resources constitute a barrier to changes that might otherwise be readily adopted. For example, in the United States, most everyone would readily accept the desirability of more effective controls on pollution, cheaper and more convenient systems of public transportation, and adequate health care for all. The fact that improvements in these areas come very slowly is a matter not only of priorities but also of cost. Cost, perceived profitability, and economic resources in a society can act as effective barriers to change, as will be shown on the following pages.

Cost

The cost of acquiring or using a novelty can be prohibitive, as far as some potential acceptors are concerned. This is an important deterrent to the widespread adoption of a variety of modern innovations in both the technological and the ideological domains. A large number of people in the world today are ready to accept—in fact, psychologically they have already accepted—electric lights, television, computers, dishwashers, central heating, sanitation programs, modern house design, and many other changes, but they are simply unable to afford them. The willingness to accept is present, but the economic sacrifice is either too great or completely beyond the scope of realization. In some cases, the cost of an innovation is so great that no one can afford it. The idea is acceptable and it has important implications, but the returns to be expected are not commensurate with the investment required to produce it. Such is the status of a recently proposed comprehensive health insurance plan for everybody in the United States.

Perceived Profitability

The perception of economic profitability is an important consideration that involves a predisposition toward an innovation. However, profitability alone would not ensure the adoption of an innovation. For example, even if the price of beef were to be reduced by 99 percent in India, Hindus would not begin eating cows. Nevertheless, there are many novelties that do not run so counter to cultural and social norms, and in these cases the rate of acceptance is likely to be more rapid if the innovation is more economically or socially profitable. Even in these instances, however, it should be noted that the increase in profitability needs to be rather spectacular to affect the rate of adoption. Students of rural life feel that the relative economic advantage of a new idea must be at least 25 to 30 percent higher than existing practice for economic factors to affect adoption. When an innovation promises only a 5 to 10 percent advantage, a farmer probably cannot even distinguish that it is advantageous (Rogers & Shoemaker, 1971:143). His limited skills with figures, elementary accounting ability, and lack of experience with the scientific method of reaching conclusions all act to limit the farmer's comparing ability. In some instances, as noted by Rogers and Shoemaker (1971:143), to induce farmers to change, the potential payoff must be very high—not 5 to 10 percent, but 50 to 100 percent. Occasionally, a new practice is accepted because of financial incentives but is rejected for some other reasons at a later stage. For example, when government agencies introduced hybrid corn to the Mexican-American farmers of the Rio Grande Valley a few years ago, they readily adopted it because of its superior yield and high profitability; but within three years they had all returned to the old corn. The reason was that the hybrid corn did not make good tortillas (Apodaca, 1952).

Limited Economic Resources

In many underdeveloped and developing countries, changes are desired but cannot be adequately implemented because of other economic pressures. In such countries, from 70 to 90 percent of the labor force is in agriculture; there is a lack of employment opportunities outside of agriculture; there is very little capital per head, and, for most people, existence is near the "subsistence" level; and savings practically do not exist for the large mass of the people. Whatever savings do exist are usually achieved by a land-holding class whose values are not conducive to investment in industry or commerce. A major proportion of expenditures is spent on food and basic necessities. There are poor credit facilities and a very low volume of trade per capita (World Bank, 2003).

These economic characteristics in underdeveloped countries tend to hinder capital formation, which, in turn, is considered a principal obstacle to change. These countries seem to face more difficulties than the now-advanced countries when they began their industrialization. Simon Kuznets (1965) points to six major differences that are still quite pronounced:

1. The present level of per capita product in the underdeveloped countries in their preindustrial phase is much lower than it was in the now-advanced countries, with the single exception of Japan.
2. The supply of land per capita is much smaller in developing countries today than it was in the presently advanced countries when they began their industrialization.
3. Agricultural productivity in developing countries today is probably lower than it was in advanced countries in the past.
4. The inequality in the distribution of income is wider today than in the past, but not in a way that favors accumulation of productive capital.
5. The social and political structure of the low-income countries today is a much greater barrier than it was in the past.

6. Most of the present-day underdeveloped countries are launching development after a long period of colonial status, whereas the European countries began industrialization after a long period of political independence.

At times, nations that are scarcely emerging from the stage of feudalism are quite unwilling to go through the stage of laissez-faire capitalism. They see and emulate social security programs in the advanced nations, along with minimum wage legislation, factory-safety and maximum-working-day legislation, trade union movements, and the like. These programs are carried out in the context of an insufficient system of taxation and are usually of relatively short duration. Moreover, expenditures on these types of activities, admirable as they are in principle, take away funds from more essential matters such as basic health care, education, and the like.

In addition, the limited savings and investment patterns are not conducive to national development or large-scale changes. For example, in India, too much of the limited savings goes to the hoarding of gold and of jewelry imported legally or illegally into the country, thus using up its scarce foreign exchange. Many underdeveloped countries also suffer from chronic inflation. Hence, there is a natural tendency for people to invest in real estate and in the holding of inventory. Finally, there is the frequent tendency of the rich in underdeveloped countries to pile up their savings abroad, legally or illegally, thereby making it unavailable to the nation for its internal development.

Other change-inhibiting economic factors include the lack of natural resources, such as oil, timber, coal, uranium, gas, and agricultural acreage. Obviously, the natural resources available to a society's economy can vary; some have a plentiful supply, others very few. However, more important than the level or abundance of indigenous resources is the degree of access a society has to natural resources, whether its own or those of another society. When availability of and access to natural resources are limited, in most cases, the economic structure of a society will not be able to support large-scale changes. Related to natural resources is labor, which can be viewed in both quantitative and qualitative senses. The number of people who can participate in the economy (quantity) always affects economic processes, but more important, the level of skill, knowledge, expertise, and motivation (quality) is an equally significant influence on the economy. Both labor and natural resources are closely associated with a society's ability for capital formation, a prerequisite for industrialization and modernization (Krugman, 1994).

In sum, cultural, social, and psychological barriers and stimulants to change exist essentially in an economic context which, in many instances, sets the absolute limits to change. Quite often people are aware of the value of change and are anxious to modify their traditional ways, but the economic conditions prevent them from doing so. In such situations, economic factors constitute a formidable barrier to change.

SUMMARY

In every society, there are factors that promote change, and there are those that strive to maintain the status quo. The former are considered as stimulants to change, whereas the latter are seen as barriers; they can be separated only in an analytical sense. In reality, stimulants and barriers operate simultaneously. In this chapter, they were examined in social, psychological, cultural, and economic terms.

One of the principal social stimulants to change is the desire for prestige. Societies in contact with one another are more likely to accept novelty than those in relative isolation. Strong friendship obligations in developing societies are also considered factors in the acceptance of change. Different social classes react to change in different ways, and in general, those in the middle classes are more likely to accept an innovation. Authority influences receptivity to change, and at times it is required over the beliefs of a dissident minority. Acceptance of change is enhanced when it can be integrated into the existing configuration of society. The timing of an innovation is also important. Under certain circumstances, competition acts as a stimulant to change, and, in general, a novelty will be more readily accepted if the people who are to change are involved in its planning and implementation.

On the other side of the token, social barriers to change are often manifested in the form of vested interests and status interests. In such situations, change is resisted by individuals or groups who fear a loss of power, wealth, or prestige should an innovation gain acceptance. Rigid class and caste patterns also tend to hinder the acceptance of the new. Resistance can also be based on ideology and rational conviction. Societies with a high degree of social solidarity and diffuse authority patterns will be resistant to change. At times, individuals are afraid of social dislocation and apprehensive of the unknown. On many occasions, prevailing moral sentiments provide a sound basis for resistance. Resistance may also be irrational and covert and, on occasions, change may meet with organized opposition.

Acceptance of or resistance to change is also conditioned by a number of psychological factors. Favorable motivational dispositions, perceived needs, clear-cut lines of communication, positive attitudes, and personal influence tend to facilitate the acceptance of change. By contrast, habit, ignorance, forms of selective perception, and unclear communication hinder change.

As Ralph Linton suggested, "If we know what a society's culture is, including its particular system of values and attitudes, we can predict with a fairly high degree of probability whether the bulk of its members will welcome or resist a particular innovation" (Linton, quoted by Allen, 1971:288). In a society where there is a high degree of emphasis on tradition, a fatalistic outlook on life, a strong sense of ethnocentrism, highly traditional norms of modesty, prevalence of superstitions, and inflexible motor patterns, there will be, in general, resistance to change. By contrast, where these conditions are absent or present to a lesser degree, the culture will be less tightly integrated and more receptive to novelty.

Of the four sources of acceptance or resistance, the economic factors are perhaps the most decisive. Perception of economic advantage and reasonable costs can, in most cases, facilitate the acceptance of change. On the other hand, regardless of the desirability of a given change, its compatibility with the recipient culture and many other considerations, it will not be accepted if the economic sacrifice is too great. In other words, regardless of how much people in a society want something, if they cannot afford it, the chances are that they will not be able to get it. However, once a novelty is affordable, its perceived profitability will facilitate its acceptance. In the following chapter, the strategies of change will be considered.

SUGGESTED FURTHER READINGS

FLEISHMAN, AVROM. *New Class Culture: How an Emergent Class Is Transforming America's Culture*. Westport, CT: Praeger, 2003. A short but informative book on a new class that is emerging in the wake of the information economy and how it is altering American culture.

FOSTER, GEORGE M. *Traditional Societies and Technological Change*, 2nd ed. New York: Harper & Row, 1973. Chapters 4 and 9 represent a most comprehensive treatment of the various barriers and stimulants to change. Many of the examples used in the present chapter came from this book.

HARRIS, PHILIP R., AND ROBERT T. MORAN. *Managing Cultural Differences*, 5th ed. Houston: Gulf, 2000. A nontechnical discussion of cultural impacts on international business, with many useful and practical hints on various stimulants and barriers to change.

HEINZE, RUTH-INGE (ed.). *The Nature and Function of Rituals: Fire from Heaven*. Westport, CT: Greenwood Press, 2000. A collection of essays on the nature and function of rituals in human society from earliest times to present and on the implications of ritual in social change.

KUSHNER, GILBERT, MICKEY GIBSON, JOHN GULICK, JOHN J. HONIGMANN, AND RICHARD NONAS. *What Accounts for Socio-Cultural Change? A Propositional Inventory*. Chapel Hill: University of North Carolina, Institute for Research in Social Science, 1962. A collection of some 400 hypotheses under thirteen categories concerning the conditions under which change will be accepted or rejected.

PATAI, RAPHAEL. *The Arab Mind*, rev. ed. New York: Hatherleigh Press, 2002. A fascinating and possibly controversial account of the way of life in Arab countries. A very helpful resource in trying to understand current events in the Middle East.

SINGER, PETER. *One World: The Ethics of Globalization*. New Haven, CT: Yale University Press, 2003. A provocative book by a renowned philosopher on the need to subjugate local interests and views to the welfare of the broader community.

WASHBURN, PHILO C. *The Social Construction of International News; We're Talking about Them, They're Talking about Us*. Westport, CT: Praeger, 2003. The book compares

U.S. commercial news reports on a wide variety of major political events with those produced by the news media of several other nations.

ZALTMAN, GERALD, AND ROBERT DUNCAN. *Strategies for Planned Change.* New York: Wiley, 1977. See, in particular, Chapter 3 on the various barriers to change. The discussion is a useful supplement to the material presented in this chapter.

REFERENCES

AGHION, PHILIPPE, AND JEAN TIROLE. "Formal and Real Authority in Organizations," *Journal of Political Economy,* 105 (1) February 1997, pp. 1–30.

AINSWORTH, SCOTT, AND ITAI SENED. "The Role of Lobbyists: Entrepreneurs with Two Audiences," *American Journal of Political Science,* 37 (3) August 1993, pp. 834–867.

ALBRECHT, STAN L., BRUCE A. CHADWICK, AND CARDELL K. JACOBSON. *Social Psychology,* 2nd ed. Englewood Cliffs, NJ: Prentice Hall, 1987.

ALLEN, FRANCIS R. *Socio-Cultural Dynamics: An Introduction to Social Change.* New York: Macmillan, 1971.

APODACA, ANADETO. "Corn and Custom: The Introduction of Hybrid Corn to Spanish American Farmers in New Mexico." In Edward H. Spicer (ed.), *Human Problems in Technological Change.* New York: Russell Sage, 1952, pp. 35–39.

ARENSBERG, CONRAD, AND ARTHUR M. NIEHOFF. *Introducing Change: A Manual for Community Development.* Chicago: Aldine-Atherton, 1971.

AXELROD, ROBERT. "The Dissemination of Culture: A Model With Local Convergence and Global Polarization," *Journal of Conflict Resolution,* 41 (2) April 1997, pp. 203–227.

BARNETT, HOMER G. *Innovation: The Basis of Cultural Change.* New York: McGraw-Hill, 1953.

BENNIS, WARREN. "Using Our Knowledge of Organizational Behavior: The Improbable Task." In Jay W. Lorsch (ed.), *Handbook of Organizational Behavior.* Englewood Cliffs, NJ: Prentice Hall, 1987, pp. 29–49.

BENSMAN, JOSEPH, AND ARTHUR J. VIDICH. *American Society: The Welfare State & Beyond,* rev. ed. South Hadley, MA: Bergin & Garvey, 1987.

BIERSTEDT, ROBERT. *Power and Progress: Essays on Sociological Theory.* New York: McGraw-Hill, 1974.

BOCHNER, STEPHEN (ed.). *Cultures in Contact: Studies in Cross-Cultural Interaction.* Elmsford, NY: Pergamon, 1982.

BRANDES, STANLEY. "Maize as a Culinary Mystery," *Ethnology,* 31 (4) October 1992, pp. 331–337.

BRODY, STUART, HARALD RAU, NIKLAS FUHRER, HEIKO HILLERBRAND, DANIELA RUDIGER, AND MANUEL BRAUN. "Traditional Ideology as an Inhibitor of Sexual Behavior," *The Journal of Psychology,* 130 (6) November 1996, pp. 615–627.

BROWN, MICHAEL F. "On Resisting Resistance," *American Anthropologist,* 98 (4) December 1996, pp. 729–736.

COHEN, ARTHUR R. *Attitude Change and Social Influence.* New York: Basic Books, 1964.

COMSTOCK, GEORGE. "The Mass Media and Social Change." In Edward Seidman (ed.), *Handbook of Social Intervention.* Beverly Hills, CA: Sage Publications, Inc., 1983, pp. 268–288.

Cook, Karen S. (ed.). *Trust in Society*. New York: Russell Sage Foundation, 2000.

Dally, Ann. "The Lancet and the Gum-Lancet: 400 Years of Teething Babies," *The Lancet*, 348 (9048) December 21, 1996, pp. 1710–1712.

Davison, Charlie, Stephen Frankel, and George Davey Smith. "The Limits of Lifestyle: Re-assessing 'Fatalism' in the Popular Culture of Illness Prevention," *Social Science & Medicine*, 34 (2) March 15, 1992, pp. 675–686.

Dunn, William N. "Probing the Boundaries of Ignorance in Policy Analysis—Initiating Change: Theory and Practice," *American Behavioral Scientist*, 40 (3) January 1997, pp. 277–299.

Economist. "Stitch Ups," October 29, 1994, p. 99.

Economist. "France's Bottin Line," June 15, 1996, p. 50.

Eriksen, Thomas Hylland. "Multiple Traditions and the Question of Cultural Integration," *Ethnos*, 57 (1–2) 1992, pp. 5–30.

Faison, Seth. "Any Omens? Colony's Soothsayers Won't Say," *The New York Times*, June 23, 1997, p. A4.

Fershtman, Chaim, and Yoram Weiss. "Social Status, Culture and Economic Performance," *Economic Journal*, 103 (419) July 1993, pp. 946–960.

Festinger, Leon. "Behavioral Support for Opinion Change," *Public Opinion Quarterly*, 28, Fall 1964, pp. 404–417.

Fleishman, Avrom. *New Class Culture: How an Emergent Class Is Transforming America's Culture*. Westport, CT: Praeger, 2003.

Fliegel, Frederic C., and Joseph E. Kivlin. "Attributes of Innovation as Factors in Diffusion," *American Journal of Sociology*, 72, November 1966, pp. 235–248.

Foster, George M. *Traditional Societies in Technological Change*, 2nd ed. New York: Harper & Row, 1973.

Gamson, William A. *The Strategy of Social Protest*, 2nd ed. Belmont, CA: Wadsworth, 1990.

Germani, Gino. *The Sociology of Modernization*. New Brunswick, NJ: Transaction Books, 1981.

Graham, Saxon. "Class and Conservatism in the Adoption of Innovations," *Human Relations*, 9, 1956, pp. 91–100.

Hall, Edward T. *Beyond Culture*. New York: Anchor Books, 1989 (orig. pub. 1976).

Hall, Richard. *Organizations: Structures, Processes, and Outcomes*, 8th ed. Upper Saddle River, NJ: Prentice Hall, 2002.

Harris, Philip R., and Robert T. Moran. *Managing Cultural Differences*, 5th ed. Houston: Gulf, 2000.

Heinze, Ruth-Inge (ed.). *The Nature and Function of Rituals: Fire from Heaven*. Westport, CT: Greenwood Press, 2000.

Helmer, Olaf. "Adversary Delphi," *Futures*, 26 (1) January–February 1994, pp. 79–88.

Heyemoto, Lisa. "'Positive' Spaces Aid Office Energy," *The Seattle Times*, November 12, 2002, pp. C1 and C6.

Hofmeister, Sallie. "Used American Jeans Power a Thriving Industry Abroad," *The New York Times*, August 22, 1999, pp. A1 and C3.

Holli, Melvin G. "E Pluribus Unum: The Assimilation Paradigm Revisited," *The Midwest Quarterly*, 44 (1) Autumn 2002, pp. 10–28.

Hovland, Carl I., A. A. Lumsdaine, and F. D. Sheffield. *Experiments on Mass Communication*. Princeton, NJ: Princeton University Press, 1949.

Jaspars, Jos, and Miles Hewstone. "Cross-Cultural Interaction, Social Attribution and Inter-Group Relations." In Stephen Bochner (ed.), *Cultures in Contact: Studies in Cross-Cultural Interaction*. New York: Pergamon, 1982, pp. 127–156.

Jensen, Michael. "Overcoming the Fear of Change," *Forbes*, 158 (13) December 2, 1996, pp. 57–59.

Katz, Elihu, and Paul F. Lazarsfeld. *Personal Influence*. New York: Free Press, 1955.

Keating, Paul. "Entrepreneurship and Economic Development in Ireland: Does Culture Matter?" *World Futures*, 33, 1992, pp. 35–48.

Keesing, Felix M. *Cultural Anthropology: The Science of Custom*. New York: Holt, Rinehart & Winston, 1958.

Keesing, Roger M. "Chiefs in a Chiefless Society: The Ideology of Modern Kwaio Politics," *Oceania*, 38, June 1968, pp. 276–280.

Kelman, Herbert C. "Processes of Opinion Change," *Public Opinion Quarterly*, 25, Spring 1961, pp. 57–58.

Kerr, Clark, John T. Dunlop, Federick H. Harberson, and Charles A. Myers. *Industrialism and Industrial Man*. New York: Oxford, 1964.

Klein, Donald. "Some Notes on the Dynamics of Resistance to Change. The Defender Role." In Warren G. Bennis, Kenneth D. Benne, and Robert Chin (eds.), *The Planning of Change*, 4th ed. New York: Holt, Rinehart & Winston, 1985, pp. 98–105.

Kroeber, A. L. "Diffusionism." In Amitai Etzioni and Eva Etzioni-Halevy (eds.), *Social Change: Sources, Patterns, and Consequences*, 2nd ed. New York: Basic Books, 1973, pp. 140–144.

Krugman, Paul. "Does Third World Growth Hurt First World Prosperity?" *Harvard Business Review*, July–August 1994, pp. 113–121.

Krusell, Per, and Jose-Victor Rios-Rull. "Vested Interests in a Positive Theory of Stagnation and Growth," *Review of Economic Studies*, 63 (215) April 1996, pp. 301–330.

Kuznets, Simon S. *Economic Growth and Structure: Selected Essays*. New York: W. W. Norton, 1965.

LaPiere, Richard T. *Social Change*. New York: McGraw-Hill, 1965.

Lewin, Kurt. "Group Decision and Social Change." In H. Proshansky and B. Seidenberg (eds.), *Basic Studies in Social Psychology*. New York: Holt, Rinehart & Winston, 1965, pp. 423–486.

Manners, R. A. "Cultural and Personality Factors Affecting Economic Growth." In Bert Hoselitz (ed.), *Progress of Underdeveloped Areas*. Chicago: University of Chicago Press, 1952, pp. 72–88.

Mead, Margaret (ed.). *Cultural Patterns and Technical Change*. Paris: UNESCO, 1953.

Mekay, Emad. "Egyptians Find Status in Costly Cellular Phones," *The New York Times*, February 24, 1997, p. D6.

Merton, Robert K. *Social Theory and Social Structure*. New York: Basic Books, 1957.

Miller, Henry I. "Overcoming Consumers' Fear of Technology," *Food Technology*, 50 (11) November 1996, pp. 140–141.

Montagu, Ashley. *Man Observed*. New York: Putnam, 1968.

Moody-Adams, Michele. "Culture, Responsibility, and Affected Ignorance," *Ethics*, 104 (2) January 1994, pp. 291–309.

Moschis, George P. *Consumer Socialization: A Life-Cycle Perspective*. Lexington, MA: D. C. Heath, 1987.

Moxley, Robert L., and Charles Proctor. "Community Solidarity, Political Competitiveness, and Social Rigidity: Relationships with Social and Health Services," *Rural Sociology*, 60 (2) Summer 1995, pp. 310–323.

Nadler, David A. "The Effective Management of Organizational Change." In Jay W. Lorsch (ed.), *Handbook of Organizational Behavior*. Englewood Cliffs, NJ: Prentice Hall, 1987, pp. 358–369.

Nair, K. N. "Animal Protein Consumption and the Sacred Cow Complex in India." In Marvin Harris and Eric B. Ross (eds.), *Food and Evolution: Toward a Theory of Human Food Habits*. Philadelphia: Temple University Press, 1987, pp. 445–454.

Naisbitt, John, and Patricia Aburdene. *Megatrends 2000: Ten New Directions for the 1990s*. New York: Morrow, 1990.

Newsweek. "Down & Dirty," November 7, 1994a, pp. 22–42.

Newsweek. "Time to Call a Shaman?" December 12, 1994b, p. 10.

Nimkoff, Meyer F. "Obstacles to Innovation." In Francis R. Allen, Hornell Hart, Delbert C. Miller, William F. Ogburn, and Meyer F. Nimkoff (eds.), *Technology and Social Change*. New York: Appleton, 1957, pp. 56–71.

Patai, Raphael. *The Arab Mind*, rev. ed. New York: Hatherleigh Press, 2002.

Perkins, J. J., R. W. Sanson-Fisher, A. Girgis, S. Blunden, and D. Dunnay. "The Development of a New Methodology to Assess Perceived Needs Among Indigenous Australians," *Social Science & Medicine*, 41 (2) July 15, 1995, pp. 267–276.

Popkin, Barry M. "Nutritional Patterns and Transitions," *Population and Development Review*, 19 (1) March 1993, pp. 138–158.

Rogers, Everett M., and F. Lloyd Shoemaker. *Communication of Innovations: A Cross-Cultural Approach*, 2nd ed. New York: Free Press, 1971.

Schneider, Harold K. "Pakot Resistance to Change." In William B. Bascom and Melville J. Herskovitz (eds.), *Continuity and Change in African Cultures*. Chicago: University of Chicago Press, 1959, pp. 144–167.

Singer, Peter. *One World: The Ethics of Globalization*. New Haven, CT: Yale University Press, 2003.

Specter, Michael. "In Modern Russia, a Medieval Witch Hunt," *The New York Times*, April 5, 1997, pp. 1 and 4.

Stroneger, Willibald-Julius, Wolfgang Freidl, and Eva Rasky. "Health Behaviour and Risk Behaviour: Socioeconomic Differences in an Austrian Rural County," *Social Science & Medicine*, 44 (3) February 1997, pp. 423–437.

Swisher, Kara. "Mail Pouring in to Attack OSHA's Anti-Smoking Plan," *St. Louis Post-Dispatch*, August 17, 1994, p. 5B.

Sztompka, Piotr. *The Sociology of Social Change*. Cambridge, MA: Blackwell, 1994.

Taras, Raymond. "When Fatalists Rebelled: Cultural Theory, Conflicting Ways of Life under Socialism, and Counterrevolution in Eastern Europe," *Cultural Dynamics*, 4 (1) 1991, pp. 55–89.

Teisberg, Elizabeth Olmsted, Michael E. Porter, and Gregory B. Brown. "Making Competition in Health Care Work," *Harvard Business Review*, July–August 1994, pp. 131–141.

Thompson, Joel A., William Cassie, and Malcolm E. Jewell. "A Sacred Cow or Just a Lot of Bull? Party and PAC Money in State Legislative Elections," *Political Research Quarterly*, 47 (1) March 1994, pp. 223–238.

Toffler, Alvin. *The Third Wave*. New York: William Morrow, 1980.

USEEM, JOHN. "South Seas Island Strike: Labor–Management Relations in the Carolina Islands, Micronesia." In Edward H. Spicer (ed.), *Human Problems in Technological Change*. New York: Russell Sage, 1952, pp. 149–164.

VAGO, STEVEN. "Blowing the Overseas Business Deal: Hypothetical Blunderplax Company Shows How Not to Succeed," *St. Louis Commerce*, May 1982, pp. 35–38.

WARREN, ROLAND S. *Social Change and Human Purpose: Toward Understanding and Action*. Chicago: Rand McNally, 1977.

WASHBURN, PHILO C. *The Social Construction of International News; We're Talking about Them, They're Talking about Us*. Westport, CT: Praeger, 2003.

WASTE, ROBERT J. *Independent Cities: Rethinking U.S. Urban Policy*. New York: Oxford University Press, 1998.

WATSON, GOODWIN. "Resistance to Change." In Warren C. Bennis, Kenneth D. Benne, and Robert Chin (eds.), *The Planning of Change*, 2nd ed. New York: Holt, Rinehart & Winston, 1969, pp. 488–498.

WEISSKOFF, RICHARD. "Forty-One Years of Structural Continuity and Social Change in Nicaragua, 1950–1991," *The Journal of Developing Areas*, 28 (April) 1994, pp. 379–392.

WELLIN, EDWARD. "Water Boiling in a Peruvian Town." In Benjamin D. Paul (ed.), *Health, Culture, and Community*. New York: Russell Sage, 1955, pp. 71–103.

WEYANT, JAMES M. *Applied Social Psychology*. New York: Oxford, 1986.

WILLIAMS, DAVID CRATIS. "Introduction: Communication Perspectives on Relationships Between Globalism and Localism," *Communication Studies*, 53 (1) Spring 2002, pp. 1–4.

WORLD BANK. *World Development Report, 2003: Infrastructure for Development*. Washington, DC: The World Bank, 2003.

ZAGORSKI, KRZYSZTOF. "Class, Prestige and Status Attainment in Comparative Perspective," *International Journal of Comparative Sociology*, 41 (4) November 2000, pp. 343–359.

ZALTMAN, GERALD, AND ROBERT DUNCAN. *Strategies for Planned Change*. New York: Wiley, 1977.

ZALTMAN, GERALD, ROBERT DUNCAN, AND JONNY HOLBEK. *Innovations and Organizations*. New York: Wiley, 1973.

ZELBY, LEON W. "Alibis Anyone?" *IEEE Technology and Society Magazine*, 11 (2) Summer 1992, pp. 2–4.

ZETKA, JAMES R., JR., "Mass-Production Automation and Work-Group Solidarity in the Post-World War II Automobile Industry," *Work and Occupations*, 19 (3) August 1992, pp. 255–272.

Chapter 7

Impact of Change

Social changes occurring in recent decades have had an enormous impact on the lives of people. As a consequence, there is a growing preoccupation in the social change literature with the impact of change (Brannigan & Goldenberg, 1985; Goldhaber, 1986; Finsterbusch, 1980; Finsterbusch, Llewellyn, & Wolf, 1983; Furlong & Cartmel, 1997; Zellner, 1995). The term "impact" refers essentially to the effect or influence of a particular change or innovation after its introduction. A change may have an impact at any level in society, or it could influence the course of an entire society. The impact of a change may be major or minor, important or insignificant, direct or indirect, short-term or long-term. Depending on one's particular perception, interpretation, and evaluation, the impact of a particular change may have harmful or beneficial effects, or it may be functional or dysfunctional for a given social system. In this chapter, the impact of change will be examined from the following perspectives: social impact of technology, responses to change, social disorganization, unintended consequences of change, and ways of coping with change.

More often than not, the study of the impact of change is a complicated undertaking. In some instances, it is relatively easy to identify the direct consequences of a change. In most cases, however, complications arise when attention is focused on other impacts or consequences. As an example, let us consider the 1973 Supreme Court decision that declared restrictive state abortion laws to be unconstitutional. According to the guidelines set by the Court, an abortion decision during the first trimester of pregnancy is left to a woman and her physician, free of any regulation by government. Since 1973, close to 60 million legal abortions have been performed in the United States; close to one-third of all pregnancies now end in abortion, at a rate of well over 4,000 per day. In some areas, such as New York State, the number of abortions every year nearly equals the number of live births. Almost half of American women have terminated at least one pregnancy and millions more are involved as partners, parents health care workers, counselors and friends (Reagan, 1997). In the early 1990s, the number of abortions hovered over 1.6 million per year. Since then, abortion rates have started to drop slightly because of reduced access to the procedure—more than 80 percent of U.S. counties have no abortion providers and some whole states have only one or two; increased use of condoms; increasing numbers of single women who are keeping their babies; and the fact that baby boomers are getting older. Specifically, the figures suggest that the overall abortion rate in the United States decreased by 11% between 1994 and 2000, from 24 to 21 abortions each year per 1,000 women aged 15–44. [By contrast, nearly two-thirds of Russian pregnancies end in abortion (Isachenkov, 2002).] This decline was not shared equally among all groups, and rates increased among economically disadvantaged women, according to a new analysis based on a survey of more than 10,000 women obtaining abortions in 2000–2001 (Jones et al., 2002). The study further found that:

- 56% of U.S. women who obtain abortions are in their 20s;
- 67% have never married;
- 61% have one or more children;
- 88% live in a metropolitan area;
- 57% are economically disadvantaged (living below established poverty levels); and
- 78% report a religious affiliation (43% Protestant, 27% Catholic and 8% other religions).

Certain effects flow immediately from the content of this change. The direct effect of an abortion is to terminate the fetus. The immediate effect of the Court decision was to enable women to obtain abortions legally. This resulted in an increase in the number of abortions performed; "a decline in birthrates and rates of illegitimate births; a decrease in the number of women with dependent children on welfare; lower maternal-mortality and infant-mortality rates" (Mauss, 1975:473); and a reduction of the cost of abortion.

Another impact of the abortion decision was the revitalization of the various pro-life (antiabortion) movements. Abortion remains a topic of considerable controversy, and it has been called "feticide," "war on the unborn," "baby killing," and "slaughter of the innocent" by its opponents. Specific individuals and organizations are conducting a nationwide campaign of intimidation, bombings, and other violent acts including the murder of physicians who perform the procedure (Parenti, 1995:306–307). At the same time, pro-choice proponents emphasize individual rights and the quality of life and proclaim that abortion is a merciful, humanitarian backup bearing? How subordinate they should be to men, how deeply embedded in the family, how firmly controlled by national or racial objectives?

As a *demographic* problem, abortion raises the question as to whether it provides a useful, legitimate, and desirable means of fertility regulation where such regulation is needed.

As a *psychological* problem, abortion involves highly emotional issues such as conception, pregnancy, birth, and child rearing. Some women feel exploited by abortion, and they regret having ended their pregnancies. At times, this feeling may result in depression, or in extreme cases, suicide.

Finally, as a *political* problem, abortion presents the American political system with a unique difficulty. The American political system is built, to a great extent, on interest-group bargaining, which is well suited to producing compromise. But abortion is among the very few issues that inherently does not admit compromise. Just as a woman cannot be slightly pregnant, neither can her fetus be a little bit aborted. And, if one side takes the position that life begins at conception, while the other argues that it is a gradual development achieved by degrees over nine months of gestation, there is no way to compromise between the absolutist and relativist positions. In the political arena, one is either for or against abortion. In an era of single-issue politics, candidates for political office and elected officials are well aware of this dilemma.

Thus, the impact of abortion needs to be considered in all of the domains discussed above. Additional effects, such as the consequences of more frequent abortions on infertility and premature deliveries, the effects of women's ability to exercise greater control over their reproductive lives, and its significance for the changing role of women, need to be entertained. On a global basis, abortion is considered perhaps the most widely used single method to control fertility (Petersen, 1975:205). As such, its long-term consequences need to be viewed in the context of broader population policies. Obviously, in such a context, the consequences of abortion could reverberate on many other aspects of life.

This discussion on the impact of abortion clearly illustrates the complexity of the effects of social change. In most instances, no social change leaves the rest of social life entirely unaffected. In some cases, the impact of change can be shattering. Recall the case of Caliente, which involved the introduction of a new invention in an American community, or the introduction of the steel ax to the Yir Yoront of Australia. The consequences of these innovations are dramatic, but so are the effects of a number of other innovations. Let us briefly consider some of them.

THE SOCIAL IMPACT OF TECHNOLOGY

There are many ways to consider or categorize the social impacts of technology. One common way is simply to examine specific impacts of certain technologies, such as the effect of television on violence or the effects of the introduction of computers in the office (Goldhaber, 1986:32–33). This approach was taken by William F. Ogburn (1933:153–156) in a now-classic article entitled "The Influence of Invention and Discovery." He compiled a list of 150 effects attributable directly to the introduction of the radio. These effects are listed under the following eleven broad headings:

1. Uniformity and diffusion
2. Recreation and entertainment
3. Transportation
4. Education
5. Dissemination of information
6. Religion
7. Industry and business
8. Occupations
9. Government and politics
10. Other inventions
11. Miscellaneous

Ogburn suggests that each one of the 150 items listed under these categories might be broken down into additional, particular, and more detailed effects. For example, the impact of the radio on increasing interest in sports is broken down in detail to show an additional fifteen social effects. More than two generations after Ogburn's article, a study conducted in rural Uganda underscores the multiple impacts of the radio (Robbins & Kilbride, 1987:256–259). The radio is given a prominent and visible place in the home. Often, the radio is decorated and proudly shown. Radio ownership enhances one's social position. Among the radio's effects: "It makes a person get more friends than before and the neighbors come for news and announcements. . . . To those who are not married, the radio makes women to love men. . . . It shows that the person is rich. . . . In the old days, men did not respect their wives. They could beat them. The radio has made men change. . . . The radio has given knowledge as to how to care for children and to prevent diseases. . . ." (Robbins & Kilbride, 1987:256–257).

In addition to the radio, Ogburn also analyzed a number of other inventions. For example, for the x-ray machine, he listed sixty-one influences that caused changes in industry, in medicine, in science, and in trade. Similarly, he noted 150 social effects from the use of the automobile. [Forty years later, Gabor Strasser (1973:926–928) almost doubled Ogburn's figure of social effects attributable to the automobile, and his list may well be incomplete.] But neither took into consideration the decline in public transportation; how emission controls have been canceled out by an increase in the miles driven; that salt used on ice and snow causes trees and vegetation to wither; and that Americans are fat because they drive rather than walk (Kay, 1997). And no one thinks of the 300 million or so tires that are annually discarded. As one observer noted: "You can't bury 'em. You can't put 'em in the water. No one will steal them. They're just there." But back to Ogburn.

Ogburn has distinguished three general forms of the social effects of invention. The first is *dispersion*, or the multiple effects of a single mechanical invention, as was illustrated in the case of the radio or the automobile. The second general effect is *succession*, or the derivative social effects of a single invention, which means that an invention produces changes, which, in turn, produce further changes, and so on. "Derivative effects of invention follow one another like ripples after a pebble is thrown in water . . . the invention of the tin can is said to have influenced the movement for woman suffrage. It first led to canning factories, then it reduced the time in preparing meals in the home; it thus gave women more time for activities outside the home, including participation in the movement for woman's rights and the suffrage. In turn, woman's suffrage has had a series of derivative effects" (Ogburn, 1933:124). Another illustration of the derivative social effects would be the invention of the cotton gin, which simplified cotton processing and made cotton more profitable, resulting in the encouragement of planting of more cotton, which, in turn, required more slaves. The increase in slavery and growing Southern dependence on cotton exports helped to provoke the Civil War, which greatly stimulated the growth of large-scale industry and business monopoly. These, in turn, encouraged antitrust laws and labor unions, and the chain reaction is still continuing. Obviously, not all these developments are viewed as directly related to the cotton gin, but it helped to produce them all.

The third form of the social effects of invention is called *convergence*, that is, the coming together of several influences of different inventions. For example, the automobile, the electric pump, and the septic tank helped to make the modern suburb possible.

Ogburn further notes that the effects of invention on society are of various degrees and kind. One of the first effects of invention is the change in the habits of the individuals using them, as in the case of persons who use typewriters instead of pen and ink. When there is a large number of individuals whose habits are changed, then a social class is affected. Thus, there develops a class of women typists and stenographers who have a place in society in relation to other groups and classes. This, in turn, changes certain organizations, and the organization of various business is affected by the use of typewriters. At times, inventions have far-removed effects on social institutions, such as the family, which is affected by the employment of daughters, wives, and single women in offices and factories. Additional influences are those that affect ethics and codes of conduct related to these material changes. For example, years ago "it was almost a moral precept that woman's place was in the home. The appearance of women on the streets and in places of business for many years slowly affected manners and customs closely related to ethical codes" (Ogburn, 1933:162). The final influence, he notes, is on systems of thought or social philosophies that tend to be influenced by inventions. Thus, the inventions that attract women away from home are related to the social philosophy concerning the equality of sexes and in the resulting greater social justice for women.

Technological innovations also affect wealth, power, culture patterns, gender relationships, work (Goldhaber, 1986:33–82), and even diet (Schlosser, 2002). Technological innovation is one of the principal ways of creating and redistributing wealth. Examples abound. Toward the end of the nineteenth century, elevators increased already high land values in major cities. Air conditioning has opened up areas in the South with hot and humid climates to modern commerce and industry. Mechanization of farm technology resulted in the growth of agribusiness, causing many farmers with small holdings to go bankrupt. Certain skills also lose their value when a new technology is introduced. For example, the traditional Swiss watch industry declined as a result of the transition to electronic, digital watches. The potential of labor-saving technology also reduces the value of many skills. Final, in the context of food consumption, some consumer groups are urging the public to consider a new issue: whether to buy meat that has been mechanically deboned. The most widely used method squeezes meat scraps from a carcass, ideally leaving the bones intact. Investigations revealed, however, that pieces of bone, bone marrow, and spinal cord sometimes get into the meat. This may be a cause for concern because spinal cords can carry bovine spongiform encephalopathy, commonly known as mad cow disease, which has been linked to several deaths in Britain in the late 1990s and early 2001 and resulted in a serious of measures impacting the cattle industry in the United Kingdom and beef distributors, processors and restaurants in Europe (Schlosser, 2002:271–275). Concerned consumers may now want to ask about processing methods, since mechanically deboned beef is not labeled as such (*Atlantic Monthly*, 1997).

Technology can extend the power of the already powerful, and it can increase the power of the relatively weak. For example, advances in communication technology are useful for augmenting the power of small groups of managers in multinational corporations or governmental bureaucracies. Information technologies allow organizations to have access to a far wider range of information than in the past, and to be able to use it in turn for strengthening themselves even further. By contrast, bicycles can augment the power of large groups to communicate, or to organize to resist centralized authority. Similarly, new information technologies such as video recorders, cable television, and computer bulletin boards can lessen the power of those who control the major networks to decide the flow of issues and concerns that command public attention.

New technologies alter culture patterns and ways of life. A good example is how the bicycle changed mate-selection practices in the French countryside in the late nineteenth century. Young men suddenly had the opportunity to travel longer distances, which extended the number of potential available spouses beyond one's village. This changed traditional courtship practices and a whole set of criteria to select a husband or wife. And, what was true for the bicycle is even more the case for cars and airplanes. Technology has had a profound impact on patterns of intimacy, home life, socialization practices, and leisure-time activities, in addition to many other areas.

In virtually all societies, tasks and social roles are divided along gender lines, although the divisions vary from society to society. Gender roles are often tied to particular technologies, often leaving women in a lower-status position. In traditional societies, certain tools are considered feminine, others are masculine. Similarly, in modern societies, certain technologies seem to have gender attached to them. To illustrate: The introduction of typewriters into offices coincided with the introduction of women into clerical roles; the early telephone operator or receptionist came to be identified as female. Computers are often seen as "male" tools, whereas the almost identical word processors are frequently perceived as "female" tools.

One of the most pronounced technological impacts on work is automation. As a result, old skills become obsolete, the character and the composition of the labor force change, and more and more workers who cannot obtain new skills enter lower-paid occupations or join the ranks of the unemployed or early retirees. Technology is also helpful to compensate for a skill that cannot be easily learned. For example, authentic Persian carpets are handmade individual products of particular Iranian villages. The designs are unique to areas and villages. The carpets are hand-knotted and have visible irregularities of symmetry, of color, and of shape. With the help of computers, the basic patterns can be analyzed; variations and irregularities can be programmed. As a result, modern rug-making factories can reproduce the intricate patterns with ever-greater fidelity, making it difficult to distinguish the imitations from the real thing. And the imitation can come from any place where there is a rug factory with state-of-the-art machinery.

The computer further altered the nature of the workplace by changing the kind and number of workers needed along with the type and amount of information needed and used. The computerization of an office, for example, may reduce the number of workers required, and those who are needed will have new skills, although the impact of computers on productivity is still being debated. With computers, more information can be utilized and stored, and this brings about an increase in the gathering of new information. The computer's impact reverberates in virtually all human activities. In education, computer-assisted instruction is gaining in popularity even though there is no good evidence that most uses of computers significantly improve teaching and learning (see, for example, Oppenheimer, 1997). Computers altered health care (but did not reduce waiting), and allow people to shop from their homes.

But computers can also be used in less desirable ways. Tapping into a vast trove of government, legal and medical databases, dozens of companies are into a booming business peddling personal details on anyone—to anyone willing to pay the price. One of the concerns is that personal data services could enable stalkers or spouse-abusers to find their victims (Beiser, 1997). Another concern is that personal information will be used for "identity theft," an exploding category of crime in which a crook masquerades as someone else. With your name and social security number, anyone can apply for credit cards and loans and leave you to pay the bills. Through computerized job and other forms of surveillance, companies can invade the privacy of their employees (Murphy, 2002). Credit bureaus hold and share over 200 million files on people and their consumption and spending patterns. New information is added to these files every time one applies for a personal loan, credit card, or mortgage. This is in addition to information about us that is stored in school, hospital, government, and other data banks and the rapidly emerging biometrics technologies which are used to identify people through various body characteristics such as faces, hands, voices eyes and even smells (Hansell, 1997). Any one of these sources can be a potential threat to our privacy, or what's left of it. As stated in a front-page article on cyberspace in *The New York Times*, "Indeed, as the free-flowing exchange and exploitation of information is being celebrated as the main engine of economic prosperity into the next century, individual privacy is looking more and more like an endangered natural resource" (Bernstein, 1997:A1). The question of privacy is further compounded by events flowing from the September 11, 2001, terrorist attack on the World Trade Center. The government is calling for a new security infrastructure, one that employs advanced technology to protect the citizenry and track down malefactors. Databases are being coordinated for a variety of purposes, from checking the identity of visa applicants to the establishment of a financial-crime data source. Technologies are being developed or refined for iris, retina and fingerprint scanners, hand-geometry assayers, remote video surveillance, face recognition, smart cards with custom identification chips, tiny radio implants beneath the skin that continually broadcast people's identification codes—the list goes on and on.

Finally, computers can also be used to commit crime. At the workplace, computer crime is costing business billions of dollars annually. [Black-market activity conducted online alone reached an estimated $36.5 billion in 2002, about the same amount consumers spent on the legitimate Internet (*Business Week*, 2002).] Basically, computer crime is any illegal act for which knowledge of computer technology is used to commit the offense. There are five broad categories of computer crime (Conly & McEwen, 1990:3). *Internal computer crimes* are alterations in computer programs to modify outcomes. For instance, in a brokerage house or bank, financial records can be systematically changed or deleted. *Telecommunication crimes* involve the use of telephone lines to gain illegal access to computers or to access phone companies to make illegal phone calls. This process is known among hackers as *phreaking*—a play on the words freak, phone, and free (Mungo & Clough, 1992:3). Long-distance and international access codes are sold, or, at times, given away by phreakers, and phone companies lose large sums as a result. *Computer manipulation* crimes are those that create new records or change data in a system to carry out some illegal activity. For example, embezzlers use this method to alter data in existing accounts. *Support of criminal enterprises* involves the use of computers and databases for money laundering, drug trafficking, intellectual-property piracy, creating fake identity, or running a network of call girls. Finally, *hardware and software theft* includes illegal copying of software and thefts of trade secrets and microprocessor chips. Hackers are increasingly getting a bad reputation (Schell & Dodge, 2002) and computer crimes have become so widespread that many law enforcement agencies had to create new units and task forces to deal with the continuously emerging problems. In the next section, responses to the effects of social change will be considered.

RESPONSES TO CHANGE

The effects of social change are never evenly distributed, and in a socially differentiated and heterogeneous society, the impact of a change will tend to differ for individuals, groups, and social strata variously located in the structure. However, it is possible to make some generalizations about the consequences and impacts of large-scale social changes and some of the more typical responses to them. For the first part of the discussion, the emphasis will be on the forms of alienation and their behavioral consequences that may be construed as responses to change.

The analysis will take place in the context of the influential so-called mass-society "theory," in which, according to Melvin Seeman, the major theme is that the passing of the old community has had powerful and often destructive impact. It is a theory in the sense that it states three major elements in the transition process. "It becomes a theory—at least in the sense that it can produce testable propositions through a set of independent, intervening, and dependent variables—by combining (1) a historically oriented account of contemporary social structure, (2) assertions about the psychological effects of that structure, and (3) predictions about the resulting individual behavior" (Seeman, 1972:468–469). In this theory, alienation is the principal intervening variable; it is produced by the social structure, and, in turn, it produces distinctive behavioral responses. Seeman concedes that the theory is highly debatable, and it currently has more critics than adherents. An oft-noted shortcoming of the theory is its lack of sufficient articulation of the process by which the various responses come about. It is also plausible that some students in the universities will not see the mass-society thesis as credible because it goes against their own past experience and does not reflect their present circumstances. Some may even see it as a threat to their hopes and aspirations (Hamilton & Wright, 1986:401). Still, in the present context, Seeman's thesis is important and informative.

As Table 7.1 shows, the structural features that are the independent variables are quite standard ones in the sociological literature. They demonstrate what is happening in a broad social change process from a historical perspective. The five trends that constitute the basis of this part of the argument are:

1. The decline of the importance of kinship and family in decision making and the consequent increase of anonymity and impersonality in social relations.
2. The decline of traditional social forms and the rise of secularized, rationalized forms, which include (a) the emergence of bureaucracy as an organizational form, (b) the growth of mechanization and standardization (in work and elsewhere) as a technical form, and (c) the secularization of beliefs and values, an ideological form of secularization involving the weakening of "given" standards of behavior.
3. The shift from homogeneity to heterogeneity, which entails increased social differentiation involving an increased specialization of tasks for individuals and institutions with increased division of labor and interdependency. This, of course, brings about standardization in other spheres such as in mass culture and consumption.
4. Increased physical and social mobility, which implies the waning of community ties and immediate interpersonal bonds.

TABLE 7.1 Components of Mass-Society Theory

(A) Contemporary Structural Trends	(B) Forms of Alienation	(C) Behavioral Consequences
1. Kinship to impersonality	1. Powerlessness	1. Political passivity (e.g., nonvoting)
2. Traditional to rational forms	2. Meaninglessness	2. Wildcat strikes
3. Homogeneity to heterogeneity	3. Normlessness	3. Mass movements
4. Stability to mobility	4. Value isolation (cultural estrangement)	4. Ethnic prejudice
5. Enlargement of scale	5. Self-estrangement	5. Mental disorder
	6. Social isolation	6. School absenteeism
		7. Low information level
		8. Suicide

Source: Melvin Seeman, "Alienation and Engagement," in *The Human Meaning of Social Change*, eds. Angus Campbell and Philip Converse (New York: Russell Sage, 1972), p. 468.

Note: The figure implies that the factors in column A lead to the development of one or more forms of alienation (column B) with the illustrative behavioral consequences in column C; but the figure is not constructed to be read line by line (e.g., powerlessness is not necessarily tied to kinship—impersonality).

5. Enlargement of scale, meaning that the bases of action (for example, communication, transport, politics, urbanization, etc.) have become massive in the literal sense that big corporations, cities, and nations make decisions that affect large populations. (Seeman, 1972:469–470)

These historical trends, Seeman points out, are guides to measurable variables. However, once the related indices are specified, a number of assumptions may be made between the relationship of social change and alienation. Alienation refers to the fact that there are "six related but distinguishable notions, and that these six varieties of alienation can be rather sharply defined in terms of the person's expectancies or his values" (1972:472). Therefore, to be alienated means to be characterized by one or more of the following:

1. *A sense of powerlessness:* a low expectancy that an individual's own behavior can control the occurrence of personal and social rewards; for the alienated individual control is located in external forces, powerful others, in luck, or fate.
2. *A sense of meaninglessness:* a sense of the incomprehensibility of social affairs, of events whose dynamics a person does not understand and whose future course the individual cannot predict.
3. *A sense of normlessness:* a high expectancy that socially unapproved means are required to achieve given objectives; the perspective that an individual is not bound by conventional standards in the pursuit of what may be, after all, quite conventional goals, for example, wealth, or high status.
4. *Value isolation* (or cultural estrangement): a person's rejection of commonly held values in the society; the assignment of low reward value to goals or behavior that are highly valued in a given society. An illustration of this would be the highly alienated artist or intellectual who rejects the going standards of success.
5. *Self-estrangement:* to be engaged in activities that are not rewarding in themselves. For example, the classic description of a worker carrying out unfulfilling or uncreative work.
6. *Social isolation:* a person's low expectancy for inclusion and social acceptance, typically manifested in feelings of loneliness, rejection, or repudiation. (Seeman, 1972:472–473)

The behavioral consequences of the various forms of alienation are illustrated in Table 7.1. "These consequences in turn become matters that a democratic society would find important in its accounting of the personal meaning of social change" (Seeman, 1972:474). Furthermore, each of the dimensions or forms of alienation is associated with a series of more specific and empirically demonstrated consequences. Let us select just one dimension: powerlessness. It has been associated with membership and participation in organizations that can mediate between the individual and the state or corporation, with a tendency not to engage in planned and instrumentally oriented action, and with a readiness to participate in relatively unplanned and/or short-term protest activities, with poor learning, and with a greater sense of powerlessness among minority groups. It may also be a factor in the rise of conspiracy theories and the widespread cynicism and disillusionment of Americans toward government. For example, according to a 1997 poll, 51 percent of the public believes it is either "very likely" or "somewhat likely" the federal officials were "directly responsible for the assassination of President Kennedy" in 1993; more than one-third of those surveyed suspect the Navy, either by accident or on purpose, shot down TWA Flight 800 near New York in 1996; and a majority also believe that it is possible that the Central Intelligence Agency intentionally permitted Central American drug dealers to sell cocaine to inner-city African American children (Hargrove & Stempel, 1997).

The concept of alienation has been used to account for a number of diverse responses to rapid social change. For example, Ted Gurr (1972:134) drew together a sample of incidents in which alienated groups expressed their disenchantment by resorting to violent uprisings. His focus was on discontent that resulted not from objective wants but from perceived discrepancies between human needs and opportunities to satisfy those needs. Using as his sample 1,100 occurrences of strife in 114 nations during the period of 1961–1965, he found that 93 percent originated in such discontent. The same conclusion is reiterated in a variety of historical and theoretical studies of revolution (DeFronzo, 1996; Goldstone, 2003). Mass alienation has also developed as a response to state socialism, giving rise to many sociological problems, such as a loss of respect for authority and the necessity of using black markets to survive. Such behaviors continue even as major democratic reforms take place since new social norms have not been formed, creating development problems for the functioning of newly formed democratic institutions in the former Soviet Union and Eastern Europe (Tong, 1995).

Although Seeman's conceptualization of the forms of alienation and their behavioral consequences is a good way of viewing responses to social change, it's not the only way, as evidenced by a review of the literature. For example, the Cargo cult, which was discussed in Chapter 5, can also be considered as a response to, and a way of coping with, accelerated change induced by European contact in Melanesia during the period of colonial rule. The Cargo cult is "one of the basic modes of reaction or adjustment to situations of rapid culture change characteristic of an entire area in a specific historical phase" (Schwartz, 1976:159). The cult responses are comparable to forms of religious responses to rapid culture change, crises, and domination reported throughout the world (Lanternari, 1965; Zellner, 1995). Social movements are also considered responses to changing social conditions (Oberschall, 1993).

Responses to change can also be viewed in the context of Hagen's notion of status withdrawal, which was discussed in Chapter 2 (Hagen, 1962). Hagen applied Robert K. Merton's typology of modes of individual adaptation to the analysis of individual and group responses to social changes resulting in status withdrawal brought about by conquest, colonialization, or changes within the elite. Status withdrawal was defined as the perception on the part of individuals or groups that "their purposes and values in life are not respected by groups in the society whom they respect and whose esteem they value" (1962:185). Several responses to a situation of status withdrawal are possible. Initially, aggression and rebellion may occur or attempts may be made to ignore the situation and pretend that things have not changed. According to Hagen, the usual response is retreatism, in which an attempt is made to maintain the traditional and valued ways of life, clandestinely as necessary. The adult generation experiencing this conflict retreats to a passive "safe" lifestyle, and, although behavior may change, there are no basic personality changes.

Retreatism can also be seen as a response to status withdrawal on the part of groups. As a whole, the Native Americans have been forced into a retreatist position in response to a conflict between their values and way of life and their defeat and placement on reservations by the federal government. Traditional avenues to status have been closed off, and the opportunities and means for achievement in the white society are extremely limited. The retreatist response is perpetuated by the children being raised to esteem traditional values but with no clear role model for the future (Hagen, 1962:490).

Retreatism as it has been described by Hagen is one possible response to a particular type of change situation. Other responses, following Merton's typology, could entail innovation, ritualism, and rebellion. Innovation offers a potential for responding in a fashion which is beneficial to the individuals or groups involved. Ritualism may entail the rejection of new cultural goals, and rebellion, a nonacceptance of the change and possible attempts to counteract it.

SOCIAL CHANGE AND SOCIAL DISORGANIZATION

Well over a generation ago, Robert E. Park (1975:38–39) gloomily but aptly noted:

> We are living in a period . . . of social disorganization. Everything is in a state of agitation—everything seems to be undergoing change. . . . Any form of change that brings any measurable alteration in the routine of social life tends to break up habits; and in breaking up the habits upon which the existing social organization rests, destroys that organization itself. Every new device that affects social life and the social routine is to that extent a disorganizing influence. Every new discovery, every new invention, every new idea, is disturbing. . . . Apparently anything that makes life interesting is dangerous to the existing order.

In many instances, indeed, social change is disruptive, and an underlying condition for social disorganization is change.

A widely accepted definition of social disorganization refers to "inadequacies in a social system that keep people's collective and individual purposes from being as fully realized as they could be." Obviously, the concept of social disorganization is relative; "It is not tied to any absolute standard, which would be Utopian, but to a standard of what, so far as we know, could be accomplished under attainable conditions." Quite simply stated, "When we say that a group or organization or community or society is disorganized, we mean that its structure of statuses and roles is not working as effectively as it might to achieve valued purposes" (Merton, 1976:26). Thus, social disorganization entails the breakdown of the organizational structure, the various elements in society become "out of joint," and the influence of social norms on particular groups or individuals is weakened (see, for example, Hechter & Opp, 2001). The result is that the collective purposes of society are less fully realized than they could be under a different, better organized system. Value and norm conflicts, mobility, weak primary relations, lack of group cohesiveness, and other ingredients of social disorganization can also lead to deviance such as mental illness, drug abuse, alcoholism, suicide, and crime (Clinard & Meier, 1995:64–68; Liska & Messner, 1999:63–64).

The processes of social change can provide the impetus for social disorganization by creating conditions for conflicting interest and values, conflicting status and role obligations, faulty socialization, and faulty social communication (Merton, 1976:26–27).

Conflicting interests and values are produced by the increased complexity and diversity of social life as illustrated by the different demands and expectations of workers, management, and stockholders. Individuals occupy a variety of statuses in society, and these statuses "can pull in different directions by calling for opposed modes of behavior" (Merton, 1976:26). When there is no provision of a shared set of priorities among these competing obligations, the individual's behavior becomes unpredictable and socially disruptive, and regardless of how it is judged, it remains disorganizing. For example, "Competition between obligations of home and work, of local mores and national law, of religion and state, of friendship and the 'organization' make for potential conflicts" (1976:27). Social change also brings about faulty socialization by not providing adequate resocialization of individuals involved in these processes. Individuals simply do not know how to behave in their newly acquired statuses or in radically changed social situations. Finally, faulty social communication is produced in situations of change by structural inadequacies or partial breakdown in channels of communication between people in a social system.

Social disorganization is also generated by the fact that change tends to be uneven, resulting, as was discussed in Chapter 2, in what William F.

Ogburn (1950) calls *culture lag*. Some areas of society change faster than others, with the result that the parts of the system no longer mesh as a whole. In general, technological changes take place more rapidly than changes in other institutions and values; humanity accepts new tools more readily than new ideas. For example, industrialization has proceeded much faster than the development of social controls over the pollution that industrialization generates. Similarly, although developments in medical science have contributed to a global population explosion, religious prohibitions against artificial methods of birth control have not been modified, nor in most parts of the world has there been any change in the traditional attitudes and preference systems for large families (Brown, 2001).

Social disorganization is also produced by what Philip M. Hauser (1973:430) calls the *social morphological revolution* (changes in the size, density, and heterogeneity of population and the impact of these changes on humans and society). This is the result of three developments: (1) the remarkable increase in the rate of population growth itself, often referred to as "the population explosion" (see, for example, Grant, 2001); (2) the increasing urbanization and metropolitanization of the people, which he calls the "population implosion"; and (3) the increasing heterogeneity of the population composed of different nationalities and racial groups, which he designates "population diversification." These demographic changes have in turn been affected by technological and social changes. These developments are highly interrelated and constitute the elements of the social morphological revolution.

Hauser (1973:435–436) asserts that the combined effects of these developments have profoundly altered human nature and the social order.

> . . . the social morphological revolution has modified the human aggregation as a physical construct and as an economic mechanism; it has transformed human behavior and social organization, including the nature of government; it has generated and aggravated a host of problems—physical, personal, social, institutional and governmental. . . . Examples of the physical problems are given by the problems relating to housing supply and quality, circulation of persons and goods, solid and human waste removal, air and water pollution, recreational facilities, urban design, and the management of natural resources. . . . Examples of personal, social and organizational problems are given by the incidence of delinquency and crime, alcoholism, drug addiction, and mental disorders. . . . It is revealed also in unemployment, poverty, racism, bigotry, intergroup conflict, family disorganization, differential morbidity and mortality, labor-management conflict, the conservative-liberal debate, the maladministration of criminal justice; and in corruption, malapportionment and inertia in government, and the fragmentation and paralysis of local government.

In short, the social morphological revolution has transformed the "little community" (a concept used by Redfield) into the "mass society."

Hauser suggests that much of the chaos and disorganization of contemporary society may be understood as frictions in the transition still under way from the little community to the mass society, and he cites governmental, racist, and other "lags" that have taken place. Without a doubt, population growth has affected all social institutions. Judah Matras (1977:251–256) cites a number of instances, in support of Hauser's contentions, in which population growth or changing age, class, or ethnic composition may render political institutions and community decision-making processes ineffective by forcing them to form coalitions, political machines, and political exchange and trade-off routines. These, in turn, become disorganized under changing population composition and need to be periodically revamped. Similarly, various forms of population pressures, such as the influx of large groups of immigrants in a short period, can affect and disorganize educational institutions, churches, voluntary organizations, police forces, business and industry, communications, recreational institutions and even the Social Security system (Huddle & Simcox, 1994).

Social disorganization is often associated with personal demoralization. For example, Vine Deloria, Jr. (1988) notes that the extermination of the buffalo highly demoralized the native Americans of the Great Plains. As it was described earlier, the buffalo provided food, clothing, and shelter, and dozens of parts of the buffalo carcass were used by the tribespeople. The buffalo hunt provided the principal object of their religious ceremonials and the main avenue to social status and recognition. Other status-conferring activities, such as warfare, were also dependent on a large supply of dried buffalo meat. The government's attempt to pacify the tribes through the extermination of the buffalo resulted in their demoralization. The integrating and status-conferring functions of the war party and the buffalo hunt have disappeared. Religious ceremonials became empty and meaningless. The hunting economy was destroyed, and the native Americans lived, and at times starved, on government handouts. The traditional goals and values that gave meaning to their lives were now unavailable; they found it extremely difficult to substitute the white man's goals and values for their own. In a few instances in which they did successfully adopt the white man's economy, this, too, was soon destroyed by the white man's "need" for their land. They suffered from the destruction of their own culture, but they were denied full access to the white man's culture. Moreover, they were subjected to unknown diseases and corrupted by alcohol. Thus, it is no surprise that many of the tribes became deeply demoralized. Depopulation became widespread, and only in recent decades has the Native American population begun to grow again.

Developing countries have perhaps the highest disorganization rate because they are undergoing accelerated changes that are compounded by population pressures, sporadic food shortages, scarcity of resources, and environmental problems (Harf & Trout, 1986). Modernization and "progress" bring new hardships to many in developing countries (Scott & Kerkvliet,

1973). Robert H. Bates (1974) points out that modernization promotes new systems of social stratification and encourages increased ethnic competition within developing countries, thus contributing to disorganization. It should be noted, however, that although modernization is generally associated with social disorganization, there is no empirical evidence that modernization directly contributes to personal disorganization and psychic strain (Inkeles, 1973:358–359).

It is important to note that under some circumstances, disorganization can be both the cause and the effect of social change. The notion of disorganization is based on the assumptions that at some point in the past, a given problem did not exist or was not recognized and that society had a fairly stable equilibrium in which practices and supporting values were in harmonious agreement. For example, prior to the dissolution of the Soviet Union and Yugoslavia, trafficking of women for the sex trade had not been an issue. Now there are an estimated 700,000 women transported annually, mostly involuntarily, over international borders each year for the purpose of prostitution and sex slavery from the former Soviet Union and Eastern bloc countries and the Balkans (Binder, 2002). Many even turn up in the United States—in Anchorage as well as Miami, New York, and Los Angeles.

Then social change of some kind disrupted this harmonious agreement and brought to the fore new practices or new conditions in which the old practices no longer worked properly, or new knowledge that made old practices obsolete, or new value judgments that declared old practices no longer endurable. This, in turn, created a confusion in which old rules were both debated and ignored, yet no new rules were generally accepted. In other words, change had disorganized and disrupted the organization of the former system of behavior. Eventually, however, new rules and practices will develop, and, at least for a while, a new equilibrium will appear and will be preserved until disrupted by another round of change. In brief, disorganization and reorganization are going on continuously. Moreover, as it was shown in the preceding chapter, willful, purposeful disorganization can be used as a tactic of achieving some desired change. Illustrations of purposeful disorganization would be some of the tactics used in the effort to thwart the Vietnam war or to obtain greater justice for black students through the takeover of university buildings in the late 1960s and early 1970s. Allen (1971:380) suggests that, to some extent, one could say that the use of disruption in order to obtain desired changes amounts to "disorganization for good reasons." In the examples given, "if disorganization was a 'means,' the 'ends' were stopping the Vietnam war, increasing justice for blacks, and so on."

The issue of disorganization for "good reasons" raises some interesting questions. Although individuals generally prefer social order and tend to dislike anarchy and chaos, "nevertheless organization is not inevitably linked with what is 'right' nor disorganization with what is 'wrong.' One can point out that a good example of a well-organized nation would be Germany under Hitler. Other sociocultural systems or subsystems may be well organized but open to serious criticisms. Justice is just as important as 'order,' and other values may be of prime consideration" (Allen, 1971:381). Obviously, whether or not disruption and disorganization is the "right" course of action to be followed is a value-laden issue open to considerable debate. The important point to remember for the present purpose is that disorganization can be seen both as an effect and as an instrument of social change. In the next section, the unintended consequences of change will be considered.

UNINTENDED CONSEQUENCES

Any change of a certain magnitude will disturb the prevailing and ever-temporary balance of social forces and will bring about subsequent changes, some of which can have unintended ramifications throughout the social structure. Technological innovations and attempts to solve social problems are notable examples. Consciously designed changes foster subsequent unplanned and unintended developments—unanticipated consequences that invariably differ in character and scope from the initial planned change. It should be noted, however, that many of the unanticipated consequences are not at all the results of consciously designed change efforts. Instead, as Robert M. MacIver (1942:20) presciently stated many years ago, they "are the social resultants of a great many individual or group actions directed to quite other ends, but together conspiring to bring them about." To illustrate this point, businesspeople, labor unions, and politicians may all pursue a common goal of economic prosperity, but the conjecture of their separate efforts may instead produce an economic slump.

Examples of unanticipated consequences of change efforts are almost bewildering in their abundance. Almost every effort is accompanied by them. Perhaps the best-known example is Prohibition, which was designed to end alcohol consumption in the United States. In fact, it did little to reduce consumption rates. More serious, however, was its consequence—of making potential criminals of millions of citizens and yielding vast profits for organized crime. Similarly, the efforts by the Drug Enforcement Administration to crack down on the importation of marijuana resulted in a phenomenal increase in domestic production. Currently, over 50 percent of marijuana consumed in the United States is produced domestically, and, in some states, such as Hawaii, Oregon, and California, it is the biggest cash crop (Vago, 2003:212–213). Similarly, the quota system imposed in the mid-1980s on imported Japanese cars backfired. Instead of the quota protecting American car manufacturers and workers, the Japanese benefited from it. The trade limits created a shortage of Japanese autos in American showrooms, thus enabling their makers to increase prices and boost their revenues by as much as $2 billion per year. That extra profit, which came out of the pockets of American consumers, gave the Japanese carmakers even more money for research to improve their competitive position against Detroit. The demand for Italian luxury goods also created a market for cheap counterfeits for customers who like brand names but not premium prices. For decades, Italian luxury goods makers have had to fight a flood of counterfeits made in Asian factories—a nuisance, but not a major threat, because of the shoddy quality of the bogus handbags, scarves and shoes gave them away to discerning eyes. Lately, industrial piracy has been taking place at home, with the result that one of the most skilled sectors of the Italian economy is now competing against itself on world markets. The same specialist workshops that provide goods for brand name companies also provide them for the black market. By the late 1990s, counterfeiting had become so widespread that it anchored some local economies. Its current prevalence helps explain why some areas with high unemployment, like Naples, have escaped social unrest: many jobs exist that are not on anybody's books (Tagliabue, 1997:3)

There are many other instances of politically sponsored and governmentally enforced changes that have produced unintended consequences. Many people benefited from the federal programs addressed to the alleviation of poverty. Some of these activities, however, have served to perpetuate poverty among the beneficiaries and others have not directly benefited them. In the Seattle-Denver minimum-income maintenance experiment, for example, the guaranteed payments were shown to be a disincentive to work and destructive of family bonds. In comparing the rate of marital breakups between those receiving the minimum payment and those in a control group, it was found, unexpectedly, that "those in the benefit group suffered from a higher incidence of breakups" (Institute for Socioeconomic Studies, 1979:4). Several other programs of urban renewal thus far have created further slums. One reason for that unintended result was the practice of demolishing ruined apartment houses, the renovation of which could not be financed. This, in turn, displaced slum dwellers, who were forced to move someplace else, where they created new slums.

Closer to home (or university), there are also some unintended consequences of the familiar Buckley amendment, which requires that in institutions with federal support, all records (particularly those concerning students) be open to inspection by persons concerned. Warren Bennis (1976) raised an important question in his article "Have We Gone Overboard on 'The Right to Know'?" He admitted that the Buckley amendment is laudable in its intent, but one consequence of it is already clear. College administrators are now reluctant to put any very substantial information into any student's record. "What will be set down will be so bland and general as to be useless, for example, to college-entrance officials who want to make a considered judgment of an applicant's overall merits. If, for example, he had threatened to cut a teacher's throat but had not done so, he could scarcely be described as 'possibly unstable.' The student or his parents might sue" (1976:21). The various "sunshine" laws that have been passed by numerous states prohibiting closed meetings and the Freedom of Information Act, which became effective on February 19, 1975, requiring that most records of federal agencies be provided to anyone upon request, also resulted in fewer written recorded discussions, more private meetings, and greater secrecy with "more winks than signatures ('don't write, send word') if for no other reason than the avoidance of some new capricious lawsuit" (1976:20).

In all of these illustrations, the changes were undoubtedly initiated with the best of intentions on the part of those who proposed them. Few individuals would question, for example, the intentions of sending emergency food supplies to disaster-stricken countries and even fewer would consider the possibility of unintended consequences. But even such an action can have deleterious consequences, as evidenced by the donation of emergency food supplies by the United States to Guatemala after the earthquake. According to *The New York Times* (Riding, 1977), it was entirely unnecessary, and had the effect of hurting the very farmers it was intended to help. When an earthquake struck on February 4, 1976, taking 24,000 lives and leaving 1.2 million people homeless, Guatemala had just harvested its largest grain crop in many years. The food was undamaged, and within days was recovered from the rubble of devastated homes. The United States sent thousands of tons of grain to be donated to rural victims of the quake. It knocked out the bottom of the grain market in the country, and did considerable damage to the vulnerable economies of the small farmers—Indians living in the highlands north of Guatemala City, who were worst hit by the disaster. Dependent on sales of grain to generate money to rebuild their homes, they found that the aid supplies caused the market price of corn to drop drastically so that they could not sell their own products to obtain sufficient funds for reconstruction. Moreover, with the decline of farm income, the string of small mountain cooperatives suddenly found themselves decapitalized, dangerously weakening a new and important experiment in local organization. The food aid also upset community leadership patterns. Some leaders were more successful than others in obtaining food handouts, and those who were able to produce "free things" suddenly assumed greater positions of power and influence.

On many occasions, even seemingly trivial changes forced upon people tend to produce dysfunctional consequences. For example, Christian missionaries to the South Seas were distressed by the near-nudity of the natives; to them it was an indication of sexual immorality,

> for in Western society clothing not only is a protection of the body against the elements, but is also, although perhaps only incidentally, a requisite for virtue.

On the assumption that lack of clothing stimulated sexual desire, they attempted to improve the sexual morality of the natives by inducing them to clothe their bodies. It may be doubted that putting clothes on the natives had any significant effects upon their sex conduct; but there is no doubt that it contributed along with newly introduced diseases, alcohol, and Western food practices, to the decimation and sometimes total extermination of native populations. For as is now clear, under the high temperature and humidity conditions of tropical regions, clothing has markedly adverse effects on physical welfare. (LaPiere, 1965:76–77)

It is probably inevitable that, in the short run, most change efforts will produce some unintended consequences, and, over the long run, even the most successful attempts will have some unplanned by-products. It should be noted, however, that the unintended consequences are not always deleterious. A good illustration of a positive, but unintended, consequence of a change effort has to do with the effects of the liberalization of pornography laws in Denmark on the incidence of child molestation. In the words of Bert Kutchinsky (1973:179), "The unexpected outcome of this analysis is that the high availability of hard-core pornography in Denmark was most probably the very direct cause of a considerable decrease in at least one type of serious sex offense, namely, child molestation. Between 1965 (the first year of the availability of hard-core pornographic pictures) and 1969 (the year of the repeal of the Penal Ban, and of peak production) the number of cases of this type dropped from 220 to 87. The implication of our conclusion is that a large number of such offenses have been avoided since the late 1960s, because potential offenders obtained sufficient sexual satisfaction through the use of pornography, most probably combined with masturbation." In a later study, Kutchinsky found a similar decrease in child molestation in the former West Germany, which he attributed to an increased availability of pornographic material (U.S. Department of Justice, 1986:974). Bear in mind that the intent of liberalizing pornography laws was not even remotely related to an attempt to reduce sex crimes. While discussing matters related to sex, it is worth noting that even Viagra has some unanticipated consequences. Since the drug was introduced in 1998, the trade in some wild animal parts (i.e., hooded and harp seal and tiger penises) used in the creation of "impotence cures" has fallen drastically (Talbot, 2002:133) along with a long list of animal products, including some derived from threatened or endangered species of sea horses, geckos and green turtles that are often used to alleviate sexual dysfunctions.

It is easy to go on listing unanticipated consequences of change. The important point to remember is that change has by-products both in the long run and in the short run, and, in most cases, the unintended consequences, both beneficial and deleterious, tend to increase over time. The impact of the automobile, for example, in 1895, when there were fewer than a dozen such machines on the road, is qualitatively different from today, when there are over 180 million in the United States alone. Consider the following statement from *Scientific American*, published in 1899 (quoted by Ayres, Simon, & Carlson, 1973:738): "The improvement in city conditions by the general adoption of the motor car can hardly be overestimated. Streets clean, dustless and odorless, with light rubber-tired vehicles moving swiftly and noiselessly over their smooth expanse, would eliminate a greater part of the nervousness, distraction, and strain of modern metropolitan life." As this quote illustrates, the determination of the impact of automobile technology has not been notably successful. Its by-products are too well known to warrant further reiteration here. The automobile, in turn, created a series of other changes whose unanticipated consequences could fill another volume. Again, the important point to remember is that most social and technological changes have brought in the wake of their primarily intended effect a series of unforeseen effects—some adverse and some beneficial. In the next section, ways of coping with both intended and unintended effects of changes will be examined.

COPING WITH CHANGE

In the always-eloquent and but at times overdramatic words of Alvin Toffler (1970:11): "Western society for the past 300 years has been caught up in a fire storm of change. This storm, far from abating, now appears to be gathering force. Change sweeps through the highly industrialized countries with waves of ever accelerating speed and unprecedented impact." Warren G. Bennis and Philip E. Slater (1998:124) describe modern society as *The Temporary Society*—"of temporary systems, nonpermanent relationships, turbulence, uprootedness, unconnectedness, mobility, and above all, unexampled social change." These writers take the position that in many areas accelerated social change complicates life by shifting standards, updating some behaviors as desirable, outdating others as old-fashioned and out of place. Ways of behaving that at one time may have been effective in establishing individuals' positions and identities became obsolete. Middle-class white parents, proud of their achievements in acquiring material goods and providing their children with the "best" in schooling, travel, recreational opportunities, and living conditions, find these values viewed as unimportant or as evidence of materialistic decadence. Black parents who learn to shelter their children from hostile environments through accommodation find themselves attacked as weaklings or "Uncle Toms." Men who learned to behave in protective, although patronizing, ways toward women are not only "politically incorrect" but are called "chauvinist pigs," and women who learned to play seductive and submissive roles toward men are considered "unliberated."

Change further complicates life by increasing the rate of friction between groups and within groups. As established standards of behavior break down, as efforts to develop appropriate standards for dealing with a changing order come to the fore, as underprivileged groups seek changes to improve their situation, and as new notions of appropriate identity emerge, friction increases. Moreover, change is always difficult, and it is especially difficult for those benefiting from the status quo. As was shown in Chapter 6, it is not surprising that change elicits resistance and resentment among some segments of the population. By the same token, lack or slowness of change will result in anger and protest among other segments. When change comes about in one area, it will reverberate in other aspects of social life, although it should be recalled that some aspects of social life (such as values and thought systems) change more slowly than others (such as technology). Change, in many instances, is disturbing; it upsets the routine and the predictability of everyday life.

In particular, in the domain of technological changes, as Donald Schon (1971:27–28) writes:

> Individuals must somehow confront and negotiate, in their own persons, the transformations which used to be handled by generational change . . . while technological change has been continuing exponentially for the last two hundred years, it has now reached a level of pervasiveness and frequency uniquely threatening to the stable state.

These technological changes cannot be isolated from the social relationships in which they are embedded. Even an apparently minor innovation such as the introduction of hybrid maize may undermine a whole tradition of peasant life, as it did in France when it revamped agricultural and dietary practices.

In many instances, change in every level of society is disruptive, can result in a series of unanticipated consequences, and can bring about social disorganization in its wake. When change is especially frustrating or upsetting, the question of coping with it becomes of paramount importance.

On the individual level, there is a set of rather versatile psychological defense mechanisms (such as rationalization, repression, projection, denial, reaction formation, and sublimation) that can be relied on in case of unexpected or threatening developments (Albrecht, Chadwick, & Jacobson, 1987:11). These defense mechanisms can be used to facilitate adjustment and coping. In the case of certain personal problems, for example, it is more a question of learning to live with them than of resolving them. This is particularly true in the case of adjusting to typical "private" problems such as death or divorce. The psychological literature is extensive on this topic, and it outlines the various strategies for coping (Bridges, 2001; Coelho, 1972).

Coping is required in situations of fairly drastic change that defy familiar ways of behaving and that require the production of new behavior, "and very likely gives rise to uncomfortable affects like anxiety, despair, guilt, shame, or grief, the relief of which forms part of the needed adaptation. Coping refers to adaptation under relatively difficult conditions" (White, 1974:48-49). This is particularly true for displaced persons and immigrants who have to learn new skills to cope with a foreign environment and to develop a new set of social relationships (Bun & Chiang, 1994: 197-198).

The past few decades have offered many opportunities to observe ways in which people cope in extreme situations. David A. Hamburg and his associates (1974:412-414) describe some instances of coping under extreme stress in the Nazi concentration camps. They cite the work of Eitinger, which was based on direct observations in the camps followed by semistructured interviews and medical examinations over many years. The principal question is: How it was that some people were able to survive this prolonged physical and psychological ordeal? Obviously, a certain physical minimum of survival possibilities were present, and Eitinger has been concerned with patterns of coping behavior that tended not only to foster physical survival but to maintain mental health both during the stay in the camp and after it. One of his major findings was that "identification with the aggressor" was not frequently used by inmates, and when it was used, it tended to have a damaging effect on self-esteem and interpersonal relationships in the long run. Inmates were found to be greatly helped if they felt they had something to live for. "The prisoners who fared best in the long run were those who for one reason or another could retain their personality system largely intact—where previous interests, values, and skills could to some extent be carried on during the period of incarceration. Very fortunate in this respect were some members of service professions, such as physicians, nurses, clergymen and social workers" (Hamburg, 1974:413).

Another method of coping in this extreme situation that has proved effective in the long run involved linkages with valued groups (see, for example, Bartrop, 2000). To illustrate, prisoners who were able to stay together with family members or to remain in contact with some of their prewar friends benefited from such relationships. Moreover, strong identification with ethnic or national groups also proved quite supportive. For example, when Norwegian prisoners were asked several years later what helped them to survive, their response very often conveyed a strong thrust: "Being together with other Norwegians." Basically, the maintenance of self-esteem, a sense of dignity, sense of group belonging, and a feeling of being useful to others all seemed to contribute significantly to survival, both in physical and psychological terms.

By contrast, conditions of high physical and psychological vulnerability are summarized by Eitinger (quoted by Hamburg, 1974:413) as follows: "Prisoners who were completely isolated from their family, bereft of all contact with groups to whom they were related before the war, people who very quickly abandoned themselves and their innermost values, people who were completely overwhelmed by the notion that they had nobody and nothing to struggle or live for, all felt completely passive and had lost their ability to retain some sort of self-activity. They were those who most usually succumbed." This work on coping and on survival under extreme conditions underlines the importance of both group support and of individual strategies in coping and adaptation.

Fortunately, not too many change situations result in such extreme hardship and stress threatening the survival of individuals, as in the case of the Nazi concentration camps. In the context of less drastic change on the individual level, a person can develop what David Mechanic (1974:33) calls *coping capabilities.* Such capacities entail the ability not only to react to changes, but also to influence and control the demands to which an individual will be exposed. But to do so, Mechanic suggests that the individual must be motivated to meet those demands as they become evident in a change situation. He points out that there is a way of escaping anxiety and discomfort by lowering motivations and aspirations, but there are many social constraints against this mode of reducing stress. For successful coping, the individuals must also have the capabilities to maintain a state of psychological equilibrium "so that they can direct their energies and skills to meeting external, in contrast to internal, needs" (1974:33). Defense mechanisms that may be successful in diminishing pain and discomfort may be catastrophic for personal coping if they retard enactment of behavior directed toward changing conditions. "To put the matter bluntly, such defenses as denial—a persistent and powerful psychological response—will do a drowning man no good!" (Mechanic, 1974:33).

Mechanic points out that people's abilities to cope depend on the efficacy of the solutions that their culture provides, and the skills they develop are dependent on the adequacy of the preparatory institutions to which they have been exposed. "To the extent that schools and informal types of preparation are inadequate to the task men face, social disruption and personal failure will be inevitable no matter how strong the individual's psychological capacities" (1974:33). In the same vein, the kinds of motivations that individuals have, and the directions in which such motivation will be channeled, will depend on the incentive system in a society, that is, the patterns of behavior and activities that are valued and those that are condemned. In this context, social supports are essential in maintaining an individual's psychological comfort, for "men depend on others for justification and admiration, and few men can survive without support from some segment of their fellows" (1974:33–34).

The ways in which individuals cope with changing conditions are institutionalized, and they tend to be cumulative through the generations. People learn from the experience of others, and mechanisms of coping are taught from one generation to another. The ability of people to adapt to the conditions of their lives depends in large part on the adequacy of institutionalized solutions. But institutionalized solutions to problems must change as the problems themselves change. With rapid technological and social change, "institutionalized solutions to new problems are likely to lag behind, and the probability increases that a larger proportion of the population will have difficulties in accommodating to life problems. . . . Increasingly, it is clear that major stresses on modern man are not amenable to individual solutions, but depend on highly organized cooperative efforts that transcend those of any individual man no matter how well developed his personal resources" (1974:34).

Mechanic advocates a kind of "collective" coping through group organization and cooperation that allows for the development of mastery through specialization of function, pooling of resources and information, developing reciprocal help—giving relationships, and the like. The effectiveness of people in many situations is dependent on the maintenance of viable forms of organization and cooperation that allow important tasks to be mastered. Mechanic also notes that "individuals who may be adaptive and effective persons from a psychological perspective may be unfitted because of their values and individual orientations for the kinds of group cooperation that are necessary in developing solutions to . . . problems. Thus, many effective copers may become impotent in influencing their environment because of their resistance or inability to submerge themselves into cooperative organized relationships with others" (1974:36–37).

Peter Marris (1986) presents a somewhat different perspective on coping with change at the level of individuals from that of David Mechanic. He argues that people assimilate new experiences by placing them in the context of a familiar, reliable construction of reality. This structure, in turn, rests not only on the regularity of events themselves, but on the continuity of their meaning. This is accomplished through what Marris calls the *conservative impulse,* which is a tendency of adaptive beings to assimilate reality to their existing structure and to avoid or reorganize parts of the environment that cannot be assimilated. He posits that conservatism and adaptability are interdependent, and the readiness to react to new kinds of experience depends on the ability to assimilate them into familiar principles. This is exemplified by the social dimensions and impact of AIDS on people and social institutions (McCoy & Inciardi, 1995). Coping with change by those who are infected in this instance is, in a sense, an ability to interpret new events in light of familiar principles.

Of course, coping with change is not limited to the level of individuals. At the primary group level, for example, coping with change is an essential function of the family (Leslie & Korman, 1989). In a sense, the family is a system of accommodation to social change. At the level of organizations, coping with change, among other things, entails the manipulation of the environment for the purpose of continuously attaining organizational objectives and internal adjustments in structure, procedures, and personnel (Gross & Etzioni, 1985; Hall, 2002).

At the level of society, there have been several historical illustrations of successful coping with change. For example, Everett E. Hagen (1962:350) notes that many of the samurai of Japan turned to business to recover the purpose and prestige they had lost in the disintegration of feudal society. According to Levy (quoted by Greer, 1975:132), others joined the police force because this preexisting social character fitted nicely the requirements of the function, and the dangerous samurai had a job in modern Japan. Similarly, Clifford Geertz (1963) has shown how the Balinese aristocracy exploited old feudal ties to create new large-scale commercial organizations, after Dutch rule and the Populist regime that followed had deprived them of political authority. Both these groups have in common a sense of superiority derived from pride in their social class, their ethnic culture, and a sense of frustration because their superiority could not find recognition through conventional careers. In a way, the revitalization movements, such as the Ghost Dance and Cargo cults that were discussed earlier in this text, are also attempts to cope with dramatic changes. Finally, the more recent movements of national liberation and decolonization in developing countries also seek, at least in principle, to enable the populace to adjust to changing conditions.

Undoubtedly, ways of coping with social change are an important aspect in the study of change. Thus far, much of the research on coping and adaptation has been limited to specific individual strategies in dealing with stress and disaster situations or with extreme hardships such as in prisons or concentration camps or to formal organizations such as hospitals (Powell, 1975). Certainly, we need to know more about major cultural differences in coping behavior and how coping strategies may be used under diverse situations and at different levels, and we need to further our understanding about long-term versus short-term coping strategies. Additional information about coping patterns under specified conditions could benefit individuals, organizations, and institutions challenged by crises of social change, as is the case currently, for example, in the former Soviet Union and Eastern Europe, and assist them further in anticipating typical or recurring coping exigencies. In the long run, it should be possible to identify change situations that are especially disruptive and to design coping strategies for various levels by pertinent social criteria such as age, sex, ethnic group, and the like, and to identify the risks, costs, opportunities, and benefits associated with each strategy in each situation, taking into account important considerations such as cultural and subcultural settings. It is not difficult to imagine the utility of such knowledge for educators, planners, and policymakers.

SUMMARY

This chapter considered the impact of change from the following perspectives: social impact of technology; responses to change; social disorganization; unintended consequences of change; and ways of coping with change.

Technology can have a multitude of social impacts. Ogburn, for example, compiled a list of 150 effects that are directly attributable to the introduction of the radio, and it would be safe to assume that the television has brought still more. There are three general forms of social effects of inventions: dispersion, succession, and convergence. In various ways, technology affects habits of individuals, which in turn reverberate in social classes and social institutions. Additional influences are those affecting ethics, codes of conduct, and social philosophies. Technological innovations have important implications on wealth, power, culture patterns, gender relationships, and work.

Responses to change were first considered in the context of the mass-society theory, which encompassed contemporary structural trends, forms of alienation, and behavioral consequences. The various manifestations of alienation, such as powerlessness, meaninglessness, normlessness, value isolation, self-estrangement, and social isolation, were seen as responses to change. Other forms of responses discussed included the Cargo cult, religious responses, social movements, status withdrawal (in the context of retreatism), and an expansion of Merton's typology of modes of individual adaptation.

Social change is disruptive, and underlying much social disorganization is the phenomenon of social change. The processes of change provide the impetus for disorganization by creating conditions for conflicting interests and values, conflicting status and role obligations, faulty socialization, and faulty social communication. Disorganization is also generated by the fact that change tends to be uneven, resulting in culture lag. The social morphological revolution has greatly altered individual behavior and social organization, and generated and aggravated a host of problems. Social disorganization is often associated with personal demoralization, as evidenced by the Native Americans of the Great Plains, who suffered social disorganization as a result of the extinction of the buffalo. The rate of social disorganization is perhaps highest in developing countries, for they are undergoing accelerated changes and at the same time they are relatively unfamiliar with change processes. Disorganization can be both the cause and the effect of social change, and, at times, it may take place "for good reasons."

Social change entails a series of unintended effects, some adverse and some beneficial. There is an abundance of illustrations of unanticipated consequences of change efforts. In many cases, these unanticipated consequences are deleterious to individuals affected by the change. In the short run, most change efforts will result in unintended consequences, and, over the long run, even the most successful attempts will have some unplanned by-product. The unanticipated consequences can be beneficial, as illustrated by the unintended effects of the liberalization of pornography laws in Denmark and in the former West Germany on the incidence of child molestation.

Change has become the prevailing life mode; a life rooted in constants seems a thing of the past. Social change complicates life by shifting standards, values, and behavior patterns. It also increases friction between groups and within groups. When change is especially frustrating or upsetting, the question of coping with it becomes of paramount importance. Coping is required in situations of drastic change that defy familiar ways of behaving and require the production of new behavior or new responses. Under conditions of extreme stress, as in the case of the Nazi concentration camps, individuals were greatly helped if they felt they had something to live for and when they maintained linkages with valued groups. In less extreme situations, individuals can develop "coping capabilities," which are based on socially conditioned and institutionalized patterns of responses. In many instances, the major stresses on modern people are not amenable to individual solutions, but depend on highly organized cooperative efforts in the form of "collective" coping through group organizations. Coping is also facilitated when new experiences are placed in the context of a familiar, reliable construction of reality. Our knowledge of coping strategies under diverse situations and by diverse groups requires further expansion. In the next chapter, the costs of change will be considered.

SUGGESTED FURTHER READINGS

BASU, ALAKA MALWADE (ed.). *The Sociocultural and Political Aspects of Abortion, Global Perspectives.* Westport, CT: Praeger, 2003. A collection of cross-cultural and multidisciplinary essays on factors that play a role in abortion-related policy decisions and practices around the world.

BRANNIGAN, AUGUSTINE, AND SHELDON GOLDENBERG (eds.). *Social Responses to Technological Change.* Westport, CT: Greenwood Press, 1985. A collection of papers and comments on the various responses to technological change.

COELHO, GEORGE V., DAVID A. HAMBURG, JOHN E. ADAMS (eds.). *Coping and Adaptation.* New York: Basic Books, 1974. A collection of twenty-one interdisciplinary articles on coping and adaptation.

DIDSBURY, HOWARD F., JR. (ed.). *The Years Ahead: Perils, Problems, and Promises.* Bethesda, MD: World Future Society, 1993. A series of articles on change scenarios and their anticipated impacts.

FURLONG, ANDY, AND FRED CARTMEL. *Young People and Social Change: Individualization and Risk in Late Modernity.* Philadelphia: Open University Press, 1997. A provocative discussion of the extent to which "individualization" and "risk" brought about by the restructuring of life chances impact young adults.

GOLDHABER, MICHAEL. *Reinventing Technology: Policies for Democratic Values.* New York: Routledge, 1986. See, in particular, Chapters 3 and 4 on the social impact of technology.

HECHTER, MICHAEL, AND KARL-DIETER OPP. *Social Norms.* New York: Russell Sage Foundation, 2001. A comprehensive volume on the workings and emergence of social norms in a variety of settings from monogamy to national self-determination.

MARRIS, PETER. *Loss and Change*. London: Routledge, 1986. A short, provocative essay on the ways of coping with change.

OGBURN, WILLIAM F., with the assistance of S. C. Gilfillan. "The Influence of Invention and Discovery." In *Recent Social Trends in the United States: Report of the President's Research Committee on Social Trends*. New York: McGraw-Hill, 1933, pp. 122–166. An often-quoted classic essay on the social effects on invention and discovery.

REAGAN, LESLIE J. *When Abortion Was a Crime: Women, Medicine and Law in the United States, 1867–1973*. Berkeley: University of California Press, 1997. A provocative historical review of the diverse effects of abortion policies.

SCHELL, BERNADETTE, AND JOHN L. DODGE. *The Hacking of America: Who's Doing It, Why, and How*. Westport, CT: Prager, 2002. The authors claim that hackers get a bad rap. Their skills are coveted yet they are often misunderstood and frequently despised. An informative analysis of one of the social impacts of computer technology.

SCHLOSSER, ERIC. *Fast Food Nation: The Dark Side of the All-American Meal*. New York: Perennial, 2002. A fascinating study of the impact of food growing and preparation technologies on the American diet. Not recommended for those with a queasy stomach.

REFERENCES

ALBRECHT, STAN L., BRUCE A. CHADWICK, AND CARDELL K. JACOBSON. *Social Psychology*, 2nd ed. Englewood Cliffs, NJ: Prentice Hall, 1987.

ALLEN, FRANCIS R. *Socio-Cultural Dynamics: An Introduction to Social Change*. New York: MacMillan, 1971.

Atlantic Monthly (The). "Food," July 1997, p. 12.

AYRES, ROBERT U., SUSAN C. SIMON, AND JACK W. CARLSON. "Technology Assessment and Policy-Making in the United States." In Marvin J. Cetron and Bodo Bartochas (eds.), *Technology Assessment in a Dynamic Environment*. New York: Gordon and Breach, 1973, pp. 733-763.

BARTROP, PAUL R. *Surviving the Camps*. Lapham, PA: University Press of America, 2000.

BASU, ALAKA MALWADE (ed.). *The Sociocultural and Political Aspects of Abortion, Global Perspectives*. Westport, CT: Praeger, 2003.

BATES, ROBERT H. "Ethnic Competition and Modernization in Contemporary Africa," *Comparative Political Studies*, 6, January 1974, pp. 457–484.

BEISER, VINCE. "The Cyber Snoops: How Internet Gumshoes Breach Personal Privacy," *Maclean's*, June 23, 1997, p. 42.

BENNIS, WARREN G. "Have We Gone Overboard on 'The Right to Know'?" *Saturday Review*, March 6, 1976, pp. 18-21.

BENNIS, WARREN G., AND PHILIP E. SLATER. *The Temporary Society*, rev. ed. San Francisco: Jossey-Bass, 1998.

BERNSTEIN, NINA. "On Frontier of Cyberspace, Data Is Money, and a Threat," *The New York Times*, June 12, 1997, pp. A1, A16–A17.

BINDER, DAVID. "In Europe, Sex Slavery Is Thriving Despite Raids," *The New York Times*, October 20, 2002, p. 10YNE.

BRANNIGAN, AUGUSTINE, AND SHELDON GOLDENBERG (eds.). *Social Responses to Technological Change*. Westport, CT: Greenwood Press, 1985.

BRIDGES, WILLIAM. *The Way of Transition: Embracing Life's Most Difficult Moments.* Cambridge, MA: Perseus, 2001.

BROWN, LESTER R. *State of the World 2001.* London: Earthscan, 2001.

BUN, CHAN KWOK, AND CLAIRE CHIANG SEE NGOH. *Stepping Out: The Making of Chinese Entrepreneurs.* Singapore: Prentice Hall, 1994.

Business Week. "The Underground Web. Drugs. Gambling. Terrorism. Child Pornography. How the Internet Makes any Illegal Activity More Accessible than Ever," September 2, 2002, pp. 67–80.

CALLAHAN, DANIEL. *Abortion: Law, Choice and Morality.* New York: Macmillan, 1970.

CLINARD, MARSHALL B., AND ROBERT F. MEIER. *Sociology of Deviant Behavior,* 9th ed. Fort Worth, TX: Harcourt Brace College Publishers, 1995.

COELHO, GEORGE V. *Coping and Adaptation: A Behavioral Science Bibliography.* Public Health Service Publication No. 2087. Washington, DC: National Institute of Mental Health, U.S. Department of Health, Education, and Welfare, 1972.

CONLY, CATHERINE H., AND J. THOMAS MCEWEN. "Computer Crime," *NIJ Reports,* January/February, 1990, pp. 2–7.

DEFRONZO, JAMES. *Revolutions and Revolutionary Movements,* 2nd ed. Boulder, CO: Westview Press, 1996.

DELORIA, VINE, JR. *Custer Died for Your Sins: An Indian Manifesto.* Norman, OK: University of Oklahoma Press, 1988.

FINSTERBUSCH, KURT. *Understanding Social Impacts: Assessing the Effects of Public Projects.* Beverly Hills, CA: Sage Publications, 1980.

FINSTERBUSCH, KURT, LYNN G. LLEWELLYN, AND C. P. WOLF (eds.). *Social Impact Assessment Methods.* Beverly Hills, CA: Sage Publications, 1983.

FURLONG, ANDY, AND FRED CARTMEL. *Young People and Social Change: Individualization and Risk in Late Modernity.* Philadelphia: Open University Press, 1997.

GEERTZ, CLIFFORD. *Peddlers and Princess: Social Development and Economic Change in Two Indonesian Towns.* Chicago: University of Chicago Press, 1963.

GOLDHABER, MICHAEL. *Reinventing Technology: Policies for Democratic Values.* New York: Routledge, 1986.

GOLDSTONE, JACK A. (ed.). *Revolutions: Theoretical, Comparative, and Historical Studies,* 3rd ed. Australia; Belmont, CA: Wadsworth, 2003.

GRANT, LINDSEY. *Too Many People: The Case for Reversing Growth.* Santa Ana, CA: Seven Locks Press, 2001.

GREER, SCOTT. "Urbanization and Social Character." In James A. Inciardi and Harvey A. Siegel (eds.), *Emerging Social Issues.* New York: Praeger, 1975, pp. 125–156.

GROSS, EDWARD, AND AMITAI ETZIONI. *Organizations in Society.* Englewood Cliffs, NJ: Prentice Hall, 1985.

GURR, TED. "Sources of Rebellion in Western Societies: Some Qualitative Evidence." In James S. Short, Jr., and Marvin W. Wolfgang (eds.), *Collective Violence.* Chicago: Aldine, 1972, pp. 132–148.

HAGEN, EVERETT E. *On the Theory of Social Change: How Economic Growth Begins.* Homewood, IL: Dorsey Press, 1962.

HALL, RICHARD H. *Organizations: Structures, Processes, and Outcomes,* 8th ed. Upper Saddle River, NJ: Prentice Hall, 2002.

HAMBURG, DAVID A. "Coping and Adaptation: Steps Toward a Synthesis of Biological and Social Perspectives." In George V. Coelho, David A. Hamburg, and John E. Adams (eds.), *Coping and Adaptation.* New York: Basic Books, 1974, pp. 403–440.

HAMILTON, RICHARD F., AND JAMES D. WRIGHT. *The State of the Masses.* New York: Aldine, 1986.

HANSELL, SAUL. "Is This an Honest Face? The Use of Recognition Technology Grows in Everyday Transactions," *The New York Times,* August 20, 1997, pp. C1, C3.

HARF, JAMES E., AND B. THOMAS TROUT. *The Politics of Global Resources: Population, Food, Energy, and Environment.* Durham, NC: Duke University Press, 1986.

HARGROVE, THOMAS, AND GUIDO H. STEMPEL. "Spreading Cynicism Fuels Belief in Conspiracies: Americans Blame Government for Drugs and Killings," *St. Louis Post-Dispatch,* July 4, 1997, p. 7A.

HAUSER, PHILIP M. "The Chaotic Society: Product of the Social Morphological Revolution." In Amitai Etzioni and Eva Etzioni-Halevy (eds.), *Social Change: Sources, Patterns, and Consequences,* 2nd ed. New York: Basic Books, 1973, pp. 428–442.

HECHTER, MICHAEL, AND KARL-DIETER OPP. *Social Norms.* New York: Russell Sage Foundation, 2001.

HUDDLE, DONALD, AND DAVID SIMCOX. "The Impact of Immigration on the Social Security System," *Population and Environment: A Journal of Interdisciplinary Studies,* 16 (1) September 1994, pp. 91–97.

INKELES, ALEX. "Making Man Modern: On the Causes and Consequences of Individual Change in Six Developing Countries." In Amitai Etzioni and Eva Etzioni-Halevy (eds.), *Social Change: Sources, Patterns, and Consequences,* 2nd ed. New York: Basic Books, 1973, pp. 342–361.

Institute for Socioeconomic Studies. "Flare-Up on Negative Income Tax," *Socioeconomic Newsletter,* 4 (1) January 1979. White Plains, NY: Institute for Socioeconomic Studies, 1979.

ISACHENKOV, VLADIMIR. "Nearly Two-Thirds of Russian Pregnancies End in Abortion," *The Seattle Herald,* October 19, 2002, p. A9.

JONES, RACHEL K., JACQUELINE E. DARROCH, AND STANLEY K. HENSHAW. "Patterns in the Socioeconomic Characteristics of Women Obtaining Abortions in 2000–2001," *Perspectives on Sexual and Reproductive Health,* 34 (5) September/October 2002, pp. 226–325.

KAY, JANE HOLTZ. *Asphalt Nation: How the Automobile Took Over America, and How We Can Take It Back.* New York: Crown Publishers, 1997.

KUTCHINSKY, BERT. "The Effects of Easy Availability of Pornography on the Incidence of Sex Crimes: The Danish Experience," *Journal of Social Issues,* 29 (3) 1973, pp. 163–181.

LANTERNARI, VITTORIO. *The Religions of the Oppressed: A Study of Modern Messianic Cults.* New York: New American Library (Mentor Books), 1965.

LaPIERE, RICHARD T. *Social Change.* New York: McGraw-Hill, 1965.

LESLIE, GERALD R., AND SHEILA K. KORMAN. *The Family in Social Context,* 7th ed. New York: Oxford, 1989.

LISKA, ALLEN E., AND STEVEN F. MESSNER. *Perspectives on Deviance,* 3rd ed. Upper Saddle River, NJ: Prentice Hall, 1999.

MacIVER, ROBERT M. *Social Causation.* Boston: Ginn, 1942.

MARRIS, PETER. *Loss and Change.* London: Routledge, 1986.

MATRAS, JUDAH. *Introduction to Population: A Sociological Approach.* Englewood Cliffs, NJ: Prentice Hall, 1977.

MAUSS, ARMAND L. *Social Problems as Social Movements.* Philadelphia: Lippincott, 1975.

McCoy, Clyde B., and James A. Inciardi. *Sex, Drugs, and the Continuing Spread of AIDS.* Los Angeles, CA: Roxbury, 1995.

Mechanic, David. "Social Structure and Personal Adaptation: Some Neglected Dimensions." In George V. Coelho, David A. Hamburg, and John E. Adams (eds.), *Coping and Adaptation.* New York: Basic Books, 1974, pp. 32–44.

Merton, Robert K. "The Sociology of Social Problems." In Robert K. Merton and Robert Nisbet (eds.), *Contemporary Social Problems,* 4th ed. New York: Harcourt, 1976, pp. 5–43.

Mungo, Paul, and Bryan Clough. *Approaching Zero: The Extraordinary Underworld of Hackers, Phreakers, Virus Writers, and Keyboard Criminals.* New York: Random House, 1992.

Murphy, Dean E. "As Security Cameras Sprout, Someone's Always Watching," *The New York Times,* September 29, 2002, pp. 1, 22.

Oberschall, Anthony. *Social Movements: Ideologies, Interests, and Identities.* New Brunswick, NJ: Transaction Publishers, 1993.

Ogburn, William F. "The Influence of Invention and Discovery." In *Recent Social Trends in the United States: Report of the President's Research Committee on Social Trends.* New York: McGraw-Hill, 1933, pp. 122–166.

Ogburn, William F. *Social Change.* New York: Viking, 1950.

Oppenheimer, Todd. "The Computer Delusion," *The Atlantic Monthly,* July 1997, pp. 45–62.

Parenti, Michael. *Democracy for the Few,* 6th ed. New York: St. Martin's Press, 1995.

Park, Robert E. "Social Change and Social Disorganization." In Stuart H. Traub and Craig B. Little (eds.), *Theories of Deviance.* Itasca, IL: F. E. Peacock, 1975, pp. 37–40.

Petersen, William. *Population,* 3rd ed. New York: MacMillan, 1975.

Powell, Francis P. *Theory of Coping Systems: Change in Supportive Health Organization.* Cambridge, MA: Schenkman, 1975.

Reagan, Leslie J. *When Abortion Was a Crime: Women, Medicine and Law in the United States, 1867–1973.* Berkeley: University of California Press, 1997.

Riding, Alan. "U.S. Food Aid Seen Hurting Guatemala," *The New York Times,* November 6, 1977, p. 51.

Robbins, Michael C., and Philip L. Kilbride. "Microtechnology in Rural Buganda." In H. Russell Bernard and Pertti Pelto (eds.), *Technology and Social Change,* 2nd ed. Prospects Heights, IL: Waveland Press, 1987, pp. 244–267.

Schell, Bernadette, and John L. Dodge. *The Hacking of America: Who's Doing It, Why, and How.* Westport, CT: Prager, 2002.

Schlosser, Eric. *Fast Food Nation: The Dark Side of the All-American Meal.* New York: Perennial, 2002.

Schon, Donald. *Beyond the Stable State.* New York: W. W. Norton, 1971.

Schwartz, Theodore. "Cargo Cult: A Melanesian Type-Response to Change." In George A. DeVos (ed.), *Responses to Change: Society, Culture and Personality.* New York: Van Nostrand, 1976, pp. 157–206.

Scott, James, and Ben Kerkvliet. "The Politics of Survival: Peasant Response to 'Progress' in Southeast Asia," *Journal of Southeast Asian Studies,* 4, September 1973, pp. 241–267.

Seeman, Melvin. "Alienation and Engagement." In Angus Campbell and Philip E. Converse (eds.), *The Human Meaning of Social Change.* New York: Russell Sage, 1972, pp. 467–527.

STRASSER, GABOR. "Methodology for Technology Assessment, Case Study Experience in the United States." In Marvin J. Cetron and Bodo Bartocha (eds.), *Technology Assessment in a Dynamic Environment*. New York: Gordon and Breach, 1973, pp. 905–937.

TAGLIABUE, JOHN. "Fakes Blot a Nation's Good Names: In Italy's Piracy Culture, Black Market Is Thriving," *The New York Times*, July 3, 1997, pp. C1, C3.

TALBOT, MARGARET. "Viagra Saves Wildlife," *The New York Times Magazine*, December 15, 2002, p. 133.

TOFFLER, ALVIN. *Future Shock*. New York: Random House, 1970.

TONG, YANGI. "Mass Alienation Under State Socialism and After," *Communist and Post-Communist Studies*, 28 (2) June 1995, pp. 215–238.

U.S. Department of Justice. *Attorney General's Commission on Pornography. Final Report*, vols. 1 and 2. Washington, DC: July 1986.

VAGO, STEVEN. *Law and Society*, 7th ed. Upper Saddle River, NJ: Prentice Hall, 2003.

WHITE, ROBERT W. "Strategies of Adaptation: An Attempt at Systematic Description." In George V. Coelho, David A. Hamburg, and John E. Adams (eds.), *Coping and Adaptation*. New York: Basic Books, 1974, pp. 47–68.

ZELLNER, WILLIAM W. *Countercultures: A Sociological Analysis*. New York: St. Martin's Press, 1995.

Chapter 8
Costs of Change

Social change, like everything else, has its costs. There are various types of costs, and this chapter will examine some of the more prevalent economic, social, and psychological costs of change at different levels in society. Certain outcomes of change, such as environmental degradation, are, in one way or another, costly for almost everyone. Other changes affect groups and individuals in different ways; some will find change beneficial and others disadvantageous. As Vilfredo Pareto (1935:1472–1473; Powers, 1987) pointed out a long time ago, for every choice made or imposed, some other potential good is sacrificed. Pareto was concerned with the price that individuals as members of a collectivity have to pay when conflicting and contradictory benefits are emphasized. For example, an army protects the country from the danger of foreign invasion. At the same time, it endangers the careers and even the lives of many young persons. This is the classic case of Pareto's dilemma of utility "for a community" and "of a community." The former refers to the various individual and group interests in a community in which the emphasis is on divergent personal benefits, advantages, and satisfactions. The latter refers to the interests of a community as a collectivity, to its capacity to survive in a hostile environment through collective strength and determination. Essentially, Pareto makes a distinction between what is good for some individuals and groups in a community versus what is good for the community as a whole. Often, the choice is painful.

Contemporary illustrations abound of Pareto's dilemma of utility "for a community" and "of a community." At times, a choice has to be made, for example between air pollution and employment in a community. Because of the high cost of pollution-abatement devices, a company may be forced to close down. The costs of the resulting unemployment may be juxtaposed with the costs of pollution. Continued employment can be seen as a "utility for a community," whereas elimination of the source of pollution is a "utility of a community." The choice can be especially difficult in a situation in which the polluting industrial firm is the principal employer in a community. Pareto's dilemma is further exemplified by the current transformations in Eastern Europe. In view of the urgency of economic development, the environment must wait. This policy decision underscores a fundamental question that Eastern Europe faces as it continues its shift to a Western-style market economy: Should antipollution devices, fines, and taxes be further postponed in order to protect factories and jobs? Or, will this bring health and cleanup costs in the future, not only to restore the havoc of the past but also the new damage still being caused during the early years of the twenty-first century?

Pareto's notion of conflicting utilities has obvious implications for the study of the costs of change. Different groups or communities in a society are affected by change differently, and the introduction of something new will invariably result in benefits for some and losses for others. As Peter L. Berger (1974:223) correctly observes: "There can be no social change without costs. The questions to be asked with intense seriousness are just what the particular costs are, who is being asked to pay them, and whether the putative gains make these costs acceptable." It is obvious that the costs of social change are never evenly distributed. What is not so obvious in many instances is the answer to the question: Who benefits from the change and who pays for it? Multiple objectives and values of competing social groups are noncommensurable. There is really no calculus for determining "net" pains and pleasures for widely differing groups. Equality, for example, is a uniformly relative and never an absolute condition. When a foundation for a new equality is established, some other inequality by necessity is imposed. The principal question is never equality in the abstract, but which equality, at what price of some new equality.

There are, however, several large-scale changes at the level of society that extract a toll from most of us. The potential sources of costs include rapid economic growth, environmental deterioration, increased pressures on natural resources, and population growth. The costs stemming from these and other changes can, of course, be categorized in a number of different ways. For example, they may be subsumed under the major institutions, or the costs may be analyzed under the headings of "micro" and "macro" changes. For the sake of simplicity and clarity, such costs are classified under the categories of *economic, social*, and *psychological* costs. It should be noted, though, that these three cost categories are separated only for analytical reasons, and, as may be expected, there is a fair amount of overlapping among them (see, for example, Davis, 2003). Finally, it should be recalled that the word cost, in addition to referring to the price of something, also implies a loss or sacrifice. In this sense, the term has a negative connotation, which may give an impression that parts of this chapter convey a degree of pessimism. In emphasizing the costs of social change, the discussion will obviously be one-sided and biased toward material supporting the arguments, although it will be devoid of what Nicholas Lehman (1997), a well-known journalist, refers to as "rhetorical overkill." There are, of course, other perspectives suggesting that it is erroneous to argue that growth leads to resource depletion, environmental and population problems, and a slate of other worries (see, for example, Sagoff, 1997). Certainly it is not my intention to paint a bleak picture of social change or to belabor the notion that "The history of mankind is a history of pain" (Berger, 1974:137). The purpose is simply to identify and analyze some of the more conspicuous costs associated with the process of change. Sociology is, at least ideally, value-free, and the interpretation of events is conditioned by evidence and not by notions of "good" or "bad," although it should be recognized that not all sociologists adhere to the notion of a value-free discipline. With this in mind, let us turn to the economic costs of change.

ECONOMIC COSTS

In the traditional credo of the economists, more is better. Indeed, the description of economic growth as a process that "widens the area of choice" would seem to favor an economic system that, over time, produces—among other things—a per-capita increase in goods and services. Such an increase presupposes economic growth, a highly debated subject that will be briefly examined in the context of the economic costs of change.

Economic Growth

The proponents of accelerated economic development argue that "growth is a necessary condition for social advance, for improving the quality of the total environment . . . it is still demonstrably true that growth in per-capita gross national product has been associated with rising levels of human well-being" (Heller, 1972:11, 29). This notion is supported by the view that "The pattern of growth in the United States in the postwar years yielded benefits to individuals far in excess of the costs it required of them. To that extent our material progress has had humane content" (Lampman, 1968:162). The benefits of rapid economic development, its advocates argue, entail an increased range of choices, greater control over the environment, more services and goods, improved status of women, a release from the drudgery of hard physical labor, greater humanitarianism, and steadily lower prices for foodstuffs and raw materials (Kennedy, 1987:30).

The benefits of economic development are undeniable. It brings about a remarkable improvement in the standard of living for the average person, compared with the average individual in preindustrial or early industrial societies (Lenski, Nolan, & Lenski, 1999). The concomitants of economic growth include greater educational opportunities, better health care, improved nutrition, increased availability of all types of goods and services, greater material comfort, more leisure opportunities, longer life expectancy, and so on.

The realization of the benefits of economic development is the subject of virtually all of the literature dealing with the problems of underdeveloped societies. The various accounts focus sharply on statistics that show the extent to which progress must be made in order to emerge as the equal of developed nations. Data on birth and death rates, literacy, rate of gross domestic product, per-capita income, percent of urbanization, and the like from underdeveloped countries are compared with those of developed nations. But the numbers do not take into account such factors as environmental pollution and dehumanization at the workplace and in the marketplace (Greenhouse, 1987). Furthermore, a large part of the literature on development deals with the strategies of development and concerns itself with whether a broad push is needed to ensure rising per-capita income, whether a basic level of investment is the key to emergence, how the generation of capital allows the progress of growth, and so forth.

Unfortunately, too little has been said about the costs of growing pains associated with rapid growth rates and economic development, and these costs can be great (see, for example, Mishan, 1977). Any society has at all times a number of possible growth rates that it may pursue under different "growthmanship" strategies. For each of these rates, there is a different cost involved, with higher and higher rates involving greater sacrifice on the part of the people and on the resources of the society. It may be said that the "proper" rate of growth for a society is the one in which the benefits of increasing the rate of growth slightly are weighed against and balanced with the costs of achieving that rate of increase. Ideally, the goal of a society should be that of optimization of the rate of development and not the maximization of that rate. Humans do not live by GNP alone. For development, the emphasis needs to be on what is the optimal (read: "best") and not the maximal (read: "largest") volume of goods and services. However, who will determine the optimal versus the maximal rate of development is another question.

An influential World Bank (2003) report on development shows that in many countries high growth rates are accompanied by increasing unemployment, rising disparities in incomes both between groups and between regions, and the deterioration of social and cultural conditions. Aspirations that may have been limited in the absence of development may rise rapidly with the emergence of the first signs of development when the people realize that things are not what they should be. Personal satisfaction may decline, not increase, especially when growth is associated with high rates of inflation and unemployment, as has happened in many parts of the world in the 1980s and 1990s (Bensman & Vidich, 1987; Hamilton & Wright, 1986; Young & Sachs, 1994). Ezra J. Mishan (1967:171) already correctly pointed out four decades ago that the continued pursuit of economic development in the Western world is more likely "on a balance to reduce rather than increase social welfare." Similar early warning was sounded by Barry Commoner (1971:295), who associated much of economic development with ecologically faulty and socially wasteful types of production rather than with an improvement in the actual welfare of individuals. Some authors go so far as to suggest that economic activity, as currently pursued, could be approaching a level where further growth in the gross world product costs more than it is worth (Postel, 1994:3–21).

Environmental Costs

Intentionally or unintentionally, economic activity has often had a negative effect on the environment, although there is some recent evidence to suggest that governments need not sacrifice environmental quality for economic well-being in developed countries (see, for example, Adam, 1998; Ghimire & Pimbert, 2000; Smothers, 1994). From the beginning of human history, the need for basic resources, such as wood for fire and shelter, ran counter to the preservation of the natural habitat. Overgrazing transformed hundreds of thousands of acres of fertile land into barren deserts. Improper plowing techniques caused fertile soil to wash away during heavy rains. But the threats posed to the environment in earlier years are minuscule compared with the current level of damage and destruction (Hempel, 1996). In this section are presented some examples of economic costs associated with development and change as they affect the environment. The discussion will focus on solid waste, air and water pollution, and climate modification.

Solid Waste An inevitable concomitant of economic growth is solid waste. Every step in the production process—whether food, clothing, drugs, cars, or books—creates useless material that is discarded. Growing populations, rising incomes, and changing consumption patterns combine to complicate further waste-generation and management patterns. The United States is the largest producer of wastes in the world. Per capita generation of solid waste increased 65 percent over the last 25 years (United Nations Environment Programme, 2002:103). Throughout North America, urban centers are having increasing problems finding sites for new sanitary landfills.

In his or her lifetime, the average American accounts for the use of some 540 tons of construction materials, 23 tons of wood, 16 tons of metals, and 32 tons of organic chemicals (Young & Sachs, 1994:11); much of these will be discarded in one form or another. The volume of waste expands as the size of a community grows, for as people earn more money, they increase their consumption of food, beverages, and durable goods, and they demand more convenience items. As more women enter the labor force, for example, the demand for convenience products grows. Frozen, canned, and vacuum-packed food packages are often used for the preparation of meals at home. In developed countries, packaging contributes roughly 30 percent of the weight and 50 percent of the volume of household waste. In the United States, more than $1 out of every $10 spent for food and beverages pays for packaging. For example, in 1994, Americans spent far more for food packaging than farmers received in income. Between 1960 and 1990, the volume of waste produced each year by the average American household doubled, along with the annual tonnage of municipal solid waste (Young & Sachs, 1994:19). Nowadays, each American produces, on the average, 1 ton of waste per year, and, at any given time, accounts for 11 tons of steel in personal possessions (car, refrigerator, washing machine, mattress springs, etc.), most of which are designed to become junk as soon as possible. New Yorkers, for instance, average 928 pounds of household garbage per resident each year, with comparable figures nationwide (Baker, 2003). The returnable bottle and recyclable paper had become too costly by the late 1990s, and the economic costs of the "Kleenex mentality" are practically unmeasurable (Ackerman, 1997).

Much of household waste also contains hazardous or toxic materials, such as mercury from batteries, cadmium from fluorescent lights, and toxic chemicals from cleaning solvents, paints, and wood preservatives. In addition, thousands of businesses produce the equivalent of more than 1 ton of toxic waste annually for each person in the United States (Shabecoff, 1985:31) in the form of contaminated oil, solvents, acids, and sludges. This does not include wastes from service stations, dry cleaners, photo-processing laboratories, and other "small generators." Electric power plants, hospitals, and industry also produce an estimated 100,000 tons of radioactive waste annually.

Frightening incidents, such as at New York's Love Canal region in 1979 or at Times Beach, Missouri, in 1982, focused attention on a new generation of environmental hazards that defy easy solution: dangerous wastes. Some 800 families had to leave the Love Canal area after unusually high rates of illness and death resulting from chemical leaks from an old industrial dump. The Times Beach area was contaminated with deadly dioxin—one of the most toxic substances made and a suspected cause of cancer. The cost of relocating residents and removing the contamination has already exceeded $100 million.

Only about 10 percent of toxic waste is disposed of properly. In many cases, the deadly materials have been piling up for years in dumps and pits. They have been dumped in sewers, rivers, and oceans. Most toxic waste cannot be disposed of safely because there are no available sites or else the cost of proper disposal is too great. Even for the 11 billion tons of nontoxic industrial waste, it is estimated that by 2010, roughly half of the cities in the United States will have run out of landfill space (Young & Sachs, 1994).

Air Pollution Another costly byproduct of economic growth is air pollution (Davis, 2003; Markowitz & Rosner, 2003). It is worst in big cities where smog alerts are daily occurrences (Elsom, 1996), but because of world air currents, it is rapidly becoming a global concern. Los Angeles produces over 3,500 tons of pollutants each year, London 1,200 tons, and Mexico City 5,000 (*Human Development Report*, 2002). The major source of pollutants in developed countries is from transport vehicles. Singapore plans to charge cars for every meter they travel, they are restricted in many European cities, and India is thinking of banishing them from within two miles of the Taj Mahal (*Economist*, 1994a:91). Oil, coal, and natural gas used for heating and generating electricity are also major contributors. There is also coal pollution that people generate inside their homes. For example, in winter, when a sour fog makes Eastern European cities look like they "belong in an old black-and-white movie," much soot comes from the tens of thousands of domestic heaters, stoves, and boilers (Simons, 1994:A6). In addition, chemical plants, paper and steel mills, oil refineries, smelters, and trash burning spew additional tons of pollutants into the air. There is a great deal of variation from area to area in the kind and amount of pollutants. The most common pollutants include carbon monoxide, hydrocarbons, nitrogen and sulfur oxides, ozone, and an assortment of tiny particles of soot (that penetrate human lungs, where they mix with water to form a potent acid which is damaging to the tissues), ash, and other industrial by-products. World carbon emissions from the burning of fossil fuels had already climbed to 6.25 billion tons in 1996 (Brown, Renner, & Flavin, 1997:58).

Air pollution is linked to a variety of illnesses and is a major factor in the increase of respiratory diseases, in particular asthma (Misch, 1994: 131–132). An estimated 1.3 billion people in the developing world live in areas of dangerously unsafe air and, in 1993—over a decade ago—some 4 million third-world children under the age of five had already died from acute respiratory disease, brought on in most cases by air pollution (Easterbrook, 1994:60). (This is about as many people of all ages who died of all causes that year in the United States and Western Europe.) More than two decades after the passage of the Clean Air Act in the United States, one in three Americans still lives in an area where the air is too polluted to meet federal health standards (United Nations Environment Programme, 2002:101).

Some of the costlier forms of air pollution can be seen in the effects of acid rain and ozone depletion. Pollutants from coal-burning plants, automobiles, and other industrial sources include sulfur and nitrogen oxides. They are changed by a chemical process in the atmosphere, then travel great distances and fall as sulfuric and nitric acids in rain, snow, fog, or even dry particles. Acid rain has dramatic effects on the environment. Several countries in Europe have reported significant forest damage. Over half of the trees in Germany and Austria were damaged during the late 1980s and early and mid-1990s, causing economic losses of well over $35 billion per year (*Human Development Report*, 2002). China is in the midst of a national environmental crisis whose commutative effect is an immeasurable but unmistakable threat to continued economic growth in coming years; for instance, half of the rain in Guangdong Province is now acidic, a problem that has become endemic in southern China (Tyler, 1994). In tens of thousands of lakes on both sides of the Atlantic, all aquatic life has been destroyed. One observer sardonically noted that lacking organic material, the water "of an acidified lake assumed the crystal clarity of a swimming pool—a deceptive beauty indeed" (Hillary, 1984:137). Acid rain is also harmful to exposed metal surfaces, buildings made of limestone or marble, and automobile paint. Drinking water is affected, and acid rain also contributes to soil erosion and deforestation problems. It has even been known to turn blond hair temporarily green. Acid rain also poses a difficult international problem, in that pollution generated in one country often rains down on another. For example, much of the pollution created in the United States often ends up in Canada, where it wreaks serious environmental damage.

Acid rain represents only one dimension of the pollution problem that stems from the productive process. Another serious concern is ozone depletion, which is created by the release of chlorofluorocarbons into the atmosphere. Used as propellants in aerosol cans, as foam-blowing agents, and as coolants for refrigerators and air conditioners, the gases emitted from these sources contribute to the thinning out of the ozone layer. As this protective layer of ozone diminishes, the amount of ultraviolet and cosmic radiation that reaches the earth's surface increases, which causes increased rates of skin cancer and destroys the food sources of many marine animals. It also contributes to climatic changes by warming the earth's atmosphere. Although many industrial nations have restricted the use of freon gases, which also contribute to ozone depletion, there is an increased demand for and use of them in third-world countries. As a result, an additional 10 percent depletion of the ozone layer by the middle of the twenty-first century is projected. Such a depletion could result in nearly 2 million additional skin cancer cases each year, damage to materials such as plastic and paints worth about $2 billion annually, and incalculable damage to crops and marine life (Postel, 1994).

Water Pollution The economic costs of water pollution are also inestimable. With 97 percent of the earth's water in the salty seas and three-fourths of the remainder locked up in glacial ice, the less than 1 percent of available freshwater appears a very small resource to serve the world's growing industrial and agricultural needs. Thus, it is not surprising that three-fourths of the world's population is without an adequate or safe water supply. In 2001, the world's supply of water, per capita, is only one-third what it was in 1970. Over 1.5 billion people lack access to clean water in the developing world, and water scarcity is increasingly becoming a factor in ethnic strife and political tension (*Human Development Report*, 2002). Freshwater supplies take a heavy load of pollution, because the lakes and rivers are the drainage systems into which industry, agriculture, and municipalities dump their wastes. In turn, pollution reduces marine life and fisheries and ruins recreational pleasures in many key urban areas. In addition, rural areas, especially the corn belt and California's agricultural valleys, already confront serious water-quality problems as a result of nitrate runoff from the soil in heavily fertilized agricultural areas. The nitrogen content of the Midwest's water drainage system is equal to the sewage of 20 million people, or twice that of the Lake Erie basin population. This, in turn, presents serious health problems. Although compared with other countries the United States enjoys relatively good water quality, still one out of five people receives water from a facility that violates a national safety standard (United Nations Environment Programme, 2002:99); physicians in some areas recommend bottled water for infants. The situation is much worse in developing countries. In China, for example, an estimated 25 billion tons of unfiltered industrial pollutants enter into the waterways annually, the water in rivers turns black "like soy sauce" (Tyler, 1994), and there is more toxic water pollution in that one country than in the entire Western world (Easterbrook, 1994:61).

Another kind of water pollution is thermal discharge from factories and power plants. The higher temperature of the discharge decreases the dissolved oxygen in the water, thus increasing metabolic rates while depleting oxygen supplies. As a consequence, small organisms such as fish larvae and plankton are destroyed. This, in turn, will create taste and odor problems in municipal water supplies and will contribute to the reduction of the fish supply.

Marine life is also affected by spills from oil tankers. Accidents involving huge tankers such as the well-known Exxon Valdez oil spill in Alaska are becoming quite common. This problem was further augmented during the 1991 Gulf War when the Iraqi army deliberately spilled close to 10 million barrels, or around 400 million gallons, of oil into the Persian Gulf. Dozens of ships routinely, and without much publicity, run into each other or develop accidental leaks, resulting in massive oil spills. Ruptured pipelines further contribute to pollution, and an October 1994 break in the Russian Arctic had a spill volume of eight times the amount of the leak from the Exxon Valdez, which was 240,000 barrels. [It is interesting to note that the most infamous commercial vessel to fly the nation's flag, the Exxon Valdez, was renamed after the accident and kept on hauling oil for 12 unremarkable years until it was finally mothballed in late 2002 (Little, 2002).] The oil that burst through the dam and flowed to the tributary of the Pechora was more than three feet deep, six to seven miles long and fourteen yards wide (Verhovek, 1994:1). In addition, smaller spills and oil wastes routinely flushed from the tanks of ships contribute significantly to pollution. Commercial fishing fleets each year dump some 50 million pounds of packaging material into the sea and lose some 300 million pounds of indestructible plastic fishing lines and nets. The resulting annual death toll is 1 million to 2 million sea birds, about 100,000 sea mammals, and countless fish. Moreover, about 30 percent of the fish in the world's oceans have tiny pieces of plastic in their stomach that interfere with digestion (Browne, 1987).

Climate Modification Fluctuation in the earth's temperature is another environmental problem brought about by economic activity. The climate can be affected in three ways: (1) by changing the concentration of substances such as water; (2) by releasing heat into the atmosphere; and (3) by making changes in the physical and biological properties of the earth's surface (Harf & Trout, 1986:129). In 1996, the temperature of the atmosphere at the earth's surface averaged 15.32 degrees Celsius, placing it among the five warmest years since data collection began in 1866. The highest was in 1995, 15.40 degrees Celsius (Brown, Renner, & Flavin, 1997:62).

The burning of fossil fuels causes a build-up of carbon dioxide in the atmosphere, which produces a "greenhouse effect" by holding heat in and thus raising the earth's temperature. As the consumption of fossil fuel increases, so does the amount of carbon dioxide released into the atmosphere. In this century, close to 140 billion tons of carbon dioxide have been released into the atmosphere, and half of it is still there. Massive deforestation and desertification further compound the problem because there is no vegetation to absorb the carbon dioxide. The resulting warming effect can increase the earth's temperature from 1 to 3 degrees centigrade (Postel, 1994).

The Kyoto Protocol (United Nations Framework Convention on Climate Change, not yet ratified by the United States among other industrial countries as of early 2003) calls for developed nations to reduce greenhouse gas emissions 6 percent below 1990 levels by 2012 in an attempt to stabilize the climate. If not heeded, increased temperatures could destabilize or melt polar ice caps, raising the level of the oceans. For example, as a result of a 1-meter rise in sea level (caused by global warming), the land area of Bangladesh (which produces only 0.3 percent of global emissions) could shrink by 17 percent (*Human Development Report*, 2002:32). Such a development could result in the flooding of coastal populations and agricultural areas. This, in turn, has implications for rainfall patterns, which, in turn, would have profound long-term effects on agriculture because if the trend continues, the best weather, for example, for growing food in the United States would shift northward into Canada, while farming in more southerly regions, including the Midwest and California, would require massive additional irrigation. Because of the reduction in rainfall, climate change could carry a global price tag of $200 billion for irrigation adjustments alone (Postel, 1994:11–14). A decrease in temperature could have the opposite effect, hurting agricultural areas of the temperate zones and requiring substantially higher levels of energy for heating.

There are many other unmeasurable economic costs resulting from development. Soil depletion costs us in the form of lost nutrients and lowered production; deforestation costs us in the form of soil erosion, decline in rainfall and water supply, and loss of beauty and recreational enjoyment; depletion of fish and wildlife costs us in terms of food, ecological balance, and biological richness; pollution costs us in terms of health, recreation, and productivity. The magnitude of the total cost is unknown, although we know it is already of extensive proportions (*St. Louis Post-Dispatch,* 1987a).

Dennis Gabor (1970:9) emphatically points out that "The most important and urgent problems of the technology of today are no longer the satisfaction of primary needs or of archetypal wishes, but the reparation of the evils and damages wrought by the technology of yesterday." Barry Commoner (1971:295) presciently noted over a generation ago that "Wealth has been gained by rapid short-term exploitation of the environmental system, but it has blindly accumulated a debt to nature—a debt so large and so pervasive that in the next generation it may, if unpaid, wipe out most of the wealth it has gained us. In effect, the account books of modern society are drastically out of balance, so that, largely unconsciously, a huge fraud has been perpetrated on the people of the world." The environment is undergoing a profound transformation—one with consequences that are very difficult (and painful) to grasp (see, for example, Brown, 2001).

Toward Modernity—The Costs of Transition

Economic costs stemming from environmental conditions are not the only ones that are incurred in the process of economic growth and development. There are other ways in which the costs of economic development might be considered. For example, one may compile a list of costs to the traditional society in moving toward a more modern society or one may consider the trade-offs involved in accepting a higher rate of development.

W. Arthur Lewis (1956:426–435), in a groundbreaking book on economic growth, has presented a basic list cataloging some of the costs of transition to traditional societies in the process of development:

1. The economizing spirit necessary for development may lead directly to materialism.
2. Development and growth promote individualism, but in doing so, tend to break down the social structure. An individual becomes more cognizant of his

responsibilities for himself and less aware of his responsibilities to family and tribe.
3. In the development of the new skills necessary for a technologically oriented society, the old handicrafts and skills will die.
4. The economies of scale inherent in development require the mobilization of capital and the separation of ownership from the use of capital. The individual becomes an employee, rather than an independent man, and is thus subjugated to the corporation.
5. Man becomes a slave of the clock and loses independence of action.
6. Large-scale production leads to the growth of cities. Cities become the homes of the slums of a country, and grow at the expense of the villages.
7. Growth and development are dependent on the inequitable distribution of income, and providing the incentives for hard work guarantees that inequalities will persist.

In cataloging the alleged costs of economic development, Lewis is very careful to point out that some of the things listed as costs are not necessarily costs at all. A change in social structure is not perforce evil. Development of the new skills, along with the division of labor, does not require that specifications for products be relaxed in mass production or that the older skills are redundant to society. The fact that large-scale production involves large organizations in which some people are employed who do not own the capital of the productive process does not necessarily mean that large industries are inherently bad. He also notes that these costs of modernization can be subjected to other interpretations and that a case may be made for their inherently negative consequences.

Another way of calculating economic costs in transition is by emphasizing the trade-offs involved in growth and development. At least three of these trade-offs are considered to be of prime importance:

1. In attempting to increase the rate of growth, we sacrifice current leisure for current work. "The high productivity and consequent high cost of labor have made people increasingly conscious of the fact that time is money: and this seems to have engendered the belief that time should be fully and efficiently utilized..." (Scitovsky, 1964:219).
2. In increasing the growth rate, current consumption is traded for future consumption.
3. The greater the rate of growth and change, the greater the difficulty in changeover, with resultant temporary underutilization of resources.

The important point to recall is that the incremental cost of each equal addition to the growth rate will be higher as the growth rate increases. Sacrifice of the first units of consumption for increased growth will not be particularly painful, but further sacrifices begin to strike into "necessities" and may become very painful indeed. As long as the benefits of development are greater than the costs of achieving those benefits, a transfer to growth is in order; but when the marginal benefits of the increased flow of future goods are just equal to the (rising) marginal costs of achieving them, further shifts can only reduce society's achievements, for the cost of further increases in the growth rate will be greater than the benefits arising from it. In the next section, the social costs will be considered.

SOCIAL COSTS

The preceding section emphasized the economic and environmental costs of change. There are, however, a number of social costs borne by society that do not appear in the calculus of economic costs. Social cost may be defined as the cost of economic activity that affects society as a whole or the depreciation of social capital, human labor, or the environment (Stabile, 1993). Some of the examples of social costs incurred in development and growth are painfully obvious: air that kills plant life and forces eyes to water, streams that will not support life, and the sprawl of the slum. William K. Kapp (1971:viii) is justly convinced that "the disruption of man's environment and the social costs resulting from productive activities are among the most fundamental and long-term issues mankind has ever faced."

The notion of social costs is essentially a normative concept. It cannot be satisfactorily measured. It is not reducible to single numbers and is difficult to define with any precision. It entails a wide variety of cost elements, and Kapp (1971:13–14) asserts that the term covers all direct and indirect losses suffered by third persons or the general public in the course of private economic activities. These social losses may be seen in damages to human health or in the destruction or deterioration of property values and the premature depletion of natural wealth; or they may be evidenced in the impairment of less tangible values. Some losses can be traced to individual industries, others to particular production processes or business practices. For example, the profits of the fast food industry have been made possible by losses imposed on the rest of the society. The annual cost of obesity alone is now twice as large as the fast food industry's total revenues. Obesity is now second only to smoking as a cause of mortality. About 280,000 Americans die annually as a direct result of being overweight; the health care costs of obesity approach $240 billion a year (Schlosser, 2002:261, 241–242). Other social costs, Kapp notes, arise in the operation of the competitive system within a given framework of generally accepted institutions and governmental policies. The notion of social costs is broad enough to include even certain "social opportunity costs"—that is, those social cost elements that take the form of wastes or inefficiencies of certain kinds.

In terms of social opportunity costs, Denis Goulet (1985:230) raises the issue of "sacrificed generations." He points out that throughout history, people have lived in conditions far below those objectively demanded by human dignity, and, to this extent, generations have always been "sacrificed." In the early stages of modernization and development,

> consumer goods must be rationed so as to build up infrastructure, provide a pedagogy of solidarity, and increase work input even without appreciable rewards. If this happens, generations are "sacrificed" not in any absolute sense, but in the purely relative sense that their social deprivations are prolonged. . . . Whether he is poor or rich, a man must never be allowed to become a simple object or a pure means for obtaining social goals. Underdevelopment's great misery clearly dehumanizes man; therefore, some efforts to meet minimum needs is required. But the most fundamental sacrifice of generations lies in the radical alienation, whether in abundance or misery.

Attempts are sometimes made to justify social costs, as was the case in the former Eastern bloc socialist countries, and to regard them as the short-run price paid for a high level of long-run efficiency and social performance of the economic system. The argument is that social losses are justified by the change, and that not much is to be gained from a detailed consideration of social costs (Berger, 1974:71–103). Let us now turn to some specific sources of social costs, starting with the ubiquitous automobile.

The Automobile

In discussing social costs, many authors single out the automobile to illustrate their points. In 1950, there was one automobile for every forty-six people worldwide. In the early 1990s, there was one car for every twelve (Lowe, 1994:82), and by late 2002, we were down to ten (Seabrook, 2002). While the human population doubled from 1950, the car population increased nearly tenfold (Brown, Renner, & Flavin, 1997:74). In the United States, the population has grown forty percent since 1970, while the number of registered automobiles had increased nearly a hundred percent by 2002. During the same period, road capacity has increased 6 percent. The old-fashioned traffic jam has turned into gridlock and—following post–September 11, 2001, restrictions (at least in the New York City area)—terrorlock, the latest gridlock neologism to enter New York's traffic vocabulary.

Throughout the world, people could hardly wait to give up rail, streetcar, subway, and other travel options in favor of the unprecedented mobility of a car. But is the exchange as beneficial as presumed? In the former Soviet Union and Eastern Europe, for instance, the rush for the automobile almost a decade ago has already eroded the vast network of trains, trams, subways, and buses that is one of communism's positive legacies (Simons, 1994:A6). In many cases, the greater mobility options did not provide people with better access to their destinations. In fact, as the automobile evolved from luxury to necessity, it contributed less and less to improvements in access. Further, as societies have greatly overvalued mobility, they have underestimated its true costs. Car travel has taken an enormous toll on economies, the environment, social equity, and even human relationships. It is difficult to quantify the costs that drivers impose on society as a consequence of congestion, accidents, air and water pollution, dependence on imported oil, solid waste, loss of cropland, and climate change. These external social costs account for 2.5 percent of the gross domestic budget in many European countries; it is somewhat higher in the United States (Lowe, 1994:95–96).

It is not surprising that some commentators use strong words in discussing the automobile. For example, Mishan (1967:173) is convinced that "the invention of the private automobile is one of the great disasters to have befallen the human race," and he calls it society's greatest nightmare. Barry Weisberg (1971:118) writes: "Considered by some to be one of the greatest inventions of American science and technology, in reality the automobile has been responsible for more deaths and human misery than any other single factor in American life." Weisberg is not exaggerating. In countries that are free of war, the largest cause of violent death is traffic fatalities, averaging some 500,000 annually worldwide. In Europe, car accidents kill four times as many people as homicides, and the numbers are much higher in many Latin American countries (Kane, 1994:132). The automobile is the leading cause of death for people between fifteen and thirty-four years of age. In the United States, there are over 60,000 fatal accidents annually, and some 5 million Americans are injured in auto accidents. Deaths resulting from automobile accidents exceed all the deaths from wars since 1775. The production, distribution, and care of the automobile consumes approximately 16 percent of the labor force and 13 percent of the GNP. This does not include the hospitals, police, courts, and myriad other agencies and institutions in its service. Nor does it include traffic congestion.

Traffic tie-ups, of course, are not new. There were probably chariot jams on the streets of ancient Rome. But now traffic congestion is pandemic, affecting hundreds of metropolitan areas and afflicting millions of people. In Atlanta, the time the average commuter spends annually in traffic rose from twenty-five hours in 1992 to seventy hours in 2000 (Seabrook, 2002:121). A timeless article, appropriately titled "Jam Sessions" (*U.S. News & World Report*, 1987b), paints a rather dismal picture. North of Beverly Hills, California, nearly a half-million cars per day pass the intersection of the Ventura and San Diego freeways. Afternoon rush hour across San Francisco's Bay Bridge starts at 2 P.M. and ends five hours later. Commuters spend an estimated $150 billion to travel to work and back, and time lost in traffic jams in the Los Angeles Basin amounts to some 84,000 hours each day. Put a bit more graphically, if a worker is tied up in traffic twenty minutes each working day—10 minutes each way to and from work—and stays on the job forty-five years, the person will spend nearly two working years tied up in traffic! Traffic congestion costs Americans 1.25 billion vehicle-hours and 1.4 billion gallons of gas each year. At the individual level, if the

St. Louis scene is illustrative of this problem, traffic congestion costs each driver in the city $740 a year in fuel and time (Hopgood, 1997). It is worth noting that Americans spend about 1 minute traveling for every 4 to 5 minutes spent in out-of-the-home work, leisure, and shopping activities (Schipper, 1996). If these trends continue, at least on the lighter side, the world will end not with a bang but a traffic jam.

People are beginning to react to traffic jams in strange ways. Feeling furious at the steering wheel is now a recognized part of modern life. Shootings and traffic-related assaults are becoming quite common. There is a paucity of civility, rules of the road are ignored, and drivers increasingly vent their frustration by speeding; tailgating; excessive horn honking; pounding the steering wheel; making obscene gestures; commenting about the driver's ancestry; and, in extreme cases, ramming or even shooting other motorists. Such behaviors are also involved in 28,000 or so highway deaths annually. The majority of the drivers involved in aggressive driving incidents are males between the ages of 18 and 26 and the rate of violent behavior among young women is on the rise. There are also new terms in psychiatric jargon such as traffic stress and "road rage disorder" (Wald, 1997). In its ultimate form, they can lead to physical ailments, such as neck pains, high blood pressure, and ulcers. The road ahead is even more discouraging.

The Quality of Life

Over the past few years, there has been growing concern over the quality of life in the United States and abroad. The concept of quality of life refers to subjective self-reports on such areas as well-being, happiness, satisfaction, fulfillment, fear, worrying, morale, pain and suffering, and the like (Andrews, 1986; Lawton, 1997). On both sides of the Atlantic, pollsters have been regularly measuring both short- and long-term changes in subjective well-being. In the United States, poll data indicate that the proportion of respondents reported to be "very happy" is decreasing as a result of health problems, work demands that interfere with nonworking time, and various environmental, social and economic problems (Martin, 1996; Rice, Frone, & McFarlin, 1992). Similarly in France, for example, half of the respondents polled felt that the quality of life had deteriorated in recent years. Since the mid-1970s, the various Euro-Barometer surveys carried out in Europe showed the same downward trend in long-term subjective well-being. The same pattern seems to prevail in the United States (Inglehart & Rabier, 1986). This means that fewer people have been reporting to be "very happy," and "happy." The proportion of those who are "dissatisfied" with life is on the increase, and about 50 percent of the adults believe that the future will be bleak for their children (Cornish, 1997).

There have been noticeable changes in other indicators. For example, fear "grew in waves throughout the 1960s" as a correlate of the rising crime rates (Harris, 1973:168–169). In the early 1960s, there was practically no concern with crime and violence as an important issue, and, as late as 1964, only 8 percent mentioned it. By 1968, however, 65 percent did so, and today it is a major preoccupation, even though the rate of violent crime in the United States has been falling for several years. The majority of people reportedly live in some fear, even in their own homes. Department of Justice data indicate, for example, that the majority of women in big cities are afraid to walk the streets, roughly the same proportion worry about being raped, and 82 percent of the general population feel that law and order have broken down (Maguire & Pastore, 1997:182–192). In the early 1990s, 77 percent of Americans worried about becoming violent-crime victims (Updergrave, 1994:114). There is a phenomenal growth in security-related businesses. The installation of security systems in single family homes more than doubled over the last five years, and we, now have over 30,000 gated communities in the country.

Fear management is becoming a topic for self-help books, and at least one, *The Gift of Fear* (Becker, 1997), made the best-seller lists in 1997. Whether or not this fear is justifiable is not the essential issue: the presence of fear is the reality. Fear spikes when a new or highly publicized risk appears (Ropeik & Gray, 2002). For example, five people died in the United States in 2001 as a result of anthrax attacks, in which letters were sent containing the deadly germ. For months people everywhere were afraid to open their mail. Similarly, during the summer of 2002, child abduction was in the headlines; parents refused to let their children go to the playground. After terrorists crashed two hijacked airplanes into the World Trade Center on September 11, 2001, people stopped flying and instead took long trips by car, even though the risk of dying in a car accident is far greater than the risk of dying in a plane crash. Fear is, obviously, a social cost that we unwittingly pay (Lewis & Salem, 1986).

Since the publication of an influential report more than a generation ago—*Work in America* (1973:26)—the quality of life at work has not changed much. It is as bad as ever, despite optimistic comments about improvements and safety. In 1969, exposure to industrial pollutants at the workplace caused 1 million new cases of occupational disease, including 3,600 deaths and some 800,000 cases of burns, lung and eye damage, dermatitis, and brain damage. For the same year there were also some 90,000 permanent impairments, and 2 million temporary disabilities. Between 1980 and 1984, a total of 32,342 Americans died traumatic deaths at work (*St. Louis Post-Dispatch*, 1987b). Mining and construction ranked as the two riskiest occupations. Although men account for 52 percent of the labor force, 95 percent of all on-the-job deaths occurred among males. Among female workers, 42 percent of all on-the-job deaths resulted from homicide, compared to 11 percent for males. In the United States, work-related accidents and illnesses account for twice as many losses as strikes and walkouts. The most significant aspect of work-related accidents is the fact that they are avoidable. "Competent authorities have estimated that from 70 to 90 percent of all work injuries could be prevented by proper safety devices" (Kapp, 1971:65). For example, every year more than a quarter of the meat-packing workers in the United States (over 40,000) suffer an injury or work-related illness that requires medical attention beyond first aid (Schlosser, 2002:172).

In addition, violence at the workplace has also increased. In 2000, well over 2 million workers in the United States were physically attacked, more than 6.5 million others were threatened with violence, and over 17 million were harassed in some way. About one-sixth of the deaths on the job in 2000 were homicides (*Human Development Report*, 2002), second after workplace injuries.

In addition, more and more workers are claiming—and getting—compensation for psychological disabilities caused by stress on the job. Stress-related compensation cases have risen by at least 50 percent since 1980. The cost to insurance companies and employers more than doubled in that time, to $50 million in 1986. In California, for example, though the absolute number of stress claims remains relatively small, such claims grew 462 percent from 1980 to 1986, to about 7,200 claims (Forbes, 1987:12). Finally, the long-term trend of reducing the average working week—from seventy hours in 1850 to fewer than forty hours by the 1950s—has been reversed. Since the 1970s, the number of hours clocked by American workers has risen, to an average of forty-two in manufacturing in 1994 (*Economist*, 1994b:20). In many families both spouses put in much longer hours than just the husbands had back in the 1950s. Ten- to eleven-hour workdays are common, and family life is brutally squeezed. In her controversial 1992 book, *The Overworked American*, economist Juliet B. Schor (1992) estimates that, in attempting to maintain their standards of living in the face of declining compensation, workers spent the equivalent of four weeks more per year on the job in 1989 than they did two decades earlier—although at least one influential sociologist would argue that we work more because we want to because we like it better at work than at home (Hochschild, 1997). Others note that for many professional people—lawyers, consultants, managers, engineers—working longer hours has become the way to impress the boss and get promoted (Uchitelle, 1997). A large part of the increase came from the flood of women into the labor force in that time: their participation increased to more than 57 percent, from 42 percent. In many families, that has more than compensated for a decline in earnings. But the addition, clearly, has brought its own pressures, including a decline in leisure time. By contrast, although Europe is going through a "mid-life crisis" economically (*Economist*, 1997) in several countries such as France, Germany and Italy, the average working week is thirty-five hours, and most workers get six weeks' paid annual vacation and ten days of paid sick leave (Rhoads, 2002); even the Japanese now take three weeks. American workers still make do with two weeks of paid vacation. One result is that the average full-time American worker now toils for more hours a year than his Japanese counterpart, and for as much as 15 percent longer than a typical Western European.

Environment and Social Costs

In addition to the decline in the quality of life, there are more specific social costs associated with change. The more disturbing ones include the rising incidence of environmentally induced illnesses, the lengthening list of endangered species, soil erosion, and the ecological undermining of the world food economy.

Environmentally Induced Illnesses Environmentally induced illnesses are the consequence of the introduction of toxic materials into the environment and the creation of conditions conducive to the rapid spread of certain infectious diseases. Air pollution, which is rapidly becoming a global problem, has reached serious levels in many urban areas (Davis, 2003). School children in Los Angeles are cautioned against vigorous play because of air pollution. In Tokyo, traffic police officers inhale pure oxygen from oxygen tanks every two hours to avoid carbon monoxide poisoning. In many parts of the world, air pollution is a major health problem, contributing to many chronic diseases and killing a substantial number of people each year. In the United States, the current mix of sulfates and particulates in ambient air may cause 50,000 premature deaths annually—about 2 percent of general mortality. As many as four out of ten Americans are exposed to high concentrations of ozone, which is associated with skin cancer. High sulfur dioxide concentration is primarily responsible for a higher rate of lung cancer deaths (Postel, 1994). Four million one- to six-year olds in the United States—including two-thirds of poor, minority, inner city preschool children—have levels of lead in their blood high enough to cause brain damage. Toxic lead exposure costs the country tens of billions of dollars in health expenditure and productivity loss (United Nations Environment Programme, 2002:102).

Another source of concern is the rapidly increasing level of toxic compounds now circulating in the biosphere. Some 70,000 chemicals are presently in everyday use, with some 500 to 1,000 new ones added to the list each year. The estimates of cancer deaths caused by these substances range from 1 percent to 10 percent. There is a lack of information on the toxic effects of an estimated 79 percent of chemicals now used. Less than one-fifth have been tested for acute effects, and fewer than a tenth for chronic (that is, cancer-causing), reproductive, or mutagenic effects. Given how little is known about the extent of people's exposure to these substances, their introduction to the environment is similar to playing Russian roulette with human health.

Another serious health hazard is radiation pollution. In large doses, radiation is associated with a high incidence of leukemia and other cancers. One of the long-term effects is genetic mutation. Environmentalists are concerned that nuclear pollution will further increase as the nuclear industry expands. In spite of elaborate safeguards, accidents can occur, as evidenced by the 1979 Three Mile Island and the 1986 Chernobyl nuclear accidents. Although the long-term effects are not known, it is estimated that the Chernobyl accident will cause up to 135,000 additional cancer cases and over 35,000 deaths in the long run (Flavin, 1997:60). It was the worst nuclear accident in history. As recently as 2000, the Ukraine government was spending 5 percent of its gross domestic product to mitigate the consequences of the disaster. Work has started in 2003 on a massive 20,000-ton hangar-shaped steel arch shell to cover the remains of Chernobyl to contain the site of the nuclear accident, with an anticipated completion date of 2007 (Gugliotta, 2003).

Endangered Species Humans are not the only species threatened by the deterioration of the environment. Because of its irreversibility, the loss of species represents a fundamental social cost. It is estimated that more than 300 species and subspecies of animals have already vanished from the face of the earth as a result of human activities. Of the approximately 9,600 known species of birds, 6,600 are in decline and an estimated 1,000 are at the point where they are now threatened with extinction (Youth, 1994:128) and since January 2000, according to the Conversation International, this trend has just intensified (*Newsweek,* 2002). The major reasons for the decline in the bird populations include pollution, hunting, and habitat destruction in the form of reductions in rain forests and the draining of wetlands. The populations of some estuarine, inshore and offshore fisheries have been reduced to drastically low levels in North America by overfishing, loss of habitat and water- and land-based pollution. During the last decade there were more than 3,650 events with disastrous impacts on fish populations, with a loss of 407 million fish in coastal and near-coastal locations in the United States (United Nations Environment Programme, 2002:100). Extinctions and population declines, in turn, affect jobs and marine environments (Weber, 1994). In addition to animals, nearly half of the world's plant species (an estimated number of 121,000) may be in danger of extinction, according to a recent study using data on endemic plants from 189 countries and territories (McIlroy, 2002).

Soil Erosion The social costs of soil erosion, soil depletion, and deforestation are abundant. "In particular, they may give rise to social damages such as floods, the silting of streams and reservoirs, the diminution of ground-water stores, the pollution of rivers, the destruction of irrigation schemes, the harmful effects of dust storms and the disappearance of wildlife" (Kapp, 1971:127–128). For instance, despite improved conservation techniques, more acreage in the Great Plains was damaged by wind erosion in the 1950s than during the 1930s. Again, between 1976 and 1977, wind erosion damage reached levels comparable to those of the 1930s. Why? Sharply higher wheat prices, fostered by world food shortages, brought a rapid expansion of crop production on acreage that should have been left uncultivated as grassland (Lockeretz, cited in *The Wilson Quarterly*, 1979:41–42).

There are many other illustrations of human beings' abuse of the soil that sustains them. For example, North Africa, once the fertile granary of the Roman Empire, is now largely a desert, or near-desert, sustained by food imports. Even the "decline of whole civilizations can in fact be traced to an overutilization of land" (Kapp, 1971:128). Globally, over 550 million hectares are losing topsoil or undergoing other forms of degradation as a direct result of poor agricultural methods. An additional 679 million hectares are lost to overgrazing, and 579 million to deforestation (Postel, 1994:9–10). In the United States, deforestation has frequently left entire industries and whole communities stranded. For example:

> In the Pacific Northwest 76 ghost towns have resulted from disorderly forest liquidation; and in another 77 communities decline of population has kept steady pace with the closing of mills due to dwindling timber supply.... Millions of acres of cutover land have become tax delinquent and abandoned....
>
> The Ozark region of Missouri contains 35 counties originally covered with splendid stands of pine, oak, and hickory. With the cutting out of timber, forest industries moved out, leaving a large dependent population unable to support itself in decent fashion. The farmers lost both nearby markets for farm produce and the opportunity for profitable winter employment. More than 20 percent of the rural families went on relief, with the remainder eking out a sorry existence.... (Kapp, 1971:144)

In developing countries, 90 percent of the population depends on wood for cooking and heating. In the tropics, 80 percent of all wood harvested is used for fuel (Hillary, 1984:67–68), and half the wood is burned as fuel in developing countries in other parts of the world (Durning, 1994:34). In these areas, firewood is as vital to the local economy as oil is to the global economy. The depletion of forests has dramatically increased the price of wood in many regions. The high cost of firewood, in turn, diminishes the prospects for improved livelihood among the poor, who are forced to spend more of their small incomes on cooking fuel. This often reduces families to one hot meal per day. In India, for example, this is becoming a chronic problem. The combined effects of fuel wood need and the conversion of forests into farmlands threaten to destroy entire forest systems in some developing areas. This, in turn, brings about other unanticipated complications. For example, deforestation often results in the loss of important commodities, many of them non-timber forest products. Over half of the prescriptions method of birth control that is necessary in population growth. Regardless of one's position on the controversy, the abortion question is at once a moral, medical, legal, sociological, demographic, psychological, and political problem (Callahan, 1970:1–2). Let us consider each of these briefly.

As a *moral* problem, abortion raises the question of the nature and control of incipient human life. Pro-life morality tends to subordinate all other considerations to the fetus's right to life. Pro-choice proponents contend that the mother's rights are prior to all other considerations. In this view, a woman's freedom rests finally on her control of her own reproductive processes. Thus, she alone has the right to decide to abort. A third position tries to balance the relative rights of mother and fetus.

As a *medical* problem, abortion affects the doctor's conscience and medical skills. Should medical technology designed to improve human life be used for this purpose? There are also questions about the viability of the fetus and the unsettled issue of when life begins. From a different perspective, many physicians who perform abortions are now concerned about harassment, personal safety, increased litigation, and rising malpractice insurance and fewer and fewer medical schools teach first-trimester abortion as a routine aspect of gynecology.

As a *legal* problem, abortion raises the question of the extent to which society should concern itself with the unborn life, with motherhood, with family, use of law-enforcement personnel, and with public control of the medical profession.

Sociologically, abortion touches on the woman's role in society, family organization and disorganization, national demographic policy, and the role of formal and informal sanctions (see, for example, Basu, 2003). Pro-choice proponents tend to be highly educated, well-paid careerists with few children, almost no ties to formal religion, and a strong vested interest in their work roles. These women see themselves as equal to their husbands, and the unavailability of abortion would limit their competitive chances in the world. Thus, abortion is perhaps as much an economic issue as a psychological and physical one. By contrast, pro-life advocates generally tend to be practicing Roman Catholic women with large families and low-paying or no outside jobs. They believe in traditional sex roles and see motherhood as the highest mission in life. For the first group, loss of the right to abortion would threaten their place in the world of work; for them, motherhood is an option and children a project. For the second group, motherhood is a calling and children a gift. These different views are shaped by divergent social and economic expectations. In an insightful book on abortion in American history, Leslie J. Reagan (1997) suggests that the abortion debate is really an ideological struggle over the position of women. How free should they be to have sexual experiences, in or out of marriage, without paying the price of pregnancy, childbirth, and motherhood? How much right they should have to consult their own needs, interests and well-being regarding child

Croplands, two-thirds of which are used to produce grains, are also becoming unsustainable in many parts of the world, leading to extensive soil erosion (Brown, 1994:20). Deforestation is another concern. For example, ecological overstress is quite evident in much of the Indian subcontinent. During the last generation, as human and livestock populations have expanded, the subcontinent has been progressively deforested. Deforestation, in turn, can undermine food-producing capability by contributing to the incidence and severity of flooding. This is what happened in 1973, when the worst flood in Pakistan's history destroyed a large share of the spring wheat crop in storage on farms as well as much of the standing crops. "Entire communities were washed away. Since the deforestation is continuing, the incidence and severity of flooding in Pakistan, India, and Bangladesh seems certain to worsen in the future" (Brown, 1974:73). Lester Brown's prediction was correct. Over a period of two months, in September and October 1978, four successive floods affected much of northern India. In West Bengal, the worst-hit state, an area of about 21,000 square miles (more than four times the area of Connecticut) was ravaged. Some 15 million Bengalis had to leave their homes; the floods ruined 6.5 million tons of wheat and rice in the fields and godowns, and killed 1.5 million cattle. In Bangladesh, one of the most flood-prone countries in the region, as many as 80 million people still remain vulnerable to flooding each year. In India, 40 million hectares remain at risk annually at an average estimated damage of $1.5 billion (United Nations Environment Programme, 2002:57) There is a growing body of evidence to suggest that human activities are responsible for the severity of the floods (Brown, 2001).

Reduction of Options

Another way of looking at the social costs is in terms of the reduction of options open to individuals. As a result of resource limits, abuses, and mismanagement, the need to regulate and coordinate human activity increases. The regulation of options, in turn, affects lifestyles, including what we eat, where we live, and where we travel.

There is a great deal of consensus in the social science literature that economic development inevitably brings about dietary changes (see, for example, Schlosser, 2002; Stevens, 1994). The trend during the course of development is from a diet heavily dependent on a few starchy staples to one greatly enriched with high-protein livestock products. However, this trend may be arrested by the growing pressures on food resources and an unprecedented rise in feed-grain prices (Brown, Renner, & Flavin, 1997:30). Already, some nations are experiencing at least a temporary downturn per-capita intake of livestock products. In Argentina, for example, a country famous for its meat products, per-capita consumption of beef has declined from nearly 200 pounds to less than 140 pounds in recent years. Whether or not less beef consumption can be construed as a social cost is secondary. The cost comes about in terms of the reduction of options.

The choice of where one lives is also beginning to diminish throughout the world. Not long ago, opportunities for migrating from one country to another were quite plentiful. In recent years, however, migration has become increasingly subject to various restrictions as nations become concerned with security, overcrowding, unemployment, and more selective about the immigrants they consider economically and socially unacceptable (*Economist*, 2002). In some areas, even the movement from rural to urban communities is becoming more difficult (Adler & Gielen, 2002). Even in the United States, there are calls for measures to stem the growth of big cities, to check and reverse the decades-old trend of migration from rural areas to the cities and from smaller cities to larger ones. In policy-making circles, nowadays the terms "national population dispersal policy" and "population distribution policy" (Sundquist, 1975:6–12) are being used increasingly.

Social costs are also incurred from the restrictions on human mobility—how frequently and how far we are able to travel from home. Restrictions on the automobile already impinge on mobility. In terms of international travel, some countries are already unwilling or unable to accommodate the large influx of people that unrestricted international travel brings them. Even in the United States, in terms of domestic travel, some states, such as Oregon, have stepped up psychological campaigns to discourage visitors from lingering too long. Those having a second home at a lake, the seashore, or in the mountains face problems that did not exist a few years ago. There is also a decrease in the opportunity to own land and the freedom to utilize it in a way one desires. Inevitably, there will be little choice but to restrict various individual freedoms.

There are also social costs involved in the choices and trade-offs that stem from emerging pressures on resources of various kinds. At the community level, it is increasingly necessary to make choices as to how freshwater lakes are used. In many instances, the choice is between recreation, irrigation, waste absorption, or the production of fish. Obviously, not all of these uses are compatible. If a lake is used for waste absorption, it is not suitable for fish production or recreation purposes. Similarly, strip-mining coal desolates the countryside and is an abomination, but strip mining is four times safer for the miner than shaft mining; hence, its direct cost in human life is only one-fourth that of shaft mining. Macklin Fleming (1974:7) raises the question, "Do we outlaw strip mining at the cost of the extra expenditure of human life that shaft mining entails?" This is only one of the questions involved in the trade-off between the destruction of the natural topography and the desire for cheap energy. Such balancing of relative values and weighing of the costs of alternatives takes place in all human activity. Obviously the decisions are hard, and in many instances judgmental righteousness does not coincide with the exigencies of a situation.

There are no easy answers to this dilemma. In a now-classic essay, "The Tragedy of the Commons," Garrett Hardin (1975:250–264) captures the essence of the problem. According to Hardin, humankind is caught in a situation akin to a classic tragedy. Although each individual apparently has no ill will toward others, all humans acting in self-interest move inexorably toward self-destruction. Hardin uses the example of animals being kept on a commons, an area open to all villagers for pasturing their stock. There are no problems on the commons as long as the number of animals is small in relation to the size of the pasture. From the perspective of each herder, however, the optimal strategy is to enlarge one's herd as much as possible. If one herder's animals do not eat the grass, someone else's will. Thus, the size of each herd grows and the density of stock increases until it exceeds the carrying capacity of the commons. The result is that everyone eventually loses, as the animals die of starvation. The sum of a set of apparently rational individual strategies equals social irresponsibility, leading to disaster. The tragedy is that even though the eventual result should be perfectly evident, no one acts to avert disaster. As yet, there are no socially acceptable ways to keep the size of the herd in line.

Urban Living

Although the social costs are more pronounced in the domain of changes brought about in the environment as a result of increased size, affluence, and energy requirements, there are many other areas of social life that have been also affected. For example, most urban areas in the United States are faced with a high crime rate, vandalism, relatively poor-quality public schools, lack of adequate mass transportation, and the already-mentioned serious traffic congestion. As a result of the dismal state of many cities' finances (caused in large part by the mass exodus of large employers that reduces the tax base), public services such as street cleaning, garbage removal, street repair and maintenance, and fire and police protection are being reduced (Spates & Macionis, 1987:359–400). The plight of urban areas is further compounded by the presence of abandoned cars and buildings not yet demolished and the poor property maintenance and upkeep of many occupied structures. For many people, housing is at a premium, and there is a high concentration of households on welfare. There are households that exist in a non-child-oriented environment that lacks open space suitable for playgrounds because of the high-rise dwellings that make watching over children difficult. Such an environment is generally more oriented to adult activities than to those of children. There is tension between whites and ethnic and minority groups (Takaki, 1994). The proportion of ethnic and minority groups, fueled by large waves of Asian and Latin American immigrants, is increasing in urban areas, accompanied by a downward shift in average incomes, which is most pronounced when neighborhoods undergo a transition from middle-income to low-income residents. There is a growing concern with social marginalization of Native Americans and Alaskan Natives in urban areas. Both groups have much higher death rates from injuries and alcohol-related causes than other urban residents (World Resources Institute, 1999:48).

At the same time, selected urban areas are being revived through the process of *gentrification* (the movement of more affluent Americans back into older, often decaying, parts of the city). This increases property values, which, in turn, often forces poorer residents in the area to relocate. Urban dwellers, regardless of where they live, pay higher insurance rates than do their suburban or rural counterparts, as well as higher security costs that stem from the use of burglary systems and other crime-control devices.

A balance sheet of costs and benefits to individuals, families, and society that took into account the changing conditions in urban areas would be exceedingly complex even if all the factors could be identified and measured. The calculation is further complicated by the presence of many factors that defy quantification. For example, no figure has been placed on many important costs, including the time lost by millions of workers in their daily commuting, limited access to outdoor recreation, high levels of air and noise pollution, and the consequences of crowding. The social costs of these conditions have yet to be measured by social scientists. As Claude S. Fischer (1984:201) observes, "Perhaps the psychic or social pains of city life are too subtle, too camouflaged, or too spiritual in character to be measured by the crude instruments of social science. Plausible arguments along this line can be constructed. But plausibility is promiscuous, and will couple readily with most theories that come by, no matter how incompatible the theories are with one another."

Reasonable arguments about social costs could be made concerning the consequences of the lack of social ties, the prevalence of fear that was previously noted, isolation, and the friction among heterogeneous populations in urban areas. Urban living adversely affects social well-being by undermining traditional primary group relations, especially those based on the family, extended kinship ties, and the neighborhood (Milgram, 1970; Wirth, 1938). Urbanism as a way of life is characterized by anomie and an absence of both moral consensus and social responsibility. Louis Wirth (1938) suggests that such conditions of social disorganization give rise to individual psychological disturbances and to increased crime, delinquency, and corruption. Urbanites have contact with many people, most of them strangers, and public encounters are usually formal, brief, and superficial. By way of protecting themselves from becoming involved, city dwellers often discourage interaction by being formal, unfriendly, and brusque. But the cost of this disengagement from others is high. It results in a tendency to disregard the personal needs of people encountered in public places, especially when the burden of social responsibility is shifted to formal agencies.

For example, the police are expected to respond to the injured in a traffic accident, and welfare agencies are expected to deal with the poor and the homeless. Two highly publicized classic examples of the absence of social responsibility and the tendency of most city dwellers to not involve themselves in the affairs of others will illustrate this point. The first involves the murder of Catherine Genovese in Queens, New York, in 1964. She was repeatedly stabbed for an extended period of time. Investigators discovered that thirty-eight neighbors either heard her screams or actually witnessed the attack. But no one did anything to help her. The second involves the gang-rape of a woman in a bar in New Bedford, Massachusetts, in 1983. Again, no one came to the woman's aid, although many customers witnessed the attack. Only when she ran out naked into the street did a motorist call the police. There are, of course, many similar examples.

Underutilization of College-Educated People

Social costs stemming from changes in the domain of education are becoming more pronounced. During the past two decades in particular, the educational system in the United States has continued to expand and diversify, with a number of consequences. Most important is the fact that a consistently increasing proportion of the population has had the opportunity to pursue higher education. These educational experiences have significantly influenced levels of aspiration and expectation in a number of areas, including lifestyles and satisfaction derived from work. Although the educational system has expanded and diversified, the occupational pyramid has remained relatively rigid in terms of the capability of offering the range of options that could effectively provide "interesting work" to all. There are now more qualified people looking for jobs in the upper echelons of organizations than the present occupational pyramid could possibly accommodate. The bachelor's degree, like the high school diploma before it, is no longer the ticket to a rising standard of living (Uchitelle, 1994). While aspirations and expectations about work have been generally rising, it is obvious that ongoing technological change has served to imbue much work with routine and repetitive qualities. The price of this is work dissatisfaction and alienation.

Greater social costs result, however, from the underutilization of the educated population. As Ivar Berg and Marcia Freedman (1977:30) comment: "A significant degree of underutilization is undoubtedly inevitable in a society in which the occupational structure has stabilized while educational achievements have bounded upward; neither the occupational structure's shape nor the educational achievements of the work force are realistically amenable, at this late date, to much amelioration by the nation's employers." Depending on the assumptions and standards used, underutilization at the present time ranges between a quarter and one half of the college graduate labor force. The plausible social costs of this underutilization of educated people include alienation and political cynicism and a "kind of intellectual atrophy in which people whose education is underutilized, who are not challenged by the work they do, fall to the level of their jobs" (1977:28). The problems stemming from this underutilization are enormous; as of the late-1990s, there were no indications of major changes at the workplace to accommodate the growing number of college-educated workers.

The Dilemmas of Scientific Specialization

Even those college-educated workers who are not underutilized are confronted with a series of dilemmas. In general, more education is associated with greater specialization. Scientists, in particular, whether they are employed in institutes, research establishments, or universities, are subjected to a growing pressure on their time and on their ability to keep up with developments in their fields. Not only are they expected to keep abreast of the avalanche of journal literature, in which, inevitably, the writing is increasingly concentrated and increasingly technical, but, in most instances, they are also expected to contribute an article or two from time to time to the accumulating weight that is bearing down on them. Perhaps more than other professions, "the ordinary academic tends to become overextended, his faculties too polarized to respond fully to other aspects of life, be they intellectual, aesthetic or emotional. Like all too many of us today, he may seek gaiety but is hard put to generate any" (Mishan, 1967:139). We recall from an earlier chapter that contemporary academics are expected to contribute to their discipline in the form of research or publication as a condition for better jobs, promotions, raises, and for many the most sought-after objective, tenure. Consequently, they package their résumés with publication credits and count their published works "as a miser counts his gold. They are his kudos, his claims to recognition. Above all, they are his certificates encashable in the world he moves in" (Mishan, 1967:140–141).

The pressure for research and publication further reinforces specialization and has the unsurprising consequences that only a handful of people know more than a fraction of the broader discipline in which they work, or are competent to judge the work of their colleagues over a wide field. Editors of scholarly journals already find it difficult to find scholars able to appraise the quality of some of the highly specialized papers submitted to them. Moreover, because of the demands upon one's time and capacity, no scholar is able to read more than a fraction of the output of professional papers in one's own field. Mishan (1967:140) mentions an estimate that "the average scientific paper is read by about 1.3 people—while many are read by several people and a few by hundreds, a large number are read by nobody but their authors (if we exclude the editors)." Often, five or six scholars write for each other and nobody knows or cares what it is all about

(Honan, 1994). The emphasis on the number of publications is so great that many people use the "salami method"—slicing every paper into six or seven separate papers before publication. Uncoordinated knowledge is growing at a rapid rate. The number of technical journals in the world exceeds 100,000, and the annual output of books is rapidly approaching that number. Some 18,000 professional journals are published in the United States (Honan, 1994). In a sense, we are faced with an overload of information (Klapp, 1986). Some 142 periodicals are now available in the United States on the subject of sociology alone (*The New Republic*, 1987:7). In sociology and related fields, there are more than 350 journals in English (Sussman, 1978). One could indulge in a bit of rough calculation, assuming that each of these 350 journals appears four times a year containing, on the average, a dozen articles annually. That would come to 16,800 articles a year, averaging about 46 articles a day. Obviously, Professor Mishan's observation is not too far-fetched. Even dedicated graduate students preparing for their Ph.D. qualifying examinations would find the digestion (or even the reading) of that many possibly "relevant" articles a task beyond their endurance. In the next section, the psychological costs of change will be considered.

PSYCHOLOGICAL COSTS

In addition to the economic and social costs, change also entails a series of psychological costs. Perhaps most noticeable is the loss of the individual's ability to understand and control his or her environment. People have become utterly dependent upon the operation of complex technological and social organizations that they can neither understand nor control. Generalized knowledge and practical problem-solving abilities are being undermined, leaving in their absence the specialists and experts with their set of instructions and push-button solutions. "We may use many materials of whose provenance we know next to nothing; we are surrounded by household implements we know how to operate but whose working principles we ignore; and we are more and more at a loss when trying to answer the simplest questions of our children concerning the nature of the everyday objects around them. This applies not only to the atom but even to the shirts on our backs. Hence man's feeling today of the utter dependence of his everyday life on a complex technical and social organization about whose working, outside his own narrow sphere, he is largely in the dark; and this, too, contributes to his feeling of impotence in relation to organized society" (Scitovsky, 1964:227). As a result of people's loss of control and utter dependence, Samar Amin (1974:1) offers an extreme view, which is nevertheless worth noting, of the personality in the making: "These beings no longer speak—they have nothing to say, since they have nothing to think or feel. They no longer produce anything, neither objects nor emotions. No more arts. No more anything. The electronic machine produces—the word itself has lost all meaning—everything, these beings included."

Although Amin's description of the personality in the making is a bit far-fetched, there are many other "psychological victimization syndromes" of social change in the literature. Theodore Roszak (1973) talks about the "automatization of personality" as a result of technological changes. Jacques Ellul (1964) argues that technological changes lead to the "systematization" of all aspects of social life, and humans will be alienated not only from their work but from their recreation as well, as that is also becoming increasingly technical. Others contend that the realization of victimization with the ability to identify and verbalize the symptoms that bring about certain deleterious psychological or social conditions (real or imaginary) which can be used to excuse behavior—anything from insanity and alcoholism to depression, post-traumatic stress disorder, battered woman syndrome, football widow syndrome, nicotine withdrawal syndrome, premenstrual syndrome, parental alienation, black rage and even "rotten social background" (Dershowitz, 1994; Wilson, 1997).

These voices are merely the latest additions to a tradition that includes such names as Herbert Marcuse and even Sigmund Freud, the general point being that modern technological civilization fragments human personality, forces people to repress essential needs, deprives people of the experiential gestalt enjoyed by primitive beings, and thus reduces individuals to a mechanized and dehumanized entity. Anton C. Zijderveld's (1971:64–68) concept of "intellectual Taylorism" eloquently summarizes the modern individual's intellectual predicament as perceived by many authors. He posits that automation is taking place not only in industry, but also in thought. It is a characteristic of modern science. As Western societies become automated, bureaucratized, and pluralized (that is, fragmented), Zijderveld argues, they move away from "the common human pattern." As a consequence, human experience in Western societies is becoming increasingly unnatural or abstract.

Robopathology

An image of the ideal type of humanistic personality is what psychologist Abraham Maslow calls a *self-actualized person*. Such a person, Maslow suggests (1959:127), has the following attributes: clear and efficient perception of reality; an openness to new experience; integration; wholeness and unity of the person; spontaneity; expressiveness; aliveness; a firm identity; autonomy; uniqueness; objectivity; detachment; creativeness; ability to fuse concreteness and abstractness; a democratic character structure; and ability to love. The attainment of these ideal characteristics is, however, hampered by the conditions created by accelerated technological and social change. Instead of self-actualization, Lewis Yablonsky (1972:16) argues that we have robopathology, which emerges when people "cop out or sell out their humanistic drives of excitement, joy, and courage to the cultural press of social machines because of fear and often an instilled sense of inadequacy. They often trade their more spontaneous creative potentials for familiar regularized rituals. . . . In the process of a dehumanized society they live in familiar, routine, and predictable patterns of behavior. Thus they cop out on their humanistic motivations and become part of the social machine." In 1990s parlance, they become "politically correct" and succumb to the "dictatorship of virtue" (Bernstein, 1994). An example of this would the proclivity of the publishing industry to reject works of great academic importance and integrity because they violate some politically correct tenets. A controversial illustration of this is Arthur Jensen's *The G Factor*, which examines racial differences in intelligence levels (Lamb, 1997). (And there are, of course, other examples, and the most notable are euphemisms. There is no more plagiarism, only unacknowledged repetition. A lover is a spouse equivalent, and criticism is verbal abuse. Quotas are race-sensitive programs and a censor is multicultural issues editor. And so on. See, for example, Leo, 2002.)

Robopathic behavior, Yablonsky contends, is found in many aspects of life. Many creative people are often corrupted by the rewards of the plastic society. They find a comfortable place and stay there. A multitude of writers, teachers, and artists, after an initially courageous and creative productive life, "cop out and become robopathic in their later creative attempts. They find a successful mold, receive their rewards, and ritualistically stick to it for the rest of their lives. . . . Their fears and lack of courage freeze them into static, uncreative roles, where they lock into a robopathic existence" (1972:18).

A number of social roles in contemporary society lack opportunities for humanistic expression, spontaneity, creativity, and compassionate action. These include such roles as file clerk, assembly line worker, and the like. Yablonsky calls these "robot roles" whose monotony, boredom, and dehumanizing qualities are exemplified "by the daily monotony of work on an assembly line in a factory. The robot role occupants rise at the same time, go through their ritualized breakfast, turn the screws at work, watch TV, make ritualistic love on a prescribed night, take their two-week vacation—and become increasingly frustrated and bored by their routinized life style. Increasingly their zest for life, and capacity for spontaneity and creativity, is reduced to zero. One common consequence of this malaise is a simmering, underlying feeling of hostility and aggression toward others" (1972:19).

Yablonsky concedes that modern societies have produced enormous advantages for people. Time and space dimensions have been changed for their benefit; leisure time possibilities have increased; the health, wealth, and welfare of many people have been grossly improved by technocratic systems, and this is reflected in a longer life span. But, "Despite these and other apparent gains from modern technology, a chorus of questions and issues have been posed and amplified about the price paid for 'technological' progress" (1972:57).

Yablonsky contends that the psychological costs of progress are indeed high. Individuals' coherent self-identities have been fragmented or rendered anonymous by their work roles in modern society. Their relationship to nature, their natural state of existence, and their enjoyment of nature's beauty have been seriously impaired by the overdeveloped machine society. The dehumanizing aspects of contemporary life have escalated crime and various forms of alienation. Current conditions are largely responsible for the acceleration of various routes of escape from self through drugs, alcohol, mysticism, superreligions, and growing fantasy states of existence. Finally, the mass media have confused people's sense of reality and personal identity, and there is a confused blur between mass media news, drama, and live experience (see, for example, Haag, 1994). According to this view, life has increasingly become a spectator sport.

Anxiety and Insecurity

To what extent people's emotions, spontaneity, creativity, personal identity, and ability to become compassionate are reduced to a set of robopathic responses is hard to tell. Much of the literature supports these impressions, and indeed there seems to be an escalation of tension, discontent, and anxiety in the face of social change. For example, Robert H. Lauer and Rance Thomas (1976) investigated the relationships among change in individual life circumstances, perceived rate of social change, and anxiety level in England and in the United States. In both societies, the authors found a positive correlation between both kinds of change and anxiety level, with the perceived rate of social change being more significant as a predictor of anxiety level than change in life circumstances. In particular, the greater the number of changes in life circumstances in a year and the greater the perceived rate of change, the greater the likelihood of a high anxiety level. The data in general support the argument that a high rate of change generates psychological reactions, which, in turn, require adjustment on the part of individuals. They point out, however, that when the changes are defined as desirable, the deleterious effects are minimized.

At times anxieties produced by change may carry over into group relations and when there are no agreed-upon measures to mediate the stress, there is a possibility that hostility will erupt within or among groups. Cyril E. Black (1966:24) observes, for example, that insecurity and anxiety may also interfere in the relationship between countries: ". . . the growing sense of insecurity . . . can be traced to the tensions resulting from the simultaneous development of nationalism and interdependence. Indeed, this sense of insecurity has been such a pervading force that one may venture to interpret the various forms of imperialism, alliance relationships, wars, and experiments in political integration that have characterized international relations in modern times as a search for security that is significantly more urgent than in earlier times." Insecurity and anxiety may also explain, in part, the rise of ethnic tensions in several nations, resulting in ethnic clashes with brutal results. For example, since the late 1980s, over 130,000 people were killed in what is called "ethnic cleansing"; in Somalia in 1993, there were more than 10,000 casualties; in 1994 in Rwanda, close to 1 million lives were lost as a result of clashes between rival ethnic factions; and by the end of the 1990s, tens of thousands had died in the former Yugoslavia.

The rise of anxiety and insecurity in modern society is generally attributed to the increased emphasis on competition and achievement [for example, affluent parents spend in excess of $15,000 a year and are willing to pledge $1 million just to get a child into a coveted nursery school in Manhattan's Upper East Side to ensure admission to the best high schools and then colleges (Hemphill, 2002)]; the sacrifice of individuality to organizational purposes; to the demand for emotional constraint and self-control; and to the inability of comprehending one's material surroundings. As a consequence, Tibor Scitovsky (1964:228) points to "man's need to compensate for his increasing remoteness from the material world around him." This compensation may take several forms. For example, there is a renewed interest in the United States in handicrafts, in a country where they have become the most obsolete and unprofitable. He notes that schools put the greatest stress on the teaching of handicrafts, and handicrafts as a hobby are becoming the most popular. He remarks: "Let us hope that making one's own ashtrays, finishing one's own furniture, and doing one's own plumbing, painting and papering accomplish this. But even if they do, they do it at the cost of time—and a lot of time—being diverted from more intellectual pursuits. This is especially true of school, where pottery, weaving, glove making, etc., divert time and energy not only from the humanities but probably also from the three Rs" (1964:228).

There are other signs of compensation for the increased sameness and homogeneity of contemporary life. For example, the notion that a house reflects the personality of its occupant is new to this century. Traditionally, houses reflected the class of their occupants. With all the utensils, artifacts, and folk art we put in our homes, we cannot hide the fact that we are living not in a farm house, or Greek peasant huts, or potty Victorian collectors' parlors, but in a technologically developed society where things do seem to be getting more and more the same. As our habitations grow more and more alike (our clothes are already alike), does it necessarily follow that we ourselves will be less individual and distinguishable from one another? Most authors discussed in this section would tend to agree that the answer is yes. One, of course, can always question this interpretation.

Mental Illness

Thus far, it has been noted that social change is associated with a number of psychological costs such as anxiety, insecurity, stress, a reduction in spontaneity, creativity, personal identity, and the ability to be compassionate. It is now appropriate to raise the question: Does social change lead to a variety of debilitating kinds of states and of behavior, and does it extract a cost in terms of mental health? Marc Fried (1972:451) notes that only a few epidemiological studies dealt directly with the effects of social change on mental illness. He describes one important group of studies that investigated the changes over periods of time in rates of psychiatric hospitalization. The studies considered admissions between 1840 and 1940 and showed that, with appropriate adjustments, age-specific first-admission rates for ages under fifty were just as high during the last half of the nineteenth century as they are today. There were some short-term fluctuations associated with wars and depressions, but the long-term trends revealed no marked increase that might correspond to this century of urbanization and industrialization in Massachusetts. He points out that other longitudinal studies draw a similar conclusion. The frequency of hospitalization for psychosis, for example, has remained strikingly constant over time. In spite of the evidence that rates of psychiatric hospitalization have not risen substantially in the United States over long periods of time, Fried notes that there are suggestions of increased rates of other forms of emotional disturbances (1972:453). Fried refers to studies that make an excellent case for both the rise of psychosomatic disorders and changing distributions of physical illness according to age and sex, which "suggest the increasing importance of stress in impaired functioning" (1972:453). His observation is supported by data that indicate that rates of some disorders are going up and the incidence of depression among the baby boomers, those who were born after World War II, is particularly serious. Over the past two generations, the rates of depression have increased about tenfold, and it is striking the younger generation at an earlier age (Klerman, 1986). However, a rise in rates for one disorder caused by the stress of social change may be, hypothetically, offset or compensated by a decline in other types of disorders. It is worth noting in this connection that studies on mental health indicate that in the United States there is no difference between rural and urban residence in terms of mental disorders (see, for example, Fischer, 1984; Robins & Regier, 1991).

Fried also refers to several comprehensive reviews of the literature on mental illness in developing societies that support the view that acculturation to Western patterns leads to increased rates of psychopathology, and suggests that "we cannot dismiss the possibility that acculturation experiences, particularly those entailing a very rapid and uncoordinated change only for some members of a society, may lead to increased impairments in functioning" (1972:453). This possibility indeed exists, and accelerated change conceivably disrupts basic social ties, breaks down social controls, and thus produces a train of personal disorientation, confusion, and uncertainty, which, ultimately, leads to misery and could produce mental breakdown among some individuals.

On the other hand, there is evidence in the literature that modernization does not produce mental disorders and does not lead to mental breakdowns. Alex Inkeles and David H. Smith (1974:262), in a study of modernization in six countries, found:

> Of the modernizing experiences frequently identified as likely to induce individual disorganization by disrupting personality, creating strain, introducing disturbed stimuli, and the like, none consistently and significantly produced increased maladjustment as measured by the Psychosomatic Symptoms Test. In contrast to our experience in studying the impact of the same independent variables on other psychological scales, such as our measures of modern attitudes, the patterns observed in relation to adjustment were not only weak but decidedly lacking in consistency across six countries.

They also wrote, "Whatever may cause psychosomatic symptoms in younger men in developing countries, it is apparently something other than the exposure to the modernizing institutions such as the school, factory, the city and the mass media" (1974:263). They have, furthermore, found no evidence that migration itself brings about psychic distress in developing countries.

The modernization experience may cause some emotional problems, but, based on the Inkeles and Smith study at least, it can safely be assumed that the experience is not associated with mental disorders or breakdowns. In some instances, as in the case with India, increased exposure to modernizing influences actually brought with it a decrease in the number of psychosomatic symptoms. In this sense, one may even argue that modernizing influences actually improved personal adjustment. As the authors say, "Quite contrary to popular expectation, therefore, one is forced to conclude that, if anything holds in this realm, it is that the more modern the individual, the better his psychic adjustment as measured by the Psychosomatic Symptoms Test" (Inkeles & Smith, 1974:264).

It should be noted in the context of social change and mental illness that often the medicalization of certain behaviors are the result of interest group pressures. For example, less than two decades ago, there were 106 mental disorders listed in the *Diagnostic and Statistical Manual of Mental Disorders*, known as the *D.S.M.* It is prepared by the American Psychiatric Association and used by psychiatrists and other therapists to identify a set of behaviors as a mental illness. The current fourth edition of the *D.S.M.* contains more than 300 disorders certified as mental diseases. One of the major reasons for the increase is that many new disorders develop powerful lobbies in the therapeutic and political worlds because of the *D.S.M.*'s significant influence on health care spending. Insurance companies and health maintenance organizations require inclusion of disorders in the manual before they compensate health care providers. This provides a motive for defining new mental disorders and marketing psychotropic medications (Kutchins & Kirk, 1997).

SUMMARY

This chapter examined the economic, social, and psychological costs of change. It was noted that the costs of social change are never evenly distributed and that it is very difficult to determine the "net" pains and pleasures for widely differing groups. There are, however, several broad societal changes that extract a toll from most of us.

The proponents of economic development argue that growth is an essential condition for social advance and for improving the standard of living. The realization of economic benefits is a major preoccupation of the literature dealing with the problems of underdeveloped societies. However, too little has been said about the costs of growing pains associated with rapid growth rates. It has been noted that continued pursuit of economic development is more likely to reduce than to increase social welfare, and development, in many instances, entails ecologically faulty and socially wasteful types of production. Progress often comes about at the cost of environmental deterioration and an increase in air and water pollution. However, there are few individuals who would give up a convenient airport or their automobile for the sake of cleaner atmosphere. Not many people would endure for long a decrease in standards of income or return to more primitive economic forms in exchange for either a clean atmosphere or clean water. In addition to environmental considerations, there are economic costs incurred in the transition from traditional to a more modern society, and such a transition invariably entails a number of trade-offs.

The notion of social costs is essentially a normative concept and it cannot be satisfactorily measured. Many authors single out the automobile in their illustrations of social costs. More pronounced, however, is the decline in the quality of life as evidenced by a number of indicators and poll data. Social costs are also brought about by the rising incidence of environmentally induced illnesses, the lengthening list of endangered species, the progressive pollution and depleting of lakes and streams, and the ecological undermining of the world food economy. In addition, environmental changes result in the reduction of options in terms of what we eat, where we live, and where we travel. Such changes often pose difficult dilemmas involving complex choices and trade-offs. It was noted also that social costs are incurred from urban living, the increased underutilization of college-educated people, and scientific specialization.

There are many psychological costs of change in addition to economic and social costs. Perhaps most noticeable is the loss of the individual's ability to comprehend and control his or her own environment. Dehumanization, automatization of personality, and systematization of all aspects of social life are recurrent themes in the literature. The symptoms of "robopathology" are becoming more pronounced as many social roles lack opportunities for humanistic expression, spontaneity, creativity, and compassionate action. The psychological costs of change are also evidenced in increased anxiety and insecurity, and, at times, they may carry over into group relations, increasing the possibility of hostility. Finally, it was noted that change is not associated with an increase in mental disorders, although there are good possibilities for other forms of emotional disturbances, such as depression. The experience of modernization does not lead to mental breakdowns, and, in some instances, modernizing influences actually result in a decrease in the number of psychosomatic symptoms. In the final chapter, the assessment of change will be considered.

SUGGESTED FURTHER READINGS

ADLER, LEONORE LOEB, AND UWE P. GIELEN (eds.). *Migration, Immigration and Emigration in International Perspective.* Westport, CT: Prager, 2002. A collection of current influential articles on worldwide configurations and complications of migration.

ANDREWS, FRANK M. (ed.). *Research on the Quality of Life.* Ann Arbor: Survey Research Center, Institute for Social Research, The University of Michigan, 1986. A series of articles on cross-cultural changes in the quality of life.

BROWN, LESTER R. (ed.). *State of the World 2001.* London: Earthscan, 2001. A Worldwatch Institute report on the various costs associated with economic development.

BROWN, LESTER R., AND HAL KANE. *Full House: Reassessing the Earth's Population-Carrying Capacity.* New York: W. W. Norton, 1994. A sober discussion of the many consequences of global population increases and a series of suggestions to restore food security.

ELSOM, DEREK. *Smog Alert: Managing Urban Air Quality.* London: Earthscan, 1996. A clear and comprehensive account of the problems of urban air pollution and the ways they can be tackled.

FISCHER, CLAUDE S. *The Urban Experience,* 2nd ed. New York: Harcourt, 1984. A highly readable summary of existing knowledge on the social and psychological consequences of urban life.

FLAVIN, CHRISTOPHER, AND NICHOLAS LENSSEN. *Power Surge: A Guide to the Coming Energy Revolution.* Washington, DC: Worldwatch Institute, 1994. A discussion of more efficient, decentralized, and cleaner energy systems and their costs.

GHIMIRE, KRISHNA B., AND MICHEL P. PIMBERT (eds.). *Social Change and Conservation: Environmental Politics and Impacts of National Parks and Protected Areas.* London: Earthscan, 2000. A series of articles on current trends in conservation in various parts of the world and a call for the overhaul of current thinking and practice on the subject.

KUTCHINS, HERB, AND STUART A. KIRK. *Making Us Crazy: DSM—The Psychiatric Bible and the Creation of Mental Disorders.* New York: The Free Press, 1997. A good discussion on how to influence trends in mental disorders.

MARKOWITZ, GERALD, AND DAVID ROSNER. *Deceit and Denial: The Deadly Politics of Industrial Pollution.* Berkeley, CA: University of California Press, 2003. A review of how the lead and plastic industries produce toxic pollution and the costs involved.

MISHAN, E. J. *The Economic Growth Debate: An Assessment.* London: Allen & Unwin, 1977. A widely cited timeless source on the costs of economic growth.

ROPEIK, DAVID, AND GEORGE GRAY. *Risk: A Practical Guide for Deciding What's Really Safe and What's Dangerous in the World Around You.* Boston: Houghton Mifflin, 2002. An excellent overview of risks that rivet attention and raise anxiety levels as part of the costs of change.

SAGOFF, MARK. "Do We Consume Too Much?" *The Atlantic Monthly,* June 1997, pp. 80–96. A provocative article in support of economic growth and a continued high rate of consumption. The arguments are quite different from the ones presented in this chapter, and the article should be consulted for other perspectives.

UNITED NATIONS ENVIRONMENT PROGRAMME. *Global Environment Outlook 3.* New York: Oxford University Press, 2002. A comprehensive United Nations report on the status of the global environment as part of the ongoing world-wide environmental assessment process.

WORLD RESOURCES INSTITUTE. *World Resources: A Guide to the Global Environment: The Urban Environment, 1998–99.* New York: Oxford University Press, 1999. An overview of economic, social and environmental trends of urban areas. A good source for comparative data on a variety of issues.

REFERENCES

ACKERMAN, FRANK. *Why Do We Recycle? Markets, Values, and Public Policy.* Washington, DC: Island Press, 1997.

ADAM, BARBARA. *Timescapes of Modernity: The Environment and Invisible Hazards.* New York: Routledge, 1998.

ADLER, LEONORE LOEB, AND UWE P. GIELEN (eds.). *Migration, Immigration and Emigration in International Perspective.* Westport, CT: Prager, 2002.

AMIN, SAMAR. "In Praise of Socialism," *Monthly Review,* 26, September 1974, pp. 1–16.

ANDREWS, FRANK M. (ed.). *Research on the Quality of Life.* Ann Arbor: Survey Research Center, Institute for Social Research, The University of Michigan, 1986.

BAKER, KEVIN. "Recycling in New York," *The New York Times,* January 5, 2003, p. 12WK.

BECKER, GAVIN DE. *The Gift of Fear: Survival Signals That Protect Us From Violence.* New York: Little, Brown, 1997.

BENSMAN, JOSEPH, AND ARTHUR J. VIDICH. *American Society: The Welfare State & Beyond,* rev. ed. South Hadley, MA: Bergin & Garvey, 1987.

BERG, IVAR, AND MARCIA FREEDMAN. "The American Work Place: Illusions and Realities," *Change,* November 1977, pp. 24–30.

BERGER, PETER L. *Pyramids of Sacrifice, Political Ethics, and Social Change.* New York: Basic Books, 1974.

BERNSTEIN, RICHARD. *Dictatorship of Virtue: Multiculturalism and the Battle for America's Future.* New York: Knopf, 1994.

BLACK, CYRIL EDWIN. "Change as a Condition of Modern Life." In Myron Weiner (ed.), *Modernization: The Dynamics of Growth*. New York: Basic Books, 1966, pp. 17–27.

BROWN, LESTER R. *In the Human Interest: A Strategy to Stabilize World Population*. New York: W. W. Norton, 1974.

BROWN, LESTER R. (ed.). *State of the World 2001*. London: Earthscan, 2001.

BROWN, LESTER R., MICHAEL RENNER, AND CHRISTOPHER FLAVIN. *Vital Signs—1997. The Environmental Trends That Are Shaping Our Future*. New York: W.W. Norton & Company, 1997.

BROWNE, MALCOLM W. "World Threat of Plastic Trash Defies Technological Solution," *The New York Times*, September 6, 1987, p. 16E.

COMMONER, BARRY A. *The Closing Circle*. New York: Knopf, 1971.

CORNISH, EDWARD. "Deliver Us From Gloom," *The Futurist*, 31 (1) January–February 1997, pp. 8–9.

DAVIS, DEVRA. *When Smoke Ran Like Water: Tales of Environmental Deception and the Battle Against Pollution*. New York: Basic Books, 2003.

DERSHOWITZ, ALAN M. *The Abuse Excuse, and Other Cop-outs, Sob Stories, and Evasions of Responsibility*. Boston: Little, Brown and Company, 1994.

DURNING, ALAN THEIN. "Redesigning the Forest Economy." In Lester R. Brown (ed.), *State of the World 1994*. New York: W. W. Norton, 1994, pp. 22–40.

EASTERBROOK, GREGG. "Forget PCB's. Radon. Alar. The World's Greatest Environmental Dangers are Dung Smoke and Dirty Water," *The New York Times Magazine*, September 11, 1994, pp. 60–63.

Economist. "Take a Deep Breath," September 17, 1994a, pp. 91–93.

Economist. "Workaholics Anonymous: Why Do Americans Work So Hard?" October 22, 1994b, p. 20.

Economist. "Europe's Mid-life Crisis: A Survey of the European Union," May 31, 1997, pp. 1–18.

Economist. "The Longest Journey: A Survey of Migration," November 2, 2002, pp. 1–16.

ELLUL, JACQUES. *The Technological Society*. New York: Knopf, 1964.

ELSOM, DEREK. *Smog Alert: Managing Urban Air Quality*. London: Earthscan, 1996.

FISCHER, CLAUDE S. *The Urban Experience*, 2nd ed. New York: Harcourt, 1984.

FLAVIN, CHRISTOPHER. "Reassessing Nuclear Power." In Lester R. Brown (ed.), *State of the World 1997*. New York: W. W. Norton, 1997, pp. 57–80.

FLEMING, MACKLIN. *The Price of Perfect Justice*. New York: Basic Books, 1974.

Forbes. "The High Cost of Stress," July 27, 1987, p. 12.

FRIED, MARC. "Effects of Social Change on Mental Health." In David R. Heise (ed.), *Personality and Socialization*. Chicago: Rand McNally, 1972, pp. 451–468.

GABOR, DENNIS. *Innovations: Scientific, Technological, and Social*. New York: Oxford, 1970.

GHIMIRE, KRISHNA B., AND MICHEL P. PIMBERT (eds.). *Social Change and Conservation: Environmental Politics and Impacts of National Parks and Protected Areas*. London: Earthscan, 2000.

GOULET, DENIS. *The Cruel Choice: A New Concept in the Theory of Development*. Lanham, MD: University Press of America, 1985.

GREENHOUSE, STEVEN. "Comparing Wealth as Money Fluctuates," *The New York Times*, August 23, 1987, p. 3E.

GUGLIOTTA, GUY. "Massive Shell to Cover Remains of Chernobyl," *The Seattle Times*, January 3, 2003, pp. A1, A10.

HAAG, BERNADINE (ed.). *Sham: Social Change Through Contrived Crises*. Sahuarita, AZ: Sahuarita Press, 1994.

HAMILTON, RICHARD F., AND JAMES D. WRIGHT. *The State of the Masses*. New York: Aldine, 1986.

HARDIN, GARRETT. *Exploring New Ethics for Survival: The Voyage of the Spaceship Beagle*. Baltimore: Penguin, 1975.

HARF, JAMES E., AND B. THOMAS TROUT. *The Politics of Global Resources: Population, Food, Energy, and Environment*. Durham, NC: Duke University Press, 1986.

HARRIS, LOUIS. *The Anguish of Change*. New York: W. W. Norton, 1973.

HELLER, WALTER W. "Coming to Terms with Growth and the Environment." In Sam H. Schurr (ed.), *Energy, Economic Growth, and the Environment*. Baltimore: Johns Hopkins University Press, 1972, pp. 3–29.

HEMPEL, LAMONT C. *Environmental Governance: The Global Challenge*. Washington, DC: Island Press, 1996.

HEMPHILL, CLARA. "Admissions Anxiety," *The New York Times*, November 17, 2002, p. WK11.

HILLARY, EDMUND (ed.). *Ecology 2000: The Changing Face of Earth*. New York: Beaufort Books, 1984.

HOCHSCHILD, ARLIE RUSSELL. *The Time Bond, When Work Becomes Home and Home Becomes Work*. New York: Metropolitan Books/Henry Holt and Company, 1997.

HONAN, WILLIAM H. "Acorns Sprout Where Mighty Oaks Grew," *The New York Times*, October 16, 1994, p. E3.

HOPGOOD, MEI-LING. "Growth's Cost: Stuck in Traffic, Congestion's Price in Area Estimated at $1 Million a Day," *St. Louis Post-Dispatch*, July 7, 1997, pp. 1–2B.

Human Development Report, 2002. Published for the United Nations Development Programme. New York: Oxford, 2002.

INGLEHART, RONALD, AND JACQUES-RÉNEE RABIER. "Aspirations Adapt to Situations—But Why Are the Belgians So Much Happier Than the French? A Cross-Cultural Analysis of the Subjective Quality of Life." In Frank M. Andrews (ed.), *Research on the Quality of Life*. Ann Arbor: Survey Research Center, Institute for Social Research, The University of Michigan, 1986, pp. 1–56.

INKELES, ALEX, AND DAVID H. SMITH. *Becoming Modern: Individual Change in Six Developing Countries*. Cambridge, MA: Harvard University Press, 1974.

KANE, HAL. "Traffic Accidents Taking Many Lives." In Lester R. Brown, Hal Kane, and David Malin Roodman (eds.), *Vital Signs—1994*. New York: W. W. Norton, 1994, pp. 132–133.

KAPP, WILLIAM K. *The Social Costs of Private Enterprise*. New York: Schocken Books, 1971.

KENNEDY, PAUL. "The (Relative) Decline of America," *The Atlantic Monthly*, August 1987, pp. 29–38.

KLAPP, ORRIN E. *Overload and Boredom: Essays on the Quality of Life in the Information Society*. Westport, CT: Greenwood Press, 1986.

KLERMAN, GERALD L. (ed.). *Suicide and Depression Among Adolescents and Young Adults*. Washington, DC: American Psychiatric Press, 1986.

KUTCHINS, HERB, AND STUART A. KIRK. *Making Us Crazy: DSM—The Psychiatric Bible and the Creation of Mental Disorders*. New York: The Free Press, 1997.

LAMB, KEVIN. "IQ and PC (Intelligent Quotient, Political Correctness)," *National Review*, 49 (1) January 1997, pp. 39–43.

LAMPMAN, ROBERT. "Recent U.S. Economic Growth and the Gain in Human Welfare." In Walter W. Heller (ed.), *Perspectives on Economic Growth*. New York: Random House, 1968, pp. 143–162.

LAUER, ROBERT H., AND RANCE THOMAS. "A Comparative Analysis of Psychological Consequences of Change," *Human Relations*, 29 (3) 1976, pp. 239–248.

LAWTON, POWELL M. "Measures of Quality of Life and Subjective Well-Being," *Generations*, 21 (1) Spring 1997, pp. 45–48.

LEHMAN, NICHOLAS. "It's Not as Bad as You Think It Is: Misguided Handwringing About Our Society's Decline Distracts Us from the Real Crises," *Washington Monthly*, 29 (3) March 1997, pp. 12–14.

LENSKI, GERHARD, PATRICK NOLAN, AND JEAN LENSKI. *Human Societies: An Introduction to Macrosociology*, 8th ed. New York: McGraw-Hill Book, 1999.

LEO, JOHN. "Put on a Sappy Face," *U.S. News & World Report*, November 25, 2002, p. 52.

LEWIS, DAN A., AND GRETA SALEM. *Fear of Crime: Incivility and the Production of a Social Problem*. New Brunswick, NJ: Transaction Books, 1986.

LEWIS, W. ARTHUR. *The Theory of Economic Growth*. London: Allen & Unwin, 1956.

LITTLE, ROBERT. "The Former Exxon Valdez Faces Retirement," *The Seattle Times*, October 17, 2002, pp. A12, A13.

LOWE, MARCIA D. "Reinventing Transport." In Lester R. Brown (ed.), *State of the World 1994*. New York: W. W. Norton, 1994, pp. 81–98.

MAGUIRE, KATHLEEN, AND ANN L. PASTORE (eds.). *Sourcebook of Criminal Justice Statistics—1996*. Washington, DC: U.S. Department of Justice, Bureau of Justice Statistics, 1997.

MARKOWITZ, GERALD, AND DAVID ROSNER. *Deceit and Denial: The Deadly Politics of Industrial Pollution*. Berkeley, CA: University of California Press, 2003.

MARTIN, T. R. "In Pursuit of Happiness: Sources of American Discontent," *Commonweal*, 123 (4) February 23, 1996, pp. 15–17.

MASLOW, ABRAHAM. "Psychological Data and Value Theory." In Abraham Maslow (ed.), *New Knowledge in Human Values*. New York: Harper & Row, 1959, pp. 119–136.

MCILROY, ANNE. "Extinction Estimate for Plants Surges. Old Figure Left Out Species in Tropics," *The Globe and Mail*, November 1, 2002, p. A5.

MILGRAM, STANLEY. "The Experience of Living in Cities," *Science*, 167, March 13, 1970, pp. 1461–1468.

MISCH, ANN. "Assessing Environmental Health Risks." In Lester R. Brown (ed.), *State of the World 1994*. New York: W. W. Norton, 1994, pp. 117–136.

MISHAN, EZRA J. *The Costs of Economic Growth*. New York: Praeger, 1967.

MISHAN, EZRA J. *The Economic Growth Debate: An Assessment*. London: G. Allen, 1977.

Newsweek. "Primates Family Report," October 14, 2002, p. 10.

PARETO, VILFREDO. *The Mind and Society*, vol. 4, trans. Andrew Bongiorno. Arthur Livingston (ed.). New York: Harcourt, 1935.

PLATT, ANNE E. "Fish Catch Stable." In Lester R. Brown, Hal Kane, and David Malin Roodman (eds.), *Vital Signs—1994*. New York: W. W. Norton, 1994, pp. 32–33.

POSTEL, SANDRA. "Carrying Capacity: Earth's Bottom Line." In Lester R. Brown (ed.), *State of the World 1994*. New York: W. W. Norton, 1994, pp. 3–21.

POWERS, CHARLES H. *Vilfredo Pareto*. Beverly Hills, CA: Sage Publications, 1987.

Rhoads, Christopher. "Short Work Hours Undercut Europe in Economic Drive. Culture That Values Leisure Now Finds It an Obstacle; Jobs Are Going Elsewhere. Taking 9½ Weeks of Vacation," *The Wall Street Journal*, August 8, 2002, pp. A1, A5.

Rice, Robert W., Michael R. Frone, and Dean B. McFarlin. "Work–Nonwork Conflict and the Perceived Quality of Life," *Journal of Organizational Behavior*, 13, March 1992, pp. 155–168.

Robins, Lee N., and Darrel A. Regier. *Psychiatric Disorders in America*. New York: Free Press, 1991.

Ropeik, David, and George Gray. *Risk: A Practical Guide for Deciding What's Really Safe and What's Dangerous in the World Around You*. Boston: Houghton Mifflin, 2002.

Roszak, Theodore. *Politics and Transcendence in Postindustrial Society*. New York: Doubleday (Anchor Books), 1973.

Sagoff, Mark. "Do We Consume Too Much?" *The Atlantic Monthly*, June 1997, pp. 80–96.

Schipper, Lee. "Life-Styles and the Environment: The Case of Energy," *Daedalus*, 125 (3) Summer 1996, pp. 113–139.

Schlosser, Eric. *Fast Food Nation: The Dark Side of the All-American Meal*. New York: Perennial, 2002.

Schor, Juliet B. *The Overworked American: The Unexpected Decline of Leisure*. New York: Basic Books, 1992.

Scitovsky, Tibor. *Papers on Welfare and Growth*. Stanford, CA: Stanford University Press, 1964.

Seabrook, John. "The Slow Lane. Can Anyone Solve the Problem of Traffic?" *The New Yorker*, September 2, 2002, pp. 120–129.

Shabecoff, Philip. "Toxic Waste Threat Termed Greater Than U.S. Estimate," *The New York Times*, March 10, 1985, pp. 1, 31.

Simons, Marlise. "Capitalist or Communist, the Air Is Still Bad. Eastern Europe Breathes the Air of Freedom, and Chokes," *The New York Times*, November 3, 1994, pp. A1, A6.

Smothers, Ronald. "Study Concludes That Environmental and Economic Health Are Compatible," *The New York Times*, October 19, 1994, p. C18.

Spates, James L., and John J. Macionis. *The Sociology of Cities*, 2nd ed. Belmont, CA: Wadsworth, 1987.

St. Louis Post-Dispatch. "Changing Rainfall Patterns May Signal Agriculture Shift," July 12, 1987a, p. 9B.

St. Louis Post-Dispatch. "Study Calls Mining Riskiest Job in U.S.," July 24, 1987b, p. 4B.

Stabile, Donald R. "Accountants and the Price System: The Problem of Social Costs," *Journal of Economic Issues*, 27 (1) March 1993, pp. 171–189.

Stevens, William K. "Green Revolution Is Not Enough, Study Finds," *The New York Times*, September 6, 1994, p. B9.

Sundquist, James L. *Dispersing Population: What America Can Learn from Europe*. Washington, DC: Brookings, 1975.

Sussman, Marvin B. (ed.). *Author's Guide to Journals in Sociology and Related Fields*. New York: Haworth Press, 1978.

Takaki, Ronald (ed.). *From Different Shores: Perspectives on Race and Ethnicity in America*, 2nd ed. New York: Oxford, 1994.

The New Republic. "The Case for Book Burning," September 14/21, 1987, pp. 7–8.

TYLER, PATRICK A. "A Tide of Pollution Threatens China's Prosperity," *The New York Times,* September 25, 1994, p. 16.

UCHITELLE, LOUIS. "A Degree's Shrinking Returns, College-Educated Men Slipping in Pay," *The New York Times*, September 5, 1994, p. Y17–18.

UCHITELLE, LOUIS. "How to Succeed in Politics Without Really Working," *The New York Times*, June 22, 1997, p. E3.

UNITED NATIONS ENVIRONMENT PROGRAMME. *Global Environment Outlook 3.* New York: Oxford University Press, 2002.

UPDERGRAVE, WALTER L. "You're Safer than You Think," *Money,* June 1994, pp. 114–124.

U.S. News & World Report. "Jam Sessions," September 7, 1987b, pp. 20–27.

VERHOVEK, SAM HOWE. "Pipeline Rupture Spreading Hot Oil in Russian Arctic, 2-Million-Gallon Spill," *The New York Times,* October 25, 1994, pp. A1, A6.

WALD, MATTHEW L. "Anger Cited in 28,000 Road Deaths a Year," *The New York Times*, July 18, 1997, p. A10.

WEBER, PETER. *Net Loss: Fish, Jobs, and the Marine Environment.* Worldwatch Paper 120. Washington, DC: Worldwatch Institute, July 1994.

WEISBERG, BARRY. *Beyond Repair: The Ecology of Capitalism.* Boston: Beacon Press, 1971.

WILSON, JAMES Q. *Moral Judgement: Does the Abuse Excuse Threaten Our Legal System?* New York: Basic Books, 1997.

Wilson Quarterly. "Eroding the Great Plains," 3 (1) Winter 1979, pp. 41–42.

WIRTH, LOUIS. "Urbanism as a Way of Life," *American Journal of Sociology,* 44, July 1938, pp. 1–24.

Work in America. Cambridge, MA: MIT Press, 1973.

World Bank World Development Report 2003: Infrastructure for Development. Washington, DC: The World Bank, 2003.

WORLD RESOURCES INSTITUTE. *World Resources: A Guide to the Global Environment: The Urban Environment, 1998–99.* New York: Oxford University Press, 1999.

YABLONSKY, LEWIS. *Robopaths.* Indianapolis: Bobbs-Merrill, 1972.

YOUNG, JOHN E., AND AARON SACHS. *The Next Efficiency Revolution: Creating a Sustainable Materials Economy.* Worldwatch Paper 121. Washington, DC: Worldwatch Institute, September 1994.

YOUTH, HOWARD. "Birds Are in Decline." In Lester R. Brown, Hal Kane, and David Malin Roodman (eds.), *Vital Signs—1994.* New York: W. W. Norton, 1994, pp. 128–129.

ZIJDERVELD, ANTON C. *The Abstract Society: A Cultural Analysis of Our Time.* New York: Doubleday (Anchor Books), 1971.

Chapter 9
Strategies of Change

This chapter considers the ways of bringing about change at various levels in society. At no other period in history has there been so much preoccupation with social change as at the dawn of the twenty-first century. Accompanying this preoccupation with change is a marked theoretical and practical interest in change strategies and tactics. In many areas of social life in which change is not occurring, or taking place too slowly, there is often a great concern about how to stimulate or accelerate change. Demands for social change come from a variety of sources, and there is a growing emphasis on creating, guiding, directing, and managing change. There are also demands to develop new methods, to refine existing ones, and to translate theoretical knowledge into practical applications. At the outset, it should be remembered that strategies and tactics are neutral processes, with value judgments entering into the picture during their applications. More often than not, leading social change at any level can be a difficult and politically dangerous act. These risks increase if a change effort under consideration challenges established societal or organizational norms and values or is considered controversial (see, for example, Austin, 1997). Finally, the various ways of creating changes in society may be approved or deplored (Is revolution "good" or "bad"?), or considered with scientific detachment. But there is no way of denying their importance.

The consequences of a particular change may be beneficial to one party and detrimental to another. The concepts of benefits and detriments are often relative and are also value judgments on someone's part, and "any manipulation of human behavior inherently violates a fundamental value, but . . . there exists no formula for so structuring an effective change situation that such manipulation is totally absent" (Kelman, 1972:575). People often feel that things are just not quite the way they ought to be and advocate and express a need for change. Invariably there will be others who oppose that advocated change. For example, population control is debated, advocated, and resisted both at the village level in underdeveloped countries and in high government offices. In some areas, court-ordered school desegregation is found to reinforce what it was intended to abolish. Heated and emotional discussions abound on both sides of the gun control and abortion issues. At the same time, as a result of purposeful, directed change efforts, important strides have occurred in the delivery of health care; there is a noticeable decline in sex discrimination and in infant mortality; and important advancements have been made in reducing racial discrimination, at least in the United States.

This chapter will examine a series of social-change strategies (plans of action or policy) and tactics (specific means or techniques that stem from a strategy) used in a variety of change efforts at several levels. This chapter is designed to provide a greater understanding of the general targets, agents, and methods of planned social change and to analyze the roles of violence and nonviolence, social movements, and the law in creating change.

TARGETS, AGENTS, AND METHODS OF PLANNED SOCIAL CHANGE

Planned social change refers to deliberate, conscious, and collaborative efforts by change agents to improve the operations of social systems (Bennis, Benne, & Chin, 1985:3). In the social-change literature, planned change has been referred to as social planning, social engineering, change management, or social marketing (Zaltman, Kotler, & Kaufman, 1972:2). Three fundamental issues are involved in the analysis of planned social change. The first has to do with the target of the change, the second with the agents of the change effort, and the third with the methods that will be utilized in the change effort. In the following pages, these three components of planned social change—targets, agents, and methods—will be examined.

Targets of Change

Planned social change usually begins as an effort to solve a problem or to rectify a situation. After the identification of the type of change desired, it is necessary to give attention to the system level on which the change is sought. Change may be sought on the individual level, or, at the other extreme, it may be change of social structural arrangements rather than simply of individuals. There is an infinite number of gradations between the individual and societal levels, and it is therefore helpful to designate the level of the system that is to be changed—that is, to identify the target system. Obviously, the nature of the target system is related to the methods to be used in bringing about change. For example, strategies used to effect change in an organization may be utterly ineffective in producing changes in individual behavior.

Various target systems have been identified for planned social change. Roland L. Warren (1977:56) incorporates four target systems—individuals, organizations, communities, and societies—in his widely used model of purposive change. Harvey H. Hornstein and associates (1971) discuss a number of change targets, including individuals and organizational structures. They have identified five aspects of individual functioning that are frequent targets of change strategies: feelings, values, attitudes, perceptions, and skills, and actions (overt behavior) (1971:15). They broke down the target system of organizational structure into three common targets of change: (1) social characteristics, including group size and composition in terms of identifiable individual features such as intelligence, manual dexterity, and authoritarianism, structure of authority, status hierarchy, incentive systems, and formal channels of communication; (2) environmental characteristics, including spatial relations among group members and other features of physical setting; and (3) task characteristics, such as special task demands (that is, manual skill, knowledge, or creative ability), task difficulty, and the degree to which the task is specific or vague in prescribing behavior necessary for its completion (1971:149).

Gerald Zaltman and Robert Duncan (1977:10–11), in *Strategies for Planned Change*, include time dimension in addition to the level of society that is the target of the change. The time dimension is obviously arbitrary, and can range from a short term of a few days or months to a long term of several months or years. Table 9.1 recapitulates the six types of change identified on the basis of these two dimensions.

At the micro, or individual, level, there may be short-term changes in attitudes and behavior (Type 1). An illustration of this change would be the use of sensitivity training to alter a person's attitudes. An illustration of a

TABLE 9.1 Time Dimensions and Target Levels

	Level of Society		
Time Dimension	Micro (Individual)	Intermediate (Group)	Macro (Society)
Short term	Type 1 (1) Attitude change (2) Behavior change	Type 3 (1) Normative (2) Administrative change	Type 5 Invention or innovation
Long term	Type 2 Life-cycle change	Type 4 Organizational change	Type 6 Sociocultural evolution

more long-term type of change at the microlevel (Type 2) is the training and socialization process of new recruits in an institution. Priests, for example, when they start their training program, learn a new set of attitudes and behavior that affects their entire lives. At the group or intermediate level of short-term change, normative or administrative change may be brought about. *Normative changes* take place when a group alters its norms temporarily to experiment with an innovation (Type 3). For example, in a corporation a team sets up a novel computerized information bank. Team members are given freedom to experiment, and they can bend established organizational rules. The change agent—in this case, the manager responsible for the innovation—encourages the team. Once the innovation has been tried and found useful, it is institutionalized (Kanter, 1983:234). At this point, it will become a more long-term change (Type 4) at the organizational level. The original participants in the change effort will be rewarded, this process then providing incentives for others to experiment.

At the societal level of change, short-term (Type 5) change is often the result of innovations or inventions. For example, the introduction of birth-control technology in a receptive society can alter birth rates and population size in a relatively short time. In the long run, these changes could result in major changes in the social structure of the society. The long-term consequences are (Type 6) sociocultural change—that is, the facilitation of the modernization process in an underdeveloped nation.

In the literature on planned social change, there is also a distinction between the *change target system* and the *change client system*. The former is seen as the unit in which the change agent is trying to alter the status quo such that the individual, group, or organization must relearn how to perform its activities. The latter is the individual or group requesting assistance from a change agent in altering the status quo. At times they are identical. In other instances, they can be separate entities, such as parents seeking psychiatric help for their child. In this case, the parents represent clients, the therapist the change agent, and the child the change target. The important point in distinguishing between the change target system and the change client system is that change agents may try to influence some system in which there is no support or wish for assistance in any change (Zaltman & Duncan, 1977:18).

There is no commonly accepted typology of change targets in the literature. Most typologies, however, include an individual level; an intermediate level dealing with groups, communities, and organizations; and macrolevel target systems. Let us consider each of them separately.

Individuals as Change Targets There are two ways of looking at individuals as change targets. In the first instance, it can be assumed that individual change is the principal mediator of social and organizational change. Changing of the various aspects of the individual is considered as a stepping-stone to other types of changes—particularly in groups and organizations. The assumption is that, because groups and organizations are made up of individuals, it is individuals who can bring about change in the systems in which they are members. Thus, a change on an individual level can be evaluated in terms of its possible benefits and usefulness to the system of which they are members.

When the individuals are the target of planned change, a number of diverse strategies may be deployed. As an extreme illustration, "At Atascadero State Mental Hospital in California, homosexual child molesters are trained to cruise in gay bars so they will not have to resort to children; heterosexual child molesters are taught to pick up women at parties; and rapists are coached in sex techniques to improve their relationships with their wives" (Sage, 1977:79). This strategy of planned change is labeled behavior modification. Three general techniques are involved in *behavior modification:* those that work with negative reinforcers (punishments for undesirable behavior); those that use positive reinforcers (rewards for desirable behavior); and those that attempt to undermine the subject's character structure. In addition, behavior-modification programs may include drugs, hypnosis, electroconvulsive shock, brainwashing, and, in extreme cases, psychosurgery. Behavior modification is being used in a variety of institutional settings, such as schools, mental hospitals, and prisons, to change a large assortment of behavior "with remarkable success" (Albrecht, Chadwick, & Jacobson, 1987:17).

Behavior modification is obviously only one of the many strategies for changing individuals. Depending on the kind of change desired, and whether it is to be implemented on a one-to-one basis or in a small-group situation, one may choose from the arsenal of psychoanalytical, social-psychological, or educational strategies. The social sciences can offer a broad spectrum of technologies, stemming from several theoretical assumptions, which can be used with varying effectiveness with individual change targets.

Intermediate Target Systems The group has come to occupy an increasingly strategic place, both as a medium and as a target of planned social change (Benne, 1985:75). The link between the individual and the larger social system is the group. This is particularly true in a formal organization such as the army. The individual's membership in a squad or tank crew is one's link to the larger army. Similarly, students are linked to the larger school system through the classroom, student government, or a varsity sports team. In a less obvious fashion, the same is true of individuals' linkage with less formally organized systems such as the community, and racial and ethnic groupings. Therefore, the group is a medium for influencing both the individuals who are its members and the larger system of which their group is a part.

Kenneth D. Benne (1985:75) points out that larger social systems usually depend on small groups in formulating and shaping their policies and programs, whether a committee, cabinet, or board. Change in the composition and functioning of such a group can also produce change in the wider social system that is dependent upon that group for direction and guidance. Consequently, the management of small-group activities and processes is an important target in planned social change.

At the community level, intergroup relations are often the target of planned social change (Kettner, Daley, & Nichols, 1985). In many instances, the object is to change the relations between racial, ethnic, and religious groups. These relationships are often marked by strong feelings of fear and hostility and by historically embedded stereotypes. At times, changes can be effective in such intergroup relations by changing the composition of group members. For example, an important study on interracial housing by Morton Deutsch and Mary Evans Collins (1965) shows that integrated housing projects had a positive impact on relations between the races and on the attitudes of white women toward their black neighbors. White women in the integrated projects were more likely to have contact with black women, to have black friends, and to engage in neighborhood activities with blacks than were white women in segregated projects. In addition, women in the integrated projects were more likely to express positive attitudes toward blacks and, on the basis of recall, were more likely to report a positive change in attitude since living in the projects. Deutsch and Collins note that the success of such changes is enhanced when supportive attitudes from the wider community are forthcoming.

In many cases the target of planned change is the organization, where attempts are made to improve internal communications, increase efficiency, work satisfaction, and productivity (Hall, 2002). Of course, the various organizations can have specific client systems as change targets. For example, family-planning associations see the mothers and the public at large as the target, and the various antidrug groups view actual and potential users as the target. The American Heart Association sees smokers and overweight people, among others, as the target.

Macrolevel Target Systems Affecting changes in macrosystems or in the structure of society is obviously much more difficult than in microlevel or intermediate-level target systems. Targets at that level would include attempts to change national policies, cultural patterns, resolving issues between nations, attempts at modernization, industrialization, urbanization, nation building, altering statuses of minority groups, and the like. At the macrolevel, in many instances, there are highly complex target systems. In many cases it is very difficult to identify such complex target systems except in the most general terms. This dilemma is epitomized in the popular expression, "Let's change the whole system." In some instances, however, target systems at the macrolevel may be clearly identified. This is the case, for example, with national policies dealing with certain aspects of society, such as agriculture, the economy, or formal educational systems. At times, efforts are directed only at a segment of one of these factors, for example, energy policy, aid to the unemployed, the minimum wage, child health programs, and farm mortgage policies. In other instances, there are efforts to deal with a segment of the society, such as the poor, as evidenced by a multitude of legislative undertakings on poverty. Additional macrolevel target systems will be further discussed under the headings of Social Movements, and Law and Social Change, in this chapter.

Change Agents

In planned social change, change agents are professionals who influence, promote and implement innovation decisions in a direction considered desirable by an organization or a community (Indergaard, 1997). Change agents may be external or internal to the social system in which change is desired, and the change desired may also be classified as external or internal in origin (Zaltman & Duncan, 1977:187). To achieve change, there must be organization. Ideally, the change effort should be compatible with the values of the target population, and the organization itself should be accepted by society (Hall, 2002).

Philip Kotler (1972:177–178) points out that change agents fall into two groups: leaders and supporters. The leaders include six types of persons: (1) the *directors*, who started or head the organization and wield the power; (2) the *advocates*, who wield the pen rather than the power but are close to those in power; (3) the *backers*, who provide the purse and supply the financial resources to keep the organization going; (4) the *technicians*, who, as employees or volunteers, provide professional advice or service, for example, public relations specialists, professional fundraisers, advertising practitioners, community organizers, lawyers, and management consultants; (5) the *administrators*, who run the day-to-day affairs of the organization; and, finally, (6) the *organizers*, who have effective skills in enlisting supporters and running the programs and campaigns.

The supporters include: (1) the *workers*, who are committed enough to the particular change efforts to give their time to it; (2) the *donors*, who make contributions of money rather than time to the cause; and, finally, (3) a much larger group of *sympathizers*, who neither work nor give much money to the cause but talk about it supportively.

Everett M. Rogers (1972:196–197) identifies several functions of the change agent, including developing a recognition for need for change among the clients; establishing a change relationship with them; diagnosing the client's problem; examining the client's goals and alternatives, then creating the intent to change in the client; encouraging the client to innovate;

stabilizing the change behavior so as to prevent discontinuance; and, finally, achieving a terminal relationship with the client.

In addition, Zaltman and Duncan (1977:185–224) note that in situations where an organization has defined the problems for the change agent and established the objectives of the change effort, the change agent should be sensitive to the needs and perspectives of the change target system in seeking solutions to change situations; should always seek the simplest solution when working with a change problem; should have administrative capabilities; should strive to maintain good interpersonal relations with persons and the change target system; should be sensitive to and tolerant of constraints; should have self-confidence and a positive self-image to accept setbacks; should be able to define the change program in a fashion that is effective to the various participants of the change program; and, finally, should try to maximize cooperation with members of the change target system.

Methods of Planned Social Change

In the literature on planned social change, there is no definitive method for categorizing the various strategies of change. Consequently, various authors on the topic use labels that are somewhat arbitrary and, on many occasions, overlap. Moreover, in many change situations, the change agent is likely to utilize multiple change strategies to accomplish the desired objective in the context of unique configurations and characteristics of change targets (see, for example, Robertson and Seneviratne, 1995). It is also conceivable that a change agent may resort to a sequence of strategies over time, again depending on the particular change situation. With this in mind, let us now examine some of the principal change strategies.

A most comprehensive review of change strategies for affecting changes in human systems is presented by Robert Chin and Kenneth D. Benne (1985). They emphasize that a common element in all approaches to planned change is the conscious utilization and application of knowledge as an instrument for altering patterns and institutions of practices. Although their orientation is primarily toward educational change, the strategies they discuss are applicable to many different types of planned change situations. They identify three broad categories of strategies: empirical-rational, normative-reeducative, and power-coercive.

The *empirical-rational strategies* are based on the assumption that people are rational and that they follow their rational self-interests once these are revealed to them. The emphasis of this category is on changing individuals. With regard to educational change, empirical-rational strategies include such activities as basic research and dissemination of knowledge to general education, personal selection and replacement, the use of systems analysts as staff and consultants, and applied research and the development of linkage systems for diffusing its findings. They also include utopian thinking as a strategy of change in the form of future scenarios and an emphasis on more adequate communication in interpersonal relationships.

The *normative-reeducative* strategies are based on the assumption that change will occur only as the individuals involved are brought to change their normative orientations to old patterns and develop commitments to new ones. Such changes involve changes in attitudes, values, skills, and significant relationships. Such approaches to effecting change "bring direct interventions by change agents, interventions based on a consciously worked out theory of change and of changing, into the life of a client system, be that system a person, a small group, an organization, or a community" (Chin & Benne, 1985:32). These change strategies have a number of common elements. For example, the emphasis on the client system and its perception of its own problem and the need for change; an assumption that such problems are seldom purely technical, having a group dynamic component; the notion of a change agent collaborating with the client who is the change target; the attempt to uncover nonconscious elements that are impeding the problem solution, so that they may be dealt with; and the selective use of knowledge from the behavioral sciences. "These approaches center in the notion that people technology is just as necessary as thing technology in working out desirable changes in human affairs" (Chin & Benne, 1985:33). They are used, for example, at the organizational level to improve problem-solving capabilities, methods of conflict resolution, and communication, and to increase organizational effectiveness and efficiency.

The *power-coercive* strategies are based on the application of economic, political, or moral power. Although the accent is more often on political and economic sanctions, Chin and Benne point out that strategies of nonviolence fit this category through the application of moral power. They also include the use of political institutions and law to achieve change. Similarly, they include efforts to manipulate or reconstitute "power elites." It is suggested that this last approach is justified only when it is necessary to remove barriers to accomplishing change through democratically and scientifically oriented methods.

As a refinement of one of the three strategies discussed by Chin and Benne, Ronald Lippitt and his associates (1958) apply the normative-reeducative strategy to four different types of client systems: individuals, small groups, large organizations, and communities. It should be noted that their method of change is limited to situations in which an individual, group, organization, or community engages a consultant as change agent in order to help it change itself. They developed a model to fit this relationship between a client system and a change agent acting as consultant. It is based on five phases: (1) development of a need for change ("unfreezing"); (2) establishment of a change relationship; (3) working toward change ("moving"); (4) generalization and stabilization of change ("freezing"); and (5) achieving a terminal relationship (Lippitt, Watson, & Westley, 1958:130).

From a different perspective, Richard E. Walton (1972) distinguishes between the power strategy and the attitude change strategy. The *power* strategy is based on the assumption that the way to bring about change is to build a power base and manipulate that power strategically. The *attitude change* strategy is based on the notion that the desired behavior change will be best produced through attitude change, based on a growth of trust and goodwill.

In an approach to develop strategies for social action, Philip Kotler (1972:183–184) identifies three basic ways in which a change agent can attempt to influence a change target: by coercion (power), persuasion, or education.

The *power* strategy attempts to bring about change in the target through the use of agent-controlled sanctions. In such situations, change agents are primarily concerned with changing the behavior rather than the beliefs or values of the change target. They seek changes through sanctions such as authority, force, or payment. Change agents in a position of authority (managers over workers, army officers over draftees, judges over defendants) attempt to bring about change by withholding rewards or administering punishment. If the change agent has no authority over the change target, two possibilities exist. If the agent views the target as an enemy, the power strategy may take the form of force or threat of force—demonstration, noncooperation, or violence. The second option entails the use of payment (gifts or bribes) to bring about the desired behavior.

Kotler's second way of bringing about change is through a *persuasion* strategy, which attempts to induce the desired behavior in the target through identifying the social object with the change agent's existing beliefs or values. The change agent seeks to find arguments that indicate that the desired behavior serves the natural interests of the change targets. Based on the Aristotelian approach, three persuasive arguments are possible: *logos*, or appeals to logic; *pathos*, or appeals to emotions; and *ethos*, or appeals to values. For example, in television campaigns to discourage smoking all three appeals have been used. "Logic-laden commercials attempted to prove that cigarette smoking was harmful to health, affect-laden commercials sought to activate smokers' fears of death, and value-laden commercials implied that the smoker was immoral or irresponsible to his family because his death would hurt them" (Kotler, 1972:184).

Kotler's *reeducative* strategy attempts to induce the desired behavior in the change target through the internalization of new beliefs or values. In such a situation, the change agent seeks a deep and lasting change in the behavior of the change target that he believes cannot be produced through power or persuasive approaches. It is used by psychotherapists in individual situations or milieu therapists in group situations.

By now, it is obvious that there are many ways to categorize the strategies of planned change. In an influential book, *Strategies for Planned Change*, Gerald Zaltman and Robert Duncan (1977) recapitulate and combine many of the previously discussed approaches. They then suggest that the various strategies can be depicted on a continuum by degree of external pressure exerted on the targets. They identify four general strategies: facilitative, reeducative, persuasive, and power—that range from minimum to maximum outside pressure.

Facilitative strategies are the ones that make easier the implementation of changes by and/or among the target group. It is based on the assumption that the target group: (1) already recognizes a problem; (2) is in general agreement that remedial action is necessary; and (3) is open to external assistance and willing to engage in self-help (Zaltman & Duncan, 1977:90). The effectiveness of the strategy is enhanced when the target groups are aware of the availability of assistance, committed to seek and accept assistance, and willing to remedy a situation. For example, on Native American reservations, children do poorly in school and have a high dropout rate. The problem is recognized, and funds are made available to rectify the situation by trying to create an environment more conducive to learning.

Reeducative strategies are used when time is not a pressing factor. In such a strategy, the relatively objective presentation is intended to provide a rational justification for action. It is based on the assumption that humans are rational beings and capable of modifying their behavior when information is presented to them. Reeducation, rather than education, is used because the strategy involves the unlearning, or "unfreezing," of something that was internalized before the change target learned the new attitude and behavior. Such reeducation strategies have been found very effective in third-world countries in a number of areas such as sanitation, increased use of hygiene facilities, and in various public health campaigns.

Persuasive strategies try to bring about change through bias in the way in which a message is structured and presented. Attempts to create change may be based on reasoning, or on rational or emotional appeals. Most advertisers and many nonprofit organizations rely on these strategies. In planned change efforts, persuasive strategies are used frequently in family planning programs and in marketing.

Power strategies involve the use of coercion to secure the target's compliance. Zaltman and Duncan suggest that the ability to exercise power is founded on an obligatory relationship between the change agent and change target. It is indicative of a situation in which the target is dependent on the change agent for satisfaction of its goals. "The strength of power is related to the degree of dependency, which in turn is a function of several factors: (1) the goals controlled by the change agent and the target's motivational investment in those goals, (2) the availability of alternatives to satisfy the target's goals, and (3) the cost of alternative modes of goal attainment" (Zaltman & Duncan, 1977:153). In some instances, the exercise of power has a cost to its user. There may be a cost involved in rewarding the target for compliance or punishing the target for noncompliance. Cost may also incur in the form of retaliation on the part of the target. An illustration of the use of the power strategies would be the various regulatory agencies in the domain of the environment, energy use, advertising, and auto safety. In general, power strategies are desirable when the change sought must be immediate and when the commitment by the target is low to a particular change.

On occasion, the use of *multiple* strategies is desirable. A good illustration of the use of multiple strategies is the case of a massive vasectomy campaign in Kerala, India, in 1970. It lasted for one month, and over 15,000 sterilizations were performed. Various persuasive strategies were used in the form of house-to-house visits by family-planning educators, public meetings, press releases, special newspaper supplements, and a variety of entertainments and cultural performances with particular reference to the campaign. The use of incentives (payment or bribe) can be called a form of power strategy according to Kotler (1972:183). Finally, the location and the physical layout of the camp and the transportation system established to bring in persons for the operation reflect considerable concern with facilitative strategies (Zaltman & Duncan, 1977:179).

VIOLENCE

In the previous section, references were made to the various power strategies of change in the context of legitimate authority manifested through institutional channels. The intent of this section is to examine the use of violence and coercion as extralegal strategies to effect change. Violence is conceptualized as direct or indirect action applied to restrain, injure, or destroy persons or property. The discussion in this section will be limited to those change efforts in which violent methods are deliberately used in the formulation and implementation of social change.

The use of violent strategies of social change is as old as humankind. Samuel P. Huntington (1972:282) points out that in no society do significant social, economic, or political changes take place without violence or the imminent likelihood of violence. At times, as H. L. Nieburg (1972:161) asserts, "The threat of violence and the occasional outbreak of real violence—which gives the threat credibility—are essential elements in peaceful social change not only in international, but also in national communities."

Violent strategies of change include ghetto riots, university confrontations, guerrilla warfare, oppressive measures by the state, various forms of insurrection, terrorism, and, in its ultimate form, revolution (see, for example, Denmark & Adler, 2003). Decentralized and spontaneous violence is a common means through which disadvantaged groups call attention to their grievances and their demands for social change (Alder, 1992). There appear to be some periods or situations in which violence succeeds more often than nonviolence. As it was noted previously, William A. Gamson (1990) studied fifty-three American groups and movements that promoted various social changes between 1800 and 1945. He claims that those that gained their goals were generally the ones that used violence (or, more correctly, had violence thrust upon them through police or mob attack), while all the nonviolent victims of attack failed to achieve their goals.

At times, the use of violence is a necessary stimulus for change. For example, "The history of reform in the United States—from the Jeffersonians down through abolitionists, populists, the labor movement, and the civil rights movement—is studded with instances of violence and other forms of disorder which helped to trigger changes in governmental policy" (Huntington, 1972:282). The riots of the early 1830s and other violence in England played an important role in consolidating Whig support for the Reform Act of 1832. Similarly, in India, middle-class groups in the mid-1950s used violence on occasions to wrest concessions from the government. In the United States, following the Birmingham riots in 1963, President Kennedy declared that passage of his civil rights bill was necessary "to get the struggle off the streets and into the courts." Failure to pass the bill, Kennedy warned, would lead to "continued, if not increased, racial strife—causing the leadership on both sides to pass from the hands of reasonable and responsible men to the purveyors of hate and violence" (Huntington, 1972:283).

The effectiveness of violence as a strategy of social change lies in the willingness of certain segments of the population to go beyond the accepted patterns of action to promote change. The use of violent strategies represents a threat to existing political organization and procedures. However, it should be noted that the repeated use of violent strategies depreciates their value. "In 1963 racial riots in the United States and monkish self-immolation in Vietnam helped to produce significant changes in governmental policy and political leadership. Three years later similar events failed to produce similar consequences" (Huntington, 1972:284).

There are certain common elements in the use of violent strategies for effecting social change. Ted Gurr (1967) outlines the principal strategic steps that are used to induce violent social change. As the first step, the change agent must increase the perception of relative deprivation among the potentially violent group. This can be done by minimizing the group's perceptions of the rewards and benefits to be gained at its current social position while enhancing the perceived discrepancy between the group and other segments of society. This perceived discrepancy, in turn, would lead to feelings of frustration and anger.

The second step entails the maximization of the intensity of anger of the group. The change agent, according to Gurr, should argue that: (1) the social goals are desirable, for example, economic benefits, improved well-being, and increased status; (2) the deprivation to which the group is subjected is indeed illegitimate, for example, by underscoring instances of social discrimination; (3) the deprivation is severe, for example, by pointing to the discrepancies between the group and its desired state while minimizing the similarities; and (4) by emphasizing the occurrence of continuous and unjust deprivation.

In the third step, the change agent must emphasize the social facilitation variables and minimize the social control variables that transform anger into violence. The accentuation of social facilitation variables entails: (1) giving examples that society is violent in other spheres, for example, violence is as American as apple pie; (2) amplifying racial, communal, and other in-group ties by emphasizing shared states of deprivation and indicating harassment by other groups; and (3) giving critical incidents that will trigger violence at optimal points in time. Gurr points to two ways for the change agent to minimize social control variables: (1) create conditions that will evoke either no retribution or an overreaction; and (2) create conditions that cut off the availability of mechanisms that discharge anger nonviolently. The first instance is illustrated by overreaction by the police to ghetto and campus violence, thus helping to increase violence. The second might entail the creation of certain incidents that bring about curfews, a temporary cessation of mass gatherings, and similar events.

Obviously, not all of these steps were present in the more than 300 outbursts of collective racial violence that occurred in major central cities between 1963 and 1969 in the United States (Downes, 1970). Many of the participants of these racial riots saw their grievances rooted in the existing arrangements of power and authority in contemporary society, and their action was—on a direct or symbolic level—an attempt at altering these arrangements (Skolnick, 1969:7). However, not all violent activities are aimed at achieving either specific or symbolic objectives. Many individuals participated because food, liquor, clothing, appliances, and other goods could be procured through looting, or they participated to vent their anger against specific merchants and police who had harassed or exploited them.

During the initial stages of the riots of the 1960s, racial violence was relatively spontaneous and unorganized. The riots were black-dominated and property-oriented. By 1968, however, the police were becoming more effective in controlling or repressing violent events. The development of improved control capabilities led to more organized small-scale terrorism or guerrilla warfare by black extremist groups such as the Revolutionary Action Movement and the Black Panthers. This violence took the form of arson and attempts to kill police, firefighters, and merchants in the ghetto. This new pattern of violence was black-dominated but person-oriented, and it also involved more systematic attacks on whites. In many instances, the violent outbursts were precipitated by specific incidents that involved the police, and on other occasions were linked to a variety of urban grievances (Wilson, 1968:23).

Martin Oppenheimer (1969) points out that violence can be a successful change strategy in the long run only if those using it have mass support or majority neutrality. After the violent outbursts and turmoil of the 1960s, blacks had neither. This is not to say, however, that their efforts were in vain.

The unrest contributed to a series of efforts to improve the plight of blacks and the underprivileged, including model city programs, the "war against poverty," black studies programs in universities, and so on.

In addition to riots, there are other forms of violence aimed at bringing about change. They include the various types of revolutions discussed in Chapter 3, such as civil wars, wars of national liberation, *putsch*, and coup d'états. Regarding the latter, Edward Luttwak (1979) notes that in the twentieth century, coups are more common than elections as a means of changing governments in many countries. There are many more military governments in existence than parliamentary democracies, and, since the end of World War II, there have been hundreds of coups worldwide. The major sources of coups include ethnic antagonisms stemming from cultural plurality and political competition and the presence of strong militaries with fractionalized office corps (Kposowa & Jenkins, 1993).

Terrorism is a special form of violence that is used to effect radical change. In 1996, 311 people died in terrorist attacks, countless injured, with incalculable social, psychological and economic costs (Weiner, 1997). By the beginning of the twenty-first century, that number has increased significantly. Some recent examples:

October, 2002, Kuta Beach, Bali, Indonesia: almost 200 killed in a night club bombing;
October, 2002, Moscow, Russia: close to 200 died in the Chechen hostage situation;
September, 2001, World Trade Center, New York: almost 3,000 killed;
September, 2001, Pentagon, Arlington, Virginia: almost 190 killed.

Scholarly interest in terrorists and terrorism has been expanding ever since the late 1960s, when a wave of dramatic incidents—hijackings, kidnappings, bombings, and hostage-taking—began (see, for example, Clutterback, 1994; Griset & Mahan, 2003; Kushner, 2003; Ross, 1993). Terrorism is a politically charged concept, and scholars trying to define it encounter practical and theoretical dilemmas, perhaps best reflected by the oft-cited adage, "One person's terrorist is another person's freedom fighter." In essence, there is a conflict of different ideologies, and what constitutes terrorism depends on one's political views. To illustrate: former President Reagan referred to the U.S.-backed Contra rebels who were trying to overthrow the Nicaraguan government as "freedom fighters." Others, in particular the Sandinistas, called the rebels terrorists, arguing that Contra violence against a civilian population constitutes terrorism. Similarly, Ilich Ramirez Sanchez, the elusive terrorist known to the world as "Carlos the Jackal," who was captured and tried in France in late 1994, is considered a hero to be emulated by Islamic fundamentalists (Hunter, 2002; Riding, 1994). Osama bin Laden, considered to be the mastermind behind the September 11, 2001 attack on the World Trade Center in New York, is idolized in many parts of the world.

Part of the lack of consensus also stems from the vast differences among "terrorist" groups themselves. They range from the Irish Republican Army to Hamas and the various other factions of the Palestinian Liberation Organization, and from the Basque nationalists in Spain to the Baader-Meinhof gang in Germany and the Red Brigades in Italy to al Qaeda, almost worldwide. The Sunnis, Shiites, Sikhs, Serbs, and Salvadorans, among many others, have causes and terrorist groups peculiar to them (Kushner, 2003). As a tactic, terrorism has been used by groups on the far right and on the far left. Terrorist acts have been committed by groups that have been vindicated by history, as well as by those that have been condemned by it.

But what is terrorism? It may be defined as a type of surreptitious warfare based on the indiscriminate use or threat of violence, a warfare in which the most important result is not the physical or mental damage of the victims, but the psychological effects produced for the purpose of altering the state of mind or policy of a nation or group whose members are directly assaulted or intimated (Grosscup, 1991:13; Turner & Killian, 1987:319).

Indiscriminate violence against innocent people is used for a variety of objectives (see, for example, Jervis, 2002). One is to coerce a nation into taking some specific action to carry out the terrorists' goal. As an example, the Arab "skyjackers" of a TWA plane in 1985 killed one passenger and held thirty-nine American tourists hostage in Lebanon for seventeen days while demanding that Israel release over 700 Shiite Muslims. Almost a decade later, an Islamic militant on a suicide mission blew up a bus in Tel Aviv, killing twenty-two and wounding forty-six others in an attempt to call attention to detained Hamas supporters (Haberman, 1994:1). On the domestic scene, the Earth Liberation Front, for example, an environmental organization considered by the FBI to be one of America's most prolific domestic terrorist groups, routinely engages in vandalism such as slashing tires, defacing businesses and damaging construction equipment. They use a corrosive cream to etch the letters ELF on the windows of SUVs and fast food restaurants. The group has no formal leadership, just a Web site and a virtual press office to handle inquiries. The loosely structured group has only a shared commitment to take aim at "anyone who is destroying the environment for the sake of profit" (Bacon, 2002). ELF began in England in 1992 as an offshoot of Earth First, an environmental advocacy group. While Earth First promoted mainstream ecological campaigns, elves, as they are often called, take a more direct approach, sabotaging research, burning buildings and placing spikes in trees to fend off loggers' chainsaws. The group says it has caused $50 million in damage in the United States. The group first went to work in the United States in 1996, claiming responsibility for the torching of a Forest Service truck in the Willamette National Forest in Oregon. Within a few months, the group said it had joined forces with the Animal Liberation Front to destroy millions of dollars in commercial and government buildings and research. In 1997, the two groups burned wild horse corrals overseen by the Bureau of Land Management in Oregon, causing nearly a half-million dollars in damage to structures and equipment. The next year, the front claimed responsibility for the largest act of eco-terrorism in United States history, burning three buildings and four ski lifts at a Vail, Colo., resort. Damages were estimated at $12 million to $24 million. The group's actions do not always succeed. In an October 2001 firebombing at a Federal Bureau of Land Management corral near Susanville, Calif., vandals caused about $80,000 in damage but failed to free the 160 horses. The group has set minks free from mink farms, only to see them run over by cars. After one such raid in Sweden, when group members painted minks' fur so that they would be useless to profiteers, the minks died of exposure.

Another objective is to demoralize and intimidate the opposition. For example, Arab terrorist incidents in the Vienna and Rome airports in 1985 and terrorist acts against the United States in 1986 adversely affected the willingness of Americans to live and work in Lebanon, created unrest among Americans working abroad, and discouraged many American tourists from going to Europe. A third objective is to call attention to the terrorist cause. Terrorists create newsworthy events; they mobilize the news media to disseminate a message that otherwise would not capture public attention. This manipulation of the media is often successful. It gives the terrorists publicity and the power to instill fear that is out of proportion to their real numbers and strength (Turner & Killian, 1987:321–322). It can have also some unintended consequences: the atmosphere surrounding terrorist incidents decreases the rates of luggage theft in mass transit stations. This may have to do both with the fear of possible thieves of picking up an item of luggage containing an explosive and with heightened police vigilance after such an event (Trivizas & Smith, 1997).

In many parts of the world, terrorist activities are highly organized and well financed (Grosscup, 1991; Kushner, 2003) as evidenced, for example, by the Al Qaeda activities (Frantz, 2002; Jervis, 2002). Manuals on terrorist strategies and tactics abound (Marighella, 1985) and can even be found on Internet. In a cookbook-like fashion, among other things, they spell out techniques of raids and infiltrations, ambushes, street operations, bomb making, executions, kidnappings, sabotage, conducting a war of nerves, obtaining weapons, and negotiating for hostages. Terrorists are also getting technologically more sophisticated, and the threat from terrorist groups could escalate dramatically were they to use nuclear weapons or chemical or biological warfare agents. Ironically, advances in science and technology could turn the whole of modern society into a potential victim of terrorism, creating a state of the world in which there is no immunity for the noncombatant segment of the population or for those who have no direct connection to particular conflicts or grievances that instigate acts of violence. The bombing of the federal building in Oklahoma City on April 19, 1995, killing 165 people, is a telling example of this point.

The Internet itself can become the target for terrorists. Today's society is becoming more dependent on electronic storage, retrieval, analysis, and transmission of information, giving the new generation of terrorists a very attractive target. With vital national activities such as banking, defense, trade, transportation and scientific research all carried out online, mischief or sabotage by any hacker with a keyboard and a cause could create major problems (Laqueur, 1997; Thomas, 2002).

In most of the literature on planned social change, the use of violent strategies is not considered a desirable means for inducing social change. For example, after examining numerous violent attempts to bring about change, Oppenheimer concludes that the use of violence tends to subvert or inhibit the emergence of a truly democratic and humanistic regime (1969:55–68). The use of violence, Oppenheimer argues, tends to foster the worship of action. Rational thought is denigrated. Moreover, in spite of Franz Fanon's (1968) arguments about the liberating effects of oppressed people engaging in violent acts, Oppenheimer asserts that violence negatively affects individual mental health and personality. The survivors of successful attempts to bring about change are usually incapable of creating a humanistic order because they are conditioned to use violence both to solve problems and against enemies of the new order. This, in turn, further subverts democratic processes and humanistic values. To change society, Oppenheimer argues that the only appropriate strategy is a "protracted nonviolent struggle."

Before examining nonviolent and direct action strategies of change, one should note that violence need not be directed toward other groups. Nieburg (1972:170) describes the Dukhobor Sons of Freedom (of Vancouver, B.C.), who have adopted a novel technique of displaying violence as they conduct their immemorial campaign against compulsory public education. They set fire to their own homes and barns, standing by and watching the blaze. They also parade naked in the middle of city streets. The unusual nature of these demonstrations is plain. Their religion forbids them to threaten or use violence against others. Instead, they demonstrate symbolically their discipline and passionate commitment to their own way of life by inflicting violence upon their own property. The naked marches result in arrests and imprisonment, and the house burnings force welfare authorities to provide temporary shelter. In the process, however, the demonstrations garner public attention and sympathy for the believers. This may well give the local authorities incentive to ignore their defiance of school attendance laws. As a matter of fact, this is what has happened during the past two generations. The law has been circumvented and there have been no concentrated efforts on the part of authorities to enforce it.

NONVIOLENCE AND DIRECT ACTION

There are many contemporary images of nonviolence as a strategy for social change: consumer boycotts, rent strikes, civil rights demonstrations, labor pickets, sitting in front of abortion clinics to prevent entrance, or pouring of blood as a symbolic act (MacQueen, 1992; Mallick & Hunter, 2002). This strategy has a long history. Socrates practiced civil disobedience as a form of nonviolent resistance over 2,000 years ago. Centuries ago, in the Far East creditors fasted on a debtor's doorstep until they were paid. Christ and his disciples embraced many nonviolent practices. Americans threw English tea into Boston Harbor to protest British taxes. In the nineteenth-century United States, Henry David Thoreau stated his philosophy of civil disobedience, which still serves as an inspiration for nonviolent action (Hornstein et al., 1971:533–534).

Chin and Benne (1985:41) consider nonviolence one of the power-coercive strategies. It is a way of forcing the change target to give in, to make concessions, and, occasionally, to cooperate with the change effort. Nonviolence is based on "moral power," and "Part of the ingredients of the power of the civilly disobedient is in the guilt which their demonstration of injustice, unfairness, or cruelty of the existing system of control arouses in those exercising control or in others previously committed to the present system of control" (Chin & Benne, 1985:41). The strategy of nonviolence is likely to be effective, other things being equal, according to the value orientation of the change target and of the pertinent third parties. When the change target, in the form of established authority, is relatively immune to the moral appeal involved, the reaction to nonviolence may be brutal repression. "Unless there are third parties with power to intervene and who are deeply impressed by the moral issues and the brutal repression, the efforts may be ruthlessly squelched" (Warren, 1977:156). On the other hand, in situations in which the target and third parties are susceptible to the moral appeal of the nonviolent action, nonviolence may be highly effective.

Hornstein and his associates (1971:537–542) suggest that the choice of nonviolent strategy and tactics can reflect either an indirect or a direct approach to the opponent's power. The indirect approach is based on the decision to meet the violent style of the opponent with nonviolence. The direct approach is based on attempts to upset the opponent's power base, attitudes, availability of resources, public image, and opinion of third parties. In such instances, the conflict is external to the opponent, not internal.

The Indirect Approach

In the indirect approach, an important assumption shared by nonviolent change agents is that the amount, duration, and intensity of violence is minimized by nonviolent change tactics. It is based on the notion that "using nonviolence against a violent attacker acts like a 'moral jujitsu'; the nonviolent behavior throws the attacker off guard, and exhausts him through an internal conflict between his needs to vent aggressive behavior and the situational inappropriateness of attacking a passive other" (Hornstein et al., 1971:538). However, the reality of the situation does not always support this assumption. For example, in many instances, physical harm is present; witness the beatings of student demonstrators by police at Berkeley, Columbia, and other campuses as they protested the war in Vietnam in the late 1960s and early 1970s.

From a related perspective, Gene Sharpe (quoted by Hornstein et al., 1971:538–539) shows that nonviolence is selected as a strategy because it technically disconfirms the opponent's expectations of violence. "The opponent, in his disconfirmed state, will now be responsive to a nonviolent strategy and agree to play the game 'in kind.'" In reality, whether or not the opponent will respond this way, however, depends on a number of factors. Some of these are as follows:

1. If the nonviolent behavior is seen as appropriate
2. If the nonviolent tactic is new
3. If the nonviolent action is seen as resulting from a strategy or a way of life
4. If the opponent can trust the nonviolent actor
5. If the nonviolent actor is valued as a human being.

It is obvious that the outcome of an indirect approach is highly speculative, particularly in view of the number of factors that could make it fail.

The Direct Approach

In the direct approach, there are two factors involved: techniques of attitude change and the use of third parties. Hornstein and his colleagues suggest that both are used to manipulate the political position of the opponents as well as to change their behavior and/or attitudes toward the issues.

Gene Sharpe (1971:546–577) advocates three mechanisms of *attitude change:* conversion, accommodation, and nonviolent coercion. *Conversion* takes place when the opponents change both their attitudes and their behavior toward the nonviolent actor. It takes place in situations in which the opponents are persuaded by a variety of messages as well as situations of identification with the nonviolent actor. Illustrations of tactics in this category of nonviolent protest would include petitions, pickets, declarations, teach-ins, and marches. *Accommodation,* according to Sharpe, is a mild form of coercion involving a willingness to go along with the nonviolent demonstrators without measurably changing one's attitude. An illustration of this would be the hunger strike, a tactic that is successful when the suffering of the participants becomes intolerable to the opponent or to third-party witnesses. *Nonviolent coercion* is present in situations in which opponents have no choice about their compliance. It is used to force opponents to behave in a certain fashion by the change agent whether or not they like it. However, it will sustain change only when the threat of continued or renewed action is present or when there are new laws to support the change. Strikes, boycotts, occupations, and sit-downs are illustrative tactics of nonviolent coercion.

In the direct approach, *third parties* often have an effect on the success of a nonviolent strategy. Their impact is based on "(1) their own attitudinal position and its correspondence to the attitudes of demonstrators or the opponent; (2) their communication to the opponent about his behavior; and (3) their availability to maintain surveillance over agreed-upon changes by either party" (Hornstein et al., 1971:541). Third parties with high prestige who support the demonstrators are likely to increase the perceived pressures on the opponent to change. By contrast, if they support the opponent's position, it will probably decrease the likelihood of change. Regarding the second point, communication that supports the nonviolent demonstrators is particularly effective when an opponent has responded violently to the nonviolence. The presence of the mass media is especially important here, as witnessed by the well-known events at the 1968 Chicago Democratic Convention. Finally, surveillance is particularly effective in accommodation and coercion strategies. The changes brought about by these approaches require impartial third parties to monitor the future course of events of both sides in the conflict.

After this overview of nonviolent strategies of change, it is appropriate to consider some of the tactics that are used. Incredible as it may seem, there are at least 146 tactics used in nonviolence (Sharpe, 1971:546). Prior to discussing some of the tactics, it should be noted that a change agent should not expect to achieve success with nonviolent tactics unless he or she has made provisions for sufficient training in their use, and planning in their application and execution. An understanding of the tactics alone is not sufficient; they need to be rehearsed extensively with those who will be involved in the action (Hornstein et al., 1971:542).

Direct-Action Tactics

Martin Oppenheimer and George Lakey (1972) discuss some of the more important direct-action tactics used in the civil rights struggle in the United States. They list them under three headings: demonstrations, noncooperation, and direct intervention.

Demonstrations are used primarily to express a position, a point of view. They are not so effective as noncooperation or direct intervention. The tactics used here include: marches and parades; picketing and vigils; fraternization; "hounding" (following and reminding officials of the immorality of their behavior); publishing leaflets, and renouncing honors. Examples would include the 1999 antiglobalization demonstrations in Seattle (Aaronson, 2001) and others such as the ones in Davos, Switzerland, in 2001 and more recently in September, 2002, in Washington, D.C. during the meetings of the World Bank and International Monetary Fund.

Noncooperation entails methods of direct action in which campaigners withdraw their usual degree of cooperation with the opponents. Depending on local laws, the tactics may be legal or illegal and include strikes; *hartal* (staying home for a day or so, leaving factories and places of business empty); consumer boycotts or selective buying; rent strikes; school boycotts; and refusal to pay taxes.

Direct, nonviolent intervention consists of physical confrontation rather than withdrawal of cooperation or demonstrating. It carries the conflict into the opponent's camp and often alters the status quo abruptly. There are several tactics involved, such as sit-ins; pray-ins in churches; wade-ins on beaches; fasting; reverse strikes (working longer hours than called for in support of certain demands); and nonviolent interjection and obstruction (such as lying down on sidewalks or in front of bulldozers, or physically occupying a site). At times, proponents of a change effort resort to shock tactics to get their message across. For example, People for the Ethical Treatment of Animals has taken its antifur campaign beyond nudes on billboards and models from various agencies created a living PETA billboard in New York in 1996 for their "fur free" cause (Luscombe, 1996).

The nonviolent strategy of *satyagraha* involves many of the tactics outlined by Oppenheimer and Lakey. "It is characterized by adherence to a stated truth by means of behavior which is not violent but which includes self-suffering" (Bondurant, 1972:303). This strategy was used during the Nationalist movement in India and involved the various methods of noncooperation and civil disobedience. Joan V. Bondurant (1972:305) outlines the various steps involved in a *satyagraha* campaign.

1. Attempt to resolve the conflict or grievance by negotiation and arbitration.
2. Prepare the group for direct action.
3. Engage in demonstrations and propaganda campaigns.
4. Try to appeal to the opponent for a final time; if there are no concessions, issue an ultimatum.
5. Engage in economic boycott and strikes of various forms.
6. Initiate actions of noncooperation with established authorities and institutions.
7. Engage in civil disobedience, but exercise care in selecting the laws to be violated.
8. Assume some of the functions of the government.
9. Establish a parallel government to handle those functions.

The *satyagraha* strategy is progressive in nature, and it can stop at any stage at which the opponents concede to the demands. In India, various groups have used this strategy, and many of the steps were incorporated in civil rights and related activities in the United States.

No discussion of nonviolent tactics (or violent tactics) of social change would be complete without some reference to Saul Alinsky (1972:138–139), a creative and often-quoted and imitated master tactician in community organization. In his words:

> I have emphasized and re-emphasized that tactics means you do what you can with what you've got, and that power in the main has always gravitated towards those who have money and those whom people follow. The resources of the Have-Nots are (1) no money and (2) lots of people. All right, let's start from there. People can show their power by voting. What else? Well, they have physical bodies. How can they use them? Now a mélange of ideas begins to appear. Use the power of the law by making the establishment obey its rules. Go outside the experience of the enemy, stay inside the experience of your people. Emphasize tactics that your people will enjoy. The threat is usually more terrifying than the tactic itself. Once all these rules and principles are festering in your imagination they grow into a synthesis . . . [for example] . . . I suggested that we might buy one hundred seats for one of Rochester's symphony concerts. We would select a concert in which the music was relatively quiet. The hundred blacks who would be given the tickets would first be treated to a three-hour pre-concert dinner in the community, in which they would be fed nothing but baked beans, and lots of them; then the people would go to the symphony hall—with obvious consequences. Imagine the scene when the action began! The concert would be over before the first movement! (If this be a Freudian slip—so be it.)

SOCIAL MOVEMENTS

Social movements generally develop among the less powerful segments in society and act outside of institutional channels (Halsey, 2001; McAdam & Snow, 1997:326). Many of the strategies and tactics discussed thus far are often deployed by social movements. In Chapter 5, social movements were discussed in a different context, and they were defined as collectivities acting with some continuity to promote or resist change. Several types were identified such as revolutionary, reactionary, reform, and expressive movements. These various types of social movements often constitute "social early warning systems" signaling dysfunction (Henderson, 1993) and they have a number of common characteristics. Luther P. Gerlach and Virginia H. Hine elaborated on five such characteristics: type of organization structure, patterns of recruitment, ideology, personal commitment, and opposition, as follows:

1. The *organizational structure* of social movements is segmentary, composed of semiautonomous cells or segments. The movement organization is decentralized and polycephalous, or "many headed." Movements generally do not have a single paramount leader who controls through a coordinated organization; instead, each cell or unit has its own leader or leaders. The various organizational units are regulated by personal, structural, and ideological ties.

2. *Patterns of recruitment* follow lines of preexisting personal relationships and are based on face-to-face contact with friends, neighbors, associates, or colleagues.
3. Every movement has its *ideology*, which codifies values and goals, provides a conceptual framework for interpreting relevant experiences and events relative to these goals, motivates and provides rationale for the changes sought, defines the opposition, and conceptually unites the fragmented groups in the movement.
4. A *commitment* is brought about by an act or experience that differentiates a participant in some important way from the established order, or his place in it, identifies him with a new set of values, and commits him to change patterns of behavior.
5. *Opposition*, which may be real or perceived, is essential to promote a movement and to offer a basis for its commitment process. It is a force against which participants of a movement can be united. (1973:169–190)

A common strategy in a social movement is usually adopted by the numerous coalitions of various organizations formed within the movement. Because movements are multicentered, coordination of the various activities is typically problematic, which is a weakness of social movements. Lack of coordination results in duplication, wasted effort, inability to carry out concerted action, inconsistent pursuit of intermediate objectives, conflicting loyalties, and internal strife (Chong, 1993). On the other hand, a movement's strengths are "in its variability, lack of rigidity, action through mutual adjustment and feedback providing resilience and flexibility, difficulty of hostile parties in finding a specific target for recrimination, and in the very redundancy of many of the efforts. These attributes make it difficult to direct and difficult to control, but also difficult to destroy" (Warren, 1977:268).

With these clarifications in mind concerning the composition of a social movement, let us consider the change strategies used by the various organizations within the social movement. The strategies used in social movements have two fundamental objectives: One is to promote the growth of a social movement as a change-promoting system, and the other is to engage the change target. For the present purpose, the emphasis will be on the strategies used to engage the target.

Change Strategies

Several principal strategies are used by social movements in their attempt to influence the actions of their target systems. The main ones include bargaining, coercion, and persuasion (Turner & Killian, 1987:297–299). *Bargaining* "takes place when the movement has control over some exchangeable value that the target group wants and offers some of that value in return for compliance with its demands." Bargaining may entail the offer of votes or other support to the target group in return for support of the movement. *Coercion* is "the manipulation of the target group's situation in such fashion that the pursuit of any course of action other than that sought by the movement will be met by considerable cost or punishment." It is a form of negative bargaining in which the threat of harm rather than actual harm is considered. When harmful action is used, it is a way of demonstrating tactically that the movement has the real potential of inflicting harm. The extreme form of coercion is the threat of total destruction when the movement has the power to do so. Lesser forms include terrorism, civil disobedience, and assassination. *Persuasion* involves the use of symbolic manipulation without substantial rewards or punishments under the control of the movement. The procedure is to identify the proposed course of action with values held by the target group. It always includes calling attention to rewards and penalties that will ensue for the target group on the basis of various courses of action. Persuasion can be *deliberative*, which encourages thought, reflection, and critical analysis, or *propaganda*, which truncates thought through the use of simplistic symbols and images that play on prejudices and emotions (Pratkanis & Turner, 1966). It should be noted that these three general types of strategies are not mutually exclusive, and various combinations of the elements in all three may be used by any given movement to engage a target system.

John Wilson (1973:226–227) notes that many social movements are often remembered more for the tactics they used than for their objectives. For example, student movements such as the Free Speech Movement and Students for a Democratic Society have achieved their notoriety through the use of disruptive and violent tactics and not through the enunciated goals and objectives, which were poorly formulated by the leaders and dimly understood by the public at large. There are two reasons, Wilson points out, why tactics contribute to the establishment of the identity of a movement. First, social movements use methods of persuasion and coercion that are, more often than not, novel, dramatic, unorthodox, and of questionable legitimacy. Second, "tactics may be all there is to 'see' in the movement. Many social movements are not much more than tactical machines, having little substance beyond their efforts to bring some cause to the attention of the public or coerce some agent of authority" (1973:227). Again, for example, the Free Speech Movement defined its priorities in terms of tactical actions, and demonstrations of a disruptive nature were given priority over other projects "such as building up a loyal following or establishing an organization" (p. 227).

Social movements employ a repertoire of strategies and tactics to influence change targets to help build up memberships, raise money, or influence politicians (Halsey, 2001; Oberschall, 1993). At this point, it should be noted again that there is a distinction between strategy, which refers to a general design or plan of action, and tactics, which refers to specific means or methods of carrying out that plan or design. Tactics are specific techniques such as strikes, boycotts, and teach-ins that are deployed to implement strategies.

Change Tactics

The tactics used predominantly by social movements are called the "politics of disorder" by Wilson to "distinguish them from the 'politics of order,' in which reliance is placed on the courtroom, the legislature, and the mass media, and from the 'politics of violence,' in which the accepted rules of bringing about social change are rejected and resort is made to mob demonstrations, bombing, and physical assault" (1973:229). The tactics used in the politics of disorder fall under the heading of "direct action" and involve, among other things, demonstrations, economic boycotts, rent strikes, and sit-ins. It should be noted, however, that social movements also use the politics of order, such as petitions, lobbies, and selective voting, as well as violence. This is evidenced by the actions of some members of the antibusing movement who tried to physically prevent the passage of school buses, and by the tactics of some members of the antiabortion movement, who firebombed abortion clinics.

There are two reasons social movements might select the politics of disorder. First, movements advocate ideas that that are not supported by mainstream groups, and movement participants lack authority and access to the media to disseminate their views; therefore, they believe they have to engage in attention-getting activities. Second, the politics of order has been tried and found wanting.

Not all tactics used by social movements are effective in advancing the movement toward its objective and maintaining, at the same time, followers as a united group. But there is no way of telling in advance which tactic will be successful, since a great deal depends on the movement's circumstances and resources and the opposition it encounters. Still, it is possible to make some general observations about the attributes of tactics. Wilson (1973:236) points out that a tactical program needs to meet three requirements: It must have breadth, simplicity, and flexibility. With regard to *breadth,* activities in which pressure is brought to bear on the target group from a number of fronts simultaneously would tend to be more effective than reliance merely on economic, political, or other measures. *Simplicity* means that the tactics should be manageable, and not too inconvenient and time-consuming for the members. *Flexibility* "means avoiding total and irrevocable commitment to any given set of tactics, and it means foresight and planning for the reactions which a given set of tactics is likely to provoke" (pp. 237–238). A movement should avoid employing all the power at its disposal in any given tactical campaign. In general, the tactics used by social movements work only so long as they contain an element of surprise.

The choice of tactics by a social movement is determined by three factors: opposition, ideology, and public opinion. With regard to *opposition,* Wilson (1973:239–241) suggests that social movements are in a subordinate position of power in facing the group they are trying to defeat or win over. He distinguishes three degrees of subordination: partial inequality, dependency, and subjugation. In a situation of *partial inequality*, a movement is composed of minorities who are granted equal status on some grounds but not on others (homosexuals), or of those agitating on behalf of a deprived group (students in California for migrant workers), or of people acting as guardians of the national conscience, trying to reverse social policies considered immoral (nuclear pacifists). In these instances, movements are reluctant to resort to tactics of "questionable legitimacy." In a *dependency* situation, the movement is made up of minority people "who feel at the mercy of the target group." They want to improve their position, but they believe they cannot do so without the help of the target group. The object is to win over the target group rather than to defeat it. The movement must use patience to educate, persuade, and set an example. The women's suffrage movement would be indicative of this situation. In the situation of *subjugation*, the minority group members are completely dominated by the majority to the extent of economic exploitation and the deprivation of civil rights. There is no value consensus with the target group, and there is no likelihood of enlisting its help. Any progress to be made will be through the group's own efforts and by means of its own resources. The object of the movement here is to defeat the opponent, and the tactics that are used include harassment, obstruction, personal assault, destruction of property, and so on. The use of illegal tactics is justified because the system itself is considered illegal. An illustration of such a movement would be the Black Panthers.

The second determinant of the choice of tactics is *ideology*. In general, the specific tactics selected will be in accord with the values a movement espouses. Most movements have a set of statements about which means are appropriate for the realization of a given set of objectives. As a result, tactics will display symbolic consistency with the movement's values even if it results in burdens on members or further difficulties in attaining objective. Ideological factors are also pronounced when issues of alliances become important.

The final determinant of the selection of tactics is *public opinion*. Movements need to establish their credentials with the public and gain the support of a sympathetic public. Without favorable public opinion and public sympathy, a movement is unlikely to attain its objectives fully.

For favorable public opinion, the choice of violent tactics is generally detrimental to movements. The public may feel threatened by the use of violent tactics, and at the same time, may also be alienated by movements using them. Public opinion can also be a factor in deciding which movements should be politically active. In such instances, care should be exercised by movements not to use tactics that might confirm the public notion that the group is socially unfit to make political or economic judgments. For example, the feminist movement suffered during the early stages because the tactics used by many groups were contrary to the popular image of ladylike conduct such as women in the steel industry during the early phases of unionization (Fonow, 2003).

In brief, the rationale for choosing a set of tactics is not necessarily reflected in the movement's objectives. The choice of tactics is conditioned by a number of social forces, including the action of the opposition, the movement's ideology, and the predominant attitudes toward social protest. The combination of these factors provides a number of options and configurations.

Accomplishments of Social Movements

Thus far, the discussion has centered on the types of social movements, the principal strategies they employ, and the conditions that determine the use of specific tactics. The remainder of this section will address the question: What are some of the specific accomplishments of social movements and their impacts on policy outcomes (Goldberg, 1991; Rochon & Mazmanian, 1993)? As Lewis Killian notes (1964), the significance of any social movement must be found in the consequences that the movement has had for the larger society or for the social order from which it emerged. That is, has the movement led to any significant social or cultural change? Unless this question can be answered affirmatively, Killian asserts that the movement is little more than a passing curiosity or a sidelight of history. In one study of fifty-three movements between 1800 and 1945, about half of the movements were unsuccessful in bringing about any of the changes they sought (Gamson, 1990). In many other cases, Killian's question can be answered affirmatively and there is a rich literature on the outcomes demonstrating *How Social Movements Matter* (Giugni, McAdam, & Tilly, 1999). Early labor movements, for example, eventually brought an end to child labor in American factories. Labor movements were also responsible for gaining shorter working hours, safer working conditions, and the right for collective bargaining. Legislation that protects the environment is another area in which social movements have been successful. As a result of these efforts, more and more people are aware of environmental issues and consider themselves environmentally active through recycling and other efforts (Stisser, 1994). The product-safety movement resulted in a variety of safety devices, including the installation of automobile seat belts (Turner & Killian, 1987:397). Let us consider briefly two other movements, the civil rights and women's movements, that have attempted to overcome social inequities that existed in the recent past.

Civil rights movements have contributed to a series of legal reforms of considerable importance and impact (Fairclough, 2001; Oberschall, 1993: 213–238). Some of the most notable of these reforms were *Brown v. Board of Education of Topeka, Kansas*, a Supreme Court case in 1954; the Civil Rights Acts of 1957, 1960, 1964, and 1968; the Voting Rights Act of 1965; and President Nixon's Executive Order 11478, issued in 1969 (U.S. Commission on Civil Rights, 1975).

In the 1954 decision, the Supreme Court reversed the *Plessy v. Ferguson* decision of 1896 (which had allowed separate-but-equal education facilities for blacks and whites to be imposed by the states), saying that "segregation, with the sanction of the law, therefore has the tendency to retard the education and mental development of Negro children and to deprive them of some of the benefits they would receive in a racially integrated system" (Marden, Meyer, & Engel, 1991). Although significant changes have flown from this case, there are still some who argue (see, for example, Irons, 2002) that the quality and outcome of the public education currently offered to blacks are both still shaped by the enduring influence of Jim Crow laws and schools. Gaps between the educational achievements of blacks and whites still reflect the effect of generations of "separate and unequal" education which kept most blacks from achieving real equality with the white majority. But such conclusions are controversial among educational reformers, many of whom no longer even cite integration as a goal.

The Civil Rights Act of 1957 followed on the heels of the early victories of the civil rights movement and constituted a countermeasure to the strong opposition in the South to the *Brown* v. *Board of Education* decision of the Supreme Court. It was the first civil rights legislation to be enacted since 1875. Its accomplishments were to establish a Civil Rights Commission, to gather data on voting violations, to empower the Justice Department to initiate action where voting violations occurred in federal elections, and to require nondiscriminatory qualifications for the selection of juries in federal courts. This relatively innocuous legislation was topped by the Civil Rights Act of 1960, which was designed to impede interracial violence without eroding the power and authority of state officials (Blaustein & Zangrando, 1968).

In 1964 and 1968, Congress enacted Civil Rights acts that were far more extensive than any such preceding laws in American history. They included detailed provisions to ensure equality in the areas of voting, public accommodations and facilities, education, and employment. Desegregation problems of school districts were to be aided by funds, and training was to be handled by the then-Department of Health, Education, and Welfare (Jackson, 2002).

The 1965 march from Selma to Montgomery led to another piece of legislation: the Voting Rights Act of 1965. This assigned federal examiners to register voters and to observe elections in states or counties where discrimination existed. Literacy tests and other discriminatory means of limiting voter participation were outlawed. The act was constructed so as to help the poor, uneducated, or other minority groups as well as blacks. In Executive Order 11478, Nixon went beyond the former, more or less passive federal support of equality of opportunity and employment and ordered that federal agencies develop affirmative programs in which minority applicants would be actively sought out and specifically trained to perform at their highest potential. The Civil Service Commission was given the power to enforce the executive order and, in particular, to consider all complaints of discrimination in federal employment based on race, color, religion, sex, or national origin (U.S. Commission on Civil Rights, 1975). These are just some of many legislative changes in which civil rights movements played an important role.

In the context of civil rights movements, the women's movement has made important strides against a series of discriminatory practices in legal, financial, political, and educational domains (Costain & Majstorovic, 1994; Goldberg, 1991:193–217). The best known advocacy organization in the women's movement is the National Organization for Women, formed by Betty Friedan in 1966 "to bring women into full participation in the mainstream of the American society now" (Gruberg, 1968:105). Others include the American Association of University Women and a series of professional groups and caucuses such as Sociologists for Women in Society.

To meet the demands of feminist advocates for equal access of women to all political and economic opportunities, Congress has passed civil rights legislation that covers women as well as ethnic minorities, and at least two executive orders (Nos. 11246 and 11375) have been issued intended to prevent discrimination on the basis of sex in government and industry. For the record, it should be pointed out that when Title VII of the proposed Civil Rights Act of 1964 was initially reported out of the House Judiciary Committee, it included prohibitions of employment discrimination based on race, color, religion, or national origin—but not sex. It was only one day before the passage of the act that an amendment was offered to include a ban on sex discrimination in an apparent attempt to kill the bill. But it passed the House and the Senate, and the sex discrimination provisions in Title VII remained as a milestone for women seeking employment opportunities equal with men (U.S. Commission on Civil Rights, 1975:20).

In addition to employment and political participation, the women's movement was instrumental in advancing a concentration of reforms in state and federal laws (Oberschall, 1993:325–338). They include remedial measures to overcome injustice and discrimination in the provisions on marriage, property, support, divorce, health, birth control, abortion, sterilization, finances, taxes, consumer credit, housing, and welfare.

In the realm of sexual behavior, there have been some movements aimed at bringing about reform. For prostitutes, there is a nationwide movement and an organization named "Call Off Your Old Tired Ethics" (COYOTE), which had its first national convention in San Francisco in June 1974 at the Glide Memorial Methodist Church. Described by its "founding mother," retired prostitute Margo St. James, as a "loose woman's organization," COYOTE works for the legalization of prostitution and for the protection of prostitutes' civil liberties. [Prostitution is legal in many European countries; the argument is that it is better to tax sin than to ban it, and Germany and the Netherlands, for example, now collect sales and income taxes from sex workers in brothels. They in turn get health care, unemployment insurance, and pensions (Business Week, 2002).] Until prostitution is legalized in a given area, however, COYOTE advocates the arrest of the customer as well as the prostitutes, not only in the interest of equal justice, but also because, as Ms. St. James has put it, "men won't change the laws unless they get their nuts caught in the cracker, too." Feminist groups such as NOW also regard antiprostitution laws and ordinances as highly discriminatory against women, and for three decades they have advocated the abolition of such laws on the grounds that a person's sexual behavior is, properly, her own private affair; they insist that as long as there are laws, they should be made to apply to male customers as well as to female prostitutes (Berman, 1974).

It is still a long way to NOW's Bill of Rights, but the changes wrought by the women's movement are evident in many areas of life and had a profound impact on American society (Blaser, 1996). This may have been a reason for the decline in NOW membership: In 1982, it had 250,000 members; by 1987, it was down to 150,000 (Pierce, 1987:3B). Another reason for the decline is that the women's agenda has ballooned far past the feminist causes that NOW traditionally stressed. Since 1982, women have moved day care, welfare reform, child-support payments, and maternal and child care into the political mainstream of state legislatures, emulating some of the European models of parental leaves and benefits (Rhoads, 2002). The years of efforts are paying off in more and more legislation that ensures equality for women on every front, from insurance to taxes, to salary and pensions. At the same time, there is a growing belief that women's rights are being abandoned in today's conservative climate. This belief is most pronounced among younger women to whom feminist struggles are seen as just history (Leslie & Korman, 1985:73). The next section will consider law as an instrument of social change.

LAW AND SOCIAL CHANGE

The relationship between law and social change is reciprocal; law can be seen as both an effect and cause of social change (Champagne & Nagel, 1983:187; Vago, 2003:302–340). In this section, law will be considered only as an active instrument for guiding and shaping future behavior and social forms—that is, as a strategy of social change.

There are many examples in which laws have been used to create changes in society (see, for example, Schissel, 1996; Vago, 2003). Since Roman times, laws have been instrumental in effecting changes at all levels in society. There are several illustrations of the idea that law, far from being simply a reflection of social reality, is a powerful means of accomplishing reality—that is, fashioning it or making it. In spite of the ideas of Marx, Engels, and Lenin that law is an epiphenomenon of bourgeois class society doomed to vanish with the advent of the Revolution, the former Soviet Union had succeeded in making enormous changes in society by the use of laws (Dror, 1968). More recently, the attempts by Nazi Germany, and, later on, by Eastern European countries to make wholesale social changes through the use of laws—such as income redistribution, nationalization of industry, land reform and introduction of collective farms, provision of free education and health care, and the restructuring of the stratification system—are examples of the effectiveness of law to induce change (Eorsi & Harmathy, 1971). When the Communists seized power in China in 1949, virtually all vices ubiquitous in Western countries—pornography, prostitution, gambling, and usury—were eliminated by government decree, along with business operations that were dependent on profits from such activities (Vago, 2003).

Recognition of the role of law as a strategy of change is becoming more pronounced in contemporary society (Lempert & Sanders, 1986:352–427). It is now generally accepted that the "law . . . increasingly not only articulates but sets the course for major social changes" (W. Friedmann, 1972:513) and "attempted social change through law is a basic trait of the modern world" (L. Friedman, 1975:277). An almost identical observation is made by Yehezkel Dror (1968:673) in stating: "the growing use of law as a device of organized social action directed toward achieving social change seems to be one of the characteristics of modern society. . . ." In an influential article entitled "Law and Social Change," Dror (1968) distinguishes between the indirect and direct aspects of law in social change.

Dror (1968:673) argues that "law plays an important indirect role in social change by shaping various social institutions, which, in turn, have a direct impact on society." He uses the illustration of the compulsory education system, which performed an important indirect role in regard to change by fostering the operation of educational institutions, which, in turn, play a direct role in social change. He points out in the discussion that law interacts, in many cases directly, with basic social institutions, constituting a direct relationship between law and social change. For example, a law enacted to prohibit polygamy has a great direct influence on social change, having as its main purpose alterations in important patterns of behavior. He warns, however, that "The distinction is not an absolute but a relative one: in some cases the emphasis is more on the direct and less on the indirect impact of social change, while in other cases the opposite is true" (Dror, 1968:674).

Dror contends that law exerts an indirect influence on social change in general by influencing the possibilities of change in various social institutions. For example, the existence of a patent law protecting the rights of inventors encourages inventions and furthers change in the technological institutions that, in turn, may bring about other types of social change.

For all modern societies, every collection of statutes and delegated legislation is "full of illustrations of the direct use of law as a device for directed social change" (Dror, 1968:676). A good example to induce social change by law directly was the enactment of Prohibition in the United States to shape social behavior. (It was also one of the most conspicuous failures, showing that there are limits to the effective use of law to bring about social change.) Others would include the use of legislative powers to bring about extensive changes in social structure and culture, as evidenced in Japan and Turkey, where large segments of Western law were received with the intention of advancing the Westernization process of these countries.

filled worldwide contain active ingredients originating from wild species, particularly from tropical plants. Some 80 percent of people living in developing countries rely on traditional medicine for their primary health care needs, and 85 percent of traditional medicines use plant extracts. At the current rate of deforestation, about 14 percent of plant species are expected to become extinct (Brown, Renner, & Flavin, 1997:97).

Ecological Undermining of the Food Economy The continued degradation of natural resources, shortcomings in environmental responses, and renewable rescue constraints are likely to lead to food insecurity and conflict situations (United Nations Environment Programme, 2002:3) Some 800 million people around the world go hungry. In sub-Saharan Africa, 240 million people, about 30 percent of the total, are undernourished. In south Asia, over 30 percent of infants are born underweight, the highest ratio in the world, and a sad measure of inadequate access to food is that women are often last to eat in the household (*Human Development Report*, 2002). The growing pressure for food is beginning to undermine each of the three food-producing systems in a number of widely separated areas around the world with increasing frequency.

Increasing human demands on the world's supply of fish are becoming excessive in most parts of the world. The earth's seventeen major oceanic fishing areas have either reached or exceeded their natural limits, and nine are in serious decline (Platt, 1994:32–33). Most countries face the effects of overfishing, overpollution, and coastal habitat destruction, not only in the form of shrinking seafood supplies but also in the decreasing number of jobs in the fishing industry as well. For example, evidence now shows that the heavy offtake from the anchovy fishery off the western coast of Latin America, ranging from 10 to 12 million tons in the late 1970s and 1980s, has exceeded the capacity of the fishery to regenerate itself, resulting in its collapse. Some 200 million people worldwide depend on the fishing industry for their livelihood, and many are concerned about their jobs. In 1992 and 1993, 50,000 Canadian fishers were laid off as a result of the vanishing cod stocks in the north Atlantic waters, and there were multiple waves of lay-offs in 2001 and 2002. Evidence suggests that the current level of fishing in many areas is environmentally unsustainable. If the trends of overexploitation continue, fish will no longer be "the protein of the poor" (Brown, Renner, & Flavin, 1997:32).

Like fisheries, the world's rangelands, which support livestock such as cattle, sheep, and goats, are being grazed at or beyond their sustainable yield almost everywhere. In areas where livestock demands exceed carrying capacity, rangeland is being converted into wasteland. This is most pronounced in the pastoral economies of Africa and central Asia, where rangeland degradation is depriving herdsmen of their livelihood and reducing available meat supplies.

as "the strongest condition," the fact that in the United States, "Elites—the power holders—must accept the results of disruptive litigation, like it or not" (L. Friedman, 1975:278). Clearly, no socialist or authoritarian country will tolerate anything like the American form of judicial review. Their legal structures are not designed to accommodate these patterns.

In the context of litigation, the role of the Supreme Court in social change invites attention. While discussing the Supreme Court's ability to influence social change, Grossman (1970:545) suggested that the Court can "offer some limited support to social change by not deciding a case where its refusal to decide upholds or reinforces a lower court decision which itself favors change by legitimizing a governmental change policy, and also by refusing to decide a case in which a lower court decision has gone against forces seeking to preserve the status quo." There are, however, several momentous ways in which the Court, indeed, can influence social change; such as: (1) by a conscious and explicit program of innovation that may specify particular behavior changes; (2) by reinforcement of prior policy decisions seeking change against challenges to their authority or legitimacy; (3) by reinforcement or legitimization of the change-oriented policies of other governmental agencies or of important groups in society; (4) by specific invalidation of symbolic challenges to social change processes or policies (Grossman, 1970:545).

A good illustration of the role of the U.S. Supreme Court in social change is its 1973 decision on abortion, striking down most state laws prohibiting abortion and providing specific guidelines regulating lawmaking in this area. This decision is an important one, not only because of the sweeping consequences it has for most states, and despite the reputed conservatism of some of the newer appointees to the Court, but also because of the role the Court continues to play in social change. The Court is able to act on controversial questions of law when the legislatures cannot or will not act on controversial social issues. In this manner, it relieves one kind of build-up of political and social pressure through changes in the interpretation of law at precisely the times when most legislatures prefer to ignore the problems or heed them much more slowly.

Few sociologists and legal scholars today would accept the notion of Sumner (1906) that folkways and mores change slowly in response to modifications in conditions of social existence and in the interests of various groups. A body of research is accumulating, and theoretical perspectives have been presented that attempt to establish when and under what conditions law can "not only codify existing customs, morals, or mores, but also . . . modify the behavior and values presently existing in a particular society" (Evan, 1965:286). As William M. Evan (1965:286–287) lucidly articulates this position:

> As an instrument of social change, law entails two interrelated processes: the institutionalization and the internalization of patterns of behavior. In this context, institutionalization of a pattern of behavior means the establishment of a norm with provisions for its enforcement, and internalization of a pattern of

behavior means the incorporation of the value or values implicit in a law. . . . Law can affect behavior directly only through the process of institutionalization; if, however, the institutionalization process is successful, it, in turn, facilitates the internalization of attitudes or beliefs.

However, the extent to which the impact of law is felt and the degree to which it can be efficient vary according to the conditions present in a particular situation. The following stipulations can have great bearing on the effectiveness of law as a strategy of social change: (1) the law must emanate from an authoritative and prestigeful source; (2) the law must introduce its rationale in terms that are understandable and compatible with existing values; (3) the advocates of the change should make reference to other communities or countries with which the population identifies and where the law is already in effect; (4) the enforcement of the law must be aimed at making the change in a relatively short time; (5) those enforcing the law must themselves be very much committed to the change intended by the law; (6) the implementation of the law should include positive as well as negative sanctions; and (7) the enforcement of the law should be reasonable not only in terms of the sanctions used but also the protection of the rights of those who stand to lose by violation of the law (Evan, 1965:288–291).

Chin and Benne (1985:41–42) justly include law under the power-coercive approaches to effecting social change. Law in society is backed by legitimate authority, which has the mechanisms to enforce compliance in several ways. For example, in the context of analyzing incentives for compliance with environmental law, Stuart S. Nagel (1975:341–356) discussed the following methods: (1) sliding fees that go down as a reward for high compliance and go up for low compliance; (2) contingent injunctions that enjoin certain activities subject to the possibility of jailing for contempt if the noncomplying behavior is not changed; (3) the use of tax deductions, credits, exemptions, and subsidies to encourage compliance; (4) civil penalties, whereby private persons can bring lawsuits for damages caused by noncompliance; (5) adversely publicizing wrongdoers; (6) the use of selective government buying power to reward high compliers and thereby punish some noncompliers; (7) fines and jail sentences; and (8) conference persuasion.

Thus far, the discussion highlighted some of the general conditions in which law can be considered as a strategy of social change. Perhaps the best way to illustrate how law can be used as an instrument of change is to turn to a concrete case.

As part of a broader project on debtor-creditor relations, the author undertook a study of wage garnishment (a process that enables a creditor, upon a debtor's default, to seize his wages in the hands of his employer before they are paid to the debtor) of low-income families. The findings indicated that existing wage garnishment laws in Missouri at that time were more counterproductive than functional as a collection device. It was shown, among other things, that a number of employers had immediately dismissed employees upon the receipt of the first garnishment suit and that such an action was detrimental not only to the debtor but also to the creditor, the employer, and society at large. Moreover, in many cases, the judgment debtors were often "judgment-proof," in the sense that they had few, if any, tangible assets. Under the former system, garnishment proceedings may be instituted to attach wages due to the debtor by an employer and have the employer pay these wages to the creditor through the court. The objective of the proposed reform was to present a procedure to provide the judgment debtor who is being garnished protection from possible dismissal from his job or from bankruptcy and, at the same time, to enable creditors to maintain an effective collection method.

On the basis of the author's data and recommendations, House Bill 279 was designed and introduced in the 74th General Assembly of the State of Missouri. Under the proposed bill, the service of the writ would be made upon the defendant only, and the employer of the defendant would not be involved in the litigation process. Upon entry of the judgment, the court may order the judgment debtor to make payments to the clerk of the court. The payments would be dispersed in turn by the clerk. In settling the amount of these payments, the court would take into consideration the circumstances of the defendant, including his or her income and other obligations or considerations bearing on the issue. If the judgment debtor fails to obey the order of the court, then and only then may the creditor summon the employer as a garnishee. The primary intention of the bill was to prohibit employers from discharging employees upon the receipt of the first garnishment suit, thus saving thousands of jobs for low-income individuals annually in Missouri. It was estimated that on the national level, approximately 500,000 individuals are fired each year as a direct result of the practice of wage garnishment. The societal implications of the proposed change are obvious (Vago, 1968:7–20). Today, wage garnishment is regulated nationally. This is the result of the Consumer Credit Protection Act (P.L. 90-321), passed in 1968. The act protects consumers from being driven into bankruptcy by excessive garnishment of wages by limiting the amount of wages subject to garnishment to 25 percent of the employee's weekly disposable income. It also prohibits an employer from firing an employee solely because of wage garnishment (Vago, 2003:174–175).

SUMMARY

This chapter considered several social change strategies and tactics used in a variety of change efforts. Three aspects of planned social change were discussed—targets, agents, and methods. The target for planned change may be conceptualized on several levels, and, for the present purposes, individual, intermediate, and macrolevel target systems were discussed. Change agents are usually professionals who influence the change effort in a direction deemed desirable by a change agency. There are two broad categories of change agents: leaders and supporters. There are many categorizations in the typologies of planned-change strategies, and the principal methods can be subsumed under facilitative, reeducative, persuasive, and power strategies.

The use of violent strategies of social change is as old as human history. Their effectiveness is based on the willingness of certain segments of a society to go beyond the accepted patterns of action to promote change. The use of such a strategy entails the perception of relative deprivation among a potentially violent group, the maximization of the intensity of anger, and the emphasis of social facilitation variables. In most instances in the literature, violent strategies are not considered as desirable means for including social change.

Nonviolent strategies of change also have a long history. They are based, to a great extent, on "moral power," and they are likely to be effective when they are in accord with the value orientation of the change target and pertinent third parties. The choice of nonviolent strategy can reflect either an indirect or direct approach to the opponent's power. The former is based on the decision to meet the violent style of the opponent with nonviolence. The latter is founded on attempts to upset the opponent's power base, alter the opponent's attitudes and public image, and the opinion of third parties. The tactics of nonviolence can be classified under the headings of demonstration, noncooperation, and direct intervention. The nonviolent strategy of satyagraha involves many of these tactics.

The various types of social movements discussed have a number of characteristics in common, including an organizational structure, patterns of recruitment, ideology, personal commitment, and an opposition or target system. A common strategy in a social movement is generally adopted by the numerous coalitions of various organizations formed within the movement. The principal strategies used by movements in their attempts to influence the actions of their target systems are bargaining, coercion, and persuasion. Many of the movements are remembered more for the tactics they have deployed rather than for their objectives. The tactics used by social movements have been referred to as the "politics of disorder." A tactical program should have breadth, simplicity, and flexibility. The tactics used in a social movement are determined, to a great extent, by three factors: opposition, ideology, and public opinion.

There is a growing recognition of the role of law as a strategy of social change in contemporary society. Law can play an indirect role in social change by altering various social institutions, which, in turn, have a direct impact on society. Law can also exert a direct influence by legitimizing certain programs or procedures and delegitimizing traditional practices. In the United States, change through law may originate in one of four arenas: the judiciary, the legislature, the executive branch, and administrative agencies. Law is categorized under power-coercive approaches to social change, and it is backed by legitimate authority, which has the mechanisms to enforce compliance. The chapter concluded with a concrete illustration of how law was used to induce change in the context of wage garnishment.

SUGGESTED FURTHER READINGS

BENNIS, WARREN G., KENNETH D. BENNE, AND ROBERT CHIN (eds.). *The Planning of Change*, 4th ed. New York: Holt, Rinehart & Winston, 1985. A good collection of articles on the various aspects of planned social change.

DENMARK, FLORENCE L., AND LOEB ADLER (eds.). *International Perspectives on Violence*. Westport, CT: Praeger, 2003. An anthology of the similarities and differences in the use of violence in countries around the world. Many types and varieties of violence are covered.

FAIRCLOUGH, ADAM. *Better Day Coming: Blacks and Equality, 1890–2000*. New York: Viking, 2001. A survey on the struggle for racial equality with an emphasis on the civil rights movement and its accomplishments. A good source material.

GIUGNI, MARCO, DOUG MCADAM, AND CHARLES TILLY (eds.). *How Social Movements Matter*. Minneapolis, MN: University of Minnesota Press, 1999. A comprehensive overview of theoretical, methodological, and empirical work on social movement outcomes. The title nicely captures the theme of the compendium.

GRISET, PAMELA, AND SUE MAHAN (eds.). *Terrorism in Perspective*. Thousand Oaks, CA: Sage Publications, 2003. A general reference text on the various facets of contemporary terrorism in the United States and abroad.

HALSEY, RICHARD S. *The Citizen Action Encyclopedia: Groups and Movements That Changed America*. Westport, CT: Praeger, 2001. Containing nearly 300 cross-referenced entries, the book presents individuals, groups, and movements that achieved both national standing and significant success in altering the political, legal, social and economic structure of the United States.

HORNSTEIN, HARVEY A., BARBARA BENEDICT BUNKER, W. WARNER BURKE, MARION GINDES, AND ROY J. LEWICKI (eds.). *Social Intervention: A Behavioral Science Approach*. New York: Free Press, 1971. A classic and widely cited anthology of articles on diverse change strategies which are still being used today. The introduction to the various selections and the discussions are all highly comprehensive, and the sections on violent and nonviolent strategies are particularly recommended.

IRONS, PETER. *Jim Crow's Children: The Broken Promise of the Brown Decision*. New York: Viking, 2002. A controversial and provocative book on what happened after the victory in *Brown v. Board of Education*.

JACKSON, JOHN P., JR. *Social Scientists for Social Justice: Making the Case Against Segregation*. New York: NYU Press, 2002. A review of how social scientists struggled to impact American law and policy on race and poverty.

KETTNER, PETER M., JOHN M. DALEY, AND ANN WEAVER NICHOLS. *Initiating Change in Organizations and Communities: A Macro Practice Model*. Monterey, CA: Brooks/Cole, 1985. A presentation of an integrated model for initiating and carrying out changes in organizations and communities.

KUSHNER, HARVEY W. *Encyclopedia of Terrorism*. Thousand Oaks, CA: Sage Publications, 2003. A 523-page Abbas-to-Zubaydah guide to the world's most sinister terrorists and the destruction they have wrought. A most comprehensive and up-to-date reference on terrorism.

MALLICK, KRISHNA, AND DORIS HUNTER (eds.). *An Anthology of Nonviolence, Historical and Contemporary Voices.* Westport, CT: Prager/Oryx Press, 2002. A selection of historical and contemporary sources on the use of nonviolence as a realistic alternative.

OBERSCHALL, ANTHONY. *Social Movements: Ideologies, Interests, and Identities.* New Brunswick, NJ: Transaction Publishers, 1993. A comprehensive discussion of social movements and collective behavior and the strategies and tactics they deploy.

SEIDMAN, EDWARD (ed.). *Handbook of Social Intervention.* Beverly Hills, CA: Sage Publications, 1983. A compendium on the ways of creating change in a variety of settings.

TURNER, RALPH H., AND LEWIS M. KILLIAN. *Collective Behavior*, 3rd ed. Englewood Cliffs, NJ: Prentice Hall, 1987. See Part Four for an up-to-date, comprehensive review of social movements and their change strategies and tactics.

VAGO, STEVEN. *Law and Society*, 7th ed. Upper Saddle River, NJ: Prentice Hall, 2003. See, in particular, Chapter 7 on the role of law in social change.

REFERENCES

AARONSON, SUSAN ARIEL. *Taking Trade to the Streets: The Lost History of Public Efforts to Shape Globalization.* Ann Arbor: University of Michigan Press, 2001.

ALBRECHT, STAN L., BRUCE A. CHADWICK, AND CARDEL K. JACOBSON. *Social Psychology*, 2nd ed. Englewood Cliffs, NJ: Prentice Hall, 1987.

ALDER, CHRISTINE. "Violence, Gender and Social Change," *International Social Science Journal*, 44 (2) May 1992, pp. 267–276.

ALINSKY, SAUL. *Rules for Radicals.* New York: Vintage, 1972.

AUSTIN, JOHN R. "A Method for Facilitating Controversial Social Change in Organizations: Branch Rickey and the Brooklyn Dodgers," *Journal of Applied Behavioral Science*, 33 (1) March 1997, pp. 101–119.

BACON, LISA. "Rash of Vandalism in Richmond May Be Tied to Environment Group," *The New York Times*, November 18, 2002, pp. 1 and 7.

BENNE, KENNETH D. "The Current State of Planned Changing in Persons, Groups, Communities, and Societies." In Warren G. Bennis, Kenneth D. Benne, and Robert Chin (eds.), *The Planning of Change*, 4th ed. New York: Holt, Rinehart & Winston, 1985, pp. 68–82.

BENNIS, WARREN G., KENNETH D. BENNE, AND ROBERT CHIN (eds.). *The Planning of Change*, 4th ed. New York: Holt, Rinehart & Winston, 1985.

BERMAN, HARRIET KATZ. "Quarantine: Policing Prostitution," *Civil Liberties*, 301, March 1974, p. 1.

BLASER, KENT. "Apocalypse Now? Social Change in Contemporary America," *American Studies*, 37 (2) Fall 1996, pp. 117–131.

BLAUSTEIN, ALBERT P., AND ROBERT L. ZANGRANDO. *Civil Rights and the Black American: A Documentary History.* New York: Simon & Schuster, 1968.

BONDURANT, JOAN V. "Satyagraha as Applied Socio-Political Action." In Gerald Zaltman, Philip Kotler, and Ira Kaufman (eds.), *Creating Social Change.* New York: Holt, Rinehart & Winston, 1972, pp. 303–313.

Business Week. "Taxing the Wages of Sin," October 7, 2002, p. 12.

CHAMPAGNE, ANTHONY, AND STUART S. NAGEL. "Law and Social Change." In Edward Seidman (ed.), *Handbook of Social Intervention*. Beverly Hills, CA: Sage Publications, 1983, pp. 187–211.

CHIN, ROBERT, AND KENNETH D. BENNE. "General Strategies for Effecting Changes in Human Systems." In Warren G. Bennis, Kenneth D. Benne, and Robert Chin (eds.), *The Planning of Change*, 4th ed. New York: Holt, Rinehart & Winston, 1985, pp. 22–45.

CHONG, DENNIS. "Coordinating Demands for Social Change," *Annals, AAPSS*, 528, July 1993, pp. 126–143.

CLUTTERBUCK, RICHARD. *Terrorism in an Unstable World*. New York: Routledge, 1994.

COSTAIN, ANNE N., AND STEVEN MAJSTOROVIC. "Congress, Social Movements and Public Opinion: Multiple Origins of Women's Rights Legislation," *Public Research Quarterly*, 47 (1) March 1994, pp. 111–136.

DENMARK, FLORENCE L., AND LOEB ADLER (eds.). *International Perspectives on Violence*. Westport, CT: Praeger, 2003.

DEUTSCH, MORTON, AND MARY EVANS COLLINS. "Interracial Housing." In William Peterson (ed.), *American Social Patterns*. New York: Doubleday, 1965, pp. 7–62.

DOWNES, BRYAN T. "A Critical Reexamination of the Social and Political Characteristics of Riot Cities," *Social Science Quarterly*, 51 (2) 1970, pp. 349–360.

DROR, YEHEZKEL. "Law and Social Change." In Rita James Simon (ed.), *The Sociology of Law*. San Francisco: Chandler, 1968, pp. 663–680.

EORSI, GYULA, AND ATTILA HARMATHY. *Law and Economic Reform in Socialistic Countries*. Budapest: Akademiai Kiado, 1971.

EVAN, WILLIAM M. "Law as an Instrument of Social Change." In A. W. Gouldner and S. M. Miller (eds.), *Applied Sociology: Opportunities and Problems*. New York: Free Press, 1965, pp. 285–293.

FAIRCLOUGH, ADAM. *Better Day Coming: Blacks and Equality, 1890–2000*. New York: Viking, 2001.

FANON, FRANZ. *The Wretched of the Earth*. New York: Grove Press, 1968.

FONOW, MARY MARGARET. *Union Women: Forging Feminism in the United Steelworkers of America*. Minneapolis, MN: University of Minnesota Press, 2003.

FRANTZ, DOUGLAS. "'They're Coming After Us.' But Who Are They Now?" *The New York Times*, October 20, 2002, p. 12WK.

FRIEDMAN, LAWRENCE M. "General Theory of Law and Social Change." In J. S. Ziegel (ed.), *Law and Social Change*. Toronto: Osgoode Hall Law School/York University, 1973, pp. 17–33.

FRIEDMAN, LAWRENCE M. *The Legal System: A Social Science Perspective*. New York: Russell Sage, 1975.

FRIEDMANN, WOLFGANG G. *Law in a Changing Society*, 2nd ed. New York: Columbia University Press, 1972.

GAMSON, WILLIAM A. *The Strategy of Social Protest*, 2nd ed. Belmont, CA: Wadsworth, 1990.

GERLACH, LUTHER P., AND VIRGINIA H. HINE. *Lifeway Leap: The Dynamics of Change in America*. Minneapolis, MN: University of Minnesota Press, 1973.

GIUGNI, MARCO, DOUG MCADAM, AND CHARLES TILLY (eds.). *How Social Movements Matter*. Minneapolis, MN: University of Minnesota Press, 1999.

GOLDBERG, ROBERT A. *Grassroots Resistance: Social Movements in Twentieth Century America*. Belmont, CA: Wadsworth, 1991.

GRISET, PAMELA, AND SUE MAHAN (eds.). *Terrorism in Perspective*. Thousand Oaks, CA: Sage Publications, 2003.

GROSSCUP, BEAU. *The New Explosion of Terrorism*. Far Hills, NJ: New Horizon Press, 1991.
GROSSMAN, JOEL B. "The Supreme Court and Social Change: A Preliminary Inquiry," *American Behavioral Scientist*, 13, 1970, pp. 535–551.
GRUBERG, MARTIN. *Women in American Politics: An Assessment and Sourcebook*. Oshkosh, WI: Academia Press, 1968.
GURR, TED R. *The Conditions of Civil Violence: First Test of a Causal Model*. Monograph 28, Princeton, NJ: Princeton University Press, Center for International Studies, 1967.
HABERMAN, CLYDE. "22 Killed in Terrorist Bombing of Bus in Tel Aviv; 46 Wounded," *The New York Times*, October 20, 1994, pp. A1, A7.
HALL, RICHARD H. *Organizations: Structures, Processes, and Outcomes*, 8th ed. Upper Saddle River, NJ: Prentice Hall, 2002.
HALSEY, RICHARD S. *The Citizen Action Encyclopedia: Groups and Movements That Changed America*. Westport, CT: Praeger, 2001.
HENDERSON, HAZEL. "Social Innovation and Citizen Movements," *Futures*, 25 (3) April 1993, pp. 322–339.
HORNSTEIN, HARVEY H., BARBARA BENEDICT BUNKER, W. WARNER BURKE, MARION GINDES, AND ROY J. LEWICKI (eds.). *Social Intervention: A Behavioral Science Approach*. New York: Free Press, 1971.
HUNTER, SHIREEN T. (ed.). *Islam, Europe's Second Religion. The New Social, Cultural, and Political Landscape*. Westport, CT: Praeger, 2002.
HUNTINGTON, SAMUEL P. "Reform and Political Change." In Gerald Zaltman, Philip Kotler, and Ira Kaufman (eds.), *Creating Social Change*. New York: Holt, Rinehart & Winston, 1972, pp. 274–284.
INDERGAARD, MICHAEL. "Community-Based Restructuring: Institution-Building in the Industrial Midwest," *Urban Affairs Review*, 32 (5) May 1997, pp. 662–683.
IRONS, PETER. *Jim Crow's Children: The Broken Promise of the Brown Decision*. New York: Viking, 2002.
JACKSON, JOHN P. JR. *Social Scientists for Social Justice: Making the Case Against Segregation*. New York: NYU Press, 2002.
JERVIS, ROBERT. "An Interim Assessment of September 11: What Has Changed and What Has Not?" *Political Science Quarterly*, 117 (1) Spring 2002, pp. 37–55.
KANTER, ROSABETH MOSS. *The Change Masters: Innovations for Productivity in the American Corporation*. New York: Simon & Schuster, 1983.
KELMAN, HERBERT C. "Manipulation of Human Behavior." In Gerald Zaltman, Philip Kotler, and Ira Kaufman (eds.), *Creating Social Change*. New York: Holt, Rinehart & Winston, 1972, pp. 574–584.
KETTNER, PETER M., JOHN M. DALEY, AND ANN WEAVER NICHOLS. *Initiating Change in Organizations and Communities: A Macro Practice Model*. Monterey, CA: Brooks/Cole, 1985.
KILLIAN, LEWIS. "Social Movements." In Robert E. L. Faris (ed.), *Handbook of Modern Sociology*. Chicago: Rand McNally, 1964, pp. 426–455.
KOTLER, PHILIP. "The Five C's: Cause, Change Agency, Change Target, Channel, and Change Strategy." In Gerald Zaltman, Philip Kotler, and Ira Kaufman (eds.), *Creating Social Change*. New York: Holt, Rinehart & Winston, 1972, pp. 172–186.
KPOSOWA, AUGUSTINE J., AND J. CRAIG JENKINS. "The Structural Sources of Military Coups in Postcolonial Africa, 1857–1894," *The American Journal of Sociology*, 99 (1) July 1993, pp. 126–164.
KUSHNER, HARVEY W. *Encyclopedia of Terrorism*. Thousand Oaks, CA: Sage Publications, 2003.

LAQUEUR, WALTER. "Terrorism via the Internet," *The Futurist*, 31 (2) March–April 1997, pp. 64–66.

LEMPERT, RICHARD, AND JOSEPH SANDERS. *An Invitation to Law and Social Science: Desert, Disputes, and Distribution*. New York: Longman, 1986.

LESLIE, GERALD R., AND SHEILA K. KORMAN. *The Family in Social Context*, 6th ed. New York: Oxford, 1985.

LIPPITT, RONALD, JEANNE WATSON, AND BRUCE WESTLEY. *The Dynamics of Planned Change*. New York: Harcourt, 1958.

LUSCOMBE, BELINDA. "Alarming News! Models Prepared to Show Off Their Bodies," *Time*, November 4, 1996, p. 99.

LUTTWAK, EDWARD. *Coup d'État: A Practical Handbook*. Cambridge, MA: Harvard University Press, 1979.

MACQUEEN, GRAEME. "Marking and Binding: An Interpretation of the Pouring of Blood in Nonviolent Direct Action," *Peace and Change*, 17 (1) January 1992, pp. 60–81.

MALLICK, KRISHNA, AND DORIS HUNTER (eds.). *An Anthology of Nonviolence, Historical and Contemporary Voices*. Westport, CT: Prager/Oryx Press, 2002.

MARDEN, CHARLES F., GLADYS MEYER, AND MADELINE H. ENGEL. *Minorities in American Society*, 6th ed. New York: HarperCollins, 1991.

MARIGHELLA, CARLOS. *The Terrorist Classic: Manual of the Urban Guerrilla*. Chapel Hill, NC: Documentary Publications, 1985.

MAYHEW, LEON H. "Stability and Change in Legal Systems." In Bernard Barber and Alex Inkeles (eds.), *Stability and Social Change*. Boston: Little, Brown, 1971, pp. 187–210.

MCADAM, DOUG, AND DAVID A. SNOW (eds.). *Social Movements: Readings on Their Emergence, Mobilization, and Dynamics*. Los Angeles: Roxbury Publishing Company, 1997.

NAGEL, STUART S. *Improving the Legal Process*. Lexington, MA: D.C. Heath, 1975.

NIEBURG, H. L. "The Threat of Violence and Social Change." In Gerald Zaltman, Philip Kotler, and Ira Kaufman (eds.), *Creating Social Change*. New York: Holt, Rinehart & Winston, 1972, pp. 161–171.

OBERSCHALL, ANTHONY. *Social Movements: Ideologies, Interests, and Identities*. New Brunswick, NJ: Transaction Publishers, 1993.

OPPENHEIMER, MARTIN. *The Urban Guerrilla*. Chicago: Quadrangle Press, 1969.

OPPENHEIMER, MARTIN, AND GEORGE LAKEY. "Direct Action Tactics." In Gerald Zaltman, Philip Kotler, and Ira Kaufman (eds.), *Creating Social Change*. New York: Holt, Rinehart & Winston, 1972, pp. 313–319.

PIERCE, NEAL. "Women Advocates Are Now in System," *St. Louis Post-Dispatch*, August 14, 1987, p. 3B.

PRATKANIS, ANTHONY R., AND MARLENE E. TURNER. "Persuasion and Democracy: Strategies for Increasing Deliberative Participation and Enacting Social Change," *Journal of Social Issues*, 52 (1) Spring 1996, pp. 187–206.

RHOADS, CHRISTOPHER. "Short Work Hours Undercut Europe in Economic Drive. Culture That Values Leisure Now Finds It an Obstacle; Jobs Are Going Elsewhere. Taking 9½ Weeks of Vacation," *The Wall Street Journal*, August 8, 2002, pp. A1, A5.

RIDING, ALAN. "The Hooking of Carlos Opens a Can of Worms," *The New York Times*, August 22, 1994, p. A4.

ROBERTSON, PETER J., AND SONAL J. SENEVIRATNE. "Outcomes of Planned Organizational Change in the Public Sector: A Meta-Analytic Comparison to the Private Sector," *Public Administration Review*, 55 (6) November–December 1995, pp. 547–558.

ROCHON, THOMAS R., AND DANIEL M. MAZMANIAN. "Social Movements and the Policy Process," *The Annals of the American Academy of Political and Social Science*, July 1993, pp. 75–88.

ROGERS, EVERETT M. "Change Agents, Client, and Change." In Gerald Zaltman, Philip Kotler, and Ira Kaufman (eds.), *Creating Social Change*. New York: Holt, Rinehart & Winston, 1972, pp. 194–213.

ROSS, JEFFREY IAN. "Structural Causes of Oppositional Political Terrorism: Toward a Causal Model," *Journal of Peace Research*, 30 (3) August 1993, pp. 317–329.

SAGE, WAYNE. "Crime and the Clockwork Lemon." In Charles H. Swanson (ed.), *Focus: Unexplored Deviance*. Guilford, CT: Dushkin Publishing Group, 1977, pp. 79–84.

SCHISSEL, BERNARD. "Law Reform and Social Change: A Time-Series Analysis of Sexual Assault in Canada," *Journal of Criminal Justice*, 24 (2) March–April 1996, pp. 123–139.

SHARPE, GENE. "Mechanisms of Change in Nonviolent Action." In Harvey A. Hornstein, Barbara Benedict Bunker, W. Warner Burke, Marion Gindes, and Roy J. Lewicki (eds.), *Social Intervention: A Behavioral Science Approach*. New York: Free Press, 1971, pp. 546–557.

SKOLNICK, JEROME H. *The Politics of Protest*. New York: Ballantine, 1969.

STISSER, PETER. "A Deeper Shade of Green," *American Demographics*, 16 (3) March 1994, pp. 24–30.

SUMNER, WILLIAM G. *Folkways*. Boston: Ginn, 1906.

THOMAS, DOUGLAS. *Hacker Culture*. Minneapolis, MN: University of Minnesota Press, 2002.

TRIVIZAS, EUGENE, AND PHILIP T. SMITH. "The Deterrent Effect of Terrorist Incidents on the Rates of Luggage Theft in Railway and Underground Stations," *British Journal of Criminology*, 37 (1) Winter 1997, pp. 63–75.

TURNER, RALPH H., AND LEWIS M. KILLIAN. *Collective Behavior*, 3rd ed. Englewood Cliffs, NJ: Prentice Hall, 1987.

U.S. COMMISSION ON CIVIL RIGHTS. *Twenty Years After Brown: Equality of Economic Opportunity*. Washington, DC: Government Printing Office (630–354/396, July 1975).

VAGO, STEVEN. "Wage Garnishment: An Exercise in Futility Under Present Law," *Journal of Consumer Affairs*, 2, 1968, pp. 7–20.

VAGO, STEVEN. *Law and Society*, 7th ed. Upper Saddle River, NJ: Prentice Hall, 2003.

WALTON, RICHARD E. "Two Strategies of Social Change and Their Dilemmas." In Gerald Zaltman, Philip Kotler, and Ira Kaufman (eds.), *Creating Social Change*. New York: Holt, Rinehart & Winston, 1972, pp. 352–359.

WARREN, ROLAND L. *Social Change and Human Purpose: Toward Understanding and Action*. Chicago: Rand McNally, 1977.

WEINER, TIM. "Terrorism's Worldwide Toll Was High in 1996," *The New York Times*, May 1, 1997, p. A9.

WILSON, JAMES Q. "Why Are We Having a Wave of Violence?" *The New York Times Magazine*, May 19, 1968, p. 23.

WILSON, JOHN. *Introduction to Social Movements*. New York: Basic Books, 1973.

ZALTMAN, GERALD, AND ROBERT DUNCAN. *Strategies for Planned Change*. New York: Wiley, 1977.

ZALTMAN, GERALD, PHILIP KOTLER, AND IRA KAUFMAN (eds.). *Creating Social Change*. New York: Holt, Rinehart & Winston, 1972.

Chapter 10

Assessment of Change

This chapter will examine the various measurements and methodologies used in the study of social change. It is organized around five themes: technology assessment, methodologies for change evaluation, use of social indicators, methodologies for forecasting change, and policy implications of change assessment. Prior to the discussion of these topics, let us briefly consider some of the more general ways sociologists go about studying change, such as the use of various survey methods, and the employment of historical data, personal documents, and records and the kinds of research objectives to which individual research objectives are suited (see, for example, Dale & Davies, 1994, for a comprehensive overview).

The repertoire of social science methodology enables us to assess change at various levels (see, for example, Klandermans & Staggenborg, 2002). Although the majority of the studies in sociology deal with events at only one point in time (see, for example, Czaja & Blair, 1996), survey methods exist that can be used to measure change over time. They are employed in longitudinal studies (Babbie, 2001) designed to permit observations over an extended period and include panel, recall, and trend surveys.

ASSESSMENT TECHNIQUES

Panel Surveys

Panel surveys are used to compare the same measurements for the same sample at several different points in time. The sample in this case is called the *panel*. Panel analysis is useful in the study of the processes of change in a person's life. A classic example of this type of survey design is found in *The People's Choice*, by Paul Lazarsfeld and associates (1944). The researchers interviewed a panel of 600 residents of Erie County, Ohio, once per month between May and November of 1940 with respect to how they intended to vote in the presidential election of 1940. Of particular interest to these investigators was the process by which panel members decided to vote in the way they eventually did. Another classic illustration of such a study is the Survey Research Center's (1972) *A Panel Study of Income Dynamics (PSID)*. In this survey, approximately 5,000 households throughout the United States were interviewed during the spring of each year from 1968 to 1972. The survey obtained detailed information about various sources of income and documented the changes in the characteristics of those moving into and out of poverty during the five-year period. Although PSID was initiated in 1968 as a short-term study, the annual sampling has continued as of 1996 with lavish funding from official and nonofficial sources. The database is continuously updated to reflect the vast economic and demographic realities in the United States (Brown, Duncan, & Stafford, 1996). Other studies on income dynamics dealt with job tenure changes over various time-horizons (Brown & Light, 1992). Data from a panel study were also used to describe alterations in occupational aspirations of high school graduates who experienced unemployment during the first year after graduation (Empson-Warner & Krahn, 1992). In a similar vein, the Medical Expenditure Panel Survey was created in recent years to provide the health services research and health policy community with facts that discuss health care use, expenditures, payment sources and health insurance status of the U.S. population (Cohen et al., 1997).

A special type of panel analysis is called *cohort analysis*. Such a study deals with more specific subpopulations (cohorts) as they change over time. Generally, a cohort is an age group, such as those born during the 1930s, but it can also be based on some other time grouping, such as people attending college during the Vietnam War, people who got married in 1969, and so on. An example of cohort analysis would be a series of national surveys, at ten-year intervals, to study the changes in economic attitudes of the cohort born during the Great Depression of the early 1930s. A sample of individuals twenty to twenty-five years of age would be surveyed in 1950; another sample of those thirty to thirty-five years of age in 1960; up to the age group sixty to sixty-five years in 1990. Although the people studied in each of the surveys would be different, each sample would represent the survivors of the cohort born between 1930 and 1935 (Babbie, 2001). Another example of cohort analysis is the nationwide panel surveys undertaken in Sweden on the decline in adherence to religious beliefs from older to younger birth cohorts (Hamberg, 1991).

Roberta Ash Garner (1977) notes that a well-designed panel study allows the researcher to draw conclusions about causality. Thus, one can study change in terms of cause and effect if a study has the following design: "(1) There should be two groups, initially similar (for instance, both selected by random sampling from the same population); (2) one group only is exposed to the possible causal factor; (3) the groups are then compared with the expectation that the one exposed to the factor ('the cause') will be in some way different from the other group" (1977:71). But she also points out that it is difficult and often unethical to establish an experimental situation of this nature for studying human beings. At times, however, such a situation is approximated. For example, in the well-known study of how the political and economic attitudes of young women changed as a result of their attendance of Bennington College would be an illustration of this design (Newcomb, 1943). In this study, the similar political attitudes of women was the dependent variable and the four years at Bennington College was the independent variable. As a control, data were gathered from students of similar background who attended two other colleges. It was found that women at Bennington College developed liberal and radical political and economic views more than did the students from the other two colleges. It can thus be concluded that something about the Bennington experience caused the changes in attitude.

There are both advantages and limitations to panel studies. Many of the advantages relate to being able to interview the same subjects repeatedly over a period of months or years. If the researcher finds shifts in attitudes or reported behavior, he or she is in a better position to argue that there has been a real change in the population of interest than a researcher who undertakes a different kind of approach, such as the "one-shot," or cross-sectional, analysis (that is, obtaining data at only one point in time). In cross-sectional surveys, researchers know that any difference they find can be attributed either to a real change in attitude or behavior in the population of interest or to a difference caused by a sampling error (that is, even if two samples are drawn from the same population, there will be some differences in observed values due to random fluctuation). This sampling error difference can be ruled out when a panel design is used. Another advantage of panel studies is that they permit much more information to be collected about each respondent than is feasible with a cross-sectional survey design. They also avoid a heavy dependence on the memory of respondents for information about the time period covered by the panel; however, they may still rely on memory for questions about subjects' past.

Panel studies, like all research techniques utilized in social science, are obviously not without their limitations (Dooley, 2001:128–129). One difficulty is that over a period of time there is bound to be some sample mortality; that is, there will be a loss of panel members because of the difficulty in reaching them, lack of cooperation, or death. It was pointed out elsewhere in the text, for example, that approximately one out of every five Americans change residence every year. The record-keeping problems caused by such mobility for a panel study are substantial. For example, in a panel study of income dynamics, a substantial effort went into minimizing sample loss, but still only

62 percent of those in the original sample remained at the end of five years. Another limitation of panel analysis is that it takes a long time to collect data. It is also more expensive than other types of designs. Still another problem with repeated interviews with the same group is *panel conditioning;* that is, the risk of repeated contacts may sensitize the subjects. For instance, members of a panel may want to be consistent with the views they express on consecutive occasions. If this happens, the panel becomes atypical of the population it was selected to represent (Nachmias & Nachmias, 2000:155).

Recall Surveys

Another form of quasi-longitudinal design is the recall survey. Such a survey conducts an observation at one point in time and has respondents remember information to establish a prior observation. Such an approach is practically useless as evidence for inferring causality. Still, studies based on recall surveys occasionally appear in the literature to describe events that result in changes in perceptions, practices, or attitudes (Midanik, 1993; Scott & Zac, 1993). For example, after the United States recognized China, an investigator may want to study the impact of recognition on attitudes toward China. The investigator takes a survey of present attitudes and also asks respondents to recall their attitudes before recognition of China. He or she then compares the remembered attitudes with present attitudes to determine how much they have changed. The recall survey is the weakest kind of longitudinal design. It attempts to approximate the pretest-posttest, one-group design by recalling the pretest observation. Obviously, lacking control over history, maturation, and experimental mortality, recall designs provide a very weak basis for causal inferences. In addition, memory decay and distortion are forms of the maturational factor that is particularly likely to contribute to survey invalidity.

Trend Surveys

Trend surveys are useful for describing changes. Trend surveys sample a population at two or more points in time. The population is the same but different samples are drawn for different observations. Examples would be a comparison of U.S. censuses over time to determine growth in the national population, or an examination of a series of National Opinion Research Center polls to note trends in attitudes over time concerning, for instance, abortion, pornography, satisfaction with work and financial situation, sexual behavior among teenagers, AIDS awareness, or the spread of TB cases (Kilborn, 1994; Naticka-Tyndale, 1991). Trend surveys are also used to determine changes in income and wealth, work time required to buy certain consumer goods and services (*Fortune*, 1987), and, in general, to "monitor" social change in the form of social indicators (Moore & Sheldon, 1965; Harris, 1987), which will be discussed shortly.

Historical Analysis

In addition to panel, recall, and trend surveys, sociologists interested in the study of social change often use *historical data* to establish long-term trends or to test theories on a variety of topics such as race relations (Luckett, 2002); women's role in the British Industrial Revolution (Tilly, 1994); abortion and adoption policies over time (Brigham, Rifkin, & Solt, 1993; Hall & Stolley, 1997); attitudes toward migrants in the U.S. since the 1880s (Simon, 1993); the concept of privacy from Plato to the modern times (Peterman, 1993); and the review of the Italian parliament's efforts to deal with problems posed by the Mafia (Marotta, 1993).

In a well-known attempt to study long-term trends, Pitirim A. Sorokin (1957) used content analysis (a technique to determine the content of a recorded communication by systematic, objective, and quantitative analysis) of paintings. He classified paintings of the various historical periods into two categories, religious and secular, in an attempt to learn what changes had occurred in the world view. He found that 94.7 percent of the known European paintings of the tenth and eleventh centuries were of a religious nature and only 5.3 percent were secular. By the fourteenth and fifteenth centuries, the percentage of paintings of a religious nature had dropped to 85, by the seventeenth century to 50.2, by the nineteenth century to 10, and by the twentieth century to 3, with corresponding rises in the secular category.

On occasion, historical case studies are used to test theories. In such instances, the emphasis is not so much on documenting trends over time as on examining in detail one reasonably limited set of historical events. One of the best illustrations of this in the literature is Kai Erikson's (1966) analysis of American Puritanism. Ever since Émile Durkheim first formulated the notion that deviance served certain social functions in a society, sociologists have looked for evidence to support this contention. Durkheim had the idea that a society needed its deviants in order to reaffirm continually the boundaries of propriety. The arguments for the importance of deviants are intriguing. They provide a novel way of showing how certain institutions in a society, if not the society itself, continue to operate. Durkheim argues, for example, that without the existence of sinners, a church could not exist. The very existence of sin provides the opportunity for believers to reaffirm the faith that has been offended by the sinner. So the worst thing that can happen to a church is to eliminate sin completely from the world and completely propagate the faith to society.

By selecting a specific case, Erikson hoped to demonstrate how, to the extent that a common morality exists in a society, the society comes to depend on its deviants for the maintenance of its social boundaries. In *The Wayward Puritans*, he shows how these theoretical notions can be applied to understand the witch hunts of colonial America. Relying primarily on secondary sources, he describes how the "moral entrepreneurs" of early Massachusetts colonial society, in their zeal to maintain religious purity, launched full-scale attacks on alleged Salem witches. This particular attack on "deviants" is only one of several that Erikson documents and analyzes. Although he does not draw these parallels himself, one could, on the basis of causal historical knowledge, assume that a number of historical cases might be used as additional historical illustrations of the functional view of deviance: the McCarthyism of the 1950s, the events leading up to the laws of discrimination against Jews in Nazi Germany, the internment of Japanese-Americans during World War II, the brutal attempts at "ethnic cleansing" by Serbs in the former Yugoslavia in the mid-1990s, or the aftermath of the September 11, 2001, events.

The use of *personal documents*, such as diaries, letters, and biographical statements, has long been considered useful in sociological research aimed at studying social change. Perhaps the best-known example of this form of primary data in sociological research is W. I. Thomas and Florian Znaniecki's (1918) study, *The Polish Peasant in Europe and America*. In this investigation, the authors were concerned with the adaptation of individuals to new forms of social organization. The Polish peasant in America provided an excellent opportunity for understanding the modes of adaptation and assimilation of persons transplanted from a largely agrarian to a modern industrial society. Their research was based on letters that these immigrants sent to their families in the "the old country." The data obtained from these letters, in fact, provided a continuous history of their New World experience. These letters, constituting actual interaction between persons, allowed the researchers to assess dynamics of attitude change, changing relations within primary groups, and the development of community life. Their insights about the assimilation of immigrants remain influential in adaptation studies (Conzen, 1996; Taylor, 2003)

Sociologists interested in historical experiences of large groups or population aggregates often turn to available records that provide systematic historical data on large numbers of individuals. For example, when demographers seek to document rates of fertility, patterns of immigration and migration, changing food resources in society, and birthrates and death rates, they utilize existing statistical records. These records enable them to examine trends of changes on a number of levels—for a selected part of society, for a whole society, for several societies; indeed, even for the world.

Of course, historical records can be used for other types of studies of change. For example, Frances Fox Piven and Richard Cloward (1993) traced the welfare system in the United States from the Great Depression to the present, revealing a distinctive pattern of relief policy—at certain times, relief policy has been quite liberal and at other times highly restrictive. Their major thesis, which is convincingly documented through their historical investigation, is that the welfare system has been used to control and regulate the poor. "Historical evidence suggests that relief arrangements are initiated or expanded during occasional outbreaks of civil disorder produced by mass unemployment, and are then abolished or contracted when political stability is returned" (Piven & Cloward, 1993:xiii). In a different vein, another study analyzed the presentation of abortion and adoption in marriage and family textbooks published from 1951 to 1987. The depiction of adoption and abortion changed over time, showing influences of societal and disciplinary orientations. Marriage and family texts show abortion as a macro, societal issue and depict adoption as a micro issue. Early texts viewed abortion as an issue of morality and ethics (Hall & Stolley, 1997).

These general comments on methodological tools for social change research are not intended to replace the more detailed discussions found in books about methods of social research. They are simply intended to provide a brief exposure to some of the strategies utilized in the study of social change. Let us now consider the subject of technology assessment.

TECHNOLOGY ASSESSMENT

In Chapter 1, it was shown that technology is one of the principal sources of social change. Technological developments have certainly brought society to an unprecedented level of comfort and prosperity, but they also have all too often brought unanticipated and undesirable consequences (see, for example, Jasanoff et al., 1994; Konstadakopulos, 2002). From environmental pollution to urban congestion, many of the major problems in society are strongly influenced by modern technology. The concern with the growing impact of technology on society and some of its deleterious effects gave rise to technology assessment. It is defined by one of its most influential practitioners and spokesmen, Joseph E. Coates (quoted by Alan Porter et al., 1990:155), as "a class of policy studies which systematically examine the effects on society that may occur when a technology is introduced, extended or modified. It emphasizes those consequences that are unintended, indirect, or delayed." Such studies should also offer alternative solutions to a problem based on their social costs, and make recommendations for policy changes or for new initiatives.

Over two decades ago, in a provocative book, *Technology and Society*, David M. Freeman (1974) stated the following reasons that remain valid for the necessity of increased technology assessment:

1. The new technologies advanced and diffused in recent times have shown enormous power to alter society and affect the environment on previously unknown scales. Supersonic aircraft, pesticides, nuclear wastes with half-lives of thousands of years, the decline and growth of industries relocating populations, transportation systems contributing to suburban sprawl, mind- and body-altering drugs—all these and many more produce effects felt over great space and time.
2. Nowadays there is a trend of diminishing lead times between initial technological invention and widespread diffusion and application leaving less time to make analysis and adjustment.

3. Various technologies are impacting on a human population of increasing size, diversity, and differentiation—developments that make technological impacts more diverse, uneven, and difficult to sort out.
4. Formerly, a small group of elites made strategic decisions unencumbered by interests of outsiders, peasants, and the urban poor. However, political revolutions of the last two centuries have all posited the ideal of participatory decision making on the part of the affected. The world is full of conflicting and cooperating groups who seek access to decisions that affect their lives and those of their children.
5. Both the beneficial and detrimental impacts of technologies are felt with increasing rapidity ever more powerfully and unevenly on diverse sectors of the population. Our technical powers, as in the past, exceed our capacity to make fully intelligent social choices with full awareness of the consequences. (1974:2–3)

In recent years, the spread of concerns with technological impacts has led governments of industrialized nations to begin thinking about new modes of technological planning and decision making (see, for example, Schot, 1992; Konstadakopulos, 2002). In the United States, the Technology Assessment Act was passed in 1972, establishing within the legislative branch an Office of Technology Assessment (OTA)—a move that greatly enhanced the capacity of Congress to deal with technological issues and the implications and effects of applied research and technology. Over the years, OTA has grown increasingly influential as a policy advisory body to Congress, greatly expanded its scope, and gained increasing currency among executive agencies of the federal government, corporations, and academic researches (Teich, 2002). Similarly, in Europe, technology assessment is seen as a vital part of national and international technology policies prompted by the growing free-market mentality and demand-oriented technology policy (Smits et al., 1995).

The scope of technology assessment ranges from broad problem-oriented investigations, which may consider a major social problem (for example, energy shortage) through technology-oriented studies designed to anticipate the effects of a particular technology (videophone, for example), to the most specific form, the project assessment, which concentrates on a single application of technology (for instance, power-plant sitting) (Porter et al., 1990:155).

The approaches to technology assessment may be future-oriented, present-oriented, or past-oriented. There are two types of *future-oriented* approaches: anticipatory and responsive. The former entails forecasting new trends and their possible effects—for example, genetic engineering. The latter responds to already perceived problems—for example, new nuclear power plants. There are also two types of *present-oriented* assessments: reactive and corrective. The reactive deals with problems of unknown causes or disasters such as large-scale oil spills or earthquakes. The corrective is concerned with known problems whose effects are felt, their causes traced, and for which corrective actions are possible, such as air or water pollution. *Past-*

oriented assessments are retrospective in nature. They examine the circumstances and facts of why a project was successful (for example, sperm banks), rejected, or abandoned—for example, nuclear power plants or strip mining technologies.

Recurrent Steps in Technology Assessment

In five technology assessment studies (of automotive emissions, computers and communications, industrial enzymes, mariculture, and water pollution by domestic wastes), Gabor Strasser (1973:915) identified seven general steps that still guide research and are comprehensive enough to fit most circumstances.

>   *Step 1:* Define the assessment task—discuss relevant issues and any major problems; establish scope (breadth and depth) of inquiry; and develop project ground rules.
>
>   *Step 2:* Describe relevant technologies—describe the major technology being assessed; other technologies supporting the major technology; and the ones that are competitive to the major and supporting technologies.
>
>   *Step 3:* Develop state-of-society assumptions—identify and describe major nontechnological factors influencing the application of the relevant technologies.
>
>   *Step 4:* Identify impact areas—ascertain those societal characteristics that will be most influenced by the application of the assessed technology.
>
>   *Step 5:* Make preliminary impact analysis—trace and integrate the process by which the assessed technology makes its societal influence felt.
>
>   *Step 6:* Identify possible action options—develop and analyze various programs for obtaining maximum public advantage from the assessed technologies.
>
>   *Step 7:* Complete impact analysis—analyze the degree to which each action option would alter the specific societal impacts of the assessed technology discussed in Step 5.

Methods of Technology Assessment

Technology assessment has no defined set of tools to be applied in a definite predetermined way and is most effective when applied in the early stages of research and development (Tepper, 1996). The tools are borrowed from all fields—the econometrician, the statistician, the sociologist, and the operations research analyst. These techniques include qualitative and quantitative appraisal techniques such as those used for the selection of research projects; systems analysis; decision aids, such as relevance trees and evaluation matrices; economic, technological, social, and, if it were possible, political forecasts; simulation and operations research models, especially those that are able to cope with random phenomena; questionnaires; public participation hearings; and, finally, and not to be overlooked, sheer "gut-feeling" and intuition.

As it may be expected, there are several deficiencies in the use of technology assessment. Bodo Bartocha (1973:347–348), is still correct is suggesting that the most critical voids in our knowledge regarding technology assessment are:

1. Criteria for choice and priorities.
2. Reference standards and pacing parameters sensitive to end objectives.
3. Indications and new values systems to express "worth" in other than just monetary terms.
4. Better simulation techniques and dynamic models.
5. Skilled interdisciplinary personnel and adequate resources.
6. Popularization and public understanding of long-range risk, expected values, and uncertainty.
7. Imagination.

These limitations are further compounded by the high cost of technology assessment programs. Joseph F. Coates (1977:269–270) reported in an early investigation that the costs of conducting the Alaska Pipeline study are alleged to have run about $9 million. Smaller assessment studies range from $125,000 to $300,000. A study conducted by the now-defunct Department of Health, Education, and Welfare on "violence and television" cost $1.5 million. As may be expected, the cost of carrying out comparable work is much higher today.

Environmental Impact Statement

An independent examination of methods and techniques for assessing the impacts of technology stemmed from the requirements of the National Environmental Policy Act of 1969 for the preparation of environmental impact statements (Dooley, 2001:299). According to Section 102 of the act, each agency "must include in every recommendation or report on proposals for legislation and other major federal actions significantly affecting the quality of the human environment, a detailed statement by the responsible official on: (i) the environmental impact of the proposed action; (ii) any adverse environmental effects which cannot be avoided should the proposal be implemented; (iii) alternatives to the proposed action; (iv) the relationship between local short-term use of man's environment and the maintenance and enhancement of long-term productivity, and (v) any irreversible and irretrievable commitments of resources which would be involved if the proposed action should be implemented" (Coates, 1977:261).

This requirement to prepare environmental impact statements has created a general demand throughout the federal system for systematic exploration of the secondary impacts of projects, and a consequent demand for the development of methodology, techniques, approaches, and procedures.

During the first three years of the act, some 3,500 impact statements have been prepared, at an aggregate cost of about $65 million.

The 1972 World Environmental Conference in Stockholm was instrumental in creating an international awareness about the protection of environment and the conservation of natural resources. Following the model of the United States, many countries drafted legislation to create new departments on environmental protection and mandated environmental impact requirements (C. Porter, 1985:27–29). In the years since the conference, there has been a trend toward the gradual acceptance of thorough environmental investigation and evaluation of projects in most industrial countries of the world (see, for example, Therivel & Paridario, 1996 a&b). There has also been a growing concern with social impacts. In Australia, for example, there were many instances in which white workers were introduced into a remote or rural area with a small population. Aboriginal communities were particularly vulnerable to intrusions, and hostility often developed between an existing black community and the new white population. Even without racial conflicts, the introduction into a poorer settlement of a new highly paid work force, associated with, for instance, strip-mining ventures, can result in tensions resulting from envy of the more affluent lifestyle of the newcomers. In addition, when hundreds, if not thousands, of workers descend on a small isolated community, severe pressures are exerted on existing social organizations (schools, recreation facilities, hospitals), and conflict is likely to ensue between members of the community and the workers. Even with an urban environment, certain types of developments need attention. For instance, a major highway may geographically divide a community, as a lack of access across the highway would interfere with shopping patterns or children's movements to and from school. It is part of the environmental impact statement to consider the results of the development on the existing social environment and for the necessary commitments to be made to mitigate any adverse impacts.

Social Technology

It should be noted that the methods of technology assessment can also be used for the study of the effects of "social" technologies. The definition of technology assessment is capable of embracing changes in institutions and organizations—changes such as the invention of mass armies and the related invention of the military draft, the Land Grant Act establishing the state college system in the United States, the acceptance of farmers of twentieth century technologies (Kline, 2000), the invention of pay-as-you-go income tax, the phenomenal increase in information technology (Laszlo, 1993), and the implications of new reproductive technologies such as the *in vitro* fertilization of women over sixty years of age (Shore, 1992). Social technology policy making is becoming a major issue (Sclove, 1994). One may consider legislation as a principal means of institutionalizing and regulating certain social inventions and, therefore, clearly in need of continuing assessment. In fact, some assessments of this nature have been already carried out; for example, studies of the impact of marijuana on society, the consequences of heavy daily doses of TV violence, and the 1986 study by the Attorney General's Commission on Pornography (Vago, 2003:418).

METHODOLOGIES FOR CHANGE EVALUATION

In political, social and organizational contexts, there has been a noticeable rise of interest in applying social science methodologies to the evaluation of change over the years. This concern is reflected in the increasing use of social science methods to monitor the impact of social legislation under the heading of evaluation research (Ewalt, 1996). It is further seen in the rapid growth of the number of social science journals that are either devoted specifically to publishing evaluation research or accept such research material for publication. Prominent among them are the *Evaluation Review, New Directions in Program Evaluation, Evaluation Practice, Evaluation and Program Planning,* and *Evaluation and the Health Professions,* besides several others (Berk, 1995).

Evaluation research is a form of applied research (see, for example, Valach, Young, & Lynam, 2002) (in contrast to pure research) whose objective is to assess the effectiveness of ongoing programs and activities intended to bring about some kind of planned change. The aim of evaluation research is to establish how successful a particular planned change effort is in achieving its goals of improving conditions for some groups or individuals (Boruch, 1996; Rossi, Freeman, & Lipsey, 1999). There have been many attempts for planned change to eliminate some negative condition or create some positive condition that affects the lives of people by instituting various programs. The federal government, for instance, initiated a large variety of programs during the 1960s, with the purpose of eventually eliminating poverty. Similar examples of planned change efforts can be cited in the areas of school reform (Baizerman & Compton, 1992), programs for the homeless (Cohen et al., 1993), or attempts at local economic development (Hughes, 1991). A basic objective of evaluation research is to answer the question of whether or not such improvement-oriented programs achieve what they set out to achieve. The outcome of such research can be used in policy making to determine which programs should be changed in what way, which programs should be eliminated, and so on.

Technically speaking, there are no formal methodological differences between evaluation and nonevaluation research (see, for example, Patton, 2002). Both have in common the techniques and the basic steps that must be followed in the research process. The difference is in the intent and purpose of the investigator (Smith & Glass, 1987:33). Evaluation research uses the deliberately planned introduction of some independent variable. Unlike nonevaluation research, evaluation research assumes that program goals and objectives are desirable, and its purpose is to determine the extent to which these objectives have been attained. Essentially, "evaluative research asks about the kind of change the program views as desirable, the means by which this change is to be brought about, and the signs according to which such change can be recognized" (Suchman, 1967:15).

Carol Weiss (1972:6–8) identifies several additional specific criteria that distinguish evaluation research from other types of research: (1) evaluation research is generally conducted for a client who intends to use the research as a basis for decision making; (2) the investigator deals with his or her client's questions as to whether the client's program is accomplishing what the client wishes it to accomplish; (3) the objective of evaluation research is to ascertain whether the program goals are being reached; (4) the investigator works in a situation where priority goes to the program as opposed to the evaluation; (5) there is always a possibility of conflicts between the researcher and program staff because of the divergences of loyalties and objectives; and (6) in evaluation research there is an emphasis on results that are useful for policy decisions. Consequently, some special problems are associated with evaluation research. There might be resistance to it by administrators of programs who feel that negative results might terminate their programs. The investigator might also be subjected to time constraints because he or she must deal within the time structure of the program being studied.

Identifying Evaluation Goals

In evaluating change, a number of areas must be taken into consideration. For ascertaining the program objectives, Suchman (1967) provides a guideline for questions that should be raised:

1. *What* is the nature of the content of the objective? Are we interested in changing knowledge, attitudes or behavior? Are we concerned with producing exposure, awareness, interest, or action?
2. *Who* is the target of the program? At which groups in the population is the program aimed?
3. *When* is the desired change to take place? Are we seeking an immediate effect or are we gradually building toward some postponed effect?
4. Are the objectives *unitary* or *multiple*? Is the program aimed at a single change or at a series of changes?
5. What is the desired *magnitude* of effect? What is the extent of anticipated results?
6. *How* is the objective to be attained? What methods, procedures, and techniques will be used in realizing program objectives? (1967:39–41)

To this list, one should add: What are the unintended effects of the program objectives? How much does it cost? And what are its costs relative to its effectiveness and benefits? (Rossi, Freeman, & Lipsey, 1999:18).

Design Considerations

A number of research approaches can be used for evaluating the effectiveness of a program (Yin, 1992). One approach might be the study of a group of individuals from the target population after it has been exposed to a program that had been developed to cause change. This approach is referred to as the *one-shot study*. Another possible approach is to study a group of individuals both *before and after* exposure to a particular program. Still another possibility would be the use of some kind of *controlled experiment.* There are many different kinds of controlled experiments, and the simplest kind for evaluation research may be set up in the following way. A number of individuals are selected from the target population with the use of probability sampling. The object is to create two groups as nearly similar as possible. The usual way to do this is through the random assignment of half the selected individuals to one group and the other half to the second group.

The key aspect of experimentation is that one group, the experimental group, participates in the program under consideration while the second group, the control group, does not. Measurements of the desired goals and outcomes of the program are made both before and after the program is conducted to see whether the program produces its desired changes. This is done for both the experimental and the control group. Ideally, the measurements should show no difference between the two groups before the program commences. If, however, the program is effective, the "after" measurements should show that the experimental group has experienced a change in the desired direction, which is noticeably greater than any change registered for the control group. The "after" measurement for the control group is the means by which we take into account any of the "other changes" related to the desired outcome of the program, which may be occurring for both the experimental and control groups. If we subtract the change experienced by the control group from the change evidenced in the experimental group, the result is a measure of the program's impact.

At this point, it should be obvious that an experiment is clearly superior to either a one-shot study or a before-and-after study. The control group in an experiment eliminates the possible interpretation that "other changes" are not accounted for in the one-shot and before-and-after approaches. However, in actual situations, the use of control groups is not always feasible. In some instances, the use of control would involve the denial of certain program treatments (for example, clinical) or benefits (for instance, welfare) to individuals.

At times, these research designs are supplemented by cost-benefit analysis and social audits. *Cost-benefit analysis* is basically a method for discovering the value of a good for which no market price exists. In social research, the difficulty with cost-benefit analysis is that there are no objective criteria with which to measure costs and benefits. More important, no provisions exist for incorporating nonmonetary elements into the calculations of cost-benefit analysis. For example, how does one assign a value to "marital happiness" or "work satisfaction"? Moreover, because a change in one part of the social system will affect other parts in the same system, it is essential to make decisions about which effects are the important ones. For example, a program for reducing speech problems may in turn create the need to retrain speech therapists for other occupations. Although there are limitations to cost-benefit analysis, at times it has proved to be a useful supplemental method in evaluation studies and there is growing political pressure for its utilization in policy making (Swanson, 1996).

Perhaps the easiest types of costs to estimate are "extra expenditures needed to add a particular supplemental service to an ongoing program" (Glaser, 1973:25). For example, the cost per client can be determined by adding up the costs of operating the entire supplemental services needed and dividing by the number of clients per year. Benefits may be measured by "estimated reductions in social costs" (Glaser, 1973:27). But Daniel Glaser (1973:36–39) also notes that many social costs are purely speculative. For example, there is no way of expressing the anguishes of rape or the emotional costs of mugging. Still, some social costs can be dealt with rationally. For instance, the costs of heavy drug usage may be viewed from the point of view of society's loss of the drug user's work power and the loss of his or her potential tax dollars.

Social audits are also used to supplement other forms of research design and are helpful in determining the efficiency of a program (Johnson, 2001). In the social audit, "resource inputs initiated by policy are traced from the point at which they are disbursed to the point at which they are experienced by the ultimate intended recipient of those resources" (Coleman, 1972:18). Social audit is obviously related to research outcomes. Lack of social change may be due to two factors: (1) The resource inputs may have been ineffective, or (2) they may never have reached their intended recipients. As an illustration of social audits, one may consider the tracing of resource inputs from the point of dispersement in voluntary organizations such as the United Fund to the point at which those inputs are experienced by the intended recipients.

Data Collection

In addition to considerations of objectives and research designs, evaluation research also includes plans for data collection, sampling, and measurement. Concerning data collection sources for evaluation research, Weiss (1972:53) compiled the following list:

> Interviews, questionnaires, observation ratings (by peers, staff, experts), psychometric tests (of attitudes, values, personality preferences, norms, beliefs), institutional records, government statistics, tests (of information, interpretation, skills, application of knowledge), projective tests, situational tests

(presenting the respondent with simulated life situations), diary records, physical evidence, clinical examinations, financial records, and documents (minutes of board meetings, newspaper accounts of policy actions, transcripts of trials).

As far as sampling is concerned, probability sampling plans are generally preferred for choosing people from the target population, but they are not always possible in evaluation research (Rossi, Freeman, & Lipsey, 1999:235–263). In reality, more often than not a sample will consist of self-selected volunteers. The purpose of measurement in evaluation research is to develop measures of variables that validly and reliably reflect what the investigator is trying to measure. It is important for a program to have clear and explicitly stated goals if it is to permit valid and reliable measurements.

Problems of Research Implementation

It is important to note that the effectiveness of a program is often considered by administrators and program personnel to be secondary to the implementation of the program. Clearly, conflicts exist between the two goals. For example, as a program is being carried out, the strategies for dealing with the problem area may change because of the decisions of program administrators. It is also possible that program personnel may change or participants may drop out during the program. To cope with these and similar problems, Weiss makes the following suggestions:

1. Take frequent periodic measures of program effect (for example, monthly assessments in programs of education, training, therapy) rather than limiting collection of outcome data to one point in time.
2. Encourage a clear transition from one program approach to another. If changes are going to be made, attempt to see that A is done for a set period, then B, then C.
3. Clarify the assumptions and procedures of each phase and classify them systematically.
4. Keep careful records of the persons who participated in each phase. Rather than lumping all participants together, analyze outcomes in terms of the phase(s) of the program in which each person participated. (1972:98)

Utilization of Results

The final consideration of evaluation research involves the utilization of results. As James Coleman (1972:6) states, "the ultimate product is not a 'contribution to existing knowledge' in the literature, but a social policy modified by the research results." In many instances, however, the clients fail to utilize results of evaluation research, the negative results of evaluation are ignored (Posavac, 1992), or the results have no visible impact on subsequent policy decisions (Weiss, 1986:216). They may feel committed to particular ways of doing things despite evidence that the program is ineffective. (This is particularly true in instances when programs were instigated by political pressures such as the various endeavors in model city programs, war against poverty, drug and alcohol rehabilitation, and corrections. As public interest waned in the later stages of these programs, there was no pressure to incorporate the results of evaluation studies into the ongoing activities.) The utilization of results could also bring about changes in relationships with funding agencies, clients, or other organizations. It is also plausible that the recommendations are economically unfeasible for the organization, and as a result, it cannot change its practices.

Obviously, there are a number of ways an organization can respond to the results of evaluation research. If the results are negative or anticipated to be so, an organization can attempt to use evaluation research in the following ways:

1. *Eyewash:* an attempt to justify a weak or bad program by deliberately selecting only those aspects that "look good." The objective of the evaluation is limited to those parts of the program evaluation that appear successful.
2. *Whitewash:* an attempt to cover up program failure or errors by avoiding any objective appraisal. A favorite device here is to solicit "testimonials" which divert attention from the failure.
3. *Posture:* an attempt to use evaluation as a "gesture" of objectivity and to assume the pose of "scientific" research. This "looks good" to the public and is a sign of "professional" status.
4. *Postponement:* an attempt to delay needed action by pretending to seek the "facts." Evaluative research takes time, and, hopefully, the storm will blow over by the time the study is completed. (Suchman, 1967:143)

The common feature of all these techniques is the attempt by the organization to manipulate evaluation research for its own interests. Evaluation researchers must be aware of this possibility and act accordingly.

In some instances in which the results of evaluation research are negative, the clients can discard the negative findings. In the field of corrections, for example, the following list of rationalizations of negative results has been used by professionals (Ward & Kassebaum, 1972:302):

The therapeutic relationships examined or the impact of the program is "too subtle to measure with statistics."

Even though they may come back to prison, they are better or happier or more emotionally stable people for having participated in the program.

The effects of the program can only be measured in the long run, not just during the first six months or year after release.

The program or the technique is OK but it is not designed for this particular individual.

The reason that the program failed was that it wasn't extensive enough or long enough or applied by the right people.

The program is worth it if it saved one person.

It is not too surprising to see such rationalizations from individuals and organizations whose programs are subjected to criticism as a result of evaluation research. On the other hand, dismissing the findings of evaluation research may be the result of methodological weaknesses and design irrelevance because policymakers are more likely to rely on their own experience than trust results of poorly executed studies. Finally, even if the study is methodologically sound and well carried out, it may not bear on the "critical issues." In spite of these limitations, evaluation research should be perceived as an important way of making the knowledge of the social sciences relevant to the study of social change, and social scientists need to be encouraged to devote more attention to it (Rossi, Freeman, & Lipsey, 1999: 389–398). In the next section, the use of social indicators in the study of change will be examined.

SOCIAL INDICATORS

There is a striking difference between how we as a nation assess our economic well-being and how we assess our social well-being (Land, 2001). We are greatly concerned with economic performance. Hourly, daily, weekly, monthly and quarterly, we observe precise fluctuations in a variety of economic barometers, from the Dow Jones Average to the Consumer Price Index. We have a Gross Domestic Product, an Index of Leading Economic Indicators, and an Index of Consumer Confidence. The economy's performance is continuously being monitored and data are being generated and presented to us in the form of economic indices and indicators that tell us how we are doing.

In contrast, the social well-being of the nation is reported much less frequently and without an overall view of the nation's social performance. To reduce the gap between economic and social reporting, social scientists have long felt the need to develop valid statistical measures to monitor levels and changes over time in fundamental social concerns. Since the 1960s, there has been a growing interest in the United States and abroad in measures of social conditions to supplement economic indicators with information on the quality of life and subjective well-being (Diener, 1994; Estes, 1996; Henderson, 1994). This interest resulted in proposals for social indicators that allow researchers to assess changes in the condition of a nation over time from some point in the past to the present. Measures of social indicators basically involve the identification of certain key aspects of social life such as health, crime, housing, satisfaction, use of time, and so on. These categories, in turn, are broken down into specific contents for which data are gathered over time. Generally, social indicators are conceived of as long-term measures in that the same data are gathered consistently at specific intervals to allow for an analysis of changes which have taken place. Indicators range from broad measures of societal performance to specific neighborhood-level activities (Sawicki & Flynn, 1996).

The social indicators "movement" is relatively recent, although there were earlier attempts. For example, in 1929 a presidential committee was appointed to undertake a quantitative analysis of American society and the changes that were occurring. It resulted in the publication of *Recent Social Trends* in 1933 (de Neufville, 1975:40). Much of the resurgence of interest in social indicators was due to the success of economists using economic indicators to predict the advantages of a tax cut upon the economy in the early 1960s. The question was posed by Raymond A. Bauer: "If we have highly organized economic indicators, why can't we set up a system of social indicators as well?" (quoted by Gross & Springer, 1969:18). The same question was in the minds of the President's Science Advisory Committee when, in 1962, it called for "the systematic collection of basic behavioral data for the United States . . . data that are comparable, systematic and periodically gathered" (Gross & Springer, 1969:18). By 1972, more than a thousand books and articles on social indicators had appeared. In the early 1980s, there was widespread reduction of funding for social research, which included social indicator work, and an apparent decline in interest by government officials in monitoring perceptions of well-being. By the late 1990s, funding for social indicators research was partially restored by both the government and private organizations, and the major journal of the social indicators movement, *Social Indicators Research*, remains vigorous, and important conceptual and empirical contributions continue to be made. Social indicators research concentrates on attempts to develop and refine measures of the quality of life, on indicator systems for monitoring an existing situation in society at a particular administrative or geographic level (for example, housing needs of low-income people), on the development of performance measures of public service delivery (for instance, health care for the elderly), and on comparative techniques (for example, analysis of predictors of life satisfaction and well-being in a number of countries or comparing specifics, such as health data, cross-culturally) (Diener et al., 1994; Land, 2001; McPheat, 1996; Rothenbacher, 1993).

Approaches to Social Indicators

There are several approaches to social indicators. They all have in common attempts to provide guidelines for the development of measures to fill the gaps in existing knowledge about social conditions; to try to link various measures so as to provide a picture not only of relevant phenomena but also of the relationships between them; and they all try to reduce information overload through concentration on relevant indicators and supporting data. It is obvious that whatever merit these various approaches have is determined by the criteria used to establish "relevance," what should be measured, what should be related to what, and how it should be presented. Let us now illustrate some of the more widely used approaches to social indicators (de Neufville, 1975:45–54; Land, 2001; World Bank, 2003).

One approach to social indicators is to work on new methods for measuring hard-to-quantify aspects. Illustrations for this approach would entail the search for new ways to measure socioeconomic status, underemployment, or poverty. Experimental work is also under way to quantify and measure aspects of life such as work and housing satisfaction, housing and neighborhood quality, inequality, alienation and the use of the satisfaction concept in the wider conceptions of welfare (see, for example, Larson, 1993; Travis, 1993; Veenhoven, 1996).

Another approach to social indicators entails replication studies. In this approach, the argument is that social indicators are supposed to measure social change, but in reality very little is known about how to do that. Here the emphasis is on one-time surveys, not on longitudinal time-series data. What is required is a set of measures taken in a carefully controlled way over time. To save time, the effort is to replicate studies that have already been done at least once. The objective is both to learn more about ways of collecting and interpreting indicators over time and more about the social processes themselves. Studies of social change in communities would be illustrative of this approach.

In still another approach, the emphasis is on indicators in their specific ideological, political, and organizational context. The accent is on how information can be used in a decision-making process. For example, contrary to dominant ideology, a comparative, continent-by-continent study of health data concludes that socialism is more efficient than capitalism in addressing health care needs, and in underdeveloped countries the socialist system has a clear advantage as measured by global health indicators such as infant mortality, life expectancy, birth weights, etc. (Navarro, 1993). In political and organizational contexts, United Nations agencies are searching for indicators that will help redirect particular policies of developing countries and the international organizations that influence them. Some organizations such as the World Bank and the United Nations Commissions for Trade and Development provide loans and aid to nations at least in part in relation to their performance on certain indicators. For instance, nations in the lowest quartile of the gross domestic product, literacy levels, and percentage urban population are eligible for special aid. International loans are generally given for projects perceived to increase the gross domestic product (Lengyel, 1986).

Data Collection

The principal methods of data collection for social indicators include interviews, self-reports, observations, and archives research.

The interview is the dominant technique because it is the most flexible. However, it is also the most expensive way of gathering data. Self-reports, in which individuals or organizations provide information on themselves according to certain established formats, provide a less expensive means of getting some of the information otherwise obtainable only through interviews. It has obvious limitations, however, such as incomplete answers to questions, or failure to return the forms. Observation means getting information through watching, hearing, or otherwise directly sensing something. Its disadvantages include difficulties in interpretation and possible reactions in the observed. Finally, using existing documents is probably the easiest and least expensive way of collecting data. However, it should be noted that vital statistics, crime, and health and welfare data, which provide much of the background for social indicators, have initially been collected for other purposes. Documentary information is generally more useful in performing the activity it was designed for rather than analyzing it for other purposes.

There are many social indicators in use both internationally and nationally. International organizations, in particular the Organization for Economic Cooperation and Development (OECD) and the World Bank, have been active in developing social indicators to measure the quality of life among its member countries. The OECD social indicators concentrate on general social concerns common to the twenty-four member nations and the World Bank surveys some eighty countries. The indicators include demographic, income and poverty trends; health; individual development through learning; employment and quality of working life; time and leisure; commands over goods and services; physical environment; personal safety and the administration of justice; and social opportunity and participation (World Bank, 2003). These indicators provide opportunities for intergroup, intertemporal, and international comparisons. Intergroup comparisons reveal relative levels of well-being of various population categories and thus provide guidance with regard to priorities for policy attention. Intertemporal comparisons give indications of changes that have taken place and show the quality of past government interventions. Finally, in addition to their inherent normative interests, international comparisons can throw light on how alternative schemes and institutional frameworks can effectively contribute to improve levels of quality of life in a society. The next section will consider the methodologies for forecasting change.

Methodologies for Forecasting Change

The future has always had a fascination for humankind. From the earliest times, humans have sought means for predicting the future. Kings and at least one late twentieth century U.S. president (and former film star) had astrologers, while others relied on tools ranging from chicken entrails to complex mathematical models and computers—all with various degrees of success unrelated to sophistication of the tools they used. To a great extent, the ability to control the effects of change depends on being able to forecast the likely course of its development.

Current interest in forecasting methodologies can be attributed to the confluence of a number of factors. The downfall of communism in the former Soviet Union and Warsaw Pact countries brought about historically unprecedented economic, social, and political transformations that came as a surprise to most social scientists. Rapid changes in population, depletion of natural resources, and overproduction of scientific manpower have created an awareness of the importance of ascertaining optimal rates for consumption and technological growth and anticipating supply and demand levels in the advanced skills provided for youth. Forecasting of changes is also needed in social planning, in the setting of national goals, and in establishing priorities for governmental intervention and manipulation. For planning purposes, for example, it is important to estimate with some degree of accuracy what the population of a society will be ten, twenty, or thirty years later and the earth's agricultural capacity to provide for human needs (Bongaarts, 1994). The business world is preoccupied with planning for the future ranging from market conditions, leadership and competition to rethinking principles, controls and complexity (Gibson, 1997; Glenn & Gordon, 2002). (Organizing and being part of the growing circuit for seminars on planning and forecasting methods for business is a lucrative undertaking. The futurist gurus, including such names as John Naisbitt, Warren Bennis and Alvin and Heidi Toffler [all mentioned in the book] are an elite group of university professors, economists and consultants who often conduct such seminars for business and industry.) Casual reading of newspapers also suggests the importance of knowing what energy needs and natural resources will be in the future. We might also want to know whether significant changes will occur in employment opportunities in the future or whether welfare case loads or crime rates will increase or decrease.

There is no shortage of forecasting methods. In an early Organization for Economic Cooperation and Development survey, Erich Jantsch (1967) already identified more than 100 distinguishable techniques—although many of these are only variations in the choice of certain statistical or mathematical methods. In the same, 1967, the premier issue of the *Futurist* appeared and since then there has been steady parade of predicting technologies, many of them captured in the 1996 *Encyclopedia of the Future* (Cornish, 1997). For present purposes, however, only a few of the more common (and not too mathematical) methods will be considered to illustrate briefly some of the ways in which change may be forecasted.

Extrapolative Forecasting The foundation of all forecasting is some form of *extrapolation*, namely, the effort to read some continuing tendency from the past into a determinant future in an attempt to aid rational decision making (Chalkley, 1993). The most common, and deceptive, technique is the straight projection of a past trend plotted on a line or curve. Linear projections represent the extension of a regular time series—productivity or expenditures—at a constant rate. Most of economic forecasting is still based on linear projections because the rates of change in the economy seem to be of that order. In other areas, such as population, one cannot make simple predictions based on past trends. Instead, those interested in population changes talk about ranges of growth or decline that are based on a number of forecasts, and each forecast is based on a different assumption about future fertility rates. For example, a demographer might say, "If the fertility rate is 2.9 births per woman, we can expect the population to grow this way; if the rate is 2.4 births, population growth will assume a different direction," and so on. In other words, demographers will not make one flat prediction but, instead, will present a number of forecasts based on alternative assumptions about key rates.

Intuitive Forecasting It has been recognized in the scientific literature that intuition plays an important role in decision-making, which provides the rationale for *intuitive forecasting* (Vogel, 1997) There are two popular forms: scenario writing and the Delphi technique. The technique of *scenario writing,* popularized by Herman Kahn and Anthony Wiener (1967) and the Hudson Institute, is used widely for sociological, political, and environmental forecasting (Coyle, Crawshay, & Sutton, 1994). A scenario attempts to describe, in systematic and exhaustive but hypothetical and largely qualitative terms, the future sequence of events that would appear logically to evolve, step by step and through cause-and-effect relationships, from any given set of conditions or recognized trends. Emphasis is placed on those critical decision points from which alternative chains of events might arise and on the simultaneous interactions between events and their environment. A single set of assumed initial circumstances can generate an entire family of related scenarios (or alternative futures), any one of which may be plausible. Military strategists in the Pentagon, medical researchers, businesspeople, demographers, and many others rely on the technique of scenario writing. For example, the Pentagon continuously prepares, revises, and updates scenarios for nuclear attack in view of the changing nature of weapons technology. Medical research and planners concerned with the AIDS epidemic use scenarios that supplement other forms of projections about the future based on different assumptions about the spread of the disease (Bongaarts, 1996).

The *Delphi technique* was developed by Olaf Helmer (1966, 1994), a mathematician at the RAND Corporation. Since its introduction, it has experienced ever-increasing utilization, variants, praise and criticism (Neiger et al., 2001; Passig, 1997). It is designed to apply the collective expertise and intuition of a panel of experts by developing a consensus through several steps of systematic questioning and polling about future events. The polling process is carefully organized so as to minimize the biases that might otherwise arise from interacting personalities or other psychological influences within the expert panel. A feedback system is used to sharpen or narrow the forecast through successive rounds of polling that are designed to call the attention of the panelists to factors they might have initially overlooked or dismissed and to force them to rethink or defend responses that differ markedly from the panel's overall views. The outcome typically is an approximate schedule of future occurrences. Delphi exercises can be particularly useful for exploring the future when adequate historic data are unavailable or when future developments are likely to be strongly influenced by such considerations as changing social values or political feasibility. Scenario writing and the Delphi technique have been applied to a variety of topics such as automation, electric and hybrid vehicles (Ng, Anderson, & Santini, 1996), space exploration, probability and prevention of war, and population growth.

Modeling Forecasting In *modeling forecasting*, researchers increasingly use computer technology to simulate future social trends such as population growth from 1988 to 2087 in China (Shen & Spence, 1996). It is one of the most difficult forecasting techniques, and the outcomes usually tend to be rather controversial (Li & Hinich, 2002; Van Steenburgen, 1994). Still, models built on assumptions of discontinuity and nonlinearity hold promise for analyzing contemporary social change and have analytic value for testing new change theories (Hallinan, 1997).

One of the most publicized debates is the controversy precipitated by the publication of *The Limits of Growth,* in 1972, by Donella Meadows and her colleagues (1972). In their book they raised the question: What will happen to the world if current economic and demographic trends continue to increase at present rates? On the basis of data from 1900 to 1970, Meadows and her associates constructed a model composed of five key variables central to the world's ecological system—population, food supply, natural resources, industrial production, and pollution. They then constructed a set of mathematical equations detailing the processes through which the five variables interact with each other. These equations, constructed from available data, describe a feedback system in which a change in any one of the variables effects changes in the other variables, which, in turn, modify the variable that started the change process. One of the several equations describing the dynamic interactions between the variables might, for example, detail a feedback process that is set in motion by a change in population growth rates resulting in changes in demands for natural resources. This produces changes in productivity; these changes, in turn, affect the food supply, resulting in changes in population growth. After describing mathematically how the variables have interacted with each other in the past, they were prepared to simulate that same process into the future. The results are quite gloomy. They have predicted that the limits to growth on earth will be reached within the next 100 years and most likely will result in a rather sudden and uncontrollable decline in both population and industrial capacity (Meadows et al., 1972:23).

A more recent attempt in global forecasting was the *Global 2000 Report to the President.* It was commissioned by the Carter administration as an attempt to employ the huge amount of data and modeling techniques available to the federal government to develop a comprehensive and authoritative series of projections concerning the world's population, environment, and resources. It was a massive three-year study with rather gloomy conclusions. In the dramatic words of the study's summary:

> If the present trends continue, the world in 2000s will be more crowded, more polluted, less stable ecologically, and more vulnerable to disruption than the world we live in now. Serious stresses involving population, resources, and environment are clearly visible ahead. Despite greater material output, the world's people will be poorer in many ways than they are today. (Teich, 2002:136)

Survey Forecasting *Survey forecasting* entails the use of survey instruments in either a panel design (using the same respondents in successive surveys) or in a cross-sectional design (using samples of individuals drawn at successive points in time), both with a view to identifying emerging trends in or estimates of attitudes. It is used primarily to forecast for a limited time horizon in areas such as political campaigns (Who would you vote for?) and consumer behavior (Do you plan to buy . . . ?). As a rule, political pollsters do not consider their polls to be valid for more than a week or so, and, similarly, consumer buying and economic confidence forecasts tend to have a rather short time horizon.

Clinical Prediction In *clinical prediction,* the emphasis is on what individuals, groups, or societies will do, given information about attitudes, beliefs, past experiences, and so on, and observations on their or its behavior. "The transfer of this procedure from the clinic to the society at large is referred to as 'social psychiatry'—an enterprise that is generally subject to severe criticism as being too superficial and anthropomorphic" (Harrison, 1976:7). On the individual level, fairly accurate predictions may be made based on performance on intelligence tests, standardized personality tests, other measurements and instruments (such as the various college and professional school entrance examinations), and the analysis of existing biographical information. The usefulness of this method is, however, highly questionable for the prediction of social events.

Intuitive Planning Technically speaking, *intuitive planning* is not a method of forecasting; rather, it is a subjective, nonexplicit, nonreproducible estimation of a likely course of events in a plan (Harrison, 1976:8). It is based on a combination of past experience, common sense, and a touch of self-attributed clairvoyance and is mentioned here simply because some policymakers use this fast, inexpensive, and methodologically sloppy approach in their work.

Multimethod Forecasting Quite frequently, one finds a number of the preceding types of forecasting methods combined in various ways to produce a forecast such as, for example, involving the prediction of criminal behavior (see Harris, 1994). Obviously, it is very difficult to formulate guidelines for the best mix of methods to use for a given social forecasting problem. One may assume that if several different forecasting methods are used with the same set of data it may be more accurate than if only one method is used. However, there is no information on how much more accurate a forecast will be as to the use of combination or multiple methods.

Accuracy of Forecasts Those doing most forecasting research—think tanks, corporate planning offices, government agencies, and the like—are subjected to strong economic, time, and professional prestige motivations to produce social forecasting studies that look good. Daniel P. Harrison (1976:56) notes that with the various kinds of forecasting methods, the amount of error ranged between just a few percentage points (for example, with econometric models, survey forecasting) to over 40 percent (clinical prediction), depending on the method and time horizon used. He comments that "In almost every instance where forecast accuracy was assessed in terms of estimated user needs in particular contexts of use none of the methods could be said to perform at an adequate level; this may help to account for the modest impact forecasts have had on decision making" (1976:57). The state of the art of forecasting change clearly provides vast opportunity and need for research on forecasting methods in addition to the substantial amount of work that has been done on forecasting methodology to date. In the final section, policy implications of change assessment will be considered.

POLICY IMPLICATIONS

In the preceding sections several methodologies have been discussed that are used in the assessment of social change. In a sense, the development of these methodologies can be seen as a response to the growing demand for the quantification of social phenomena for decision-making purposes. Many of these methodologies are capable of generating information that can have policy or applied implications. Such information is helpful in transferring the basic knowledge and techniques for use in policy decisions or in evaluating current policies or proposed policy alternatives (see, for example, Maxfield & Babbie, 2001:322–330). Data generated through research provide policymakers with means for identifying problems and grounds for their discussion. Availability of hard data also helps in reducing the judgmental elements in decision making and thus the personal responsibility of decision makers.

Research findings also filter through to policymakers indirectly. Often, they hear about generalizations and ideas in the mass media or pick up information during conversations with colleagues and consultants. In this sense, research enlightens them and modifies the definition of problems they face (Weiss, 1986:218–219). This does not mean, it should be noted, that policymakers always rely directly or indirectly on data in making decisions. Often political considerations, personal experience, interest-group pressures, and a host of other phenomena enter into the picture.

Still, the methods of technology assessment are being increasingly used in policy making. Technology assessment is policy- and action-oriented, and the results are being used to change or influence policy decisions. This orientation stems from the milestone events that have contributed to the establishment of technology assessments as legitimate and substantive programs within the realm of governmental activities, both in the United States and elsewhere. As was pointed out, the recognition of the need for technology assessment resulted in the formal establishment of the Office of Technology Assessment in the United States Congress.

Technology assessment may be seen as part of a rational process of policy making with four steps: (1) identification of possible outcomes of policy alternatives; (2) estimation of the valency or probability of each of the possible outcomes; (3) estimation of the utility or disutility of each of the outcomes to the interested parties; and (4) weighing the utilities and disutilities to the interested parties and deciding whether the policy alternative is better than other alternatives (Folk, 1977:243). The importance of the methods and techniques of technology assessment for decision making is also reflected in the requirements of the National Environmental Policy Act of 1969 for the preparation of environmental impact statements for federally sponsored projects.

The use of quantitative information is increasingly built into legislation, and there are specific requirements for the evaluation of many federal programs and activities designed to induce change in some area. As it was noted, evaluation research is characterized by explicitness of policy implications in the design and execution of the research plan and the incorporation of variables specifically relevant to the problem at hand. Evaluation research allows policymakers to determine the effectiveness of a program, whether or not it should be continued or phased out, and what in-course adjustments, if any, are needed to make it more effective. But care needs to be exercised to avoid reducing outcomes to what may be called "one-number" summaries of complex and multi-dimensional programs (Broder, 1997).

Social indicators for some time now have been used for measuring and reporting changes in the quality of life and related social concerns. Lately there has been a growing reliance on social indicators in decision making and policy debates, both at the national and international levels (see, for example, Land, 2001; McPheat, 1996). Policymakers increasingly find it desirable to issue information designed to estimate or evaluate the state of society and in varying degrees to assess alternative courses of action. Social indicators are also used as a vehicle to focus on public discussion of changes in the quality of life, increasing the level of awareness of the public, who, in turn, can exert some pressure on decision makers to engage in alternative courses of action.

Forecasting methodologies are essential for long-term planning and decision-making efforts. As with other methodologies of change assessment, governmental and nongovernmental policymakers at various levels are increasingly relying on the use of estimates and projections for future trends so that decisions and policies can be as future-proof as possible (Coyle, 1997). With improvements in forecasting technologies, this reliance is anticipated to grow.

It should be noted, however, that once these various social science methodologies become relevant to and influential on policy, they become part of politics by definition. In such a situation, data can become tools for immediate political ends; politicizers of data are not interested in them for their information content, but for propaganda. Ideally, the objective should be to insulate, but not isolate, the statistics from the immediate vagaries of day-to-day politics, to strike some sort of balance between political and technical considerations, permitting neither to dominate, and to concentrate on accuracy and not on advocacy

In contributing to decisions of technological, economic, administrative, and social welfare policy, social scientists can provide skills and perspectives related to an enriched appreciation of human needs, a fuller anticipation of the consequences of new technological inventions or new policies, and a greater respect for basic human values. In order to do so, however, there is a need for a greater dialogue between social scientists and decision-making bodies.

SUMMARY

This chapter examined the various measurements and methodologies used in the assessment of change. Longitudinal designs conduct observations at two or more points in time. There are two major types: panel and cohort. Panel analysis involves the observation of the same sample at two or more points in time. Cohort analysis is the observation of a specific cohort (age group) at two or more points in time. A form of quasi-longitudinal design is the recall survey, which conducts an observation at one point in time and has respondents remember information to establish a prior observation. Trend surveys also sample a population at two or more points in time. In addition to these types of analyses, sociologists interested in the study of change often use historical data to establish long-term trends or to test theories. The use of personal documents such as diaries, letters, and biographical statements has long been considered useful in the study of change. Researchers interested in historical experiences of large groups often turn to the use of available documents and records, which provide systematic data on large numbers of individuals.

The concern with the growing impact of technology on society gave rise to technology assessment to provide methods for identifying the implications and effects of technology on society. The methods of technology assessment may be future-, present-, or past-oriented. The common steps in assessment entail the definition of assessment task, description of relevant technology, development of state of society assumptions, identification of impact areas, preliminary impact analysis, identification of possible action options, and impact analysis. The methods of assessment are borrowed from different fields, for technology assessment has no defined set of tools. Comprehensive technology assessment programs can be very expensive. Methods of technology assessment are used also for the preparation of environmental impact statements and in the study of social technologies.

In recent years, there has been a considerable rise of interest in applying social science methodologies to the evaluation of planned change efforts. This interest is reflected in the growing emphasis on evaluation research. The object of evaluation research is to establish how successful a particular planned change effort is in achieving its goals. The designs of evaluative research include one-shot studies, before-and-after studies, and controlled experiments, supplemented by cost-benefit analysis and social audits. They also include plans for data collection, sampling, and measurement. The differences in emphases between program administrators and researchers is a potential source of problems. If the results of the evaluation program are negative, the client might attempt to dismiss the findings or rationalize the conclusions.

The social indicator "movement" is relatively recent. Three rationales for social indicators have been described: social policy, social change, and social reporting. The approaches to social indicators include the design of "the best set of measures for a society," devising new methods for measuring the hard-to-quantify, the design of theoretical frameworks, replication studies, and the use of indicators in their specific political and organizational contexts. After a brief review of the social indicator models, methods of data collection for indicators were considered, which include interviews, self-reports, observations, and the use of existing documents. The section concluded with a discussion of the use of social indicators by the World Bank and the Organization for Economic Cooperation and Development.

The methodologies discussed for forecasting change included extrapolative, intuitive, modeling, and survey forecastings, clinical prediction, intuitive planning, and the use of multimethod forecasting. In spite of the considerable amount of research that has been done on social forecasting methodology to date, the state of the art of forecasting warrants additional research to increase the accuracy of both short- and long-term horizon forecasts.

The methodologies discussed in this chapter have important policy implications. Technology assessment is policy- and action-oriented, and the results are being used to alter or influence policy decisions. Evaluation research is increasingly built into legislation, and there are specific requirements for the evaluation of federal programs and activities dealing with deliberate social change. There seems to be a growing reliance on social indicators in decision making, both at the national and international levels. Forecasting methodologies are essential for long-term policy planning and decision-making activities. Policymakers at various levels are increasingly relying on the methods of change assessment, and this reliance can only expand in the future as the government undertakes more responsibility and wants more information.

SUGGESTED FURTHER READINGS

DALE, ANGELA, AND RICHARD DAVIES (eds.). *Analyzing Social and Political Change: A Handbook of Research Methods.* Thousand Oaks, CA: Sage Publications, 1994. A comprehensive discussion of the various methods available for the analysis of social change over time, the research objectives to which the techniques are suited, and the limitations and constraints of individual methods.

DOOLEY, DAVID. *Social Research Methods*, 4th ed. Upper Saddle River, NJ: Prentice Hall, 2001. A lucidly written survey of social science methodologies with a discussion on how to use various computer technologies.

GLENN, JEROME C., AND THEODORE J. GORDON. *2002 State of the Future.* Washington, DC: American Council for the United Nations University, 2002. A series of distilled prospects for technology, human security, economic development, crime, decision making, and various global scenarios. An outstanding research source for background material.

HELLER, FRANK (ed.). *The Use and Abuse of Social Science.* London: Sage Publications, 1986. A collection of articles by noted international authors on the utilization of social research.

JASANOFF, SHEILA, GERALD E. MARKLE, JAMES C. PETERSEN, AND TREVOR PINCH (eds.). *Handbook of Science and Technology.* Thousand Oaks, CA: Sage Publications, 1994. A summary and synthesis of the multidisciplinary field and an excellent resource on the interplay between technology and change research.

MORRIS, PETER, AND RIKI THERIVEL (ed.). *Methods of Environmental Impact Assessment*, 2nd ed. New York: Spon Press, 2001. Using detailed international case studies, the authors show how to carry out environmental assessment work.

PATTON, MICHAEL QUINN. *Qualitative Research & Evaluation Methods*, 3rd ed. Thousand Oaks, CA: Sage Publications, 2002. A valuable resource for the use of qualitative inquiry with hundreds of timely examples.

PORTER, COLIN F. *Environmental Impact Assessment: A Practical Guide.* St. Lucia, Australia: University of Queensland Press, 1985. A cross-cultural review of environmental assessments and concerns.

Rossi, Peter H., Howard E. Freeman, and Mark W. Lipsey. *Evaluation: A Systematic Approach*, 6th ed. Thousand Oaks, CA: Sage Publications, Inc., 1999. A sophisticated discussion of the various facets of evaluation research with a minimum of technical jargon.

Teich, Albert H. (ed.). *Technology and the Future*, 9th ed. New York: St. Martin's Press, 2002. See, in particular, Part II on forecasting, assessing, and controlling the impacts of technology.

Valach, Ladislav, Richard A. Young, and M. Judith Lynam. *Action Theory: A Primer for Applied Research in the Social Sciences*. Westport, CT: Praeger, 2002. A review of some of the major issues involved in applied research.

REFERENCES

Babbie, Earl. *The Practice of Social Research*, 9th ed. Belmont, CA: Wadsworth, 2001.

Baizerman, Michael, and Donald Compton. "From Respondent to Consultant and Participant: The Evolution of a State Agency Policy Evaluation," *New Directions for Program Evaluation*, 53, Spring 1992, pp. 5–15.

Bartocha, Bodo. "Technology Assessment: An Instrument for Goal Formulation and the Selection of Problem Areas." In Marvin J. Cetron and Bodo Bartocha (eds.), *Technology Assessment in a Dynamic Environment*. New York: Gordon and Breach, 1973, pp. 337–356.

Berk, Richard A. "Publishing Evaluation Research," *Contemporary Sociology*, 24 (1) January 1995, pp. 9–13.

Bongaarts, John. "Can the Growing Human Population Feed Itself?" *Scientific American*, 270 (3) March 1994, pp. 36–43.

Bongaarts, John. "Global Trends in AIDS Mortality," *Population and Development Review*, 22 (1) March 1996, pp. 21–46.

Boruch, Robert F. *Randomized Experiments for Planning and Evaluation*. Thousand Oaks, CA: Sage Publications, 1996.

Brigham, John, Janet Rifkin, and Christine G. Solt. "Birth Technologies: Prenatal Diagnosis and Abortion Policy," *Politics and the Life Sciences*, 12 (1) February 1993, pp. 31–44.

Broder, John M. "Keeping Score: Big Social Change Revive the False God of Numbers," *The New York Times*, August 17, 1997, pp. E1, E4.

Brown, Charles, Greg J. Duncan, and Frank P. Stafford. "Data Watch: The Panel Study of Income Dynamics," *Journal of Economic Perspectives*, 10 (2) Spring 1996, pp. 155–169.

Brown, James N., and Audrey Light. "Interpreting Panel Data on Job Tenure," *Journal of Labor Economics*, 10 (3) 1992, pp. 219–258.

Chalkley, Tom. "Technological Forecasting," *The Futurist*, 27 (4) July–August 1993, pp. 13–17.

Coates, Joseph F. "Technology Assessment." In Albert H. Teich (ed.), *Technology and Man's Future*, 2nd ed. New York: St. Martin's Press, 1977, pp. 251–270.

Cohen, Evan H., Carol T. Mowbray, Deborah Bybee, Susan Yeich, Kurt Ribisl, and Paul P. Freddolino. "Tracking and Follow-Up Methods for Research on Homelessness," *Evaluation Review*, 17 (3) June 1993, pp. 331–352.

COHEN, JOEL W., ALAN C. MONHEIT, KAREN M. BEAUREGARD, STEVEN B. COHEN, DORIS C. LEFKOWITZ, D. E. B. POTTER, JOHN P. SOMMERS, AMY K. TAYLOR, AND ROSS H. ARNETT III. "The Medical Expenditures Survey: A National Health Information Resource," *Inquiry*, 33 (4) Winter 1997, pp. 373–390.

COLEMAN, JAMES S. *Policy Research in Social Science*. Morristown, NJ: General Learning Press, 1972.

CONZEN, KATHLEEN NEILS. "Thomas and Znaniecki and the Historiography of American Immigration," *Journal of American Ethnic History*, 16 (1) Fall 1996, pp. 16–26.

CORNISH, EDWARD. "The Next 30 Years: Our Editor Offers His Personal View of What Is Likely to Happen Over the Next Three Decades," *The Futurist*, 31 (2) March–April 1997, pp. 7–9.

COYLE, GEOFF. "The Nature and Value of Future Studies or Do Futures Have a Future?" *Futures*, 29 (1) February 1997, pp. 77–94.

COYLE, R. G., R. CRAWSHAY, AND L. SUTTON. "Futures Assessment by Field Anomaly Relaxation: A Review and Appraisal," *Futures*, 26 (1) January–February 1994, pp. 25–44.

CZAJA, RONALD, AND JOHNNY BLAIR. *Designing Surveys: A Guide to Decisions and Procedures*. Thousand Oaks, CA: Pine Forge Press, 1996.

DALE, ANGELA, AND RICHARD DAVIES (eds.). *Analyzing Social and Political Change: A Handbook of Research Methods*. Thousand Oaks, CA: Sage Publications, 1994.

DE NEUFVILLE, JUDITH INNES. *Social Indicators and Public Policy: Interactive Processes of Design and Application*. New York: Elsevier, 1975.

DIENER, ED. "Assessing Subjective Well-Being: Progress and Opportunities," *Social Indicators Research*, 31 (2) February 1994, pp. 103–158.

DOOLEY, DAVID. *Social Research Methods*, 4th ed. Upper Saddle River, NJ: Prentice Hall, 2001.

EMPSON-WARNER, SUSAN, AND HARVEY KRAHN. "Unemployment and Occupational Aspirations: A Panel Study of High School Graduates," *The Canadian Review of Sociology and Anthropology*, 29 (1) February 1992, pp. 38–55.

ERIKSON, KAI. *The Wayward Puritans: A Study in the Sociology of Deviance*. New York: Wiley, 1966.

ESTES, RICHARD J. "Social Development Trends in Asia, 1970–1994," *Social Indicators Research*, 37 (2) February 1996, pp. 119–149.

EWALT, PATRICIA L. "Research Responds: Monitoring the Impact of Social Legislation," *Social Work*, 41 (1) January 1996, pp. 5–7.

FOLK, HUGH. "The Role of Technology Assessment in Public Policy." In Albert H. Teich (ed.), *Technology and Man's Future*, 2nd ed. New York: St. Martin's Press, 1977, pp. 243–251.

Fortune. "Do We Live As Well As We Used To?" September 14, 1987, pp. 32–46.

FREEMAN, DAVID M. *Technology and Society: Issues in Assessment, Conflict, and Choice*. Chicago: Rand McNally, 1974.

GARNER, ROBERTA ASH. *Social Change*. Chicago: Rand McNally, 1977.

GIBSON, ROWAN (ed.). *Rethinking the Future*. London: Nicholas Brealey Publishing, 1997.

GLASER, DANIEL. *Routinizing Evaluations: Getting Feedback on Effectiveness of Crime and Delinquency Programs*. Washington, DC: Government Printing Office, 1973.

GLENN, JEROME C., AND THEODORE J. GORDON. *2002 State of the Future*. Washington, DC: American Council for the United Nations University, 2002.

GROSS, BERTRAM M., AND MICHAEL SPRINGER. "Developing Social Intelligence." In Bertram M. Cross (ed.), *Social Intelligence for America's Future: Exploration in Societal Problems*. Boston: Allyn & Bacon, 1969, pp. 3–44.

HALL, ELAINE J., AND KATHY SHEPHERD STOLLEY. "A Historical Analysis of the Presentation of Abortion and Adoption in Marriage and Family Textbooks: 1950–1987," *Family Relations*, 46 (1) January 1997, pp. 73–83.

HALLINAN, MAUREEN T. "The Sociological Study of Social Change," 1996 Presidential Address, *American Sociological Review*, 62 (1) February 1997, pp. 1–12.

HAMBERG, EVA M. "Stability and Change in Religious Beliefs, Practice, and Attitudes: A Swedish Panel Study," *The Journal for the Scientific Study of Religion*, 30 (1) March 1991, pp. 63–89.

HARRIS, LOUIS. *Inside America*. New York: Vintage, 1987.

HARRIS, PATRICIA M. "Client Management Classification and Prediction of Probation Outcome," *Crime and Delinquency*, 40 (2) April 1994, pp. 154–174.

HARRISON, DANIEL P. *Social Forecasting Methodology: Suggestions for Research*. New York: Russell Sage, 1976.

HELMER, OLAF. *Social Technology*. New York: Basic Books, 1966.

HELMER, OLAF. "Adversary Delphi," *Futures*, 26 (1) January–February 1994, pp. 79–88.

HENDERSON, HAZEL. "Paths to Sustainable Development: The Role of Social Indicators," *Futures*, 26 (2) March 1994, pp. 125–138.

HUGHES, J. T. "Evaluation of Local Economic Development: A Challenge for Policy Research," *Urban Studies*, 28 (6) December 1991, pp. 909–918.

JANTSCH, ERICH. *Technology Forecasting in Perspective*. Paris: Organization for Economic Cooperation and Development, July 1967.

JASANOFF, SHEILA, GERALD E. MARKLE, JAMES C. PETERSEN, AND TREVOR PINCH (eds.). *Handbook of Science and Technology*. Thousand Oaks, CA: Sage Publications, 1994.

JOHNSON, HOMER H. "Corporate Social Audits—This Time Around," *Business Horizons*, 44 (3) May 2001, pp. 29–39.

KAHN, HERMAN, AND ANTHONY WIENER. *The Year 2000: A Framework for the Next Thirty-Three Years*. New York: Macmillan, 1967.

KILBORN, PETER T. "Alarming Trend Among Workers: Survey Finds Clusters of TB Cases," *The New York Times*, January 23, 1994, p. 1N.

KLANDERMANS, BERT, AND SUZANNE STAGGENBORG (eds.). *Methods of Social Movement Research*. Minneapolis, MN: University of Minnesota Press, 2002.

KLINE, RONALD R. *Consumers in the Country: Technology and Social Change in Rural America*. Baltimore: The Johns Hopkins University Press, 2000.

KONSTADAKOPULOS, DIMITRIOS. "The Challenge of Technological Development for ASEAN: Intraregional and International Co-operation," *ASEAN Economic Bulletin*, 19 (1) April 2002, pp. 100–111.

LAND, KENNETH C. "Social Indicator Models: An Overview." In Kenneth C. Land and Seymour Spilerman (eds.), *Social Indicator Models*. New York: Russell Sage, 1975, pp. 5–36.

LAND, KENNETH C. "Models and Indicators," *Social Forces*, 80 (2) December 2001, pp. 381–411.

LARSON, JAMES S. "The Measurement of Social Well-Being," *Social Indicators Research*, 28 (3) March 1993, pp. 285–296.

LASZLO, ERVIN. "Information Technology and Social Change: An Evolutionary Systems Analysis," *Behavioral Science*, 37 (4) October 1993, pp. 237–249.

LAZARSFELD, PAUL, BERNARD BERELSON, AND HAZEL CAUDET. *The People's Choice.* New York: Columbia University Press, 1944.

LENGYEL, PETER. "The Misapplication of Social Science at Unesco." In Frank Heller (ed.), *The Use and Abuse of Social Science.* London: Sage Publications, 1986, pp. 54–63.

LI, TA-HSIN, AND MELVIN J. HINICH. "A Filter Bank Approach for Modeling and Forecasting Seasonal Patterns," *Technometrics,* 44 (1) February 2002, pp. 1–15.

LUCKETT, JUDITH. "Local Studies and Larger Issues: The Case of Sara Bagby," *Teaching History: A Journal of Methods,* 27 (2) Fall 2002, pp. 86–98.

MAROTTA, GEMMA. "The Mafia and Parliamentary Inquiries during the First Fifty Years of State Unifications" (in Italian), *Sociologia,* 27 (1–3) 1993, pp. 423–464.

MAXFIELD, MICHAEL G., AND EARL BABBIE. *Research Methods for Criminal Justice and Criminology,* 3rd ed. Belmont, CA: Wadsworth, 2001.

MCPHEAT, DAVID. "Technology and Life-Quality," *Social Indicators Research,* 37 (3) March, 1996, pp. 281–302.

MEADOWS, DONELLA H., DENNIS L. MEADOWS, JORGEN RANDERS, AND WILLIAM W. BEHRENS III. *The Limits to Growth.* New York: Universe Books, 1972.

MIDANIK, LORRAINE T. "Two Random Repeat Methods to Assess Alcohol Use," *The American Journal of Public Health,* 83 (6) June 1993, pp. 893–896.

MOORE, WILBERT E., AND ELEANOR BERNERT SHELDON. "Monitoring Social Change: A Conceptual and Programmatic Statement," *Social Statistical Proceedings of the American Statistical Association,* 1965, pp. 144–149. Washington, DC: American Statistical Association.

NACHMIAS, DAVID, AND CHAVA NACHMIAS. *Research Methods in the Social Sciences,* 6th ed. New York: Worth Publishers, 2000.

NATICKA-TYNDALE, ELEANOR. "Notifications of Sexual Activities in the Area of AIDS: A Trend Analysis of Adolescent Sexual Activities," *Youth & Society,* 21 (1) September 1991, pp. 31–50.

NAVARRO, VINCENTE. "Has Socialism Failed? An Analysis of Health Indicators under Capitalism and Socialism," *Science and Society,* 57 (1) Spring 1993, pp. 6–30.

NEIGER, BRAD L., MICHAEL D. BARNES, ROSEMARY THACKERAY, AND NATALIE LINDMAN. "Use of the Delphi Method and Nominal Group Technique in Front-End Market Segmentation," *American Journal of Health Studies,* 17 (3) Summer 2001, pp. 111–120.

NEWCOMB, THEODORE M. *Personality and Social Change.* New York: Dryden Press, 1943.

NG, H. K., J. L. ANDERSON, AND D. J. SANTINI. "Electric and Hybrid Vehicles: A 25-year Forecast," *Automotive Engineering,* 104 (2) February 1996, pp. 66–71.

PASSIG, DAVID. "Imen-Delphi: A Delphi Variant Procedure for Emergence," *Human Organization,* 56 (1) Spring 1997, pp. 53–62.

PATTON, MICHAEL QUINN. *Qualitative Research & Evaluation Methods,* 3rd ed. Thousand Oaks, CA: Sage Publications, 2002.

PETERMAN, LARRY. "Privacy's Background," *The Review of Politics,* 55 (2) Spring 1993, pp. 217–247.

PIVEN, FRANCES FOX, AND RICHARD CLOWARD. *Regulating the Poor: The Function of Public Welfare,* rev. ed. New York: Vintage Books, 1993.

PORTER, ALAN L., FREDERICK A. ROSSINI, STANLEY R. CARPENTER, AND A. T. ROPER. "An Introduction to Technology Assessment and Impact Analysis." In Albert H. Teich (ed.), *Technology and the Future,* 5th ed. New York: St. Martin's Press, 1990, pp. 153–163.

PORTER, COLIN F. *Environmental Impact Assessment: A Practical Guide.* St. Lucia, Australia: University of Queensland Press, 1985.

POSAVAC, EMIL J. "In Response to Welch and Sternhagen's 'Unintended Effects of Program Evaluation'," *Evaluation Practice*, 13 (3) October 1992, pp. 173–174.

ROSSI, PETER H., HOWARD E. FREEMAN, AND MARK W. LIPSEY. *Evaluation: A Systematic Approach*, 6th ed. Thousand Oaks, CA: Sage Publications, 1999.

ROTHENBACHER, FRANZ. "National and International Approaches to Social Reporting," *Social Indicators Research*, 29 (1) May 1993, pp. 1–63.

SAWICKI, DAVID S., AND PATRICE FLYNN. "Neighborhood Indicators: A Review of the Literature and an Assessment of Conceptual and Methodological Issues," *Journal of the American Planning Association*, 62 (2) Spring 1996, pp. 165–184.

SCHOT, JOHAN W. "Constructive Technology Assessment and Technology Dynamic: The Case of Clean Technologies," *Science, Technology, & Human Values*, 17 (1) Winter 1992, pp. 36–57.

SCLOVE, RICHARD E. "Democratizing Technology," *The Chronicle of Higher Education*, 40 (19) January 12, 1994, pp. 81–83.

SCOTT, JACQUELINE, AND LILLIAN ZAC. "Collective Memories in Britain and the United States," *Public Opinion Quarterly*, 57 (3) Fall 1993, pp. 315–332.

SHEN, J., AND N. A. SPENCE. "Modeling Urban-Rural Population Growth in China," *Environment & Planning*, 28 (8) August 1996, pp. 417–445.

SHORE, CRIS. "Virgin Births and Sterile Debates: Social Impact of Fertility Method and Birth Control," *Current Anthropology*, 33 (3) June 1992, pp. 295–315.

SIMON, RITA J. "Old Minorities, New Immigrants Aspirations, Hopes and Fears," *Annals of the American Academy of Political and Social Sciences*, 530, November 1993, pp. 61–73.

SMITH, MARY LEE, AND GENE V. GLASS. *Research and Evaluation in Education and the Social Sciences*. Englewood Cliffs, NJ: Prentice Hall, 1987.

SMITS, RUUD, JOS LEYTEN, AND PIM DEN HERTOG. "Technology Innovations and Technology Policy in Europe: New Concepts, New Goals, New Infrastructures," *Policy Sciences*, 28 (3) August 1995, pp. 271–300.

SOROKIN, PITIRIM A. *Social and Cultural Dynamics* (one-volume ed.). Boston: Porter Sargent, 1957.

STRASSER, GABOR. "Methodology for Technology Assessment, Case Study Experience in the United States." In Marvin J. Cetron and Bodo Bartocha (eds.), *Technology Assessment in a Dynamic Environment*. New York: Gordon and Breach, 1973, pp. 905–937.

SUCHMAN, EDWARD A. *Evaluative Research: Principles and Practice in Public Service and Social Action Programs*. New York: Russell Sage, 1967.

SURVEY RESEARCH CENTER. *A Panel Study of Income Dynamics*. Ann Arbor, MI: Institute for Social Research, 1972.

SWANSON, K. C. "Umpiring the Environmental Wars," *National Journal*, 28 (7) February 1996, pp. 377–378.

TAYLOR, DONALD M. *The Quest for Identity: From Minority Groups to Generation Xers*. Westport, CT: Praeger, 2003.

TEICH, ALBERT H. (ed.) *Technology and the Future*, 9th ed. New York: St. Martin's Press, 2002.

TEPPER, AUGUST. "Controlling Technology by Shaping Visions," *Policy Sciences*, 29 (1) February 1996, pp. 29–41.

THERIVEL, RIKI, AND MARIA ROSARIO PARIDARIO. *The Practice of Strategic Environmental Assessment*. London: Earthscan, 1996a.

THERIVEL, RIKI, AND MARIA ROSARIO PARIDARIO. *Strategic Environmental Assessment.* London: Earthscan, 1996b.

THOMAS, W. I., AND FLORIAN ZNANIECKI. *The Polish Peasant in Europe and America.* Chicago: University of Chicago Press, 1918.

TILLY, LOUISE A. "Women, Women's History and the Industrial Revolution," *Social Research,* 6 (1) Spring 1994, pp. 115–138.

TRAVIS, ROBERT. "The MOS Alienation Scale: An Alternative to Srole's Anomie Scale," *Social Indicators Research,* 28 (1) January 1993, pp. 71–79.

VAGO, STEVEN. *Law and Society,* 7th ed. Upper Saddle River, NJ: Prentice Hall, 2003.

VALACH, LADISLAV, RICHARD A. YOUNG, AND M. JUDITH LYNAM. *Action Theory: A Primer for Applied Research in the Social Sciences.* Westport, CT: Praeger, 2002.

VAN STEENBURGEN, BART. "Global Modeling in the 1990s: A Critical Evaluation of a New Wave," *Futures,* 26 (1) January–February 1994, pp. 44–57.

VEENHOVEN, RUUT. "Developments in Satisfaction-Research," *Social Indicators Research,* 37 (1) January 1996, pp. 1–46.

VOGEL, GRETCHEN. "Scientists Probe Feeling Behind Decision-Making; Role of Intuition in Decision-Making," *Science,* 275 (5304) February 28, 1997, p. 1269.

WARD, DAVID, AND GENE KASSEBAUM. "On Biting the Hand That Feeds: Some Implications of Sociological Evaluations of Correctional Effectiveness." In Carol Weiss (ed.), *Evaluating Action Programs.* Boston: Allyn & Bacon, 1972, pp. 300–310.

WEISS, CAROL. *Evaluation Research: Methods of Assessing Program Effectiveness.* Englewood Cliffs, NJ: Prentice Hall, 1972.

WEISS, CAROL HIRSCHON. "Research and Policy-Making: A Limited Partnership." In Frank Heller (ed.), *The Use and Abuse of Social Science.* London: Sage Publications, 1986, pp. 214–235.

WORLD BANK. *Social Indicators of Development—2003.* Washington, DC: The World Bank, 2003.

YIN, ROBERT K. "The Case Study Method as a Tool for Doing Evaluation," *Current Sociology,* 40 (1) Spring 1992, pp. 121–138.

Index

A

Aaronson, S.A., 34, 377
Abel, T., 204
Abernethy, V., 146
Abortion, 129, 279–282
Aburdene, P., 15, 172, 233
Acculturation, 95–98
Acculturative modernization, 105
Acid rain, 321
Ackerman, F., 319
Adam, B., 4, 318
Adler, L.L., 337, 368
Adler, P.S., 173
Adopters, 92
Adoption, 90–91
Age-sex composition, 146–148
Aghion, P., 256
Agrarian societies, 155
Aguirre, B.E., 203
AIDS, 138, 140, 205, 305
Ainsworth, S., 258
Air pollution, economic costs associated with, 320–321
Albrecht, S.L., 242, 302, 361
Alder, C., 368
Alderson, A.S., 150
Alienation, 291
Alinsky, S., 378
Allen, F.B., 9
Allen, F.R., 255, 272, 296, 297
Altbach, P.G., 168, 169
Althaus, F.A., 144
Amani, M., 114
Amason, J.P., 22
American Psychiatric Association, 348
American Sociological Society (ASS), 69
Amin, S., 342
Ancient Society (Morgan), 53
Anderson, C.H., 175
Anderson, J.L., 423
Andrews, F.M., 329
Annez, P., 114
Anxiety, 345–346
Apodaca, A., 270
Appelbaum, R.P., 54, 69
Applebaum, P., 161
Apter, D.E., 104
Arensberg, C., 174, 240, 248
Arenson, K.W., 164, 167
Aries, P., 158
Armbruster, F.E., 163
Arnold, A.J., 90
Assessment of change, 400–427

Assessment techniques, 400–406
  historical analysis, 404–406
  panel surveys, 400–403
  recall surveys, 403
  trend surveys, 403
Atlantic Monthly (The), 285
Atomic age, 192
Attitude change strategy, 366
Austin, J.R., 357
Authority, 154, 237, 256–257
Automobiles, social costs associated with, 327–329
Awareness stage of adoption, 90
Axelrod, R., 244
Ayres, R.U., 301

B

Babbie, E., 400, 425
Baby boomers, 133
Bacevich, A., 34
Bachrach, P., 29
Bacon, L., 372
Baizerman, M., 411
Baker, K., 319
Baker, R., 89
Baradat, L.P., 15, 19
Baratz, M.S., 29
Barber, B., 17, 18, 149
Barnes, J.A., 162
Barnes, M.D., 422
Barnet, R.J., 35, 94
Barnett, H.G., 248
Bartocha, B., 409
Bartrop, P.R., 303
Basu, A.M., 281
Bates, R.H., 296
Battle of Wounded Knee, 221
Beauregard, K.M., 401
Becker, G.D., 330
Becker, H.P., 56
Behavior modification, 361
Beiser, V., 287
Bell, D., 72
Bellah, R.N., 73, 87, 104
Bell Curve, The (Herrnstein & Murray), 150
Bengtsson, M., 90
Benne, K.D., 18, 358, 361, 362, 364, 365, 375, 391
Bennis, W.G., 250, 254, 265, 298, 299, 301, 358
Bensman, J., 204, 206, 233, 318
Berelson, B., 401
Berg, I., 167, 340, 341
Berger, P.L., 148, 315, 316, 317

437

Berk, R.A., 411
Berman, H.K., 387
Bernard, H.R., 15
Bernstein, N., 287
Bernstein, R., 344
Betts, R.K., 26
Bhagwati, J., 165
Bhalla, A., 108
Bianchi, S.M., 26, 165, 173
Bierstedt, R., 153, 253
Bikhchandani, S., 196
Binder, D., 296
Birman, D., 95
Birth Dearth, The (Wattenberg), 145
Black, C.E., 104, 345
Black Panthers, 370
Blair, J., 400
Blaser, K., 387
Blau, P.M., 20, 151
Blauner, R., 15
Blaustein, A.P., 385
Blumer, H., 196
Bochner, S., 235
Bodley, J.H., 95
Bogenhold, D., 204
Bondurant, J.V., 378
Bongaarts, J., 422
Boruch, R.F., 411
Boskoff, A., 190
Bottomore, T., 158
Boulding, K.E., 175
Bowers, B., 168
Boyd, R., 86
Boyer, E.L., 164, 166, 169
Brandes, S., 251
Brannigan, A., 279
Bride price, 129
Bridge, C., 102
Bridges, W., 302
Brigham, J., 404
Brinton, C., 102
Broder, J.M., 426
Brown, C., 401
Brown, D.L., 13
Brown, E., 194
Brown, G.B., 239
Brown, J.N., 401
Brown, L.R., 37, 95, 111, 138, 142, 294, 320, 323, 324, 327, 335, 336
Brown, M.F., 251
Browne, M.W., 323
Brown v. Board of Education (1954), 384, 385
Buckley amendment, 298
Buenting, J.A., 207
Bultman, M., 133
Bumpass, L., 137
Bun, C.K., 303
Bunker, B.B., 359, 375, 376, 377
Bureaucratic authority, 154

Bureaucratization, 116–119
Bureaucratization of the World, The (Jacoby), 116
Burgess, E.W., 131
Burke, W.W., 359, 375, 376, 377
Burr, J.A., 95
Burtless, G., 160
Business Week, 5, 36, 167, 175, 287, 386
Bybee, D., 411

C

Callahan, D., 281
Campbell, E., 132
Caniglia, J., 208
Capitalism, 27
Caplovitz, D., 178
Cargo cults, 222–224, 306
Carleheden, M., 78
Carlson, J.W., 301
Carman, J.M., 197
Carnegie Foundation, 166
Carpenter, S.R., 406, 407
Cartmel, F., 279
Carty, A., 21
Carvajal, D., 177
Cassidy, J., 146
Cassie, W., 258
Caste stratification system, 148
Caudet, H., 401
Cavanagh, J., 35, 94
Cernea, M.M., 90
Chadwick, B.A., 242, 302, 361
Chalkley, T., 421
Champagne, A., 387
Change
    agents, 363–364
    client system, 360
    coping with, 301–306
    costs of, 314–349
    duration of, 190–224
    impact of, 279–306
    reactions to, 232–271
    resistance to, 251–252
    responses to, 288–292
    strategies of, 357–392
    targets of, 358–363
    target system, 360
Change, spheres of, 128–180
    economy, 170–178
    education, 158–170
    family, 128–139
    population, 139–148
    power relations, 153–158
    stratification, 148–153
Charismatic authority, 154
Chattoe, E., 86
Chen, L.C., 143
Chen, Y.P., 108
Chin, R., 18, 358, 364, 365, 375, 391

Chirot, D., 7, 103, 105
Chodak, S., 30, 104, 105
Chong, D., 380
Christianity, 94
Chronicle of Higher Education Almanac, 164, 165, 166, 167
Chua, A., 35
Church of Scientology, 210
Civil Rights Act (1957)(1960)(1964)(1968), 384, 385
Claeys, G., 18
Class, 236, 254–255
    lifestyles and, 204–207
Clean Air Act, 320
Climate modification, economic costs associated with, 323–324
Clinard, M.B., 293
Clinical prediction, 424
Close, D., 102
Clough, B., 288
Cloward, R., 405, 406
Clutterbuck, R., 371
Coalescence stage, 218–219
Coates, J.F., 409
Cockerham, W.C., 204
Coelho, G.V., 302
Coelho, P.R.P., 195
Cohabitation, 137, 138
Cohen, A.R., 242
Cohen, E.H., 411
Cohen, J.W., 401
Cohen, R., 34
Cohort analysis, 401
Coitus reservatus, 215
Colamosca, A., 35
Coleman, J.S., 118, 414, 415
Collective behavior, 217
Collins, M.E., 362
Colonialism, 94
Comfort, A., 138
Commoner, B.A., 318, 324
Communal living arrangements, 137
Communication, 241–242, 263–264
    ineffective, 263–264
    patterns, 241–242
Communism, 27, 94, 143
Communist Manifesto (Marx & Engels), 85
Compatibility, 91
Competition, 19–20, 239
Complexity, 91
Complex marriage, 213–217
Compliance, 243
Compton, D., 411
Computer crimes, 287–288
Comstock, G., 263
Comte, Auguste, 52
Conflict, 20–28
    in Eastern Europe and former Soviet Union, 26–28
    gender, 25–26
    international, 26
    racial, 24–25
    in the university, 22–24
    in the workplace, 22
Conflict theories of change, 58–64
    Coser, Lewis A., 61–62
    Dahrendorf, Ralf, 62–64
    Marx, Karl, 59–61
Conly, C.H., 287
Consciousness, 208
Conservative impulse, 305
Consumer Credit Protection Act, 392
Consumption, 175–178
Convergence, 284
Conzen, K.N., 405
Cook, K.S., 236
Cook, R.J., 129
Cooperman, A., 5
Copernicus, Nicholas, 99
Coping with change, 301–306
Cornish, E., 329, 421
Coser, Lewis A., 21, 61–62
Costain, A.N., 386
Cost-benefit analysis, 413
Costs of change, 314–349
Cottrel, W.F., 32, 33
Counterculture lifestyles, 207–211
Cowley, G., 138
Coyle, G., 427
Coyle, R.G., 422
COYOTE, 386
Craik, J., 196, 198
Crawshay, R., 422
Crenshaw, E.M., 114
Crispell, D., 178
Critical Legal Studies Movement, 63
Crossette, B., 27, 140
Cults, 217–220
    Cargo, 222–224
    Ghost Dance, 220–222
    Heaven's Gate, 219
Cultural barriers to change, 264–268
    ethnocentrism, 265–266
    fatalism, 264–265
    incompatibility, 266–267
    integration, 266
    motor patterns, 267
    norms of modesty, 266
    superstitions, 267–268
Cultural creatives, 204
Cultural stimulants to change, 244–247
    high/low context cultures, 244–245
    integration, 245–247
Cultured academic lifestyle, 206–207
Culture lag, 294
Current family trends, 131–133
Currie, E., 33
Curtis, J.M., 217

Curtis, M.J., 217
Cvitkovic, E., 19
Czaja, R., 400

D

Dahl, R., 6
Dahrendorf, Ralf, 30, 36, 62–64
Daley, J.M., 362
Dally, A., 262
Dalton, D., 222
Darroch, J.E., 280
Daugherty, H.G., 109
Davis, D., 315, 320, 332
Davis, F., 209
Davis, K., 9, 66, 70, 111, 115, 200
Davison, C., 265
Decentralization of power, 157
Decision making, participation in, 238–239
DeFronzo, J., 99, 103, 291
Deloria Jr., V., 295
Delphi technique, 422
Demographic transition, 142–148
Demos, J., 129, 130
de Neufville, J.I., 418
Denmark, F.L., 368
Dershowitz, A.M., 343
Deutsch, M., 362
DeVos, G.A., 96
DeVries, J., 114
Dewitt, M.R., 67
DeWitt, P.M., 135
Dictionary of Occupational Titles (1992), 31
Diener, E., 417, 418
Diffusion, 88–95
Diffusion of Innovations (Rogers), 90
Dispersion, 284
Distribution, 174–175
Division of Labor in Society, The (Durkheim), 65
Divorce, 133–135
Dodge, J.L., 288
Dooley, D., 402, 409
Dornbusch, S.M., 144
Downes, B.T., 370
Dowry, 129
Dror, Y., 387, 388
Drug Enforcement Administration (DEA), 297
DSM (Diagnostic and Statistical Manual of Mental Disorders), 48
Dudley, K.M., 33
Duke, J.T., 19, 60
Duncan, G.J., 401
Duncan, O.D., 151
Duncan, R., 249, 250, 251, 255, 256, 263, 359, 360, 363, 366, 367, 368
Dunlop, J.T., 108, 260
Dunn, W.N., 260
Duration of change, 190–224
    historical perspective of, 191–193

Durkheim, Emile, 65
Durning, A.T., 334
Dye, T.R., 157

E

Early majority, 92
Easterbrook, G., 320, 322
Eastern Europe and former Soviet Union, conflict in, 26–28
Eaton, L., 178
Ecological undermining of food production, 335–336
Economic barriers to change, 268–271
    costs, 269
    limited resources, 270–271
    perceived profitability, 269–270
Economic communism, 212
Economic costs, 248–250, 269, 316–326
    of change, 248–250, 269, 316–326
    in transition, 324–326
Economic growth, 316–318
Economic inequality, 149–151
Economic Opportunity Act (1964), 164
Economic resources, limited, 270–271
Economic stimulants to change, 247–251
    advantages, 248
    cost, 248–250
    vested interests, 250–251
Economic system, structure, based on, 170–178
    consumption, 175–178
    distribution, 174–175
    production, 171–174
Economist, 15, 35, 36, 118, 142, 145, 146, 149, 159, 160, 161, 165, 196, 234, 250, 320, 331, 337
Economy, 31–34, 170–178
Edari, R., 9
Edmonds, R.G., 90
Education, 158–170
    credentials, importance placed on, 167–168
    elementary and secondary, 160–163
    higher, 163–167
Ehrlich, A.H., 139
Ehrlich, P.R., 139
Einstein, Albert, 99, 100
Eisenstadt, S.N., 10, 73, 79, 106, 107
Eisenstein, H., 217
Ellerson, A., 206
Ellul, J., 343
Elsom, D., 320
Empirical-rational strategies, 364–365
Empson-Warner, S., 401
Encyclopedia Americana, 199
Encyclopedia of the Future, 421
Endangered species, 333
Engel, M.H., 385
Engels, F., 60

Environmental costs of change, 318–324
 air pollution, 320–321
 climate modification, 323–324
 endangered species, 333
 soil erosion, 333–335
 solid waste, 318–320
 water pollution, 321–323
Environmental impact statement, 409–410
Environmentally induced illnesses, 332–333
Eorsi, G., 388
Epstein, J., 151
Eriksen, T.H., 245
Erikson, K., 404
Eshleman, J.R., 131
Estate stratification system, 148–149
Estes, R.J., 417
Ethnocentrism, 265–266
Etzioni, A., 305
Etzioni-Halevy, E., 29
Evaluation of change, methodologies for, 411–417
 data collection, 414–415
 design considerations, 413–414
 identifying goals, 412
 research implementation, 415
 utilization of results, 415–417
Evaluation stage of adoption, 91
Evan, W.M., 390, 391
Evolution, 85–88
Evolutionary theories of change, 51–58
 Comte, Auguste, 52
 Morgan, Lewis Henry, 52–54
 Spencer, Herbert, 54–55
Evolution of Societies (Parsons), 67
Ewalt, P.L., 411
Executive Order 11478 (1969), 384, 385
Expressive movements, 218
Exxon Valdez oil spill, 322–323
Eyetsemitan, F.E., 147

F

Facilitative strategies, 367
Fads, 194–195, 200–203
Fairclough, A., 384
Faison, S., 200, 268
Family, 128–139
 changing functions of, 129–131
 current trends in, 131–133
 divorce and, 133–135
 religious function of, 130
 sexual revolution and, 135–139
Fanon, F., 374
Farrell, J.J., 208
Fashion, 195–200
Fatalism, 264–265
Feagin, J.R., 111
Fear of the unfamiliar, 257–258
Feldman, S.D., 204
Feminist Legal Theory, 63

Fershtman, C., 234
Fertility, 144–145
Festinger, L., 243
Feuer, L.S., 15
Finsterbusch, K., 279
Fischer, A.J., 90
Fischer, C.S., 339, 347
Fischer, F., 119
Flavin, C., 320, 323, 327, 333, 335, 336
Fleishman, A., 205, 236, 255
Fleming, J., 21, 58
Fleming, M., 337
Fliegel, F.C., 247
Flynn, P., 417
Folk, H., 426
Fonow, M.M., 383
Food economy, ecological undermining of, 335–336
Foran, J., 99
Forbes, 331
Forcasting change, methods, 420–425
 accuracy, 425
 clinical prediction, 424
 extrapolative, 421–422
 intuitive, 422–423
 modeling, 423–424
 multimethod, 425
 planning, 424–425
 survey, 424
Force, 153
Fortune, 191, 403
Foster, G.M., 218, 235, 236, 240, 252, 254, 261, 262, 263, 264, 266, 267, 268
Fragmentation, 219
Frank, S.E., 164
Frankel, S., 265
Frantz, D., 373
Freedman, M., 340, 341
Freedom of Information Act, 299
Freeman, D.M., 11, 406, 407
Freeman, H.E., 411, 412, 415, 417
Free Speech Movement, 381
Freidl, W., 236
Freire, P., 16
Fried, M., 87, 347
Friedan, Betty, 386
Friedman, L.M., 30, 388, 389, 390
Friedmann, J., 111
Friedmann, W.G., 388
Friendly, A., 114
Friendship obligations, 236
Frone, M.R., 329
Fukuyama, F., 26, 73
Functions of Social Conflict, The (Coser), 61
Funderburk, C., 15, 19
Fun-lover lifestyle, 207
Furlong, A., 279
Furnham, A., 94
Futurist, 421

G

Gabor, D., 324
Gabriel, T., 138
Gagnon, J.H., 136
Galbraith, J.K., 33, 177
Gamson, W.A., 217, 259, 368, 384
Gans, H., 113
Gappa, J.M., 170
Gargan, E.A., 167
Garner, R.A., 401, 402
Gartner, A., 178
GATT (General Agreement on Tariffs and Trade), 36
Geertz, C., 306
Gelles, R.J., 128
Gender conflict, 25–26
Gentrification, 339
Gerlach, L.P., 99, 379, 380
Germani, G., 103, 106, 110, 111, 250, 255
Gerth, H.H., 8, 153, 154
G Factor, The (Jensen), 344
Ghimire, K.B., 318
Ghost Dance cult, 220–222, 306
Gibbs, M., 90
GI Bill, 164
Gibson, R., 421
Gielen, U.P., 337
Gift of Fear, The (Becker), 330
Gilbert, D., 148, 152, 204, 206
Ginsberg, M., 8
Gire, J.T., 147
Girges, A., 240
Giugni, M., 384
Gladwell, M., 201
Glaser, D., 414
Glass, G.V., 411
Glenn, J.C., 191, 421
Globalization, 34–37
Global 2000 Report to the President, 424
Gluckman, Max, 99
Gober, P., 145
Goldberg, R.A., 384, 386
Goldenberg, S., 279
Goldhaber, M., 279, 283, 285
Goldstone, J.A., 12, 98, 102, 291
Gomez, C.A., 95
Goode, W.J., 17, 110, 128, 129
Goodenough, W.H., 223
Gordon, T.J., 191, 421
Gorer, G., 144
Gould, S.J., 49
Gouldner, A.W., 15
Goulet, D.A., 30, 326
Graham, S., 246
Grant, L., 37, 140
Graves, P.E., 114
Gray, G., 330
Gray, L., 135
Great Depression, 204, 401

Greeley, A., 199
Greenhouse, S., 22, 317
Greening of America, The (Reich), 208
Greer, S., 306
Grigsby, J.S., 143
Griset, P., 371
Gross, B.M., 119, 418
Gross, E., 305
Grosscup, B., 372, 373
Grossman, J.B., 390
Group marriage, 137
Group solidarity, 255–256
Gruberg, M., 386
Grubler, A., 92, 191
Gu, Y., 108
Gugliotta, G., 333
Gulati, U.C., 108
Gurr, T.R., 291, 369
Gutenberg, Johann, 99
Gutierrez-Rexach, J.J., 16

H

Haag, B., 345
Haberman, C., 372
Habit, 259–260
Hacker, A., 150
Hagen, Everett E., 73–76, 291, 292, 305
Hagopian, M.N., 101
Hakim, D., 206
Hall, E.J., 404, 406
Hall, E.T., 244, 250
Hall, P., 108, 115
Hall, R.H., 20, 239, 249, 253, 305, 362
Hallinan, M.T., 423
Halpern, J., 115
Halsey, R.S., 217, 379, 381
Hamberg, E.M., 401
Hamburg, D.A., 303
Hamilton, R.F., 289, 318
Hansell, S., 287
Hanson-Harding, B., 39, 169
Harberson, F.H., 260
Hardin, G., 338
Hardoy, J.E., 111
Harf, J.E., 142, 146, 295, 323
Hargrove, T., 291
Harmathy, A., 388
Harris, L., 330, 403
Harris, M., 197
Harris, P.M., 425
Harris, P.R., 236, 265
Harrison, B.T., 208
Harrison, D.P., 424, 425
Harrison, F.H., 108
Harrison, P., 35
Hauser, P.M., 111, 294
"Have We Gone Overboard on 'The Right to Know'?" (Bennis), 298
Hays, S.P., 94

Hayt, E., 136
Heartlanders, 204
Heaven's Gate cult, 219
Hechter, M., 293
Heckscher, C., 116, 119
Heer, D.M., 143
Heinze, R-I., 233
Heller, W.W., 316
Helmer, O., 238, 422
Hempel, L.C., 318
Hemphill, C., 346
Henderson, H., 379, 417
Henshaw, S.K., 280
Hernnstein, R.J., 150
Hershey Jr., R.D., 159, 172
Hertog, P.D., 407
Hertzler, J.O., 157
Heterophily, 263
Hetzler, S.A., 20, 118
Hewstone, M., 236
Higher Education Act, 164
High/low context culture, 244–245
Hillary, E., 321, 334
Hine, V.H., 99, 379, 380
Hinich, M.J., 423
Hintze, Otto, 119
Hirshleifer, D., 196
Historical analysis, 404–406
Hittman, M., 220
HIV, 138, 140–141
Hochschild, A.R., 331
Hockenos, P., 26
Hodgson, G., 57
Hoffman, A., 209, 210
Hofmeister, S., 235
Holbek, J., 249
Holden, C.P., 198
Hollander, A., 196
Hollander, S., 61
Holli, M.G., 245
Holmes, S.A., 131, 132
Homophily, 263
Homo sapiens, 112, 139
Honan, W.H., 162, 342
Hopgood, M-L., 329
Hornstein, H.H., 359, 375, 376, 377
Horticultural societies, 154–155
Howard, J.R., 21
Howells, J.R.L., 88
Huddle, D., 295
Hughes, J.T., 411
Human Development Report, 320, 321, 322, 323, 331, 335
Hunt, M., 202
Hunter, A., 34
Hunter, D., 375
Hunter, S.T., 371
Hunter/gatherer societies, 154
Huntington, S.P., 368, 369

Hymowitz, C., 173

I

Identification, 243
Ideological resistance to change, 255
Ideologies, 15–19, 383
  and change, 16–17
  of the conjugal family, 17
  political, 18–19
  utopian, 18
  Zionist, 18
Ignorance, 260–261
Impact of change, 279–306
Inciardi, J.A., 138, 305
Incipient stage, 218
Incompatibility, 266–267
Indergaard, M., 363
Induced modernization, 105
Industrialization, 108–111, 150
Industrial modernization, 105
Industrial societies, 155, 156
Infant mortality, 142, 143
"Influence of Invention and Discovery, The" (Ogburn), 283
Information highway, 202
Inglehart, R., 329
Ingold, T., 190
Ingrassia, L., 135
Inkeles, A., 103, 106, 296, 348
Inner sensibilities, exploring, 209
Innes-Smith, J., 196
Innovation, 238, 295
Innovators, 92
Insecurity, 345–346
Institute for Socioeconomic Studies, 298
Institutionalization stage, 219
Integration, 245–247, 266
Interest stage of adoption, 90
Internal computer crime, 287
Internalization, 243
International conflicts, 26
International Society for Krishna Consciousness, 219
Intuitive forecasting, 422
Intuitive planning, 424–425
Irons, P., 385
Isachenkov, V., 280
Issel, W., 29
Iverson, N., 111

J

Jackson J.P., Jr., 385
Jacobs, D.J., 22
Jacobsen, M.H., 78
Jacobson, C.K., 242, 302, 361
Jacoby, H., 116, 117, 119
James, J., 108
Janssens, A., 128
Jantsch, E., 421

Jasanoff, S., 406
Jaspars, J., 236
Jeffrey, P., 57
Jejeebhoy, S.J., 129
Jencks, C., 113
Jenkins, J.C., 371
Jensen, M., 254
Jervis, R., 372, 373
Jewell, M.E., 258
Johnson, C., 100
Johnson, H.H., 414
Johnson, H.M., 9
Johnson, K., 135
Jones, G.W., 129
Jones, J.M., 24
Jones, M.A., 197
Jones, R.K., 280
Journal of the American Medical Association, The (JAMA), 143
Jovanovic, B., 90
Joy of Sex, The (Comfort), 138

K

Kahl, J.A., 148, 152, 204, 206
Kahn, H., 422
Kammeyer, K.C.W., 109
Kando, T.M., 175
Kane, H., 37, 138, 328
Kanter, R.M., 360
Kapp, W.K., 326, 331, 334
Kasarda, J.D., 114
Kassebaum, G., 416
Katz, E., 194, 195, 202, 203, 247
Kaufman, I., 358, 364
Kay, J.H., 283
Keating, P., 264
Keesing, F.M., 235
Keesing, R.M., 237, 257
Keiser, L.R., 116
Keller, S., 156
Kelley, T., 178
Kelman, H.C., 243, 357
Kempf, W., 222
Kennedy, P., 34, 35, 316
Kephart, W.M., 211, 213, 214, 215
Kerkvliet, B., 295, 296
Kerr, C., 108, 260
Kettner, P.M., 362
Kibbutz, 18
Kids as Customers (McNeal), 175
Kilborn, P.T., 403
Kilbride, P.L., 283
Killian, L.M., 200, 201, 217, 372, 373, 380, 384
Kim, S.H., 20
Kimmel, M.S., 99
Kirby, E.G., 90
Kirby, S.L., 90
Kirk, S.A., 349

Kivlin, J.E., 247
Klandermans, B., 400
Klapp, O.E., 342
Klein, D., 232
Klerman, G.L., 347
Kline, R.R., 410
Konstadakopulos, D., 406, 407
Korman, S.K., 128, 129, 131, 132, 137, 305, 387
Koten, J., 151
Kotler, P., 358, 363, 364, 366, 368
Kposowa, A.J., 371
Kracht, B.R., 220
Krahn, H., 401
Kriesberg, L., 20, 22, 24
Krinopathy, 213
Kristof, N.D., 98, 224
Kroeber, A.L., 88, 196, 266
Krugman, P., 149, 271
Krusell, P., 250
Ku Klux Klan, 210, 259
Kushner, H.W., 371, 372, 373
Kutchins, H., 349
Kutchinsky, B., 300
Kuznets, S.S., 142, 270

L

La Ferla, R., 198
Laggards, 92
Lakey, G., 377
Lamb, K., 344
Lampman, R., 316
Lancaster, J., 129
Land, K.C., 417, 418, 427
Land Grant Act, 410
Landis, J.R.9
Lanternari, V., 222, 291
LaPiere, R.T., 193, 194, 196, 200, 217, 251, 253, 255, 257, 259, 300
Laqueur, W., 374
Larson, J.S., 419
Lassonde, L., 141
Lasswell, H., 28
Laszlo, E., 410
Late majority, 92
Lattuca, L.R., 199
Lauer, R.H., 9, 21, 39, 57, 88, 118, 345
Laumann, E.O., 136
Law and power, 157–158
Lawton, P.M., 329
Lazarsfeld, P.F., 195, 247, 401
Leach, W., 175
League of Deliverance, 259
Leatherman, C., 170
Lebow, R.N., 29
Lee, E., 35
Lehman, N., 316
Lemann, N., 78

Lempert, R., 388
Lengyel, P., 419
Lenski, G.E., 17, 32, 57, 86, 108, 149, 154, 192, 317
Lenski, J., 57, 86, 108, 192, 317
Leo, J., 344
Leslie, D.W., 170
Leslie, G.R., 128, 129, 131, 132, 137, 305, 387
Levy Jr., M., 104
Lewellen, T.C., 36
Lewin, K., 238, 260
Lewin, T., 25, 136
Lewis, D.A., 324, 330
Lewis, G.H., 209
Lewis, L.S., 168, 169
Leyten, J., 407
Li, Ta-Hsin, 423
Liang, Z., 108
Liebow, E., 113
Lifestyles, 203–204, 207–211
    counterculture, 207–211
    social class and, 204–207
Light, A., 401
Limits of Growth, The (Meadows), 423
Lin, Hui-Sheng, 128
Lind, M., 205
Lindblom, C.E., 7
Linder, S.B., 15, 38
Linn, J.F., 111
Linton, R., 88, 89, 97
Lippitt, R., 365
Lipset, S.M., 118
Lipsey, M.W., 411, 412, 415, 417
Liska, A.E., 293
Little, R., 322
Llewellyn, L.G., 279
Lobao, L., 31
Lockwood, D., 118
Lorsch, J.W., 116
Losyk, B., 205
Lowe, M.D., 327, 328
Lowi, T.J., 29
LSD, 202
Lu, Hsien-Hen, 137
Lulops, R.S., 21
Lurie, A., 197
Luschen, G., 204
Luscombe, B., 378
Luttwak, E., 371
Lynam, M.J., 411

M
MacDonald, G.M., 90
Macedo, D., 16
Macewan, A., 34
Machine age, 192
Macionis, J.J., 9, 10, 338
MacIver, R.M., 9, 297

Mackenzie, D., 11
MacQueen, G., 375
Maguire, K., 330
Mahan, S., 371
Maines, J., 133
Majstorovic, S., 386
Malinowski, B., 65
Mallick K., 375
Mandel, M.J., 150, 152
Mandlebaum, D.G., 148
Manegold, C.S., 162
Mann, C.C., 7
Manners, R.A., 266
Marano, H.E., 136
Marden, C.F., 385
Marighella, C., 373
Marijuana, 297
Marin, B.V., 95
Mark, J.A., 172
Markle, G.E., 406
Markowitz, G., 320
Marks, J., 210
Marotta, G., 404
Marriage, 129, 131, 135, 137
Marris, P., 305
Marsh, R.M., 9
Martin, T.R., 329
Marx, Karl, 59–61
Maryanski, A.R., 65, 71
Masland, T., 26
Maslow, A., 343
Massey, D.S., 151
Mass-society theory, 288
Matras, J., 295
Mauss, A.L., 218, 219, 280
Maxfield, M.G., 425
Mayhew, L.H., 389
Mazmanian, D.M., 384
McAdam, D., 90, 217, 379, 384
McCarthy, D.E., 15
McClelland, David C., 76–79
McClure, J.E., 195
McClusky, J.E., 158
McCord, A., 21
McCord, W., 21
McCoy, C.B., 138, 305
McEwen, J.T., 287
McFarlin, D.B., 329
McIlroy, A., 333
McKeon, E., 143
McKie, C., 147
McLaughlin, P., 176
McMichael, P., 35
McNeal, J.U., 175
McNeil, L.D., 220
McPheat, D., 418, 427
McQuarie, D., 61
Mead, M., 98, 265

Meadows, D.H., 423
Meadows, D.L., 423
Meadows, P., 107
Mechanic, D., 304, 305
Medical Expenditure Panel Survey, 401
Medoza, J.L., 203
Meier, K.J., 116
Meier, R.F., 293
Meisel, J.B., 90
Mekay, E., 234
Mendelsohn, O., 148
Menken, J., 147
Mental illness, 347–349
Merik, S., 170
Merton, R.K., 38, 64, 66, 244, 293
Messner, S.F., 293
Mesthene, E.G., 12
Metcalf, A., 202
Meusner, N., 159
Meyer, G., 385
Meyer, M.W., 119
Meyer, R.E., 202
Meyersohn, R., 194, 202, 203
Michael, R.T., 136
Michel, R., 118
Michelson, R.A., 168
Midanik, L.T., 403
Migration, 145–146
Milgram, S., 339
Millennium bug, 202
Miller, D.C., 192
Miller, H.I., 257
Miller, J.C., 86
Miller, S.M., 152
Mills, C.W., 8, 64, 153, 154
Misch, A., 320
Mishan, E.J., 317, 318, 328, 341
Modeling forecasting, 423
Modern craft age, 192
Modernists, 204
Modernization, 103–107
Modesty, norms of, 266
Mohrbacher, B.C., 220
Moland, J.R., 24
Monheit, A.C., 401
Montagu, A., 246
Montgomery, R.L., 94
Moody-Adams, M., 261
Mooney, J., 220, 221
Moore, W.E., 8, 38, 39, 49, 103, 108, 403
Moran, R.T., 236, 265
Morbidity and Mortality Weekly Report, 142
Morgan, Lewis Henry, 52–54
Morrill Act, 164
Morris, K.T., 24
Morrison, D.E., 198
Mortality, 142–144
Mosca, Gaetano, 156
Moschis, G.P., 244

Motivating Economic Achievement (McClelland), 78
Motivation, 260
Motivations to change, 239–240
Motor patterns, 267
Mott, P.E., 157
Mowbray, C.T., 411
Moxley, R.L., 255
Muller-Willie, L., 13
Multimethod forecasting, 425
Mungo, P., 288
Murdock, G.P., 88, 89
Murphy, D.E., 287
Murray, C., 150
Murray, D.W., 132
Mutchler, J.A., 95
Mutual criticism, 212–213
Myers, S.L., 27
Myrdal, G., 107

N
Nachmias, C., 403
Nachmias, D., 403
Nadler, A., 154
Nadler, D.A., 239
NAFTA (North American Free Trade Agreement), 36
Nagel, S.S., 387, 391
Nair, K.N., 247
Naisbitt, J., 15, 172, 233
Naroll, R., 87
Nathawat, S.S., 78
Natick-Tyndale, E., 403
National Center for Health Statistics, 132
National Environmental Policy Act (1969), 409, 426
National Labor Relations Act (1935), 157
National Opinion Research Center, 403
National Organization for Women, 386
National Rifle Association (NRA), 258
NATO, 28
Navarro, V., 419
Needs, 240–241
Neiger, B.L., 422
Nemeth, M., 132
Neumann, S., 98
Neumark, D., 7
Newcomb, T.M., 402
Newman, R., 90
The New Republic, 342
Newsweek, 146, 203, 205, 219, 241, 268, 333
Newton, Isaac, 99, 100
The New York Times, 162, 235, 287, 299
Ng, H.K., 423
Ngoh, C.C.S., 303
Nichols, A.W., 362
Nieburg, H.L., 368, 374
Niehoff, A.M., 240, 248
Nielsen, F., 150

Nimkoff, M.F., 252
Nisbet, R.A., 9, 51, 56
Nolan, P., 17, 57, 86, 108, 192, 317
Nonviolence/direct action as change strategy, 374–379
  direct-action tactics, 377–379
  direct approach to, 376–377
  indirect approach to, 375–376
Normative changes, 360
Normative-reeducative strategies, 365

O

Oberschall, A., 217, 291, 381, 384, 386
O'Brian, A., 138
Observability, 91
Occupational Safety and Health Administration (OSHA), 258
Ockey, J., 118
Office of Technology Assessment (OTA), 407, 426
Ogburn, William F., 69–71, 129, 283, 284, 293, 294
Olsen, M.E., 153, 219
Oneida community, 211–217
  complex marriage in, 213–216
  economic communism in, 212
  mutual criticism in, 212–213
On the Revolutions of the Celestial Orbs (Copernicus), 253
Open class stratification system, 148
Opp, K-D., 293
Oppenheimer, M., 370, 374, 377
Oppenheimer, T., 286
Organization for Economic Cooperation and Development (OECD), 420
Organization Man, The (Whyte), 205
Organized opposition, 258–259
Origins of the Family, Private Property and the State, The (Morgan), 53
Ottenheimer, M., 54
Overworked American, The (Schor), 331

P

Page, C.H., 9
Panel Study of Income Dynamics (PSID) (Survey Research Center), 401
Panel surveys, 400–403
Parenti, M., 280
Pareto, V., 314
Paridario, M.R., 410
Park, R.E., 292
Parsons, Talcott, 66–69, 110
Passig, D., 422
Pasteur, Louis, 100
Pastore, A.L., 330
Patai, R., 246, 254, 255, 265
Patterns of change, 85–120
  acculturation, 95–98
  bureaucratization, 116–119
  diffusion, 88–95
  evolution, 85–88
  industrialization, 108–111
  modernization, 103–107
  revolution, 98–103
  urbanization, 111–116
Pattnayak, S.R., 106
Patton, M.Q., 411
Pearce, F., 112
Pearson, H., 174
Pelto, P.J., 13, 15
Peng, Y., 201
People's Choice, The (Lazarsfeld), 401
Perceived economic profitability, 269–270
Perception, selective, 261–263
Perkins, E.J., 11
Perkins, J.J., 240
Perlez, J., 27
Perlmutter, H.V., 86
Perrolle, J.A., 173
Persuasion, 381
  strategy, 366, 367
PETA (People for the Ethical Treatment of Animals), 378
Peterman, L., 404
Petersen, W., 97, 282
Peterson, J.C., 406
Pettit, P., 64
Pfeiffer, J.E., 111
Phreaking, 288
Phrenological Journal, 199
Phrenology, 199
Piddington, R., 222
Piel, G., 112, 114
Pierce N., 387
Pimbert, M.P., 318
Piven, F.F., 405, 406
Planned social change, 358–368
  methods of, 364–368
Platt, A.E., 335
Plessy v. Ferguson (1896), 384–385
Polanyi, K., 174
Policy implications, 425–427
Polish Peasant in Europe and America (Thomas & Znaniecki), 405
Political ideologies, 18–19
Politics, as source of change, 28–31
Politics of Modernization, The (Apter), 104
Popkin, B.M., 259
Population, 139–148
  change in patterns, 109
  demographic transition, 142–148
  implosion, 111
  rapid growth rates, consequences of, 140–142
Population dynamics, 142–148
  age-sex composition, 146–148
  fertility, 144–145

Population dynamics (*continued*)
  migration, 145–146
  mortality, 142–144
Population Reference Bureau, 111, 139, 140, 143, 146
Porter, A.L., 406, 407
Porter, C.F., 410
Porter, M.E., 239
Posavac, E.J., 415
Postel, S., 318, 321, 323, 324, 332, 334
Powell, F.P., 306
Power, 157–158
  decentralization of, 157
  definition of, 153
  law and, 157–158
Power and Privilege (Lenski), 154
Power-coercive strategies, 365
Power relations, 153–158
  dynamics of, 154–157
Powers, C.H., 314
Powers, M., 134, 135
Power strategy, 366
Pratkanis, A.R., 381
Pregnancy, 136–137
Prestige, 234–235
Pridham, G., 26
Principles of Scientific Management, The (Taylor), 199
Pritchett, L., 143
Proctor, C., 255
Production, 170–174
Prohibition, 297
Propaganda, 381
Protestant Ethic and the Spirit of Capitalism, The (Weber), 16, 71, 76
Pruitt, D.G., 20
Psychological barriers to change, 259–264
  habit, 259–260
  ignorance, 260–261
  ineffective communication, 263–264
  motivation, 260
  selective perception, 261–263
Psychological costs of change, 342–349
  anxiety/insecurity, 345–346
  mental illness, 347–349
  robopathology, 343–345
Psychological stimulants to change, 239–244
  attitudes, 242–243
  communication, 241–242
  motivation, 239–240
  perceived needs, 240–241
  personal influence, 243–244
Publish or perish, 168–169
Purdum, T.S., 219

Q

Quality of life, social costs associated with, 329–332

Quarantelli, E.L., 203

R

Rabier, J-R., 329
Racial conflict, 24–25
Radcliffe-Brown, A.R., 65
RAND Corporation, 422
Randers, J., 423
Rao, M., 165
Rapid population growth, consequences of, 140–142
Rasky, E., 236
Rationalization, forms of, 258
Rational legal authority, 154
Ravitch, D., 161
Ray, C.A., 168
Ray, P.H., 204
Reactionary movements, 218
Reactions to change, 232–271
Reagan, L.J., 280, 281
Rebellion, 101
Recall surveys, 403
Recent Social Trends, 418
Redfield, R., 56, 113
Reeducative strategies, 366, 367
Reese II, W.A., 150
Reform movements, 218
Regier, D.A., 347
Reich, C., 208
Rein, M., 93
Relative advantage, 91
Religion, 87, 130
"Religious Evolution" (Bellah), 87
Remnick, D., 27
Renner, M., 320, 323, 327, 335, 336
Resistance to change, 251–252
Responses to change, 288–292
Retreatism, 292
Revolution, 98–103
  six patterns of, 100–101
Revolutionary Action Movement, 370
Revolutionary movements, 218
Rhoads, C., 170, 331, 387
Rice, R.W., 329
Richerson, P.J., 86
Riches, D., 8
Riding, A., 299, 371
Riessman, F., 178
Rifkin, J., 404
Riggs, F.W., 118
Rinehart, J., 20
Rios-Rull, J-V., 250
Riots, 370, 371
Rise, C.S., 18
Ritzer, G., 34, 173
Rivers, C., 136
Robbins, M.C., 283
Roberts, S., 25

Robertson, P.J., 364
Robins, L.N., 347
Robinson, D.E., 197
Robopathology, 343–345
Rochon, T.R., 384
Roehling, P.V., 133
Roentgen, Conrad Wilhelm, 100
Rogers, C.R., 153
Rogers, E.M., 90, 241, 262, 263, 270, 363
Roodman, D.M., 138
Ropeik, D., 330
Rose, S.J., 152
Rosen, C.M., 113
Rosen, L.D., 15
Rosner, D., 320
Ross, J.E., 371
Rossi, P.H., 411, 412, 415, 417
Rossides, D.W., 148
Rossini, F.A., 406, 407
Rostow, W.W., 57, 58, 192
Roszak, T., 208, 343
Rothenbacher, F., 418
Rubin, J.Z., 20, 209
Rucht, D., 90
Rudofsky, B., 197, 198
Ruggles, S., 128
Rulli, J., 31
Russell, C., 131
Ryckman, L., 27

S

Sachs, A., 318–320
Sage, W., 361
Sagoff, M., 316
Sahlins, M.D., 87
Salem, G., 324, 330
Sanders, B., 149–151
Sanders, J., 388
Sandole-Stratoste, I., 22
Sanson-Fisher, R.W., 240
Santini, D.J., 423
Sarno, A., 135
Satyagraha, 378
Savelsberg, J.J., 103
Sawicki, D.S., 417
Sawyer, J., 22
Scenario writing, 422
Schaeffer, R.K., 34, 57
Schaer, R., 18
Schafer, P.D., 57
Schafer, S., 199
Schatz, S., 16
Schell, B., 288
Schipper, L., 329
Schissel, B., 387
Schlosser, E., 285, 326, 331, 336
Schneider, H.K., 233
Schneider, L., 144
Schodolski, V.J., 159
Schon, D.A., 92–94, 302
Schor, J.B., 331
Schot, J.W., 407
Schupack, D., 135
Schwartz, J., 150
Schwartz, M.A., 128, 131
Schwartz, R., 86
Schwartz, T., 291
Schwendener, P., 207
Science of Culture, The (White), 87
Scientific American, 301
Scientific specialization, 341–342
Scitovsky, T., 325, 342, 346
Sclove, R.E., 410
Scott, B.M., 128, 131
Scott, J., 295, 296, 403
Seabrook, J., 327, 328
Secondary education, 160–163
Seeman, M., 288, 290
Self-actualized person, 343
Semmelweis, Ignaz Philipp, 100
Sened, I., 258
Seneviratne, S.J., 364
September 11, 2001, terrorist attacks, 287, 327, 330
Serrill, M.S., 219
Sexton, R.L., 114
Sexual revolution, 135–139
Shabecoff, P., 319
Shannon, M., 7
Shapiro, J., 169
Sharp, R.L., 13
Sharpe, G., 376, 377
Sheldon, E.B., 403
Shell, E.R., 5, 138
Shellenbarger, S., 173
Shen, J., 423
Shenk, D., 15
Sherman, H.J., 61
Shoemaker, F.L., 241, 262, 263, 270
Shore, C., 410
Shultz R.H., Jr., 26
Silk, L., 36
Simcox, D., 295
Simmel, G., 195
Simon, S.C., 301
Simons, M., 320, 327
Singer, H.W., 21
Singer, P., 264
Singh, B., 78
Singh, R., 78
Sirianni, C., 119
Sivard, R.L., 26
Sjoberg, G., 111
Skinner, B.F., 153
Skolnick, J.H., 33, 370
Slater, P.E., 301

Smelser, N.J., 14, 68, 69, 79, 171, 174, 200
Smith, A.D., 58, 101
Smith, D.H., 106, 348
Smith, G. Elliot, 88
Smith, G.D., 265
Smith, M.L., 411
Smith, P.T., 373
Smith, R., 200
Smith, S.S., 151
Smith, T.L., 146
Smits, R., 407
Smock, P.J., 138
Smothers, R., 318
Snow, D.A., 217, 379
Social audits, 414
Social barriers to change, 252–259
    authority, 256–257
    fear of unfamiliar, 257–258
    forms of rationalization, 258
    group solidarity, 255–256
    ideological resistance, 255
    organized opposition, 258–259
    social class, 254–255
    status interests, 253–254
    vested interests, 252–253
Social change, 4–9
    conceptualizations of, 7–10
    definition of, 10–11
    law and, 387–392
    nature of, 4–7
    planned, 358–368
    and social disorganization, 292–297
    transitory, 193–194
Social change, sources of, 11–39
    competition, 19–20
    conflict, 20–28
    economics, 31–34
    globalization, 34–37
    ideology, 15–19
    politics, 28–31
    structural strains, 37–39
    technology, 11–15
Social class barriers to change, 254–255
Social costs of change, 326–342
    automobiles, 327–329
    quality of life, 329–332
    reduction of options for individuals, 336–338
    underutilization of college-educated people, 340–341
    urban living, 338–340
Social disorganization, 292–297
    definition of, 293
Social impact of technology, 282–288
Social indicators, assessing, 417–425
    approaches to, 418–419
    data collection, 419–420
Social Indicators Research, 418
Social mobility, 151–153

Social morphological revolution, 294–295
Social movements, 217–224, 379–387
    accomplishments of, 384–387
    strategies used by, 380–381
    tactics used by, 382–384
Social-psychological theories of change, 71–79
    Hagen, Everett E., 73–76
    McClelland, David C., 76–79
    Weber, Max, 71–73
Social relationships, 9–10
Social stimulants to change, 234–239
    acceptance, 237–238
    authority, 237
    competition, 239
    contact with other societies, 235–236
    decision making, participation in, 238–239
    friendships, 236
    prestige, 234–235
    social class, 236
    timing, 238
Social structure, 9–10
Social System, The (Parsons), 67
Social technology, 410–411
Societies: Evolutionary and Comparative Perspectives (Parsons), 67
Society, 8–9
    change in structure of, 8–9
Soderholm, A., 90
Soil erosion, 333–335
Solid waste, economic costs associated with, 318–320
Solt, C.G., 404
Sorokin, P.A., 404
Spain, D., 26, 165, 173
Spake, A., 5
Spates, J.L., 338
Specter, M., 267, 268
Spector, A.J., 148
Spence, N.A., 423
Spencer, Herbert, 54–55
Spencer, J., 194
Spengler, J.J., 145
Speth, J.G., 32
Spindler, L.S., 89, 97, 98
Spiro, M.E., 18
Springer, M., 418
St. Louis Post-Dispatch, 324, 330
Stabile, D.R., 326
Stack, S., 136
Stafford, F.P., 401
Staggenborg, S., 400
Stansky, L., 37
Stark, J.S., 199
Starke, L., 144
Starnes, C.E., 32
State of World Population 2002: People, Poverty and Possibilities (United Nations), 140
Statistical Abstracts of the United States, 4

Status interests, 253–254
Steele, V., 197
Steinberg, J., 166
Steinmetz, R.C., 18
Stempel, G.H., 291
Stevens, W.K., 336
Stevenson, M., 34
Stewart, J., 57
Stiglitz, J., 37
Stirpiculture, 215
Stisser, P., 384
Stolley, K.S., 404, 406
Strain, 68
Strang, D., 90
Strasser, G., 283, 408
Strategies for Planned Change (Zaltman & Duncan), 359, 366
Strategies of change, 357–392
Stratification, 148–153
    economic differences and, 149–151
    mobility and, 151–153
    systems, types of, 148–149
Streaking, 202–203
Stroneger, W-J., 236
Structural-functional theories of change, 64–71
    Ogburn, William F., 69–71
    Parsons, Talcott, 67–69
Structural strains, 37–39
Succession, 284
Suchman, E.A., 412, 416
Summers, L., 143
Sumner, W.G., 55, 390
Sundquist, J.L., 337
Superstitions, 267–268
Survey forecasting, 424
Survey Research Center, 401
Survivalists, 210
Sussman, M.B., 342
Sutton, L., 422
Swanson, K.C., 414
Swisher, K., 258
System of Modern Societies, The (Parsons), 67
Szalai, A., 110
Szreter, S., 142
Sztompka, P., 78, 99, 233

T

Tagliabue, J., 298
Takaki, R., 338
Talbot, M., 135, 300
Taras, R., 265
Targets of change, 358–363
    individuals as, 360–361
    intermediate target systems, 361–362
    macrolevel target systems, 362–363
Taro cult, 223
Tarrow, S., 218
Taxation, 118
Taylor, D.M., 405
Taylor, F.W., 199
Technology, 11–15, 406–411
    positive/negative features of, 12–13
    social impact of, 282–288
    and work, 14–15
Technology and Society (Freeman), 406
Technology assessment, 406–411
    methods of, 408–409
    recurrent steps in, 408
Technology Assessment Act, 407
Teich, A.H., 407, 424
Teisberg, E.O., 239
Teitelbaum, M.S., 140, 143, 145
Telecommunication crimes, 287
Telles, E.E., 109
Tepper, A., 408
Terrorism, 371–374
Thackeray, R., 422
Theories of change, 49–79
    conflict, 58–64
    evolutionary, 51–58
    social-psychological, 71–79
    structural-functional, 64–71
Therivel, R., 410
Thielbar, G.W., 204
Thobaben, R.G., 15, 19
Thomas, D., 374
Thomas, R., 345
Thomas, W.I., 405
Thompson, J.A., 258
Thomson, S.C., 166
Thornton, A., 128
Tibbitts, C., 129
Tilly, C., 99, 103, 384
Tilly, L.A., 404
Timasheff, N.S., 51, 54
Time, 136, 137, 203
Tirole, J., 256
Toennies, F., 55, 56
Toffler, A., 233, 301
Tong, Y., 291
Tooker, E., 53
Traditional authority, 154
Traditionalists, 204
"Tragedy of the Commons, The" (Hardin), 338
Trahair, R.C.S., 18
Transition, economic costs associated with, 324–326
Travis, R., 419
Trend surveys, 403
Trial stage of adoption, 91
Trickett, E.J., 95
Trinkhaus, J., 200
Trivizas, E., 373
Trout, B.T., 142, 146, 295, 323
Trow, M., 118
Trust (Fukuyama), 73

Tryability, 91
Tsai, M., 202
Tschann, J.M., 95
Tuma, N.B., 90
Tumin, M.M., 153, 204
Turner, J.H., 32, 55, 65, 71
Turner, M.E., 381
Turner, R.H., 200, 201, 217, 372, 373, 380, 384
Tyler, P.A., 321, 322

U

Uchitelle, L., 177, 331, 340
U.N. Commissions for Trade and Development, 419
Unification Church, 210
Unintended consequences, 292–301
United Nations Environment Programme, 318, 320, 322, 323, 332, 333, 335, 336
United Nations Population Fund, 140
University, conflict in, 22–24
Updergrave W.L., 330
Urbanization, 111–116, 150
Urban living, 338–340
U.S. Bureau of the Census, 131, 145, 159, 165, 172, 176
U.S. Commission on Civil Rights, 384, 385, 386
U.S. Department of Health and Human Services, 165
U.S. Department of Justice, 300
U.S. Department of Labor, 172
U.S. News & World Report, 328
Useem, J., 264
Utopia (More), 18
Utopian ideologies, 18

V

Vago, S., 23, 63, 245, 297, 387, 388, 392, 411
Vailala Madness, 222
Valach, L., 411
Valente, T.W., 90
Van den Berghe, P.L., 66
Vanhanen, T., 26
Van Steenburgen, B., 423
Veblen, T., 194, 197
Veenhoven, R., 419
Vega, W.A., 95
Verhovek, S.H., 322
Vested interests, 250–253
Vidich, A.J., 204, 206, 233, 318
Vinokurov, A., 95
Violence, 368–374
Violent strategies for effecting change, 369–370
Vogel, G., 422
Voting Rights Act (1965), 384, 385
Vulgarian lifestyle, 207

W

Wacquant, L.J.D., 39
Waheeduzzaman, A.N.M., 19
Walczak, D., 173
Wald, M.L., 329
Wall Street Journal, 7, 129
Walt, S., 26, 99
Walton, R.E., 366
Ward, D., 416
Ward, L.F., 55
Ward, S.C., 71
Warren, R.L., 359, 375, 380
Warren, R.S., 258
Wascher, W., 7
Washburn, P.C., 263
Waste, R.J., 256
Water pollution, economic costs associated with, 321–323
Watson, G., 259, 261
Watson, J., 365
Wattenberg, B.J., 140, 145, 147
Wayward Puritans, The (Erikson), 404
Webb, H., 196
Weber, Alfred, 116
Weber, Max, 16, 71–73, 77, 116, 204
Weber, P., 333
Weicher, J.C., 149
Weil, M.M., 15
Weiner, T., 371
Weinert, F., 72
Weisberg, B., 328
Weismann, R., 140, 149
Weiss, C.H., 412, 414, 415, 426
Weiss, Y., 234
Weisskoff, R., 269
Wejnert, B., 22, 26
Welch, I., 196
Wellin, E., 261
Westley, B., 365
Westwood, J.N., 26
Weyant, J.M., 241
"What Goes Up May Stay Up" (Harris), 197
White, C.C.R., 178
White, J.R., 211
White, L., 87
White, R.W., 303
Whyte W.H., Jr., 205
Wiener, A., 422
Wilensky, H., 32
Wilkins, V.M., 116
Williams, D.C., 5, 241
Williams, J.H., 133, 135, 137
Willigan, J.V., 219
Wilson, J.Q., 220, 221, 224, 343, 370, 381, 382
Wilson Quarterly, 334
Winch, R.S., 131

Winter, D.G., 78
Winter, J.M., 140, 143, 145
Winter, S.K., 78
Wirth, L.B., 112, 339
Wittgenstein, F., 143
Witwer, M., 131
Wolf, C.P., 279
Wolman, W., 35
Work, technology and, 14–15
Work in America, 330
Workplace conflict, 22
Workplace violence, 331
World Bank, 270, 418–420
World Bank World Development Resources Report 2003, 317
World Environmental Conference, 410
World Health Organization (WHO), 142
World Population News Service, 136
World Resources Institute, 112, 339
World Trade Center, terrorist attack on, 287, 330, 371
Worsley, P., 222
Wright, J.D., 289, 318
Wright, L., 220
Wudunn, S., 202

Y

Yablonsky, L., 343–345
Yagoda, B., 199
Yin, R.K., 413
Yippies, 209–210
Yir Yoront tribe, 13–14
Young, J.E., 318, 319, 320
Young, R.A., 411
Youth, H., 333

Z

Zac, L., 403
Zagorski, K., 234
Zaltman, G., 249, 250, 251, 255, 256, 263, 359, 360, 363, 366, 367, 368
Zangrando, R.L., 385
Zarnowski, A., 129
Zeitlin, M., 155
Zelby, L.W., 258
Zellner, W.W., 210, 211, 213, 214, 215, 279, 291
Zernike, K., 160
Zetka J.R., Jr., 256
Zijderveld, A.C., 343
Znaniecki, F., 405
Zopf, Paul E. Jr.,, 146

培文书系·社会科学·英文影印系列

政治社会学导论
Introduction to Political Sociology
Anthony M. Orum 著

（第4版）

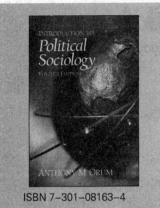

ISBN 7-301-08163-4
定价：31.00元
（16开 303页）
原著书号：0139271538
（Prentice Hall 2004）
原著定价：$53.00元

■ 内容简介

本书对政治的广泛社会基础进行了描述，分析了政府的政策和行为影响其国家和人民命运的方式。从经济和政治、国家和社会、公民社会和政治等多个方面介绍了政治社会学的基本原理，提供了近期的政治社会学理论和社会主流对当今有关议题的认识和理解。在丰富的理论文献基础上关注现时的社会和政治变革，有关的重要原理和发现有助于学生深入理解当今世界发生的许多社会和政治变化及其意义。

审视自我：社会学经典、当代和跨文化阅读
Seeing Ourselves: Classic, Contemporary, and Cross-Cultural Readings in Sociology
John J. Macionis, Nijole V. Benokraitis 著

（第6版）

ISBN 7-301-08162-6
定价：50.00元
（16开 534页）
原著书号：0-13-111557-X
（Prentice Hall 2004）
原著定价：$48.00

■ 内容简介

本书是一本社会学选集，包括了77篇社会学经典、当代和跨文化研究的代表性作品，多方面反映了社会学的多元观点和方法，内容涉及社会学原理、社会问题、女性研究、婚姻家庭、动物权利等广泛的议题和领域。其中经典代表作选取了大部分社会学奠基者如迪尔凯姆、马克斯·韦伯等大家的作品；当代部分则主要以当今众多社会学议题、争论和应用为主；跨文化理解启发了学生对北美文化多样性的批判性理解，由此扩展了对其他文化领域的认识。

培文书系·社会科学·英文影印系列

社会科学：社会研究导论
Social Science: An Introduction to the Study of Society
Elgin F. Hunt, David C. Colander 著

（第12版）

ISBN 7-301-08048-4
定价：50.30 元
（16开 534页）
原著书号：0-205-40847-8
（Allyn and Bacon 2005）
原著定价：$75.33

■ 内容简介

　　本书是一本经典的社会科学介绍性教科书，作者以客观的立场进行了多学科的探索与研讨，全面涵括了人类学、经济学、政治科学、社会学、历史和地理等学科的内容。同时，不断回应社会现实进行全面的修订和适时更新，第12版尤其对近年来席卷世界的戏剧性政治和经济变化进行了关注，例如对911恐怖袭击事件的考察等，为学生和研究者提供了课堂教学的生动题材和资料。另外，其平易的写作风格以及每章节后互联网资源的提供为学生深入理解章节内容提供了有效的帮助。

大众传媒
The Media of Mass Communication
John Vivian 著

（第7版）

ISBN 7-301-08217-7
定价：50.00 元
（16开 520页）
原著书号：0-205-41848-1
（Allyn and Bacon 2005）
原著定价：$76.67

■ 内容简介

　　大众传播领域日新月异，对教科书的写作者来说，要想跟上如此迅速的发展步伐无疑是一个巨大挑战。本书打破了出版界的传统局限，将最新的版本送到了学生们手中。书中既有2004年学术奖的相关内容，还提到了美国在线（AOL）从时代华纳的名称中剥离出去，以及默多克收购DirecTV的重大新闻事件。在书中您还可以找到有关大众传播媒介发挥作用的途径的最新学术成果。

　　本书在进一步发展的基础上，继续弘扬了本书以往各版本重视图片效果的优良传统，通过图片使读者加深了对书中的基本要点的认识。

培文书系·最新书目

← 人文科学系列

英文影印版

历史人文系列

全球通史:从史前到21世纪(第7版)(上)
全球通史:从史前到21世纪(第7版)(下)
西方文明遗产(第9版)(上)
西方文明遗产(第9版)(下)
世界文明的源泉(第3版)(上)
世界文明的源泉(第3版)(下)
伦理学:理论与实践(第8版)
世界宗教(第9版)

艺术人文系列

艺术:让人成为人(第7版)
西方文化中的音乐简史

中文翻译版

历史人文系列

全球通史:从史前到21世纪(第7版)(上)
全球通史:从史前到21世纪(第7版)(下)

艺术人文系列

艺术:让人成为人(第7版)
西方文化中的音乐简史

社会科学系列 →

英文影印版

社会学系列

审视自我:社会学经典、当代和跨文化阅读(第6版)
社会变迁(第5版)
社会与政治原理:经典读本
社会科学:社会研究导论(第12版)
医学社会学(第9版)
政治社会学导论(第4版)

文化研究系列

文化研究导论(第1版)
文化原理与通俗文化导论(第3版)
女性与学术研究
男性的世界(第6版)
女性的世界

心理学系列

心理学:大脑,人,世界(第2版)
心理学的历史与体系(第6版)
心理学史:观点与背景(第3版)
教育心理学:理论与实践(第7版)
社会心理学(第11版)
语言心理学
变态心理学(第12版)
心理学与生活(第17版)
发展心理学:婴儿、孩童与青春期(第5版)
心理测量(第4版)
终身发展心理学(第3版)
应用心理学与人力资源管理(第6版)

中文翻译版

心理学系列

社会心理学(第5版)
心理学的邀请(第3版)
投资心理学(第2版)

市场营销中心联系名录

主任：张涛
副主任：潘建 刘宗彦

地区	联系人	电话
北京	经理：潘建（兼）	62752018
	经理：刘梓盈	62767313
	助理：宋诗安	62752018
	助理：黄英	62767313
陕西、河南、天津	经理：饶勇	62757439
	助理：陈志国	62752935
广东、浙江、湖南	经理：刘宗彦（兼）	62759712
	助理：宗秀菊	62757317
江苏、东三省、内蒙古	经理：王林冲	62767314
	助理：郗雨	62757438
上海 安徽 四川 重庆	经理：谢尚楹	62757299
	助理：李瑞芳	62752954
山东、福建、海南、江西	经理：张志国	62752013
	助理：许秀文	62757295
河北、山西、新疆、甘肃、青海、宁夏	经理：梁滨	62757298
	助理：陈志国	62752935
湖北、云南、贵州、广西	经理：张继承	62757295
	助理：许秀文	62750694

北京大学出版社培文教育文化公司

地址：北京市海淀区中关村北大街118号1号楼1209室
邮编：100871　　　　　　　　联系人：孙明卉
网址：http://cbs.pku.edu.cn　　电子信箱：pw@pup.pku.edu.cn
电话：010-58874097　　　　　传真：010-58874098

北京大学出版社人文社科类图书重点经销商

省份	店名	电话	地址
北京	北大书店	010-62757515 010-62752015	北京大学校内博实商场2楼
	海淀图书城北大读者服务部	010-62534449 010-62523168	北京市海淀图书城5号2层
	三联书店	010-64002710	北京市东城区美术馆东街22号
	涵芬楼书店	010-85117603	北京市东城区王府井大街36号
	风入松书店	010-62625941	北京大学南门外资源东楼地下室
	国林风书店	010-82618384	北京市海淀区西大街36号 昊海楼地下一层
	万圣书店	010-62768750	北京海淀区清华北大教师楼4—5号楼二层
	北京大学新华书店	010-62753275	北京大学三角地
	清华大学新华书店	010-62782410	清华大学校内
	人民大学出版社读者服务部	62510566-230	北京市中关村大街31号
	北京师范大学出版社读者服务部	010-58808104	北京市新街口外大街19号
天津	天津南开大学出版社书店	022-23507092	天津市卫津路94号南开大学校内
	天津南开区书香缘书店	022-23509858	南开大学新图书馆一楼外跨楼梯间书香缘书店
	天津市新华书店高等教育书店	022-23526801	天津大学院内（老图书馆西侧）
河南	郑州二七区新世纪法律书店	0371-6955389	郑州市大学路33号付4号
	三联书店郑州分销店	0371-5367851	郑州市文化路56号（文化路与农业路交汇处金国商厦3楼）
	河南大学出版社书店	0378-2825010	开封市明伦街85号
陕西	西安科技法律书店	029-85218448	西安市长安南路280号
	陕西万邦文化传播有限公司	029-82222531	西安市东大街383号方汇大厦一层万邦书城
广东	汕头三联商务文化中心	0754-8165365	汕头市长平路105号1-2楼
	深圳市新文海图书有限公司	0755-25910358	深圳市八卦三路522栋一楼
	珠海市文华书城有限公司	0756-8881203	珠海市拱北迎宾南路1013号国际大厦负一层国际大厦书城
	广东学而优书店有限公司	020-89027101	广州市海珠区新港西路91-93号
湖南	湖南弘道文化传播有限公司	0731-4431522	长沙市解放中路定王台文化广场15H
浙江	杭州华宝斋古籍书社	0571-88256044	杭州市登云路639号杭州文化商城B区228号
	生活.读书.新知三联书店杭州分销店	0571-88989020	杭州市文三西路沁雅花园康恒大厦
	杭州博大教育图书发行有限公司	0571-86721090	杭州下沙高教园区2号大街18号月雅苑10-1-102号
甘肃	甘肃纸中城邦书业有限公司	0931-8831085	兰州市城关区东岗西路462号
	兰州安宁高教书店	0931-7766637	兰州市安宁东路935号
	兰州学源理工科技图书有限公司	0931-8840555	兰州市七里河区兰工坪路1号
河北	河北大学出版社书店	0312-5033223	河北保定合作路1号
	石家庄学步书店	0311-3800874	石家庄市红旗大街389号

省份	书店	电话	地址
山西	山西尔雅书店有限公司	0351-7231473	山西省太原市双塔西街130号
	太原市文杰大学书店有限公司	0351-4132420	太原市并州路东坡斜巷1号
	山西省外文书店—学府购书中心	0351-7018919	太原市坞城路36号山大旧校门
宁夏	银川市新华书店—宁大店	0951-5018005	银川市解放东街47号
	银川周末文汇书店	0951-5042547	银川市解放西街111号（公安厅对面）
山东	三联书店济南分销店	0531-6096766	济南市院前大街泉城路商业设施F3-8号
江西	南昌市青苑书店	0791-8592290	南昌市洪都北大道图书城1号
福建	厦门华文图书有限公司	0592-2185998	厦门大学图书馆一楼（厦门大学963号信箱）
	福建省厦门市晓风书屋	0592-5816123	厦门市思明南路416-12号
	厦门对外图书交流中心	0592-5054027	厦门市湖滨南路809号
安徽	安徽省导航图书有限公司	0551-5107801	合肥市东至路5号炮院招待所
	合肥考试书店－格致书店	0551-3600141	中国科技大学东区活动中心
	中国科技大学出版社读者服务部	0551-3607380	安徽省合肥市金寨路96号科大东区出版社一楼
四川	西南书局	028-86511882	成都市梨花街2号四川书市2楼7号
	弘文书局	028-86129612	成都市人发西路101号
重庆	重庆大学出版社书店	023-65111509	重庆市沙坪坝正街174号
	重庆精典文化传播有限公司精典书店	023-63734260	重庆市渝中区民权路17号
上海	上海交大昂立图书有限公司	021-32260589	上海市徐汇区广元西路43号惠谷电脑城地下室
	上海季风图书有限公司	021-32260589	上海市陕西南路215号
	上海复旦经世书局	021-65642857	上海杨浦区国权路579号
	上海财大书店	021-65163862	上海中山北路369号
	上海鹿鸣书店	021-65647139	上海国权路334号
广西	广西师范大学出版社大学书店	0773-5806955	桂林市普陀路44号
	广西南国书店	0771-2615485	广西南宁市中山路99号
贵州	贵阳西南风文化发展有限公司	0851-5933050	贵阳市延安东路130号
	贵州西西弗	0851-5811504	贵州市富水南路196号金林广场A栋11楼4号
湖北	湖北政博书刊发行有限公司（图书）	027-87388263	武汉市楚雄大道268-A13号
	湖北三新图书公司	027-87870493	武汉市洪山区楚雄大街龙家湾270号
云南	云南清华实业公司	0871-5314348	昆明12.1大街158号(云南师大)
	昆明新知图书城有限责任公司	0871-4184679	云南省昆明市新闻路348号（云南省图书批发市场四楼）
吉林	长春学人书店	0431-5676686	长春市人民大街4696号
	长春联合图书城	0431-2722234	长春市宽城区芙蓉路1号
	吉林大学出版社书店	0431-5676648	长春市朝阳区永昌路9号
内蒙古	内蒙古大学出版社书店	0471-4990657	呼和浩特市赛罕区昭乌达路凯旋广场88号
辽宁	东北财经大学出版社图书代办站	0411-84712239	大连市黑石礁
江苏	南京大学出版社书店	025-83320583	南京市汉口路22号
	南京先锋书店	025-83325082	南京市广州路12号2楼
黑龙江	哈尔滨工业大学出版社书店	0451-6412461	哈尔滨市南岗区教化街21号

Another way of looking at the role of law in social change is in terms of Mayhew's (1971:195) notion of the possibility of either redefining the normative order or creating new procedural opportunities within the legal apparatus. He calls the first an "extension of formal rights," illustrated by the pronouncement of the Supreme Court that the defendant accused of serious crimes has the right to professional representation. The second is termed the "extension of formal facilities" and is illustrated by the establishment of a system of public defenders who provide the required professional representation. The extension of formal rights and of formal facilities has definite implications.

A rather different perspective on law in social change is presented by Lawrence Friedman. He refers to change through law in terms of two types: "planning" and "disruption." *Planning* "refers to architectural construction of new forms of social order and social interaction. *Disruption* refers to the blocking or amelioration of existing social forms and relations" (L. Friedman, 1973:25). Both operate within the existing legal system and can bring about "positive" or "negative" social change, depending on one's perspective.

Lawrence Friedman (1975:277) infers that revolution is the most distinct and obvious form of disruption. But

> milder forms are everywhere. Judicial review is frequently disruptive. American courts have smashed programs and institutions from the Missouri Compromise to the Alaska pipeline. Activist reformers have played a sensational role in American life in the last decade. Ralph Nader is the most well-known example. . . . He stimulates use of legal processes as a lever of social charge.
>
> Much of his work is technically disruptive; it focuses on litigation and injunctions, on stopping government dead in its tracks, when it fails to meet his ethical and policy standards. Legal disruption can . . . include lawsuits; particularly after *Brown v. Board of Education,* reformers have frequently gone to court to upset many old and established arrangements.

Social change through litigation has always been an important feature in the United States. Whether or not the change brought about by such action is destructive or constructive depends on one's interpretation. The fact remains that law can be highly effective in producing social change. For example, when the California Supreme Court destroyed the legal basis for the system of financing schools in the state, Friedman (1973:27) succinctly observed: "Many a coup d'état in small countries have achieved less social change than this quiet coup d'état in the courts."

Friedman refers to this as an American phenomenon and raises the question: Will this spread to other countries? His response is that creative disruption of the judicial type presupposes a number of conditions that rarely coincide and are apparently not present in other countries to the same degree. These conditions include an activist legal profession, financial resources, activist judges, a genuine social movement, and what he describes